International Directory of

COMPANY HISTORIES

International Directory of
COMPANY
HISTORIES

VOLUME 53

Editor

Tina Grant

St-J

ST. JAMES
PRESS®

THOMSON
━━━━━✦━━━━━ ™
GALE

Detroit • New York • San Diego • San Francisco • Cleveland • New Haven, Conn. • Waterville, Maine • London • Munich

THOMSON

GALE

International Directory of Company Histories, Volume 53

Tina Grant, Editor

Project Editor
Miranda H. Ferrara

Editorial
Erin Bealmear, Joann Cerrito, Jim Craddock, Stephen Cusack, Peter M. Gareffa, Kristin Hart, Melissa Hill, Margaret Mazurkiewicz, Carol A. Schwartz, Christine Tomassini, Michael J. Tyrkus

Imaging and Multimedia
Randy Bassett, Dean Dauphinais, Robert Duncan, Lezlie Light

Manufacturing
Rhonda Williams

LIBRARY OF CONGRESS CATALOG NUMBER 89-190943

ISBN: 1-55862-483-X

BRITISH LIBRARY CATALOGUING IN PUBLICATION DATA

International directory of company histories. Vol. 53
I. Tina Grant
33.87409

Printed in the United States of America
10 9 8 7 6 5 4 3 2 1

CONTENTS

Company Histories

PREFACE

The St. James Press series *The International Directory of Company Histories (IDCH)* is intended for reference use by students, business people, librarians, historians, economists, investors, job candidates, and others who seek to learn more about the historical development of the world's most important companies. To date, *IDCH* has covered over 5,950 companies in 53 volumes.

Inclusion Criteria

Most companies chosen for inclusion in *IDCH* have achieved a minimum of US$25 million in annual sales and are leading influences in their industries or geographical locations. Companies may be publicly held, private, or nonprofit. State-owned companies that are important in their industries and that may operate much like public or private companies also are included. Wholly owned subsidiaries and divisions are profiled if they meet the requirements for inclusion. Entries on companies that have had major changes since they were last profiled may be selected for updating.

The *IDCH* series highlights 10% private and nonprofit companies, and features updated entries on approximately 45 companies per volume.

Entry Format

Each entry begins with the company's legal name, the address of its headquarters, its telephone, toll-free, and fax numbers, and its web site. A statement of public, private, state, or parent ownership follows. A company with a legal name in both English and the language of its headquarters country is listed by the English name, with the native-language name in parentheses.

The company's founding or earliest incorporation date, the number of employees, and the most recent available sales figures follow. Sales figures are given in local currencies with equivalents in U.S. dollars. For some private companies, sales figures are estimates and indicated by the abbreviation *est.* The entry lists the exchanges on which a company's stock is traded and its ticker symbol, as well as the company's NAIC codes.

Entries generally contain a *Company Perspectives* box which provides a short summary of the company's mission, goals, and ideals, a *Key Dates* box highlighting milestones in the company's history, lists of *Principal Subsidiaries, Principal Divisions, Principal Operating Units, Principal Competitors,* and articles for *Further Reading.*

American spelling is used throughout *IDCH*, and the word ''billion'' is used in its U.S. sense of one thousand million.

Sources

Entries have been compiled from publicly accessible sources both in print and on the Internet such as general and academic periodicals, books, annual reports, and material supplied by the companies themselves.

Cumulative Indexes

IDCH contains three indexes: the **Index to Companies**, which provides an alphabetical index to companies discussed in the text as well as to companies profiled, the **Index to Industries**, which allows researchers to locate companies by their principal industry, and the **Geographic Index**, which lists companies alphabetically by the country of their headquarters. The indexes are cumulative and specific instructions for using them are found immediately preceding each index.

Suggestions Welcome

Comments and suggestions from users of *IDCH* on any aspect of the product as well as suggestions for companies to be included or updated are cordially invited. Please write:

The Editor
International Directory of Company Histories
St. James Press
27500 Drake Rd.
Farmington Hills, Michigan 48331-3535

ABBREVIATIONS FOR FORMS OF COMPANY INCORPORATION

A.B.	Aktiebolaget (Sweden)
A.G.	Aktiengesellschaft (Germany, Switzerland)
A.S.	Aksjeselskap (Denmark, Norway)
A.S.	Atieselskab (Denmark)
A.Ş.	Anomin Şirket (Turkey)
B.V.	Besloten Vennootschap met beperkte, Aansprakelijkheid (The Netherlands)
Co.	Company (United Kingdom, United States)
Corp.	Corporation (United States)
G.I.E.	Groupement d'Intérêt Economique (France)
GmbH	Gesellschaft mit beschränkter Haftung (Germany)
H.B.	Handelsbolaget (Sweden)
Inc.	Incorporated (United States)
KGaA	Kommanditgesellschaft auf Aktien (Germany)
K.K.	Kabushiki Kaisha (Japan)
LLC	Limited Liability Company (Middle East)
Ltd.	Limited (Canada, Japan, United Kingdom, United States)
N.V.	Naamloze Vennootschap (The Netherlands)
OY	Osakeyhtiöt (Finland)
OAO	Otkrytoe Aktsionernoe Obshchestve (Russia)
OOO	Obshchestvo s Ogranichennoi Otvetstvennostiu (Russia)
PLC	Public Limited Company (United Kingdom)
PTY.	Proprietary (Australia, Hong Kong, South Africa)
S.A.	Société Anonyme (Belgium, France, Switzerland)
SpA	Società per Azioni (Italy)
ZAO	Zakrytoe Aktsionernoe Obshchestve (Russia)

ABBREVIATIONS FOR CURRENCY

$	United States dollar	KD	Kuwaiti dinar
£	United Kingdom pound	L	Italian lira
¥	Japanese yen	LuxFr	Luxembourgian franc
A$	Australian dollar	M$	Malaysian ringgit
AED	United Arab Emirates dirham	N	Nigerian naira
B	Thai baht	Nfl	Netherlands florin
B	Venezuelan bolivar	NIS	Israeli new shekel
BFr	Belgian franc	NKr	Norwegian krone
C$	Canadian dollar	NT$	Taiwanese dollar
CHF	Switzerland franc	NZ$	New Zealand dollar
COL	Colombian peso	P	Philippine peso
Cr	Brazilian cruzado	PLN	Polish zloty
CZK	Czech Republic koruny	PkR	Pakistan Rupee
DA	Algerian dinar	Pta	Spanish peseta
Dfl	Netherlands florin	R	Brazilian real
DKr	Danish krone	R	South African rand
DM	German mark	RMB	Chinese renminbi
E£	Egyptian pound	RO	Omani rial
Esc	Portuguese escudo	Rp	Indonesian rupiah
EUR	Euro dollars	Rs	Indian rupee
FFr	French franc	Ru	Russian ruble
Fmk	Finnish markka	S$	Singapore dollar
GRD	Greek drachma	Sch	Austrian schilling
HK$	Hong Kong dollar	SFr	Swiss franc
HUF	Hungarian forint	SKr	Swedish krona
IR£	Irish pound	SRls	Saudi Arabian riyal
ISK	Icelandic króna	TD	Tunisian dinar
K	Zambian kwacha	W	Korean won

International Directory of

COMPANY
HISTORIES

A-dec, Inc.

2601 Crestview Drive
Newberg, Oregon 97132
U.S.A.
Telephone: (503) 538-7478
Toll Free: (800) 547-1883
Fax: (503) 538-5911
Web site: http://www.a-dec.com

Private Company
Incorporated: 1966 as Austin Dental Equipment
    Company
Employees: 900
Sales: $134.4 million (2001)
NAIC: 332912 Fluid Power Valve and Hose Fitting
    Manufacturing; 339112 Surgical and Medical
    Instrument Manufacturing; 339114 Dental Equipment
    and Supplies Manufacturing; 333995 Fluid Power
    Cylinder and Actuator Manufacturing, 339114 Dental
    Equipment and Supplies Manufacturing

Located on the A-dec Technical Park campus in Newberg, Oregon, A-dec, Inc. is one of the largest dental equipment manufacturers in the world. A-dec designs, builds, and markets much of the furniture and equipment used in the dental office, including chairs, stools, delivery systems, dental lights, cabinetry, handpieces, and a full line of accessories, such as vacuum pumps, water sprays, and controls—everything except X-ray machines. With an extensive global network of authorized dealers and customers in more then 100 countries, A-dec covers more than 40 percent of the domestic dental equipment market. It provides equipment for 52 of the 53 dental schools in the United States.

Early 1960s: Rapid Innovation in Dental Equipment

The husband and wife team of Joan and Ken Austin founded A-dec (an acronym for Austin Dental Equipment Company) in 1964 with a $2,400 loan from Ken Austin's father and a local dentist, and the goal of having ten employees in five years.

Austin, a life-long tinkerer, had trained as an engineer at Oregon State University, from which he graduated in 1954. Upon graduation, Austin served in the Air Force, first as a radar controller, then as a radar site repair crew supervisor, on active duty in Korea, and, finally, as an aircraft maintenance officer in the United States.

Back in civilian life, Austin found himself unable to fit his inventive nature to the restrictions of the work place. He went through a series of seven or eight jobs in eight years. "I thought my ideas were better than anyone else's," he explained in the *Oregon Stater*'s September 2002 issue, attributing his repeated firings to his own arrogance. In the 2001 special edition of the company's magazine *ON-DEC*, he recalled that he "saw a tremendous need to be able to help the dentist, but my employers kept reminding me that my concerns were not in my job description." Among the businesses where Austin worked before founding A-dec were: Tektronix of Beaverton, Oregon; Research Engineering and Manufacturing of Portland, Oregon; Williams Air Company of Portland, Oregon; Power Brake Equipment of Portland, Oregon; and DENSCO of Colorado, a dental equipment manufacturing company where Austin was chief engineer and learned about oral evacuation systems.

The 1960s were a period of intense innovation in the dental equipment industry. The high-speed air drill had revolutionized the industry in the mid-1950s, creating the need for an oral evacuation device that cleaned debris from a patient's mouth fast enough to keep the working area clean for continued drilling. According to Austin in a 1972 *Oregonian* article, "The first evacuation systems were composites of existing products and very clumsy. . . . The vacuum equipment was manufactured in Salt Lake City, the controls in Portland. The syringe came from Buffalo and the water heater from Ohio."

Austin's personal credo, developed while still in college, was "dream it, design it, draw it and do it"—which seemed to him to be the opposite of what most engineers did; they drew up plans and turned them over to someone else to construct. "An engineer doesn't really know the 'how to do it part'," he was quoted in the *Oregon Stater* in 2002. Austin became convinced that he could create a new simple piece of equipment designed to do the job the dentist wanted done. When his lack of tact once again led to unemployment, he went to work for Kelly Temporary Services as a temporary draftsman, and began building his first oral evacuator in his home in Broomfield, Colorado. ''I built a better version of something that was already being used,'' he was quoted in *ON-DEC*. ''Mine was smaller, less expensive and more reliable.''

By 1964, Austin had perfected a more efficient air-powered system than the industry standard and A-dec was founded. Its A.V.S. (air-vacuum system) was purchased by the S.S. White Company of Philadelphia in 1965, the nation's largest dental manufacturing company, and the Austins moved to Newberg, Oregon, where they set up business in a World War II vintage Quonset hut. Both Austins had grown up in Newberg and welcomed the chance to return to the place they still called home.

The Dec-Et followed the A.V.S. in 1965; this was the first miniature delivery unit designed specifically for the new reclining chair, the first equipment break-through of sit-down dentistry. The reclining patient chair had created the need for units for holding tools that were handier for the dentist to use from a seated position. The Dec-Et was followed by the complementary Tray-Cart, the first mobile dental assistant's work surface.

Late 1960s–70s: Growth at Home and Abroad

A-dec was incorporated in 1966 and began introducing other pieces of equipment at a very rapid pace, including an air operated amalgam condenser, a light post, a small mobile dental cart for both doctor and assistant, and preformed disposable oral evacuator tips.

Mobile dental equipment was a key to the early success of the company. ''When we started the company, no one was making mobile dental equipment,'' Joan Austin noted in the September 2002 *Oregon Stater*. Prior to meeting her husband, she worked in the insurance industry and had plans to open her own business. At A-dec, she took charge of A-dec's administrative, legal, and personnel departments, eventually becoming the company's executive vice-president and treasurer. ''Chairs and movable work tables that could be adjusted to any height and for left-handed or right-handed dentists—these were new and dentists could see the advantage,'' she recalled.

Dentists also liked A-dec because of the simplicity of its designs. If a unit broke down, a dentist could usually fix it himself. The company avoided equipment obsolescence by using standard parts and components, ensuring that the latest attachment was adaptable to an earlier produced model. When a breakdown did occur, A-dec parts were readily available because A-dec made most of its component parts itself.

By 1969, A-dec was the world's largest manufacturer of oral evacuation equipment, commanding 53 percent of the sales market. The company entered into a verbal marketing agreement with Den-Tal-Ez Manufacturing Company to market A-dec products nationally and internationally. In 1971, it began building a new plant and offices on 150 acres secured for the A-dec Technical Park. The company was also aggressively seeking overseas business with distribution in 23 countries. Domestically, it instituted a distribution plan involving regional representatives. By 1973, A-dec's sales were $7 million.

Dental schools also began to take an interest in A-dec products in the 1970s because of its use of interchangeable components. In 1970, the company developed the Student Unit, a completely portable unit in a case that students could carry to class and later install in a Denta-Cart. The company also completed its first major installation of equipment for teaching at the dental school of the University of Missouri.

The first half of the 1970s was a period of steady growth and advancement for A-dec. In 1972, the company moved into its A-dec Technical Park offices and plant, and by 1975 it occupied three buildings. As the number of its catalog items increased, A-dec discontinued its domestic marketing relationship with Den-Tal-Ez in 1974 in favor of expanding its own domestic marketing team to 16 people. As A-dec entered the second half of the 1970s with sales of $10 million, it appointed its first international territory manager to oversee the distribution of its items in upward of 20 countries, and in 1976 A-dec International began operations.

With more than 600 items in its catalog by the by 1977, A-dec built and produced more dental equipment items than its two next largest competitors combined. Beginning in 1976, with a government contract to produce Porta-Carts for the nation's armed forces, A-dec had begun producing all military dental units as well as 90 percent of all units sold to missionaries. Also that year, A-dec International assumed control of the company's international marketing, while A-dec severed its marketing ties with Den-Tal-Ez. In 1978, the company expanded again to occupy its fourth building in A-dec Park. Employees that year purchased the company's original Quonset hut, which they gave to the Austins as a Christmas present.

1980s–90s: Organizational Innovation

By the early 1980s, A-dec offered a full line of doctors' and assistants' controls, or instrument delivery systems. In subsequent years, it added chairs and stools and dental lights. A-dec entered 1980 strong, with $32 million in sales. It controlled approximately 40 percent of the domestic dental equipment market, but only about 2 percent of the international market. In 1981, the company widened its focus, forming a new division, Air Lock, to manufacture and market air-actuated security locks for commercial industrial buildings and correctional institutions. In 1983, it added a Dental Furniture division as well as DecTron equipment division. The following year, A-dec Australia began operations.

Such expansion necessitated organizational changes, which began in 1980 when A-dec adopted the new practice of ''group manufacturing technology,'' whereby manufacturing ''fami-

Key Dates:

1964: Ken and Joan Austin start A-dec in Colorado.
1965: A-dec and the Austins move to Newberg, Oregon.
1966: A-dec is incorporated.
1969: Company enters into an agreement with Den-Tal-Ez to market A-dec products nationally and internationally.
1972: A-dec moves into a new plant and offices in A-dec Technical Park.
1974: The company discontinues its domestic marketing relationship with Den-Tal-Ez.
1976: A-dec International begins operations.
1981: The company forms Air Lock, a new division.
1984: A-dec Australia begins operations.
1986: DecTron and Air Lock merge to form the A-dec Commercial Products Division.
1998: A-Dec Dental U.K. moves into new headquarters.

lies,'' or business units, assumed responsibility for developing new design ideas and ensuring the quality of equipment items. Group technology was followed by a more product-line-focused arrangement to enhance employees' sense of ownership in the production process. Instead of a common machining area to serve all product lines, product units operated on their own, with employees assuming responsibility for seeing a part through to completion. The same was instituted in assembly and other operations.

Despite staff reductions of 100 people in 1982, the company continued to expand through the mid-1980s, adding additional square footage in 1982, 1985, and 1986. By that time, A-dec was the largest dental equipment manufacturer in the nation. DecTron and Air Lock were then merged to form the A-dec Commercial Products Division, and by 1988 this division had sales of more than $1 million. In 1989, A-dec, with about $70 million in sales, exported to 66 countries and more than 200 dental supply houses in the United States and Canada. It also had direct sales to government agencies and dental schools and was the sole source of military dental field equipment for the Armed Forces. By 1990, sales were estimated at $75 million.

The 1990s were a decade of ongoing reorganization and redesign for A-dec. Production was again restructured, adopting a product-unit system that functioned much like an agglomeration of smaller, independent companies. At the same time, the company embarked on a major restyling of its products, addressing in particular the need for infection control by making equipment easier to clean. The company expanded its product line to include modestly priced chairs for sale in foreign markets

in 1996, the same year it won the American Dental Association's Distinguished Service Award. By 1997, A-dec did business in 102 countries, earning one-third of its $100 million in revenues from export sales. In 1998, A-Dec Dental U.K. moved into new headquarters.

A-dec turned its attention to streamlining production and delivery as it entered the new century. In 2001, the company purchased new software that could move from the design desk to the shop floor, in anticipation of significantly reduced production time. A-dec also began enhancing Internet sales, implementing an online tool that allowed international dealers to quote prices for customers 24 hours a day, seven days a week, thereby overcoming the obstacle of time zones.

Although the market for dental equipment had become increasingly competitive, A-dec was at the top of its field, covering more than 40 percent of the domestic dental equipment market and enjoying an extensive global network of authorized dealers and customers in more then 100 countries. The company that had helped revolutionize its industry by developing products for sit-down dentistry, now in its mature years, looked forward to a future of continued expansion in its domestic and international markets.

Principal Subsidiaries

A-dec International, A-dec Trading Company of Australia, A-dec Dental UK Ltd.

Principal Competitors

Planmeca; Royal Dental Group; Sullivan Schein Dental; Air Techniques, Inc.; JB Dental Supply Co.; Patterson Dental Supply Co.

Further Reading

''Celebrating 35 Years,'' *ON-DEC*, Special Edition 2001.
Edmonston, Jr., George P., ''Building a Better Mousetrap,'' *Oregon Stater*, September 2002.
Gutierrez, Max, ''Dental Gear Firm Flourishes,'' *Oregon Journal*, March 4, 1975, p. C5.
Johnson, Angela, ''Success With One's Self,'' *Oregon Business*, January 1989, p. 34.
Khermouch, Gerry, ''A-dec Finds Success in Thinking Small; Dental Equipment Producer is Being Run Like Family Shop,'' *Metalworking News*, March 19, 1990, p. 4.
Magmer, James, ''Newberg Dental Equipment Plant Grows,'' *Oregonian*, June 27, 1972, p. I15.
Olmos, Bob, ''They Must Be Doing Something Right Down in Newberg,'' *Oregonian*, July 6, 1980, p. E2.

—Carrie Rothburd

Adventist Health

Adventist Health

Adventist Health

2100 Douglas Boulevard
Roseville, California 95661-9002
U.S.A.
Telephone: (916) 781-2000
Fax: (916) 783-9909
Web site: http://www.adventisthealth.org

Not-for-Profit Corporation
Incorporated: 1980 as Adventist Health System/West
Employees: 16,500
Sales: $2.87 billion (2001)
NAIC: 622100 General Medical and Surgical Hospitals

Adventist Health is a non-profit healthcare system affiliated with the Seventh-Day Adventist Church and part of an international network of 160 Adventist facilities. The organization's headquarters is located in Roseville, California, where Adventist Health has no facilities, the site chosen because it provided a central location for most of the system's 15 California hospital. All told, Adventist Health controls, manages, or leases 20 acute-care hospitals, totaling more than 3,200 beds, located in the states of California, Hawaii, Oregon, and Washington. In addition, the organization operates Adventist Health/Home Care Services, four hospices, nine personal care agencies, six home medical equipment agencies, and five home infusion therapy services. Despite the financial difficulties facing hospitals in recent years, Adventist Health has been able to succeed as a niche player, concentrating on smaller hospitals in single-hospital markets. It also has a solid reputation for providing consistent services and adhering to the mission laid out by the Adventist Church.

Seventh-Day Adventist Movement Established in 1800s

The Seventh-Day Adventist Church grew out of the efforts of Baptist preacher William Miller, a former military man who in the 1830s was instrumental in an evangelical wave known as the "great second advent awakening." According to Miller's reading of biblical prophecy, Jesus would return sometime during 1843 or 1844. His followers soon pinned down the Second Coming to October 22, 1844, a date which ultimately became known as the "Great Disappointment" when Jesus failed to appear. The movement quickly dwindled to just a handful of followers, among them a 17-year-old girl named Ellen Harmon who helped reinvigorate the Adventists when she experienced a vision of its people traveling to the city of God. She married an Adventist preacher named James White and the couple became instrumental in the growth of the church. As Ellen G. White, she also became an author, publishing her first book in 1851. In 1860, several Adventist congregations assumed the name Seventh-Day Adventist and formally organized a church in 1863. During that same year, White had another vision, this one emphasizing the connection between physical health and spirituality and the importance of proper diet, exercise, and natural remedies. Health, which had never been an Adventist concern, now became a focal point.

At the behest of White, in 1866 the church established the Western Health Reform Institute in Battle Creek, Michigan, to care for the sick as well as disseminate health instruction. At first it was little more than an eight-room clinic. Renamed the Battle Creek Sanitarium in 1877, when it was under the direction of Dr. John Harvey Kellogg, it would become as famous as some of its wealthy clientele, which included the likes of J.C. Penney, Henry Ford, Thomas Edison, Amelia Earhart, William Jennings Bryan, Dale Carnegie, and John D. Rockefeller. Kellogg had moved to Battle Creek at the age of four and was raised in a Seventh-Day Adventist family. White and her husband recognized that Kellogg held great potential and groomed him from an early age to take over the institute. They helped to finance his education at New York's Bellevue Medical College, from which he graduated in 1875. Kellogg then became medical superintendent of the Institute and quickly put his stamp on the operation, changing its emphasis from hydrotherapy to medical and surgical treatment. He also coined the word "sanitarium" and formulated what he called was the "Battle Creek Idea," an emphasis on good diet, exercise, proper rest, good posture, and the value of fresh air. Kellogg was not paid for his work at the Sanitarium, earning his income from the royalties of some 50 books he authored in his lifetime. He also made money from the manufacture of breakfast cereal following the discovery of a

Company Perspectives:

Adventist Health is a family of caring people reaching out to those in need. We follow Christ's example of servanthood, as we promote physical, mental, and spiritual health and healing. Through creative partnerships, we enhance the quality of life of the communities we serve.

way to make crispy wheat and corn flakes. Acting as his right-hand man in building the sanitarium and the cereal business for more than 20 years was his disgruntled brother, Will Keith Kellogg, who patiently bought up shares of the institute's corn flake business until he gained control. He then broke from his brother and in the early 1900s applied the Kellogg's name to the cereal, creating one of the world's most recognizable trademarks as well as a successful international company. While the Kellogg Company prospered throughout the twentieth century, the Battle Creek Sanitarium reached its high water mark in the 1920s. After the stock market crash of 1929, many of the sanitarium's clientele could no longer afford their annual pilgrimage, and the fortunes of the institution began to fade. In 1942, the main building was sold to the federal government, and a year later, at the age of 91, John Kellogg died.

Adventist Health Forms from 1980 Merger

The popularity of the Battle Creek Sanitarium in the 1800s led to the foundation of other Adventist sanitariums around the country, which numbered 27 by the turn of the century. Over the next 50 years, the sanitariums evolved into hospitals, forming the backbone of the Adventists' medical network. The medical headquarters of the church also moved from Battle Creek to Loma Linda, California, site of another sanitarium founded by Ellen White. In the 1960s, ownership of the hospitals was transferred to local Adventist organizations known as conferences. In 1972, the church decided to centralize the management of its healthcare institutions on a regional basis, forming Adventist Health Systems. Conferences ceded control to the system, forming several entities at the union (multi-state) level, based on the way the church itself was organized. In the North Pacific Union of the Adventist Church, Northwest Medical Foundation was established, and in the Pacific Union region Adventist Health Services was created. The Western divisions merged in 1980 to create Adventist Health System/West (which in 1995 shortened its name to Adventist Health). Originally the headquarters for Adventist Health was located in Los Angeles, close to some of the division's largest institutions. Wary that small facilities might be neglected, management moved its operations in 1982 to more centrally located Roseville, California, a city where Adventist Health had no healthcare presence at all. In 1985, a headquarters was built in Roseville to provide financial management for system hospitals and perform other administrative functions.

In 1982, the regional operations formed a national organization, Adventist Health System/U.S., which management called the largest not-for-profit, multi-institutional healthcare system in the United States. The purpose of consolidation was to achieve economies of scale, but it soon became apparent that AHS/US

also brought with it the problem of ascending liability for the church. Bankruptcy of any division in AHS/US, or a lawsuit, held the potential of putting all of the church's assets at risk. Legal counsel for the church convinced its leadership that ascending liability made it imperative that the consolidated healthcare organization be dissolved. A system reorganization was completed in 1991, and regional divisions began operating on their own.

In 1990, Adventist Health was sued by the Arizona conference of the Seventh-Day Adventist Church in connection with a long-term dispute over Tempe Community Hospital. The suit alleged that Adventist Health had been hired to manage the facility but improperly took control, sold the hospital, and kept all the proceeds. Moreover, Adventist Health was accused of continuing to charge the conference $15,000 per month for management fees for more than seven years after the sale of Tempe Community. When the matter was finally resolved in 1994, the courts ruled in favor of Adventist Health. This litigation, as well as other law suits with AHS divisions, was an indication of an ongoing rift between the church and the healthcare institutions it had founded. Increasingly, AHS entities began to operate like any other hospital organizations, although continuing to maintain an affiliation with the church. More outspoken Adventist church members, however, expressed a sense of betrayal, maintaining that the church's medical work had been intended as an instrument for spreading the church's beliefs. According to these dissidents, AHS operations were now in business simply to stay in business, as well as to lavishly reward the executives who ran them.

Whether or not the criticism was valid, Adventist Health took steps to grow its operations in the manner of a secular enterprise. In 1988, it acquired Ukiah General Hospital, in California's Mendocino County, for $5.9 million. Already operating Ukiah Adventist Hospital as well as another facility in nearby Willits, Adventist Health came under scrutiny by the Federal Trade Commission (FTC), which was concerned that the organization had violated antitrust laws governing nonprofit companies because it now controlled 17 percent of the Ukiah healthcare market. The matter took five years to resolve, and in the end the FTC decided that there was insufficient evidence that the acquisition of Ukiah General had harmed area consumers. This conclusion had national ramifications, opening the door for more hospital mergers and acquisitions. With the advent of managed care, which greatly reduced inpatient revenues, many smaller-market hospitals, by necessity, sought out partners like Adventist Health.

Strategies for Prosperity in the Mid-1990s and Beyond

In the mid-1990s, Adventist Health ran 18 hospitals with 2,800 beds, 18 home health agencies, four hospices, and eight home care services, in addition to various clinics, outpatient facilities, and medical foundations. Eleven of its hospitals were located in California, with another four in Oregon and single facilities in Washington, Utah, and Hawaii. Adventist Health was older and more stable than most healthcare operations in the West, but it too was forced to contend with the rise of managed healthcare organizations that paid fixed rates for care. In 1994, Adventist Health established a managed care contracting enterprise, Pacific Integrated Healthcare, in order to help

---

Key Dates:

1863: Seventh-Day Adventist Church is organized.
1866: Western Health Reform Institute, later known as the Battle Creek Sanitarium, opens.
1972: Adventist Health Systems is formed.
1980: The merger of two AHS divisions results in Adventist Health System/West.
1982: AHS/West moves its headquarters to Roseville, California.
1991: The national organization is dissolved.
1999: Donald Ammon becomes president of Adventist Health.

---

member Southern California institutions negotiate better rates in a prepaid healthcare environment. Adventist Health also took part in a similar initiative for Fresno-based Community Hospitals of Central California, called Center California Health Partners, which in turn was linked to the California Health Network, consisting of 81 hospitals and 50 physicians' organizations. While other area healthcare organizations were losing money, in 1994 Adventist Health reported net revenues of $916 million and net income of $90.2 million. Results fell off somewhat over the next two years, but the organization remained relatively healthy. Nonetheless, it was forced to close its Utah facility, Monument Valley Hospital, in 1996.

In the mid-1990s, Adventist Health began to focus on strengthening its position in California's Central Valley region. A long-term effort to acquire the 156-bed Delano Regional Medical Center was dropped in 1997, but the organization was successful elsewhere. In April of that year, it assumed management of the 57-bed Selma District Hospital in Fresno County and immediately began working with the board of directors to acquire the 35-year-old institution. The deal was not completed until two years later, following approval from area voters in a special election held in June 1999. In the end, Adventist Health agreed to assume the hospital's outstanding liabilities of $4 million in addition to a 1984 $4.2 million bond taken out for expansion. Adventist Health further solidified its presence in the Central Valley area with the acquisition of Clearlake's 32-bed Redbud Community Hospital and 49-bed Central Valley General Hospital, located in the town of Hanford. In the era of managed care, these facilities were forced to find a larger partner in order to simply survive and continue providing healthcare in their rural communities. While often serving as a savior of such institutions, Adventist Health was not immune to financial pressures. In 1998, it was forced to institute some cost-cutting measures, including the closure of two skilled nursing units and cutbacks in its home care program. It was also forced to cancel some HMO contracts and renegotiate others. Adventist Health posted net income of $20.5 million in 1998, the result of $25 million in investment income, so that the organization actually suffered a $4.5 million operating loss for the year.

Adventist Health also faced a change in leadership in 1998 when its president, Frank Dupper, announced his retirement. The board decided to look within the ranks of the organization for a replacement and quickly settled on Donald Ammon, who had been an executive vice-president with Adventist Health for 18 years and whose experience in the healthcare field dated back to 1964. Moreover, Ammon and his wife were lifelong members of the Seventh-Day Adventist Church. He assumed his new position on January 1, 1999, and faced a challenging healthcare industry environment at the close of the century. Recognizing that regional delivery systems and medical foundations that had worked well in the 1990s were no longer efficient, Ammon scrapped them and returned to a more centralized approach that resulted in significant savings. While keeping an eye on costs, he also initiated building efforts throughout the system, providing enhanced earthquake safety at many facilities, and also looked to add more private rooms and deliver expanded services. Although a solid enterprise, Adventist Health faced an uncertain future, especially in light of Medicaid cuts and state budget deficits that were likely to have an adverse impact on revenues. The organization would have to remain vigilant about costs and enhancing income, while at the same time attempting not to lose sight of the century-old mission of the Seventh-Day Adventist Church.

Principal Competitors

Catholic Healthcare West; Tenet Healthcare.

Further Reading

Carlson, Eugene, "American Entrepreneurs: For the Kellogg Boys, No Brotherly Love Lost," *Wall Street Journal,* April 4, 1989, p. 1.
Davis, Kurt, "Roseville Hospital Firm Fights the FTC," *Business Journal Serving Greater Sacramento,* January 1, 1990, p. 1.
Robertson, Kathy, "Adventist Health Altering $926 Million Empire," *Business Journal Serving Greater Sacramento,* August 28, 1995, p. S15.
——, "Adventist Health Grows Big While Keeping a Low Profile," *Business Journal Serving Greater Sacramento,* February 6, 1998.
——, "Adventist Health Reaches into the Valley," *Business Journal Serving Greater Sacramento,* May 20, 1996, p. 5.

—Ed Dinger

Advo, Inc.

One Univac Lane
Windsor, Connecticut 06095-2668
U.S.A.
Telephone: (860) 285-6100
Fax: (860) 285-6393
Web site: http://www.advo.com

Public Company
Incorporated: 1929
Employees: 4,700
Sales: $1.14 billion (2001)
Stock Exchanges: New York
Ticker Symbol: AD
NAIC: 541860 Direct Mail Advertising

Advo, Inc., is America's largest direct mail marketer, dispatching 16 million pieces of advertising to American homes every week. With an address list of over 126 million, comprising virtually every household in the United States, the company can deliver materials to a huge array of consumers. Advo deploys advertising in bundled packets of coupons or circulars for many different retailers. This saves money for Advo clients, who can share the cost of mailing. Advo does most of its own sorting and processing of its mail. It counts itself the nation's largest private client of the United States Postal Service. The company has 22 production facilities for printing and processing its advertising circulars, and it maintains 65 sales offices in the United States. Advo sells its services to many of the country's largest retailers, restaurants, and grocery chains. Its clients include Kmart, J.C. Penney, Wal Mart, McDonald's, Pizza Hut, CVS pharmacy, the grocery chains Safeway and Acme, and many others. Advo also provides on-line advertising through its ShopWise.com web site. The company's MailCoups, Inc. subsidiary produces advertising for small neighborhood businesses. Advo is also known for operating a missing children program. Its widely distributed pictures of missing children have led to the recovery of over 100 children since the program's inception in 1985.

Growth from the 1920s to the Mid-1970s

Advo was founded in 1929 by Paul Siegel, who offered a private service delivering printed advertising fliers by hand for retail stores in the Hartford, Connecticut, area. The privately owned company limited its activities to this modest field until 1946, when Advo switched from hand delivery to delivery by mail. The company sent out materials for Hartford's insurance companies, and also dispatched individual pieces of advertising for retail stores to selected households, a practice known as ''solo mail.''

By the mid-1970s, Advo had changed hands twice since 1969 and had expanded the scope of its operations beyond the Northeast, opening additional plants in Atlanta and Miami. The company's annual sales had reached $7 million, on which it was losing $1 million a year. In 1976, the company's latest set of owners, a group of companies headed by the Travelers Insurance Company, sold the company to two partners, Jack A. Valentine and Robert Stucki. Although Stucki, a Minneapolis real estate developer, acted simply as an investor, Valentine's professional background was in the direct mail business, and he set out to revamp Advo's operations.

New Owners in the Late 1970s and 1980s

Valentine's first move was to expand Advo's base of operations from just three areas to over six, opening facilities in Chicago, Dallas, and selected locations on the West Coast. In this way, Advo hoped to reap higher profits through higher volume on its fixed expenses. Within a year, however, the company had run out of money, and its precarious financial situation made borrowing from a bank impossible. To raise funds, Valentine sold one-third of the company to the Allstate Insurance Venture Capital Group, a subsidiary of Sears, Roebuck & Company.

Advo had a new lease on life, but it was shortly to face an even greater peril, when the United States Postal Service raised its third class bulk mailing rate, dramatically increasing Advo's costs. With postage exceeding $50 for 1,000 pieces of mail, mailers could no longer afford to deliver an individual advertisement to a household for less money than a newspaper charged to

Company Perspectives:

We're a company you already know! ADVO is ... the nation's largest full-service targeted direct mail marketing services company ... the company behind the ShopWise brand and the Missing Child Program ... the single largest private customer of the United States Postal Service ... known for serving and satisfying over 23,000 clients each year ... the distributor of the most successful and most visible "shared mail" advertising program in the country.

fold the advertisement into its publication and deliver it along with the paper. The effect on Advo's business was "catastrophic," Valentine later told *Advertising Age*. "Our volume fell right off the table, and the newspapers owned virtually 100 percent of the market. The only mail we were left with was in small-town, rural America, where there was no alternative."

Convinced that "solo mail ... was dead," as Valentine further recounted, Advo began to experiment with various forms of joint mailings. The company tried a "shopper" packet and failed. Next, it offered something called the "Value Parade," with four pages of ads wrapped around retail fliers. This, too, failed. Then it set up a co-op program, in which two merchants committed to advertising together on the same day in the same market, but store owners chafed under the lack of flexibility, and this also failed.

Finally, Advo was contacted by the owner of a small Los Angeles direct mail firm who was trying to sell his company, Marriage Mailers. The company was losing money on its shared mail operations, in which advertisers were guaranteed a certain rate to place materials in the company's package, regardless of the number of advertisers joining any given effort. Since the company covered only one market, it frequently found that it had too few customers signed up for a mailing, which nevertheless went out, with the company taking a loss. "It gave the company a flat rate to deal with, and they could then make commitments," Valentine explained to *Advertising Age*. "In effect, what he was doing was creating a publication without a cover." The idea later began to work because it allowed direct mailers to exploit a change in the bulk-mailing regulations, which had gone into effect in 1979. The new rules stipulated that mail would be priced by weight, rather than by the number of pieces it contained. In this way, a company could put together a package of fliers for different merchants that would cost only 7.4 cents to mail, as long as it weighed less than 3.9 ounces.

Advo purchased Marriage Mailers and combined its guaranteed rate pricing plan with the company's existing practice of wrapped packaging. The company signed on several large stores in Los Angeles and within 18 months began to expand to other markets, competing with newspaper delivery systems by offering more complete coverage in a given area. Although newspapers got advertising only to homes that subscribed to the paper, Advo's mailing lists, compiled with the assistance of postal service route carriers, covered every address in a zone.

With this new program, Advo first turned a profit in 1980, when the company was given a large boost by the United States Census Bureau, which purchased its near-inclusive list of American households. This success launched Advo on a rapid expansion, and the company doubled its sales every year for the next several years. In 1981, the company launched Advo Publications, Inc., a company operating independently of the direct mail operations, whose purpose was to create a national chain of free newspapers that would carry advertising. In addition, the company endeavored to build a nationwide network of printing businesses. The company bought the Western Offset Publishing in San Diego, and also purchased two presses to be installed in a facility in Columbia, Maryland, near Washington, D.C. Advo also took over *Grit*, a weekly newspaper designed to get advertisements into rural areas that had long been unprofitable.

This expansion was not without its costs, however. In addition to the start-up expenses of the company's new ventures, maintaining Advo's essential database of addresses siphoned off capital, as did the ever-present search for new clients, who, once found, proved slow to sign on. By the end of 1982, Valentine had grown weary of the constant fund-raising necessary to keep Advo afloat. "The more we borrowed, the more we needed," he told *Advertising Age*. In that year, outsiders estimated that Advo lost $5 million, despite its growing sales.

By early 1983, Advo's efforts had earned it 12,500 retail clients, including Sears, Roebuck & Company, Kmart, and the Kroger grocery store chain. The company's mailing list, arranged in "carrier-route" sequence for easy delivery by the post office, contained 83 million residences, making up 97 percent of the households in America. Advo operated 14 distribution centers, sending out shared mail packages to 60 different markets. Through its aggressive spending, Advo had expanded to become the country's largest commercial bulk mail distributor.

In June 1983, Advo put these resources to use in a partnership with John Blair Marketing, a division of the New York-based John Blair & Company, a marketing firm that was the country's largest distributor of national brand coupons. The joint venture, in which Blair provided a four-to-eight-page spread of coupons to wrap around Advo's promotional circulars, was called Network Mail. The program was designed to reach 40 million customers and draw them into stores with its combination of coupons and promotions.

Despite its gains in revenue, which doubled again in 1983, Advo had trouble becoming profitable. The company's attempt to start up several free-circulation newspapers had failed, and it also lost money on *Grit*. Armed with the Blair partnership, as well as regional contracts to deliver advertising circulars throughout several states, Advo went head-to-head with the newspaper industry in an effort to gain a third of the $2.5 billion a year business of distributing promotional materials. The company won a decisive battle in this war in September 1983, when it announced that it had won a contract with the Kmart Corporation, a major user of newspaper distribution facilities, to deliver 10 million promotional fliers each week in a four-state area of the Midwest. The retailer cited Advo's more complete coverage of the area involved in explaining its switch to direct mail.

At this time Valentine and his two co-owners announced that they had decided to sell Advo to their Network Mail partners, John Blair & Company, for $40 million, and the sale was finalized in March 1984. Valentine stayed on as the company's president and also became Blair's senior vice-president in charge of marketing services and coupon operations.

With the resources of the Blair operation, Advo continued its rapid expansion, installing its fourth major new computer system in three years, at a cost of $16 million, adding six new handling and distribution centers and augmenting its sales force by 350 people and more than 12 new offices. At the end of 1984, Blair posted a decline in earnings, reflecting the high costs of its Advo acquisition and expansion. Advo itself posted losses of $20 million at the end of the year.

In February 1985, as Blair continued to pour money into Advo, Valentine resigned. By the end of that year Blair had sunk $150 million into its subsidiary, expanding its reach into 238 different markets. Despite this growth, however, Advo continued to have problems. Confused by the similarity of Blair's free-standing inserts of coupons in newspapers and its coupon wrappers for Advo's Network Mail, clients for both services withered away. In an effort to woo them back, Advo introduced Coupon Feature Plus, designed to combine direct mailing with trade advertising. Beset by poor management and little control over spending, the company racked up another $30 million in losses. "Under Blair, the company grew out of control," one analyst told *New England Business* magazine. "They tried to grow too fast and bled Blair to death."

Reorganization in the Late 1980s

Weakened by its experiment with Advo, Blair became the object of a hostile takeover by McFadden Publishing in 1985. McFadden proposed to justify its investment by disposing of Advo at a fire-sale price: $100,000. Rather than effectively close the company down, Blair sold Advo to a group of investors led by the investment house Warburg, Pincus & Company, which purchased 28 percent of the company for $11 million and sold the rest of its stock to Blair shareholders.

In its new incarnation, the company was run by former Blair executive Hugh R. Beath, who became Advo's chief executive officer. Under its new management, Advo was reorganized. The company abandoned its quest for growth, withdrawing from markets in which it failed to make money, and focused instead on profitability. In addition, the company took steps to cut its costs, thereby stabilizing its bottom line.

Advo aggressively sought new clients, inaugurating marketing efforts designed to attract national advertisers and ad agen-

cies. The company built on its strengths of market saturation and selectivity to offer joint national and local campaigns to potential clients such as McDonald's and General Electric, with national rebates or coupons linked to customized promotions for local franchises or dealers. With its ZIP code indexes, Advo was able to key its mailings to the areas surrounding local businesses.

In its continuing battle with the newspaper industry, Advo filed an anti-trust suit against the *New York Times*, charging that the company used economic leverage to infringe on Advo's attempts to do business. In addition, the company charged that the American Newspaper Publishers Association had used undue influence in arranging for anti-junk mail editorials to be run when deliberations over third class mail rates, which had a major impact on the viability of Advo's operations, were taking place within the U.S. Postal Service. Despite all its efforts at change, Advo continued to lose money in 1986, posting losses of $47.8 million. By 1987, however, its first full year as a publicly held company, Advo's sales of $520.5 million allowed it to move into the black, notching profits of $9.6 million.

In the following year, Advo suffered the implementation of higher third class mailing rates, which upped the company's postage costs by 26 percent. In addition, the company received a second blow when Kmart announced that it would stop sending advertising circulars through Advo's distribution channels, concentrating on television advertising instead. With the loss of this large account, Advo racked up about $600 million in sales, but its earnings suffered. By 1989, however, Advo had regained its profitable status, and the company posted earnings of $5.3 million.

In the early 1990s, Advo continued to increase its net income, despite a general recession in the American economy and an associated cutback by most advertisers. The company's earning power was curtailed again in 1991, however, when a 40 percent hike in third class postage rates took effect in February. To lessen the impact of this, the company developed a "drop-ship" system, using more than 700 rented trucks to deliver its mailings to the appropriate U.S. Post Office mail facilities. This practice allowed Advo to qualify for discounted mailings.

In addition to its shared mailings of promotional fliers, Advo also introduced several more elaborate direct mail initiatives in an effort to retain its market share. The company began producing *Savers*, a magazine-like publication of advertisements. *Savers* had an artistic cover and a calendar of upcoming local events, a feature designed to encourage consumers to keep it around the house for handy reference. In addition, Advo launched *Celebrando*, a publication geared to the Hispanic population, and *International Style Report*, a fashion magazine and catalogue.

Advo also developed a strategic plan to broaden its activities, moving into the developing field of micromarketing, which identified discrete parts of the market and then targeted them for specialized, and presumably more effective, advertising efforts. Convinced that micromarketing represented the wave of the future in the advertising field, Advo hoped to reposition itself as a growth company that dominated this special niche of the advertising market. The company foresaw a movement from saturation marketing, in which it blanketed every household in the country with a given mailing, to segmented marketing, in which only certain neighborhoods, selected by ZIP code, received a certain advertisement, and afterward to even more highly targeted efforts in which specific households were chosen to receive a mailing.

To achieve this goal, Advo formed a number of alliances with other firms in its field. In late 1990, the company bought the majority of RM Marketing, a Los Angeles-based marketing concern that created customized publications to carry the advertising of supermarkets and other retailers.

In addition, Advo moved to tap the potential of one of its greatest assets, its mailing list of virtually every household in the United States. The company formed Decision Base Resources, a joint venture with worldwide advertising giant Young & Rubicam to sell marketing databases. Advo also entered into an agreement with a company called Acxiom to form Infobase Services. The goal of this joint venture was to develop name-specific lists, with data on behavioral characteristics, lifestyle, and the demographic nature of a large segment of the population. This represented a significant augmentation of Advo's name-blind address files.

In the same vein, Advo formed a strategic alliance with VNU/Claritas, a marketing research company that had developed a series of demographic, psychographic, and product-oriented profiles of the American populace arranged according to ZIP codes. Claritas classified areas into 40 different consumer "clusters," giving them names such as "Blue Blood Estates," "God's Country," and "Pools & Patios." With this information, designed to tell advertisers which products residents might want to buy, marketers could attempt to target their appeals to the most receptive audience.

Along with these futuristic advances, Advo reverted to its earliest incarnation when it formed Door-to-Door, a hand-delivery service that operated in three small Michigan cities. The company was a joint venture with Alternate Postal Delivery, which Advo undertook as an experiment, to explore possible alternatives to delivery by the U.S. Postal Service should third-class mail become prohibitively expensive. In this way, the company also hoped to mollify investors who felt that Advo's future prosperity was a hostage to postal rates, a factor largely beyond the company's control. In April 1991, Advo moved in on its newspaper competitors when it bought the Chicago Sun-Times Distribution Systems.

Turning the Corner in the 1990s

Advo had been led since 1988 by Robert Kamerschen, who had been hired by Warburg Pincus for his skill in turning around failing companies. By the early 1990s, Kamerschen had succeeded in bringing the company's profit margin up, principally by introducing automation that cut costs. By 1993, Advo had revenues of around $845 million, and it had managed to quadruple its profits, which sent its share price way up. Direct mail was a fast-growing industry, as many clients shifted from other types of advertising. Growth had been particularly strong in the 1980s, at about 12 percent a year, and was predicted to continue at roughly 4 percent a year in the 1990s, setting up Advo comfortably. The company also emphasized its ability to focus

on smaller niches in the marketplace. It had begun compiling more targeted consumer data in the late 1980s. By the mid-1990s, Advo's database included information on consumers' lifestyle choices, such as what kind of cars they preferred and what their favorite sports were. Advo hooked clients with claims that this more precise information gave a higher probability of success for its advertising. Advo also reached out to companies in new industries. In 1990, almost all of Advo's clients were retailers. But by the mid-1990s, 10 to 15 percent of the company's clients were in other categories, such as financial services, telecommunications, and entertainment.

Advo stepped up its competition with newspapers in the mid-1990s, only to enter into cooperative agreements with them in some cities by the end of the decade. The company filed suit in Philadelphia in 1993, claiming that the *Philadelphia Inquirer* and the *Philadelphia Daily News* were trying to monopolize the market for advertising circulars and that the papers offered clients free or deeply discounted advertising in order to cut Advo out. The case was dismissed in 1994, and Advo lost again on appeal in 1995.

The Philadelphia newspapers were owned by Knight-Ridder, and Advo particularly objected to the papers' tactics because they were distributing circulars not only to subscribers but to non-subscribers as well. Despite the outcome of the suit, the Philadelphia papers eventually stopped trying to reach non-subscribers, finding it too difficult and expensive. Then, in 1997, Advo made an arrangement with Knight-Ridder's St. Paul, Minnesota, newspaper the *Pioneer Press* to work jointly to distribute advertising circulars in the city. With Advo reaching non-subscribers and the *Pioneer Press* distributing to its readers through its Sunday paper, the two blanketed St. Paul with ads, achieving what in advertising parlance was known as TMC—Total Market Coverage. This development seemed to bring an end to the bitter competition between Advo and newspapers. Advo subsequently entered into similar arrangements with newspapers in other cities, aiming for TMC in Denver with the *Denver Post* in 2000 and in Detroit with Gannett News's *Detroit Free Press* in 2001.

A new force that emerged at Advo during the mid-1990s was Gary Mulloy, who became president and chief operating officer in 1996 and soon succeeded to chairman and chief executive officer. Mulloy continued to tout the company's database capabilities. By the late 1990s, Advo was sorting its mailings, at least in some areas, by so-called targeting zones instead of by zipcode, grouping thousands of households by shopping patterns and demographics. In 2000, Advo began to advertise for itself for the first time ever, promoting its ShopWise mailer in a nationwide television campaign. The company hoped to build a brand image for ShopWise, and the campaign emphasized how much a family could save using the ShopWise coupons. Advo's weekly mailing reached 60 million households a week by 2000, and the company counted 24,000 clients.

Both revenue and net income grew appreciably for the five years ending in 2001. Sales for 2001 were at an all-time high of $1.14 billion. Then the U.S. economy began to falter, and advertising was one of the industry's hit first and hardest. Yet Advo's revenue held relatively steady, and in some areas the company gained market share, where newspapers and other media lost ground. Advo planned to continue its new policy of cooperation with its former competitors, newspapers, which was a promising source of growth. Advo also worked to keep costs reined in as it weathered the recession.

Principal Subsidiaries

ShopWise.com Inc.; Advo Investment Co. Inc.; Mail Coups, Inc.; Mail Marketing Systems Inc.

Principal Competitors

ACG Holdings, Inc.; Harte-Hanks, Inc.; Valassis Retail Marketing Systems; Vertis Inc.

Further Reading

"Advo Pitches ShopWise with National TV Effort," *Advertising Age*, August 21, 2000, p. 12.

"Appeals Court Upholds Dismissal of Advo Lawsuit," *Editor & Publisher*, June 3, 1995, p. 31.

Beeler, Amanda, "Advo Lures Dot-Coms to Realm of Direct Mail," *Advertising Age*, May 8, 2000, p. 76.

——, "Denver Dailies Fight for Insert Lead; Advo Partners with 'Post' for Total Market Coverage," *Advertising Age*, May 8, 2000, p. S20.

Brownlee, Lisa, "Advo Hopes to Increase Its Earnings by Broadening Direct-Mail Client List," *Wall Street Journal*, February 14, 1997, p. A9A.

——, "Two Combatants in Battle for Ads Cooperate in Direct-Mail Effort," *Wall Street Journal*, February 27, 1997, p. B9.

Colford, Steven W., "Ad Circular Row Flares," *Advertising Age*, October 31, 1994, p. 35.

Edwards, Paul L., "Blair Ducks FSI Confusion," *Advertising Age*, April 7, 1986.

Gloede, William, "Blair Now Shares Success of Advo," *Advertising Age*, August 9, 1984.

Jervey, Gay, "Blair, Advo to Debut 'Network Mail' Plan," *Advertising Age*, May 16, 1983.

Jones, Alex S., "Competition in Ad Circulars," *New York Times*, November 24, 1983.

McGurrin, Lisa, "A Nemesis to Newspapers, Advo Pulls in First Rate Revenues via Third-Class Mail," *New England Business*, May 2, 1988.

Oliver, Suzanne L., "You've No Place to Hide," *Forbes*, April 29, 1991, p. 88.

Radolf, Andrew, "Direct Mail Firm Seeks Marriage to Newspapers," *Editor & Publisher*, August 14, 1982.

Stark, Ellen, "This Junk Mailer Has First-Class Profits," *Money*, April 1993, p. 76.

Welles, Chris, "What's Free, Full of Ads, and Read All Over," *Business Week*, November 2, 1987.

—Elizabeth Rourke
—update: A. Woodward

AES Corporation

1001 North 19th Street
Arlington, Virginia 22209
U.S.A.
Telephone: (703) 522-1315
Fax: (703) 528-4510
Web site: http://www.aesc.com

Public Company
Incorporated: 1981 as Applied Energy Sources
Employees: 38,000
Sales: $9.3 billion (2001)
Stock Exchanges: New York
Ticker Symbol: AES
NAIC: 221122 Electric Power Distribution; 221121
 Electric Bulk Power Transmission and Control;
 221111 Hydroelectric Power Generation; 221112
 Fossil Fuel Electric Power Generation; 221119 Other
 Electric Power Generation

AES Corporation is one of the largest independent producers of electrical power in the world, with an ownership stake in 177 facilities in Argentina, Australia, Bangladesh, Brazil, Canada, China, the Dominican Republic, El Salvador, Hungary, India, Kazakhstan, the Netherlands, Mexico, Pakistan, Panama, the United Kingdom, Venezuela, and the United States. The company supplies more than 59 gigawatts of electricity worldwide to 16 million customers through its electricity distribution network. The company's operations are grouped into four major business segments: Contract Generation; Competitive Supply; Large Utilities; and Growth Distribution. AES experienced remarkable growth during the 1990s and into 2000, with assets growing from $11 billion in 1997 to $37 billion in 2001. Due to an economic slowdown and volatile overseas markets, AES began a major restructuring effort in 2002 that included the sale of certain assets.

The Development of PURPA: Late 1970s

AES was the invention of Roger W. Sant and Dennis W. Bakke, who had served together in the Federal Energy Adminis-

tration (FEA) during the Nixon and Ford administrations in the early to mid-1970s. Sant had been a lecturer at the Stanford School of Business; Bakke, a Harvard MBA and career government employee, was his assistant. As part of their work at the FEA, the two had been instrumental in drafting preliminary versions of the Public Utility Regulatory Policies Act (PURPA).

The law was part of the federal government's attempt to deal with America's energy crisis, which, according to prevailing opinion at the time, was caused largely by American dependence on foreign oil. Seeking to reduce this dependence, PURPA mandated that electrical utilities fulfill any need they might have for new power by seeking out qualified cogenerators and independent, small-scale, private-sector power producers. The law further stipulated that the cost of power provided by these facilities be less than a utility's "avoided cost"—that is, the cost incurred by the utility if it generated the power itself.

Prior to PURPA, by contrast, utilities typically secured additional power by building a new power-generating facility, which was usually oil dependent. Otherwise they purchased new power on the open market from yet another oil-dependent utility. PURPA, however, changed that, since it effectively required utilities to fulfill their energy needs by turning instead to cogenerators and other oil-independent power producers.

PURPA was enacted into law in 1978—four years after Sant and Bakke had left the government to found an energy research institute, or "think tank," at Carnegie Mellon University. That was also the year in which President Carter declared America's energy crisis to be the "moral equivalent of war," as Americans experienced oil and gas shortages, long lines at the gas pumps, and fear of what the crisis portended for its future. Because of their formative work experience in government at the height of this crisis and their subsequent related work experience in academe, Sant and Bakke were well familiar with the contours of this problem—and familiar as well with the rapidly emerging business opportunities spawned by the new law.

What Sant and Bakke were quick to realize—and, at the time, were virtually alone in recognizing—was that PURPA had the paved the way for a burgeoning market in independent, private-sector power production. In part this was because of the new law's mandate that outside purchases of power be made from cogenerators and independent, small-scale, private-sector power producers. It also stemmed, however, from the fact that PURPA shielded new producers from costly state government regulation and subjected them instead to less onerous federal rules and strictures. In practice, this meant that new producers typically could undercut a utility's "avoided cost."

Applied Energy Sources Is Established: 1981

AES was founded in 1981 as Applied Energy Sources, and it took several years for Sant and Bakke to taste real success. The novelty of their idea and the untested nature of the market in which they sought to do business made it difficult to attract capital financing. Investors were understandably wary and skeptical of the firm's chances for success. One year's worth of effort netted the firm only $1.1 million in venture capital—a inadequate sum on which to build an electric power company. "From 1981 to 1985," reported the *Washington Post,* "one potential project participant after another—including ARCO, IBM, Bechtel Corp. and other large companies—marched in and then backed out of agreements with tiny AES."

The firm's luck took a turn for the better in 1985, when Sant and Bakke invested all of AES's assets in a single deal: a Beaver Valley, Pennsylvania, coal-burning plant. The deal was closed in September 1985 and the plant commenced production in 1987, marking a turning point for the company, which would never again have to depend upon the success of a single project for its very survival.

By then, in fact, AES had two plants up and running: its Beaver Valley facility supplied 125 megawatts of electricity to residents and commercial outfits in the Pittsburgh area; its Deepwater, Texas, power plant, which, fueled by petroleum coke, went on line in June 1986, supplied 143 megawatts of electricity to homeowners and businesses in the Houston area. Financial arrangements for Deepwater had been completed on December 30, 1983, and, in addition to AES, involved 12 other companies: ARCO, Bechtel, J.P. Morgan, eight supporting banks, and the General Electric Credit Corporation.

It was an auspicious start for the struggling company, which, over the course of the next 11 years (1984–94), proceeded to build or acquire ten new power plants. According to an article in a 1993 issue of *Financial World* magazine, the average utility, by contrast, might "build one large facility every 10 or 15 years." AES sales, consequently, more than tripled in two years, rising from only $55.4 million in 1988 to $190.2 million in 1990. Sales grew an additional 75 percent the following year, while net company income witnessed similarly spectacular growth, soaring from $1.6 million in 1988 to $42.6 million in 1991.

AES Goes Public: 1991

Buoyed by its success, the company changed its name from Applied Energy Sources to AES and became a publicly traded company on the NASDAQ stock exchange in 1991—the company listed on the New York Stock Exchange in 1996. Company stock began and closed the year priced at $22.18 a share, with investors earning 66 cents per share. Sant assumed the position of company chairman, while Bakke became the firm's president and CEO. Together, they owned approximately 27 percent of all AES stock.

In these early growth years, AES's primary source of profits and revenue was the domestic U.S. power market. Bakke, for instance, estimated that up until about the mid-1992, 70 percent of the money that AES spent on new business activity was spent in the United States. The remaining 30 percent, he noted, was spent in the United Kingdom.

These investments yielded very good results. A November 1993 report by the investment banking firm of Kidder Peabody, for example, found that from 1988 to 1992 AES revenues grew at an annual compounded rate of 64 percent. Company earnings during that same time period, the report noted, likewise soared at an annual rate of 136 percent. In 1991, AES was recognized by the leading chronicler of American business, *Forbes* magazine, as one of "America's fastest growing companies," an honor it again earned in 1992 and 1993.

Promoting a Socially Conscious Image

In conjunction with this success, AES staked out a reputation as one of the world's most socially conscious and organizationally innovative companies. Such distinctions were a legacy of Sant and Bakke and a direct consequence of their backgrounds. Bakke was a devout Christian who readily acknowledged that his religious beliefs formed the basis of his world view. Sant, too, was raised a Christian, specifically a Mormon, and was an ardent environmentalist. Moreover, Bakke and Sant shared a common formative work experience in the federal bureaucracy, which inspired in them a deep and abiding distrust of centralized bureaucracies in either the public or private sector. Nevertheless, their youthful and idealistic desire to work for the government resulted in a strong and life-long commitment to public service.

Such principles and beliefs made AES a rather unique company. Indeed, Bakke and Sant maintained that the firm's primary goal was to build and nurture a firm that embodied their shared values, specifically integrity, fairness, fun, and social responsibility. A company that embodied these values, they felt, would in all likelihood make money. For AES, however, profits were neither an end in and of themselves nor the chief reason for the firm's existence. Rather, according to Bakke and Sant, money was the natural and inevitable byproduct of the firm's shared values. As Bakke told *CFO* magazine in 1995: "The most socially responsible thing we can do is to do a really good job of fulfilling our business mission, which is to provide clean, reliable, safe, low-cost electricity around the world."

By conscious design, in fact, AES plants were among the safest and cleanest in the world, with pollution-emissions rates, accident rates, and "plant availability" time all setting the standard for the electric power industry. "Plant availability" referred to the percentage of total potential capacity at which a plant was able to operate; taken as a group, AES power-generating facilities consistently averaged at least 90 percent availability. Moreover, *Financial World* magazine reported in 1993 that "the company's number of lost-time accidents is 44 percent below the national average." Regarding its pollution-emissions rates, AES plants were reportedly running an estimated 58 percent below permitted emission levels for sulphur dioxide and nitrogen oxide, averaging nearly one-sixth the rate reported by the majority of American plants.

To further protect the environment, AES committed itself to a tree planting and preservation program, whereby the company agreed to plant or preserve enough trees to offset the carbon dioxide emissions from its power-generating facilities. Study into such a program was initiated in 1987 after growing concern by company executives that such emissions were contributing to global warming and therefore having a deleterious effect on the environment. The program got underway in earnest two years later when AES committed itself to planting more than 52 million trees in Guatemala over roughly a ten-year period. The project cost the company an estimated $2 million, an amount that reportedly nearly equaled AES profits for that year.

Similar company efforts to plant and preserve trees, woodlands, and forests followed, including a $3 million effort undertaken in conjunction with Oxfam America, an international development group, to preserve 3.7 million acres of South American forest. The program was unique in that to save this land from development and exploitation, AES and Oxfam were helping pioneer a private property-rights approach to environmental protection by helping indigenous peoples in South America establish ownership rights to their territorial homelands. It also involved developing land-management programs that would help keep this land in good condition for decades to come.

Other company-sponsored social programs included the funding and construction of a $1.5 million public elementary school in Panama, Oklahoma, the site of one of its power-generating facilities. According to AES's chief financial officer, Barry Sharp, this was done to give something back to the town,

which had given AES generous tax breaks to build the facility. In 1994, when construction of the school was completed, it was dedicated and turned over to the local school district. AES also established a consulting arm, AES Greenhouse Offset Group, to help other electric power companies be environmentally responsible and progressive. In recognition of these efforts, Harvard University honored AES in 1994 with its George S. Dively Award for Corporate Public Initiative.

Organizationally, AES established a decentralized corporate culture that gave company employees responsibility for most all aspects of business management. "Frequent and intensive cross-training, role rotation, and finance education for everyone are the rule," reported *CFO* magazine. At AES, no more than three layers of management separated an AES entry-level employee from the firm's plant supervisor, each power-generating facility was responsible for its own affairs, and there were no company-wide departments for finance, human resources, operations, purchasing, or public relations. Consequently, the few company officers assigned to these areas acted typically as distant in-house advisors to the plant project management team responsible for a given project rather than as more conventional hands-on corporate facilitators. For plant financing, for example, CFO Barry Sharp raised less than 10 percent of the estimated $3.5 billion needed for AES's first ten power plants; most of the necessary financing was raised by each plant's own multidisciplinary project team, composed of a broad cross-section of AES employees. By all accounts, this management system worked spectacularly well for AES. By giving workers a greater sense of involvement in, and responsibility for, their own professional destiny, employee morale was boosted. In 1995, annual employee turnover was averaging less than 1 percent, according company executives.

Like all management systems, however, the AES program faced challenges. One of the earliest and most significant breakdowns occurred in 1992 when the company disclosed that employees at its plant in Oklahoma had falsified the results of wastewater test samples in order to retain pollution permits from the Environmental Protection Agency (EPA). The workers responsible for the infraction said they feared losing their jobs if their violation of EPA pollution standards became known. In fact, the infraction actually had little substantive impact on AES since the pollution effect being covered up proved negligible and the company itself disclosed to the government that it had broken the law. The workers responsible were fined, demoted, and placed on probation, but not fired. Sant and Bakke voluntarily cut their own bonus pay for that year by 65 percent and 85 percent, respectively. The company publicly apologized for the incident and paid a $125,000 EPA fine. In addition, employees at the Oklahoma plant imposed upon themselves another layer of management supervision and environmental monitoring before eventually re-adopting AES's standard management system.

Also in 1992, the state of Florida charged AES with misleading state officials about the environmental impact of a coal-fired power plant then under construction in Jacksonville. A subsequent state investigation cleared AES of any wrongdoing. By the time the state eventually concluded its investigation, however, the banks providing financing for the facility had cut off funding for the power plant, thus forcing AES to sell off its financial interest in the facility, cut its losses, and abandon the project, despite the fact that construction was nearly complete.

In spite of these difficulties, AES appeared to have a bright and promising future. In the early 1990s, independent, small-scale, private-sector power producers generated only 9 percent of electricity in the United States. The U.S. Department of Energy estimated, however, that they would account for nearly 40 percent of all new electrical generating capacity added in the United States by the turn of the century. Certainly, AES's growth record bore this out, as company profits grew by some 650 percent from 1990 to 1994, and earnings per share during that same time period also grew dramatically, by approximately 500 percent.

International Expansion: Mid- to Late 1990s

Despite the opportunities for continued growth in the U.S. power market, however, AES began to look abroad for most of its new business ventures in the early 1990s. In fact, by 1995, the firm was spending an estimated 85 percent of its venture capital abroad. Six AES divisions worldwide emerged: AES Electric, which serviced Europe, the Middle East, and Africa; AES Enterprise; AES Chigen, which serviced China; AES Transpower (Asia, Hawaii, and the American West Coast); AES Shady Point; and AES Americas (Latin America).

The company's shift to the developing world was in part a natural reaction to its experience with its defunct Jacksonville power plant. The plant's failure underscored the relative difficulty independent power producers had doing business in the United States as opposed to overseas, where environmental restrictions were more flexible in part because the cost of pollution there was more easily offset by the benefits of electrical power. As AES company executive Sheryl Sturges told the *Washington Post* in 1995: "In the developing world, electricity produced from coal and other sources can make the difference between life and death. It can mean refrigeration for medicines and light for schoolchildren to study by."

AES's U.S. government tax levy rose sharply in the mid-1990s, from an effective rate of taxation of 23 percent in 1993 to 40 percent in 1996. In the developing world, by contrast, which was hungry for electrical energy, governments were eliminating tax and regulatory barriers that stymied the efforts of independent power producers.

In fact, the developing world's heightened need for electrical power was the chief reason AES shifted most of its new business ventures abroad. Electricity consumption in the United States, for instance, was expected to grow at an average annual rate of 1.9 percent until the year 2010, according to the Edison Electric Institute. The demand for electricity in the rest of the world, however, was projected to grow at nearly twice that rate, at an estimated annual rate of 4 percent during that same time period, according to the International Energy Agency.

According to Sant, the world needed $30 billion worth of new power plants a year through the year 2000. China and India alone, he suggested, would need three times more generating power over the next ten years than all of North America combined, and thus would require some $500 billion in power plant financing. As such, AES began an international expansion effort

that would position it as the world's largest independent power company. As overseas governments began privatizing their utilities sectors, AES stepped in by making acquisitions and constructing new plants.

By 1999, the Virginia-based company operated in 24 countries and over half of its profits stemmed from its operations outside the United States and Europe. That year, AES paid National Power plc $3 billion for the Drax power station, which supplies power to England and Wales. The company also began diversifying into telecommunications and investing in fiber optic networks in Brazil and Bolivia.

While the company completed a series of acquisitions during the late 1990s and 2000 as part of its global strategy, it made several key moves on the home front as well. In 1998, it announced its $885 million purchase of U.S.-based Cilcorp Inc., which was completed the following year. The firm also acquired California-based NewEnergy Inc. in July 1999. AES then took advantage of deregulation in the U.S. energy sector by creating Power Direct, a retail subsidiary that served U.S. consumers in deregulated markets. Then, in 2000, the firm acquired Indiana-based IPALCO Enterprises Inc. for $3 billion.

Success for AES continued into the new century. The company acquired Venezuelan utility C.A. La Electricidad de Caracas in a $1.7 billion hostile takeover. The firm also set plans in motion to acquire a stake in Chilean utility Gener S.A., and expanded into Bolivia, Nigeria, and Oman. In 2000, revenues climbed to $7.5 billion, up from $2.2 billion in 1997. In early 2001, AES's growth and expansion appeared to be unflappable.

Overcoming Hardships in the New Century

By this time, the majority of the firm's revenues stemmed from its South American operations. The firm's reliance on global economies, however, eventually caught up with it. An economic slowdown, which worsened after the terrorist attacks of September 11, 2001, threatened future growth at AES. Falling power prices in Britain, a political and social crisis in Argentina, and faltering currency exchange rates in Brazil also caused earnings to plummet. Overall, earnings fell to $273 million in 2001, down from $795 million in 2000.

In order to combat falling electricity prices, tumultuous emerging markets, and a slowdown in capital, AES announced a major restructuring and cost cutting effort in early 2002, which included a possible sale of various Latin American holdings. Select construction projects were put on hold and capital spending was reduced by $490 million. The company announced plans to sell Cilcorp, an interest in IPALCO, a portion of Dominican Republic-based Itabo, and certain AES facilities. The firm also began to divest its merchant generation businesses and in June 2002 announced the sale of its NewEnergy arm to Constellation Energy Group.

That month, Paul Hanrahan took over as president and CEO after Bakke announced his retirement. "The entire power sector has undergone a crisis of confidence, and investors are demanding change. Although AES has grown a great deal during my tenure, it became clear to me that this is a time for a new CEO. Different times require different leaders," proclaimed co-founder Bakke in a June 2002 company press release. The new leader indeed had his work cut out for him and pledged to restore and maximize shareholder value. While AES appeared to have some tough times ahead, its remarkable history of success left it on a solid platform for future growth.

Principal Subsidiaries

IPALCO Enterprises Inc.; Eletropaulo Metropolitana (Brazil); Companhia Energetica de Minas Gerias (CEMIG) (Brazil); C.A. La Electricidad de Caracas (Venezuela).

Principal Competitors

Duke Energy Corp.; Endesa S.A.; Mirant Corporation.

Further Reading

"AES: Back to Basics," *Project Finance*," March 2002, p. 6.

"The AES Corporation (AESC)," *Wall Street Transcript*, February 27, 1995.

Birchard, Bill, "Power to the People," *CFO: The Magazine for Senior Financial Executives*, March 1995, pp. 38–43.

Buchanan, Leigh, "The Way We Work," *CIO: The Magazine for Information Executives*, August 1994, pp. 33–77.

"Cilcorp Sold for $1.4 Billion, *Crain's Chicago Business*, May 6, 2002, p. 58.

Cropper, Carol M., "A Four-Letter Dirty Word," *Forbes*, January 17, 1994, p. 83.

Egan John, "Power Plays," *Financial World,* February 4, 1992, pp. 28–29.

Markels, Alex, "A Power Producer Is Intent on Giving Power to Its People," *Wall Street Journal*, July 3, 1995.

McDonald, Duff, "Why AES Is a Smart Power Play," *Money*, April 1, 1999, p. 56A.

Rubino, John, "Powering the Planet—and Saving It," *Virginia Business*, September 1993, pp. 49–52.

Southerland, Daniel, "The International Power Generators: Arlington's AES Corporation Leads a Battery of U.S. Energy Companies Expanding Overseas," *Washington Post*, May 22, 1995, Bus. Sec., pp. 1, 12–13.

Waterman, Jr., Robert H. "Values from the Start: Culture Is Strategy at the AES Corporation," in *What America Does Right*, New York: Penguin Books, 1994, pp. 111–36.

Webb-Vidal, Andy, "The Predator Strikes Again," *LatinFinance*, November 2001, p. 48.

Wee, Heesun, "AES: A High-Powered Utility With a Conscience," *Business Week*, March 29, 2001.

——, "A Nasty Short-Circuit as AES," *Business Week*, October 4, 2001.

—John R. Guardiano
—update: Christina M. Stansell

Affiliated Foods Inc.

1401 Framers Lane
Amarillo, Texas 79118
U.S.A.
Telephone: (806) 372-3851
Toll Free: (800) 234-3661
Fax: (806) 372-3647
Web site: http://www.afima.com

Cooperative
Incorporated: 1968
Employees: 1,000
Sales: $854 million (2002)
NAIC: 42221 Drugs and Druggists' Sundries Wholesalers;
42241 General Line Grocery Wholesalers; 42243 Dairy
Product (Except Dried or Canned) Wholesalers; 42247
Meat and Meat Product Wholesalers; 42248 Fresh Fruit
and Vegetable Wholesalers

Affiliated Foods Inc., headquartered in Amarillo, Texas, is a grocers' cooperative provisioning over 700 independent, member-owned stores in seven states: Arizona, Colorado, Kansas, New Mexico, Oklahoma, Texas, and Wyoming. The cooperative receives and distributes over two million pounds of groceries daily. It owns and operates the Plains Dairy and has a "sister company," the Tri-State Baking Co., located next door that shares board members with Affiliated. Respectively, the bakery and dairy produce over five million loaves of bread per year and about 60,000 gallons of milk per day. The dairy also bottles water, juice, and fruit beverages. In addition, the co-op owns an interest in Western Family Foods, which produces private label goods under the Western Family and Shurfine brand names. Besides providing its member-owned retail stores with both foods and non-food items, the co-op has helped them in other ways, notably in implementing computer-based accounting and stock-control systems. In addition to provisioning its member stores, Affiliated Foods also operates a food service division that conducts business with over 1200 vendors, including restaurants, kitchens, and cafeterias at hospitals and other institutions.

Becoming a Major Regional Cooperative: 1946–84

Although it was not until 1968 that Affiliated Foods came into existence through the key merger of South Plains Associated Grocers, Inc. and the Panhandle Associated Grocers, Inc., its origins extend back to the boom period following World War II with the founding of the latter organization. Panhandle started out in Amarillo, Texas, in 1946, housed in a 4,000-square-foot building close to the downtown area of that small but rapidly growing city. It was created by a group of charter members of independent grocers in the area who wanted to establish a centralized cooperative that could purchase and distribute food products from a single distribution point or warehouse using its own fleet of trucks. Growth was slow at first, but by 1960 Panhandle had moved its operation to the site that it and then Affiliated would occupy for the rest of the century. By that time, the impact of national retail chains was beginning to hit independent grocers fairly hard, and increasing numbers signed on with Panhandle to survive.

Affiliated Foods officially came into existence on November 1, 1968, when the boards of South Plains Associated Grocers and the Panhandle Associated Grocers, Inc. merged to form the new company. The merger proved to be a fortuitous step, one allowing for steady growth and a widening market range.

Gradually, the cooperative took on members beyond its epicenter in Amarillo, moving into Colorado, Kansas, and New Mexico. In addition, in 1977, it added food-service supply to its business, that is, the direct sale of foodstuffs to restaurants and cafeterias. Thereafter, Affiliated enjoyed substantial growth in that segment every year.

The Cooper Era Begins and Affiliated Updates Its Operations: 1985–93

In 1985, Benny Cooper became Affiliated's president. Cooper, from McLean, in the Texas Panhandle, had grown up in the grocery business. Members of his family owned and operated stores both in Texas and New Mexico, and his father and one of his uncles were charter members of the cooperative back in 1946. For years he lived in Canyon, Texas, where he first worked at his uncle's grocery store and eventually bought his uncle out. In

Company Perspectives:

Affiliated Foods meets the needs of grocery stores and restaurants in Texas, Oklahoma, Kansas, New Mexico, Colorado, Arizona, and Wyoming. We've been supplying only the freshest produce, meats, bread, and dairy products for over 50 years. With 700 member stores as part of our family, we're committed to bringing quality service and goods to the Southwest.

1979, while on Affiliated's board of directors, he was invited to join the company, and in 1983, two years before being elected president, he was named the company's general manager.

During the 1990s, a good bit of Affiliated's focus was on adapting to rapidly changing technologies. Although Affiliated had installed its first computer in 1963, by 1990 its system was badly overloaded, and its response time in managing the company's distribution needs had become badly outmoded and inefficient. To remedy the situation, Affiliated began automating its warehouse operations. In 1991, it installed a high power IBM computer using a full-function software package developed by BACG/Marwood Distribution Systems. At that stage, Affiliated, with an annual revenue of about $450 million, was servicing over 600 member stores and 2,500 institutional accounts from its single 700,000-square-foot, full-line distribution warehouse and center. The new program enhanced the company's limited automation technology, which, until that time, had been largely limited to placing orders and picking documents. The new software computerized the receiving, storage, and letdown functions, and it gave notice that Affiliated was not going to fall victim to the enhanced efficiency of its competitors by a failure to adapt to changing technologies.

Affiliated Expands Merchandising and Ventures into Food Production: 1994–97

Change accelerated more quickly through the decade, prompting Cooper, in 1997, to note that over the previous five years the company had experienced more changes and a greater need to incorporate technological advances than it faced in the previous 40 plus years of its development.

In roughly that same five-year period, from 1993 through 1997, Affiliated found it necessary to step up its non-food sales in order to compete more successfully with the growing number of alternative format stores in its market area. In 1994, the company had set a goal of boosting its non-food sales by one percent at some of the 300 full-fledged supermarkets it was then servicing. To accommodate new non-food items, Affiliated's retailers expanded some of their departments, increasing both their size and their variety. They also undertook some in-store promotional measures to increase the sale of non-food items. By April 1994, about 60 retailers had adopted Affiliated's non-food merchandising program. The stores involved reported that their sales had gone up from .05 percent to 1 percent.

While expanding its non-food merchandising program, through demographic analyses, Affiliated gave careful consideration to the regional demands of its member stores in order to

provision them with items that their particular customers needed or wanted. This resulted in a different product mix for stores in, say, Colorado as opposed to those in south Texas or New Mexico. For example, in Colorado it proved more appropriate to stock plastic snow shovels than in Texas, where metal shovels were more serviceable because winter was more likely to produce ice than the type of deep snow covering the Colorado landscape.

By the end of 1997, Affiliated was receiving and delivering about two million pounds of groceries each day. It had 210 stockholding members, owners, and operators of about 650 stores. These, located for the most part in West Texas, New Mexico, and parts of Colorado, Kansas, and Oklahoma, were all within about a 500-mile radius of Affiliated's distribution center. From its single warehouse and distribution facility, just south of Amarillo, Affiliated ran about 180 trucks and 200 trailers round the clock and covered the company's entire trade area.

Affiliated had also expanded its facility from 700,000 to 750,000 square feet, and it was undertaking another 22,000-square-foot increase to its dry-grocery warehouse at its center. In addition, the company maintained its own motor pool facility to service its fleet of trucks. Altogether, Affiliated had over 1,000 employees. With its improving stocking, inventory, and ordering systems, the company was able to establish a 24-hour turnaround schedule for any member store in its network, and it was working on a new buying and networking system designed to make it operate in a more efficient manner while providing its member stores with greater product information than had been previously available to them.

It was also during the 1990s that Affiliated Foods undertook expansion into the production end of the grocery business. It took one important step when it acquired the Plains Dairy, a business that enjoyed both a local habitation and an established name. Lindsay Nunn, a prominent Amarillo citizen, started up the dairy in 1934 and brought in A.F. Mason, later Amarillo's mayor, to manage it. The pair sold it in 1955 to National Dairy, which marketed milk under the Sealtest name and was a division of Kraft Foods. Ten years later, National sold the dairy to L.B. Parker, who owned it for 30 years before selling it to Affiliated Foods in 1996.

Affiliated's Growth Continues: 1998–2000

By 1998, Plains was the last commercial dairy left in town. Servicing parts of West Texas, most of New Mexico, as well as parts of Oklahoma, Kansas, and Colorado, the dairy was producing 60,000 gallon of milk a day. The dairy obtained most of its milk from large dairy farms in New Mexico, but some of it came from Texas farms. In any case, all of it was brought into the Plains operation by the tanker load, and about 70 percent of the goods it processed were sold to Affiliated, its parent, which marketed milk and milk products under its own brand, ''Frosty Acres.'' The dairy also sold milk and milk products to other businesses in the Amarillo marketing area. Dub Garlington, Plains Dairy's president, believed that the company's purchase by Affiliated would lead to an expansion of the dairy, both in its size and product line. It had already begun producing bottled water under the Culligan name as well as fruit drink items; it had also become a distributor of Blue Bunny Ice Cream. Fur-

Key Dates:
1946: Panhandle Associated Grocers is organized in Amarillo, Texas.
1960: The company moves to its South Washington location in Amarillo.
1968: Panhandle is merged with South Plains Associated Grocers, Inc. of Lubbock, Texas to form Affiliated Foods Inc.
1977: Affiliated begins provisioning food service operators.
1996: Plains Dairy is acquired.
1998: Affiliated purchases Tri-State Baking.

thermore, Garlington had anticipated that the dairy would quickly package its milk in a wider range of container sizes and types, including single-serving plastic bottles suited to the needs of some of Affiliated's vendors. Over the next few years, Affiliated Foods would promote the dairy's "Snack Attack Line" of beverages and add new items, including tea bag-brewed Red Diamond Tea bottled in gallon and pint containers.

In that same year, 1998, Affiliated took another important step into the food production business when it acquired the Tri-State Baking Company, a "sister company" which, like the Plains Dairy, had a well-established place in Amarillo and had become the only operating commercial bakery in that city. Founded in the 1950s, the bakery sold bread and other baked goods under the locally familiar "TenderCrust" and "Always Fresh" labels. Using both its own fleet of tractor-trailers as well as trucks from Affiliated Foods' fleet, the company distributed its Frontier line of baked goods, which, in addition to breads, included buns, rolls, coneys, cakes, tortillas, and cookies. In 2000, the bakery moved six million loaves of bread into the marketplace.

By the end of the century, Affiliated Foods was venturing into the e-commerce world with its characteristic deliberation. In 2000, for example, it entered an agreement with Networld Exchange, Inc., a business-to-business e-commerce service for food-service and hospitality providers. Affiliated wanted an advanced but economical Web-based system capable of providing immediate product and pricing information to its 1,200 plus food-service clients, one that could provide easy-to-access and accurate information for its customers. Convinced that Networld offered what it needed, Affiliated began steps to place 30,000 products online. Then, in order to improve its order-filling efficiency, in early in 2001 Affiliated Foods contracted SPS Commerce to provide e-commerce supply chain automation and optimization services. Affiliated selected SPS because

that company's hosted model allowed Affiliated to do business with each of its vendors no matter what their size.

New Century Brings Changes in Affiliated's Management: 2000–01

In 2001, there was a change in the company's upper management when George Lankford, who had been serving as president and COO since October, 2000, also became Affiliated's CEO. He had started out with the company in 1990, when he took the post of vice-president of merchandising and marketing. Before being named COO, he had served as the company's executive vice-president.

Over its history, reflecting its business growth, the physical plant of Affiliated foods has grown by over one million square feet. Its business had been steady and determined, despite increased pressure from giant supermarket chains that have been largely successful in driving independent grocers out of business. Affiliated took well-conceived steps to avoid that fate. In addition to the acquisition of a dairy and a bakery, the cooperative bought a share of Western Family Foods, Inc., a company founded in 1934 that provides private label products to over 3,500 independent grocers. Affiliated and a handful of other wholesale grocers own it and distribute its Western Family and Shurfine branded foods. Also, Affiliated's members have been very loyal, and all indications are that they will continue to be so for the foreseeable future, in part because the cooperative has successfully met the competitive challenges in range and depth service provided by the industry's giants.

Principal Subsidiaries

Plains Dairy; Tri-State Baking; Western Family Foods (25%).

Principal Competitors

Associated Wholesale Grocers. Inc.; Fleming Companies, Inc.; Nash Finch Company; SUPERVALU INC.

Further Reading

Browser, David, "Grocery Supplier Takes Care of Affiliates," *Amarillo Business Journal*, November 3, 1997.
——, "Plains Dairy Is the Last One Standing," *Amarillo Business Journal*, July 21, 1998.
Elson, Joel, "Affiliated Meeting Goal to Boost Nonfood Sales," *Supermarket News*, April 18, 1994, p. 16.
"Info Systems Tackle Warehouse Problems," *U.S. Distribution Journal*, October 15, 1991, p. 15.
"SPS Commerce to Provide E-Commerce Services to Affiliated Foods, Inc.," *Supply Chain Press Releases*, January 22, 2001.

—John W. Fiero

Ahlstrom Corporation

Eteläesplanadi 14
00101 Helsinki
Finland
Telephone: (+358) 10-8880
Fax: (+358) 10-888-4709
Web site: http://www.ahlstrom.com

Private Company
Incorporated: 1851
Employees: 7,302
Sales: EUR 1.80 billion ($1.88 billion) (2002)
NAIC: 322121 Paper (Except Newsprint) Mills; 322130
 Paperboard Mills; 322211 Corrugated and Solid Fiber
 Box Manufacturing; 322214 Fiber Can, Tube, Drum,
 and Similar Products Manufacturing; 325221
 Cellulosic Manmade Fiber Manufacturing; 325520
 Adhesive and Sealant Manufacturing

Ahlstrom Corporation celebrated its 150th anniversary in 2001 by breaking up. Formerly known as the multi-faceted industrial conglomerate A. Ahlstrom Corporation, the company has refocused itself around a single core of specialty paper products, shedding nearly all of its diversified industrial operations. As part of its restructuring, Ahlstrom has regrouped around three key divisions: FiberComposites, which produces a range of nonwoven and filtration technology-based products and accounted for 32 percent of the company's sales in 2001; LabelPack, which produces packaging, labeling, and release papers (that is, the backing for labels) and provided 29 percent of sales in 2001; and Specialties, which includes cores, coreboards, and other products for technical applications and earned 19 percent of sales in 2001. The remaining 20 percent of sales were generated by non-core operations that were slated for disposal throughout 2002. Ahlstrom's focus on niche and specialty products has enabled it to capture world-leading shares in many of its product markets. Based in Finland, Ahlstrom generates only 4 percent of its revenues at home. The United States is the company's single largest market, at 27 percent of total sales. Germany and France are also strong markets for Ahlstrom, representing 14 percent and 10 percent of sales respectively. In all,

Ahlstrom operates production and sales facilities in more than 20 countries, including the extension of its manufacturing base into Spain in 2002. A private company still controlled by the founding Ahlstrom family, Ahlstrom has announced its intention to go public by as early as 2004. This transition has been led since 1999 by CEO Juha Rantanen.

Origins in the 19th Century

Farmer's son Antti Ahlström founded what was to grow into one of Finland's largest conglomerates in the middle of the 19th century. In 1851, Ahlstrom took over a business with holdings that included a paper mill, a grain mill, and part of a saw mill. Then just 24 years old, Ahlstrom quickly began seeking new business opportunities, turning toward shipping at the beginning of the 1860s. At first plying ports between the Finnish coast and other ports on the Baltic Sea, Ahlstrom built up one of Finland's largest shipping fleets by the 1890s, with destinations as far away as Singapore.

The strong cash flow generated by his shipping operations enabled Ahlstrom to build up a portfolio of industrial interests back home, including an entry into ironworks, starting with the purchase of the Kauttua ironworks in 1873. Originally constructed in 1689, the Kauttua works was to remain a central facet of the Ahlstrom empire into the 21st century.

Iron quickly became one of the company's largest production areas. Yet Finland's iron industry, which relied heavily on the country's forests for providing needed charcoal, had been overtaking by advancing technology elsewhere in the world. In the 1880s, however, Ahlstrom had recognized that the company's ironworks holdings, which included vast forest holdings, provided a different opportunity. Over the next decade, Ahlstrom began converting his operation to concentrate on forestry products, buying up some 18 sawmills, expanding the company's forestry holdings, and converting most of the company's ironworks to wood and wood products production. By the turn of the century, the Ahlstrom name had become synonymous with its sawmill operations.

Antti Ahlstrom died in 1896, and the company's operations were taken over by his son Walter. The younger generation proved

Company Perspectives:

Ahlstrom's vision is to be the most successful global company in high performance fiber solutions and be at the forefront in leadership quality.

as ambitious as the first. In 1907, Ahlstrom converted the Kauttua ironworks into wood pulp and paper production. Then, as World War I approached, Ahlstrom made two new ambitious expansion moves to step up its pulp and paper and other industrial operations. The first came with the purchase of Varkaus, which the company converted to sulphite pulp and paper production. The second came in 1915, when the company acquired Karhula, which had started out as a wood pulp producer in 1888 before adding board production at the turn of the century. Both purchases placed the company dangerously in debt as its European market bogged down in an protracted war. The company continued to expand, however, adding the Iittala glassworks in 1917.

Finnish Industrial Conglomerate in the 1930s

The soaring inflation rates of the postwar period proved a boon for the company, as it paid off its debts using the inflated currency, securing financial control of its expanding empire. Ahlstrom now turned toward paper production, launching the new operation at the Varkaus mill in 1921 on what was then the largest paper production machine in Europe. The company also converted its Kauttua mill to support its expanding paper interests, switching from low-grade brown papers to higher-grade sulfite papers.

Finland raised protective trade barriers following World War I, sealing off the domestic market from foreign competition. This situation encouraged companies like Ahlstrom to diversify into a variety of other business areas. Starting in the 1920s, Ahlstrom began adding on a number of businesses, including engineering, forest technology equipment, and industrial pumps, as well as glassmaking. At one point the company was internationally known for its art glass production under the Karhula and Iittala names. By the beginning of the 1930s, Ahlstrom had grown into Finland's largest industrial conglomerate.

The outbreak of World War II led the company to convert much of its production to support the Finnish war effort. Following the war, the company played a major role in the country's reconstruction and in its war reparations obligation. Ahlstrom alone accounted for nearly 15 percent of the country's total reparations. The company continued to expand into the 1950s, stepping up its engineering operations while also expanding into chemical wood processing technology.

Ahlstrom continued its diversification through the 1960s and 1970s, building up a portfolio of some 60 different businesses. The company also began making its first moves onto the international scene. In 1963, the company acquired majority control of Cartiere Giacomo Bosso SpA, a paper producer based in Turin, Italy, originally founded in 1841. Under Ahlstrom, Bosso began targeting the specialty papers market, and particularly the market for specialty filter papers, becoming a European leader in that niche market. In 1976, Ahlstrom turned to Germany,

where it joined with fellow Finnish company Kemi Oy to acquire Kammerer, another specialty paper maker focused on production of release papers—silicon-based papers used as the backing for adhesive labels and papers. In 1979, Ahlstrom took full control of Kammerer, which by then had a gained a 40 percent share of the European market for release papers.

Restructuring for a New Century

Yet for the most part Ahlstrom remained focused on the Finnish market. And by the early 1980s, Ahlstrom's fortunes had begun to slip. The company's highly diversified nature had also left it highly vulnerable to changes in the international marketplace. The opening of Finland to foreign competition, the emergence of new technologies, and a long decade of economic decline combined to cut deeply into the company's growth. Ahlstrom found itself unable to provide the necessary investments to maintain the competitiveness of its diversified portfolio of companies. At the same time, Ahlstrom's continued commitment to its private, family-owned status meant that the company was unable to call on outside investors to provide backing. Nearly all of the company's businesses were struggling, and a large number had begun to fail.

In 1982, fourth-generation family member Krister Ahlstrom, who had been working for another Finnish conglomerate, Wartsila, was brought in as the company's CEO. Ahlstrom immediately brought in consultants to perform an analysis of the company's operations. The result was disheartening—more than half of the company's businesses were labeled as mediocre, and the company was advised to take immediate steps to divest as many as 15 of its worst performers. Of its existing operations, only three companies were deemed strong enough to bring the company into the future.

Krister Ahlstrom met with a great deal of resistance from other Ahlstrom family owners—which by then numbered nearly 200—as he began to restructure the company's operations. Among the most controversial of the Ahlstrom's moves was the sell-off of its money-losing bulk paper operation—the company's symbolic core. By 1986, however, Krister Ahlstrom had managed to convince a majority of the family that the sell-off was necessary. The company exited other operations as well during this time, including its Varkaus forestry products unit and the company's newsprint production. By the end of the decade, Ahlstrom's operations had come to focus more and more around two new core areas—engineering and specialty papers.

While restructuring its other operations, Ahlstrom continued investing in its specialty papers division. The United States had become a primary focus market for the company as it began building a portfolio of paper products holdings in that country in the late 1980s and early 1990s. Ahlstrom's U.S. acquisitions included Knowlton Brothers and its Mt. Holly Springs, Pennsylvania site, as well as the 1989 purchases of Filtration Sciences Inc, based in Chattanoga, Tennessee, and Clark and Vicario, based in St. Petersburg, Florida. In the early 1990s, the company also added United States-based filter paper manufacturer Taylorville.

While building up its position in the United States, Ahlstrom also continued to build up its European network, including the purchase of Germany's Lippke in 1989. In 1991, Ahlstrom bought another German company, Jagenberg, adding its paper production plant in Altenkirchen. That plant was then converted to focus on production of gasket materials and other specialty paper products. Both the United States and Germany remained major international markets for Ahlstrom, accounting for 27 percent and 14 percent of its total sales, respectively, by the end of the decade. Ahlstrom continued to expand its production facilities, acquiring Swedish packaging specialist Akerlung & Rausing and French specialty paper maker Sibille-Dalle.

By the mid-1990s, Ahlstrom had decided to restructure itself around its core paper and packaging operations. The company began selling off its newly non-core businesses, including Ahlstrom Pyropower and its glassworks, and divested its stake in Lexel, an electrical products business, as well as its various holdings in the Finnish utilities industries.

In 1999, Krister Ahlstrom ceded the CEO position to Juha Rantanen as the fifth generation of the Ahlstrom family emerged as the primary owners of the company. In that year, however, Ahlstrom nearly ended its nearly 150-year history as an independent company when it announced an agreement to merge its operations with the those of the British-Danish group Kvaerner. Yet that merger eventually collapsed following scrutiny by the European Commission's mergers and monopolies body.

Instead, Ahlstrom stepped up its restructuring into the new century, selling off more of its holdings, including its 50 percent share of the Andritz-Ahlstrom paper production systems partnership with Austria's Andritz in 2001, and merging its flexible packaging operations into a new joint-venture company with Danisco and Amcor that same year.

In recognition of its restructuring, Ahlstrom, until then known as the A. Ahlstrom Corporation, split up into three entities: Ahlstrom Corporation, which took over the company's paper production operations; Ahlstrom Capital, which acquired the company's investment-related operations; and A. Ahlstrom Osakeyhtio, which served as a vehicle for the Ahlstrom family's holdings. Ahlstrom Corporation, amidst its 150th anniversary celebrations, then announced its intention to go public as early as 2004.

Ahlstrom meanwhile continued to expand its operations, notably into Spain, in April 2002, when it acquired that country's Papelera del Besos, a filtration and specialty paper maker, and into the United states, when it bought up the specialty filtration operations of FiberMark Inc. in December of that year. With sales of more than EUR 1.7 billion and operations in more than 20 countries, Ahlstrom had successfully completed a transition into one of the world's leading specialty papers manufacturers at the start of the new century.

Principal Subsidiaries

Ahlstrom Finance Canada Inc.; Ahlstrom Holding GmbH (Germany); Ahlstrom Altenkirchen GmbH (Germany); Ahlstrom Cores GmbH (Germany); Ahlstrom Osnabrück GmbH (Germany); Ahlstrom Nümbrecht GmbH & Co. KG (Germany); Ahlstrom Industries SA (France); Ahlstrom Australia Pty Ltd (74.0%); Ahlstrom Benelux S.A. (Belgium); Ahlstrom Brignoud SA (France); Ahlstrom Tampere Oy; Ahlstrom Chantraine (France); Ahlstrom La Gère (France); Ahlstrom Neu-Isenburg GmbH (Germany); Ahlstrom Packaging SA (France); Ahlstrom Dexter Belgium; Ahlstrom Research and Competence Center (France); Ahlstrom Spain SL (Spain); Ahlstrom Specialties SA (France); Ahlstrom United Kingdom Ltd. (75.0%); Ahlstrom Italia S.p.A. (Italy); Ahlstrom Turin S.p.A. (Italy); Ahlstrom Ascoli S.r.l. (Italy); Nordica S.r.l. (Italy, 60.0%); Ahlström Karhulan Palvelut Oy (58.0%); Ahlstrom Kauttua Oy; Ahlstrom Milano S.r.l. (Italy); Ahlstrom Norrköping AB (Sweden); Ahlstrom Finance Ireland; Ahlstrom Paper Group Oy; Ahlstrom Chirnside Limited (United Kingdom); Ahlstrom Cores Oy; Ahlstrom Alcore B.V. (Netherlands); Ahlstrom Asia Holdings Pte Ltd (Singapore, 70.0%); Ahlstrom Paper Korea Co., Ltd (Korea, 56.0%); Ahlstrom Paper Shanghai Co., Ltd (China, 70.0%); PT. Ahlstrom Indonesia (70.0%); Ahlstrom Cores AB (Sweden); Ahlstrom Cores AS (Norway); Ahlstrom Cores Oü (Estonia); Ahlstrom Cores SA (France); Ahlstrom Cores Sp.z.o.o. (Poland); ZAO Ahlstrom Cores (Russia); Ahlstrom Glassfibre Oy; Ahlstrom Korea Co., Ltd (Korea); Ahlstrom Louveira Ltda (Brazil); Ahlstrom Nordic Oy; Ahlstrom South Africa (Pty) Ltd (South Africa, 60.0%);

Ahlstrom Ställdalen AB (Sweden); Ahlstrom USA Inc.; Ahlstrom Capital Corporation (United States); Ahlstrom U.S. Industries, Inc. (USA); Ahlstrom Engine Filtration, LLC. (United States); Ahlstrom Mount Holly Springs, LLC. (United States); Ahlstrom Windsor Locks, LLC. (United States); Ahlstrom Tokyo, Inc (Japan); Kamtech, Inc. (United States); Akerlund & Rausing S.p.A. (Italy); Norrmark Insurance Company Limited (Isle of Man); ZAO Akerlund & Rausing Kuban (Russia).

Principal Divisions

FiberComposites; LabelPack; Specialties.

Principal Competitors

Procter and Gamble Co.; International Paper Co.; Kimberly-Clark Corp.; Stora Enso Oyj; Weyerhaeuser Co.; UPM-Kymmene Corp.; Oji Paper Company Ltd.; Svenska Cellulosa AB; Metsaliitto Group; Boise Cascade Corp.; M-real Corp.; Orkla ASA; Eastern Pulp and Paper Corp.; Nippon Unipac Holding; Brascan Corp.; Jefferson Smurfit Group PLC; SAPPI Ltd.; Norske Skogindustrier ASA; Abitibi-Consolidated Inc.; Hitachi Zosen Corp.; Daio Paper Corp.; Domtar Inc.; Tembec Inc.

Further Reading

"Ahlstrom Acquires FiberMark's Specialty Filtration Business," *Nordic Business Report*, December 20, 2002.

Ahlstrom Corporation Expands into Spain," *Nordic Business Report*, April 2, 2002.

"Ahlstrom Is Learning the Importance of Timing," *Tekniikka & Talous*, November 28, 2002.

"Ahlstrom to Invest EUR 16m in German Plant," *Nordic Business Report*, November 4, 2002.

Magretta, Joan, "Governing the Family-owned Enterprise: An Interview with Finland's Krister Ahlstrom," *Harvard Business Review*, January–February 1998, p. 112.

—M.L. Cohen

Air Methods Corporation

7301 South Peoria Street
Englewood, Colorado 80112
U.S.A.
Telephone: (303) 792-7400
Fax: (303) 790-0499
Web site: http://www.airmethods.com

Public Company
Incorporated: 1980 as Cell Technology, Inc.
Employees: 686
Sales: $92 million (2001)
Stock Exchanges: NASDAQ
Ticker Symbol: AIRM
NAIC: 481211 Nonscheduled Charter Flight
    Transportation; 446199 All Other Health and Personal
    Care Stores; 488190 Other Support Activities for Air
    Transportation

Air Methods Corporation is one of the world's leading airborne healthcare companies, providing air medical emergency transport services and systems using both a hospital-based and community-based model throughout the United States. The company's Air Medical Services Division (hospital-based model), based in Denver, Colorado, provides emergency air medical transportation services to hospitals. This division provides hospital clients with helicopters and airplanes, which it operates and maintains in accordance with Federal Aviation regulations. Hospital clients are responsible for providing medical personnel and all medical care. The company's community-based model, operated by its wholly-owned subsidiary Mercy Air Service, Inc., based in Los Angeles, California, provides air medical transportation services in California, Nevada, Missouri, and Illinois. These services include operation and maintenance of helicopters and fixed-wing aircraft, medical care, 24-hour communications and dispatch, and medical billing and collections. This division's aircraft are typically based at fire stations or airports. Air Method's Products Division designs, produces, installs, and maintains aircraft medical interiors and other aerospace products for domestic and international customers. The company's medi-

cal interiors range from basic life support systems to intensive care units, while its engineering and production capabilities have enabled the division to design and integrate aerospace products that include aircraft navigation systems, environmental control systems, and structural and electrical systems.

Company Beginnings

Air Methods Corporation was founded in Colorado in 1982 as a research and development company then doing business as Cell Technology. On November 12, 1991, Cell Technology completed the acquisition of Air Methods Corporation, a Colorado corporation incorporated in 1980, which was involved in providing life-saving emergency air medical services. The company issued approximately 600,000 restricted shares of common stock for all of Air Method's outstanding common stock. Upon the merger, the company changed its name to Air Methods Corporation. From its inception until the completion of this transaction, the company was primarily involved in the development of biological response modifiers (BRMs), naturally occurring substances designed to alter the body's immune system and its reaction to cancer and other diseases. In late 1990, the Food and Drug Administration (FDA) notified the company of the need to construct a full-scale commercial production plant prior to initiating Phase III clinical trials. Up to this point, the company had completed various multi-center Phase II clinical trials of its BRMs for the treatment primary adult brain cancer. As a result of the FDA's notification, the company terminated the internal development of its BRMs, subsequently out-licensing these development responsibilities to other pharmaceutical and biotechnology companies.

Company Alters Its Business

With the acquisition of Air Methods Corporation, the company transformed itself into a provider of aeromedical emergency services and systems to hospitals throughout the United States. The company also designed, manufactured, and installed proprietary aircraft medical interiors and equipment for third parties, which allowed each aircraft to operate as an airborne intensive care unit. As a result, the company began to play a significant role in pioneering the integrated use of helicopters and airplanes equipped with patient life support systems to transport patients requiring intensive medical care from the scene of an accident or general care hospitals to highly specialized trauma centers, tertiary care centers, or university research and teaching hospitals. In an attempt to expand operations and raise profits, on September 14, 1993, the company acquired Golden Eagle Aviation, Inc., an airplane charter business.

Restructuring and the Pursuit of Strategic Acquisitions

By 1994, the company was losing money, leading to the appointment of a new CEO, George Belsey, an outside director and former hospital administrator. In leading the turnaround, on September 21, 1994 Belsey sold the money-losing Golden Eagle as part of a company-wide restructuring plan stemming from more than $7 million in losses for the fiscal year ended June 30, 1994. He also cut staff by 30 percent, reduced officers' salaries, sold off under-utilized aircraft, and guided the company back to its core business. To ensure future growth, Belsey began pursuing strategic acquisitions, joint business ventures, and branching out beyond simple transportation. In 1995, the company formed it first international franchise with Unimed Air de Sao Paulo of Brazil, a member of Brazil's largest healthcare cooperative, with the aim of creating an integrated air medical transportation and delivery system for the entire continent of South America. Under the franchise agreement, the Brazilian company purchased the right to use the trademarks and expertise of Air Methods in providing air medical services in Brazil for an acquisition price of $2,250,000, payable over ten years, plus annual royalties based on gross revenues. The franchise began air medical operations in January 1996.

In 1996, Air Methods believed that demand for comprehensive medical transportation would continue to grow with the closing and consolidation of rural hospitals. In response to increasing cost pressures and other changes within the healthcare industry, the company also began pursuing innovative approaches to aeromedical transportation, such as the turn key or independent provider (IP) model. Under the IP model, the operator provided the medical care, communications center, and medical billing resources as well as flight and maintenance capabilities. The company also planned to market its three aircraft interior product lines to domestic and international customers. In 1996, Air Methods secured a contract to provide medical interior systems for two U.S. army UH-60Q medical evacuation helicopters. The company considered the government aeromedical industry an important area for future growth.

As of December 31, 1996, Air Methods employed 109 pilots, 122 aviation machinists, engineers, and other manufacturing and maintenance positions, and 38 business and administrative personnel. Net income totaled $308,000 compared to $959,000 in the previous year. The decrease in net income stemmed from investment in the development of a new modular medical interior and in the design of a medical interior system for the HU-60Q helicopter for the U.S. Army.

In July 1997, the growing financial success of the company's flight operations enabled it to acquire all of the common stock of Mercy Air Service, Inc., and the net assets of Helicopter Services, Inc., both California corporations. These acquisitions fit with Belsey's strategy of saving money by buying competitors, tying them together into regional services, and serving entire communities of hospitals with air transport staffed with paramedics and nurses. The company acquired Mercy, a California-based independent provider of air medical services, for around $6 million. The transaction also included a separate maintenance facility in Rialto, California, which provided all maintenance services to Mercy and engaged in third party sales of helicopter spare parts. Mercy's operations for the five months following the acquisition produced $7 million in revenue and $892,000 in net income, generating a 24 percent increase in revenue and a 290 percent increase in net income for the year. As an independent provider since 1988, Mercy's operations included medical care, aircraft operations and maintenance, FAA training and support, 24-hour communications and dispatch, and medical billing and collections. The company saw the addition of these core capabilities as not only providing a new model for the delivery of air medical transportation services but also a new model for delivering emergency air medical care, thus expanding Air Method's market from $330 million to almost $1 billion. At the time of the acquisition, Mercy operated eight helicopters in southern California and Las Vegas and served as a leading provider of aeromedical transport services in Orange, Riverside, San Diego, Kern, San Bernadino, and Los Angeles counties. All of the aircraft were based either at fire stations or airports and served community hospitals. Revenue from Mercy's flight operations derived primarily from flight fees billed directly to patients, their insurers, and governmental agencies. Mercy's community-based model stemmed largely from the managed care environment of southern California in 1989. With the emphasis by hospitals on cutting costs and under growing pressure to justify or terminate noncore functions, many hospital-based programs in the region were eliminated. Mercy utilized its neutral locations at fire stations and airports and its computer-aided dispatch system to provide independent service to community healthcare institutions. Mercy's experience with medical billing also enabled it to establish preferred provider status with managed care groups.

In 1997, the company's product division delivered four multimission medical evacuation systems for the U.S. Army UH-60Q helicopter. The multi-mission system, which can be quickly converted from medical evacuation to personnel or cargo transport, was considered critical for modernizing the Army's helicopter fleet. Following Operation Desert Storm, the Army set the modernization of medical evacuation forces as a top priority for the medical corps. The need to provide medical care en route from the battle field led to the development of the UH-60Q medical evacuation helicopter. Because the Army planned on producing

Key Dates:

1980: The company is incorporated in Delaware as Cell Technology, Inc.
1991: Air Methods Corporation is acquired.
1993: Golden Eagle Aviation, Inc. is acquired.
1994: The company sells all outstanding common shares of Golden Eagle Charters, Inc.
1995: An international franchise with Unimed Air de Sao Paulo of Brazil is established.
1997: The company acquires Mercy Air Services, Inc. and all of the net assets of Helicopter Services, Inc.
2000: Subsidiary Mercy Air acquires the business assets of Area Rescue Consortium of Hospitals.

447 UH-60Q units over the next 20 years, contingent on Congressional funding, the company hoped to profit from securing continuing contracts with the U.S. armed forces.

By the end of 1997, the company's flight division was also providing air medical transport services in 16 states under 21 long-term operating agreements using a fleet of 35 helicopters and 3 airplanes. In addition, the flight division delivered five Bell 407's to its various hospital programs. Known for its speed, performance, and patient care facilities, the Bell 407 proved increasingly popular with the company's air medical transport customers.

In 1998, Air Methods continued to expand operations within a multi-billion dollar market for specialized medical transportation services and technology. Revenue increased 25 percent to a record $48.7 million compared to $38.9 million in 1997. The company's rapid expansion, however, came at a cost as Air Methods invested in hiring and training new personnel and in acquiring additional aircraft to service new locations. As a result, net income declined to $257,000 from $1.7 million in 1997. Increased revenues stemmed primarily from expansion of the company's flight services division and Mercy Air Service, Inc. into new geographic markets as well as expansion of sales from its products division.

The flight services division secured new contracts for its operations in Flagstaff and Bullhead City, Arizona, and Columbia, South Carolina. In 1998, Mercy expanded its operations in Las Vegas, Nevada, and introduced a second helicopter in San Diego. In addition, Mercy formed a joint venture with Aspen Helicopters, Inc. to expand its air emergency helicopter ambulance unit into Ventura, Santa Barbara, and San Luis Obispo Counties in California. The 50/50 venture—operating as Mercy Air, Tri-County, LLC—began operations on August 30, 1998. Under the agreement, Mercy would provide medical staffing, dispatch, marketing and public relations and administrative support services. Aspen Helicopters, a local helicopter service provider headquartered in Ventura County, would provide a medically equipped Bell 222 UT/SP helicopter as well as pilot staffing and aircraft maintenance. The company considered the joint venture a significant addition to its service, adding seven tertiary care centers to the already 20 that were being served in southern California.

In 1998, the company formed another joint venture servicing Catholic Health Services of Long Island (CHS), a large consortium of hospitals, nursing homes, diagnostic and treatment centers, and home health agencies in Nassau and Suffolk counties, New York. With more than 1,600 beds, CHS constituted the second largest healthcare consortium on Long Island. Air Methods formed the joint venture with EMX LLC of New York City, creating EMX Emergency Medical Services, LLC. The joint venture operated under a 5-year administrative service contract with CHS to operate CHS Ambulance Services, Inc. Air Methods was a 50/50 partner in the venture and owned 5 percent of privately held EMX, which developed information services and products for improving the delivery and efficiency of healthcare services. The venture enabled Air Methods to enter the ground services business, which began operations in late June with six ambulances servicing various hospitals.

On September 15, 1998, Air Methods also announced that the U.S. Airforce's Health Systems Center had selected the company as a prime contractor to develop and manufacture a new generation Spinal Cord Injury Transport System (SCITS). The new system signified the product division's first entry into the healthcare medical device market. One of Air Method's business strategies had been to diversify into new, complementary markets by utilizing its core competencies in emergency air medical systems for commercial and government applications.

Growth in 2000 and Beyond

In 2000, Air Methods' business strategy of growth through strategic acquisitions continued unabated. On April 25, Air Method's wholly-owned subsidiary, Mercy Air Service, acquired through a newly formed company all of the assets of Area Rescue Consortium of Hospitals (ARCH), a Missouri nonprofit organization, for $11 million plus two fixed wing aircraft and related equipment and inventory from Skylife Aviation, LLC for around $1.7 million. Because the acquisition was funded with proceeds from debt and lease financing and from existing treasuries, the company avoided issuing any additional shares of common stock outstanding, thus eliminating dilution to shareholders. The newly formed company, ARCH Air Medical Service, Inc., operated as a Missouri corporation and a wholly-owned subsidiary of Mercy Air. Following this transaction, Air Methods moved to acquire ownership of Rocky Mountain Holdings, LLC (RMH), one of the largest private companies providing air medical transport services in the country. RMH had pioneered more than 30 years earlier the first hospital-based air medical service program. Like Air Methods, RMH provided air medical services under both the community-based and hospital-based models, utilizing a fleet of 80 helicopters and fixed-wing aircraft. Headquartered in Provo, Utah, RMH also ran maintenance and overhaul operations in Provo and Greenville, South Carolina. In addition, it maintained a national dispatch and communications center in Omaha, Nebraska. Air Methods purchased RMH for $28 million. This transaction made Air Methods the largest provider of air medical services in the United States with operations in 31 states and a fleet of 136 helicopters and 19 fixed-wing aircraft.

Despite the economic downturn in 2001 and 2002, Air Methods continued to demonstrate substantial growth. Revenues had increased an average of 25 percent annually over the previous three years to $98.4 million, and profits grew by an average of 169 percent to $7.7 million. This rate of growth attracted the attention of the financial media. In 2002, the company was named number 30 on the ''100 America's Fastest Growing Small Companies'' list in the July–August issue of *Fortune Small Business Magazine*. The company was also profiled in *Business Week* as one of the magazine's ''Hot Growth Companies,'' listing as number 57.

Financial analysts anticipated the company would see future growth from its products division in light of the September 11, 2001 terrorist attacks in New York and Washington, D.C. After securing the contract with the U.S. Army in 1996, Air Methods developed a system that could transform a cargo helicopter into an airborne ambulance in two minutes. The helicopters were outfitted with lights, oxygen, medical supplies, and stretchers, comprising a small intensive care unit. The Army contract may conceivably generate $200 million over the next 20 years. Nonetheless, the inherent risks and unpredictability of the company's airborne missions, sometimes plagued by unscheduled delays and inclement weather affecting the bottom line, had kept investors at a distance until June 2002, when Wall Street took notice of the company's growth. In the midst of the worst bear market since the Great Depression, the company's stock increased from approximately $4 a share to more than $10 by June 2002. With this kind of performance, Air Methods appeared well positioned to take advantage of additional growth opportunities in the future.

Principal Subsidiaries

Mercy Air Service, Inc.; ARCH Air Medical Service, Inc.

Principal Divisions

Air Medical Services Division; Products Division.

Principal Operating Units

Air Medical Transportation Services; Aerospace and Air Medical Technologies; Air Management Services.

Principal Competitors

Corporate Jets, Inc.; OmniFlight, Inc.; Petroleum Helicopters, Inc.; Rocky Mountain Helicopters, Inc.

Further Reading

''Air Methods Announces Agreement to Acquire Rocky Mountain Holdings, LLC,'' *PR Newswire*, June 7, 2002.

''Air Methods Corporation Announces Completion of Area Rescue Consortium of Hospitals (ARCH) Acquisition,'' *PR Newswire*, April 26, 2000.

''Air Methods Forms Venture to Expand Mercy Air in California,'' *PR Newswire*, September 10, 1998.

''Air Methods' Joint Venture Increases Number of Ambulances in New York,'' *PR Newswire*, August 26, 1998.

''Air Methods Wins U.S. Air Force Contract to Develop Spinal Cord Injury Transport System,'' *PR Newswire*, September 15, 1998.

Todd, Aaron, ''Air Methods Corporation Completes Acquisition of Mercy Air Services, Inc.,'' *PR Newswire*, 20, no. 31, 1997

——, ''Air Methods Corporation to Acquire Mercy Air Services, Inc., *PR Newswire*, 18, no. 28, 1997.

Weintraub, Arlene, ''Air Methods Gets A Lift,'' *Business Week*, June 10, 2002.

—Bruce P. Montgomery

Alain Afflelou SA

Alain Afflelou
104, avenue des Champs Elysees
F-75008 Paris
France
Telephone: (+33) 45 61 69 69
Fax: (+33) 45 61 69 09
Web site: http://www.alainafflelou.com

Public Company
Incorporated: 1972 as Optica
Employees: 304
Sales: EUR 445 million ($400 million)(2001)
Stock Exchanges: Euronext Paris
Ticker Symbol: AAF
NAIC: 339115 Opthalmic Goods Manufacturing

Alain Afflelou SA is one of the leading optical retailers in France, with a network of more than 475 largely franchised stores owned by more than 220 franchisees. Led by the charismatic Alain Afflelou, himself an optician, the company owns 27 stores and receives fees of 4.5 percent per year from each franchised store. Afflelou stores average 100 square meters, and some two-thirds of the network's stores are located in downtown locations, while the rest are found in shopping malls. In addition to its retail network, Afflelou markets its own eyeglass and sunglasses designs under brand names Le Forty d'Afflelou, Tchin Tchin, and Afflelou Les Fatales, as well as licensed brands that include Agatha, Carita, Célio, Grès, and Lolita Lempicka. Much of Afflelou's success has been due to its innovative advertising. The company was one of the first in France to run ads featuring its own CEO, a tactic which has gained it a recognition rate of more than 95 percent. Most of Afflelou's sales, which topped EUR445 million in 2001 across the entire network, including more than EUR90 million generated by the parent company itself, come from its French home base. Afflelou intends to extend its French implantation to nearly 700 stores by the end of the 2000s. Yet Afflelou is pegging its biggest growth prospects on international expansion. (The company is already present in Belgium, Luxem-

bourg, Morocco, and Lebanon.) In order to provide funding for this expansion, which the company expects to come through extending its franchise network as well as through targeted acquisitions, Afflelou went public in April 2002, listing on the Euronext Paris Stock Exchange's Secondary Market. Alain Afflelou continues to head the company, seconded by deputy chief executive Pascal Derry.

Pied Noir *Origins in the 1970s*

Alain Afflelou was born in Algeria in 1948, a member of what was later called the *pied noir* (''black foot'') community of French living in the country's former North African colonies. His introduction to retail sales came in the bakery run by his parents, and he appeared destined to take up a retail trade as well. As he told *L'Entrepreneur:* ''I loved helping my parents in the store, it was true pleasure. In reality, I discovered at that time that I couldn't live in an office.''

After Algeria's declaration of independence and the resulting war, Afflelou's family moved to Bordeaux when he was 14 years old. Afflelou gave little thought to his future career throughout his teenage years. At the age of 18, however, he became more serious about his future, telling *L'Entrepreneur:* ''I'd met a woman. I was 18 years old. I didn't want to get involved in long studies because I was planning to get married.'' In that light, Afflelou chose become an optician, moving to Paris to study at the École Supérieure d'Optométrie, from which he received his optician's degree in 1972.

Afflelou returned to Bordeaux to open his own optician's shop that same year, using the trade name Optica. The optical trade in France in the early 1970s remained a staid market of traditional, clinical shops; at the time, wearing eyeglasses was still stigmatized and far from the fashion statement it was to become starting in the 1980s. Afflelou himself was to take part in the change in attitude toward eyeglasses and toward opticians themselves. With his background in retailing and a flair for marketing, Afflelou began planning his first advertising campaign. Because a single store did not give him sufficient revenues for mounting an advertising campaign, he opened two more stores in the Bordeaux suburbs in the mid-1970s. Then, in

Company Perspectives:

Always listening to the consumer, Alain Afflelou develops new concepts to improve glasswearers' daily life.

1978, Afflelou bought up the Maison Larghi shop, one of the oldest and most-well known French opticians. The store's location, in the heart of Bordeaux itself, gave Afflelou the visibility he sought.

In 1978, Afflelou used the equivalent of a year's profits to launch his first advertising campaign, offering frames at half-price. The slogan used for the campaign—"La moitié de votre monture à l'oil," ("half of your frame for free")—already demonstrated the company's gift for word play. The ploy worked, and Afflelou was soon selling more than 100 frames per day. He also attracted a good deal of media attention, particularly among optician trade journals. Before long, Afflelou began receiving letters from other opticians wishing to copy his sales techniques.

Franchising Success in the 1980s

In 1979, Afflelou decided to set up a franchise business to capitalize on the interest in his business model. By the end of that year, the company had signed up its first three franchisees—some of whom came from among Afflelou's former optician's school classmates—in Bayonne, Pessac, and Rouen. Through this network, Afflelou was able to introduce a number innovations into the French retail optical market, establishing a standardized store format, offering a wide selection of frames, as well as bargain prices and other marketing initiatives.

Advertising remained a strong component of Afflelou's business, and in 1980 the company once again attracted attention—and customers—when it announced it would begin selling certain frames at cost. The campaign was a success, attracting growing numbers of customers and franchisees. By 1985, the company's franchise network had opened its 100th store.

Afflelou had begun seeking a new name for the franchise network but had been unsatisfied with the possibilities. As he told *L'Entrepreneur:* "Everything we found was hackneyed: Lynx Optique, Cornée Optique. . . . One day in a café someone said to me: 'I don't understand why you don't call yourself Alain Afflelou.' " Afflelou took the idea to advertising firm RSCG, which created the slogan "On est fou d'Afflelou" ("We love Afflelou").

Once again, Afflelou succeeded in raising eyebrows, becoming one of the first French business leaders to place himself in his company's advertising campaign. Nevertheless, Afflelou's advertising strategy met with success. Even more so, the charismatic Afflelou quickly proved one of the company's strongest marketing assets. The brand and Afflelou himself soon enjoyed strong recognition on a national scale.

In 1987, the company merged its two existing operations, Optica and Maison Larghi into a new company called Alain Afflelou SA. By then, the group counted more than 140 franchise outlets. An important moment for the company followed the next year, when Afflelou acquired Paris-based Leroy SA Optician, which ran a network of ten stores in the Paris area, including a store on the famed Champs-Elysées. Following the acquisition, Afflelou moved its headquarters to Paris and made the Champs-Elysées site its flagship store. The company's Paris-area stores—which, because of the difficulty of extending the franchise network into the expensive Paris market, remained company-owned—became a laboratory of sorts as the company continued to seek new innovation opportunities.

Innovative Leadership in the 1990s

Afflelou continued to build its franchise network, which expanded rapidly at the end of the 1980s to nearly 400 stores by 1992. The company continued to roll out new advertising and marketing successes, such as the campaign launched in 1989, "Quand on a une gueule, on y tient" ("When you've got a look, love it"). In 1990, the company created its Contrat Lentilles Liberté, offering special deals for contact lenses purchases.

Afflelou, which had built much of its early success on its aggressive pricing policies, now sought to emphasize the range of services provided at its network's stores, rolling out a new campaign, "Alain Afflelou et moi, ce n'est pas que pour l'argent" ("It's not just for the money"). The company boosted its services offering again in 1991 when it began promoting one-hour eyeglasses preparation. Then, in 1993, the company began selling a new series of frames that were guaranteed for life.

With the rapid expansion of the franchise network, which had topped 400 stores, and his own growing media fame, Afflelou brought in Pascal Derrey to serve as the company's chief financial officer (and later as deputy chief executive). Derrey took over the day-to-day management of the company and restructured the franchise network, while adding new accounting and financial procedures. Afflelou had also brought in new capital to the group, selling 23 percent of the company to bank Credit Lyonnais's investment subsidiary Clinvest.

By the mid-1990s, Afflelou's franchise network was largely in place. The company also enjoyed a high loyalty rate among its more than 200 franchisees, with more than 96 percent remaining in the network. Afflelou now began seeking new ways to expand sales. The company decided to begin developing its own product line to be sold throughout its network, and in 1993 launched its first line of Afflelou-branded eyeglasses. In 1994, the company reached a distribution agreement with Orcolite of the United States, later acquired by Vision Eyes, which gave Afflelou the exclusive European distribution rights to that company's new polycarbonate lenses, which were both significantly lighter and more resistant to breakage than traditional lenses. Afflelou began marketing the lenses under the brand 2AI.

In 1995, Afflelou gained exclusive French distribution rights to a new progressive lens produced by Shamir. The company then launched the new product as the "Cent pour Cent" ("100 percent"), which became another strong sales success for the company. That year also, the company launched its Price Contract, offering to reimburse the price if a customer found cheaper eyeglasses elsewhere.

Key Dates:

1972: Alain Afflelou opens his first optical shop, Optica, in Bordeaux.
1978: Afflelou acquires Maison Larghi and begins advertising eyeglass frames at half price.
1979: The optical firm establishes a franchise network.
1985: The Optica stores are rebranded as Alain Afflelou.
1987: The company changes its name to Alain Afflelou SA.
1988: Leroy SA Optician is acquired, with 10 stores in Paris area.
1993: The company creates it own label of eyeglasses and sells a 23 percent stake to Credit Lyonnais.
1997: Alain Afflelou reacquires 100 percent control, then sells 70 percent to investment fund group Alpha.
1998: The company's first international franchises open in Belgium and Luxembourg.
2000: Alain Afflelou, with Apax Partners, reacquires control of the company.
2002: The company goes public with a listing on Paris Bourse's Secondary Market.

New Strategies in the Late 1990s and Beyond

Afflelou hit on a new formula in the late 1990s, that of package deals. The first of these was "La Forty d'Afflelou," a set of four matched reading glasses, launched in 1997. These were followed in the next year with "La Funny d'Afflelou," featuring a pack of four sunglasses.

By then, Afflelou had changed ownership. In 1997, the company had bought back 100 percent control of the company as Credit Lyonnais began disposing of much of its holdings. Afflelou then sold the 23 percent share to investment fund group Alpha, which specialized in investing in family-run businesses before re-launching them as public companies. That purchase gave rise to suggestions that Afflelou was preparing to take his company public.

Instead, however, Afflelou sold control of the company to Alpha and another investment group Marine Wendel, reducing his own stake to just 30 percent. Part of Afflelou's motivation came from difficulties surrounding his purchase of the Bordeaux soccer team in 1990, which resulted in Afflelou becoming involved in a fraud investigation into the soccer team's finances. The negative publicity surrounding the case had dashed hopes of taking Afflelou public—and Afflelou himself left the country to take up residence in Switzerland.

Despite its founder's legal difficulties, Afflelou continued to grow, and in 1998 the company began its first efforts to expand internationally. New franchise stores opened in Belgium, Morocco, Lebanon, and Luxembourg, backed by a new subsidiary, Alain Afflelou International. That year the company also began introducing a new range of designer fashions in its stores, selling sunglasses and frames by Célio, Carita, Lolita Lempicka, and others.

Afflelou bounced back in 1999 with the launch of another highly successful marketing campaign, the "Tchin-Tchin,"

which offered a second pair of eyeglasses for just one additional French franc. The company followed that campaign up the following year with a Tchin Tchin for sunglasses. In 2000, Afflelou also expanded the range of its own label eyeglasses with the license to produce a new line of products under the name of famed French actor Alain Delon.

By then, the company had hit a new setback in its domestic growth drive. In July 1999, the company had reached an agreement to acquire rival optical chain Lissac, which headed a franchise network of more than 100 stores. Despite Afflelou's intention to leave the Lissac brand and franchise network intact, a revolt by a number of Lissac franchisees forced the two sides to break off the purchase agreement at the beginning of 2000.

Instead, the company was forced to look beyond the more or less mature French market and begin to pursue its international expansion. At the end of 2000, Afflelou bought back control of the company, joined by capital investment group Apax partners. Afflelou's personal stake was raised to 58 percent of the company, while Apax's share reached 39 percent.

By the end of 2001, Afflelou's franchise network had topped 475 stores, with total revenues of EUR445 million. The company announced its intention to continue to expand its retail network in France by as many as 100 stores and also indicated its interest in pursuing new acquisitions, both in France and elsewhere in Europe, especially in Germany and Spain. In order to fuel its new growth ambitions, Afflelou at last went public in April 2002, taking a listing on the Paris Bourse's Secondary Market. Alain Afflelou's own stake in the company remained at more than 48 percent, with more than 55 percent of the company's voting rights. Afflelou, who had become one of France's most recognized media figures, continued to be one of his company's primary assets.

Principal Subsidiaries

Les Boutiques d'Alain Afflelou SA; JR & F SA; AASE SARL; SCI 169 Rue de Rennes; Alain Afflelou International SA (Luxembourg).

Principal Competitors

Fielmann GmbH; Grandvision SA.

Further Reading

"Alain Afflelou Raises Eu60m as Penauille Offer Flounders," *Euroweek*, April 12, 2002, p. 24.
"Alain Afflelou reprend le contrôle de sa société," *Le Telegramme*, May 4, 2000.
"Alain Afflelou retrouve ses lunettes, *Challenges*, October 1, 2000.
"Alain Afflelou se prépare pour la Bourse," *Le Figaro*, December 13, 2001.
"Apax's Vision for Alain Afflelou," *European Venture Capital Journal*, June 2000 p. 42.
Bonnet, Nathalie, "L'entrepreneur qui voit loin," *L'Entrepreneur*, November 8, 2001.
Ferron, Aurelien, "Le pari fou d'Afflelou," *Newsbourse,* March 24, 2002.

—M.L. Cohen

Amedysis, Inc.

11100 Meade Road
Suite 300
Baton Rouge, Louisiana 70816
U.S.A.
Telephone: (225) 292-2031
Toll Free: (800) 467-2552
Fax: (225) 295-9685
Web site: http://www.amedisys.com

Public Company
Incorporated: 1982 as Analytical Nursing Management
   Corporation
Employees: 1,521
Sales: $110 million (2001)
Stock Exchanges: NASDAQ
Ticker Symbol: AMED
NAIC: 561310 Employment Placement Agencies; 621610
   Home Health Care Services

Amedisys, Inc., with its main office in Baton Rouge, Louisiana, operates 60 home-care nursing locations in nine southern and southeastern states: Alabama, Florida, Georgia, Louisiana, North Carolina, Oklahoma, South Carolina, Tennessee, and Virginia. In addition to providing expert, regular nursing care, the company offers several specialized, home-health programs, including physical, speech, and occupational therapy as well as pain management, wound care, cardiac, infusion therapy, oncology, pediatric, and psychiatric services. When needed, Amedisys also provides medical social workers. Founder William F. Borne, who owns close to 10 percent of Amedisys, is the company's chairman and CEO.

Founding a Network of Nursing and Home Health Care Services: 1982–92

William F. Borne was the founder of Amedisys, which he started up in Baton Rouge, Louisiana, in 1982, as Analytical Nursing Management Corporation (ANMC). A graduate of the Charity Hospital School of Nursing in New Orleans, Borne, a registered nurse, worked clinically in medical-surgical areas with supplemental staffing agencies in that city from 1979 to 1980. Between 1980 and 1983, he served as director of nursing at West St. James Hospital in Vacherie, Louisiana. At the time he started up ANMC, he was also an intensive care supervisor for Key Nursing Corporation, a position he had taken in June 1982.

Initially, the company focused on providing nurses and nursing services for both home health care and other health care facilities. The focus was reflected in the fact that some of Borne's early associates were also trained nurses, including current board members William Hession and Lynne S. Bernard. Hession, who has served as a director of the company since 1983, holds a nursing degree from Nicholls State University in Thibodaux, Louisiana. He was president of Key Nursing Corporation at the time Borne founded ANMC. Bernard, who holds a nursing degree from Southern Arkansas University and now holds the post of president of the company's nursing services division, joined the company in 1988 and held various posts with an ANMC subsidiary. Prior to joining the company she had served as director of home health care services for Medical Personnel Pool in Baton Rouge.

Although nurse staffing services and home health care were the central focus of ANMC during its first decade, it soon diversified its business, developing allied areas that would become the company's primary divisions when it underwent reorganization in 1993. In December of that year, in a reverse acquisition arrangement, M & N Capital Corp., created as a blind investors' pool registered with the Securities and Exchange Commission (SEC) as a public corporation, obtained ANMC. The upshot was that ANMC became M & N's wholly owned subsidiary and received a capital infusion of $1.265 million. M & N, initially incorporated in New York, was reincorporated in Delaware, changed its name to ANMC, and began trading on the NASDAQ small cap market. Subsequently, ANMC changed its name to Amedisys, Inc. The company consolidated the holdings of it various subsidiaries via stock transfers so that these were then wholly owned by Amedisys.

Company Perspectives:

Our Purpose: To serve and care for people at home. Our Strategy: To offer low-cost, outcome driven health care at home as an alternative to facility based care. Our Mission: To become the home care agency of choice in the markets we serve.

Growth through Acquisition in the Mid-1990s

When the reorganization was completed, Amedisys's network of subsidiaries consisted of a group of companies that evolved somewhat amorphously through mergers and acquisitions. Among these were Amedisys Staffing Services, Inc. (ASS), Amedisys Nursing Services, Inc. (ANS), Amedisys Specialized Medical Services, Inc. (ASM), Amedisys Home Health, Inc., Amedisys Home Health, Inc. of Texas, Amedisys Surgery Centers, L.C. (ACS), and Amedisys Physician Services, Inc. (APS). ASS, the staffing service, provided registered and licensed practical nurses to all kinds of health care facilities. ANS, an employee-based staffing agency, also provided nurses and aides as relief personnel in the same sort of facilities. In 1996, another staffing agency, Amerinurse, Inc., previously a separate subsidiary, was merged into ANS. Amerinurse supplied highly trained nurses to health care facilities on a contract basis.

A wide range of health care services were provided by Amedisys Specialized Medical Services, Inc., Amedisys Home Health, Inc., and Amedisys Home Health, Inc. of Texas. In addition to providing nursing care in the home, they provided other home health aid, including physical therapy, occupational therapy, speech therapy, and medical social workers.

Through its Amedisys Surgery Centers subsidiary, Amedisys operated two outpatient surgery centers in Houston, Texas, and another, which began operations in Hammond, Louisiana, in 1996, as St. Luke's SurgiCenter, a joint venture undertaken with physicians practicing in Hammond. In addition, through Amedisys Physician Services, the company provided management for both practitioners and networks, including Independent Practice Associations, and for home health agencies. APS evolved from the Rural Health Provider Network, Inc., which had been formed in 1994 as a corporation to manage both an internal medicine clinic and rural health clinics. That corporation, jointly owned by a group of physicians and Amedisys, became Amedisys Physician Services in 1995. In 1996, Amedisys entered an agreement with the Louisiana Health Care Authority, which governs public hospitals in Louisiana, to manage physician services at a public hospital in Lake Charles. The agreement gave Amedisys the responsibility of integrating the inpatient staff's services with those of outpatient clinics in the Lake Charles community. In addition, APS operated a laboratory, though by 1997 its chief focus was on providing management services to practitioners and networks through its physician services division.

In October 1996, Amedisys announced plans to merge with Complete Management Inc. of New York, an expansion plan that initially seemed promising but ended up falling through the following March because the two companies could not reach a final agreement on the buyout price that Complete Management would pay for absorbing Amedisys. Initially, Complete Management offered $23.3 million in stock for Amedisys, but over the next five months its stock fell in value from around $15 to $11.88 per share, souring the proposed merger. Its failure meant that Amedisys looked to alternative expansion plans, including the purchase of additional outpatient surgery centers and managing doctors' group practices in other regions. More closely linked to its shifting business focus, the company began acquiring home-care service companies, including, in September 1997, Allgood Medical Services Inc., a Louisiana enterprise that conducted business as Care Medical and Mobility Equipment Co. Allgood provided medical equipment in home-health settings as well as HMO's and medical facilities in both Louisiana and Mississippi.

Takeover Attempt in the Late 1990s

Major changes in Amedisys's core business began in earnest in 1998, when it purchased 116 home heath sites from Columbia/HCA Healthcare Corp., which, at the time, was undergoing a major downsizing. The facilities were located in six states: Alabama, Georgia, Louisiana, North Carolina, Oklahoma, and Tennessee. The acquisition was the first major step in a restructuring plan that chairman and CEO William Borne had announced in August of that year. Under that plan, Amedisys was to focus on its home-health nursing and infusion therapy.

The restructuring plan was in part prompted by new government guidelines, which, in 1998, left Amedisys in financial turmoil. The company took a big bottom line hit from new payment rules for home health care afforded Medicare beneficiaries. Its revenues for the first nine months of 1998 dropped 22 percent below those of the same period in the previous year, and in November it announced a third-quarter loss of $4 million. Further, the company was forced to delist its stock with NASDAQ and trade over the electronic Bulletin Board, where its stock fell to half the $4.88 peak it had reached the previous year.

In order to refocus its energies almost exclusively on home health care, Amedisys began retrenching services in other areas. In September 1998, for an undisclosed selling price, the company sold its staffing services division to Nursefinders Inc. of Arlington, Texas. The sale included offices in Florida, Louisiana, Minnesota, Mississippi, North Carolina, Oklahoma, Tennessee, and Texas, and involved about 90 employees.

Amedisys's corporate make-over efforts were complicated by the fact the company was mired in legal battles with some of its former executives. The principal dispute was with James Cefaratti, whom the company had hired as president in August 1997 but then fired on the grounds that Cefaratti had misrepresented himself with regards to his prior employment accomplishments and reasons for his previous terminations. Under legal siege and financially reeling, Amedisys was very vulnerable. Its condition prompted William Smith, a New Orleans investor, to attempt a leveraged buyout of the company. Smith tendered an $23.5 million offer to buy Amedisys's 4.7 million shares of common stock at $5 per share. It was an unsolicited and unwanted offer, and, as the Baton Rouge *Advocate* reported, one that William Borne described as a "less than up

Key Dates:

Key Dates:

1982: Analytical Nursing Management Corporation (ANMC) is founded in Baton Rouge, Louisiana.
1992: ANMC is reorganized.
1994: M & N Capital Corp. (M & N), established as a blind pool, completes reverse acquisition of ANMC, and goes public.
1995: M & N changes its name to Amedisys, Inc and acquires Surgical Care Services of Texas.
1997: A proposed merged with Complete Management Inc. falls through.
1998: Amedysis divests its supplemental staffing, home care management, and primary care services; the company acquires Columbia/HCA Healthcare Corp.'s facilities in Alabama, Georgia, Louisiana, North Carolina, Oklahoma, and Tennessee.
1999: The company shifts its primary focus to home health care nursing.
2000: Amedisys completes its divestment of five ambulatory surgery centers and its infusion therapy division; the company sells it infusion pharmacy operations in Dallas and San Antonio, Texas and St. Petersburg, Florida.
2001: The company sells a controlling interest in Hammond Surgical Care Center.

front way of going about getting what you want.'' The company dodged the buyout bullet, however, helped by its restructuring moves and the fact that it secured a $25 million line of credit arranged with an Ohio finance company. Although Amedisys denied that the capital infusion was related to Smith's takeover move, it did shore up the company's sagging fortunes. It also allowed it to continue its restructuring, and, among other things, acquire a 67 percent interest in another business, the Tanglewood Surgery Center in Odessa, Texas.

At the time, Amedisys appeared committed to maintaining its surgery centers. It owned and operated three surgery centers in Houston and one in Hammond, and it was also building one in Lafayette, Louisiana, that opened in March 1999. However, it would soon divest itself of these operations as, in 1999, it continued to shift its basic focus still further away from providing alternate site provider health care services to concentrate almost strictly on home health care nursing services. That change was prompted by the company's major investment in home health care, namely the 83 home care offices it acquired from The Healthcare Company; changes in Medicare's home-care reimbursement allowances, which made such care profitable; and the company's by then well established reputation for home care nursing expertise and innovation.

Returning to Financial Stability: 2000 and Beyond

As a result of the decision to shift its operational focus, Amedisys entered a new restructuring phase and began divesting its non-home health care nursing divisions. Between September 1999 and December 2000, it sold five of its six surgery centers and the three infusion centers making up its infusion division. In August 2000, the company sold its infusion pharmacy operations in Dallas and San Antonio in Texas and in St. Petersburg in Florida. These, which combined generated $6.5 million in revenues in 1999, were acquired by Park Pharmacy Corp. That company planned to make them part of its wholly owned Park Infusion Services L.P. subsidiary. Terms of the sale were not made public.

With its new strategy firmly in place, Amedisys set out to achieve market dominance in the South and Southeast through expanding its referral base, using a highly trained sales force, as well as by making additional acquisitions and offering an array of specialized services, such as wound care, for example. In July 2001, for an undisclosed sum, the company bought HealthCalls from East Cooper Regional Medical Center, a Tenet Healthcare hospital. At the time of the acquisition, HealthCalls was servicing three counties in South Carolina. Meanwhile, to tighten its focus yet further, Amedisys continued to sell off some of its other holdings. In September 2001, for about $1 million, Amedisys sold off its controlling interest in the Hammond Surgical Care Center to the Surgery Center of Hammond.

Amedisys still faced major problems, however. Although it had benefited from a new Medicare reimbursement system, which had sent its stock climbing in 2000, in June 2001 the company disclosed that it had overstated its revenue through a six-month period through clerical errors on its Medicare paper work. That temporarily sent its stock value plummeting, right at a time when the company was trying to get reinstated with NASDAQ. Amedisys reimbursed Medicare and was not charged with any wrongdoing, and subsequent earnings sent its stock back up. By March 2002, it had reached a sufficient level to get relisted with NASDAQ. Perhaps to buffer itself against any hint of shadiness, Amedisys fired its accounting firm, Arthur Anderson, a company that was then reeling from its role in the infamous Enron scandal.

According to a statement on its Web site, Amedisys perceived 2002 as a year that would bring new changes. The health care industry would become outcome driven, with a focus on ''defining and accomplishing specific patient outcomes in the most cost efficient manner.'' The company was convinced that it was positioning itself appropriately by focusing on home health nursing services, ''strategically separating itself from other competitors in the industry,'' most of which continued to offer services in categories that Amedisys had been jettisoning, including infusion therapy and home medical equipment provision services. The company was confident that its more narrow focus would allow it ''to emerge as a leader in home health nursing.''

Principal Subsidiaries

Amedisys Physician SVC; Amedisys Specialized Med SVC.

Principal Competitors

Almost Family, Inc.; Apria Healthcare Group Inc.; Coram Healthcare Corporation; Gentiva Health Services, Inc.; Home Health Corporation of America, Inc.; National HealthCare Corporation; Option Care, Inc.

Further Reading

Griggs, Ted, "Amedisys Inc. Sells Division on Staffing to Nursefinders," *Advocate* (Baton Rouge), September 24, 1998, p. 1D.

McClain, Randy, "Amedisys Ends Merger Plans Over Price Tag," *Advocate* (Baton Rouge), March 22, 1997, p. 1C.

Ngeo, Christine, "Columbia in Four Home-Care Deals," *Modern Healthcare*, June 8, 1998, p. 21.

Shinkle, Peter, "Amedisys Secures Credit Line," *Advocate* (Baton Rouge), December 31, 1998, p. 1D.

Smith, William, "Investor Makes Offer for Ailing Amedisys," *Advocate* (Baton Rouge), September 18, 1998, p. 8C.

—John W. Fiero

Amerock Corporation

4000 Auburn Street
Rockford, Illinois 61101
U.S.A.
Telephone: (815) 963-9631
Fax: (815) 959-6138
Web site: http://www.amerock.com

Division of Newell Rubbermaid Inc.
Incorporated: 1909
Employees: 1,178
Sales: $200 million (2001 est.)
NAIC: 332510 Hardware Manufacturing

Based in Rockford, Illinois, Amerock Corporation is a leading U.S. manufacturer of cabinet hardware and storage systems. The company is part of Newell Rubbermaid Inc.'s Levolor Hardware Group. Amerock manufactures products under a number of different brand names, including Accentz, Accuride, Hint of Heritage, Inspirations, Marathon, Pro-Glide 5850, Radiance, Reflections, Royal Family/Natural Elegance, Storage & Convenience, System 2000, and System 3200. Its product offerings fall into several broad categories. In addition to decorative hardware, the company's line of functional hardware includes drawer slides, brass items, and both concealed and decorative hinges. Amerock's storage and convenience product offerings include blind corner shelves, turn-a-shelf sets, storage systems for pantries, organizers, and media storage products.

Starting Strong: 1928–49

Like many American manufacturing companies, what eventually became Amerock began modestly, resulting from the efforts of a few determined people and a pioneering idea. In 1928, two Swedish immigrants named Reuben and Gedor Aldeen left Rockford's formidable National Lock Co. to establish the Aldeen Manufacturing Co. Trained as mechanics before they came to America, Reuben Aldeen had served as National Lock's superintendent of tool, machine, and maintenance, and Gedor was the firm's vice-president of engineering.

Along with the Aldeens came a select group of other National Lock workers. Together, these ten men comprised what some believe to be the first U.S. manufacturing company to concentrate solely on the production of cabinet hardware. Until that time, the hardware in most American kitchens was relatively basic and highly functional. Aldeen and his counterparts were convinced that Americans would buy more decorative matching hardware that enhanced the appearance of their kitchens and homes.

The new enterprise first rented space in the city's knitting district, on the 12th floor of a 13-story structure on South Main Street known as the William Ziock Building. Constructed in two phases between 1918 and 1924, the Ziock Building was long recognized as the first "skyscraper" in Rockford. It was owned by knitting company Ziock Industries Inc. Aldeen Manufacturing Co. initially occupied half of the 12th floor of this structure, which was sometimes referred to as the Tower Building. According to Amerock, the equipment used to manufacture products during the company's first year was especially crude, consisting of "porcelain iceboxes and car batteries for plating." However, the operation was a success, resulting in first-year sales of approximately $69,000.

When the 1930s arrived, Aldeen's company changed its name to American Cabinet Hardware Corp. The prosperity that Americans had enjoyed during the 1920s gave way to unfortunate times during the 1930s. The stock market crashed in October 1929, and the Great Depression followed. Building permits in Rockford fell from roughly 6,000 in 1928 to 11 in 1931, and a mere two in 1934. As factories closed and workers lost their jobs, more than 8,000 families went on work relief by 1935.

Amidst these difficult times, American Cabinet Hardware found success. By 1933, the company unveiled a solid lineup of matched kitchen hardware. According to the December 13, 1955 *Rockford Register Republic*, "Amerock introduced new, modern designs of drawer pulls, knobs, hinges, and 'push button' catches in beautiful 'matched' ensembles. Improved mechanical features made the hardware easier to install and operate."

The company's first customers were cabinet manufacturers like American Central, Boro Wood, Curtis, Del-Mar, Farley &

Loetscher, Geneva Modern, Hot-Point, Kitchen Maid, Lyon, Morgan, Mutschler, Shirley, Coppes Inc., and Youngstown Steel. However, hardware dealers soon wanted the company's products to sell at retail. Thus, American Cabinet Hardware's two main market niches were established.

In addition to its success through these channels, the manufacturer received its first order from Andersen Windows in 1932. This initial order developed into a strong business relationship that was critical to the company's early growth, helping sales to reach $3 million by the end of the 1930s. By this time, things were going so well that the company purchased 15 acres of land in the southeastern part of the city. Even though plenty of capacity was still available in the Ziock Building, American Cabinet Hardware bought the acreage with future expansion in mind.

In 1940, American Cabinet Hardware combined portions of the words "American" and "Rockford" to create a new brand name called "Amerock." The brand's patriotic ring could not have come at a better timer: by the end of the following year, America was at war. World War II created a challenging environment for U.S. manufacturers, as the military demanded large amounts of resources for wartime production. However, despite these conditions American Cabinet Hardware found continued prosperity. In 1941, the company obtained a small, 40,000-square-foot manufacturing plant on Seminary Street from the Old Colony Furniture Co. By 1942, the manufacturer occupied all 13 floors of the Ziock Building, which it purchased three years later for about $300,000.

In 1947, American Cabinet Hardware built a one-story warehouse on the Harrison Avenue property it had acquired in the late 1930s. The following year, the company was recognized by the state employment commission of the American Legion for its commitment to employing handicapped people, especially disabled veterans. The award came after the commission reviewed 422 Rockford-area employers. According to the October 7, 1948 *Rockford Morning Star*, at the time more than 22 percent of the manufacturer's 1,112 employees were veterans. Approximately 5 percent (57) of all employees were handicapped, 22 of whom were veterans. By the end of the 1940s, annual sales had climbed to $7 million, more than doubling in ten years.

Major Expansion Begins: 1950–64

After establishing a strong foothold during its first two decades of operation, American Cabinet Hardware entered a period of rapid growth and expansion in the 1950s. In March 1950, the company announced plans to build a six-story, $400,000 addition to its 13-story plant. At this time, American Cabinet Hard-

ware relied on a number of specialized machines—many of which it designed and manufactured in-house—to produce a broad offering of cabinet hardware. These machines were part of a highly organized manufacturing process that created beautiful finished hardware from raw material such as steel coils.

Also in 1950, American Cabinet Hardware expanded internationally by establishing American Cabinet Hardware Limited. The new Canadian company was based in Meaford, Ontario, and employed about 125 workers who produced for the Canadian market the same hardware manufactured in Rockford. A major development occurred in late 1953 when the Aldeens announced plans to build a new, $3 million plant on Auburn Street. In addition, they revealed that operations at the other two facilities in Rockford (Seminary Street and Harrison Avenue) would be moved to the new facility, and that the Ziock Building would be sold for $500,000 to L.C. Miller and Associates.

In 1954, another member of the Aldeen family joined American Cabinet Hardware's executive ranks. Norris G. Aldeen, who joined the company in 1933 as an apprentice toolmaker and gradually assumed positions involving greater responsibility, was named vice-president of manufacturing. Prior to this role, he had served as the company's personnel director.

American Cabinet Hardware continued to lease the Ziock Building from its new owners until 1956, when construction of the new Auburn Street facility was complete. The company's new plant was built on a $44,000 tract of land spanning almost 95 acres. The facility itself included ten acres of floor space, a 300-seat cafeteria, and 1,000 parking spaces for the firm's 1,800 workers. Shortly before the company moved into its new physical plant, another major change took place in 1956 when American Cabinet Hardware Corp. adopted the name of its flagship brand and officially became Amerock Corporation. The change was made because the Amerock name had become more recognizable than the company's name.

It was not long before Amerock announced plans to expand its new plant. The need for more manufacturing space led to construction of a 40,000-square-foot addition, built at the cost of $250,000. Construction was to be completed by early 1960. It also was in 1959 that Amerock repurchased the former Ziock building for storage purposes.

When the 1960s arrived, the Aldeen family was still very much in control of Amerock. Gedor Aldeen remained chairman and Reuben Aldeen was president. Norris Aldeen had been promoted to administrative vice-president in 1961, and then executive vice-president the following year. By this time, the company's offerings fell into one of three hardware categories: appliance, cabinet, and window. Amerock had developed an excellent reputation within the industry. In 1961, *American Builder* magazine presented the manufacturer with a quality award at the National Association of Home Builders show. The award was given per the recommendation of a San Diego-based construction firm, which claimed Amerock's products increased homes' salability.

In 1964, Amerock announced yet another addition to its enormous Auburn Street plant. That September, the company revealed plans to add 98,000 square feet at a cost of $800,000, relieving overcrowding and increasing manufacturing space by

Key Dates:

1928: Reuben and Gedor Aldeen leave Rockford's National Lock Co. to establish the Aldeen Manufacturing Co.

1930s: The company name changes to American Cabinet Hardware Corporation.

1933: A solid lineup of matched kitchen hardware is introduced.

1939: Annual sales reach $3 million.

1940: American Cabinet Hardware combines portions of the words ''American'' and ''Rockford'' to create a new brand name called Amerock.

1949: Annual sales reach $7 million.

1956: American Cabinet Hardware Corp. adopts the name of its flagship brand and officially becomes Amerock Corporation.

1965: Norris Aldeen becomes president of Amerock.

1966: Amerock becomes a subsidiary of Stanley Works in a $32 million merger.

1971: The Federal Trade Commission instructs Stanley to sell Amerock, having deemed the merger illegal.

1974: Ohio-based Anchor-Hocking Corp. acquires Amerock for $32 million.

1982: Larry E. Gloyd, a long-time Amerock employee, is named president.

1986: Don Sell, president of Amerock's Canadian operation, replaces Gloyd.

1987: Newell Co. acquires Amerock parent Anchor Hocking Corp.

1994: Amerock achieves sales of $200 million.

2002: New leadership ensues as Robert W. Bailey is named Amerock's president.

roughly 25 percent. Part of the addition, totaling 28,000 square feet, was made to finish off the east end of the plant where two previous additions had been made. Besides this, a two-story structure was planned for the northeast corner of the plant. The upper level was to be used for manufacturing and the bottom for additional storage. At this time, an expansion effort also was underway at Amerock's Canadian plant. The fourth since 1950, the addition increased that facility's size by almost one-third.

Ownership Changes: 1965–87

In February 1965, Norris Aldeen became president of Amerock. He was at the company's helm when it announced a $32 million merger with New Britain, Connecticut-based toolmaker Stanley Works. Effective August 1, 1966, Amerock became a subsidiary of Stanley. In addition to his role at Amerock, Norris Aldeen became vice-president of the Stanley Works and a member of its board and executive committee. On April 30, 1968, almost two years after the merger occurred, the Federal Trade Commission ''filed a complaint charging the merger violated the Clayton Anti-Trust Act and had the potential for cornering the general hardware and cabinet hardware market,'' as explained in the November 24, 1969 *Rockford Register Republic*. Amerock contested the FTC's claim, and the issue was not resolved until the 1970s.

Amerock ended the 1960s with another expansion of its physical plant. This time, the addition totaled 95,000 square feet and cost $1 million. The project, which involved several phases, increased the company's office space by 15,000 square feet while boosting manufacturing space by 80,000 square feet. Overall, the total size of the Auburn Street facility grew to 650,000 square feet.

Amerock started the early 1970s at a fast pace, achieving record sales in 1971 thanks to a number of new product introductions, as well as strong housing starts. In addition, employment increased at the manufacturer, reaching levels of about 1,900 workers. It also was in 1971 that the Federal Trade Commission instructed Stanley to sell Amerock by 1973, and to refrain from acquiring a similar company for a period of ten years without first getting the commission's blessing. Although Stanley made an appeal to the U.S. Supreme Court in 1973, the high court refused to hear the matter. Thus, a lower court decision that Amerock should be sold remained intact.

In 1973, Amerock achieved yet another year of record sales. The company also expanded again, acquiring a 60,000-square-foot manufacturing plant in Winnebago, Illinois, and adding 90,000 square feet of shipping and warehouse space at the Auburn Street plant. By 1974, Norris Aldeen had become Amerock's chairman, and Roger Linderoth was serving as president. In November, Lancaster, Ohio-based Anchor-Hocking Corp.—a manufacturer of kitchenware with sales of $367 million—announced that it had acquired Amerock for $32 million. The change in ownership became effective in October of 1975, after the Federal Trade Commission (FTC) and the Canadian government approved the acquisition.

By the late 1970s, a strong housing market had benefited Amerock considerably, leading to a 30 percent sales increase in 1976 and an estimated 12 percent increase in 1977. Massive market penetration also had been attained; about 70 percent of American kitchens included Amerock products. The following year, Amerock received industry-wide recognition for its promotional programs and innovative in-store packaging when *Building Supply News* presented the manufacturer with three industry awards. According to the company, during the 1970s Amerock's promotional efforts had grown to include mobile marketing tactics. Vans were used to showcase Amerock's product lines, which included display units, drawer systems, and items incorporating combinations of porcelain, metal, and wood.

During the 1980s, Amerock was challenged by an economic recession. As a securities analyst explained in the December 2, 1984 *Rockford Register Star*, a poor housing market between 1979 and 1982 took a heavy toll on the company's profits. Thus, during the early 1980s Amerock began implementing measures to save money, including layoffs. Guiding the manufacturer during these difficult times was Larry E. Gloyd, a long-time Amerock employee who was named president in 1982.

In 1983, the housing market began to improve and Amerock diversified its product line to offset dependence on cyclical housing starts. Part of its diversification strategy included the acquisition of Safe Hardware in 1982, as well as a Missouri-based lock manufacturer in 1984. However, despite better profitability, times were still tough. In late 1984, Amerock announced a number of cuts to its compensation program. No cost-of-living increases were given to workers that year, and bonuses for supervisors also ceased.

Despite these difficult conditions, Amerock continued to invest in its future. In the mid-1980s, the company revealed plans to enhance quality control initiatives and make production processes more modern and efficient. It also began implementing strategies to help offset the effects of competition from Asian firms. As the 1980s progressed, Amerock was forced to be more flexible with customers in what had become a highly competitive environment. Along with these measures, the company kept rolling out new products in tandem with effective merchandising strategies.

In September 1986, Gloyd left Amerock to become president and chief operating officer of J.L. Clark Co., a Rockford-based packaging company. Don Sell, who had been serving as president of Amerock's Canadian operation, replaced Gloyd. However, even bigger changes took place when, in July 1987, Freeport, Illinois-based Newell Co. (which eventually became Newell Rubbermaid Inc.) acquired Amerock parent Anchor Hocking Corp. for $340 million.

Life With Newell: 1988 and Beyond

As part of the Newell acquisition, Richard F. Krug replaced Sell as Amerock's president. However, Krug left the organization in October 1989, leaving Newell executive Tom Ferguson in charge. Amerock benefited from its new ownership arrangement, which provided strong financial backing. The company continued to introduce new products, including a new line of concealed hinges in 1993. That year, Amerock forged a joint agreement with Lama d.d., in which Amerock would market the Slovenia-based firm's concealed hinges in the United States. On the financial front, Amerock achieved sales of $200 million by 1994, a healthy increase over levels of $180 million in 1988.

According to Amerock, during the 1990s the company also increased the efficiency of its manufacturing processes, further consolidated operations, and received ISO 9001 certification.

By 1998, Richard Krause was serving as Amerock's president. At this time, the company was targeting home improvement retailers such as Lowe's and Menard's with a strategy to cross-sell Amerock cabinet hardware with cabinetry from other manufacturers. As part of the strategy, Amerock began developing special order displays that eliminated inventory requirements for retailers.

In September 2002, Robert W. Bailey was named Amerock's president. By this time, the company had changed considerably from the days of the Aldeen brothers. It had weathered numerous challenges and ownership changes. Likewise, Amerock's products—which began with a simple, yet innovative idea—had evolved with the times. They remained in-demand with consumers and builders alike, boding well for the company's future.

Principal Competitors

Hunter Douglas Inc.

Further Reading

''Amerock's Answer Man. New Company President Looks to Bright Future,'' *Rockford Register Star*, December 8, 1986, 1D.

''Amerock Approves Merger,'' *Rockford Morning Star*, July 30, 1966.

''Amerock Divestiture Completion By November 3,'' *Rockford Register Republic*, October 27, 1975.

''Amerock Fights Back,'' *Rockford Register Star*, December 2, 1984.

''Amerock Name is Official Now,'' *Rockford Morning Star*, April 6, 1956.

''Amerock Plans Economy Moves,'' *Rockford Register Star*, November 27, 1984.

''Amerock Sold for $32 Million,'' *Rockford Morning Star*, November 21, 1974.

''Heading for a Billion: Major Acquisition Bringing Newell Toward a Record Sales Mark,'' *Barron's*, August 24, 1987, pp. 39–40.

Lundin, Jon W., *Rockford: An Illustrated History*, Tarzana, California: American Historical Press, 1996.

''Sale of Amerock Highlight of Year,'' *Rockford Morning Star*, January 23, 1975.

—Paul R. Greenland

Anaheim Angels Baseball Club, Inc.

2000 Gene Autry Way
Anaheim, California 92806
U.S.A.
Telephone: (714) 940-2000
Fax: (714) 940-2205
Web site: http://angels.mlb.com

Wholly Owned Subsidiary of The Walt Disney Company
Founded: 1961
Employees: 100 (est.)
Sales: $102.6 million (2001)
NAIC: 711211 Sports Teams and Clubs

The Anaheim Angels Baseball Club, Inc. is the American League franchise of the two Major League baseball teams located in the Los Angeles, California, market. Much less celebrated than the National League's Los Angeles Dodgers, the Angels have known little financial success operating in the shadow of their neighbors, and on the field have provided their fans with few contending teams. Since the Walt Disney Company acquired the franchise in 1999, however, the fortunes of the Angels have improved. Municipally-owned municipal Anaheim Stadium has been completely renovated and renamed Edison Field, complete with luxury boxes that are so important to the finances of contemporary professional sports. In addition, a more favorable lease with the city of Anaheim has been negotiated. With the deep pockets of Disney behind it, the Angels have also developed a winning ball club.

Gene Autry Becomes Original Angels' Owner

The Angels first owner was Gene Autry, famed movie and television singing cowboy star, who was able to make the successful transition from celebrity to businessman, accumulating a wide range of properties, from radio and television stations to cattle ranches—and, almost by accident, a baseball team. Love of baseball was actually a lifelong affair for Autry, whose childhood dream was to become a professional baseball player, not an entertainer. He was born in a small Texas town named Tioga in 1907 and raised on a farm in Oklahoma, where at the age of five he began singing in the choir of his grandfather's Baptist Church. He was taught by his mother to play the guitar at the age of 12 and gained exposure to show business for three months as a teenager when he sang ballads with the Fields Brothers Marvelous Medicine Show. To help support his family he had to return home, taking a job as a railroad baggage handler in Chelsea, Oklahoma. In the meantime, he honed his skills as a shortstop, playing for several semi-pro baseball teams, as well as learning Morse Code. By the age of 19, he was working the evening shift as a railroad telegrapher, often finding ample time to sing and play the guitar. Autry had a chance to sign a professional contract with the St. Louis Cardinals' Tulsa minor league team but turned down the offer, opting instead for more secure employment with the railroad. During that same summer he met Will Rogers, who was visiting his sister in Chelsea. As usual, Autry was singing and playing to pass the time, and Rogers encouraged the young man to keep at it while he composed a telegraph. Rogers was so impressed with Autry's ability that he encouraged him to travel to New York to try to get work on the radio. A year later, Autry followed Rogers' advice, but instead of breaking into radio in the big city he ended up working at a Tulsa station where he was billed as Oklahoma's Yodelin' Cowboy. In 1929, he returned to New York to sign a recording contract with Victor and two years later released "That Silver-Haired Daddy of Mine," which sold more than a million copies and established the practice of awarding "gold records" to artists for topping the million mark in sales. He also began to develop a national following through his appearances on a popular radio show, National Barn Dance, produced by WLS radio. The station was owned by Sears, which began to feature Autry records, songbooks, and guitars in its catalogs.

Autry made his debut in movies in 1934, singing a number in a western, *Old Santa Fe.* He was soon cast as a singing cowboy in *Tumblin' Tumbleweeds,* establishing the role he would play in scores of B westerns over the years. Little known in the major cities, Autry was pure box office in the West and Southwest during the Depression years. He shrewdly invested the money he made from singing and acting into an array of businesses and by the 1940s owned five ranches, three western radio stations, a pair of cowboy music publishing houses, a chain of movie

---

Key Dates:

1960: A Los Angeles American League baseball franchise is awarded to Gene Autry and investors.
1961: The Angels begin play.
1966: The California Angels begin play in Anaheim.
1974: Autry and Signal Companies become the only investors in the team.
1982: Autry becomes the team's sole owner.
1996: The Walt Disney Company acquires the Angels.
1998: A renovated stadium is opened.
2002: Disney retains Lehman Brothers to sell the team.

---

theaters in Texas, and even a flying school. In 1947, he established Gene Autry Productions, splitting profits with Columbia Pictures on a deal that called for him to star in four pictures a year. Unlike many in Hollywood at the time, he embraced television early on, creating Flying A Productions, which not only produced "The Gene Autry Show" from 1950 to 1956 but other series as well.

Autry Loses Dodger Radio Rights in 1960

It was Autry's interest in radio that would lead to his involvement in major league baseball. He purchased his first station in 1948, which formed the basis of Golden West Broadcasting, a chain of media assets that became the crown jewel of the cowboy tycoon's business empire. By the mid-1950s, he was well on his way to making the transition from entertainer to businessman. One of the radio stations he owned, KMPC in Los Angeles, broadcast the games of the Los Angeles Dodgers, which in 1958 had abandoned Brooklyn for the West Coast. In 1960, Autry was shocked to learn from the pages of *Variety* that Dodger owner Walter O'Malley intended to grant the radio rights to another station. Around the same time, the American League decided to expand from eight teams to ten and to tap into the lucrative Los Angeles market. Hoping to maintain KMPC's reputation as the top sports station in southern California, Autry felt he had to secure the radio rights for the new American League team. He reached a tentative deal with the frontrunners for the franchise, former baseball player Hank Greenberg and former baseball owner Bill Veeck. The Dodger's O'Malley, however, scuttled the deal, demanding $450,000 in territorial indemnification, what Autry would characterize as "grazing rights." In order to guarantee the radio rights for KMPC, Autry and partner Robert Reynolds, who owned 30 percent of the station and served as president of Golden West, decided to make a last minute bid on the franchise themselves. It was a Friday when Autry called American League president Joe Cronin, an old friend, who had no objections to their application but laid out some basic requirements, which included a $1.5 million letter of credit due on Monday. Autry secured the letter, then made his pitch at a joint American and National League meeting in St. Louis that was called to settle the nettlesome issue of expansion in both leagues. Once the American League agreed to permit a National League franchise in New York for 1962, the National League allowed the American League's Los Angeles franchise to go forward. Not only was Autry an American icon and the idol of millions of children, he had also

cultivated relationships in baseball for decades, befriending both owners and players. He had built up so much good will that awarding the Los Angeles franchise to him was almost a foregone conclusion. Official approval was granted on December 7, 1960. As part of the deal, the new owners agreed to pay $350,000 in indemnification to the Dodgers.

O'Malley wasted no time in buttonholing Autry, inviting him up to his hotel suite in St. Louis where he convinced the new owner to become a tenant of Dodger Stadium, which was under construction and scheduled to open in 1962. During its inaugural season in 1961, Autry's team would have to play in undersized Wrigley Field, the 20,500-seat home of the former Pacific Coast League franchise, the Los Angeles Angels. Without asking permission, Autry had already appropriated the Angels' name, which the Dodgers owned as part of the buyout of the Pacific Coast League Angels' franchise and its Wrigley Field facility, a transaction that paved the way to relocating in Los Angeles. O'Malley was annoyed but said nothing, then hammered out as restrictive an agreement with his new tenants as possible. The Angels agreed to play in Dodger Stadium for four years with an option to renew for three more. For rent, the team was to pay 7.5 percent of gross attendance revenues. In addition, the Dodgers received half of the Angels' concession gross and all of the parking revenues. O'Malley also insisted that the Angels compensate for reduced attendance at Dodger Stadium caused by the 20 Angels' road games that would be televised, and he even forced Autry to agree to use the Dodgers' pay-TV company, which was under development, should the Angels ever decide to try pay-TV. Although the pay-TV company never materialized, O'Malley proved once again that he was a true visionary, as well as a skinflint. Shortly after he left O'Malley's suite around three in the morning, Autry confided to Reynolds that he had no intention of renewing the Dodger Stadium lease after four years, realizing at once that a joint tenancy arrangement would never work.

Before Autry could even think about finding a permanent home for the Angels, he first had to hire a general manager and manager and field a team for the 1961 season, which was scheduled to start in just four months. Only a day after being awarded the franchise and minutes before a press conference was scheduled to discuss the new team, Autry and Reynolds decided that they could not meet the media without a general manager on the dais. They quickly offered the job to Fred Haney, who had been serving as their advisor at the league meetings. Although well qualified, Haney was under contract to NBC as an analyst on the *Game of the Week* show. Despite realizing that the construction of a baseball team and organization from scratch was a daunting task, he agreed.

While Haney and the manager he hired, Bill Rigney, assembled a club, acquiring 28 players for $2.1 million in an expansion draft, Autry looked for more capital. He signed a number of limited partners, including Joseph Thomas, a senior partner in Lehman Brothers; Thomas's associate J.D. Stetson Coleman; and Leonard K. Firestone of Firestone Tires. Team offices were set up in downtown Los Angeles close to Wrigley Field, and unlike all the other major league teams, which opted for Florida or Arizona, the Angels decided to set up their spring training camp in the desert resort of Palm Springs, some 120 miles from Los Angeles. The team would return there for the next 30 years.

The Angels surprised everyone with their initial success in the American League, posting a respectable 70 wins and finishing seventh in 1961. The following season, playing in Dodger Stadium, the team fared even better, winning 86 games and finishing third in the league. The Angels quickly regressed, however, and soon became a consistent second division team in the American League. In the meantime, the organization had to endure the difficulties of playing in someone else's stadium. The Dodgers, according to Autry, "dollared us to death." The Angels were billed for half the landscaping, which the Dodgers would have contracted whether they had a tenant or not, and half the toiletries, despite drawing far fewer fans than the Dodgers. The Angels were charged for window cleaning, yet the only windows at the stadium belonged to the Dodgers' offices. Although receiving none of the parking revenues, the Angels were also billed for improvements to the parking lot. The most egregious slight from the Angels' perspective, however, was the location of the team's ticket office, which was situated in an out-of-the-way corner of Dodger Stadium where the groundskeeper maintained large piles of manure.

That the Angels were unhappy in Dodger Stadium was no secret, and Autry was soon contacted by a number of cities offering to build a stadium if he would relocate the team. In order to have a place to play and not be forced to renew the Dodger Stadium lease, the Angels began to make serious efforts at finding a new home in 1963. The leading candidate was Long Beach, located 30 miles south of Los Angeles, but negotiations ultimately broke down when the city insisted the club be known as the Long Beach Angels. Autry, knowing the marketing difficulties the name would cause, refused to call the team anything other than the Los Angeles Angels or California Angels.

Angels Relocate to Anaheim in 1964

It was when the Angels reached an impasse with Long Beach in late 1963, and only months before the team would have to renew the Dodger Stadium lease, that the mayor of Anaheim, Rex Coons, stepped into the picture. Anaheim, best known for Knott's Berry Farm and Disneyland, had a population of just 150,000. Nevertheless, the city was expanding rapidly, as was the county in which it was located (Orange County), and Coons was eager to spur that growth and add legitimacy to the region by boasting a professional sports team. Despite its small population, Anaheim was attractive to the Angels because 7 million people lived within 50 miles of the stadium, and studies indicated that in the future Anaheim would sit at the center of a massive population belt that reached from Santa Barbara to Mexico. Moreover, Coons did not care what the Angels called themselves: he knew that Anaheim would be put on the map regardless. And so the Los Angeles Angels became the California Angels. Coons ushered a stadium deal through the Anaheim city council, the Angels gave notice to the Dodgers, and in August 1964 groundbreaking ceremonies were held for the team's new ballpark. Under the Angels' lease, rent was a $160,000 minimum or 7.5 percent of the admission gross up to $2 million. After $2 million the Angels paid 10 percent. The club also received half the parking and two-thirds of the concessions net revenues. What appeared to be a generous lease in 1964, however, would become one of the worst in all of baseball some 30 years later.

In 1968, Autry signed a deal with the Signal Companies, a Los Angeles conglomerate, which acquired a 49.9 percent stake in Golden West Broadcasting and a significant interest in the Angels. Unhappy with Signal's participation, Autry's partners in the ball club began to sell out, and by 1974 Autry and Signal were the only remaining shareholders. In a deal to buy out Signal engineered by Kohlberg Kravis Roberts & Company in 1982, Autry paid $225 million to Signal, which also received KTLA, an independent Los Angeles television station. Not only did the aging Autry tidy up his estate, he became the sole owner of the Angels and retained a string of media assets.

After a promising start to their history in the American League, the Angels proved to be a disappointment on the field more often than not, leading to continuous changes in club management. Nevertheless, the team usually drew more than two million fans a year. The Angels' product was also adversely affected by changes made to Anaheim Stadium to accommodate a new tenant in 1980, the Los Angeles Rams of the National Football League. The facility was enclosed and seating expanded to 70,000, but extra seats and the new luxury suites built for the Rams offered little additional revenue to the Angels and hardly compensated for the loss in the stadium's appeal. It was far from an attractive football venue as well, and after the 1994 season the Rams left for St. Louis, where a new domed stadium awaited them.

Baseball underwent significant changes in the decades since Autry was awarded the Angels franchise. With the advent of player free agency in the 1970s, the economics of the game changed dramatically. Once dominated by family ownership, major league baseball increasingly turned into a corporate enterprise. Autry was one of the last holdouts, and despite his personal wealth he found it increasingly difficult to compete, a situation complicated by an outmoded stadium and a poor lease. By the late 1980s, the Angels began to consistently lose money and were forced to cut costs. With one of the smallest front office operations in baseball and limited funds for marketing, the team was essentially trapped in a losing cycle.

Autry and his wife Jackie, a banker for many years who helped run the team, finally decided in the early 1990s that they had no choice but to sell the Angels. A group of investors headed by Peter Ueberroth negotiated a deal to purchase the team for $130 million but refused to assume any debts or cover operating losses while Major League Baseball approved the transaction. It was at this point, in February 1995, that Michael Eisner and Disney decided to become involved. By May 1995, Disney had struck a deal with the Autrys in which the company agreed to assume $10 million in losses. For Disney, buying the Angels insured that the team stayed in Anaheim and continued to lend the area major league status, which in turn helped to protect Disney investments in the Mighty Ducks National Hockey League Franchise as well as Disneyland. For Autry, who had been a personal friend of Walt Disney, selling the club to Disney seemed like a natural fit. He would pass away at age 91 at the end of the 1998 season.

Major League Baseball approved the sale of the Angels to Disney in January 1996. There was no agreement in place with Anaheim, however, and Eisner wasted no time in announcing that unless the city worked out a new stadium deal within 60 days, Disney would withdraw from the agreement. Although it would take twice as long for the two sides to come to an agreement, and it appeared at times that the sale was off, Anaheim and the Angels ultimately worked out a deal that called for a $100 million renovation of Anaheim Stadium, with Disney contributing 70 percent of the financing and agreeing to all cost overruns. A 33-year lease was also worked out, and the California Angels now became known as the Anaheim Angels.

The Angel's renovated park, renamed Edison International Field, opened for the 1998 season. Attendance immediately increased to 2.5 million but over the next couple of years began to slip as high-priced free agents did not produce the kind of results the fans expected. The team had better success in developing its own talent, making significant progress in the early years of the new century. The fortunes of the Angels may have improved on the field, but Disney lost close to $100 million since its purchase of the club and periodically indicated that it was willing to part with the Angels and Mighty Ducks in order to concentrate on its core entertainment business. Ironically, on the very day in 2002 that the Angels secured their first playoff berth in 16 years, Disney announced that it retained investment bank Lehman Brothers to find a potential buyer for the team. Several weeks later the Angels surprised the sporting world, not only by making it to the World Series but by winning it, defeating the San Francisco Giants in seven games.

Principal Competitors

Oakland Athletics; Seattle Mariners; Texas Rangers.

Further Reading

Klayman, Gary, ''Boys of Summer Out, Accountants of Winter Arrive,'' *Orange County Business Journal,* November 2, 1992, p. 1.

Newhan, Ross, *The Anaheim Angels: A Complete History,* New York: Hyperion, 2000.

Powell, Tom, ''Disney Has Big Plans for California Angels,'' *Amusement Business,* May 29, 1995, p. 1.

Thorn, John, et al, *Total Baseball*, Kingston, NY: Total Sports, 1999.

Whitcomb, Dan, ''Disney Hires Broker to Sell Playoff-Bound Angels,'' *Reuters,* September 26, 2002.

—Ed Dinger

@nker

Anker BV

Crompton House
Barrs Fold Road
Wingates Industrial Park
Westhoughton
Bolton
Lancashire BL5 3XP
United Kingdom
Telephone: (+44) 0 870 905 1300
Fax: (+44) 0 870 905 1301
Web site: http://www.anker-systems.com

Private Company
Incorporated: 1995
Employees: 1,861
Sales: EUR 243.6 million ($240 million) (2001)
NAIC: 423430 Computer and Computer Peripheral
    Equipment and Software Merchant Wholesalers;
    541512 Computer Systems Design Services

Bolton, England-based (but Netherlands registered) Anker BV has transformed itself into a leading supplier of electronic point of sales systems to the European market. The company, which combines the electronic cash register business of the former BTR (now merged with Siebe into Invensys), and the EPOS business of Riva Group PLC, as well as the European distribution network of Japan's Omron, claims an installed base of more than 900,000 systems throughout Europe. The company accounts among its many clients such retailing heavyweights as Germany's Aldi, France's Carrefour and Auchan Group, Harrods and Granada in the United Kingdom, as well as other clients requiring intensive customer/retail contact, such as the Legoland theme park. Anker operates through three primary divisions: Software, which includes its flagship products OSCAR EpoS, Power, and emPower; Services, providing consulting, integration services, and aftermarket support; and Hardware, including the company's Anker-branded cash drawers, electronic cash registers, modular POS systems, touch screens, and other peripherals, as well as third-party peripherals and printers. Anker operates throughout Europe, with 11 subsidiaries. Europe West, including the United Kingdom, France, and the Benelux countries provided more than half of the company's EUR 244 million in sales in 2001. Europe Central, including Germany, Austria, and Switzerland, added nearly EUR 85 million in sales, while Scandinavia generated revenues of more than EUR 35 million. Anker is led by CEO John Foulkes, who, backed by European Acquisition Capital, bought out the company from BTR in 1995.

Origins

Anker's origins can be traced to Germany in the middle of the 19th century. Carl Schmidt and Nickolaus Durkopp had founded a partnership to manufacture sewing machines in 1867. In 1876, Schmidt left the partnership to found his own company, Bielefelder Nähmaschinenfabrik Carl Schmidt, in the town of Bielefeld. Schmidt's company began production of a specific type of sewing machine, called the "circular-elastique" machine, which was used in the shoemaking industry at the time. Schmidt then added production of other types of sewing machines, including long bobbin and shuttle-type sewing machines.

Schmidt was joined by Hugo Hengstenberg in 1878, and the company began producing machines under the combined name Carl Schmidt & Hengstenberg. After Schmidt left the company in 1883, it was renamed as Bielefelder Nähmaschinenfabrik Hengstenberg & Co. The company continued manufacturing sewing machines as its main product line for the next decade. Then, in 1894, the Bielefelder plant added a second production line, that of bicycles. By 1895, production of bicycles had grown sufficiently for the company to modify its name to Bielefelder Nähmaschinen- und Fahrrad-Fabrik Hengstenberg.

By the end of the decade, the Hengstenberg company had found a new product category: cash registers. The first cash registers had been invented in the United States some 20 years earlier by James Ritty, who called his invention the "Incorruptible Cashier." But Ritty's invention met with little enthusiasm from retailers. It was not until John H. Patterson bought Ritty's company, renaming it National Cash Register (NCR) in 1884, that the cash register began to find acceptance in the retail market. The addition of new features, including paper

---

Company Perspectives:

Anker provides IT solutions for shopping—wherever, whenever, or however that shopping takes place. We offer complete solutions that support all aspects of the consumer/retailer interface—in hospitality, food, and specialist retail segments. We support not only the initial order taking process but the subsequent supply of back and head office management information for retailers. Our range of products and services for retailers includes software, consulting and support, and hardware. As part of our commitment to deliver complete IT solutions for shopping, we are working alongside retailers and selected partner companies to help deliver the best of breed solutions for next generation retailing.

---

readouts and, at the turn of the century, electric motors, helped spread the popularity of the new machine.

Success and Struggles in the 20th Century

Hengstenberg began production of cash registers under the brand name Anker ("anchor" in English) in 1900. By 1906, the company decided to change its name to Anker Werke AG. Anker went on to become one of the most prominent manufacturers of cash registers in Europe, and one of the few companies to resist the market dominance of NCR. Over the next decades, Anker leveraged its cash register brand into the wider category of office machinery, introducing its first accounting machines in 1912. The company also set up a wide-ranging sales network which enabled it to counter the growing influence of NCR in Europe.

Anker grew steadily throughout the 1920s and 1930s despite the economic collapse of its home market. With 1,000 employees at the start of the 1920s, the company grew to more than 2,000 by the end of the 1930s. In order to meet the growing demand for its products, which continued to include sewing machines and bicycles, the company opened a second factory in Bieleberg.

At the end of World War II, Anker decided to refocus its production to concentrate on its cash registers and office machinery. The company's bicycle production was transferred under a licensing agreement. Anker held onto its sewing machine manufacturing operation for some time longer. In 1958, the company spun off that business into a newly formed subsidiary, Anker-Nähmaschinen AG, which was then merged the following year with another company, Baer & Rempel, as Phoenix Nähmaschinen AG. Anker finally sold off that subsidiary in 1969.

By then, Anker was struggling as a business. The company had attempted to enter the electronic age in the 1950s, launching its first electro-mechanical accounting machines in 1956. By the 1960s, Anker fully entered the rising new market for computer- and electronics-based machinery by setting up a dedicated subsidiary, Anker Data Systems (ADS). Yet by the mid-1970s, Anker was sinking financially. An attempt to restructure the company failed, and Anker, which by then employed some 8,000 people, ended in bankruptcy in 1976.

Anker was picked up by the United Kingdom's Thomas Tilling Group, which had been one of the pioneers of Britain's public

transportation sector in the late 19th century and had grown to become a diversified conglomerate with a portfolio of nearly 200 business throughout the United Kingdom, Australia, the United States, and Europe. Anker returned to production under its new owner, which retained its subsidiary's respected brand name.

Thomas Tilling was itself bought up by another fast-growing British conglomerate, BTR (formerly British Tyre & Rubber). Anker itself remained in production, with its focus now restricted to manufacturing electronic cash registers. While its head offices were now located in Bolton, the company retained its original manufacturing site in Bieleberg.

Returning to Independence in the New Century

BTR began restructuring its operations in the 1990s, and Anker's management, then led by John Foulkes, was presented with the opportunity to return the company to independence after nearly 20 years as a small subsidiary within a giant conglomerate. Foulkes partnered with the investment group European Acquisition Capital to buy Anker from BTR in 1995. The company was then reincorporated under a holding company, the Netherlands-registered Anker BV, although the company's headquarters remained in Bolton.

The "new" Anker began restructuring its operations in the late 1990s, shutting down a number of its manufacturing plants and reducing its reliance on electronic cash registers by striking out into the broader and fast-growing market for electronic point of sales (EPoS) systems. In order to support this strategy, Anker continued to develop its own in-house software while at the same time targeting the acquisition of related businesses, such as that of GPI, acquired in 1996.

Early in 1999, the company also reached an agreement with Japan's Omron Nohgata Co. to acquire its manufacturing subsidiaries Omron Systems Europe, based in Germany, and Omron Systems UK, as well as the exclusive European distribution license for Omron systems. The company also began building up its service arm, acquiring the service division of the U.K. firm MDIS in 1999.

During that same year, the company made a still more significant acquisition. In October 1999, Anker paid £42 million to acquire Riva Group Plc. The integration of Riva's internationally operating network boosted Anker into the European leadership for EPoS systems.

Riva represented the combination of two businesses. Riva Computer Services Ltd. was founded in 1978 as a development company using Hewlett-Packard hardware. Riva's original business centered on developing point of sales systems for the U.K. hospitality market. Riva went public in 1988 and changed its name to Riva Group Plc. The following year, Riva acquired the Hugin Sweda (a company specialized in manufacturing cash registers), which had been founded in 1928 in Sweden and which had been acquired by the U.S. firm Litton Industries in 1963.

The acquisition of Hugin Sweda helped broaden Riva's geographic base. It also marked Riva's transition into the broader point of sales (POS) market, especially the retail sector. In the early 1990s, Riva extended its focus to include software solutions, and in 1994 the company became one of the first to

Key Dates:

1867: Carl Schmidt and Nickolaus Durkopp found a partnership to manufacturer sewing machines in Germany.

1876: Schmidt establishes his own sewing machine business in Bielefeld, Germany, Bielefelder Nähmaschinenfabrik Carl Schmidt.

1878: Joined by Hugo Hengstenberg, the company begins producing machines under the combined name Carl Schmidt & Hengstenberg.

1894: The company begins producing bicycles and changes its name to Bielefelder Nähmaschinen- und Fahrrad-Fabrik Hengstenberg the following year.

1900: The company begins production of cash registers.

1906: The company changes name to Anker Werke AG.

1912: Anker Werke begins production of accounting machines and other office equipment.

1948: The company ends production of bicycles to concentrate on cash registers and accounting machinery.

1956: Anker Werke launches its first electro-mechanical accounting machines.

1958: Sewing machine production is spun off into a separate subsidiary.

1967: Subsidiary ADS Anker Data Systems is created.

1976: Anker declares bankruptcy and is acquired by the U.K. company Thomas Tilling.

1978: Riva Computer Services Ltd. is founded in the United Kingdom.

1983: Thomas Tilling Group acquired by BTR.

1988: Riva goes public as Riva Group Plc.

1989: Riva acquires Hugin Sweda cash register group.

1995: Anker is bought from BTR by European Acquisition Capital and John Foulkes.

1996: Anker acquires GPI and begins restructuring, shutting manufacturing facilities and focusing on software development.

1999: Anker acquires OMRON Europe and the exclusive license to distribute Omron products in Europe; Riva Group plc is also acquired.

2001: Unicos BV of the Netherlands is acquired.

In 2000, Anker signed a strategic alliance with Viewlocity, a provider of business-to-business integration and systems solutions for the burgeoning online trading market, to combine Viewlocity's AMTrix hub software with Anker's new emPower real-time retail and supply chain database software for the European retail market. Meanwhile, the company's flagship software, OSCAR, was enjoying strong success on the European market. In 2001, the company unveiled a new integrated software and hardware product, called Media Network, which permitted retailers to position multi-media POS displays, including video and sound support, in their stores. In that year, Anker acquired Dutch company Unicos BV, a specialist in retail automation software. In 2002, Anker signed a new OEM (original equipment manufacturer) partnership agreement with ProClarity. The agreement allowed Anker to integrate ProClarity's web-based analytical software into Anker's own eToolbox product group.

By then, Anker's sales had topped EUR 243 million—more than double its revenues in the mid-1990s, and the company had strengthened its leadership position in the European POS market. Anker had come a long way, successfully making the transition from manufacturing to software development while inheriting a tradition of supporting retailers begun more than a century before.

Principal Subsidiaries

Anker Systems Ltd (United Kingdom); Anker Systems AG (Switzerland); Anker Systems OY (Finland); Anker Systems A/S (Denmark); Anker Systems A/S (Norway); Anker Systems AB (Sweden); Anker Systems B.V. (Netherlands); ADS Anker Data Systems BV (Netherlands); Anker Systems S.A. (France); Anker B.V.B.A. (Belgium); Anker Systems GmbH (Germany); Anker Systems GesmbH (Austria); Compcas Kft (49%, Hungary).

Principal Competitors

IBM Corporation; NCR Corporation; Aspeon, Inc.; BancTec, Inc.; Fujitsu Services Limited; Hewlett-Packard Company; Hypercom Corporation; Groupe Ingenico; JDA Software Group, Inc; MAI Systems Corporation; MICROS Systems, Inc; PAR Technology Corporation; Radiant Systems, Inc.; Retalix Ltd.

Further Reading

''Aldi Weighs Anker,'' *Super Marketing*, September 1, 2000, p. 3.

''Anker Agrees 42 mln stg Bid for Riva,'' *Reuters*, September 24, 1999.

''Beatties Weighs Anker up for Terminal Upgrade,'' *Computer Weekly*, July 13, 2000, p. 14.

''MDIS to Transfer EPOS Business to Anker Data Systems for 3.9 mln stg,'' *AFX* (UK), April 8, 1999.

—M.L. Cohen

incorporate the Microsoft operating system as the basis for their POS software systems. By the late 1990s, Riva had decided to refocus itself entirely as a software-driven business. In support of its new direction, Riva made a series of acquisitions, including France's Aurique, the Netherlands' Unisoft, and Infocare, based in the United Kingdom. Meanwhile, the company spun off a number of its previous businesses, including its Spanish and Australian subsidiaries, as independent companies.

Antonov Design Bureau

Tupoleva Street 1
03062 Kiev
Ukraine
Telephone: +380 (44) 442-60-75
Fax: +380 (44) 442-41-44
Web site: http://www.antonovaircargo.com

State-Owned Company
Incorporated: 1946 as Antonov Design Bureau
Employees: 7,500
NAIC: 336411 Aircraft Manufacturing; 481212
    Nonscheduled Chartered Freight Air Transportation;
    54133 Engineering Services; 54171 Research and
    Development in the Physical, Engineering, and Life
    Sciences; 611512 Flight Training

Ukraine-based Antonov Design Bureau, a scientific and technical complex named after Oleg Konstantinovich (O.K.) Antonov, designs transport, regional, and special purpose aircraft. The bureau is engaged in designing and building new prototype aircraft and modifications of earlier designs, providing their operational support and follow-up engineering work on the aircraft service life extension. Specifically, Antonov offers basic and conversion training of flight and maintenance crews, sends high-skilled specialists to render assistance in mastering the aircraft and training local personnel, provides international air transportation of cargoes including oversized ones on a charter basis, participates in the international co-operation in the field of aircraft and equipment design and manufacture, and develops land transit vehicles. Among its designs are the An-124 and the An-225, the world's largest plane, which can carry things no other aircraft can. The An-124 was originally designed for military use, while the An-225 was designed to carry the Soviet space shuttle. These giants have been marketed in the West since the late 1980s. Besides enjoying a corner on the outsized air freight market, Antonov aircraft have made possible previously inconceivable logistical undertakings, and their ability to quickly transport huge pieces of equipment across the world has saved mining, construction, and manufacturing industries from costly downtime.

1930s Origins

O.K. Antonov had a line of basic training gliders under production even before he graduated the Leningrad Polytechnical Institute in 1930. His very first glider was named the OKA-1 Golub. Antonov then joined the Moscow Glider Factory as chief engineer, and was later named its chief designer. His first powered glider design to enter production was 1937's OKA-33 (LEM-2).

The glider factory closed in 1938. After being rejected by the Zhukovskii Military Air Academy, Antonov began working for A.S. Yakovlev, an eminent Soviet designer, where he was given the task of developing the Fieseler Fi 156 Storch, a German utility aircraft being produced under license in Lithuania. Later, during World War II, Antonov saw his A-7 assault glider produced before rejoining the Yakovlev design bureau in 1943 to oversee production of the Yak-3 fighter in Novosibirsk.

On May 31, 1946, Antonov established his own design bureau after being given the task of developing a new utility plane to be powered by a 730-horsepower engine. The resulting design, the An-2, first flew in August 1947 and was a monumental success, in spite of its antiquated styling (a biplane with fixed landing gear). For the An-2, Antonov and his assistants were awarded a Stalin Prize and 100,000 rubles in 1952. The An-2 was exported mostly throughout the Eastern Bloc and Third World, and examples would remain in use for at least another 50 years. The aircraft was unique in being the only biplane made in large numbers anywhere after the war. By 1960, 5,000 An-2s had been built in the Soviet Union; the plane was also in production under license in China and Poland. Its production run lasted nearly 20 years.

In the Soviet system, aircraft manufacturing facilities were typically separate from the firms that designed them. However, the Antonov bureau did make its own prototypes and did production runs of certain types (the An-26, An-30, and An-32) in Kiev at the Aviant aviation plant. Plants producing Antonov aircraft included Ulyanovsk on the Volga (the An-124) and the

Kharkov plant in the Ukraine (the An-72 and An-74). The An-28 transport was built in Poland.

Furthering Soviet Transport in the 1960s–70s

Having moved to Kiev, Antonov continued to work on gliders after World War II to some extent, but became best known for developing transport aircraft. Most Antonov aircraft, like the twin-engine An-8 and its the four-engine successors, the civil An-10 Ukraine and military An-12, were designed to operate from concrete and unpaved runways, including grass landing strips.

Antonov started developing the An-10 and An-12 aircraft in 1955. The An-10 airplane flight tests were begun on March 7, 1957. On December 16 of the same year, the AN-12 transport performed its maiden flight at Irkutsk aviation plant. The An-12 was a phenomenally successful mid-sized military turboprop transport which began operations in 1956. In 1962 the creators of the An-12 airplane were awarded with the Lenin Prize and O.K. Antonov was given the rank of General Designer. The resulting An-12 was very similar in appearance to the Hercules and a little less capable. Nevertheless, it represented a huge leap forward in Soviet transports.

The An-14 Pchelka ("Little Bee"), first produced in 1958, was a smaller twin-tailed, twin-engine utility aircraft with short take-off and landing capability. However, most of Antonov's subsequent output would be large planes, some of them true behemoths.

Antonov began an oversized cargo service in the late 1960s using the An-22 Antei ("Anteus"). Their first cargo deliveries contained equipment necessary for oil drilling and mining. The An-22 Antei, which debuted at the Paris Air Show in 1965, had a capacity of 180,000 pounds and a wingspan of 211 feet. It would remain the world's largest aircraft until Lockheed unveiled its C-5A Galaxy in 1968. The An-22 Antei could carry the largest pieces of equipment in the Soviet arsenal, including tanks and SAM launchers. It also carried its own cargo handling equipment on board, which greatly extended its flexibility in military operations. An-22 production was curtailed in 1974 after 64 were built.

The An-24 was a medium-haul, mid-sized twin-engine turboprop transport comparable with those found in the West. This plane incorporated advanced welding techniques and other manufacturing refinements. Developed in the late 1950s, the An-24 would be used by many airlines in the Soviet Bloc, Africa, and the Middle East. A total of 1,335 were built, and the An-24 performed more than 30 percent of passenger transportation volume in the former Soviet Union. This exceptionally successful aircraft became the basis for such derivatives as the An-26 freighter, the An-30 aerial photography airplane, the An-32 high-mountain aircraft, and others.

In the 1970s, the Soviet Union not only attained parity with but surpassed the West in its ability to transport troops, at least as far as Eurasia and the Middle East were concerned. However, an Ilyushin-designed aircraft, the jet-powered Il-76, replaced the An-12 as the leading Soviet heavy transport. Antonov was more successful during this time with smaller transports. The high-wing, twin-engine An-72 was developed for military uses in the 1970s, and it would remain in production for more than 20 years.

Growing Capacity in the 1980s

In the 1980s, Antonov designed and built a huge military transport that would eventually extend the barriers of commercial air freight. Named after Pushkin's mythical giant, the four-engine An-124 Ruslan (called the Condor by NATO, after the largest flying bird) had a wingspan of almost 242 feet, a length of 228 feet, and a height of 70 feet.

With a maximum payload of 120 metric tons, the An-124 was the world's largest plane and had a greater capacity than the American-made C-5 or the Boeing 747, the next largest commercially available freighter at the time. Using the An-124 aircraft as its basis, Antonov specialists developed and certified its civil version—an An-124-100 aircraft intended for commercial cargo carriages. Typical cargoes included locomotives, boats, jet engines, other aircraft components, and a variety of industrial and mining equipment. In time, the An-124 payload was increased to 150 metric tons, and by 2000 over 50 of the aircraft had been built.

Piotr Vasilyevich Balabuyev succeeded Oleg Antonov as the bureau's General Designer in 1984. Balabuyev headed the An-225 design team, which was working on a carrier for the Soviet space shuttle *Buran*. The An-225 would become the world's largest operational aircraft, with a maximum payload capacity of 551,000 pounds—twice that of a C-5. Loads that would not fit inside the An-225, such as the space shuttle, could be carried on its back.

The An-225 Mriya (Dream) first flew on December 21, 1988, and made its international debut at the 1989 Paris Air Show carrying the *Buran* in piggyback fashion. The novel aircraft's design was actually based on the An-124: the fuselage was stretched 40 feet and the number of engines was raised from four to six. The wingspan was 290 feet, nearly a football field in length. The cargo bay was 141 feet long.

Another unique feature of the An-225 was its landing gear, which had a maximum gross takeoff weight of 1.4 million pounds. Thirty-two wheels were used; the rear 16 wheels of the main gear were steerable as well as the four that made up the nose gear, which could be lowered, allowing the plane to "kneel." The *Buran* program was cancelled in 1993 due to a lack of funds, however, and the An-225 was shelved for seven years.

Antonov's outsized cargo business intensified in the late 1980s. Charters were at first arranged directly with Antonov or through the Soviet Union's Aviaexport import/export organization. A British firm, AirFoyle Ltd., became Antonov's general sales agent for An-124-100 leases in Europe, North America, and the Persian Gulf in July 1989. This territory was expanded to include the entire world in September 1993, with An-22 and An-12 freighters added to the agreement. In 1990, Antonov was awarded an Air Operator's Certificate, clearing the way for it to start its own cargo airline, which became known as Antonov Airlines. An air maintenance business was soon launched as well; this and the airline would soon account for an estimated 70 percent of annual revenues. An-124-100s were also operated by Russia's Volga-Dnepr Airlines and Polyot Air Cargo.

Coping with Change in the 1990s

Antonov continued to develop regional airliners. In April 1989, the firm's designers began work on a stretched version of the 17-passenger An-28. The result, the An-38, had its first flight five years later. Its development was made more pivotal to the company given cutbacks in military budgets following the collapse of the Soviet Union. Also on the drawing board at that time was a large civil airliner called the An-218.

The An-74, a civil modification of the An-72 designed for extreme conditions, began production in 1991 with Antonov maintaining high hopes for the export market. A successful range of multipurpose aircraft was developed from the An-74, including the An-74TK-300 passenger-cargo aircraft, which could carry up to 68 passengers or ten metric tons of cargo.

The An-140 regional passenger turboprop aircraft, developed to replace the An-24, made its first flight in 1997. Having close to the An-24's passenger capacity (52 seats), the An-140 surpassed its predecessor in passenger comfort level and performance: flight range was 75 percent greater; flight speed was 20 percent higher; and fuel efficiency was almost twice as great. The An-140 also required 30 percent less runway. It was manufactured at the Kharkov State Aviation Manufacturing Company (KSAMC), the Samara AVIACOR Joint Stock Company, and the HESA plant in Isfahan, Iran, and started regular passenger service in March 2002.

An end to government subsidies in the early 1990s plunged the Antonov bureau into a period of crisis. To raise cash, the bureau turned to making trolley buses, in partnership with the Kiev-based Aviant Aviation Factory. "Our task is to preserve our scientific brains until all this craziness is over," said General Designer Piotr Balabuyev in *The Economist,* which reported that the company was also making equipment for dyeing leather and making false teeth.

Development work on the An-70, a replacement for the mid-sized An-12 military transport, extended from the mid-1970s to mid-1990s. The An-70 aircraft comprised the best features of Antonov transports to date. The Ivchenko Progress Design Bureau designed a D-27 propfan engine especially for the An-70, which, when combined with a contra-rotating propfan specially designed by Aerosila Joint Stock Company, ensured 30 percent less fuel consumption than other turbofan engines.

The An-70 performed its maiden flight on December 16, 1994. The first prototype was lost in a collision, however, and the second model did not fly until April 1997. The aircraft entered the bidding to become a new military transport for Germany, France, Italy, and Spain; in the end, however, these countries went along with their NATO allies and settled on the Airbus A400M. Still, Russia and the Ukraine were buying the An-70, whose components were being sourced from factories in Russia as well as the Ukraine; in fact, Russia was to account for most of the plane's equipment. The first customer was the Czech military. In 2002, it was announced that the Czech Republic would receive three An-70s, partly in exchange for Soviet-era debts owed by Russia.

A Dream Reborn in 2001

In 2001, Antonov, the Kharkov State Aviation Manufacturing Co. (HGAPP), and Motor-Sich JSC, manufacturer of the An-225's IVCHENKO Progress Design Bureau jet engines, joined to bring the Mriya out of retirement. Ironically, the An-225's first commercial flight, on January 2, 2002, was to carry 216,000 MREs (meals ready-to-eat) from Germany to U.S. military personnel in the Persian Gulf.

A number of near-rivals were appearing to challenge the market for very large cargo aircraft. The Airbus A380, scheduled for launch in 2006, was a bit smaller than the An-225, but was not expected to be able to carry outsize cargo. Boeing was working on a commercial version of its C-17 transport, with a projected $200 million price tag.

Antonov was also developing a line of regional jets (small airliners) in cooperation with a number of partners in Russia and Ukraine. The An-148 was expected to fly in 2004.

Principal Subsidiaries

Antonov Airlines.

Principal Competitors

Airbus Industrie; Boeing Co.; Ilyushin; Lockheed Martin Aeronautical Systems; Tupolev; Volga-Dnepr Airlines.

Further Reading

"Aircraft Design and Production Facilities Traditionally Kept Separate in Soviet Union," *Aviation Week & Space Technology,* June 5, 1989, p. 37.

Alexander, Jean, "Antonov," *Russian Aircraft Since 1940,* London: Putnam, 1975, pp. 22–53.

"An-124 Offered to International Customers on Charter Basis," *Aviation Week & Space Technology,* June 5, 1989, p. 77.

"Antonov Seeks Help with An-225," *Flight International,* May 13, 1998, p. 19.

"Antonov to Start Regional Jet Family," *Flight International,* March 12, 2002, p. 15.

"Antonov Swoops on West's Air Freight Market," *East European Markets,* January 25, 1991.

"Antonov's Teething Troubles," *The Economist,* March 19, 1994, p. 80.

Barnard, Bruce, "Antonov 124: Ukraine's High Flier," *Journal of Commerce,* November 23, 1999, p. 8.

Cottle, Michelle, "How the Jet Brought Christmas (and a Profit)," *New York Times,* November 15, 1998, Sec. 3, p. 4.

Doke, DeeDee, "Future Imperfect," *Flight International,* November 6, 2001, p. 46.

Done, Kevin, "Six-Engine Giant Is a Dream Come True for Antonov," *Financial Times* (London), Cos. & Finance Europe, June 21, 2001, p. 32.

Duffy, Paul, "Antonov Ascending," *Flight International,* August 27, 1997, p. 41.

Eisenstein, Paul, "World's Biggest Plane," *Popular Mechanics,* Extreme Machines, January 2003, pp. 34–35.

"Giant Aircraft Move Mighty Mining Payloads," *Engineering & Mining Journal,* September 2000, p. 132.

Greenwood, John T., "The Designers: Their Design Bureaux and Aircraft," *Russian Aviation and Air Power in the Twentieth Century,* Robin Higham et al., eds., London: Frank Cass, 1998.

Gunston, Bill, *Aircraft of the Soviet Union,* London: Osprey, 1983.

Hastings, Phillip, "Antonovs Hungry for Big Loads," *Journal of Commerce,* July 29, 1991, p. 4.

Komarov, Alexey, "An-225 Refurbished After Seven-Year Sleep," *Aviation Week & Space Technology,* July 2, 2001, p. 73.

Lenorovitz, Jeffrey M., "Freighter Specialist Antonov Broadens Focus by Developing Passenger Aircraft," *Aviation Week & Space Technology,* September 16, 1991, p. 44.

Norris, Guy, "Soviets Team Up on 550-Seater," *Flight International,* July 10, 1991, p. 6.

Olearchyk, Roman, "Antonov Trolley Buses Roll on Kyiv's Streets," *Kyiv Post,* April 13, 2000.

——, "Czech Acquire Three Antonovs; Deal Struck to Supply 3 An-70s in Exchange for Soviet-Era Debt," *Kyiv Post,* July 18, 2002.

Velovich, Alexander, "Against All Odds," *Flight International,* February 9, 1994, pp. 34f.

——, "Antonov An-70: Heir Apparent," *Flight International,* January 18, 1995, pp. 24f.

Wings of the Red Star: Russian Giants, The Discovery Channel, 1993.

Zavarskiy, Leonid, "Ambitious International Modernization Project Involving An-124-100 Heavy Transport Is Hardly Feasible," *Kommersant* (RusData DiaLine-BizEkon News), April 7, 1999.

—Frederick C. Ingram

Atwood Mobil Products

4750 Hiawatha Drive
Rockford, Illinois 61103-1298
U.S.A.
Telephone: (815) 877-5700
Fax: (815) 877-7469
Web site: http://www.atwoodmobile.com

Division of Dura Automotive Systems Inc.
Incorporated: 1909 as Atwood Vacuum Machine Co.
Employees: 500
Sales: $150 million (2002 est.)
NAIC: 336332 Other Motor Vehicle Electrical and
    Electronic Equipment Manufacturing; 336360 Motor
    Vehicle Seating and Interior Trim Manufacturing

Based in Rockford, Illinois, Atwood Mobile Products manufactures a wide variety of products—including chassis components, cooking appliances, gas alarms, heating systems, seating, water heaters, windows and doors—for boats, recreational vehicles, and towed equipment. Founded in 1909, the company has served a number of different commercial and industrial markets throughout its history including the automotive and agricultural sectors. According to the company, its products are found in 90 percent of recreational vehicles (RVs) in America.

Origins

Arguably, Atwood Mobil Products' foundation was laid during the childhood of James Thomas Atwood. In the eighth grade, Atwood constructed models of two miniature engines from one toy steam engine. By his freshman year of high school, he had constructed a three-horsepower steam engine and his physics teacher had arranged for him to experiment in a nearby manufacturing shop. After graduating from high school in 1899 and earning a degree in mechanical engineering from the University of Illinois four years later, Atwood obtained a faculty position in the University of Wisconsin's engineering department. There, he developed a stationary vacuum cleaner intended for use in buildings.

Finding it difficult to ignore his entrepreneurial spirit, Atwood left the academic world in 1908 to produce and market his vacuum cleaner system, which consisted of a central unit and many tubes that allowed hoses to be attached at different points throughout a building. Established in 1909, his new enterprise initially was located in Madison, Wisconsin. However, by 1910 James Atwood had moved Atwood Vacuum Machine Co. to his native Rockford, Illinois, where his brother Seth B. Atwood—who had been a student at the University of Wisconsin when the elder Atwood was a professor there—joined him in the venture. This was a dream come true for the Atwood brothers, who had always wanted to go into business together.

Experimentation and Enterprise: 1909–49

In the beginning, the Atwoods rented space in what used to be Rockford's Water Power District, where a dam on the Rock River once provided power for area manufacturers. As the young company expanded, it moved to other locations, including sites on South Church Street and North Water Street.

It was not long before the Atwood enterprise changed direction. The impetus came when a rattling door in Seth Atwood's automobile led to the development of an adjustable door bumper in 1915. Eventually, the bumper became a standard automotive industry product. Production levels skyrocketed to 21 million units by the mid-1920s. Inspired by the success of their door bumper, the Atwoods began offering additional products to the automotive industry, including hinges for doors, trunks, and hoods. As the brothers succeeded in the automotive arena, they moved away from vacuum cleaner production, stopping it completely by 1919. The Atwoods pioneered many innovative automotive products such as telescoping props for holding open trunk doors and forward-aft seat adjusters that eventually became commonplace in most automobiles.

In 1925, the Atwood enterprise continued to prosper, leading to the construction of a new, 30,000-square-foot plant on North Main Street. Recalling this period of the company's history in an early news article, Seth B. Atwood commented: ''During that period we worked day and night shifts at the N. Water St. plant and two shifts at the new building before it was even enclosed.''

Company Perspectives:

Customer service is paramount at Atwood. Whatever the situation, customer service is the primary concern. That means meeting your delivery schedules and product specifications, monitoring installation and solving any difficulties that may occur, and actively participating in trade associations and standards development in all markets that we serve.

Midway through the 1930s, the company continued to expand. It became the first manufacturer to produce concealed hinges for car doors, which were unveiled on the 1937 Graham-Page. In 1936, a division was established to manufacture automobile and tractor clutches. In 1938, this division moved to Auburn, Indiana, where Atwood operated the Auburn Manufacturing Co. This operation served a vital production role during World War II, supplying both Ford and Willys with clutches for U.S. military jeeps. Atwood's clutch unit was acquired by the Toledo, Ohio-based Spicer division of Dana Corp. in 1947.

In addition to the clutches it manufactured for military use, Atwood also supplied other parts to the U.S. Army and Navy during the war for use in tanks, amphibious vehicles, gun mounts, and in the Flying Fortress bomber. On several occasions, the company received the E Award from the military for excellence in the area of production. Sometime in the late 1940s, the Atwoods' partnership officially became a corporation.

Growth through Acquisition: 1950–69

By the early 1950s, Seth G. Atwood, son of Seth B. Atwood, had joined the firm as executive vice-president. Atwood's employee base had increased to 700 workers. This growth was mirrored in the company's physical infrastructure. In approximately 25 years, the North Main plant had grown to include nine different buildings. Linked together, these facilities represented some 300,000 square feet of manufacturing space. It was around this time that a new, 100,000-square-foot plant in nearby Stockton, Illinois, was constructed.

The company's explosive growth was fueled by demand for its expanding array of 2,500 products, which, according to the November 7, 1952, *Rockford Register Republic*, included house trailer couplings, rotary lawn mower housings, electric motor bases and radios, brakes, items for tractors, and parts used by the railroad industry. Atwood also supplied products for the defense industry that were used in jeeps, tanks, planes, transport vehicles, and ammunition boxes.

The company's manufacturing diversity did not stop there. Atwood was also a supplier to the bicycle industry, for which it had pioneered the development of kick-stands (the Atwood Kick-Up Steel Stand) and training wheels (the Atwood Stabilizer). Among Atwood's other product offerings were items made of sheet metal, including cabinets and junction boxes. In addition to its depth of product offerings, the company's reach was also growing, extending to international markets such as England, where items were manufactured under the Atwood name.

In 1952, Atwood constructed a new manufacturing plant at 1400 Eddy Avenue. Within two years, the company established a Canadian affiliate called Lake Simcoe Industries in Beaverton, Ontario. In October of 1954, Seth G. Atwood was named president upon his father's elevation to chairman, and James T. Atwood became chairman emeritus.

It was around this time that Atwood began acquiring other companies, beginning with Royal Oak, Michigan-based Press Products Inc. and Chicago-based A.B.T. Manufacturing Corp. in 1955. The latter firm, which became a wholly owned subsidiary of Atwood, manufactured items like change-making devices, coin chutes, and slug rejectors. In mid-1958, Atwood announced that A.B.T. would remain a separate corporation but that all operations would move to Rockford. In 1956, Atwood acquired the trailer hardware division of Maywood, Illinois-based H.W. Crane Co., expanding its offering of couplers.

The arrival of the 1960s was characterized by more acquisitions. In February 1961, Atwood bought the assets of Pontiac, Michigan-based American Forging & Socket Co. and transferred production of the company's products—which included various kinds of automobile locks and latches, as well as parking brakes and seat adjusters—to Atwood's Rockford and Stockton plants. The acquisition created about 100 new jobs in northern Illinois and involved only business assets and certain pieces of equipment.

In September 1961, the company suffered a loss when James Atwood died. His inventive spirit and entrepreneurial drive was responsible for the formation of Atwood Vacuum Machine Co. However, growth and success continued with Seth G. Atwood at the helm. By 1963, Atwood had established a manufacturing facility in Havana, Illinois, expanded its engineering and manufacturing departments, and increased the company's presence in the European market through additional licensing agreements.

In December 1964, Atwood acquired Wixom, Michigan-based Hemco Inc., a manufacturer of both electric and gas heaters for use in trailers and mobile homes. As a result of the acquisition, a new organization called Atwood-Bowen Co. was formed. Led by Seth G. Atwood as president and Hemco's Max E. Bowen, the new firm combined the product offerings of Hemco with those that Atwood Vacuum Machine already provided to the trailer industry, including couplers, hitches, hydraulic trailer brakes, and jacks. In early 1966, Atwood established the General Products Division to serve the automotive, trailer, and mobile home markets from the company's plants in Wixom, Michigan, and Rockford, Illinois (North Main Street).

In 1967, Atwood constructed a new foundry in Havana, Illinois, to make iron castings used mainly for non-automotive purposes. The new plant included high-speed molding machines as well as a lab with x-ray capabilities for conducting metallurgical analyses. In July of that year, long-time Atwood employee Robert B. Rosecrance was promoted from executive vice-president to president, succeeding Seth G. Atwood, who became Atwood's chairman. Seth B. Atwood was subsequently appointed senior chairman.

By 1968, Atwood had established itself as the world's "largest independent manufacturer of internal auto body hardware," according to the February 15, 1968, *Rockford Register Repub-*

Key Dates:

1909: Brothers James and Seth Atwood establish Atwood Vacuum Machine Co.

1915: Seth Atwood develops an adjustable door bumper, which eventually becomes a standard automotive industry product.

1919: The company ceases production of vacuums and concentrates on serving the automotive market.

1925: A new 30,000-square-foot plant is constructed.

1936: A division is established to manufacture automobile and tractor clutches.

1952: Explosive growth is fueled by demand for Atwood's expanding array of products; company constructs a new manufacturing plant.

1954: A Canadian affiliate called Lake Simcoe Industries in Beaverton, Ontario, is established.

1963: Atwood establishes a manufacturing facility in Havana, Illinois.

1970: Atwood reorganizes, establishing the Automotive and Contract Division and the Mobil Products Division.

1971: Sales reach approximately $50 million.

1985: The Atwood family sells its enterprise to Anderson Industries.

1986: Atwood Vacuum Machine Co. changes its name to Atwood Industries Inc.

1989: Sales reach approximately $200 million.

1996: Elkhart, Indiana-based Excel Industries Inc. acquires Atwood Industries.

1997: Excel closes Atwood's automotive division and consolidates operations into existing Florida and Tennessee plants.

1999: Excel Industries is acquired by Dura Automotive Systems Inc., and Atwood Mobil Products becomes a division of Dura.

2001: Atwood Mobil devotes resources to the development of new technology, including innovative fuel cell systems for RVs.

lic. At this time, the organization employed about 2,500 workers at six different plants that collectively represented manufacturing space of approximately 750,000 square feet.

Operating as Two Divisions: 1970–98

Atwood began the 1970s by reorganizing. In May 1970, the company announced that the newly named Automotive and Contract Division would serve the automotive market and the Mobil Products Division would serve the trailer and mobile home markets. In 1971, total company sales were approximately $50 million, $40 million of which was attributed to the Automotive and Contract Division and the remainder to the Mobil Products Division. Approximately 80 percent of Atwood's workers were employed in the former division.

In 1971, record sales and optimistic projections for the Mobil Products Division prompted Atwood to announce construction of a new 48,000-square-foot facility for the division on Hiawatha Drive in Rockford, along with a 10,000-square-foot office building. Completed in fall 1972—another record year for the Mobil Products Division—the new facilities were located on a 14-acre site.

In 1973, Atwood made several acquisitions. In April, the company acquired Oakland, California-based Gilro Stamping Co. and made it a wholly owned Atwood subsidiary under the Automotive and Contract Division. The newly acquired firm had established relationships in the heavy-duty trucking sector. In December, Atwood sold its high-tech foundry in Havana, Illinois, to automotive part maker Dana Corp. By 1975, the Automotive Division had established a new plant in Oregon, Illinois, to make parking brakes, adding to the company's overall lineup of plants in Illinois, Michigan, and California. The following year, construction of yet another plant—a 40,000-square-foot facility situated on 29 acres—was announced in Western Union, Iowa.

Business continued at a steady, uneventful pace until 1985. That year, after 75 years of continuous operation, the Atwood family sold its enterprise to Anderson Industries, a local holding company operated by Rockford businessman John R. Anderson. According to the February 22, 1985 *Rockford Register Star*, Anderson Industries was selected from a group of several potential buyers. Commenting on the transaction, in which Atwood became a wholly owned subsidiary of Anderson Industries, John Anderson remarked that the quality of Atwood's 1,800 workers was a key factor in the acquisition. At the time of the acquisition, Atwood's annual sales totaled $138 million.

Following the sale to Anderson, long-time Atwood employee John R. Henriksen was named president. In 1986, the company added air conditioners to its line of mobile products and acquired Greenbriar, Tennessee-based Wedgewood Industries. In December of that year, the company's name changed from Atwood Vacuum Machine Co. to Atwood Industries Inc. According to comments from Henriksen in the December 12, 1986, *Rockford Register Star*, the ''change was made to give the name a broader scope and image consistent with the company's products and markets.''

Progress continued into the late 1980s. In December 1987, Atwood purchased Jonesville, Michigan-based Mark I Molded Plastics Inc. Then an $18 million company, Mark I manufactured molded automotive body parts and trim, as well as plastic cabinets and hardware for the electronics sector. According to Atwood President John Henriksen in the December 18, 1987, *Rockford Register Star*, the acquisition put the company in a stronger position to compete in the market for foreign automobiles manufactured in the United States.

In 1988, Henriksen was named Atwood's chairman. James H. Rilott, a long-time employee who had been serving as president of the Mobil Products Division, was named president of Atwood Industries. These and other executives were at the company's helm as it began to concentrate more heavily on international markets like Italy, the Netherlands, and Japan. That year, Atwood entered into a partnership with Yokohama, Japan-based Ohi Seisakusho Co. Ltd. that, like the Mark I acquisition, strengthened Atwood's ability to prosper in the market for U.S.-made foreign automobiles. In addition to the prospect of international sales, the aging Baby Boomer demographic held great promise for Atwood in the recreational vehicle sector.

Together, these factors led to projected annual sales of approximately $200 million in 1989. In August, it purchased Travel Star Inc.'s line of cooking appliances, giving Atwood a market share of 50 percent in the recreational vehicle market for slide-in range ovens and drop-in ranges, according to the August 29, 1989 *Rockford Register Star*. Atwood also acquired the Marvel line of trailer couplers and jacks from Franklin, Kentucky-based Dayton Walther.

Atwood's Mobil Products Division continued to prosper in the early-to-mid-1990s. In late 1992, the division acquired Hydro Flame, a Salt Lake City, Utah-based manufacturer of heaters for recreational vehicles, in a deal worth roughly $9 million. In June 1994 the Mobil Products Division also acquired Better Products Inc. of Elkhart, Indiana, allowing Atwood to add seat frames to its line of RV products. Finally, in 1996, the division announced its intention to purchase Greendale, Wisconsin-based The Compliance Group.

Meanwhile, Atwood's Automotive Division was suffering from a reduction in orders, forcing the layoff of roughly 185 workers in December 1993. Conditions continued to worsen for the division. When Elkhart, Indiana-based Excel Industries Inc.—a manufacturer of automotive window systems with annual sales of approximately $888 million—acquired Atwood Industries in March 1996, it announced that the division's technical and engineering staff would be relocated to Detroit. By May 1997, Excel closed the entire automotive division in Rockford and moved operations to its plants in Florida and Tennessee.

1999 and Beyond

In March 1999, Excel Industries was acquired by Rochester Hills, Michigan-based Dura Automotive Systems Inc., a $2.5 billion company with approximately 20,000 employees. Atwood Mobil Products then became a division of Dura. By the early 2000s, the company that John and Seth B. Atwood started

in the early 20th century continued to offer a wide array of products to the recreational vehicle market. Following in John Atwood's entrepreneurial footsteps, Atwood Mobil also devoted resources to the development of new technology, including innovative fuel cell systems for RVs, allowing the company to evolve with the needs and demands of its customers.

Principal Competitors

Teleflex Inc.; Ventra Group Inc.

Further Reading

"As Rain Falls, Atwood Begins Shutting Down," *Rockford Register Republic*, May 3, 1997, pp. 1A, 4A.

"Atwood Grows in New Plant," *Rockford Register Republic*, January 4, 1972.

"Atwood Names New President, Board Chairman," *Rockford Register Republic*, June 28, 1988.

"Atwood Utilizes 5,000 Parts in Marketing 2,500 Products," *Rockford Register Republic*, November 7, 1952.

"Atwood Vacuum Adds New Division," *Rockford Register Republic*, December 27, 1966.

"Atwood Vacuum Changes Name," *Rockford Register Star*, December 12, 1986, p. 11A.

"Atwood Vacuum Is Sold," *Rockford Register Star*, February 22, 1985, p. 1A.

"Atwood Vacuum Machine Co," *Rockford Register Republic*, February 15, 1968.

"Atwood World Leader in Seat Adjusters," *Rockford Register Star*, January 29, 1974.

"Autos, Trucks Use Atwood Products," *Rockford Register Republic*, February 1, 1972.

"Honor 3 Atwoods As Firm Marks 50th Anniversary," *Rockford Morning Star*, September 20, 1959.

"Ideas to Aid Production Reward Atwood Employees," *Rockford Register Republic*, May 25, 1955.

"James Atwood Dies," *Rockford Register Republic*, September 11, 1961.

"Trailer Firm is Formed by Atwood," *Rockford Register Star*, December 27, 1964.

"VEHICLE: Firms Work on RV Systems," *Fuel Cell Technology News*, March 2001.

—Paul R. Greenland

Barton Protective Services Inc.

11 Piedmont Center
Suite 410
Atlanta, Georgia 30305
U.S.A.
Telephone: (404) 266-1038
Toll Free: (800) 866-1122
Fax: (404) 364-6373
Web site: http://www.bartonsolutions.com

Private Company
Incorporated: 1977
Employees: 12,500
Sales: $305 million (2002)
NAIC: 561611 Investigation Services; 561612 Security
    Guards and Patrol Services; 561621 Security Systems
    Services (Except Locksmiths)

Headquartered in Atlanta, Barton Protective Services Inc. provides security and emergency services through 33 offices in the United States, the United Kingdom, and The Netherlands. Specifically, Barton's offerings include security officer, concierge, and patrol services as well as emergency medical and disaster response services, physical security services, intellectual asset protection services, fire and life safety services, workplace violence prevention services, and high incident management and risk management services. In line with its durable motto, "Barton provides," the company offers contracted security officers to corporations, toll plazas, and gated communities throughout the United States and the United Kingdom. The company also provides electronic integration solutions via its alliance with SecurityLink from Ameritech. In total, the company serves over 700 clients and employs over 10,000 people. Barton, which in 2001 ranked 86th on *Fortune* magazine's list of the 100 Best Companies to Work For, is principally owned by its chairman and founder, Charles Barton Rice, Sr.

Late 1970s Origins

Charles Barton Rice, Sr., long-time chairman of the company, founded Barton Protective Services Inc. in 1977. That year he opened the company's first office, what would become the Midtown Atlanta Branch, one of three Barton branches in the company's home base of Atlanta, Georgia. In that same year, with the Piedmont Center, its first customer and a loyal client throughout Barton's history, the new company began developing its expertise in the Class A office property market. That first account involved a grand total of 36.5 hours of security coverage per week, a humble beginning to be sure.

Although from its earliest years Barton established an excellent employer-employee relationship, it did have occasional problems. One involved Charles A. Kent, who began working for Barton in 1978. In October 1980, while he was working as a security guard at the United Parcel Service in Atlanta, there was an oil spill of about 4,600 gallons, for which Kent was held responsible. At the request of UPS, Barton removed Kent from his security post at that company. Kent alleged that over the next two years, Barton gave him a "bureaucratic runaround," and in 1982 he filed a discrimination complaint with the Department of Labor. He claimed that Barton engaged in retaliatory discrimination against him because he had originally reported the oil spill at UPS to the Environmental Protection Agency, a charge denied by Barton. Kent later filed for unemployment compensation, but was also denied that. Barton argued that Kent had never been dismissed but that he voluntarily ended his employment with the company. Ultimately, Kent's complaints against Barton were dismissed on the basis that they were not filed in a timely manner as required by the "whistleblower" provisions of the relevant federal law. Although Kent lost his bid for compensation, the affair left a sour taste and was probably instrumental in shaping the company's strong commitment to both its employees' training and their welfare—a commitment that would lead Barton to become a security industry leader in employee loyalty and retention.

In 1982, Barton established its National Training Center in Atlanta, one of the first training facilities for security professionals in the United States. It was originally created as a service center to meet Barton's needs in Atlanta, but it later became the national support hub for the company's entire training network, which would take in all of the company's branch offices and their personnel. Over its evolution into that national hub, Barton's National Training Center adopted relevant state-of-art technology and developed over 750 hours of training programs for use in its whole training network.

1983–95: Expansion Beyond Georgia

In 1983, Barton expanded its operations outside of Georgia for the first time. That year it opened its very successful branch in Charlotte, North Carolina. In an area of rapid growth and development, Charlotte challenged the new company to keep pace, which it managed well, over the years partnering with several of the area's most prestigious firms and major properties.

Barton opened its first Florida branch in 1988, in Miami. Later in the year it opened a second Florida branch at Deerfield Beach. A major factor in the company's decision to open branches in those two locations was the tremendous growth in the Sunshine State. The branches would eventually service 45 customers and employ 525 people in the South Florida area; they would also serve as the locus of Barton's Florida Department of Transportation Division, which by the end of the century employed over 1,100 people for Florida highway toll operations.

The company opened its first Texas branch in Houston in 1992. There, operations centered on the corporate needs for security services in the high-tech and petrochemical industries. Eventually, its client base would include Shell Oil, Equistar Chemicals, and Donohue Industries. The Houston branch also became the security provider for the Sharpstown Mall and Greenway Plaza, large, high-traffic shopping plazas. The growth of the Houston branch prompted Barton to open another training and support office in Pasadena, servicing the needs of customers operating in the Houston ship channel.

Late 1990s Overseas Expansion

A major development for Barton occurred in 1996, when the company partnered with Sun Microsystems. At the time, the company had no branch in the Silicon Valley, but Sun determined that Barton could do the job the computer giant needed, and it retained the company to provide security services for it operations in Northern California. Over the next couple of years, Sun acknowledged its satisfaction with the arrangement, bestowing on Barton its "Supplier-of-the-Year" accolade in 1997 and its "Outstanding Supplier" award in 1999.

The growth of some of Barton's clients had an important impact on its own pattern of development. In 1996, the company opened a Denver branch specifically to serve the expanding needs of two customers—Premisys and Sun Microsystems—after they themselves branched into the Denver area.

Moreover, the partnership with Sun Microsystems directly led to new opportunities for the company. Starting in 1998, when it began providing security service at Sun's facilities in the United Kingdom and The Netherlands, Barton began its expansion into overseas markets. Once in England, the company began offering people-oriented security services in London and the Thames Valley region. In 1998, Barton also opened a branch in San Francisco, looking to find customers among many potential high-rise and high-tech clients. The branch augmented Barton's presence in California, since it already had an older established branch in Los Angeles.

1999 and Beyond: Continued Growth under a Changing Guard

In February 1999, Barton opened a new branch office in Boston, once more in conjunction with the needs of Sun Microsystems, which had facilities in Chelmsford and Burlington, Massachusetts. However, in addition to providing security for Sun's operations, the new branch landed a contract to provide such services for "The Pru." Boston's downtown landmark Prudential Center, which served as the corporate headquarters of the Gillette Company and several other concerns. Late in the same year, Barton formed another branch in Austin, Texas, which was initially opened to meet the security needs of a *Fortune* 500 company in the semiconductor industry.

At the start of 2000, Rice turned Barton's operating reins over to Tom Ward, who was installed as both CEO and president. In addition to his extensive background in the security industry, Ward had served as president of Snelling & Snelling and was a partner in Management 2000, a consulting firm that specialized in strategic planning for larger companies. In the press release announcing Ward's appointment, Rice observed, "Before Tom joined us, I had spent 14 years taking Barton from zero to $44 million annually in sales. In the last eight years, Tom has taken us from $44 million to $200 million . . . and we fully expect to be a $500 million company within the next several years. But more importantly, I know that Tom will lead without sacrificing the values that got us where we are today—by *winning the customer for life*, by taking care of our people, by rewarding them and acknowledging them and by never becoming complacent."

During 2000, for the first time, *Fortune* named Barton as one of the nation's "100 Best Companies to Work For," and the following year it made the list again, moving up from number 97 to number 86. That same year, Barton opened up a branch on the 28th floor of the Empire State Building in Manhattan. Its aim, again, was to build a customer base from among Class A and B real estate buildings and *Fortune* 500 corporations. Adjacent to its offices, Barton also established a New York State approved security training school.

Barton's growth into a major security services business through the 1990s and into the first year of the next decade was slow and steady. Comparatively speaking, it compiled an excel-

Key Dates:

1977: Charles Barton Rice, Sr., founds company.
1983: Company opens an office in Charlotte, North Carolina, its first branch outside of Georgia.
1987: Barton expands in Texas, purchasing Las Colinas Security in Dallas.
1996: Barton forms partnership with Sun Microsystems in the Silicon Valley.
1998: Company expands abroad, providing security services for Sun in the United Kingdom and The Netherlands.
2000: Tom Ward is named CEO and president; New York branch opens.
2001: Rice receives Ernst & Young's Entrepreneur of the Year Award in the Business Service Category; Barton is named one of *Fortune*'s 100 Best Companies to Work For for the second year in a row.

lent record in retaining both its personnel and clients. It also widely distributed its business across its national network of branch offices, each of which developed a solid client core. For example, in 2001, the company's very first office, what became the Midtown Branch in Atlanta, with a force of 650 employees, claimed a client base of 65 customers. The company also was planning to continue its expansion abroad, hoping to form new partnerships with customers in the sizable European market.

Several factors have accounted for Barton's good employee-retention record, rare in an industry noted for its high turnover in personnel. The company provided fringe benefits similar companies simply would not offer, including medical and dental insurance, vision care, short-term disability insurance, and Bank of America direct-deposit cash-pay cards. It was also the first company in the security industry to offer a matching 401(k)

plan. In addition, the company has offered good training programs that were constantly being upgraded to help employees keep their skill levels up to par.

Barton's clients seemed no less content than the company's employees. In fact, the company has pretty much lived up to its abbreviated mission statement: "win the customer for life." In 2000, Barton claimed a 97 percent client retention rate, which way outdistanced the industry's average of 75 percent.

An additional senior-executive level change occurred in January 2001, when Baron appointed Patrick O. McNulty as chief operating officer and located him at his Barton's Global Customer and Employee Support Center command post in Atlanta. McNulty, with 20 years experience in the contract security service industry, reported directly to the company's CEO and president, Tom Ward. At the time of his selection, McNulty was serving as president of the East Central Region for Securitas/Pinkerton. He had begun his career with the Chicago-based Kane Service, a private security firm that his great grandfather has founded in 1911.

Principal Competitors

The Chubb Corporation; Command Security Corporation; Protection One, Inc.; Securicor plc; Securitas AB; The Wackenhut Corporation.

Further Reading

Harbour, Jessica, and Emmet Martin, "Take This Job and Love It," *Atlanta*, November 2000, p. 116.
"Optio Software Selected by Barton Protective Services," *Business Wire*, August 20, 2001.

—John W. Fiero

Bel Fuse, Inc.

198 Van Vorst Street
Jersey City, New Jersey 07302
U.S.A.
Telephone: (201) 432-0463
Fax: (201) 432-9542
Web site: http://www.belfuse.com

Public Company
Incorporated: 1947
Employees: 866
Sales: $96 million (2001)
Stock Exchanges: NASDAQ
Ticker Symbol: BELFA
NAIC: 335999 All Other Miscellaneous Electrical
    Equipment and Component Manufacturing

Originally an automobile fuse maker, Bel Fuse, Inc. has stayed abreast of technological changes and diversified into the manufacture of television components and the production and sale of parts used in cutting edge high-speed data transmission, telecommunications, and networking. From its corporate headquarters in New Jersey, Bel Fuse operates facilities in Massachusetts and California, as well as plants in the Far East and the United Kingdom. Although the company was hit hard by the economic downturn that struck the high-tech industry as a whole in 2000 and 2001, its cost-management efforts and strategic acquisitions left it well positioned to prosper in the coming years.

A Family Company Flourishes

In 1949, 26-year-old Elliot Bernstein founded Bel Fuse in Jersey City, New Jersey, to make fuses for automobiles. With America's love affair with the car blossoming in the postwar years, the young company did well and soon expanded its business to make fuses for another wildly popular consumer product: televisions. The company's fortunes waxed further when it collaborated with television industry giant RCA Corp. to create the first delay lines used in color television sets. (Among other functions, delay lines are used to ensure that signals are transmitted in proper order.) When RCA became one of the pioneers in the computer business in the 1960s, Bel Fuse followed in its wake, making delay lines for these newfangled products as well. In 1966, Bel Fuse began making delay lines for the mainframe computers produced by industry colossus International Business Machines Corp. (IBM).

To fund further growth, Bel Fuse held an initial public offering of stock in 1967, though Bernstein and his brother Howard, the company's vice-president and treasurer, retained a majority ownership interest, controlling more than 50 percent of the stock. (Although the family's stake was down to about 25 percent by 1995, day-to-day management still remained in the hands of the Bernstein family, particularly in the person of Elliot's son Daniel Bernstein, who became president of the company in the 1990s.) As the computer industry grew through the 1970s and then exploded in the early 1980s with the proliferation of desktop personal computers (PCs), Bel Fuse moved along with it. Counting IBM and Digital Equipment Corp. among its customers, the firm expanded its product offerings to include miniature fuses, which help prevent computer circuit boards from overheating. By 1983, Bel Fuse had revenues over $18 million and operated manufacturing plants in Hong Kong and Macao. The company had shown consistent sales growth of better than 15 percent each year since its inception, with annual profits increasing more than 35 percent yearly on average. "Our secret has been our ability to change as technologies evolve," company president (and founder Elliot's son) Daniel Bernstein told *Business News New Jersey.* "As new technologies evolve, we grow with them." Bel Fuse continued to grow throughout the 1980s, spending roughly eight to 10 percent of its annual revenues on research and development to diversify its product range and compiling a nearly 500-strong customer base that included such notable firms as 3Com Corp., Compaq Computer Corp., Philips Electronics Corp., Siemens AG, and Apple Computer, Inc.

Expansion in the 1990s

Although Bel Fuse had never stopped making products for the automotive and television industries while simultaneously moving into the burgeoning computer field, by the early 1990s it had become evident that components for high-technology products

Company Perspectives:

Bel Fuse enjoys a long-standing reputation as a financially stable, world class manufacturer—the result of its ability to engineer optimal solutions to meet changing market demands. The company continues to grow through its strategic partnerships with leading high tech companies, making Bel components an integral part of customers' new product development programs.

would be the company's main source of revenue in the coming years. Along with fuses and delay lines, Bel Fuse began to manufacture a wider set of magnetic components and power converters, essential parts for the electrical and electronics industries. To capitalize on the technological boom of the decade, Bel Fuse established an engineering facility in California's Silicon Valley, allowing it to work in closer proximity to firms that would become some of its best customers. This proved to be a distinct competitive advantage, as Bel Fuse was able to tailor its products to be compatible with products of different companies to appeal to the widest possible customer base. "Being near the 3Coms and Intels of the world, Bel Fuse is able to offer a higher level of engineering support than its competitors," Brent Bracelin, an industry analyst told *Business News New Jersey*. "That has really opened quite a few doors for the company."

Bel Fuse made another significant decision in 1996 when it decided to restructure its operations and focus most heavily on its networking components business. Networking—the ability of computers and other electronic devices to talk with one another—was becoming an increasingly important field with the rise of the Internet and the reliance on computers in the workplace, and great profits were available to firms who could succeed in facilitating it. Bel Fuse's magnetic components were integral to the field, and the company reached sales of $73.5 million in 1997, on which it realized an $8.9 million profit. Wall Street was impressed, as the company's share price more than doubled between the start of 1997 and May 1998, when it announced extremely strong first quarter profits ($2.97 million—more than double 1997's first quarter profits of $1.31 million).

The year 1998 brought a few shaky moments, as the electronics industry was effected by fallout from the Asian economic crisis. Bel Fuse—whose main overseas manufacturing plants were in Hong Kong (which had been returned by the United Kingdom to China in 1997) and Macao (which Portugal handed over to China in 1999)—sweated out the political uncertainties caused by these geopolitical shifts. However, the company continued to thrive and indeed to pursue its new interest in networking. In August, Bel Fuse announced plans to purchase Lucent Technologies, Inc.'s signal-transformer division. The deal closed in October, and Daniel Bernstein explained the acquisition's importance for Bel Fuse to *Electronic Buyer's News*. "We have to broaden our portfolio for telecommunications and power applications," he said. "With the acquisition of the signal-transformer business of Lucent, we accomplish this goal." To cut costs, Bel Fuse shifted production of the newly acquired lines from Lucent's plant in Matamoros, Mexico, to its own plants in Asia. The acquisition boosted Bel

Fuse's bottom line, as the company reported a profit of $15.2 million in 1998 on sales of over $90.8 million.

The following year proved even more successful. Sales reached nearly $120 million, and Bel Fuse netted a record $21.3 million for the year. In recognition of its achievements, *Forbes* named the firm one of its 200 best small companies in America for 1999.

Networking into the New Millennium

Bel Fuse's focus on networking continued to pay dividends in 2000, as the company posted strong sales for the first half of the year, driven primarily by "increasing demand for its products that support ADSL high-speed data transmission and voice-over-the-Internet protocols," as *Electronic Buyer's News* explained. Demand for the firm's fuse products also increased dramatically due to the explosive growth in the telecommunications sector. Fuses are essential for the proper operation of an array of products such as modems, fax and answering machines, and cellular base stations, and the strong demand for these products pushed the company's fuse sales up by more than 35 percent during the course of the year. Networking, however, still remained the firm's biggest profit source. In late 2000, Bel Fuse entered the home phone line networking market, rolling out a transformer module designed to work with Broadcom Corp.'s newly released networking chip. Broadcom's offering, itself part of a strategic partnership with budget computer vendor Gateway, Inc., was designed to enable people with multiple computers in their homes to set up in-house networks and also to afford people with portable computers the ability to have network and/or Internet access from their homes, offices, or other remote locations. With at least 25 million multiple-PC households, and millions more portable computer users, this new product line gave Bel Fuse access to a huge and potentially lucrative market.

These factors combined to make 2000 Bel Fuse's best year ever. Sales topped $145.2 million, an increase of 22 percent on 1999's then-record figure, and the company earned more than $32.2 million, 51 percent higher than the year before. To top it off, *Forbes* again named Bel Fuse one of its 200 best small companies in America. Storm clouds appeared on the horizon, however, as the U.S. economy began to weaken during the latter part of the year.

Bel Fuse's profits continued to rise during the first quarter of 2001, as the company netted $7.5 million on sales of $33.7 million during the quarter. (This was a 69 percent increase over the company's $4.4 million in profit during the first quarter of 2000, which was achieved on sales of $26.1 million). Bel Fuse, however, recognized that the global economic slowdown was about to hit the company hard, as many of its customers were already experiencing extreme difficulties in the post-bubble environment. Anticipating that its short-term profitability was likely to suffer, Bel Fuse turned an eye to the future and decided to invest much of the $63 million in cash it had on hand to acquire companies that would help it reach its long-term product development goals. As it had in 1996 with its focus on networking, Bel Fuse identified what it expected to be another growth field and concentrated its efforts there. Specifically, the company decided that it wanted to make itself into a one-stop shopping source for all of its customers' power supply needs. To this end, the company acquired the Westborough, Massachusetts, start-up firm Current Concepts, Inc. in May 2001. Although only five months old at the time, Current Concepts had been founded by two industry veterans and was regarded as an innovative designer of cutting edge DC/DC converters that could be used to power coming generations of low-voltage silicon that would be used in high-speed microprocessors and memory chips. Bel Fuse planned to turn its new purchase into the flagship of its newly formed Power Products Division, headed by Bel Fuse's strategic marketing director Marshall Miles.

The following week, Bel Fuse expanded its presence in East Asia with the purchase of Hangzou, China-based E-Power Co., Ltd., a privately held research-and-development company that concentrated on devising power conversion technologies for high volume commercial users. Bel Fuse was enthused about the deal, the terms of which (as had been the case with Current Concepts) were not disclosed. "The E-Power acquisition will significantly speed the development and introduction of cost-effective low power DC/DC converters for high volume applications typically used by Bel's established customer base in the telecommunications, networking and computing markets," Bel Fuse's President Bernstein said in a company press release. "This is Bel's first China-based design center and we look forward to their assistance in developing these new products and providing ongoing engineering and cost-control support for our new team in Massachusetts [at the erstwhile Current Concepts plant]." Industry observers were impressed. "The Point of Load segment Bel is pursuing with these acquisitions [of Current and E-Power] is the fastest growing sector of the [$5.8 billion] DC/DC market," Jeff Shepard, president of the Darnell Group, an power supply industry analyst, told *Business Wire*. "This is also an area in which their packaging capabilities should serve them well as they compete for market share."

While Bel Fuse continued to plan for the long term, its prediction about the immediate state of the economy proved correct. Due in part to expenses incurred during its spring buying spree,

and more to the overall business climate as the technology bubble of the late 1990s emphatically burst, the company lost $12.2 million in 2001 on sales of $96 million (a figure roughly one-third lower than 2000 revenues). Bel Fuse also suffered a more intimate blow in July of 2001 when its founder, Elliot Bernstein, died at age 78. (His son, company president Daniel Bernstein, had been named chief executive officer two months before.) Undeterred, the company pushed ahead during the year, rolling out several new products and seeking to position itself strongly for the recovery that the company expected would inevitably arrive. Perhaps the most important among these new product lines were three different families of transformer modules—part of the company's growing line of surface mount magnetic components. These modules are used in an array of Wide Area Network applications, such as Internet service provider servers, digital access and cross-connect systems, cellular base stations, and internetworking interfaces. Crucially, the three different sets of offerings were tailored to work with divergent systems offered by leading transceiver manufacturers such as Sierra Wireless, Inc.; Connexant Systems, Inc.; Cirrus Logic, Inc.; Exar Corp.; and Intel Corp. "These are not 'one size fits all' components," Daniel Bernstein told *Business Wire*. "Each part number within our new [product lines] is specifically engineered to optimize the performance of a specific manufacturer's chipset." In this way, Bel Fuse could offer high-quality items to serve the broadest possible customer base. "We're trying to move up the food chain to provide more value-added products to help our telecom customers," Bernstein told *Electronic Business News*.

Buoyed by offerings from its new Power Products division and efficiencies gained from internal restructuring, Bel Fuse charged into 2002. In January, the company announced a further streamlining effort, the consolidation of its telecommunications and value-added engineering operations into one San Diego facility, a move which involved shuttering plants in Dallas and Indianapolis as well as an existing one in San Diego. The company unveiled seven new lines from its Power Products division in the first five months of the year alone. And despite posting a nearly $600,000 loss in the first half of the year (on revenues of $41.2 million), Daniel Bernstein was optimistic about the firm's potential. "We believe the worst of the slowdown in the global electronics industry is now behind us," he told *Business Wire* on April 26, 2002. "While conditions remain tough, they are clearly getting better. Backlog is rising and we see signs that momentum is being reestablished in several key product areas. . . . At the same time, manufacturing overhead and variable expenses have been dramatically reduced, which should contribute to improved profitability as sales begin to recover." Indeed, by the end of the third quarter of 2002, the company was $1.2 million in the black on revenues of $69.6 million. While total sales were still down from 2001, the company was well positioned to profit in the future, so long as the technology industry as a whole managed to return to health.

Principal Divisions

Power Products.

Principal Competitors

Cooper Electronic Technologies; Littelfuse, Inc.; S&C Electric Co.

Further Reading

"Bel Acquires E-Power Corp.," *Business Wire*, May 15, 2001.

"Bel Announces Three Transformer Families for Industrial T1/E1/J1 Applications," *Business Wire*, September 5, 2001.

"Bel Enters Home Phoneline Networking Market with Transformer for Broadcom's 'Internet-on-a-Chip' Products," *Business Wire*, December 8, 2000.

"Bel Fuse to Reorganize Domestic Engineering Ops," *Dow Jones News Service*, January 9, 2002.

"Bel Reports First Quarter Results," *Business Wire*, April 26, 2002.

"Bel Reports Fourth Quarter and 2001 Results," *Business Wire*, February 8, 2002.

"Bel Second Quarter Net Income Increases," *Cambridge Telecom Report*, August 5, 2002.

Chin, Spencer, "Acquisition Improves Power Line," *Electronic Buyer's News*, May 14, 2001.

——, "Navigating in Today's IP&E World," *Electronic Buyer's News*, February 11, 2002.

Joseph, V.K., "Bel Fuse Breaks Free from the Pack," *Business News New Jersey*, May 18, 1998.

Moore, Anne, "Growth in the Middle Medium-Sized Firms Show Strength," *The Record of Northern New Jersey*, November 18, 1984.

Roos, Gina, "Telecom Drives Transformers," *Electronic Engineering Times*, June 19, 2000.

Scouras, Ismini, "Lucent to Sell Signal-Transformer Biz to Bel Fuse," *Electronic Buyer's News*, August 31, 1998.

"Special Report: Best Managed Companies—Runners Up," *Electronic Buyer's News*, October 18, 1999.

—Rebecca Stanfel

BG

BENFIELD GROUP

Benfield Greig Group plc

55 Bishopsgate
London EC2N 3BD
United Kingdom
Telephone: (44) 207 578-7000
Fax: (44) 207 578-7001
Web site: http://www.benfieldgreig.com

Private Company
Incorporated: 1973 as Benfield, Lovick & Rees
Employees: 1,700
Sales: £325 million ($520 million)(2001)
NAIC: 524210 Insurance Agencies and Brokerages

Benfield Greig Group plc is the world's third-largest reinsurance company, behind leaders Aon and Marsh & McClellan reinsurance subsidiary Guy Carpenter & Co. Benfield Greig is also the world's leading privately held reinsurance group—a distinction that will become moot after the company completes its proposed public offering in 2003. With 35 offices and 1,500 employee's worldwide, Benfield Greig's operations are split between Benfield Greig Ltd, which handles the company's international operations outside of the United States, and Benfield Blanch Inc., which represents the company in the United States. The company offers a full range of reinsurance services, including advisory, consulting and administrative support, as well as the company's pioneering ReMetrics risk modelling unit. Benfield Greig has also been one of the fastest-growing companies in the international reinsurance market, multiplying its revenues by more than ten in the second half of the 1990s. Acquisitions, including mergers with Greig Fester in 1997, and with EW Blanch in 2001, have formed a large part of the company's growth. In 2001, the company posted revenues of £325 million ($520 million). Benfield Greig is led by chairman John Coldman and CEO Grahame Chilton. The company expects to go public on the London Stock Exchange and is also contemplating a follow-up listing on the New York Stock Exchange.

1970s Origins

The Benfield Greig Group was a relative newcomer to the reinsurance market when its was founded by Ted Benfield and Michael Rees as Benfield, Lovick & Rees in 1973. Joining the firm that year was Matthew Harding, then 20 years old, who began working for the firm as an office assistant. By the end of the 1970s, Harding had risen to become one of the group's top executives. In 1980, Harding bought into the firm, acquiring a 10 percent stake. Two years later, Harding became the group's major shareholder, raising £160,000 to buy out Ted Benfield's 32 percent share.

Harding set to work to reorient the firm, which at the time had just 20 employees and revenues of just £4 million per year, with a focus on the marine reinsurance sector. The reinsurance market in the early 1980s remained underdeveloped, and largely consisted of the offshoot business of larger generalist insurance companies. Harding sought to create one of the industry's first specialist reinsurance firms, or as the company called itself, a reinsurance 'intermediary' capable of brokering reinsurance agreements among insurance companies.

1980s Expansion

One of Harding's first moves was to hire on Grahame Chilton, who had been working as a reinsurance specialist CT Bowring, which had been acquired by Marsh & McClellan in the 1970s. Chilton quickly became part of the core leadership group at Benfield, which also included founder Michael Rees. As Chilton told the *Independent:* "Joining from a large company, I saw the opportunity that lay in a specialist reinsurance intermediary. The market was in its infancy, and we all felt we could create something special. I thoroughly enjoyed Matthew's intellect and company, and I jumped at it."

Harding's and Chilton's interests focused on customer service. In 1985, Harding brought in a new member of the management team, John Coldman, who had started his career in the reinsurance area in the mid-1960s with the WT Greig insurance firm, and who became Benfield's office manager.

By 1988, Harding's management team was in place. In that year, Harding led a management buy-out of the remaining shares of the firm, renaming it the Benfield Group. Both Chilton and Coldman became owners, with 12 and 9 percent of the business, respectively, while founding partner Rees held a similar percentage of the business. By then the firm counted some 50 employees and was posting profits of more than £4 million per year.

Over the next several years, the company established its reputation in the reinsurance market. Benfield continued to serve as a pioneer in the field, particularly with the launch of what it was to call its ReMetrics team, a system of risk modeling that became an important part of the firm's consultancy toolbox. The company, while extremely profitable for its primary partners—Harding himself joined England's 100 wealthiest people list in the early 1990s—remained quite small, posting under £40 million in revenues in 1993.

A Global Reinsurance Company for the New Century

By then, however, the reinsurance market was coming of age, as the company found itself joined by a growing number of specialist firms. Reinsurance had also come to play an important part in the growth of the world's largest insurance companies, such as Aon and Marsh & McClellan, which had captured the top spots in the reinsurance category as well.

Benfield Group began to prepare for its own growth in the mid-1990s. In 1995, the firm acquired Ellinger Heath Western, a reinsurance broker that had developed a specialty focus on the non-marine market in the United Kingdom and in North America. The acquisition doubled Benfield's size and led to a name change, to Benfield Ellinger Ltd. Harding, who had made national headlines with a £25 million investment in the Chelsea football club, remained the group's chairman.

Tragedy struck the group in 1996, when Harding and another top Benfield executive died in a helicopter crash on the way home from a Chelsea soccer match. The loss of two of the firm's five principal partners threatened to devastate Benfield's business. Chilton and Coldman took over the company's leadership, with the former taking the CEO role and the latter taking the position of chairman. While Chilton secured the group's customer loyalty, Coldman began putting into place the groundwork for a larger organization, one less dependent on a handful of top people, while maintaining a relatively flat management structure.

An important step in Benfield's transition from a small-scale firm to one of the world's top three reinsurance companies came in 1997 when the firm acquired fellow U.K. group Greig Fester in a deal worth £120 million ($190 million). Greig Fester stemmed from WT Greig, founded in 1921, and Fester Fothergill and Hartung, one of the oldest U.K. insurers active in the reinsurance market, which had merged in 1974. The addition of Greig Fester brought Benfield onto the international scene, with 24 new offices around the world. Follwing the merger, both Chilton and Coldman made a point of visiting each of the group's new offices and meeting all of its new employees.

By 1999, Benfield had successfully integrated Greig Fester's operations and the company looked forward to continuing its international expansion. The United States became a primary target for the company's next growth moves. In 1999, the company, which had for the most part directed its U.S. operations from its U.K. office, set up a dedicated U.S. subsidiary, Benfield Greig LLC. By the end of that year, the company had made its first U.S. acquisition, Bates Turner Intermediaries LLC, the reinsurance business of Employers RE, itself a unit of GE Capital. The acquisition helped boost the Benfield U.S. unit's revenues past $5 million.

Benfield's new expansion in the United States came with the hiring of Rodman Fox and Paul Karon. Both men had been top producers at troubled EW Blanch, at the time the world's fourth-largest reinsurance firm, before being lured away by Benfield—in Fox's case, through a salary package worth more than $4 million per year. Fox and Karon brought a number of Blanch employees and especially a number of Blanch clients, including the company's top client, to Benfield. By the end of 2000, Benfield's U.S. branch was posting $30 million (£20 million) in revenues. Meanwhile, Benfield Greig's total sales had also gained strongly, topping £95 million in 1999 and £131 million in 2000.

The following year, however, saw Benfield leap into the top ranks of the worldwide reinsurance market. In May of that year, Benfield agreed to pay $179 million to acquire EW Blanch, a move that boosted its operations to more than 30 offices and 1,700 employees, with combined sales of some £260 million ($410 million). The acquisition also propelled the company into the leading position among privately owned reinsurance companies, and gave it the number-three spot in the total reinsurance market. The company's U.S. operation was then renamed Benfield Blanch, with Fox placed in the CEO spot.

The Blanch acquisition had brought with it a heavy debt burden for Benfield Greig, and by the end of 2001, the group had announced its interest in pursuing a public offering in order to pay down debt. As part of the approach to the public offering, the company switched its registered domicile to Bermuda, a move that gave it the choice between a listing on the London and New York stock exchanges.

Benfield's announcement caught the attention of Marsh & McClellan Cos., the world's largest insurance broker, which also held the number two position in the world's reinsurance market. In early 2002, Marsh & McClellan prepared an acquisition offer reportedly worth some $1.2 billion. Talks between the two sides reached were said to have reached an advanced stage, including an agreement on the management structure of

Key Dates:

1973: Ted Benfield leads establishment of Benfield, Lovick & Rees insurance firm, specializing in the reinsurance market; Matthew Harding joins firm as an office boy.
1980: Harding is given the opportunity to buy 10 percent of Benfield, Lovick & Rees.
1982: Harding buys Ted Benfield's share in company and becomes the largest shareholder with 32 percent; Grahame Chilton is hired.
1985: John Coldman joins Benfield as office manager.
1988: Harding, Chilton and Coldman lead a management buyout of Benfield, changing firm's name to the Benfield Group.
1995: Benfield acquires Ellinger Heath Western and changes name to Benfield Ellinger.
1996: Matthew Harding dies in helicopter crash.
1997: Benfield acquires Greig Fester and changes name to Benfield Greig.
1999: Benfield acquires Bates Turner from Employers Re (part of GE Capital).
2001: Benfield Greig acquires EW Blanch and becomes world's third-largest reinsurance group.
2002: Benfield announces plans to go public.

the new group. Yet talks broke down after Marsh & McClellan reduced its offer to just $950 million, and no formal offer was made.

Instead, Benfield Greig reset its sights on its public offering. New filing rules set up in New York following the Enron and Worldcom financial scandals had in the meantime made the New York exchange less attractive to the British group; instead, Benfield Greig announced its plans to list on the London exchange before the end of the first half of 2003. The company did not rule out an eventual listing on the New York exchange, however.

In the meantime, Benfield Greig continued to flesh out its international network. In 2002, the group acquired the Czech and Slovak offices of BMS Harris & Dixon, providing Benfield Greig with an entry into the Central European market. By the end of that year, the company's sales had topped £325 million ($520 million). As it prepared for its public offering, Benfield Greig had already successfully transformed itself into one of the world's largest reinsurance groups.

Principal Subsidiaries

Benfield Blanch Inc; Benfield Greig Ltd.; Benfield Premium Finance; Benfield Sports International Ltd.; Orbit Benefits Ltd.; Paragon; Wildnet Group.

Principal Competitors

Aon Reinsurance Worldwide Inc.; Guy Carpenter & Co. Inc.; Willis Faber Reinsurance; Jardine Lloyd Thompson Reinsurance Holdings Ltd.; Towers Perrin Reinsurance; Lambert Fenchurch Group plc; Am-Re Brokers Inc.; John P. Woods Co. Inc.

Further Reading

"Benfield Looks to Next Level with Planned IPO," *Bestwire*, December 3, 2002.
"Benfield May Float Soon, Say Analysts," *Reactions*, August 2002, p. 9.
Bolger, Andrew, "Marsh Talks with Benfield Break Down," *Financial Times*, August 14, 2002, p. 18.
Cave, Andrew, "Another Pounds 100m? It Won't Change My Life," *Daily Telegraph*, December 21, 2002, p. 28.
Souter, Gavin, "Expanding Reach," *Business Insurance*, September 25, 2000, p. 3.
Swift, Jonathan, "Interview: Playing in the Premier League," *Post Magazine*, May 9, 2002, p. 15.
Thackray, Rachelle, "Me and My Partner: John Coldman and Grahame Chilton," *Independent*, March 15, 2000, p. 8.
Vaughan-Adams, Liz, "Benfield Receives Pounds 660m Bid from US Giant," *Independent*, August 12, 2002, p. 15.

—M.L. Cohen

Big Y Foods, Inc.

2145 Roosevelt Avenue
Springfield, Massachusetts 01104
U.S.A.
Telephone: (413) 784-0600
Toll Free: (800) 828-2688
Fax: (413) 732-7350
Web site: http://www.bigy.com

Private Company
Incorporated: 1947
Employees: 7,850
Sales: $1.2 billion (2002)
NAIC: 445110 Supermarkets and Other Grocery (Except Convenience) Stores

Big Y Foods, Inc., headquartered in Springfield, Massachusetts, owns and operates a retail supermarket chain in Massachusetts and Connecticut. With almost four dozen stores, it is the largest privately owned grocery chain in the region. Half of these are Big Y World Class Markets, which in their range of goods and services rival some of their giant, mass market rivals. Besides floral shops, bakeries, and delis, some provide banking, dry cleaning, photo processing, and even baby sitting services and propane sales. Many stores also have Big Y Food Courts, where shoppers can lunch on prepared foods. Big Y also operates a Table & Vine shop, a gourmet food, fine wine, and liquor store located in its World Class Market in Northampton, Massachusetts. Ownership of the company remains in the D'Amour family, which inherited the business from its founders, Paul and Gerald D'Amour.

A Family Business on a Small Scale: 1936–50s

Big Y Foods got its start in Chicopee, Massachusetts, in 1936, when 30-year old Paul D'Amour, a Wonder Bread Baking Company route salesman, bought the Y Cash Market, a small grocery store where hamburger meat sold for 25 cents a pound and bread for a nickel a loaf. The store was so named because it was located at an intersection in the Willimansett section of Chicopee where two streets converged to form a

"Y." D'Amour opened the 900-square-foot store on December 12 and was soon joined in the business by his teenage brother, Gerald. They were thereafter joined by their two sisters, who helped out with administrative tasks, including cash handling and financial reporting. Thus, from the outset, Big Y was a family business.

By 1940, just prior to World War II, the Y Cash Market's sales had increased 20 fold, and the store had physically expanded to three times its originally size. The war slowed the store's growth somewhat, but by 1947, with the postwar boom started, the D'Amours were able to open a second store in what had previously been a bowling alley, a much larger facility than the original Y Cash Market. It was also in 1947 that the company was first incorporated.

The business was faring well, and the D'Amours made sure that it kept in step with the rapid changes in the retail food industry, accommodating, for example, the new packaging and frozen food preparation advances that were then revolutionizing the trade. The Y Cash Markets met increasing customer demands for greater variety, self-service, and one-stop-shopping convenience.

First Big Y Supermarket and Continued Growth: 1950–70

In 1952, the D'Amour family took a lease on a 10,000-square-foot store located close to the Westover Air Base in Chicopee. Because it was considerably larger than other grocery stores in the area, the D'Amours dubbed it the Big Y Supermarket. It became the first real supermarket in Chicopee. Eight years later, the company opened a much larger store in Northampton, a town in western Massachusetts. At 31,000 square feet, it was three times the size of the Big Y Supermarket in Chicopee and rivaled most any store in that area of the state. Three years later, in 1963, the D'Amours acquired a second site in Northampton, where it opened Big Y Wines & Liquors, a specialty store retailing various alcoholic beverages.

Big Y moved into what would become its operational home, Springfield, Massachusetts, in 1967, and in 1968, with six stores then it operation, it added seven more when it acquired the

Jumbo Supermarket chain. About that same time, a second generation of the D'Amour family began working in the business. The company's management also moved into a whole floor of offices in a business building in Chicopee. From there, the family and its colleagues directed the further expansion of the company.

In 1972, the company acquired two Popular Supermarkets, located in Longmeadow and the Sixteen Acres section of Springfield. By then, Big Y was established as the leading privately owned grocery chain in its area of the state. And it continued to grow through the rest of the decade, despite increasing competition from the burgeoning number of giant supermarket chains sprouting in the region.

In 1981, in a move that enhanced its image as a locally owned business, Big Y established its annual scholarship program honoring academic achievement and merit, a program that it would expand for the next several years. The company was also broadening its business horizons, and in 1984, for the first time, it expanded outside the state by purchasing a supermarket and shopping center in Stafford Springs, Connecticut. During that same year, Big Y was also expanding in its home state, where it acquired of the Adams Supermarket chain in Berkshire County, Massachusetts.

Innovations and World Class Supermarkets: 1980s–90s

By 1986, the year in which Big Y reached its 50th anniversary, it had become the top ranked private grocery chain in western Massachusetts. Although it ranked only 12th in the entire state, it had 21 stores and about 1600 employees. In order to maintain a competitive edge, it had also became a leader in the use of technology to develop efficient energy management, security, product delivery, inventory oversight, and scanning and communication systems that ranged through every aspect of its business. Its growth, which continued through the rest of the decade, dictated a need to expand its base of operations. Accordingly, in 1989, it leased new offices on Chestnut Street in Springfield, which thereafter became its corporate center.

The new decade brought many changes, one of which, sadly, was the passing of Big Y's founder, Paul D'Amour, who died at 84 in 1990. At the start of the new decade, the chain expanded into Worcester County, Massachusetts. By that time, too, Big Y began handling some of its own product distribution, thereby taking advantage of special sales and discount bulk purchasing. To facilitate this move, the company purchased a 100,000-square-foot warehouse and distribution center in Springfield. For a few years, Big Y Foods maintained a small fleet of trucks to distribute products to its various stores, but in 1994, finding it

difficult to hire and retain drivers and meet training and DOT (Department of Transportation) requirements, it turned the task over to dedicated carriage-route providers, ultimately contracting with Ryder Integrated Logistics Inc. of Miami to handle this operation exclusively. Ryder operated a fleet of ten tractor-trailers to service the Big Y stores.

In the same period, Big Y put some innovative programs into effect. For example, in 1990 the company instituted its Express Saving Club. Under the new plan, which gained national recognition, Big Y stores eliminated in-store coupons in favor of giving savings to customers who received discounts when clerks scanned customer-held cards at checkout counters. In 1993, it also tied the Express Savings Club to Education Express, one of several education programs Big Y sponsored. Education Express helped fund the purchase of equipment for local schools.

Civic involvement, particularly in school projects and support, was and is a point of pride for Big Y Foods. By June 1994, through Education Express, the company had awarded almost $2 million to over 900 schools in its market area. Big Y also developed a toll-free tutoring service for students. Dubbed Big Y's Homework Helpline, it was instituted to assist grade K thru 12 students in completing their out of class assignments.

It was also in 1993 that, in Springfield, after three years of research and development, the company opened its first World Class Market. The 64,000-square-foot store stressed true single-stop shopping, featuring several amenities not usually available in most supermarkets: a food court for in-store dining, a pizza counter, rotisserie-flamed chickens and ribs, a European-style bakery, a floral shop, a full-service bank, and an array of newspapers from around the world. The next year, 1994, it also opened another such market in Monroe, in Fairfield County, Connecticut. Further expansion continued the following year, when Big Y moved its grocery and produce distribution operations into a new 185,000-square-foot warehouse in Springfield and began its facilities management operations in an adjacent building.

Growth through Acquisition and E-Commerce in the Late 1990s

The next year, 1996, Big Y marked its 60th anniversary by purchasing five additional stores. These stores were formerly Edwards Supermarkets, all located in Connecticut. Their addition increased the number of Big Y stores in that state to 14. The company also added a new customer service in 1996, its Little Y Kids Club, a supervised play area for children in the store. The initial one opened in Big Y's Manchester, Connecticut, World Class Market. It was the first of its kind in Connecticut and only the second of the sort in all of New England.

Two years later, in 1998, Big Y opened a web site, offering to Internet browsers a range of data, including information on the individual stores in the Big Y chain, such as the various services that each of them offered to customers. That year, too, the company moved into its new corporate headquarters, a 133,000-square-foot building in Springfield. Designed by Wrenn and Pepin Associates, the structure began as just a shell office building, but over the year in which it was built it developed into a complete corporate center dubbed the Store

---

Key Dates:

1936: Paul D'Amour buys Y Cash Market in Chicopee, Massachusetts.

1947: Big Y Foods, Inc. is incorporated, and the D'Amour family opens a second Y Cash Market in Chicopee.

1952: The company opens Big Y Supermarket in leased store near Westover Air Force Base in Chicpoee.

1960: Big Y opens a supermarket in Northampton, Massachusetts.

1963: The company buys a second Northampton location and opens Big Y Wines & Liquors.

1967: Big Y opens a store in Springfield, Massachusetts.

1968: The company acquires seven-store Jumbo Supermarket chain.

1984: The company extends its operations into Connecticut with the acquisition of a supermarket in Stafford Springs; Big Y also purchases Adams Supermarket chain.

1989: Corporate headquarters are moved to Chestnut Street in Springfield.

1990: Big Y initiates its Express Savings Club; company founder Paul D'Amour dies at age 84.

1993: The company introduces new community-service programs: Education Express, Educating Kids, and the Big Y Homework Helpline; Big Y also opens its first World Class Market in Springfield.

1998: Big Y moves into new corporate headquarters and goes online with bigy.com; Big Y Wines & Liquors is refashioned as Table & Vine, a gourmet food and fine wine and liquor store.

2001: The company rolls out its new interactive, computerized register system.

Support Center. In addition to executive office suites, it housed a conference center, cafeteria, physical fitness training center, and a museum dedicated to the company's history. The year 1998 also saw the conversion of Big Y's Wines & Liquors into Table & Vine, a separate, 14,000-square-foot gourmet food, wine, and liquor shop in Northampton, Massachusetts.

A second round of Big Y's Education Express ended early in 1999. It awarded another $2.5 million to schools for funding the purchase of essential equipment, bringing the total of Big Y's first two rounds to $4.5 million. Altogether, 1,800 schools participated in the program.

Expanded Services and Upgraded Support Systems: 2000 and Beyond

Big Y ventured into another service area when, in August 2001, it opened its first in-store pharmacy at its newly remodeled supermarket in Longmeadow, Massachusetts. Although small, occupying just 400 square feet, the pharmacy was designed to accommodate two pharmacists and a technical assistant. Although the company had resisted installing pharmacies in its super stores through the 1990s, once it did decide to incorporate them it set about the task at a fair clip. Its plans called for placing pharmacies in ten additional supermarkets by June 2002.

In both 2001 and 2002, Big Y again illustrated why it could boast a reputation for quick adjustments to new technology, particularly systems that improved information retrieval and both effective routing and display. First, in June 2001, Big Y entered into an agreement with Retalix Ltd. to employ that firm's Storeline POS (point of sales) application for its promotional activities. The system displayed purchases on a screen visible to store customers during scanning along with a running, item-by-item total as well as savings. Next, in February 2002, it partnered with Cognos Finance to help fill its need to provide up-to-the-minute financial information to its department and district decision makers. Cognos allowed Big Y's IT (Information Technology) department to centralize financial information in one system and automate roll ups and roll downs in pricing.

Because of its adaptability to both technology and marketplace trends, as well as its community services, Big Y Foods earned a solid reputation in its market area. It continued to compete with national super chains in range of goods and services, which, with the advantages it enjoyed as a regional company, gave it a solid footing for future growth and longevity.

Principal Competitors

Cumberland Farms, Inc.; DeMoulas Super Markets Inc.; The Golub Corporation; Hannaford Bros. Co.; Shaw's Supermarkets, Inc.; The Stop & Shop Companies, Inc.; SUPERVALU INC.; Wal-Mart Stores, Inc.

Further Reading

Bennett, Stephen, "A World-class Effort," *Progressive Grocer*, December 1994, p. 52.

"Big Y Foods Takes Fresh Approach to Financial Reporting with Cognos Finance; Grocery Chain Turns to Cognos for Business Performance Management," *PR Newswire*, February 14, 2002.

Cockerham, Paul W. "Big Y Makes It Work," *Frozen Food Age*, December 1998, p. 4.

Misitano, Julie, "They Have Fun Too," *Progressive Grocers*, May 1994, p. 135.

Parks, Liz, "Big Y Foods Makes Moves to Branch into Pharmacy," *Drug Store News*, July 23, 2001.

"Retalix Ltd. Named as Preferred Point-of-Sale Software Provider for Big Y Foods Inc.; StoreLine to Power Big Y's Revolutionary Dual-Touch, Flat Panel Displays," *Business Wire*, June 19, 2001.

Weinstein, Steve, "Reversal of Fortune," *Progressive Grocer*, April 1995, p. 54.

—John W. Fiero

The Body Shop International plc

Watersmead Business Park
Littlehampton, West Sussex BN17 6LS
United Kingdom
Telephone: (903) 731-500
Fax: (903) 726-250
Web site: http://www.the-body-shop.com

Public Company
Incorporated: 1976
Employees: 6,304
Sales: $538.8 million (2002)
Stock Exchanges: London
Ticker Symbol: BOS
NAIC: 446120 Cosmetics, Beauty Supplies, and Perfume
Stores

The Body Shop International plc is one of England's best known retailers of cosmetics and personal care products, with over 1,900 stores in 50 countries. The company is best known for pioneering the natural-ingredient cosmetics market and establishing social responsibility as an integral part of company operations. In fact, The Body Shop has historically received more attention for its ethical stances, such as its refusal to use ingredients that are tested on animals, its monetary donations to the communities in which it operates, and its business partnerships with developing countries, than for its products. This focus, however, proved to be costly as The Body Shop lost market share in the late 1990s to product-savvy competitors that offered similar cosmetics at lower prices. The company manufactures over 600 products and claims that a Body Shop product is sold every .4 seconds. Anita Roddick, founder of the company, built The Body Shop by flouting industry conventions. In 1991, *Business Week* quoted this cosmetic industry leader as saying: "We loathe the cosmetic industry with a passion. It's run by men who create needs that don't exist." After several years of faltering profits and sales, Anita and her husband, Gordon Roddick, stepped down as co-chairs in 2002.

Beginnings

Roddick entered the industry in 1976 when she used £4,000 to open a small stand-alone shop of natural-ingredient cosmetics and personal care products. Her goal was to support herself and her two daughters while her husband spent two years riding horseback from Buenos Aires to New York. Her store design, product packaging, and marketing approach all originated from her need to economize. Roddick painted the walls dark green to hide cracks, rather than to suggest respect for the environment, and the award-winning clear plastic bottles were actually urine sample containers purchased from a local hospital. When Roddick's original supply of bottles ran out, and she did not have enough money to buy more, the Body Shop's famous refill policy was born.

Other hallmarks of the company were born during this frugal period. Handwritten labels filled with product information established the Body Shop's candid approach to customer relations. For example, one of the first products, a henna hair treatment, sported a label explaining that the product smelled like manure but was great for the hair. Also during this time, Roddick developed an aversion to advertising; not wanting to spend the time or money on advertising, she instead relied on press coverage to spread the word about the fledgling company.

Success came quickly: Roddick's cosmetics store thrived, and she opened another before the company's first year was over. Returning home in 1977, Gordon Roddick joined his wife in the enterprise. They decided to franchise the operation during the company's second year, and by 1984 The Body Shop boasted 138 stores, 87 of which were located outside of the United Kingdom. Franchising outpaced the opening of company-owned stores over the years, until franchises accounted for 89 percent of Body Shop stores in 1994. The company's fast-paced development continued when it went public in April 1984. The Roddick's kept 27.6 percent of the company's stock. Gordon Roddick became company chairperson and handled the finances as well, and Anita Roddick continued as managing director, essentially determining the course the company would take.

Company Perspectives:

The Body Shops strives to dedicate our business to the pursuit of social and environmental change; to creatively balance the financial and human needs of our stakeholders, employees, customers, franchisees, suppliers, and shareholders; to courageously ensure that our business is ecologically sustainable; to meaningfully contribute to local, national, and international communities in which we trade by adopting a code of conduct which ensures care, honesty, fairness, and respect; to passionately campaign for the protection of the environment, human and civil rights, and against animal testing within the cosmetics and toiletries industry; and to tirelessly work to narrow the gap between principle and practice, whilst making fun, passion, and care part of our daily lives.

Focus on Social and Environmental Awareness in the 1980s

During this time, Roddick decided to encourage and contribute to social and environmental change through her company. Although she first allied The Body Shop with established groups, such as Greenpeace, Amnesty International, and Friends of the Earth, she soon began her own campaigns, particularly ones that focused on recycling and on putting an end to animal testing in the cosmetics industry. Body Shops displayed posters and made petition sheets available to customers. By the mid-1990s, franchises were asked to support two to three campaigns a year for such causes as AIDS education, voter registration, and opposition to animal testing in the cosmetics industry.

In 1987, Roddick began The Body Shop's Trade Not Aid program. Combining the company's need for exotic natural ingredients with its mission of social responsibility, the program established business partnerships with struggling communities. By purchasing such ingredients as blue corn from the Pueblo Indians in New Mexico and Brazil nut oil from the Kayapo Indians of the Amazon River Basin, the Trade Not Aid program avoided exploiting native peoples and helped developing countries earn money selling renewable resources rather than destroying their habitat. The Body Shop's ethical practices also included aiding communities close to home. For example, the soapmaking factory the company founded in Glasgow returned 25 percent of after-tax profits to the economically depressed city. The retail store in New York's Harlem established a policy of giving 50 percent of store profits to local community groups. Other charitable activities included donating £230,000 in 1991 to start a weekly newspaper to be sold by the homeless in London.

The Body Shop fared just as well publicly as it had privately. In its first eight years on the London Stock Exchange, its stock price rose 10,944 percent. Between November 1986 and November 1991, investors realized a 97.2 percent annual return. In 1991, sales were up 46 percent from the year before to $238.4 million; net profits were $26.2 million, up 71 percent from the previous year. The company's notoriety also increased dramatically. Profiles of Roddick appeared in numerous magazines, from *People* to *Forbes*. The company was cited in *Business Week* as a pioneer in marketing. The magazine explained The Body Shop's appeal as follows: "Typical Body Shoppers are at the back of the baby boom, a skeptical group. They distrust advertising and sales hype, demand more product information than their elders, and are loyal to companies they consider responsible corporate citizens."

The Body Shop Enters the U.S. Market: 1988

The Body Shop opened its first stores in the United States in 1988; all were owned directly by the company. Deciding that the company needed to first adjust to the new market, particularly to selling in shopping malls, Roddick postponed franchising any stores until 1990. The first franchise opportunity prompted 2,000 applicants, whom Roddick screened through a written questionnaire, asking such unconventional questions as what books and movies the applicants liked and how they would want to die. "I want people who are politically aware and want a livelihood which is values-led," Roddick explained in *Working Woman*.

In the autumn of 1993, The Body Shop opened new headquarters in Raleigh, North Carolina, to help manufacture and distribute its U.S. product lines. The new facility was needed to reach and support the company's goal of 500 stores in the United States by the year 2000. Sales figures in 1994 supported that vision of aggressive growth. Sales in the United States had grown by 47 percent in the first half of fiscal 1994 to $44.6 million, with profits up 63 percent to $1.9 million. However, Allan Mottus, a U.S. cosmetics industry consultant, warned in *Working Woman* that The Body Shop would have difficulty in the coming years: "Opening new doors is one thing. Sustaining business is another. Americans are not as brand-loyal as Europeans. They will look at products and price."

Such competition was already challenging The Body Shop by the mid-1990s, both in the United States and elsewhere. H2O Plus, Goodebodies, Bath & Body Works, Origins, and Garden Botanika were also offering natural products in simple packaging but usually for a lower price. The company's two first major competitors appeared in 1990. That year, Estee Lauder Inc. introduced Origins, a product line with natural ingredients packaged in recycled containers. Leslie Wexner, owner of the Limited, opened Bath & Body Works in the United States in the fall of 1990; 18 months later he had 100 stores grossing $45 million. Although Roddick brushed off many of the U.S. lookalikes as too small to be a threat, she sued Wexner for copying her stores too closely. "It was becoming confusing between the two businesses," Gordon Roddick explained in *Working Woman*, noting that Body Shop customers "were bringing in Wexner's containers to be refilled." Roddick reports having settled with Wexner out of court. However, Bath & Body Works continued to pose a threat to The Body Shop in both the United States and England, where it opened its first shop in the fall of 1994.

In 1994, L'Oreal entered the natural-style product market with its Planet Ushuaia line of deodorants, shampoos, and other personal care products. Like Bath & Body Works, L'Oreal copied the bright coloring of The Body Shop packaging and emphasized exotic ingredients. The same year, Procter & Gamble, with its vast resources, also entered the fray with their purchase of Ellen Betrix, a German company that had introduced Essentials natural cosmetics early in 1994.

Key Dates:

1976: Anita Roddick opens a small shop that sells natural-ingredient cosmetics.

1977: Anita Roddick's husband Gordon Roddick joins the company, and the couple decide to franchise the operation.

1984: The Body Shop goes public with 138 stores in operation.

1987: The Trade Not Aid program begins.

1988: Body Shop stores are opened in the United States.

1993: The company files suit against a television program that claims it uses products that have been tested on animals.

1994: The Body Shop begins using traditional methods of advertising for the first time.

1998: Patrick Gournay is named CEO; the company forms a United States-based joint venture with the Bellamy Retail Group LLC.

1999: The company stops manufacturing as part of a re-structuring program.

2002: Anita and Gordon Roddick step down as co-chairs of the company.

The Body Shop's phenomenal growth slowed somewhat in 1992. Fiscal 1993 profits (the company's year ends February 28) were down 15 percent from the previous year, from £25.2 million to £21.5 million. Roddick criticized dissatisfied investors in *Working Woman* as "speculators who make their money off buying and selling. That is where the greed factor comes in. They expected us to make £23 million. Tough—we made £21 million." However, the company seemed to recover some of its momentum the following year: pretax profits for the first half of fiscal 1994 were £10 million, a 20 percent increase over the same period in 1993.

Falling Victim to Bad Press: 1993–94

The Body Shop faced other problems in the first half of the 1990s, as its reputation as a socially responsible company was repeatedly challenged. The first attack came from a British television program entitled "Body Search," which accused The Body Shop of misleading customers with its "Against Animal Testing" product label. The Body Shop's policy, designed as an incentive for companies to eliminate their animal testing, rejected ingredients that had been tested on animals in the previous five years. The television program, however, charged the company with using ingredients that had been tested on animals. The Body Shop brought suit in the summer of 1993 and won £276,000 in damages.

Although the company won their suit, the battle had focused attention on The Body Shop's ethical record and inspired additional criticism. Cosmetics competitor Goodebodies tried to distinguish themselves by pointing out that, unlike The Body Shop, they did not use any animal by-products, such as tallow from pigs to make soap. The Body Shop responded, however, that it only used by-products from the meat industry and that it

provided customers with information in the store if they wished to choose products with no animal ingredients.

Questions about the company's integrity continued in the summer of 1994, when it was reported that the U.S. Federal Trade Commission was investigating The Body Shop for exaggerated claims of helping developing nations and for alleged pollution from a New Jersey warehouse. The investigation, combined with the company's slowing growth, led Franklin Research & Development, an investment fund that dealt only with socially responsible companies, to sell 50,000 shares. That in turn led to a stock price drop of 11 percent in the next two weeks. Although the stock price stabilized soon thereafter, the company remained in a defensive position.

In the mid-1990s, the company showed signs of changing some of its long-standing policies, such as its refusal to advertise. From 1976 until 1994, The Body Shop used window displays, catalogs, and point of purchase product descriptions to attract and inform customers. In 1994, however, Anita Roddick appeared in an American Express commercial, talking about the company's Trade Not Aid program. Later that year, the company placed its first "advertorial" in the magazine *Marie Claire*. This eight-page spread offered a discussion of the *Body Shop Book* on personal care techniques and products. In addition, the company was considering further "advertorials" or television "documercials" for the Trade Not Aid products that would focus on the stories and people behind the products. Angela Bawtree, The Body Shop's head of investor relations, explained the company's apparent change of attitude toward advertising in an October 1994 article in *Advertising Age:* "It would be wrong for people to think we have some kind of moral problem with using advertising. But using glamorous images or miracle cure claims—those kinds of things you won't see us doing." As of late 1994, the company had no plans to hire an advertising agency.

In the mid-1990s, the company increased its focus on international expansion. Same-store sales in the United Kingdom, The Body Shop's most mature market, declined 6 percent in fiscal 1993 and were stagnant in fiscal 1994. New international stores seemed the key to continued growth, and Gordon Roddick specifically targeted Germany, France, and Japan for expansion. In early 1994, Germany had 39 stores and Japan had 17, and Roddick believed that each of these countries could support 200 stores. In addition, The Body Shop opened its first stores in Mexico in 1993.

"We think the limit for the number of stores we can have globally is more than 3,000," Gordon Roddick said to *Working Woman* in 1994. He also commented that "in three years we will see the company's worth hit $1 billion." This statement was supported by a 1994 report from NatWest Securities, which expressed "confidence that the international growth potential (over 2,000 stores in year 2000) cannot only be realized, but also translated into healthy profits."

The Body Shop Falters: Late 1990s and Beyond

Gordon Roddick's speculation, however, was not fulfilled. While The Body Shop had indeed experienced stellar growth throughout the 1980s and early 1990s, it appeared unable to concoct a strategy strong enough to overcome increased competition in the industry. As a result of weakening sales—especially in the United States—and faltering profits, The Body Shop spent much of the late 1990s and beyond restructuring and revamping business operations. In 1997, the firm announced that it would discontinue certain lower-priced merchandise in an attempt to attract a more upscale clientele. Then in 1998, Patrick Gournay was named CEO while Anita Roddick became co-chairman with her husband. The company commented on the management changes in a 1998 *WWD* magazine article, claiming that "the task of realizing our strategic plan and developing the brand without losing the nonnegotiables surrounding its philosophy and business ethics will be challenging. We have taken the view that this will not be achievable without substantially strengthening our top management team."

During that year the company also entered into a joint venture with the Bellamy Retail Group LLC to oversee its United States-based operations. At the time, The Body Shop had reported a loss of $2.8 million from its U.S. stores while sales fell by 2.1 percent over the previous year. Sales in the United Kingdom were also weak and its Asian operations were also suffering due to economic difficulties in the region.

The restructuring moved ahead in 1999 as the company continued to report losses. In an effort to win back profits, The Body Shop exited the manufacturing sector to focus on its retail operations. It also sought to improve its product time-to-market, slash operating costs, and decrease the number of franchise-owned stores. Management was also reorganized into four main geographical segments including the United Kingdom, Europe, the Americas, and Asia.

Despite the restructuring efforts, problems continued for The Body Shop as it entered the new millennium and the firm began feeling out possible sale and merger options. A May 2001 *Marketing* article suggested that during the 1990s the company had "rested on its laurels while top management allowed itself to be diverted by wider global issues. It is paying the price, both in the United States and the United Kingdom, where Boots, Superdrug, and new entrant Lush have made significant in-roads." As management worked to gain back this lost market share, the firm continued to report losses. In 2000, pre-tax profit fell by 21 percent over the previous year due in part to low profit margins on new products and mismanaged inventory levels that led to high warehouse costs.

Changes continued in 2002 when the Roddick's stepped down as co-chairs but remained non-executive directors. At the same time, Gournay resigned after his restructuring efforts failed to restore The Body Shop's financial record. In fact, according to a 2002 *WWD* article, Anita Roddick publicly claimed that under his leadership, The Body Shop had "lost its soul." Adrian Bellamy was named executive chairman and Peter Saunders took over as CEO—both men had led firm's North American operations. Under direction of this new management team, The Body Shop announced that it was no longer for sale. Whether or not Bellamy and Saunders would be able to boost the company's fortunes and restore it to its former glory of the 1980s and early 1990s, however, remained to be seen.

Principal Competitors

Bath & Body Works Inc.; The Boots Company plc; The Estee Lauder Companies Inc.

Further Reading

"Body Shop Aims for Bigger Spenders," *Cosmetics International*, January 25, 1997, p. 10.

"Body Shop Pulls Out of Manufacturing," *Soap & Cosmetics*, April 1999, p. 64.

"Body Shop Sees Profits Fall by Nearly a Quarter," *Cosmetics International*, May 25, 2001, p. 5.

Colin, Jennifer, "Survival of the Fittest," *Working Woman*, February 1994, pp. 28–31, 68–9, 73.

Conti, Samantha, "Body Shop Reshuffles, Roddicks to Step Down," *WWD*, February 13, 2002, p. 16.

Fallon, James, "Body Shop Reports a $25.4 Million Loss," *WWD*, May 7, 1999, p. 11.

——, "Body Shop Shakeup Brings New CEO," *WWD*, May 13, 1998, p. 3.

"Has The Body Shop Lost its Direction for Good?," *Marketing*, May 10, 2001, p. 19.

Jacob, Rahul, "What Selling Will Be Like in the '90s," *Fortune*, January 13, 1992, pp. 63–4.

Siler, Charles, "Body Shop Marches to Its Own Drummer," *Advertising Age*, October 10, 1994, p. 4.

Zinn, Laura, "Whales, Human Rights, Rain Forests—And the Heady Smell of Profits," *Business Week*, July 15, 1991, pp. 114–15.

—Susan Windisch Brown
—update: Christina M. Stansell

Boyd Coffee Company

19730 Northeast Sandy Boulevard
Portland, Oregon 97230
U.S.A.
Telephone: (503) 666-4545
Toll Free: (800) 545-4077
Fax: (503) 669-2223
Web site: http://www.boyds.com

Private Company
Incorporated: 1900 as Boyd Importing Tea Company
Employees: 500
Sales: $100 million (2002 est.)
NAIC: 311920 Coffee and Tea Manufacturing; 311999
   All Other Miscellaneous Food Manufacturing; 333294
   Food Product Machinery Manufacturing; 811412
   Appliance Repair and Maintenance

Boyd Coffee Company is a leading distributor of coffee, brewing equipment, and dry mixes for food service users. The company uses a direct sales force of 200 sales representative in 25 states. Headquartered in Portland, Oregon, their territory extends as far east as Chicago and St. Louis. Since the 1960s, Boyd's has gone from delivering three varieties of coffee to distributing more than 2000 coffee and food items, such as dry mixes for beverages and sauces. Coffee and brewing equipment account for about two-thirds of sales. Co-CEO's Dick and David Boyd and their father Percival "Rudy" Boyd are the company's sole shareholders. In the late 1980s, the firm reintroduced retail and ran two of its own Portland area stores. Altogether, the company's coffee output was the equivalent to an estimated 800 million cups a year.

Portland Origins

Percival Dewey "P.D." Boyd was born in New Zealand in 1879. The son of a Presbyterian missionary from Scotland, P.D. immigrated to the United States at the age of three. He worked at grocery and sales jobs until about 1900, when he started the Boyd Importing Tea Company in downtown Portland.

P.D. made door-to-door deliveries of tea and coffee with a horse and red wagon he had bought for five dollars. Trucks replaced horses around 1910; in another ten years, Boyd had stopped delivering to homes. Among other measures P.D. Boyd initiated to keep his company in business was the practice of loaning brewing equipment to food service customers.

Rudy Boyd took over his father's business after World War II. In December 1946, the company became known as Boyd Coffee Company. A few years later, a frost wiped out Brazil's coffee crop and nearly took Boyd Coffee with it.

Boyd introduced vacuum-packed coffee in cans in 1955. About this time, the company began manufacturing automatic coffee brewers for restaurants. The company also introduced paper coffee filters to restaurant users. A home version, the Flav-R-Flo Brewer, was rolled out a few years later. Boyd Coffee was also ahead of its time in hiring practices. Its long time coffee buyer, Veda Younger, was one of the first females in her line of work.

While Rudy Boyd never finished high school, his sons David and Dick went to the University of Oregon. Like their father, they both grew up working for the family business. David began stripping tape from cartons at age 12. Dick began at age 16, counting coffee can lids. In 1975, David took over as CEO of Boyd Coffee upon Rudy Boyd's retirement. Rudy maintained a presence as chairman.

In the late 1980s, Boyd opened five of its own Red Wagon retail stores. It also opened espresso cafés in Portland and Seattle.

Going Gourmet in the 1990s

Gourmet products would be the fastest-growing segment of the coffee market in the 1990s. In 1990, Boyd, which claimed to be the country's largest purveyor of gourmet coffee, had more than 50 gourmet varieties. Its coffee carts were supplying colleges, supermarkets, department stores, and hotels.

With annual sales of $100 million and 400 employees, Boyd Coffee was profitable and growing in the early 1990s. Its plant

---

Key Dates:

1900: P.D. Boyd begins coffee and tea deliveries in Portland.
1946: Rudy Boyd takes over his father's business.
1972: Boyd's relocates to a new factory and headquarters complex.
1975: David Boyd succeeds father Rudy as head of Boyd Coffee.
1991: Dick Boyd replaces brother at top spot.
2001: Boyd's breaks ground on plant expansion.

---

was enlarging by 60 percent and going to double shifts. However, in November 1991, Boyd's board replaced David with Richard for undisclosed reasons, reported *Fortune FSB* in a 2002 article on sustaining family businesses. The brothers eventually began sharing the position of president/CEO equally after bringing in a business/family therapist. *The Oregonian* reported that Dick Boyd also brought in Los Angeles-based Flamhlotz Management Systems Consulting Corp. to facilitate some strategic planning.

In 1991, Boyd sued the coffee businesses of Denver's Boyer family over trademark infringement. Boyd claimed the Boyer name was similar enough to confuse consumers. The next year, Boyd acquired another Denver-based business, Ambassador Office Coffee Service.

Boyd expanded its sales and service operations to Minnesota, Wisconsin, and the upper peninsula of Michigan in 1993. The company was part of the Dine-More consortium of regional roasters servicing national food service accounts such as ServiceMaster.

By the mid-1990s, Boyd was packaging 75 different types of coffee. The company had installed electronically controlled roasters and was increasing production to 19,000 tons of beans a year. Boyd was rolling out espresso entertainment centers and coffee carts under the Italia D'Oro brand. The firm also imported espresso equipment. Company executives credited Starbucks with boosting awareness and sales in this segment.

Boyd began selling organically grown coffee around 1990; it was certified organic by Quality Assurance International (QIA) in 1997. The certification process, which documents the processing as well as the growing of the coffee, took three years. Boyd claimed to be the only national distributor of certified organic coffee.

Boyd was the main supplier for Tuscany Premium Coffees, a small upscale chain that had eschewed its Seattle origins to focus on markets new to gourmet coffee, such as Cleveland, Pittsburgh, Philadelphia, Dallas, Houston, and Denver. Tuscany Inc. went bankrupt in April 1997 after a failed IPO.

Boyd was also heavily involved in the food service business, an outgrowth of its coffee packaging. It prepared packaged dry mixes for soups, sauces, beverages, and desserts, and other products. To foster ties with the food service community, Boyd prepared an educational program for Johnson and Wales Uni-

versity, a leading culinary institute. The company also sponsored a culinary competition for high school students in Washington State.

By the late 1990s, Boyd products were being distributed in Japan, Korea, and Taiwan. Boyd participated in a joint roasting venture in the Philippines. In early 2001, Boyd began a partnership with Vitality Foodservice Canada, Ltd., the largest Canadian food service beverage manufacturer and distributor.

2001 Expansion

By 2000, the expansion of Boyd's Sandy Boulevard plant had dragged on for several years. The company had scouted areas elsewhere in the country, including Utah (an odd choice, since traditional Mormon wisdom frowned upon coffee and other hot beverages). However, Boyd ultimately decided to stay in Portland. A new plan called for adding 132,000 square feet to the facility, doubling its size. Boyd aimed to have all its operations under one roof, and the space would house a new warehouse distribution facility. The company had been leasing 55,000 square feet of warehouse space near the airport. Boyd finally broke ground on the $8 million expansion in March 2001.

Oregon Business magazine named Boyd Coffee number 49 of Oregon's top 100 companies to work for in 2001. Dick and David Boyd attributed the company's success to integrity, respect for employees, and contribution to the local community. More good media coverage came from the Food Network. The cable network's ''Unwrapped'' series took a five-minute look behind the scenes at Boyd Coffee in one of its episodes.

Principal Subsidiaries

Boyd Coffee Co. (Philippines), Inc. (50%).

Principal Divisions

Boyd International Foods; Red Wagon Stores; Techni-Brew International; Today Food Products.

Principal Competitors

Farmer Brothers Co.; Superior Coffee.

Further Reading

Boyd, Richard D., and David D. Boyd, ''A Message to the People of the State of Oregon,'' *Oregonian,* December 4, 1994, p. B9.
''Checkweigher Streamlines Foodservice Dry Mix Filling,'' *Packaging Digest,* July 1999, pp. 26–31.
Faust, Fred, ''Tuscany to Jump Start Gourmet Coffee Here,'' *St. Louis Post-Dispatch,* Business Plus Sec., October 2, 1995, p. 5.
Goranson, Eric, ''Boyd Coffee Co. Plans to Expand Operations,'' *Oregonian,* February 22, 1990.
——, ''Boyd's New Roasters Erase Pleasant Aroma,'' *Oregonian,* May 5, 1994, p. M13.
——, ''Boyd's Tries to Clarify Its Stand,'' *Oregonian,* December 5, 1994, p. B2.
Irsfeld, Mitch, ''Those Who Can Teach: Educating Guests Is Elementary to Building Repeat Business,'' *Nation's Restaurant News,* December 13, 1999, p. 31.

Junia, Catherine C., "Enterprisers: Over a Cup of Coffee," *Businessworld* (Manila), August 24, 2000, p. 1.

Juttelstad, Ann, "Damage Control: When Your Product Makes the Front Page," *Food Formulating,* January 1997, pp. 24–26.

Lingle, Rick, "Automation Adds Agility to Coffee Casing Capability," *Packaging Digest,* November 1998, pp. 37–42.

Painter, John, Jr., "Boyd Coffee Sues Similarly Named Foes," *Oregonian,* November 28, 1991, p. E19.

Spaulding, Mark, "Non-Cryogenic Nitrogen Cuts CAP Costs 50%," *Packaging,* September 1993, pp. 41f.

Spector, Robert, "When Does It Pay Not to Replace a Truck?," *Purchasing,* June 21, 1990, pp. 2f.

Strom, Shelly, "Boyd Coffee to Consolidate by Expanding Sandy Facilities," *Business Journal of Portland,* August 11, 2000.

——, "Boyd Seals Major Deal for Organic Coffee Line," *Business Journal of Portland,* December 15, 2000.

——, "Local Roaster to Be Showcased on Food Network," *Business Journal of Portland,* May 15, 2001.

"Swimmer Sets Record After 20-Year Hiatus," *Oregonian,* August 28, 1988.

Whitford, David, "Century-Old Companies Built to Last," *FSB: Fortune Small Business,* June 2002, pp. 28–34.

—Frederick C. Ingram

Briazz, Inc.

3901 7th Avenue, Suite 200
Seattle, Washington 98108-5206
U.S.A.
Telephone: (206) 467-0994
Fax: (206) 467-1970
Web site: http://www.briazz.com

Public Company
Incorporated: 1995
Employees: 450
Sales: $32 million (2001)
Stock Exchanges: NASDAQ
Ticker Symbol: BRZZ
NAIC: 722211 Limited-Service Restaurant

Briazz, Inc., operates 45 cafés and kiosks selling high-end, pre-packaged sandwiches and salads in Seattle, San Francisco, Los Angeles, and Chicago. Clustered near heavy concentrations of office buildings, the company's stores target white-collar workers pressed for time on lunch break. In addition to its retail business, which accounts for approximately 72 percent of its revenue, Briazz offers box lunches and corporate catering and sells its products through grocery chains. The company went public in 2001 but has yet to turn a profit. The economic downturn of 2001 and 2002—and the subsequent increase in vacancies in the office buildings Briazz aimed to serve—has eroded Briazz's primary market.

A New Kind of Sandwich

Briazz was founded in 1995 by Victor Alhadeff. No novice at starting a business, Alhadeff, a former first lieutenant in the U.S. Army, had headed up three companies before Briazz. After a stint in the 1970s with an oil and gas partnerships venture, Equities Northwest Inc., Alhadeff founded Egghead Discount Software in 1983 and built the company into the nation's largest computer software retailer. When Egghead began to struggle with rising competition and rapid growth, Alhadeff turned the company over to a friend and focused on Catapult Corp. (formerly part of Egghead), a national business that trained office workers to use personal computers. He sold Catapult to IBM in 1993.

Briazz represented another tactical step for Alhadeff. He astutely recognized that a segment of the fast-casual dining sector was ripe for a new addition. The sandwich has been around for nearly two hundred years, ostensibly since the Earl of Sandwich encased a hunk of meat with two slices of bread so that he need not leave a card game to eat dinner. For much of its history, however, the sandwich was viewed as little more than a quick and convenient meal choice, with little verve or cachet. But the success that Starbucks had in the 1990s converting coffee, another commodity food item, into big business had a huge impact on the restaurant industry. As the industry publication, *Automatic Merchandiser* explained, "Starbucks created the model for taking an everyday, mundane 50-cent beverage and turning it into a $3.00 emotional experience." Restaurant operators soon recognized the potential of upgrading the sandwich's place on their menus, or even of centering an entire menu on sandwiches.

It was more than a love of the formerly humble sandwich, though, that propelled Alhadeff to launch Briazz. Lunch is big business—Americans spend more than $1 billion a day on this middle meal alone. While industry insiders had long believed that fast food hamburger restaurants were the unassailable leaders in the lunch market, Alhadeff and a few other entrepreneurs recognized that Americans were suffering from what the *Los Angeles Times* termed "fast food fatigue." According to *Restaurants and Institutions*, non-burger sandwich restaurants had compound annual sales growth between 1979 and 1999 of 12.4 percent, while burger chains had only 3.9 percent. The reason for this trend appeared to be the fact that consumers—especially the gigantic baby boomer generation—wanted lunch fare that they perceived to be healthier and fresher than fast food. At the same time, however, they were reluctant to sacrifice the speed and convenience fast food offered. As the *San Francisco Examiner* noted, "Briazz is based on research showing that 60 percent of office employees are doing something besides lunch during the noon hour. Most can only spare twenty minutes or so for lunch."

Key Dates:

1995: Victor Alhadeff opens the first Briazz Café in downtown Seattle.
1996: Briazz launches cafés in San Francisco and Chicago.
1998: Briazz opens its first café in Los Angeles; by year's end, Briazz has 25 cafés in four major markets.
2001: Briazz goes public and raises $16 million with initial public stock offering.
2002: Briazz reports its seventh consecutive year of losses.

The first Briazz—the name a combination of the Italian word for vivacity and the English word "jazz"—debuted in September 1995. The café featured fresh sandwiches and salads that were prepackaged and arranged supermarket-style in a floor-to-ceiling refrigerator case. Customers helped themselves to the sandwich of their choice and could be out of the store and back at their desks in a matter of minutes. Tables were available for those who were less pressed for time and wanted to eat in the café. Most sandwiches sold for about four dollars.

Briazz put a particular focus on its flavors. While it offered some standard sandwich fare such as pastrami and ham and cheese, the majority of the sandwiches had a more exotic pedigree. Recipe developers Sharon Kramis and Mary Alhadeff (the founder's daughter-in-law) introduced gourmet offerings such as the Roast Beef Palouse (sliced rare beef with red-pepper rings, lettuce, and horseradish served on Palouse potato bread) and the Roasted Veggie (roasted zucchini, eggplant, and sun-dried tomatoes, a chevre cream-cheese pesto spread, balsamic vinaigrette, and mixed field greens). Briazz paid special attention to the bread used in its sandwiches. "The basic premise is that the bread is the meat of the sandwich," Nancy Lazara, vice-president of food for the company, told *Restaurants and Institutions*. To this end, Briazz relied on Seattle bakeries to provide high quality artisan breads.

Briazz was not the only company stepping into this niche. Competitors such as Panera Bread Co. and Cosi developed sophisticated sandwiches as well. Briazz's point of distinction, though, was its centralized distribution network. The company's sandwiches were assembled elsewhere and brought, prepackaged, to the café. "There is an abundance of fast food, deli food, and, of course, sit-down restaurants," Alhadeff explained to the *Seattle Times*. "What we felt was lacking was ready-made food that is truly exceptional."

Early Success and Rapid Expansion

Alhadeff's concept was appealing to consumers, industry analysts, and investors alike. Although Alhadeff initially owned the whole company, he soon drew in some big name investors, including Starbucks Chairman Howard Schultz, Costco Chairman Jeff Brotman, and musician Kenny G. Alhadeff welcomed this support because Briazz's business plan had never involved staying small or local. "Our goal is for this to be another Seattle home-grown national success story," Alhadeff told the *Seattle Times* in November 1995, less than two months after the first café opened. Throughout 1996, Briazz unveiled new cafés and kiosks in Seattle. These shops remained true to the original plan. Sandwiches and salads were prepared at a central kitchen and delivered to the cafés and kiosks every morning. And each facility was deliberately located in a high-density commercial area within an easy walk of at least two million square feet of office space.

By the close of 1996, Briazz had tallied a brisk $2.8 million in sales. In addition to opening new cafés and kiosks across Seattle, the company had entered the potentially lucrative corporate catering and business box lunch arena. Although Briazz failed to a turn a profit after its first full year of operations, Alhadeff was unfazed. On September 26, 1997, he told the *Seattle Times* that "Briazz was prepared to go though a period of early losses as it builds its infrastructure of stores, employees, and computerized equipment while seeking to establish a reputation as the premier ready-to eat sandwich café in cities across the country."

In early 1997, Alhadeff moved toward his goal of national expansion when he took Briazz outside the Seattle market for the first time and opened two cafés in San Francisco. A few months later, Briazz launched a Chicago sandwich café as well. In each of these new markets, Briazz implemented its original strategy, building a central kitchen to deliver ready-made sandwiches to all the local shops and positioning itself to appeal to on-the-go white collar workers. Briazz did not earn a profit again in 1997, which was unexceptional given the heavy capital investment required for its expansion. The company did achieve some other important milestones, however. By the close of 1997, Briazz had grown to 22 cafés, kiosks, and mini-cafés (seven of which were in Seattle). Briazz had also managed to raise $27 million in private capital to fuel its ongoing growth.

The year 1998 proved to be eventful for Briazz. In September, the company established its first sandwich café in Los Angeles and also continued to expand its presence in Seattle, San Francisco, and Chicago. In addition, Briazz turned its attention to wholesale business. The central kitchen design that Briazz faithfully followed in each of its four markets gave the company the opportunity to realize economies of scale unavailable to its competitors that maintained a small kitchen in each sandwich shop. Briazz was thus able to establish a partnership with Delta Airlines to provide sandwiches to the airline's first-class cabins. Briazz also experimented with vending machines that dispensed its bread creations.

In 1999, Briazz accelerated its pace of expansion. Rather than enter new markets, though, the company sought to "build out" its existing four-city territory. After securing an additional $5 million in private financing, Briazz announced that it planned to field 40 sites in those markets by the end of 1999. Moreover, in an effort to lengthen the stores' business days, it introduced a menu of hot breakfast items to complement the popular lunchtime offerings.

Even more significant was the series of partnerships Briazz founded that year to broaden its wholesale business. The company began selling its branded sandwiches in QFC, a Seattle grocery store chain, as well as in 25 Ralph's Markets in southern California. Briazz also received the lucrative contract to provide ready-made sandwiches to select Seattle Starbucks stores. Starbucks wanted to expand its fare beyond coffee and muffins but did not want to involve itself directly in a lunch-making operation. Briazz's centralized distribution network made it an ideal partner.

Fueled by its growing chain of retail venues and its strategic wholesale partnerships, Briazz saw its sales for 1999 rise to $25.6 million. However, the capital-intensive investments required to build new cafés and kiosks meant that Briazz's losses continued to mount as well. Although Alhadeff confidently informed *Nation's Restaurant News* that "over the next five years the opportunity exists to add 150 cafés in our existing geographic markets," the reality was that the company's costs were increasing exponentially, and Briazz's financial backers were tiring of writing the company large checks.

Economic Downturn and Financial Challenges

Briazz's sales jumped more than 30 percent in 2000, reaching $33.7 million. In a major coup, the company also landed a major wholesale account with supermarket giant Safeway, which accounted for 20 percent of its accounts receivable for the year. In addition, it formed a partnership to sell sandwiches at Tully's Coffee and continued to add new retail outlets in its four markets. Nevertheless, expenses continued to outpace income, and Briazz reported a net loss of $6.3 million for the year. It was obvious that to proceed with its expansion, the company would need an infusion of cash.

Alhadeff decided that the best solution to this problem was to take the company public. Making an initial public offering in 2001, however, was a risky move. The American economy was weakening as the stock market plummeted and workers were laid off. A souring economy is never good news for the restaurant industry. While people always need to eat, they do not have to eat out. Typically, when people are under financial pressure, they cook at home and brown bag their lunch to conserve money. Moreover, Briazz had only a string of losses to show potential investors. To make matters worse, Briazz's auditor issued a going-concern statement prior to the initial public offering (IPO). The statement said that Briazz's operating losses and need for capital "raise substantial doubt about its ability to continue as a going concern." These facts notwithstanding, Alhadeff went ahead with the IPO and managed to raise $16 million of the $17.7 million that had originally been anticipated. The company said that it planned to use $2 million of this to repay a loan, $8 million to open new cafés, $2.5 million to upgrade computer systems, and the rest for general business purposes.

Unfortunately, Briazz's financial woes were not solved by the IPO. The company was especially hard hit by the economic downturn, which only worsened in the wake of the September 11, 2001 terrorist attacks on New York and Washington, D.C. Briazz's raison d'être was to serve lunch to busy office workers, but as companies laid off workers there were fewer customers to whom Briazz could sell its gourmet sandwiches. Moreover, as Briazz had deliberately located its stores in densely packed business districts, it was particularly affected by the depopu-

lation of those areas. Between 2000 and 2001, the vacancy rates in downtown Seattle and San Francisco, for instance, shot up from less than 2 percent to 10 percent, mainly because of the crash of dot-com companies. Largely as a result of this trend, the company's sales in 2001 fell back to $32 million. Briazz also lost its accounts with Starbucks and Safeway.

Briazz was also facing stiffer competition in its own sector. As the *Wall Street Journal* explained, "Take out sandwich shops are quite common." In addition to high-end sandwich rivals, such as Cosi and Panera Bread Co., fast food chains had entered the gourmet sandwich fray. Subway rolled out a line of "Subway Selects" in 2001. These high-end sandwiches featured the same bold flavors promoted by Briazz and cost about twice as much as Subway's standard fare. Even Arby's launched a new line of gourmet-style sandwiches that year. This increasingly crowded field faced an additional problem: despite analysts' predictions, customers were not wholeheartedly embracing the ready-made sandwich concept. It turned out that American sandwich eaters liked to watch their sandwiches being made, rather than grabbing a pre-packaged product. And they liked the option of getting a hot sandwich.

Recognizing these realities, Briazz was forced to reassess its strategy. As Alhadeff told *Restaurant Business* in April of 2002, "Our cafés have undergone a total redesign so that hot food is the merchandise focus in the store." As part of this process, Briazz introduced a hot, made-to-order sandwich called the Piadina. Hot food sales quickly came to account for a stunning 45 percent of total sales. Alhadeff also recognized that the company's cash shortage and the slumping economy necessitated backing off expansion plans. But Alhadeff did not intend for the company simply to stand still. Instead, he hoped to use wholesale partnerships to leverage the Briazz brand. Briazz reached an agreement to sell its sandwiches at freestanding kiosks in select Target department stores. In May 2002, Briazz landed a major contract to start selling its products in 20 Albertson's supermarkets in southern California. If the pilot program proved successful, Briazz would have the opportunity to sell its products in 630 Albertson's stores.

But the sandwich-maker faced an uncertain future. A year after its initial stock offering, Briazz's share price had fallen 80 percent. Many industry insiders were pessimistic about Briazz's prospects. A financial editor at the *Nation's Restaurant News* told the *Seattle Times*, "Basically, they either generate some real interest by performing or they get bought out." For Alhadeff, though, the goal is clear: "When people think of sandwiches five years from now, we want them to think of Briazz as the dominant national brand," he said to the *Seattle Times*.

Principal Competitors

Cosi, Inc.; Starbucks Corporation; Panera Bread Co.; Atlanta Bread Co.; Pret a Manger; Subway.

Further Reading

Ballon, Marc, "Cheesecake Factory Is Cooking," *Los Angeles Times*, April 23, 2002.
Batsell, Jake, "Seattle-Based Sandwich Chain Sees Year Filled with Trouble After IPO," *Seattle Times,* April 30, 2002.

Brumback, Nancy, "Well-Bred Heros: Upper Crust Sandwich Concepts Shine in the Fast-Casual Niche," *Restaurant Business*, April 15, 2002.

Cosby, Gloria, "Behold the Lowly Sandwich. Look Where It's Going!," *Automatic Merchandiser*, March 1, 2002.

Hinterberger, John, "Briazz is Halfway Between Upper-End Fast Serve and the Venerable New York Self-Service Automats," *Seattle Times*, March 3, 1996.

Molinari, Elena, "Simplex, Show IPO Market Improved, But Choosy," *Wall Street Journal*, May 3, 2001.

Moriwaki, Lee, "Seattle-Based Sandwich Maker to Open Store in University Village," *Seattle Times*, September 26, 1997.

Papiernik, Richard, "Briazz Slicing Up Some Thin Numbers As It Eyes IPO Move," *Nation's Restaurant News*, February 19, 2001.

Silver, Deborah, "Layered Ascent: Sandwich Shops Grow More Popular," *Restaurants and Institutions*, June 15, 2001.

Strauss, Karyn, "Briazz Café Aims to Beef Up Customer Base," *Nation's Restaurant News*, October 4, 1999.

Werner, Holly, "Hungry for Success, Briazz Plots Future After Rough First Year," *IPO Reporter*, May 13, 2002.

Wilson, Warren, "Out of Egghead and into Egg Salad," *Seattle Times,* November 11, 1995.

Wood, Jim, "A New Entry on Quick Lunch Scene in San Francisco," *San Francisco Examiner*, January 22, 1997.

Yee, Laura, "Upper Crust Packages," *Restaurants and Institutions*, April 1, 1999.

—Rebecca Stanfel

Cannon Express

Cannon Express, Inc.

1457 East Robinson
Springdale, Arkansas 72764
U.S.A.
Telephone: (501) 751-9209
Toll Free: (800) 846-8400
Fax: (501) 756-1857
Web site: http://www.cannonexpress.com

Public Company
Incorporated: 1981
Employees: 797
Sales: $85.8 million (2001)
Stock Exchanges: American
Ticker Symbol: AB
NAIC: 484121 General Freight Trucking, Long-Distance,
   Truckload

Cannon Express, Inc. is an irregular route trucking company operating in 48 states and in Canada. The firm maintains a fleet of approximately 775 trucks and 1,450 trailers. The company's freight primarily includes retail and wholesale goods destined for discount merchandisers, paper goods, automotive supplies and parts, and non-perishable food products. Cannon Express is managed by CFOex, Inc., a Knoxville, Tennessee, financial services company hired by Cannon Express's founder, Dean Cannon.

Origins

Cannon Express originated from the assets of a Springdale, Arkansas, trucking company named C.R. Kidd Produce. In 1981, C.R. Kidd was acquired by Dean Cannon, who had been operating as a lease operator of trucks since 1974. By the time Cannon purchased C.R. Kidd, his modestly sized fleet comprised three trucks. The acquisition of C.R. Kidd substantially increased Cannon's stature in the Arkansas trucking industry. C.R. Kidd operated as a refrigerated carrier hauling produce to retail stores, relying on a fleet of 5 trucks, 20 trailers, and 15 lease operators. Once the acquisition was complete, the newly named Cannon Express began to expand, its growth orches-

trated by Cannon, who presided as chief executive officer and president, and his wife, Rose Marie, who served as Cannon Express's secretary and treasurer.

Within five years of founding Cannon Express, the husband-and-wife team had made significant progress in expanding the trucking company. By 1986, Cannon Express had 100 trailers at its disposal and continued to operate its business under the lease-operator arrangement, contracting with truck owners for deliveries. The Cannons soon changed the way their business operated, forsaking the lease-operator arrangement for control over their own fleet. The Cannons purchased 100 trucks, replacing the owner-operated trucks they had been using. They also fashioned the company into an irregular route, truckload carrier, its mission to transport a wide range of commodities throughout the country, pursuant to nationwide operating authorities granted by the Department of Transportation. The company's sales efforts consisted of a three-pronged approach spearheaded by satellite salespeople, a telemarketing staff, and customer coordinators. Cannon Express's salespeople were situated in strategic locations, dotting the company's operating territory. The telemarketing staff drummed up new business by soliciting new customers. Cannon Express's customer coordinators arranged shipments for the company's existing customers.

A new customer's initial contact with the company was made through one of Cannon Express's salespeople. The salesperson collected pertinent information from the customer, ascertaining the its financial condition, payment history, and information related to its loads, including the volume of freight to be delivered, the origins and destinations of the shipments, the pick-up and delivery time frames, and any special needs. Once the information was recorded on a database, Cannon Express and the shipper discussed shipment rates, agreeing on a figure that was subsequently passed to one of the company's customer coordinators, who where assigned to a specific region of the country. A customer coordinator served as a matchmaker, finding a truck available for the shipper's load. Once a match was found, the customer coordinator assigned the shipment to a dispatcher, the final link in the process. Dispatchers relayed the shipment information to the selected driver, who, once on the road, communicated with the dispatcher either via telephone at

Key Dates:

1981: Dean Cannon purchases C.R. Kidd Produce.
1997: Wal-Mart begins to sever its business relationship with Cannon Express.
2000: Cannon Express reduces the size of its fleet.
2002: CFOex, Inc. is hired to manage Cannon Express.

routine stops on route or through a computer and satellite link located in the truck. The satellite link allowed the dispatcher to keep track of the shipment's progress. When the shipment reached its destination, the dispatcher assigned another shipment to the driver.

Cannon Express published its own freight rates, rather than using those published by freight rate publishing bureaus. By doing so, according to the company's belief, Cannon Express could adjust its prices more nimbly, enabling it to be more responsive to changing market conditions and to the particular needs of its customers. The cargo carried by the company's trucks consisted of a wide range of commodities, including retail and wholesale goods destined for discount merchandisers, paper goods, automotive supplies and parts, and non-perishable food products.

Growth in the Early and Mid-1990s

By the time Cannon Express celebrated its 10th anniversary, the company had developed into a genuine regional carrier. Freight traffic local to Springdale accounted for virtually none of the company's business. Instead, Cannon Express spread its presence throughout a wide territory bounded by Texas and Oklahoma to the west. To the east, Cannon Express's operating territory extended to the Atlantic Ocean. To service this territory, the company maintained a fleet of 288 trucks (referred to as tractors in the trucking industry), and 359 trailers, the extent of the Cannons' expansion efforts by mid-1991. Increasing customer demand, despite the anemic financial conditions prevalent during the early 1990s, demanded a larger, newer fleet. Consequently, the company was negotiating for a substantial upgrade and expansion of its fleet midway through 1991, planning to purchase 85 new tractors, to replace 95 of its tractors with new tractors, and to acquire an additional 100 trailers, expecting to put the acquired assets into service by the end of the year.

At this point in the company's development, it stood as a $27 million company. The total, recorded in 1991, represented a 43 percent increase over the previous year's total. The gain was indicative of the robust growth the company was enjoying at the completion of its first decade of business. The growth, which continued for much of the 1990s, transformed Cannon Express into a national freight hauler, with operations in the 48 contiguous states and in Canada. The expansion made Cannon Express the eighth-largest trucking company in Arkansas, but by the time the company's second decade of business was nearing completion, the years of growth had given way to a period of considerable frustration. A number of factors contributed to the pain suffered by Cannon Express—the publication *Arkansas Business* referred to ''an almost cataclysmic union of negative business factors'' in

a June 4, 2001 article. This situation was further exacerbated by the actions of one of Cannon Express's customers.

Much of Cannon Express's strength as it entered the late 1990s was drawn from a another Arkansas concern, Wal-Mart Stores Inc., the largest retailer in the world. Wal-Mart operated 31 of what it referred to as ''Centerpoints,'' distribution centers that served as hubs for the company's myriad stores. Cannon Express, to its great financial benefit, enjoyed a share of Wal-Mart's Centerpoint business, deriving roughly 50 percent of its $109 million in sales in 1998 from Wal-Mart. The company's reliance on Wal-Mart was massive, helping to account for the four-fold increase in annual sales Cannon Express recorded between 1991 and 1998. Dependence on Wal-Mart worked to Cannon Express's advantage, but the gains were equal to the losses when Wal-Mart rethought the distribution of its $1.5 billion worth of annual outside trucking business. For Cannon Express, the hammer began to fall in 1997.

In 1997, Wal-Mart converted to a ''price-only'' bidding system for its trucking contracts, part of the retailer's plan to consolidate its distribution processes. Cannon Express lost its share in the Centerpoint business as a result of Wal-Mart's decision, one of the effects of which was to cause Cannon Express's stock value to plunge by 70 percent. In early 2000, Cannon Express's loss was compounded when Wal-Mart handed another Arkansas-based trucking company, J.B. Hunt Transport Services Inc., a $100 million distribution contract. J.B. Hunt, the state's largest trucking concern, generated more than $2 billion in annual revenue from its fleet of 9,400 trucks and 38,000 trailers. Ted Wade, Wal-Mart's vice-president of corporate traffic, explained the decision in an April 24, 2000 interview with *Arkansas Business*. ''J.B. Hunt was selected for their ability to provide the entire scope of transportation and logistics solutions to meet our needs. The simplicity of dealing with a single source that will help us lower transportation costs to benefit our customers was a key factor.'' Cannon, two years after Wade's remarks, provided his perception in an April 1, 2002 interview with *Arkansas Business,* saying, ''We heard they were wanting to single-source a lot of that business, so they took it away from us and gave to other companies—gave it to Hunt. It's extremely difficult to recoup from that big of a hit.''

Diminishing Financial Health: Late 1990s

The blow was devastating, triggering the downward spiral of the company's fortunes. Cannon rallied to reverse the negative affects, which were aggravated by the financial troubles of the company's second-largest customer, International Paper, whose contribution to Cannon Express's annual revenue volume declined from 14.4 percent to 9.4 percent between 1998 and 2000. At roughly the same time that Wal-Mart handed $100 million in new business to rival J.B. Hunt, Cannon Express launched a Web site that, for a fee of $10, allowed trucking companies to post their loads and to coordinate hauling, providing capabilities that removed the need to pay brokerage fees. Within the first two weeks of the Web site's debut, it attracted 22,000 trucks. Hoping to compensate for the loss of Wal-Mart traffic, Cannon was endeavoring to attract business from two million trucks for his company's Web site. ''The intent at this point,'' Cannon said in an April 24, 2000 interview with *Arkansas Business,* ''is to reduce the carriers' expenses, to cut out the parasites, and keep the money in the trucking community where it belongs.''

However, Cannon's efforts to recover from the loss of Wal-Mart's business were hampered by a host of other, almost conspiratorial, obstacles. As the company entered the 21st century, it was beset by rising diesel costs and hobbled by a shortage of qualified drivers. A weakening national economy offered no salve. In response, Cannon reduced the size of his fleet, a consequence of steadily declining revenues. In June 2000, he sold 120 of his trucks and 180 of his trailers. At the same time, he began replacing many of his 48-foot trailers with 53-foot trailers in an effort to become more competitive. Cannon also implemented a new lease program for truck owner-operators, a strategy which was expected to improve Cannon Express's driver retention rate and operating results by transferring responsibility of certain costs, such as fuel costs, from the company to the owner-operators.

By the end of the company's 2001 fiscal year in June 2001, the financial figures for the previous 12 months pointed to serious problems. For the year, the company generated $85.8 million in sales, down markedly from the $109 million collected in 1998, and posted a crippling $7.3 million loss. To make matters worse, the company found itself embroiled in legal controversy as fiscal 2001 drew to an end. In May 2001, three individuals—Ed Bennett, Farish Kincaid, and Felix Pruss— filed an involuntary bankruptcy petition against Cannon Express, claiming that the company owed them more than $1.3 million for services rendered. (According to the petition for Chapter 7 liquidation, the trio claimed to have signed contracts with Cannon Express to recruit foreign drivers, primarily from Australia and New Zealand). Cannon responded to the accusation with disbelief. In a May 28, 2001 interview with *Arkansas Business,* he remarked, ''We don't know totally what the complaint says. But we know who some of the individuals are who are involved. One we've never heard of and has never had any affiliation with us, and the other two we don't owe any money to. It does not make a lot of sense.''

At the end of July 2001, Cannon's prospects brightened somewhat when the request for involuntary bankruptcy was withdrawn. According to the plaintiffs' attorneys, the lawsuit was dropped because of Felix Pruss' failing health. Cannon's respite from legal problems was all too brief, however. In February 2002, the company announced a net loss for the seventh consecutive quarter, contributing to the more than $4.5 million deficit racked up during the first six months of the company's fiscal 2002. At the same time, the Internal Revenue Service (IRS) notified Cannon Express that it owed $6 million in back taxes. Cannon brushed aside the accusation. ''We believe [the IRS position is] totally unfounded,'' he explained in a February 25, 2002 interview with *Arkansas Business.* ''It involves a leasing transaction. It's more of a question of who pays the tax.''

One month after the IRS notified Cannon Express of its tax obligations, the company began to unravel. The first major job cut in the company's 21-year history occurred in March 2002, when 50 workers were laid off, which represented one-quarter Cannon Express's non-driving work force. Concurrently, Cannon and his wife announced they would stop drawing a salary

from the company in an effort to reduce expenses. The company's precarious financial condition did not improve, however, as the summer months of 2002 resulted in further losses. By August 2002, Cannon had run out of options, save one.

In an August 26, 2002 article published in *Arkansas Business,* Cannon made what must have been a difficult announcement. ''Due to the company's lack of operating success, it is imperative that Cannon Express take immediate steps to improve its operating performance and liquidity.'' The immediate steps Cannon referred to, in effect, represented his own dismissal. Cannon hired CFOex Inc. to assume day-to-day management responsibilities over Cannon Express's operation. CFOex Inc. was a financial services company comprising former chief financial officers and senior executives from public and private trucking companies. Concurrent with the announcement, Cannon resigned as president and chief executive officer and Rose Marie Cannon resigned as secretary and treasurer.

Into the void created by Cannon's departure stepped Bruce Jones, the founder and president of CFOex. Jones, the former chief executive officer of two trucking companies, including J.B. Hunt, took on the title of interim chief executive officer. The impact of Jones's managerial reign was not determined by the end of 2002, but the first few months of his tenure pointed to continued problems for the beleaguered company. During the first fiscal quarter of 2003, revenues were down 13 percent and the company reported a net loss of $3.1 million. Ahead lay many months of arduous work to repair the damages incurred during the previous five years, a crucible for the 21-year-old company.

Principal Subsidiaries

Cannon Express Corporation.

Principal Competitors

J.B. Hunt Transport Services, Inc.; P.A.M. Transportation Services, Inc.; Werner Enterprises, Inc.

Further Reading

Bowden, Bill, ''Cannon Express Attempts U-turn,'' *Arkansas Business,* April 1, 2002, p. 1.
''Cannon Express Founder Gives Up Management,'' *Arkansas Business,* August 26, 2002, p. 10.
''Cannon Express Inc.,'' *Arkansas Business,* August 12, 1991, p. 31.
Moritz, Gwen, ''Cannon Downplays Involuntary Bankruptcy,'' *Arkansas Business,* May 28, 2001, p. 10.
''Truckload Carrier Cannon Express Lays Off 50 Workers,'' *Knight Ridder/Tribune Business News,* March 25, 2002.
Whiteley, Michael, ''Hunt Picks Up $100M Wal-Mart Contract,'' *Arkansas Business,* April 24, 2000, p. 10.
Whitsett, Jack, ''Trucking Industry still Riding Out 'Perfect Storm,' '' *Arkansas Business,* June 4, 2001, p. 1.
——, ''Plaintiffs Drop Cannon Bankruptcy,'' *Arkansas Business,* July 30, 2001, p. 11.
——, ''IRS Compounds Cannon Woes,'' *Arkansas Business,* February 25, 2002, p. 10.
Wood, Jeffrey, ''Cannon Express Posts $3.1 Million Net Loss,'' *Arkansas Business,* November 25, 2002, p. 11.

—Jeffrey L. Covell

Cardo AB

Roskildevägen 1
Box 486
SE-201 24 Malmö
Sweden
Telephone: (+46) 40-35-04-00
Fax: (+46) 40-97-64-40
Web site: http://www.cardo.se

Public Company
Incorporated: 1985
Employees: 8,179
Sales: Skr 10.8 billion ($1.19 billion)(2001)
Stock Exchanges: Stockholm
Ticker Symbol: CARD
NAIC: 332321 Metal Window and Door Manufacturing;
333911 Pump and Pumping Equipment
Manufacturing; 423390 Other Construction Material
Merchant Wholesalers; 551112 Offices of Other
Holding Companies

Cardo AB has focused its efforts on building two world-leading companies: Cardo Door and Cardo Pump. Cardo Door is the European leader in the manufacture of residential garage doors and is also one of the world's leading industrial door and door systems manufacturers, with products including doors for airplane hangars, automated and high-speed closure systems, and complete loading dock systems. Cardo Pump manufactures industrial pumps, mixers and aerators for a variety of applications, as well as high-technology measurement instruments. Linking these two unrelated business units is Cardo's commitment to pursuing holdings with strong aftermarket potential: Cardo generates as much as 30 percent of its total revenues through its aftermarket service operations, providing the company with a stable revenue base even in economic downturns. Europe accounted for more than 92 percent of the company's sales of nearly SKr11 billion ($1.19 billion) in 2001; Sweden represented seven percent of the company's sales. Cardo operates nearly 120 subsidiaries in 30 countries, including all Western European countries, Hungary, Poland, the United States, Canada, China, Singapore, and Brazil. Cardo has been growing through acquisitions, including the purchases of Amber Doors Ltd. and Nopon Oy in 2002. As part of its restructuring around Doors and Pumps, Cardo sold off its third business unit, Cardo Rail, in September 2002.

An Evolving Enterprise: 1913 to the 1990s

Cardo's origins trace back to the World War I era. The oldest component of what was to become the "first" Cardo in the mid-1980s was founded by Axel Diurson in 1913. Diurson had invented and patented the first brake regulator system for rail vehicles and established the company Svenska Aktiebolaget Bromsregulator (SAB). Although Diurson's invention initially met with resistance from the railway industry, the importance of brake regulation systems was soon recognized, becoming a railway standard. SAB rose to become one of Europe's most prominent manufacturers of railway brake systems.

SAB's success led it to diversify into the development, engineering, and production of other brake component, such as resilient wheels—another revolutionary component—as well as actuators and other equipment for trains and railroads. For the most part, SAB's sale remained limited to Europe. Its presence in that market was strongly enhanced through the acquisition of two important railway systems manufacturers at the beginning of the 1990s.

In 1990, SAB acquired the European operating division of the U.S. firm WABCO. Founded in 1869, WABCO had been the first company formed by the great American industrialist George Westinghouse. Through WABCO, which stood for Westinghouse Air Brake Corporation, had developed the automatic air brake system, which gradually imposed itself as an industry mainstay. WABCO's success in Europe had led it to establish factories in Italy and France. The WABCO acquisition established SAB as the preeminent manufacturer of railroad brake systems in Europe.

SAB quickly consolidated that position with the purchase of Lucas Girling's Rail division, also in 1990. That company traced its origins back to England in the 1880s. For the first half of the twentieth century, Lucas Girling had been known as a supplier to the British automotive industry. Starting in the 1950s, the company had formed its rail division, working with

Company Perspectives:

Cardo is to advance its position as an international engineering group and leading supplier of high-quality products and systems with a good aftermarket. The Group's competitiveness is to be continually improved by ongoing efficiency programs. Cardo is to show an annual profitable growth in sales of 15 percent, approximately half organic and the remainder provided by acquisitions. Growth is to be accomplished mainly by sharper focus on the aftermarket, development of new products, increased marketing activities in countries where market share is low, long-term expansion in eastern Europe and Asia, and acquisitions that give positive synergies.

British Rail to develop braking systems for high-speed trains, as well as ceramic disk braking systems for freight trains.

SAB WABCO, as the company was renamed in 1990, was by then just one part of Investment AB Cardo, a publicly listed industrial holding group then largely held by Sweden's industrial giant Volvo. Another significant Cardo holding, known as Cardo Pump, had been formed in 1918 by trading company Ekman & Co. as AB Pumpindustri. Producing pumps and systems for the growing European industrial community, Pumpindustri grew through the 1966 acquisitions of Gothia Piston Pumps and SIHI, a German company. A year later Pumpindustri was itself acquired by diversified Swedish industrial group Wilhelm Sonesson & Co., changing its name to Sonesson Pumpindustri.

After changing its name again in 1979, to Scanpump AB, the Sonesson division made a pair of important acquisitions. The first came in 1982, when the company bought Jönköpings Mekaniska Werkstad (JMW). That purchase enabled Scanpump to extend its range of pumps into large-scale pumping systems for the pulp and paper industries, as well as for water and waste treatment plants. Three years later, Scanpump further expanded its range with the acquisition of Vadstena Pumpar, a specialist in pumping systems for the building and construction services market, originally founded in 1918.

Shifting Ownership in the 1990s

In the mid-1980s, several Swedish companies joined in a restructuring effort that created a new industrial investment holding company, New Investment AB Cardo, controlled at nearly 45 percent by Volvo. Cardo combined a number of former Sonesson interests, including the Scanpump and SAB operations, as well as a majority shareholding in rising medical equipment manufacturer Gambro.

Another important part of the new Cardo's operations was its door manufacturing subsidiary. That operation had started up business in 1960 as Crawford Door AB and introduced the overhead garage door concept to the European market. Over the following decades, Crawford had established itself as a European market leader in overhead doors. Cardo had also expanded into the industrial door segment, chiefly through a series of acquisitions that gave it operations in Denmark, Germany, the Netherlands, France, and the United Kingdom. An important acquisition came in 1984 when Crawford acquired Utec-Porten

AB. Set up in 1971, that company specialized in large-scale doors capable of withstanding extreme weather conditions. In 1982, Utec had set up a U.S. subsidiary named Megadoor Inc. After its acquisition by Crawford, Utec itself changed its name to Megadoor AB. Following the restructuring, which grouped its operations with those of Scanpump and SAB, Cardo formed the Cardo Door subsidiary composed of its Crawford, Megadoor, and other related holdings.

By the time of the WABCO acquisition, Cardo had begun to focus its operations on three core areas: Cardo Door, Cardo Pump, and Cardo Rail. The Cardo Pump division had been growing steadily, particularly with the acquisition of Sweden's Pumpex, which specialized in submersible pumps, in 1986; Lefi, based in France, which manufactured process pumps for the chemical industry, in 1988; and ABS Pumpen, based in Germany and the number two maker of submersible pumps in Europe. That acquisition led Scanpump to change its name to ABS-Scanpump in 1990. By then, the division had become the fifth-largest pump manufacturing group in Europe. In 1993, the pump operation was restructured into separate product and sales organizations under the direction of newly created parent company Cardo Pump AB.

Volvo's failed attempt to take over French carmaker Renault in the early 1990s led the Swedish industrial giant to undergo its own restructuring. As part of that effort, Volvo sold off its Cardo holding to investment group Incentive AB, controlled by the Wallenberg family, in 1994, which then made a public offer to take over the remainder of Cardo. Over the next year, Incentive reorganized Cardo, spinning off its Pump, Rail, and Door divisions as the ''new'' Cardo AB, which placed its shares on the Stockholm exchange in 1995. Incentive, which by then had decided to focus itself as a medical equipment manufacturer, maintained control of the Gambro unit. Soon after Incentive changed its name to Gambro AB.

Cardo continued growing through acquisition, with each of its three major businesses making important purchases in the second half of the decade. In 1995, Cardo Door acquired, through its Crawford Door industrial door subsidiary, Windsor Door A/S, Denmark's fifth-largest industrial door producer, formerly part of the United Kingdom's Henderson door group. In 1996, Cardo Door acquired Alsta, based in Holland. Founded in 1980, Alsta specialized in industrial-use overhead doors and had gained a strong position in that sector in the European market. Soon after, Cardo boosted its Swedish garage door production capacity with the purchase of Carpro AB. Most of Cardo Door's business remained in Europe; in 1997, however, the company sought to expand its international operations with the creation of a joint-venture in China, with local partner Shenyang Liming taking the minority share.

Cardo Pump's acquisition during this time included the 1995 purchase of Scaba, based in Sweden, which manufactured non-submersible mixers, complementing Cardo's existing line of submersible mixers. In 1997, Carbo Pump added Germany's Frings, a specialist manufacturer of aerators for the water treatment industry. Meanwhile, Cardo Rail's growth moves included signing a distribution agreement with Japan's NABCO to introducer Cardo's electromechanical disk-brake systems into that country, and the 1996 acquisition of Transferia Tebel, a leading, Netherlands-based manufacturer of train doors. The following year Cardo Rail made a still more important acquisition when it

Key Dates:

1913: Svenska Aktiebolaget Bromsregulator (SAB) is established to manufacture brake regulators for trains.
1918: Founding of AB Pumpindustri by trading company Ekman & Co.
1960: Crawford Doors AB is founded to produce overhead residential garage doors.
1967: Wilhelm Sonesson & Co. acquires AB Pumpindustri, changing its name to Sonesson Pumpindustri.
1979: Sonesseon Pumpindustri changes its name to Scanpump.
1982: Scanpump acquires Jönköpings Mekaniska Werkstad (JMW).
1984: Crawford acquires Utec-porten and its Megadoor Inc. (USA) subsidiary.
1985: Restructuring creates New Investment AB Cardo with Volvo as its principal shareholder, grouping three primary businesses of Cardo Pump, Scanpump, and SAB; Scanpump acquires Vadstena Pumpar.
1993: Cardo Pump is formed as the parent company of ABS Scanpump subsidiaries.
1994: Incentive AB acquires Cardo and restructures the company around Cardo Doors, Cardo Pumps, and Cardo Rail.
1995: Incentive spins off Cardo AB as a public company.
1997: Cardo Rail merges with Thyseen's Rail division, BSI, forming Cardo BSI Rail.
2002: Cardo sells off its Cardo Rail subsidiary.

merged with German group Thyssen's Railway division to form the 60–40 partnership Carbo BSI Rail. Following the merger, Cardo decided to sell off the Tebel unit as part of a strategy to re-center on its core brake systems operations. In 1999, Cardo bought out Thyssen to regain full control of Cardo Rail.

Focus on Doors and Pumps in the New Century

Cardo Door remained a strong driver for Cardo's growth into the next decade, continuing its acquisition drive as it reached the top ranks of industrial and residential door makers. In 1997, the company acquired Normstahl, based in Germany, with operations in Austria and Switzerland. That acquisition quadrupled Cardo's residential garage door activity, placing it firmly in the European top three. Cardo Door had also been expanding into the loading dock equipment market, an area complementary to the company's industrial door operations. In 1998, the company took the European leadership in dock loading equipment with the purchase of Germany's Hafa-Alten Gerätebau, a move that tripled Cardo's dock loading activity.

That unit grew again in 2000, with the purchase of Miflex Miljöexpert A/S, the leading dock loading equipment company in Denmark. Also in 2000, Cardo Door had completed its acquisition of PC Henderson Ltd., the leading maker of residential garage doors in the United Kingdom. By the end of that year, Cardo Door's shares of Cardo AB's total revenues neared 50 percent.

Cardo decided to concentrate its efforts on its Pump and Doors subsidiaries, and in July 2002 announced it had to agree

to sell its Cardo Rail subsidiary to Vestar Capital Partners. The deal, worth SKr2 billion—including some SKr1.2 billion of debt—was completed in September of that year. Meanwhile, Cardo had been adding steadily to its remaining core businesses. In January 2002, Cardo Pump acquired Finland's Nopon Oy, a specialist in aeration systems for biological wastewater treatment, which followed on the December 2001 purchase of Swedmeter, a specialist in control engineering processes.

These acquisitions helped Cardo near its goal of supplying complete systems for the water and wastewater industry. At the same, Cardo continued to add to its Cardo Door division, acquiring Amber Doors Holding Ltd., a specialist manufacturer of fire safety, security, and other industrial doors based in the United Kingdom. The streamlined Cardo forecasted strong growth for both of its core components. Meanwhile the company's early commitment to aftermarket sales gave it the financial stability upon which to continue its future expansion.

Principal Subsidiaries

Allhabo AB; Cardo Door Export AB; Cardo Door Production AB; Crawford Door Försäljnings AB; Crawford Garageportar AB; Crawmator AB; International Door Automation AB; Megadoor AB; ABS Pump AB; ABS Pump Production AB; ABS Pumps International AB; Lorentzen & Wettre AB; Skandinavien AB; Pumpex AB; Pumpex Sverige AB; Swedmeter AB; SAB WABCO AB; SAB WABCO International AB; SAB WABCO Nordic AB.

Principal Competitors

Lowe's Companies Inc.; Tostem Inax Holding Corp.; Owens Corning; Williams PLC; Armstrong Holdings Inc.; Imerys; Sanwa Shutter Corp.; Royal Group Technologies Ltd.; Sankyo Aluminium Industry Company Ltd.; Hunter Douglas Group NV; Alcan Deutschland Holdings GmbH Und Co. KG; Kidde PLC; Masonite International Corp.; Okamura Corp.; Fujisash Company Ltd.; Griffon Corp.; SCHUCO International KG; Tateyama Aluminium Industry Company Ltd.; Quanex Corp.; Pella Corp; FE Petro Inc.; Beach-Russ Co.; General Electric Co.; Depco Pump Company Inc.; MAN AG; Brabazon Compressor; Alfred Conhagen Inc.; Crane Pumps and Systems Inc.; Ebara Corp.; Dover Resources Inc.; J.M. Voith AG; Pentair Inc.; Saint-Gobain Abrasives; Red Jacket Pumps; Hydromatic Pump; Hypro Corp.; Flowserve Corp.; ACD Inc.; Motion Industries Inc; ACD L.L.C.; Metaullics Systems Co.

Further Reading

"Cardo Acquires Leading Manufacturer in Biological Wastewater Treatment," *PrimeZone Media Network*, January 23, 2002.
"Cardo Completes Sale of Cardo Rail to Vestar Capital Partners," *Nordic Business Report*, Sept 25, 2002.
"Cardo Sees 2001 Sales Growth to Beat Market Despite Uncertain Outlook," *AFX EUROPE*, May 4, 2001.
"Cardo Wins Record Order for Doors in China," *HUGIN*, August 29, 2002.
"Close Brothers Walks out of Amber Doors," *European Venture Capital Journal*, February 2002, p. 36.

—M.L. Cohen

CCA Industries, Inc.

200 Murray Hill Parkway
East Rutherford, New Jersey 07073
U.S.A.
Telephone: (201) 330-1400
Fax: (201) 842-6042
Web site: http://www.ccaindustries.com

Public Company
Incorporated: 1983
Employees: 134
Sales: $42 million (2001)
Stock Exchanges: NASDAQ
Ticker Symbol: CCAM
NAIC: 325620 Toilet Preparation Manufacturing

CCA Industries, Inc. has only a small percentage of the total health and beauty aids market, yet it has several leading products and for much of its history has had an enviable profit margin. CCA distributes and markets almost 200 products altogether, selling principally to mass marketers and health and beauty aid wholesalers. Giant merchandiser Wal-Mart is a key customer, accounting for almost 30 percent of CCA's sales. CCA's products are found in many leading drugstore chains such as Walgreens and Eckerd, for a total of some 40,000 stores nationwide. The company does none of its own manufacturing and often picks up innovative product ideas from inventors who bring them to CCA. Its product range includes a slew of niche items from all different segments of the health and beauty aids spectrum. One of CCA's best known products is its Plus+White brand of tooth whiteners and tooth pastes. Other top brands include the Sudden Change line of skin care products, Nutra Nail nail polishes and treatments, Hair Off depilatories, Bikini Zone skin crème, sun care products marketed under the Solar Sense brand, and the fragrances Cherry Vanilla and Cloud Dance. Many of CCA's products are unique or unusual. Its Cloud Dance perfume, for example, is made by a special formula that contains two differently colored liquids in suspension. The product sets itself apart by being visually dis-

tinctive. CCA advertises its brands through television ads and infomercials, as well as in print media.

Getting Started in the 1980s

CCA Industries was founded in 1983 by Ira W. Berman and David Edell. Berman, the company's chairman, had a law degree from Cornell University and had been practicing law since 1955. Edell, who still serves as president and chief executive officer of the company, had extensive experience in the health and beauty business before forming his own company. He was formerly the executive director of Hazel Bishop Industries, Inc., a New Jersey-based cosmetics company with a venerable history. The company was named for its founder, Hazel Bishop, a chemist who invented what was known as the world's first ''kissproof'' lipstick—a special long-lasting, nondrying formula. Hazel Bishop, Inc. had a 25 percent share of the U.S. lipstick market in the 1950s. Bishop sold the company in 1954. By the early 1980s, the company was known as a maker of low-priced cosmetics, as well as hair and skin products it had acquired when it bought Lanolin Plus in 1981. Hazel Bishop Industries did not make its own products by the 1980s but contracted that function out to six different manufacturers. CCA Industries was formed on much the same model. It aimed to sell health and beauty aids through mass marketers and chain stores, looking to capture only a small share of what was a huge market. CCA, however, did not look only to the low-price end of the market. Instead, it debuted products which often sold for much more than the competition but which offered consumers unique characteristics that seemed worth the extra dollars. Because it contracted its manufacturing, CCA was able to move nimbly, bringing out new products and dropping unsuccessful ones with less financial risk than a company that was heavily invested in factories and equipment. And CCA could concentrate on marketing, which was its forte.

Edell's two sons joined the company, Drew in 1983 and Dunnan in 1984. Drew Edell had a degree in industrial design from the Pratt Institute in New York; he became vice-president for manufacturing. Dunnan Edell's background included working at Hazel Bishop for five years. He became vice-president for sales. By the mid-1980s, CCA already had nationwide distribu-

Company Perspectives:

CCA Industries, Inc., is ... engaged in the manufacturing and marketing of its own brand of health and beauty aid products. The Company markets directly to major mass merchandisers and drug and food retail chains throughout the United States and internationally. All of the company's products are sold under their individual brand names. The Company's brand name products are Plus+White in the oral health care field, Sudden Change skin treatments, Hair Off depilatories, Nutra Nail nail treatments, Bikini Zone medicated creme and gel, Wash 'N Curl and Wash'N Straight shampoos, IPR 3 foot products, Cherry Vanilla, Cloud Dance, and Vision fragrances, Solar Sense sun care products, and Mega 16 and Progress diets aids.

tion of several products in different categories. It was selling Nutra Nail, a nail treatment, the hair conditioner Pro Perm, and the depilatory Hair Off, among other products. By 1987, CCA was ready for nationwide television advertising. The company went to Chestnut Communications to devise a campaign for a new diet aid called Eat 'n Lose. Eat 'n Lose was one of several CCA products developed outside the company, this one by Dr. Gio B. Gori, who had worked with the diet and nutrition program of the National Cancer Institute. It was a fiber that the consumer sprinkled on food. According to Dr. Gori, the product diluted calories and moved them through the digestive system faster. CCA invested about $1.5 million on Eat 'n Lose commercials, and spent a total of some $5 million on advertising for all its products combined that year. The company continued to advertise, and by the early 1990s it was known for the light-hearted tone of its television commercials.

In 1991, CCA made a major push for two of its products, with national advertising appearing on prime time television and during popular daytime talk shows such as *Donahue*, *Sally Jesse Raphael*, and *Geraldo*. These two products both sold in low-end mass merchandisers, yet they were relatively expensive products. Sudden Change was a skin cream that was touted as being able to smooth out lines and wrinkles within minutes. Sudden Change stood out from competitors because it was not marketed as moisturizer or make up. It was something more, as it claimed to be able to make wrinkles vanish immediately and stay away for up to eight hours. A half-ounce bottle retailed for $15.99. CCA also made a big effort to promote Plus+White, a tooth whitening system that became a market leader and a big profit maker for drugstores.

Riding High on Tooth Whiteners in the Early 1990s

CCA's success came from promoting unusual products that were able to grab a small share of the huge health and beauty market. Its Plus+White brand was one of its best products, becoming a prominent name in a neglected corner of the oral care industry. Tooth whiteners became hot sellers in the early 1990s, when several brands, including Plus+White, received heavy promotion. The total market in whiteners was estimated at $36.6 million in 1990, according to research published in *Drug Topics* (March 23, 1992), and by 1991 sales had grown

over 70 percent, to $63 million. Consumers paid between $7 and $10 for Plus+White, leading to a very high profit margin for both CCA and the retailer. By 1992, sales at CCA had climbed to over $27 million. The next year, the company brought out another oral care product, a toothpaste called Triplex, which combined baking soda, hydrogen peroxide, and fluoride in one formula. Competitors had tried to present a similar product, but because the hydrogen peroxide and baking soda chemically reacted the ingredients had to be packaged separately, leading to a rather complicated and cumbersome toothpaste. A dentist approached CCA with a patented formula that encapsulated the hydrogen peroxide, so that for the first time, these three ingredients could co-exist in one tube. Triplex was soon a top seller at chain stores like Walgreens. The product again had a high profit margin, retailing for around $6, compared to $2 for most regular toothpastes.

The Food and Drug Administration (FDA) took notice of the leap in sales of tooth whiteners. The government agency thought initially that whiteners should be classified as a drug and be subject to long-term clinical studies. CCA marketed Plus+White as a cosmetic and was sure that its use of 3 percent hydrogen peroxide had already been declared safe for oral use by the FDA in 1988. CCA and another dental marketer formed the National Tooth Whitener Coalition in 1992 to argue for the safety of their products. CCA estimated it lost some $13 million in potential sales of Plus+White due to the FDA's stance, yet the company nevertheless had record sales and earnings for the year. The FDA changed its position on tooth whiteners in July 1992, and CCA resumed heavy marketing of its dental care line. The company began a joint venture with Media Dynamics in 1993 to produce infomercials for CCA's products. Infomercials are a hybrid between advertising and content, devoting usually a half hour to promoting a product and in most cases offering the item directly to consumers by telephone. The infomercial industry was growing quickly, and it offered a new outlet for CCA. The company hoped to attract first-time buyers through the television spots, which would then build to more sales through its traditional chain-store outlets. By 1993, CCA's biggest customers were Wal-Mart, Walgreens, and Kmart. ''Wal-Mart can't get enough of CCA's unique products,'' claimed an industry analyst quoted in *Business Week* (April 19, 1993), and the company's stock took off as news of its dramatic rise in sales and profits spread. CCA brought in $44.3 million in 1993, up steeply from its $27 million a year previous.

The firm was canny in its marketing, spending some $10 to $12 million on advertising in 1993. When the new cop show *NYPD Blue* premiered in 1993, many advertisers shied away from it, afraid of the controversial level of violence and nudity the drama promised. CCA, however, leapt at prime advertising spots during the show. The gamble paid off when the show became a hit. Tooth whiteners and toothpastes were not all CCA had going for it. Its wrinkle reliever Sudden Change did an estimated $10 million in wholesale volume by 1993, and its Nutra Nail 60 Second, a quick-drying nail polish, brought in about $6 million wholesale. An even bigger seller was the Wash 'n Curl hair care line. After two years on the market, Wash 'n Curl had captured about 1 percent of the total North American shampoo market. This was just a small sliver, but worth over $11 million. Wash 'n Curl was a shampoo that tended to make hair curlier. CCA followed it with Wash 'n Moist, a shampoo

Key Dates:

1983: The company is founded by a former Hazel Bishop executive and others.
1987: The company launches its first national advertising campaign.
1991: CCA brings out Plus + White and Sudden Change.
1998: The company enters the fragrance market.

that protected hair from the heat damage of blow drying, and Wash 'n Tint, which brought out natural highlights in hair.

CCA Industries filed suit against the American Dental Association (ADA) in 1995 over a video the association produced alleging dangers that may result from using over-the-counter tooth whiteners. The video showed two Plus + White products, among others. CCA demanded a retraction of the video, which had been distributed to 700 broadcast journalists, but apparently the spot had already been run by some stations. CCA filed suit for damages relating to the video, and the ADA settled several months later. By that time, tooth whiteners had become unquestionably the most profitable segment of the oral care market. Despite having prime products in that segment, CCA stumbled in 1995, with sales dropping to $36 million, from $47 in 1994, and registering a loss of $1.5 million. Apparently, the company had overspent on advertising for products that did not go over well.

New Lines in the Late 1990s

The young company had spurted enormously in the early 1990s, followed by one bad year in the middle of the decade. But CCA seemed to have a good take on the health and beauty market, with effective advertising for an array of interesting products. Though its sales and profits went up and down through the late 1990s into the 2000s, CCA held to its original business formula, and at times did very well. The company began to try to rein in its advertising costs in the late 1990s, running spots which combined several of its products. And it always had more new products coming out. According to an interview with *WWD* (April 22, 1994), CCA president David Edell said the company always had 10 to 12 products in development. Some of them were line extensions, working on the Plus + White or Sudden Change name. But the company was also able to shift gears and bring out new products where it did not already have an established brand. In 1997, CCA began selling an analgesic skin cream called Bikini Zone, which was intended for women to use after shaving. It also came out with Shape 'a Soap, a children's soap that could be molded by hand, and a children's nail polish called Young 'n Lovely that washed off with soap and water. With these new products in its line-up, CCA's revenue rose to $56 million that year. The company's gross profit margins were an astonishing 65 percent, and CCA had no debt.

In 1998, the company introduced several extensions to its popular Sudden Change line, bringing out three versions of a Sudden Change patch. CCA also came out with a related product called Magic Beauty Potion. Magic Beauty Potion claimed to revitalize skin with a vitamin-rich formula that also reduced the appearance of wrinkles. Like Sudden Change, it carried a rela-

tively high price tag—$14.95—and this gave retailers $6 profit for every jar sold. The company spent $10 million advertising these new skin care products in 1998. That year, CCA Industries also entered the fragrance market for the first time. The company acquired the manufacturing and distribution rights to the scents of Shiara Holdings, Inc., which sold Cherry Vanilla, Mandarin Vanilla, Amber Musk, and a men's cologne called Vision. CCA formed a new division, 20 percent owned by Shiara's founders, to market the new scents. It also bought the rights to a perfume that had been developed in Europe, Cloud Dance. The overall perfume market had not been particularly strong at the time, and for that reason CCA's entry into the category seemed surprising. But the new division had extensive marketing expertise in the Shiara executives, one of whom had developed the well-known Jovan Musk brand. And Cloud Dance was the kind of unique product that seemed typical for CCA. A chemist had created the scent with a new process that bottled two separate fragrance oils of different colors in the same package. One version was orange and pink, and the other was turquoise and lavender. Marketers hoped women would buy Cloud Dance to display the bottle as much as to wear the scent.

CCA received an offer to sell the company in 1999, but it refused. Sales for 2000 were just over $37 million, down substantially from several years earlier, and it took another loss of around $650,000. By 2001, CCA was bringing out more line extensions of Plus + White and had a new crop of wrinkle creams. It had several products that were in the top ten of their particular categories, including Bikini Zone, the depilatory Hair Off Mitten, and Sudden Change. Plus + White was ranked number four out of 19 top sellers in the whitener category in terms of sales growth, and the year finished better for CCA, with revenue up 12 percent to $41.7 million and net income of just over $2 million. One of its largest customers, Kmart, filed for bankruptcy in January, 2002. The chain kept operating but closed many locations, and CCA acknowledged that Kmart's status might have an impact on the company. Yet 2001 was a good year for CCA, while much of the rest of the U.S. economy suffered. It seemed possible that with CCA's eclectic mix of products, the recession and economic uncertainty of the early 2000s would not hamper the company's sales unduly.

Principal Divisions

Fragrance Corporation of America, Ltd.

Principal Competitors

Chesebrough-Pond, Inc.; The Proctor & Gamble Co.; Revlon, Inc.

Further Reading

"Beauty Line," *Forbes*, April 7, 1997.
Brookman, Faye, "CCA's Five Percent Solution," *WWD*, April 22, 1994, p. 8.
"CCA Bullish on 2001," *MMR*, February 4, 2001, p. 40.
"CCA H&BAs Bring Continued Success," *Chain Drug Review*, June 21, 1993, p. 190.
"CCA Is Planning Big Media Push," *Chain Drug Review*, June 17, 1991, p. 139.
"CCA to Post Sharp Rise in Per-Share Profit for Period," *Wall Street Journal*, December 13, 1993, p. A9C.

"Chestnut Prepares Ads for New Diet Product," *New York Times*, November 30, 1987, p. D9.

Fried, Lisa I., "Has ADA Tarnished OTC Tooth Whiteners?," *Drug Store News*, January 9, 1995, p. 25.

Marcial, Gene G., "Brush Up On This Stock," *Business Week*, April 19, 1993, p. 102.

"Niche Marketing Drives Sales at CCA," *Chain Drug Review*, April 25, 1994, p. 160.

Parks, Liz, "CCA Plans Surprising Entry into Fragrance Category," *Drug Store News*, May 25, 1998, p. 27.

Rosendahl, Iris, "Tooth Whiteners White Hot Despite Heat from FDA," *Drug Topics*, March 23, 1992, p. 96.

"Smiles All Around in Oral Care," *Discount Merchandiser*, April 1994, p. 56.

Weisz, Pam, "CCA Intros HeatSafe Challenger," *Brandweek*, July 25, 1994, p. 12.

——, "Mentadent Competitor Has Ad Bite," *Brandweek*, March 21, 1994, p. 8.

—A. Woodward

Century Casinos, Inc.

200-220 East Bennett Avenue
Cripple Creek, Colorado 80813
U.S.A.
Telephone: (719) 689-9100
Fax: (719) 689-9700
Web site: http://www.cnty.com

Public Company
Incorporated: 1993
Employees: 500
Sales: $29.6 million (2001)
Stock Exchanges: NASDAQ
Ticker Symbol: CNTY
NAIC: 713210 Casinos (Except Casino Hotels); 713290
    Other Gambling Industries; 721120 Casino Hotels

Century Casinos, Inc. operates casinos worldwide through direct ownership or management agreements. The company owns Womacks Casino and Hotel in Cripple Creek, Colorado, providing more than 675 gaming machines and game tables, casual and fine dining, and 21 hotel rooms. Century Casinos holds a 65 percent ownership in the Caledon Casino, Hotel & Spa east of Capetown, South Africa, providing over 250 gaming options. In addition to a 92-room hotel, amenities at the property include natural hot springs, tourist services, a retail center featuring local arts and crafts, conference and meeting space, and Outdoor Experience, a team-building activities program for corporate executives. Through a long-term management agreement, the company operates Casino Millennium, a 5,000-square-foot gaming area located in the five-star Marriott Hotel in Prague, Czech Republic. Century Casinos also operates gaming concessions on luxury cruise vessels for Silversea Cruises and The World at ResidenSea, providing equipment, staff, and management services for more than 200 gaming positions. The company offers consulting services for all stages of casino development, including market research, casino design, equipment selection, and operations management.

Early 1990s: Europeans Enter U.S. Gaming Market

Century Casinos formed in late 1992 when five men brought their experience in the European gaming industry to the United States. Erwin Haitzmann, chairman; James Forbes, CEO; Norbert Teufelberger, CFO; Michael Raunegger, senior vice-president of marketing; and Peter Hoetzinger, vice-chairman, were previously employed developing and managing casinos for state-owned Casinos Austria International. That company operated over 100 casinos in 17 countries on five continents, including several in Eastern Europe. Century Casinos' founders chose to start their own business in the United States to capitalize on the expansion of the gaming industry. They felt that gambling had become more acceptable as a form of entertainment in the United States and their experience had taught them how to open casinos in new places. Century Casinos chose to locate in Colorado to counter the stereotype of the Las Vegas casino manager wearing a polyester suit and cheap cologne. In 1990, Colorado passed a referendum to allow limited stakes gaming in three mountain towns. Flourishing gold mining towns during the late 19th and early 20th centuries, Central City, Blackhawk, and Cripple Creek catered to tourists by the late 20th century.

With $2 million in funds from private investors in Europe, Century Casinos Management, as the company was called originally, planned to develop a network of managed and owned casinos. Projects included an agreement to manage a gaming facility on the Soboba Indian Reservation near San Jacinto, California, and to develop riverboat casinos in Louisiana and Indiana. In September 1993, Century Casinos acquired out of foreclosure Terp's Casino in Central City, Colorado, 30 miles west of Denver, for $1.45 million. Plans involved remodeling and renaming the property under the brand Legends.

The company's first gaming operation set sail with the August 1993 inaugural voyage of the *Albatross*, a deluxe, yacht-like cruise ship operated by V. Ships of Monte Carlo. The luxurious *Silver Cloud*, operated by Silversea, a newly acquired subsidiary of V. Ships, initiated service from Civitavecchia near Rome in April 1994. Under three-year management agreements, Century Casinos supplied equipment for roulette, blackjack, and slot machines, provided personnel, and paid the expenses of the casinos; V. Ships received a portion of gaming revenues per day based on the number of adult passengers onboard.

In December 1993, Century Casinos entered into a merger agreement with Alpine Gaming, owner-operator of the Long Branch Saloon and Casino in Cripple Creek, Colorado, 45 miles west of Colorado Springs. The Long Branch opened in July 1992, offering patrons 125 slot and video gaming machines and four blackjack tables. The casino reported revenues of $2.3 million and a loss of $372,000 during its first year in operation. Alpine Gaming purchased the property in fall 1993 and became a public company that November. A merger with Alpine Gaming would allow Century Casinos to become a public company without the usual costs and procedures.

After approval from state regulators and Century Casinos' board of directors, the merger came to completion the following March. In a $10 million, non-cash transaction, Century Casinos obtained 76 percent ownership of the company and assumed all management positions. The transaction was recorded as an acquisition of Alpine Gaming with Century Casinos Management becoming a subsidiary. The following June, Alpine Gaming took the name Century Casinos, Inc. and the Long Branch was renamed Legends.

In the meantime, Century Casinos moved forward in its development of riverboat casinos in Louisiana and Indiana. In March 1994, Century Casinos obtained a gaming license from the Louisiana State Police to operate a riverboat casino near New Orleans, in St. Charles Parish. Under a management contract for St. Charles Gaming Company, Century Casinos would receive a percentage of gross revenue from gaming and a percentage of net profit. The 20,000-square-foot paddlewheel riverboat, named the Crown Casino, opened in August 1994 carrying 1,100 gaming machines.

Passage of a gaming referendum in Indiana prompted Century Casinos to purchase land on the Ohio River in Switzerland County and to apply for a gaming license there. Hospitality Franchise Systems (HFS) purchased an equity interest in Century Casinos for $2 million, forming a joint venture on the Switzerland County riverboat project, Pinnacle Gaming Development Corporation.

Shifting of resources followed as Century Casinos sold its Central City property in June 1994 for $1.9 million in order to pursue opportunities elsewhere. This proved to be a wise deci-

sion as casino development in nearby Blackhawk eventually overshadowed Central City and attracted more gamblers. The company purchased the Ranch House Casino in Wells, Nevada, for $850,000. The 18,000-square-foot facility provided 6,000 square feet of gaming space. Closed since 1992, Century Casinos had no immediate plans for the property.

Several casino projects came to fruition in 1995 as two casinos opened and a new management agreement was signed. Century Casinos began its casino concession on another Silversea cruise ship in January 1995 with the inaugural voyage of the *Silver Wind* from Mombassa, Kenya. The onboard gaming facility was named Legends at Sea to correspond with other Legends brand casinos owned or operated by the company. Also in January, the Legends Casino Soboba opened, beginning a five-year management agreement with the Soboba Band of Mission Indians. Century Casinos would receive 30 percent of net profit for management, development, and pre-opening costs. Century Casinos terminated the agreement in August, however, accepting a $3.1 million promissory note to be paid over three years.

The pursuit of international gaming opportunities resulted in a management and consulting agreement with Rhodes Casino, S.A., a consortium of businesses, including Playboy Enterprises. Signed in November, the $1.1 million contract involved oversight of the construction phase and the first three years of operation of a new casino on the Greek island of Rhodes.

In 1995, Century Casinos divested certain holdings. Crown Casino bought Century Casinos' remaining rights in a management agreement with St. Charles Gaming Company, a subsidiary of Crown Casino, for $4 million. In December, the company sold its 80 percent interest in Pinnacle Gaming to Switzerland County Development Corporation, a joint venture owned by Boomtown, Inc. and Hilton Gaming Corporation. For its activities promoting gaming in the area, Century Casinos received an initial payment of $80,000 and would be compensated upon approval of a gaming license, at groundbreaking, and when the casino began operations.

International Expansion During the Late 1990s

Finding the U.S. gaming market to be more difficult to navigate than anticipated, Century Casinos' management decided to pursue gaming opportunities internationally. To provide a financial foundation, Century Casinos expanded its share of the Cripple Creek gaming market with the July 1996 acquisition of Womacks Saloon and Gaming Parlor. The $13.5 million price included $3 million in assumed debt and $5.2 million in seller financing, with the balance paid in cash. The company preserved the Womacks name and folded the Legends casino into it. After interior remodeling to link the adjacent properties and the addition of new gaming devices, Womacks became the second largest casino in Cripple Creek, with nearly 600 gaming devices.

Marketing for the property included the Gold Club, a player tracking system that provided members with special offers on food and merchandise, as well as cash for gaming, based on previous game play. Century Casinos sought wide exposure through Western Pacific Airlines logojet program. The Womacks logo was painted on a jet serving 18 cities in the western United States from Colorado Springs. The company

Key Dates:

1994: Through a merger with Alpine Gaming, Century Casinos becomes a public company and acquires a casino in Cripple Creek, Colorado.
1996: The acquisition of Womacks Casino expands the company's presence in Cripple Creek.
1999: Casino Millennium opens in Prague, Czech Republic; Caledon Casino, Hotel & Spa opens near Capetown, South Africa.
2000: Casino concession contracts renewed for operation on Silversea ultra-luxury cruise ships.
2002: Casino concession opens with the inaugural voyage of *The World of ResidenSea*, a cruise vessel of luxury home residences.

cosponsored Ramblin' Express buses with hourly departures from Colorado Springs to Cripple Creek.

The Womacks acquisition impacted Century Casinos' revenues significantly as the company increased its market share from 4.3 percent to 17.3 percent in Cripple Creek. In 1995, the company generated $4.2 million in net operating revenue from gaming, food and beverage sales, and hotel accommodations, less promotional allowances. In 1996, Century Casinos reported $11.5 million in net operating revenue with the addition of Womacks. In 1997, after one full year of ownership in Womacks, revenues reached $19.6 million with a net loss of $543,000. In its efforts to build a financial base for expansion, the company streamlined operations at Womacks for improved cost and operating efficiency.

With Womacks as a strategic stronghold and a reserve of funds from the company's previous projects, Century Casinos sought international gaming opportunities. The company negotiated an early settlement with the Soboba Indians in 1998, receiving a final payment of $500,000 on the $2.5 million debt. When Switzerland County Development obtained a gaming license in September 1998, Century Casinos received a payment of $431,000. With groundbreaking in 1999, Century Casinos received an additional $1 million. Switzerland County Development made a final lump sum payment of $1.4 million in January 2000 when the riverboat casino opened.

Through several different partnerships, Century Casinos pursued gaming development and management opportunities in South Africa, in British Columbia, Canada, and in Prague, Czech Republic. One of the risks in Century Casinos' search for gaming opportunities involved the government licensure processes, with gaming commissions closely scrutinizing the companies offering proposals to operate casinos. In searching for casino management opportunities, Century Casinos found that the small size of the company to be a hindrance. In May 1998, this factor contributed to the failure of a consortium to obtain a gaming license in the South African province of Gauteng. The company spent $500,000 in pursuing the deal. A subsequent joint venture continued to pursue gaming opportunities in Gauteng.

Century Casinos succeeded in winning a gaming license for Casino Millennium, in central Prague, in March 1999. Located adjacent to the five-star Marriott Hotel and connected to a complex of offices, retail shops, restaurants, and other entertainment, Casino Millennium was expected to become the premier entertainment facility in Prague. Century Casinos held a 49 percent ownership interest in the project, jointly owned with B.H Centrum, a subsidiary of Bau Holdings AG, a major European construction company. An exclusive 20-year service agreement provided Century Casinos with a fee based on gross revenues and a gaming equipment lease with pay based on a percentage of net profit. The casino opened in July 1999 with 15 gaming tables, 70 gaming machines, and a VIP gaming area.

In April 2000, a Century Casinos joint venture obtained a gaming license for operations in Caledon, South Africa, the only license for the Overberg region and one of five in the province of Western Cape. Construction began immediately on the property, located near popular tourist areas along the coast east of Cape Town. By September, the main structure was completed and celebrated according to local tradition with a ''roof-wetting'' ceremony. The Caledon Casino, Hotel & Spa opened in October, offering 14 game tables and 250 slot machines. With a 50 percent ownership in the property, Century Casinos signed a ten-year management agreement with its local partner, Fortes-King Hospitality.

By December, the company completed construction on conference and meeting facilities and refurbishment of a hotel on the property, providing 92 rooms, including six luxury suites. Construction continued on facilities at the property's natural hot mineral springs. At this time Century Casinos acquired an additional 15 percent ownership in the property. While initial attendance at the casino exceeded expectations, the December 2001 opening of another casino closer to Capetown proved to be strong competition for the Caledon casino. Future prospects for the property include a golf course, residential and timeshare units, and other facilities.

Century Casinos continued to implement its long-term strategy of improvement at Womacks Casino in Cripple Creek. Providing ample parking in proximity to the property became a competitive issue which the company addressed through the strategic lease or purchase of open lots. Efforts to attract gamblers were successful as Womacks won several local awards from the *Mountain Jackpot* in November 1999. Among other accolades, Womacks won first place in the Reader's Choice Awards for ''Best Large Casino'' and ''Casino with the Best New Games.'' In 1999, the company reported an average win per day of $103 in contrast to the Cripple Creek average of $81 per day. That year, Womacks generated $22.7 million in net operating revenue, a 19.4 percent increase over 1998.

As part of the company's long-term strategic plan, Century Casinos began to develop a 500-seat events center adjacent to Womacks. Century Casinos and the City of Cripple Creek hoped to attract new clients through entertainment and special events and by offering the space for conventions and meetings. The city would operate and market the center. Century Casinos relocated its offices to the new facility, freeing space at Womack for hotel rooms, food and beverage operations, and additional gaming. Womacks Events Center celebrated is grand opening in September 2000 with the presentation of the Cripple

Creek Film Festival. Featuring 33 independent films, this event was attended by producers, directors, and film celebrities.

Building on Previous Successes in the Early 2000s

After a hiatus in which an affiliate of Silversea Cruises handled shipboard casino concessions, Century Casinos returned to the sea with a new casino concession agreement with Silversea. The five-year agreement covered the *Silver Cloud* and the *Silver Wind* as well as two new six-star, luxury vessels for a total of 160 gaming positions. The inaugural voyage of the *Silver Shadow* took place in September 2000, and the original two ships sailed in October and November, respectively. The *Silver Whisper* began sailing in June 2001. Passenger traffic declined after the September 11, 2001 terrorist attacks on the World Trade Center and Pentagon, however, leading Silversea to suspend service on the *Silver Wind* in October 2001.

In August 2000, Century Casinos signed a casino concession agreement with *The World of ResidenSea,* the first luxury resort residences aboard an ocean-going vessel. The ship offered 110 residences, from 1,000 square feet to 3,200 square feet, as well as 88 guest suites, with purchase prices starting at $2 million. The five-year agreement involved provision of gaming equipment and casino management while the ship traveled around the world year round with an emphasis on warm climates. *The World of ResidenSea* launched from Oslo, Norway, in March 2002, carrying a 40-position game room operated by Century Casinos.

Century Casinos continued to pursue international opportunities. In November 2001, the company joined a consortium to seek a gaming license in the beach resort town of Punta del Este, Uruguay. The consortium included Inter-Continental Hotels & Resorts. The project involved a resort, a convention center, and a casino with over 1,000 gaming positions. Century Casinos sought to acquire a 50 percent ownership stake in Casino Millennium, pending government approval. The company purchased a 50 percent stake in Rhino Resort Limited in September 2001 as it continued to pursue a gaming license for Gauteng Province, near Johannesburg. Rhino Resort was granted a gaming license for the $40 million project, but in February 2002 another Gauteng gaming company, Tsogo Sun Holdings, appealed to the gaming authorities to revoke license. The courts overturned the licensure the following September.

Century Casinos' long-term development strategy for Cripple Creek progressed in 2001 and 2002. In early 2001, the company transformed the second floor of Womacks into ten luxury hotel rooms, completing construction in July for a total of 18 hotel rooms. The loss of gaming space was regained through a $2.5 million expansion project. Construction began in

March 2002, adding 3,000 square feet to the casino for an overall increase in gaming space as the company added 60 new slot machines. Another 3,000 square feet provided space for back-of-the-house functions. Womacks benefited from a general increase in visitors to Cripple Creek as people chose shorter vacations closer to home in a soft economy. Future plans under consideration included the addition of 200 hotel rooms and 400 covered parking spaces.

In April 2002, Century Casinos purchased for $1.2 million the Palace Casino, an 8,500-square-foot property located across the street from Womacks. Century Casinos planned to maintain a gaming operation in the historic portion of the building, approximately 5,000 square feet, and to demolish the remaining part of the building to provide parking.

Principal Subsidiaries

Century Casinos Africa (Pty.) Ltd. (94.8%); Century Casinos Management, Inc.; Century Management u. Beteiligungs GmbH; WMCK-Venture Corporation.

Principal Competitors

Blackhawk Gaming, Inc.; Trans World Corporation.

Further Reading

"Alpine Gaming Announces Off-Track Betting," *PR Newswire*, December 15, 1993.

"Alpine Gaming to Purchase Nevada Property; Company negotiates Sale of Terp's Casino in Colorado," *PR Newswire*, June 1, 1994.

Day, Janet, "2 Casino Operators in 2 Towns Merge," *Denver Post*, December 28, 1993, p. C1.

Fletcher, Amy, "Casino Developer Plans Colorado Site Based on European Convention," *Colorado Springs Gazette*, February 14, 2000.

Heilman, Wayne, "Cripple Creek casino plans $1.53 million public stock sale," *Colorado Springs Gazette*, August 28, 1993, p. B17.

——, "Century Casinos Headquarters Leaving Denver for Colorado Springs, Colo.," *Knight Ridder/Tribune Business News*, August 23, 1996.

"Hilton Gaming Corp. and Boomtown Inc. Acquire Pinnacle Gaming Development Corp from Century Casinos Inc.," *Business Wire*, December 28, 1995.

Nesbitt, Sara, "Gambling Hotel in Cripple Creek, Colo., Plans Expansion," *Colorado Springs Gazette*, March 19, 2002.

Robinson, Robin, "Gaming Companies Expand Beyond Colo.," *Denver Post*, April 3, 1994, p. H1.

Steers, Stuart, "Century Brings European Flair to Hot U.S. Gambling Business," *Denver Business Journal*, May 20, 1994, p. 6A.

"Womacks Casino Takes to the Air," *PR Newswire*, January 22, 1997.

—Mary Tradii

Chancellor Beacon Academies, Inc.

3520 Mary Street, Suite 202
Coconut Grove, Florida 33133
U.S.A.
Telephone: (305) 648-5950
Toll Free: (800) 239-7510
Fax: (305) 648-5951
Web site: http://www.chancellorbeacon.com

Private Company
Employees: not available
Incorporated: 2000
Sales: $100 million (2001 est.)
NAIC: 611110 Elementary and Secondary Schools

Formed when Chancellor Academies and Beacon Education Management LLC merged in 2001, Chancellor Beacon Academies, Inc., is the second largest education management company in the United States. Through its 80 public charter schools and tuition-based private schools in eight states and Washington, D.C., Chancellor Beacon Academies serves more than 19,000 students from pre-kindergarten to twelfth grade. Like other players in the emerging education management industry, Chancellor Beacon has yet to turn a profit, though its hopes for the future remain undiminished.

Education Reform in the late 1980s

Chancellor Beacon Academies owes its existence to educational reform movements that began in the late 1980s. At that time, parents, students, teachers, and politicians were seized by the fear that the traditional public education system in the United States was failing. Standardized test scores were plummeting for students of all ages, and the ranking of American students compared to those of other nationalities was dropping. U.S. companies complained in newspaper editorials that job applicants emerging from the public school system were unable to read, write, or do basic arithmetic. Parents started to doubt whether American public schools were actually educating their children.

Demographic trends and budget problems fueled these concerns. Enrollment in public schools grew unexpectedly during the late 1980s and into the 1990s, driven in large part by the combination of higher than predicted birthrates and increased immigration. Class sizes seemed to expand every year, and the economic recession that hit the United States in the early 1990s made it difficult for schools to secure the funding needed to alleviate the crunch. Some schools, particularly those in lower-income urban areas, literally began to crumble before parents' eyes.

To compound matters, public schools came to be perceived as places of unchecked violence. Accounts of weapons, gangs, and drugs in public schools were all too common, and teachers and administrators seemed unable to stem the rising tide of dysfunction. In their quest to find solutions to the problems in their children's schools, parents often ran up against a tangled education bureaucracy that seemed to stymie innovation and change. Teachers' unions, some parents felt, protected incompetent teachers and rewarded educators for their seniority rather than their pedagogical skills.

From this stew of dissatisfaction emerged the idea for charter schools. Charter schools are publicly funded and regulated schools that exist outside the bureaucratic control of public school districts. While charter schools have to follow district safety and anti-discrimination codes, they are free to experiment with curricula, class sizes, dress codes, and other policies and programs that regular public schools cannot. The schools derive their name from the charter, or contract, made with a school district or state agency, which authorizes individuals or groups to launch a school. For parents, charter schools represented a chance to wrest control from often unresponsive and distant school bureaucracies and to implement approaches that made sense for a local neighborhood. As one parent advocate told the *Orlando Sentinel*, "We have to go back to neighborhoods being in control of their schools."

In 1990, Minnesota became the first state to enact legislation allowing charter schools. The first charter school opened its doors there in 1991, and the movement quickly flourished. By 1994, there were more than 100 charter schools across the United States, and the number of states accepting charter schools grew each year, encompassing states as diverse as Pennsylvania, Massachusetts, and North Carolina.

Company Perspectives:

At Chancellor Beacon Academies, we believe parents should decide where their children attend school and play an active role in their education. Most of all, we believe that parents should make the best decision for their child. Finally, you can choose a school that will give your child the personal attention every child needs. At Chancellor Beacon, all teachers are nationally recruited and share our vision of nurturing the whole child. And their performance, as well as that of the students, is continuously evaluated to ensure that each child achieves his or her personal best. Chancellor Schools offer: smaller classes for more personal attention; more teacher involvement to create a friendly, secure environment; computers and advanced technological support in every classroom; and a proprietary, comprehensive curriculum that integrates best teaching practices.

A Business Niche Is Discovered: Early 1990s

Astute observers of the changes that the charter school movement were effecting in the field of public education recognized that a potential for profit existed in school reform. While parents, teachers, and community groups might be excited and eager to launch charter schools, they had little or no experience in actually running a school. Therefore, they would need help raising funds for the actual building of new charter schools. They would need assistance hiring teachers and staff, creating curricula, managing expenses, buying textbooks, and providing school lunches. Companies that could provide these services economically and efficiently stood to reap significant gains.

Bill DeLoache and John Eason were among those excited by this prospect. Although the duo had little background in education, they recognized that the charter school movement could offer private companies access to a tremendous wellspring of public funds—the education market was estimated to be worth roughly $300 billion at this time. Although some public schools had turned to private companies on a small scale in the past, such as contracting out for janitor services, the charter school movement offered private companies an unprecedented opportunity to get into the nuts and bolts of running a public school.

With just an inkling of the changes that were to come, DeLoache and Eason founded Alternative Public Schools, Inc. (APS) in Nashville, Tennessee, in 1991, using a $2.5 million investment from a California banker as start-up capital. These self-proclaimed "citizens with a hobby" were investment counselors—not teachers or administrators. "We came at it from a business person's perspective," DeLoache told *The Nation.* "Charter laws started passing. The market was opening up." The company proposed to manage a charter school in exchange for a flat fee, which the charter school would pay out of the per-student allotment it obtained from either the state agency or local school board responsible for school funding.

APS made its first bid to run a charter school in Tennessee in 1992, but it was not until 1995 that the company actually won a contract. That year, APS inked a five-year deal with the Wilkinsburg, Pennsylvania, school board to run Turner Elementary School, an existing public school that was in the process of changing its status to a charter school. APS took total control of the school, even to the point of ousting the unionized teaching force and replacing them with its own teachers. The company received a good deal of publicity—both favorable and unfavorable—because Turner was the first public school in the nation to be operated by a for-profit company with its own teaching staff.

Alternative Public Schools Grows: Mid- to Late 1990s

Once it entered the education management sector with its contract at Turner, APS grew rapidly, buoyed by the growth of the charter school movement as a whole. (By January of 1996, 19 states had passed charter school legislation.) As *The Nation* noted, in three years APS "went from being a couple of guys looking for a school to a major force in the for-profit education industry." By early 1997, APS was managing three charter schools in Massachusetts, North Carolina, and Pennsylvania and had six other contracts in the works. The company touted its longer school year (212 days rather than the 180 day standard public school calendar), extensive day programs, and integrated curriculum.

A driving force in the growth of APS was Michael B. Ronan, who joined the company in December of 1996 as vice-president of school administration. Ronan lent the young company credibility. As the superintendent of the Uxbridge, Massachusetts, school district for 15 years, Ronan had the educational pedigree that DeLoache and Eason lacked. Even more significantly, Ronan had earned his reputation by "turning the Uxbridge school district into a national model for cost-efficient education," according to the *Worcester Telegram & Gazette.* Ronan quickly became the chief operating officer at APS.

With Ronan's guidance, APS slightly shifted its strategy for attracting new school clients. Rather than wait for a charter school to be established—and then go to the governing board to pitch APS's expertise—APS began directly to lobby parent groups to form charter schools (either by establishing a new school or by converting an existing public school to charter status). In 1997, for example, APS shepherded a parents group through the process of converting the Washington, D.C., Richardson Elementary School to a charter school. The company "help[ed] parents get organized," said the *Washington Times.* "In return, it proposes to manage school finances for a fee if the charter is approved."

As APS continued to add to its roster of schools, the company hit an obstacle involving its first client, Turner Elementary. In August of 1997, a judge declared that the privatization of the school (and the subsequent firing of its union staff) was illegal, and decreed that the 1997–98 school year would be the last in which the school was run by APS. Around the same time, an independent evaluating agency concluded that Turner's privatization had had a negative impact on students. According to the *Pittsburgh Post-Gazette,* the study found that students had declined academically on APS's watch.

APS took these developments in stride and, in 1997, moved its headquarters from Tennessee to Westboro, Massachusetts, and changed its name to Beacon Education Management LLC

Key Dates:

1990: Minnesota passes the first charter school legislation in the United States.

1993: Bill DeLoache and John Eason found Alternative Public Schools.

1994: Alternative Public Schools wins its first contract to manage a school.

1997: Alternative Public Schools changes its name to Beacon Education Management; Michael Ronan joins the company.

1999: Octavio Visiedo, Alan Olkes, John J-H Kim, and Kevin Hall form Chancellor Academies.

2000: Chancellor opens its first independent school (The Day School at Coral Springs) and enters the mid-Atlantic region by purchasing Fairfax-Brewster School in Virginia.

2001: Beacon Schools and Chancellor Academies merge to form Chancellor Beacon Academies; President Bush dedicates $375 million in his federal budget for charter schools.

(BEM) to reflect the firm's "expanded mission." And expand the company they did. By the close of 1999, BEM operated 25 charter schools in five states, and served more than 4,500 students. BEM's growth reflected the fortunes of the school management sector as a whole. The number of charter schools grew astronomically through the late 1990s, and many of these schools then turned to for-profit companies for help. Reflecting the flourishing state of the industry, BEM's largest competitor, Edison Schools, made a heavily promoted and well-received initial public offering (IPO) of stock in 1999.

Problems with Profitability

Despite the industry's rapid growth, there was a nagging concern about the education management sector: profitability. Through the turn of the millennium, no education management company—including Beacon—had turned a profit. In 2000, BEM had $27 million in revenue but reported a $6 million loss. The company remained optimistic, though. "We can break even with just 30 schools," Michael Ronan told *Business Week*, a goal the company expected to achieve within two years. The reality, however, was that BEM and its counterparts were in a capital-intensive industry, which posed significant fiscal challenges. New charter schools typically required new buildings, and state funds usually did not cover building expenses. Even existing public schools that were simply converting to charter status often still needed extra cash to operate facilities and buy equipment. As a result, BEM was frequently forced to loan its clients money for infrastructure and other projects. *Dow Jones News Service* noted that in 2000, BEM had extended almost $6 million in loans to 13 of its schools (nearly the exact amount of the company's net loss for the year). *Dow Jones* explained the logic behind this business strategy: "The schools are fledgling enterprises, in need of extra money. . . . [The loans] are almost necessary investments to ensure that the schools ultimately prosper and are in a position to more reliably pay the management fees Beacon relies on for its revenues."

BEM's solution to this conundrum was to seek additional operating capital. In 1999, venture capitalist William R. Hambrecht invested $6 million in the company; the following year, KinderCare announced an initial investment of $5.2 million. But even these infusions were insufficient to meet BEM's needs. Consequently, in May 2001 BEM announced plans to follow in Edison's footsteps and become a public company with an initial offering of $33 million in stock. BEM planned to use the proceeds from the sale to pay off loans and generate working capital. But the company cautioned in its pre-IPO Securities and Exchange Commission filing that "We have not yet demonstrated that public schools can be profitably managed by private companies, and we are not certain when we will become profitable." Furthermore, the bursting of the economic bubble of the late 1990s, along with the general downturn that began in the spring of 2001, made the investing climate much less hospitable to stock offerings from companies with uncertain prospects for profitability. In August 2002, BEM put off its IPO plans, citing poor market conditions.

Chancellor Academies Is Founded in 1999

Unlike BEM, Chancellor Beacon Academies' other progenitor, Chancellor Academies, was a relative newcomer to the industry. Backed by $35 million in venture capital supplied by Warburg Pincus, Chancellor Academies was founded in 1999 by a team of education insiders led by Octavio Visiedo, the former superintendent of Florida's Miami-Dade school district. Chancellor's selling point was its curriculum, which incorporated what was termed an "integrated" approach to education. "No one subject is taught in isolation," a company spokesperson explained to the *Boston Globe*. "They all overlap, so that kids understand how everything in life is integrated and not exclusive." Departing from the approach pioneered by BEM, Chancellor chose not to lengthen the school day or the school year, promising instead a "standards-based" approach to improve pupil performance. It most popular pledge with parents, though, was Chancellor's commitment to smaller class sizes of no more than 25 students.

With sleek new buildings, which often included high-tech computer labs, Chancellor schools seemed a far cry from regular public schools. Although capital intensive, this approach proved a wonderful marketing tool for the company. "It just looks like a private school," one parent gushed to the *South Florida Sun-Sentinel* about a Chancellor school. Indeed, what drew many parents to transfer their children to an untried and untested privately run public school involved this sort of nebulous perception rather than a specific attribute of the charter school itself. Visiedo's own assessment of the value of charter schools was candid: "The school districts are saying, 'Maybe you can do better.' The parents feel it can't get much worse."

The formula worked well for Chancellor, particularly in its home state. Charter schools had received an enthusiastic endorsement from Florida Governor Jeb Bush, who himself had once worked for an education management company. Governor Bush sought to increase public funding for charter schools. By October 2001, Chancellor was running 11 public schools in Florida, as well as eight public schools in Arizona and one in Washington, D.C. Chancellor also launched two purely private schools (collecting tuition directly from parents rather than via public funding) in Florida and Virginia.

The company followed a cluster growth strategy by concentrating on adding schools in pre-determined geographic areas, particularly Florida and Arizona. In rapidly growing states such as these, capital budgets were strained, fraying the public education system and making the concept of charter schools even more popular.

Chancellor and Beacon Join Forces: Early 2000s

Like BEM, Chancellor grew at a ferocious pace yet had not reported a profit. Both companies recognized that their best chances for profitability involved following the lead of several of their competitors (including the industry leader, Edison)—merging with another education management company. In January 2001, BEM and Chancellor agreed to join forces. "In this industry, we don't pretend that our goal is to be the absolute largest," Visiedo told *Education Week*. "But you do have to have a certain scale." The new company, named Chancellor Beacon Academies, became the second-largest education management company in the country. With its combined resources, Chancellor Beacon served 19,000 student in 81 schools.

A few weeks after Chancellor Beacon was formed, the company received a great deal of attention by playing a part in the largest school privatization in U.S. history. The public schools in Philadelphia, Pennsylvania, had long been plagued by academic and financial woes, with 75 percent of Philadelphia's students unable to meet state academic standards. Frustrated with the district's long-standing inability to show improvements, the state took control of the school district. Led by Republican Governor Tom Ridge, the state decided to turn 70 of the district's schools over to private companies in a move the *Philadelphia Daily News* called "a tremendous endorsement for the industry." Chancellor Beacon made a bid and won a contract to manage five Philadelphia schools. Despite being beset by financial problems of its own, Edison, the nation's largest school management company, was tapped to run the bulk of the schools.

Chancellor Beacon was optimistic about its future prospects. With charter schools in Arizona, Florida, Massachusetts, Maine, Michigan, Missouri, New York, North Carolina, Virginia, and Washington, D.C., Chancellor Beacon retained a secure grasp on its position as the second largest education management company in America. Despite 2002's economic downturn, the company anticipated having its first break-even year in 2003. Moreover, although the young industry continued to evolve, public schools run by for-profit companies appeared to have made themselves a permanent feature of the American educational landscape. Even though no study had ever demonstrated that privately run charter schools were even slightly better than traditional public schools at improving their students' academic performance, President Bush made funds for charter schools the centerpiece of his 2002 education budget. Industry analysts believed the charter school movement, and the private operators who had staked their fortunes on it, were just beginning to flourish. The education management industry expected to see revenues in excess of $1 billion by 2004.

Principal Competitors

Edison Schools Inc.; National Heritage Academies, Inc.; Nobel Learning Communities Inc.

Further Reading

Berry, Mike, "11 Charter Schools Proposed," *Orlando Sentinel*, October 15, 2000.

Chute, Eleanor, "Turner Initiative a Failure, Independent Report Says," *Pittsburgh Post Gazette*, May 14, 1999.

Greenberger, Scott, "For-Profit Firm Proposes New Charter Schools for Massachusetts," *Boston Globe*, October 14, 2001.

Hennessey, Raymond, "Going Public: With Beacon, Customers are Debtors," *Dow Jones News Service*, July 26, 2001.

Mandel, Michael, Richard Melcher, and Doris Jones Yang, "Will Schools Ever Get Better," *Business Week*, April 17, 1995.

O'Connor, Lona, "Luck of the Draw in Weston Fills Up New Charter School," *South Florida Sun-Sentinel*, May 17, 2001.

"Philadelphia Schools To Share $55 Million in Funding," *Philadelphia Daily News*, August 1, 2002.

"Ronan's Move," *Worcester Telegram & Gazette*, December 28, 1996.

Spellman, Karyn, "Parents See Hope in Charter Bid," *Washington Times*, June 9, 1997.

Symonds, William, Ann Therese Palmer, and Dave Lindorff, "For-Profit Schools," *Business Week*. February 7, 2000.

Vine, Phyllis, "To Market, To Market . . . The School Business Sells Kids Short," *Nation*, September 8, 1997.

Walsh, Mark, "School Managers Chancellor and Beacon Merge," *Education Week*, January 16, 2002.

—Rebecca Stanfel

CHIASSO⊙

Chiasso Inc.

1500 West Cortland Street
Chicago, Illinois 60622
U.S.A.
Telephone: (773) 342-7900
Fax: (773) 342-5490
Web site: http://www.chiasso.com

Private Company
Incorporated: 1985
Employees: 200
Sales: $20 million (2001 est.)
NAIC: 442110 Furniture Stores; 442299 All Other Home
  Furnishing Stores

Chiasso Inc. is a Chicago-based leading retailer of specialty housewares, toys, barware, bath, kitchen, and office accessories, lighting, and furniture with stores across the United States. Operating through a multichannel approach, the company has stores in upscale malls, as well as sales through catalog and Web site marketing. Chiasso distinguishes itself by offering an eclectic mix of avant-garde products that are often designed by well-known modern artists and architects. From its inception, Chiasso, which is an Italian slang expression that loosely translates as "to cause an uproar or sensation," has based its retail philosophy on creating a fun, amusing, and innovative shopping experience. A spirited twist on renowned Chicago architect Louis Sullivan's maxim that "form follows function," the company's motto "formfunctionfun" drives Chiasso's efforts to continue to offer its customers modern, design driven merchandise for the home and office.

Mid-1980s: Quirky Merchandising Sparks Success

Inspired by the gift store at the Museum of Modern Art in New York City, Keven Wilder and her husband Nicholas Wilder decided to go into business on their own. A former lawyer who worked in the cable TV and public television industries, Keven utilized her interest in art to set the tone for the innovative design of their first retail shop, while Nicholas added expertise as a designer and real estate developer. In 1985,

the couple opened Chiasso, an upscale boutique on Chestnut Street in Chicago's trendy Gold Coast neighborhood with a start-up cost of $500,000. The concept of their store was built on the notion of marketing home and office accessories that were both functional and highly appealing aesthetically.

The name Chiasso provided a touchstone for the company philosophy as well. According to the company's Web site, Chiasso, pronounced key-ah-so, is a town on the Italian/Swiss border where famed Italian designer Ettore Sottsass' Memphis Design Group first gathered. It also means "to cause an uproar or sensation" in Italian. Many commentators have noted that the name well suits the whimsical quality of the store design as well as the playful mix of merchandise that included and continues to carry products from leading architects and industrial designers such as Michael Graves and Aldo Rossi.

The first Chiasso store was designed by Paul Florian and Stephen Wierzbowski, who played off the company name to create a sense of disorder amid deceptively ordered design concepts. Described by Jerry Cooper in *Interior Design* in 1986, the 1,400-square-foot basement space was "a three-dimensional metaphor that merrily juxtaposes formal and hip, geometric and organic, serious and—well, just plain daffy. Despite all that, however, the scheme also adheres to time-tested principles considered essential to retail design." The store also distinguished itself in design with fixtures created by Ettore Sottsass. The playful aspect of the store soon caught on because customers were treated to the high-quality merchandise of design shops without the stuffy high-art feel. The store displays utilized a successful merchandising approach that encouraged customers to touch the product.

Growing the Business

Wilder also launched a catalog in the mid-1980s. As with the retail shop, Chiasso catalog invited the customer to have fun. Keven emphasized the importance of play, even for adults, and the need to supply an adult toy that, while it may be functional, nevertheless encouraged play and inspired creative energy. Chiasso began to open new, high-design concept stores in malls. Keven's eye for design, eclectic buying savvy, and fresh

Company Perspectives:

Over the years, "What are you?" has been the question we've been asked the most. It's a simple question, but we've yet to come up with a simple short answer. We can tell you this much however, the thread, or essence, that weaves its way through Chiasso is "inspired design for the home." We sell products that look great (design), work well (quality), and lift the spirit (fun). This blend of quality, design and fun combined with a dash of sophistication creates the uniqueness that is Chiasso.

Key Dates:

1985: Keven Wilder and husband Nicholas Wilder open first Chiasso store in Chicago's Gold Coast district.

1996: Company moves flagship store to Water Tower Place on Michigan Avenue; David Marshall joins company as chief executive officer.

1997: Keven sells company to Marshall and investors at Holden Capital Advisors LLC.

1998: Chiasso revamps prototype for store units, maintaining playful style at "value engineering" costs.

1999: Catalog is redesigned with much greater circulation; company introduces Internet sales with its own Web site.

2000: Chiasso increases store floor space and adds furniture and dinnerware to merchandise offerings.

approach to merchandising helped generate record mall sales per square foot, as well as several awards. The company also grabbed national media focus when Chiasso was featured on television's "Oprah Winfrey Show."

In 1996, Chiasso moved its flagship store to Chicago's Magnificent Mile in the Water Tower Place, closing its Gold Coast store. Chiasso achieved remarkable success in its new location, topping $1 million in sales in its first year and accounted for almost 8 percent of Water Tower store revenues. With an affordable price point ranging from $15 to $138, the company managed to meet $700 in sales per square foot, as compared to the industry average of $278. The challenge at this stage in the company's development was to continue to grow and still maintain its unique identity.

David Marshall joined Chiasso in 1996 as chief executive officer, working with Keven to expand into more markets and bolster its staff to include more managers and buyers. In 1997, Marshall and a group of investors from Holden Capital Advisors LLC purchased Chiasso from founder Keven Wilder. Initially, Marshall worked to close the existing stores in high-rent locations and open new stores in upscale malls. New store locations were chosen based on catalog sales. However, with the increasing success of Chiasso stores, the company was being wooed by several large mall developers. Marshall was cautious of accepting any offer and expanding too quickly, though he had managed to raise $3.6 million in venture capital.

On the verge of a national rollout, Chiasso revamped the prototype for their retail store. The Chicago firm of Bailey Edward Design was contracted to "value engineer" a new prototype to open in Troy, Michigan, in 1997. While still maintaining the playful, high-style design of the original, Bailey Edward brought down construction costs by 31 percent by using more cost-effective goods and reengineering construction details in lighting and fixtures. By the end of 1997, Chiasso had stores in Chicago, Boston, Detroit, and New York regions, as well as plans to open stores in Palo Alto and Dallas. The new prototype became the standard for stores opening in the late 1990s.

Late 1990s: Multichannel Sales

With sales at $5.5 million in 1998, the national expansion plan included 11 store locations in 1999 with plans to open four to eight more in 2000. By 1999, the company was ready to expand its catalog business as well. In 1998, Chiasso had mailed its catalog to 100,000 established customers, but the company

bought prospective customer lists in 1999 and mailed 750,000 catalogs. The catalog was redesigned by the consultancy firm of Muldoon & Baer to go from a seven- by seven-inch format to a nine- by nine-and-a-half-inch format. The larger catalog size allowed for more photos and also increased the selection of goods. In 2000, Chiasso mailed one million catalogs, and in 2001, the company distributed 3.6 million. By 2001 the changes and expansion to the catalog were expected to achieve catalog sales of more than $5.5 million. Additionally, Chiasso also began to seek Internet sales when it launched its Web site in September 1999 after a $700,000 investment. Internet and catalog sales were 30 percent of total company sales in 2000, with projected Internet and catalog sales set at 40 percent to 50 percent in 2001. In 2000, combined catalog and Internet sales reached $3.7 million. By 2001, sales from the Internet alone were expected to reach $1.8 million.

When discount stores like Target began selling less expensive goods with the same Chiasso flair, the company continued to focus on staying ahead of trends. Another important aspect of the company's plan centered on continuing to achieve growth in all three of its sales distribution categories. With combined distribution in store, catalog, and Internet, projected sales for 1999 were expected to be just below $10 million.

In 2000, Chiasso had 14 stores in malls across the United States. The company had raised $3 million through Holden Capital to finance further expansion of its catalog and Internet operations. It also planned to open a new prototype store in the fall. This new model would be bigger than the existing 1,200-square-foot store. While the company had always done well—even exceeded expectations—in its small stores, space was extremely limited to hold between 650 and 800 SKUs. The expanded prototype utilized 2,500 square feet of floor space. With a larger amount of selling space, the company also turned to offering furniture and dinnerware that maintained the same whimsical and modern style of its home and office accessory selection. Following the addition of furniture, Marshall noted in *HFN,* "I read where Gordon Segal once said that when Crate & Barrel added furniture, accessory sales went up, and we're finding that to be true." Another added outlet for sales were kiosks in every store and the launch of a bridal registry.

Within Marshall's first five years at the helm, Chiasso had increased sales from $1.4 million to $21 million in 2001. Although this represented impressive growth, Chiasso had yet to show strong profitability. Marshall initiated cost-cutting measures to bring down salary, rent, and travel expenses as a means toward higher profitability in 2002.

At the beginning of the 21st century, long range plans for the company included expanding their brick and mortar operations to 75 units through a conservative rollout of stores in premier malls on a yearly basis. Still placing importance on their stores, Marshall noted in *HFN,* "The Web and our catalog are our biggest areas of growth. We exist to be multichannel."

Principal Competitors

Euromarket Designs Inc. (Crate & Barrel); Williams-Sonoma Inc. (Pottery Barn); Sharper Image Corporation.

Further Reading

Baeb, Eddie, "Offbeat Boutique Sets Sights on Main Street: But Funding Is Key to Chiasso's Vision," *Crain's Chicago Business,* August 30, 1999, p. 4.

Balu, Rekha, "How Chiasso Masters Fine Art of Retailing," *Crain's Chicago Business,* August 4, 1997, p. 3.

"Chiasso Inc.," *Entrepreneur.com,* October 22, 2001.

"Chiasso: Raises Cash for Expansion," *Crain's Chicago Business,* May 1, 2000, p. 1.

Cooper, Jerry, "Chicago Architects Florian-Wierzbowski Combine Order and Disorder for a Contemporary Housewares Shop," *Interior Design,* May 1986, p. 268.

Knapp, Pat Matson, "Art with an Attitude," *Shopping Center World,* January 2002, p. 8.

Markoutsas, Elaine, "Grown-Up Toys," *Times Union,* June 7, 1992, p. G1.

Miller, Paul, "Bigger Better for Chiasso," *Catalog Age,* August 2001, p. 10.

Nicksin, Carole, "Chiasso Channels Its Efforts Toward Standing Out in the Crowd," *HFN: The Weekly Newspaper for the Home Furnishing Network,* May 28, 2001, p. 7.

Wilson, Marianne, "Low-Cost, High-Style Design at Chiasso," *Chain Store Age Executive,* May 1998, p. 258.

—Elizabeth Henry

Chugoku Electric Power Company Inc.

4-33, Komachi
Naka-ku, Hiroshima 730-8701
Japan
Telephone: (082) 241 0211
Fax: (082) 523 6185
Web site: http://www.energia.co.jp

Public Company
Incorporated: 1951
Employees: 10,122
Sales: ¥1.02 trillion ($7.6 billion) (2002)
Stock Exchanges: Tokyo Osaka
Ticker Symbol: 9504
NAIC: 221110 Hydroelectric Power Generation; 221112
Fossil Fuel Electric Power Generation; 221113 Nuclear
Electric Power Generation; 221119 Other Electric
Power Generation; 221122 Electric Power Distribution

The Chugoku Electric Power Company Inc. (CEPCO) generates and supplies electricity to the Chugoku region of Japan, which covers approximately 32,000 square kilometers. The region is made up of the prefectures of Yamaguchi, Hiroshima, Shimane, Tottori, and Okayama, which with local heavy industry and a total population of 7.8 million provides the sixth largest customer base of the ten electric power companies in Japan. The company operates 93 hydroelectric power stations, 12 thermal stations, and one nuclear power station. Plans are in the works to launch several new hydroelectric and coal-fired power stations, and by 2016 the company expects to have its generating capacity balanced equally between nuclear, coal-fired, and other types of facilities. As a result of industry liberalization, CEPCO has diversified its operations and established new divisions including comprehensive energy supply, information and telecommunications, environment, and business and lifestyle support.

Early History: 1945–50s

CEPCO was incorporated along with the other eight regional electric power companies in May 1951, but the story of its

foundation goes back to the start of the Allied occupation of Japan in 1945. Japan's energy-intensive, military industrial complex, centered on the production of steel, ships, and munitions, had been destroyed, in large part, at the beginning of the occupation. Although the nuclear bomb dropped on Hiroshima in August 1945 had all but destroyed the main industrial city of the Chugoku region, and enormous damage had been caused by conventional bombing of other industrial sites in the region, Chugoku's electricity-generating facilities had survived the war relatively unscathed. The first year of the Allied occupation saw an energy surplus in the region due to the wartime depletion of industrial demand. This pattern was mirrored throughout the country. As the process of postwar reconstruction gathered pace, however, demand for electricity increased dramatically and soon exceeded supply. The General Headquarters of the Allied Powers (GHQ) feared that an expansion of electricity production under the surviving and highly centralized wartime structure of the Japan Electricity Generation and Transmission Company (JEGTCO) and the nine local distribution companies could be a step in the direction of rearmament. The wartime structure itself had played a key role in Japan's military expansion in the first place. In 1948 GHQ decided to dismantle the centralized JEGTCO structure and replace it with nine regionally based, vertically integrated electricity generation and distribution companies. After a certain amount of disagreement between GHQ and the fledgling Japanese government about the precise structure, status, and organization of the new companies, the government acted to establish the nine electric power companies by implementing the Electricity Utility Industry Reorganization Order and the Public Utilities Order. A tenth electric power company, Okinawa Electric Power, was formed by the Japanese government and the Okinawa Prefecture in 1972 after Japan regained control of the Ryukyu Islands.

On May 1, 1951 operating rights and facilities of the state-run Chugoku branch of the Japan Electricity Generation and Transmission Company and the Chugoku Electric Power Distribution Company were taken over by the newly created Chugoku Electric Power Company. Under government decree, the new company was given the task of generating and supplying electric power to the entire Chugoku district.

While the demand for electricity had already caught up with supply in the late 1940s as a result of rapid reconstruction, the

---

Company Perspectives:

The Chugoku Electric Power Co. Inc. seeks to realize inherent potential of energy, rejoices in winning its customers' trust, operates with priority placed on people, contributes to the development of the region, and constantly seeks harmony with nature.

---

manufacturing economy of Chugoku was given a further boost in the 1950s by the need for components and material support for the war raging on the Korean peninsula. The resulting surge in demand for electricity from local industry stimulated CEPCO to seek the immediate stabilization and expansion of its generating capabilities. The company turned to the United States for technical assistance toward expanding generating capacity through the construction of new coal- and oil-fired thermal power stations.

Growth Fueling Demand: 1960s

By the early 1960s the Japanese economy had entered a period of unprecedented growth, and demand for electricity in Chugoku was increasing by more than 10 percent per year. This need was fueled by industrial demand from the chemicals, metals, steel, shipbuilding, and automobile industries that were growing up along the region's southern coastal corridor. New demand also came from the rapidly expanding small business sector and from private consumers. The latter were beginning to see the fruits of Japan's rapid postwar growth as an increasing number of electric household goods came on the market. The additional electricity necessary for lighting and heating, and in the summer months for air conditioning, contributed substantially to the company's business.

The surge in demand for electric power required the progressive modernization and expansion of CEPCO's electricity generation and transmission facilities. In 1962 the company completed the 81-kilometer, 220,000-volt Chugoku-West trunk line and substations, resulting in a super-high-voltage transmission system linking the Chugoku region with Kansai to the east and Kyushu to the west. By the mid-1960s the annual rate of growth in electricity demand and production was dramatic.

From the early 1960s new generating facilities developed by CEPCO were predominantly thermal plants using imported oil and coal rather than the more traditional hydroelectric power. These included a total of five coal-fired plants commissioned at Mizushima and Shin Ube between 1958 and 1964 and oil-powered facilities opened at Kudamatsu and Iwakuni in 1964 and 1966, respectively. In terms of generating volume, hydroelectric power exceeded that of thermal electric power in 1963, but a decade later the balance had changed to 88 percent thermal, 10 percent hydroelectric, and 2 percent nuclear. This was due not only to the new availability of cheap oil from overseas as an alternative source of energy, but also to technological advancements that had brought the cost of building thermal power stations substantially below that of hydroelectric equivalents.

Oil Crises and Finding Alternative Energy Supplies: 1970s–80s

By 1971, after more than 15 years of uninterrupted growth in demand for electricity in the region accompanied by the continued availability of cheap oil, the first signs of a slowdown in CEPCO's performance began to appear. In that year the Organization of Petroleum Exporting Countries (OPEC) managed to secure the first substantial increase in the price it was charging for oil. This did not cause immediate problems for CEPCO other than necessitating a slight revision of revenue projections, though this was more than offset by continued strong demand from the industrial and domestic sectors. On the expenditure side of the company's finances, rising personnel and repair costs were starting to undermine the company's annual financial performance, though not drastically. The company's investment plans also were influenced by government regulations aimed at reducing atmospheric pollution levels, which required the installation of expensive flue gas scrubbers in thermal power stations. CEPCO responded to these changing and challenging conditions by bringing forward the completion dates for a number of its new power-generating projects. These included the company's first nuclear power plant at Shimane and two oil-burning plants at Tamashima and Iwakuni.

In early 1971, with Kansaku Yamane as president and Kimio Sakurauchi as chairman, CEPCO was anticipating further steady—and by international standards, spectacular—growth in the foreseeable future. The outbreak of war in the Middle East in mid-1973 and the subsequent quadrupling of oil prices by OPEC, however, hit Japan harder than any other country in the Organization for Economic Co-operation and Development (OECD) because of the country's heavy dependence on Middle Eastern oil. The immediate effect on CEPCO was an increase in the price of fuel for its oil-powered thermal generating plants. This resulted in financial difficulties in the short term because the company, like Japan's other electric power companies, was not free to pass on the higher fuel rates to its industrial and domestic consumers without approval from the Ministry of International Trade and Industry (MITI). In December 1973 the Japanese government introduced measures to enforce conservation of electric power, but it was not until later the following year that MITI finally consented to allowing a 60 percent electricity rate increase for CEPCO and the other electric power companies. The first sharp rise in the electricity rate for 20 years, though alleviating short-term financial pressures on the industry as a whole, failed to ultimately benefit the power companies because the price of oil continued to rise. Furthermore, as higher charges were passed on to the large energy-intensive manufacturing sector, output fell, inflation rose, and the economy moved into its first real postwar recession.

The oil price hikes that continued throughout the 1970s stimulated a major reappraisal of Japan's resource security. Even though individual power and oil companies were able to meet their requirements for oil by paying inflated prices at spot markets around the world, it soon became apparent that Japan needed to diversify its supply of energy away from the Middle East and its oil. Although a number of projects had been in the planning phase for some time, the events of 1973–74 added urgency to strategic decision-making in Tokyo and at CEPCO's head office in Hiroshima.

Key Dates:

1948: The General Headquarters of the Allied Powers creates nine regionally based electricity generation and distribution companies.

1951: CEPCO incorporates and is given the task of generating and supplying electric power to the entire Chugoku district.

1962: The company completes the Chugoku-West trunk line and substations.

1973: The Japanese government begins to enforce electric power conservation during an oil crisis; CEPCO launches a 60 percent rate increase.

1980: CEPCO is forced to raise its rates by 67 percent due to rising oil prices.

1989: The firm's second nuclear reactor, Shimane No. 2, begins operation.

1991: The company launches a new marketing slogan, ''EnerGia—With You and With the Earth.''

1995: Japan partially liberalizes its electricity market.

2000: CEPCO diversifies its holdings as the electricity industry continues to deregulate.

The commissioning in 1974 of the Shimane Boiling Water Reactor (BWR) as CEPCO's first nuclear power unit, with a capacity of 460 megawatts, contributed substantially to oil-saving measures. In 1976 the diversification policy was pursued actively through a large financial commitment toward construction of the 620-megawatt pumped-storage-type hydroelectric power complex at Nabara. Both local and national economies were recovering by 1976 and CEPCO's sales for that year increased by 21 percent over the previous year.

In spite of the strenuous efforts made by CEPCO after the first oil shock in 1973–74, by the time of the second oil crisis, following the Iranian revolution in 1979, CEPCO was still heavily dependent on imported oil for electricity generation. Its vulnerability to rising oil prices was such that in 1980 CEPCO was forced to raise its rates again, this time by 67 percent, the highest rate rise of the nine other electric power companies. In the same year, in order to accelerate the diversification policy, it was decided that three existing oil-burning power stations at Shin Ube would be converted to coal power.

In 1981 CEPCO was still dependent on oil for 52 percent of its generating capacity, the highest dependency of the nine electric power companies. To reduce further the destabilizing effects of this dependency, in 1980 plans were launched by CEPCO to import coal from China and Australia, and since 1989 liquefied natural gas has been imported from Australia.

The Three Mile Island nuclear accident in the United States in 1979 led to a suspension of nuclear plant construction plans in Japan for one year, and resulted in a general distrust of all nuclear-related matters by the Japanese population, especially in the Hiroshima region. Nevertheless, the building of Shimane No. 2 started in July 1984. The plant began operations less than five years later, in February 1989, adding a further 820 megawatts of capacity to the existing output of 460 megawatts from

the Shimane No. 1 reactor. Also in 1989, plans were completed to build a third nuclear reactor in Yamaguchi Prefecture to provide electric power for the early 21st century.

Liberalization Bringing Changes: 1990s and Beyond

In 1991 CEPCO's chairman, Kenichiro Matsutani, headed a company with a much-reduced dependency on imported oil and a generating capacity well diversified between imported LNG, coal, and oil, and locally produced hydroelectric and nuclear power. As the leader of the Chugoku business community, with a regional monopoly in the supply and distribution of electricity to domestic and industrial customers, CEPCO was now better prepared for fluctuations in the price of energy resources and demand for electricity than it had been for many years.

In fact, during fiscal 1990 the company reported an increase in sales and profits for the first time in five years. The good fortune continued into the following year, as after-tax profit climbed by 42.1 percent. During 1991, the company adopted a new environmentally friendly corporate philosophy. Its key concept included the marketing tag, ''EnerGia—With You and With the Earth.''

Meanwhile, Japan's electricity sector was beginning to change. During 1995, the Japanese government partially liberalized the industry, allowing independent power producers (IPPs) to sell electric power to the regional companies. Then in March 2000, these IPPs were allowed to market directly to customers, allowing both foreign and domestic competition in the retail electricity market.

In response to the liberalization, CEPCO began to restructure its operations to prepare for the increased competition. Three new divisions were established—Energy and Marketing Services, Power Generation, and Power System. Like the other regional power companies, the firm began to cut costs and lower prices. A November 2000 *Financial Times* article claimed that Japan's electric power concerns were also ''busily building up alternative sources of income, focusing mainly on telecommunications and activities on the fringe of their core businesses, following the example set by power companies in the deregulated markets of Europe and the U.S.''

Indeed, CEPCO entered several new markets during 2000 and 2001, including energy supply, information and telecommunications, environment, and business and lifestyle support. Energia Solution & Service Company Inc. (ESS) was established as an energy supply venture in October 2001. Mizushima LNG Company Ltd., Mizushima LNG Sales Company Ltd., and Power Engineering and Training Services Inc. also were created. In early 2002, Chugoku Information System Service Co. began offering a fixed-rate Internet connection service and EnerGia Real Estate Co. Inc. was launched.

CEPCO also expanded its core business. It had plans in motion to open several new hydroelectric and coal-fired thermal power stations and in 2000 the firm was given permission to develop the Shimane Nuclear Power Station No. 3 Unit. Construction was slated to begin in March 2003.

During this time period, Japan's economy was faltering. Demand from steel and manufacturing sectors fell, and in fiscal

2002, electricity sales fell for the first time in 15 years. Overall, company revenue fell by 2.3 percent over 2001. The firm's major cost-cutting and streamlining efforts paid off, however, and net income rose to $349.4 million—an increase of 70.8 percent over the previous year.

In order to survive in its new competitive environment, CEPCO management remained focused on strengthening its core business and developing lucrative new ventures. The company also strove to maintain a healthy corporate image and targeted environmental preservation and research and development as key points in its management philosophy. Although Japan's electricity industry was certain to experience additional change, CEPCO appeared to be on track for future success.

Principal Subsidiaries

Chuden Kogyo Co. Ltd.; Chuden Plant Co. Ltd.; Chugoku Instruments Co. Inc.; Chugoku Kigyo Co. Inc.; Chugoku Electric Mfg. Co. Ltd.; Chuden Kankyo Technos Co. Ltd.; Chugoku Information System Service Co. Inc.; Ozuki Steel Industries Co. Ltd. (80%); Chuden Engineering Consultants Co. Ltd. (80%); The Chuden Access Company Inc. (80%); Chuden Life Co. Ltd. (76.4%); Tempearl Industrial Co. Ltd. (56%); Sanko Inc. (46.7%); Fukuyama Joint Thermal Power Co. Ltd. (50%); Mizushima Joint Thermal Power Co. Ltd. (50%); Chudenko Corporation (37.4%); Chugoku Telecommunication Network Co. Inc. (34.4%); Chugoku Koatsu Concrete Industries Co. Ltd. (33.3%); EAML Engineering Company Ltd. (18%); Chuden Business Service Co. Inc.; EnerGia Real Estate Co. Inc.; Power Engineering and Training Services Inc. (80%); International Standard Management Center Inc. (66%); Energia Solution & Service Company Inc. (53%); Chugoku Health and Welfare Club Co. Inc. (50%); Mizushima LNG Company Ltd. (50%); Mizushima LNG Sales Company Ltd. (40%); Houseplus Chugoku Housing Warranty Corporation Ltd. (35.6%).

Principal Competitors

Chubu Electric Power Company Inc.; Kansai Electric Power Company Inc.; Tokyo Electric Power Company Inc.

Further Reading

"Chugoku Electric Power Boosts Sales, Profits," *Jiji Press Ticker Service,* May 28, 1991.

"Chugoku Electric Power Lifts Sales, Profit," *Jiji Press Ticker Service,* May 27, 1992.

"Chugoku Electric Power's Profit Sags," *Jiji Press Ticker Service,* May 27, 1996.

"Chugoku Enjoys Higher Earnings," *Jiji Press Ticker Service,* May 26, 1995.

Davis, Paul, Anne Hung, and Hideo Ohta Baker & McKensie, "Liberalization of Japanese Electricity Industry," *Power Economics,* May 31, 2000, p. 18.

"Deregulation Opens Power Market," *Nikkei Weekly,* April 24, 1995, p. 10.

Fukuda, Takehiro, "Electric Power Industry Posts Profit," *Nikkei Weekly,* December 14, 1991.

History of Electric Power Industry in Japan, Tokyo: Japan Electric Power Information Centre, 1988.

Hutton, Bethan, "Japan's Electricity Producers Profit from Liberalization," *Financial Times London,* November 23, 2000, p. 16.

"Japanese Govt. Panel Clears Construction of Nuclear Reactor," *AsiaPulse News,* August 22, 2000.

Thomas, Steve, and Chris Cragg, *Japan Power Station Fuel Demand to 2000,* London: Financial Times Business Information, 1986.

—Stephen Christopher Kremer
—update: Christina M. Stansell

Colonial Williamsburg Foundation

P.O. Box 1776
Williamsburg, Virginia 23187-1776
U.S.A.
Telephone: (757) 220-7286
Toll Free: (800) HIS-TORY
Fax: (757) 220-7325
Web site: http://www.colonialwilliamsburg.org

Non-Profit Company
Incorporated: 1928
Employees: 3,500
Sales: $193.8 million (2000)
NAIC: 712110 Museums; 712120 Historical Sites;
    721110 Hotels (Except Casino Hotels)and Motels;
    722110 Full-Service Restaurants

The Colonial Williamsburg Foundation operates the oldest and largest (174 acres) outdoor living history museum in the United States. With 88 original and more than 50 restored historic structures, Colonial Williamsburg is often considered the epitome of the historic preservation movement. More than a million people visit Colonial Williamsburg every year. Created in the 1920s and 1930s, Colonial Williamsburg is the ancestor of all American theme parks.

Patriotic Origins

Williamsburg, named after King William III of England, was the capital of the Virginia colony from 1699 to 1780. Its orderly streets were laid out by Royal Governor Francis Nicholson. Before Thomas Jefferson relocated the Virginia capital from Williamsburg to Richmond in 1781, he and other patriots, including George Washington and Patrick Henry, frequented its streets. Williamsburg was the cultural, social, and political center of the colonial world. It is home to the second oldest college in the United States, the College of William and Mary—Jefferson's alma mater.

The leader of the movement to restore this city to a pre-revolutionary grandeur was Reverend W.A.R. Goodwin, the rector of Williamsburg's Bruton Parish Church and religion professor at the College of William and Mary. He unsuccessfully approached Henry Ford before finding a sponsor, John D. Rockefeller, Jr. By various accounts, Williamsburg was one of his most rewarding projects. He would also leave it a $60 million endowment.

The reconstruction or "restoration" of Colonial Williamsburg began in 1926. The project was organized in 1928 as two corporations. Colonial Williamsburg, Incorporated had a historical and educational mission and owned designated historic properties. The Williamsburg Holding Company was in charge of the construction, maintenance, and management of the project. It also owned and operated commercial properties. Williamsburg Holding was renamed Williamsburg Restoration, Incorporated in 1934.

Work on the landscaping began in 1931. The restored gardens, designed by Arthur Shurcliff, inaugurated the revival, though later archeological discoveries proved them too flowery to be considered truly authentic. The holly maze in the gardens at the Governor's Palace, while lacking in historical evidence, has nevertheless proved to be enormously popular with visitors.

Colonial Williamsburg Opens in 1932

The museum opened in 1932 with about 100 employees. Six "appeals"—history, research, gardens, trades, collections, and architecture—were to attract the American public. The Raleigh Tavern also opened in 1932, its hostesses dressed in colonial clothes (they were paid between 30 and 40 cents an hour). The practice of costumed interpreters plying 18th-century crafts began in 1936 with a blacksmith hammering out horseshoes for souvenirs. Attendance steadily grew: 31,000 people visited the park in 1934; this figure more than tripled in the next two years.

Williamsburg was chosen for restoration because its downtown area had been less developed than those of Boston, Philadelphia, and other cities with patriotic associations. Nevertheless, more than 450 modern buildings were demolished in the first nine years of its restoration. By 1937, an estimated $14 million and five million man-hours had been spent on the project.

Although rooted in the past, Colonial Williamsburg was already beginning to show a sense of business innovation. One source described its licensing program, which began in the 1930s, as the oldest city in the country. Buffalo, New York's Kittinger Co. Inc. began reproducing furniture from Colonial Williamsburg's collection in 1936. (It lost the license to Baker Furniture Co. of Grand Rapids, Michigan, in 1990.)

Colonial Williamsburg had more than 1100 employees at the dawn of the 1950s. Employment exceeded 1,800 by the close of the decade, when operating revenues were $9.6 million. Hostesses' wages were approaching $2 an hour in the 1960s; mostly married women held this prestigious job.

Visitors to Colonial Williamsburg numbered 600,000 visitors in 1952; more than half paid for admission to the historic buildings. The visitor count exceeded one million by 1957 as Colonial Wiliamsburg rose to national prominence as a family tourist destination. In the 1960s, CWF acquired Carter's Grove, a nearby 18th-century plantation, from Archibald and Mollie McCrea. The house at Carter's Grove is maintained as an example of the Colonial Revival of the 1930s and 1940s.

In 1969, in order to head off the development of nearby "parasitic" businesses such as low-rent pottery warehouses, CWF sold the Anheuser-Busch Corporation much of the Carter's Grove land. This would become the site of Busch Gardens, a bona fide amusement park with few historical aspirations, as well as the upscale planned community of Ford's Colony.

CWF Formed 1970

Colonial Williamsburg, Incorporated and Williamsburg Restoration, Incorporated merged in 1970 to form the Colonial Williamsburg Foundation. Colonial Williamsburg had 1.4 million visitors in 1971 when operating revenues were nearly $26 million. The number of employees soon reached 3,500.

A licensing agreement circa 1971 allowed Wedgwood to reproduce a historic plate. Colonial Williamsburg Co. was the for-profit company that supported the foundation through such deals.

Operating revenues were $46.3 million in 1976. In the previous fifty years, the Rockefeller family had given Colonial Williamsburg $100 million. However, rising costs edged CWF into massive operating deficits. Like other tourist attractions, Colonial Williamsburg suffered during the gasoline shortages of the 1970s.

In the mid-1970s, CWF began to look beyond its endowment and its admission, hotel, and restaurant sales for financial

sustenance. It solicited individuals and corporations for support, much like a private college; CWF recruited Roger Thaler, an attorney from Duke University, who led the fund raising effort.

In 1976, *Reader's Digest* founders DeWitt and Lila Bell Wallace gave CWF $5 million to fund the DeWitt Wallace Decorative Arts Gallery, which opened in 1984. To meet the requirement that only 18th-century buildings be visible, the 85,000-square-foot gallery was built almost entirely underground (the half story above ground was hidden behind the Public Hospital). The Wallaces' philanthropy was not limited to one building. They sponsored the restoration of the Public Hospital, and in 1981 they established the Wallace Fund for Colonial Williamsburg to provide annual operating funds for CWF's museums and educational programs. In 2001, the New York attorney general dissolved this fund, transferring $60 million of Reader's Digest Association Inc. stock and other assets directly to CWF.

Improving in the 1980s and 1990s

Revenues reached $64.4 million in 1981. A separate hospitality subsidiary, Colonial Williamsburg Hotel Properties, Incorporated, was formed in 1983 to operate the hotels and restaurants.

CWF launched a $75 million capital improvement program in the mid-1980s, its first in more than 25 years. This included restoration of a historic public hospital (the first mental hospital in the United States), a blacksmith shop, and a tavern; the addition of hotel rooms; and an update of the telephone and hotel reservation systems.

At the time, Colonial Williamsburg employed about 2,800 people, plus another 1,200 seasonal workers during the summer. In 1986, CWF had overall revenues of $97 million derived from ticket sales ($18 million), hotels, several restaurants, publishing ventures, reproduction furniture sales, and the Merchants Square shopping center. The Wallace Fund, which was worth $159 million, produced $18.8 million in interest income; donations accounted for $8.3 million of revenues.

Revenues were $136.1 million in 1994. Colonial Williamsburg had 3,500 employees in the mid-1990s, nearly double the town's Revolutionary period population. Some of these were historical interpreters—guides dressed in period garb. Some performed 18th-century trades in authentic shops, selling wares such as candles. Colonial Williamsburg pitched a variety of modern merchandise ranging from furniture to Christmas CDs at on-site gift shops and in a glossy catalog with a circulation of more than one million.

However, attendance was declining as the number of competing destinations multiplied. With the help of a Richmond advertising agency, Just Partners, CWF aired a series of TV ads that parodied the famous "I'm going to Disneyland" commercials with historical figures like Patrick Henry instead of celebrity jocks.

In 1998, CWF posted its first surplus since 1990. Still, at 940,000 visitors a year, attendance was down 25 percent from its peak of 1.2 million in 1988. CWF was partnering with nearby attractions like Busch Gardens to help pitch the Hampton Roads area as a family tourist destination in competition

<table>
<tr><td colspan="2"><h2>Key Dates:</h2></td></tr>
<tr><td>1926:</td><td>Restoration of Williamsburg begins.</td></tr>
<tr><td>1932:</td><td>Museum opens to the public.</td></tr>
<tr><td>1957:</td><td>Visitors per year exceeds one million.</td></tr>
<tr><td>1970:</td><td>Colonial Williamsburg, Inc. and Williamsburg Restoration, Inc. merge to form the Colonial Williamsburg Foundation.</td></tr>
<tr><td>1976:</td><td>CWF expands fund-raising effort.</td></tr>
<tr><td>1983:</td><td>A hotel subsidiary formed.</td></tr>
<tr><td>1999:</td><td>"Enslaving Virginia" exhibit garners unprecedented publicity.</td></tr>
</table>

with Myrtle Beach, South Carolina, and Disney World. The foundation was also proposing to close Colonial Williamsburg's streets to those not purchasing a one day ($25), two-day ($29), or ($33) season pass, which allowed holders to visit most indoor exhibits. However, this proved legally unworkable, since these streets were in fact public property.

The dramatic "Enslaving Virginia" program, launched in March 1999, brought Colonial Williamsburg unprecedented worldwide media attention. In the preceding years, more attention had been placed on representing the lives of all strata of colonial society. A slave market had been restored five years earlier, and slave quarters were recreated at Carter's Grove in 1989.

75th Anniversary in 2001

Colonial Williamsburg celebrated its 75th anniversary throughout 2001 and 2002. In early 2002, CWF began offering schools "electronic field trips" produced in its new TV studio.

The *New York Times* reported that CWF and other nonprofits were attending licensing trade shows alongside Hollywood studios and large corporations. During the year, the foundation licensed blueprints to some of its buildings to Wilmington, North Carolina, home designer William E. Poole. CWF's total licensing income—from 4,000 different products—was about $10 million a year. The brand had been extended into two furniture lines: the reproduction-oriented Reserve Collection and the more modern line called Pure, Simple, Today. Lane Home Furnishings was the partner in this venture.

Principal Subsidiaries

Colonial Williamsburg Co.; Colonial Williamsburg Hotel Properties Inc.

Principal Competitors

Busch Gardens; Old Salem; Plimoth Plantation, Inc.; Walt Disney Parks & Resorts; Six Flags, Inc.

Further Reading

Ashenburg, Katherine, "Williamsburg Rethinks History," *New York Times,* September 24, 2000.

Barnes, Julian E., "Nonprofits Expand Their Universe of Products," *New York Times,* June 13, 2001, p. C1.

Buchanan, Lee, "Lane to Roll Out Williamsburg Collection; Licensing Program Also Includes Accessories, Lighting, Rugs," *HFN,* June 7, 1999, p. 19.

Buchanan, Patricia, "Marketing 1000: Janet Kane," *Advertising Age,* October 8, 2001, p. 41.

Campbell, Helen J., *Diary of a Williamsburg Hostess,* New York: Putnam, 1946.

Campbell, Tom, "Kittinger Loses Prestigious Line of Furniture," *Business First of Buffalo,* June 25, 1990, pp. 1f.

Cohn, Meredith, "Colonial Williamsburg CEO to Leave in June," *Virginian-Pilot,* March 5, 1999, p. D3.

Gattuso, Greg, "Back to the Future," *Direct Marketing,* December 1993, p. 32.

Goodwin, W.A.R., "The Restoration of Colonial Williamsburg," *National Geographic Magazine,* April 1937, pp. 402–43.

Greenspan, Anders, *Creating Colonial Williamsburg,* Washington: Smithsonian Institution Press, 2002.

Handler, Richard and Eric Gable, *The New History in an Old Museum: Creating the Past at Colonial Williamsburg,* Durham, N.C.: Duke University Press, 1997.

Huxtable, Ada Louise, *The Unreal America: Architecture and Illusion,* New York: New Press, 1997.

Kopper, Philip, *Colonial Williamsburg,* New York: Harry N. Abrams, 1986.

McCaffrey, Meg, "American History Redux Via Virtual Field Trips," *School Library Journal,* April 2002, p. 32.

Straszheim, Deborah, "Blacks at Colonial Williamsburg Say They Feel Like Slaves," *Knight-Ridder/Tribune News Service,* September 8, 1999.

Whitson, Brian, "Developer Bases New Residence Patterns on Historic Williamsburg, Va. Houses," *Daily Press* (Newport News), June 19, 2001.

"Williamsburg Hotels, Restaurants Lose Money; Some Funds Help Support Nonprofit Foundation," *Roanoke Times,* June 16, 1997, p. C3.

"Williamsburg Officials Wary of Closing Area to Public But They Are Still Willing to Consider Limiting Access to the Historic Streets," *Virginian-Pilot,* May 24, 1997, p. B2.

"Williamsburg Would Not Be Alone in Charging to Enter Historic Area," *Virginian-Pilot,* May 25, 1997, p. B5.

—Frederick C. Ingram

Community Coffee Co. L.L.C.

3332 Partridge Lane, Building A
Baton Rouge, Louisiana 70809
U.S.A.
Telephone: (225) 368-3900
Fax: (225) 295-4510
Web site: http://www.communitycoffee.com

Private Company
Incorporated: 1956
Employees: 1,000
Sales: $100 million (2001 est.)
NAIC: 311920 Coffee and Tea Manufacturing

Community Coffee Co. L.L.C. is the largest family-owned coffee brand in the United States. The company was founded in Baton Rouge, Louisiana, in 1919 by Henry Norman Saurage, whose grandson, Henry Norman Saurage III, remained chairman of the board of directors in 2002. Community was the first company in North America to develop vacuum-sealed bag packaging and is now the owner of a patent on vacuum-sealed whole bean dispensers for retail outlets. Unofficially regarded as the "state coffee" of Louisiana, Community sells its signature "red bag" coffee in grocery stores across the Gulf South, through mail- and Internet-ordering, and through its subsidiary CC's Gourmet Coffee Houses in Louisiana and Texas.

Laying the Foundation for Success: 1919–76

Community Coffee began with Henry Norman "Cap" Saurage in 1919 when Saurage opened the Full Weight Grocery in Baton Rouge and began selling his own unique blend of coffee. Saurage bought a variety of freshly roasted beans from New Orleans, mixed them according to his own tastes, ground and packaged the coffee by hand, and delivered it to his local customers by horse-drawn wagon. By 1924, demand for the coffee was so great that Saurage could hardly fill all of his orders. He closed the grocery store and converted the barn in his own back yard into a coffee mill and packaging plant in order to devote himself to the coffee business full time. Saurage named his product "Community" in recognition of his devoted local

customers. As the reputation of Community Coffee grew, Saurage began delivering his coffee to stores and restaurants.

Cap Saurage was famously meticulous about the quality of his product, and his son, H. Norman Saurage, Jr., was no different. In 1941, shortly after assuming the helm of the company, H. Norman bought a Jabez Burns "Jubilee" Roaster, and Community began roasting its beans in-house. By controlling this crucial phase of coffee production, he argued, the company would be able to guarantee an even greater level of quality and freshness. In 1946, production expanded further when the family built its first modern coffee roasting and packaging plant in downtown Baton Rouge. During these years, the company also began filling orders by mail upon request.

In the 1960s, Community began importing its own beans directly from Brazil. At the time, this was highly unusual for a company of Community's size; most companies purchased their beans from brokers. The move was indicative of Community's dedication to maximizing quality control and further streamlining all phases of production. In the early 1970s, Community built a new and improved plant on the other side of the Mississippi River, in Port Allen. At the new location, Community could receive shipments of green coffee beans straight off the cargo ships that came into the port of Baton Rouge.

Innovation and Growth: 1970s–80s

Cap's grandson Henry Norman Saurage III assumed the role of president and CEO in 1977. Norman had grown up in the coffee business. During his teens, he had worked as a coffee urn repairman in the warehouse of the mail order department and also filled in as a salesman in the summer. Norman spent much of his early career in the sales department, where he developed his knowledge of the industry as well as his coffee palate. Eventually, he earned his way to management level, where he served as vice-president overseeing operations, marketing, and sales.

When Saurage III succeeded his father in July 1977, the coffee industry was in the throes of a worldwide crisis. A freeze in Brazil had ruined the bulk of that country's coffee crops. At this time, Brazil's crops accounted for about 35 percent of the world's supply of green coffee beans, so when the freeze devastated world supply, the price of coffee soared. True to his grandfather's founding values, H. Norman Saurage III led Community's management team to design a new pricing strategy that would lessen the impact of the coffee shortage on retailers and individual customers, demonstrating the company's ongoing commitment to the community it served. Through Community's efforts to offer extremely competitive prices and avoid taking advantage of its customers during the coffee shortage, the company benefited greatly: it attracted new customers, gaining greater market share and brand recognition, while redoubling the loyalty of existing customers.

During this time, Saurage III was also instrumental in pushing forward the development and marketing of new, vacuum-sealed coffee bags—the first of their kind in North America. The vacuum bags made it possible to offer customers the convenient packaging that they were accustomed to, along with a level of freshness that had previously only been available from vacuum-sealed steel cans. Further, vacuum bags were a much more cost-effective form of packaging than cans, and Community was able to pass the savings along to its customers once again.

At a time when H. Norman Saurage III was focused on revamping and reinvigorating the company's brand growth strategy, the vacuum-sealed bags were a critical innovation, enabling Community to extend its business to previously unreachable regions. Before the vacuum bag, Community could not—or would not—sell its coffee outside Louisiana or the lower Mississippi Gulf Coast, because the lower-tech packaging of that time was not sufficient to maintain optimum freshness and flavor (qualities upon which Community had built its name) over the extended shipping distance. The vacuum technology enabled Community to introduce its product to Texas and all of the Gulf states. The result was an exponential increase in sales. Later, Community would go on to patent a special, vacuum-sealed whole bean gourmet coffee dispenser called the Fresh-O-Lator, which would prove an enormous boon to grocery store sales.

With the vacuum technology in place, Community was also well poised to expand its mail-order business. In 1981, the company launched its first proactive effort to increase sales through mail order. Community developed and distributed its first extensive mail-order catalog, which included gourmet coffee, gourmet food, and kitchen equipment.

Saurage III's tenure as president and CEO ended in 1983, when his father resumed the position. In 1986, Charles E. Lee, Community's treasurer, was named president until he was succeeded by L. Patrick Pettijohn. Lee and Pettijohn were the first top executives at Community who were not members of the Saurage family.

Investing in Louisiana: 1988–99

From its first years, Community Coffee was committed to participating in and giving back to the community in which it operated. Through financial commitments, product donations, and employee volunteer work, Community contributed to civic improvement, particularly in the area of education. To this end, Community Coffee launched a program in 1988 called Community Cash for Schools, which involved community participation (and encouraged sales of the company's coffee) and resulted in monetary donations, used for equipment and supplies, to participating schools. By 2001, the 13th year of the program, Community had contributed more than $2 million and attracted the participation of 750 schools throughout the South.

By 1995, Community Coffee was selling strongly at supermarkets in six southern states, and the well-known brand was poised once again for market expansion. In September of that year, Community formed a subsidiary called Community Coffee Shop, Inc., and announced plans to start opening local coffee houses under the name CC's Gourmet Coffee House, beginning with its first location on Magazine Street in New Orleans. Community had made an appearance on the coffee house scene in the early 1980s when it opened six coupon redemption sites in Louisiana under the name Community Coffee Place. At these outlets, customers could redeem coupons for coffee and tea, as well as gourmet kitchen items. Community also used these sites to sell and serve coffee, but the venture was discontinued in 1981 due to waning consumer interest.

With the launch of CC's, Community's first wholly retail endeavor, the company staked its territory in the final frontier of distribution. This was seen as a necessary move in order to keep the company at the forefront of all avenues of industry competition. Billed as community gathering spots, CC's took pains to cater to the full spectrum of coffee drinkers—from the inquiring coffee gourmet to the regular guy seeking a plain old cup of ''joe.'' New employees were required to undergo a week-long training program that focused on developing their palate and vocabulary for the world's many varieties of coffee.

By 1997, Community was planning a major expansion of the chain—from four locations to 12 in a year's time. The stated strategy was to continue to expand into areas where the Community brand already enjoyed a grocery store presence and an established base of loyal customers. At this time, the most prevalent coffeehouse chain in the region was PJ's Coffee and Tea, founded in 1978, with 20 stores and 16 franchises from New Orleans to Mississippi and Florida.

In the following years, Community forged ties with the local arts community as a way of further distinguishing its cafes and its identity as a true Louisiana brand. In 1998, CC's began a collaboration with New Orleans' Contemporary Arts Center (CAC) whereby CC's cafes would host professionally curated exhibitions of works by local artists and crafters. By supporting the arts, Community had found a way once again to promote its own business while providing a public service.

In 1999, Community Coffee became the exclusive corporate underwriter of a New Orleans-produced, nationally syndicated radio show called American Routes. Distributed by Public Radio International, American Routes was then being broadcast weekly on 80 stations around the United States.

Community Coffee experienced astronomical growth in the 1990s. The decade had spawned a new national awareness

Key Dates:

1919: Henry Norman "Cap" Saurage begins selling his own blend of coffee to customers at his Baton Rouge country store, the Full Weight Grocery.

1924: Saurage closes the company store and converts his barn into a coffee mill to devote himself to selling coffee full time.

1941: Henry Norman Saurage, Jr. brings the roasting process in-house.

1946: The Saurage family builds a modern roasting plant overlooking the Mississippi River.

1957: Community begins importing beans directly from Brazil.

1970: Community builds a new plant across the Mississippi River in Port Allen, implementing advanced European packaging techniques.

1977: Henry Norman Saurage III becomes president and begins development of the first vacuum-sealed bags in North America.

1988: Community Coffee launches its Cash for Schools program.

1995: Community Coffee opens the first CC's Gourmet Coffee House on Magazine Street in New Orleans.

2000: Community Coffee launches its Web site and begins selling coffee online.

2001: Randall "Randy" Russ succeeds H. Norman Saurage III as president and CEO.

about the quality and varieties of coffee available. Sales of instant coffee had plummeted and Americans were now willing to pay more for gourmet grinds. Coffeehouses offering premium gourmet coffee and specialty drinks had sprung up everywhere, responding to and nurturing the craze. According to the Specialty Coffee Association of America and the National Coffee Association, these coffeehouses, CC's among them, netted $3.9 billion in sales in 1999. Over the decade, Community's staff roster had grown from around 200 employees to more than 1000, and CC's Coffeehouses had spread through Louisiana and into Texas, numbering 30 locations and still growing by 2000.

New Ideas for the 21st Century

In 2001, Randall "Randy" Russ, then acting as vice-president of operations, was elected Community's new president and CEO. Russ's stated vision was to make Community Coffee the best coffee company in the nation—not necessarily the biggest, but the best. The challenge for Russ in fostering Community's ongoing growth and success would be to hold the company true to the values and identity of its 82-year-old heritage while continuing to innovate and keep pace with the changing times.

Community Coffee continued to grow and modernize its operations as it entered the twenty-first century. In 2000, the company launched a Web site with an online store. Community also sought to extend its presence beyond the seven states it already occupied and began marketing itself to the rest of the nation (especially Louisiana expatriates) alongside other distinctive Louisiana offerings such as Tabasco sauce or Zatarain's food products.

At the public service end of the business, Community maintained its support of Louisiana and the other Gulf Coast states through programs like Cash for Schools. In 2001, the company also spearheaded a Relationship Coffee Program with the Colombian Coffee Federation in Toledo-Labteca, one of the poorest regions of that country. This program guaranteed coffee farmers a premium, fixed price for their coffee in exchange for continued top-quality crops. In addition to the pricing guarantee, Community pledged to deposit money into an endowment that would be used to build a new secondary school in the region. Randy Russ cited collaborations like this as essential to the future of the specialty coffee industry. Indeed, as consumer awareness of the politics surrounding coffee production continued to grow (as evidenced by the fair trade coffee movement), it seemed as though Community Coffee's strong values and capacity to innovate would put it ahead of the competition.

Principal Subsidiaries

Community Coffee Shop, Inc.

Principal Competitors

The Procter & Gamble Co.; Starbucks Corporation; New World Restaurant Group Inc.; Tully's Coffee Corporation.

Further Reading

King, Ronette, "Teaching the Art of Coffee; Counter Servers Must Get a Jump on Savvy Customers," *Times-Picayune*, November 20, 1996, p. C1.

LaBan, Craig, "Coffeehouses Get Even Hotter; The Community Company Plans to Triple the Number of Its Outlets By the End of the Year," *Times-Picayune*, August 26, 1997, p. F1.

Welsh, James, "Ahhhhhh, Coffee," *Times-Picayune*, February 21, 1993, p. F1.

——, "Strong Regional Sales and a Healthy Mail-Order Business Deliver Perfect Blend for Louisiana's Community Coffee: Strong Brew," *Times-Picayune*, July 23, 1995, p. F1.

——, "A Brand New Flavor; Coffee Business Brews with News of Three More N.O. Area Java Shops," *Times-Picayune*, September 9, 1995, p. C1.

—Erin Brown

COSÍ

Cosi, Inc.

242 West 36th Street, 11th Floor
New York, New York 10018
U.S.A.
Telephone: (212) 653-1600
Fax: (212) 653-1666
Web site: http://www.getcosi.com

Public Company
Incorporated: 1999 as Xando Cosi, Inc.
Employees: 1,902
Sales: $70.24 million
Stock Exchanges: NASDAQ
Ticker Symbol: COSI
NAIC: 722110 Full-Service Restaurants

Cosi, Inc. operates more than 80 casual restaurants under the "Cosi" and "Cosi Downtown" banners. Cosi's restaurants are all-day cafes featuring coffee drinks, exotic sandwiches, and alcohol. The restaurants change menus, service, music, and lighting throughout the day, transforming at five points during the day: breakfast, lunch, afternoon coffee, dinner, and dessert. At 5:00 p.m., the chain begins offering alcohol and table service. The company's restaurants are located in 11 states and the District of Columbia.

Origins

The 21st-century version of Cosi was created by the combination of two business concepts. In 1999, Cosi Sandwich Bar, Inc. and Xando Incorporated merged, uniting two companies that "served a similar customer, but focused on different parts of the day," according to the Cosi corporate web site. Of the two companies, Xando Inc. was founded first, formed in October 1994 by three childhood friends. Cosi Sandwich Bar was founded roughly 18 months later, when two brothers opened their first store in February 1996. Xando Inc. began operating in Hartford, Connecticut. Cosi Sandwich Bar got its start in New York City. The corporate marriage of the two concerns created one of the most talked about concepts in the restaurant industry.

The inspiration for Xando came from a film. When Andy Stenzler was 25 years old, he and longtime friends Nick Marsh and David Kaufman went to see *Reality Bites,* a film featuring a cast in their 20s who spent much of their time hanging out in coffee bars and night clubs. In an October 2000 interview with *Sales & Marketing Management,* Stenzler explained the inspiration triggered by watching *Reality Bites.* "We were in the movie and it kind of snapped," he said. "We realized it was right under our nose—that the same place that we might enjoy getting coffee at in the morning was not a place where we wanted to be in the evenings. And the original concept was born: to transform from day to night." The three friends walked out of the movie with a business plan, aiming to create an establishment that catered to both daytime and nighttime crowds.

Stenzler, by his own admission, knew virtually nothing about the food business when the inspiration for Xando struck him, but he was pursuing his M.B.A. degree at New York University at the time. The day after he graduated from New York University, Stenzler quit his day job as a sales engineer and moved to Hartford, Connecticut, the location chosen for the first Xando unit. Hartford was chosen because the community had yet to be added to the ever-expanding network of stores operated by Starbuck's, the national coffee shop chain. Hartford, according to Stenzler, also possessed the proper mix of day-and-night business, offering a viable proving ground for his coffeehouse/bar concept. Stenzler and his two friends borrowed money from friends and charged their credit cards to the limit to raise the $400,000 in start-up capital they needed to open the first unit. In October 1994, Stenzler and his friends unveiled their concept, which at first was called ZuZu. The name of the restaurant concept soon was changed to Xando Coffee & Bar, the name derived from the hugs-and-kisses symbol "X" and "O." The concept proved to be an instant success, drawing a flood of customers and earning distinction as the Innovative Concept of the Year by the Connecticut Restaurant Association.

The first Xando, like the other stores that followed, morphed at selected periods during the day. The stores observed a daily schedule defined by what the company referred to as "dayparts." There were five dayparts in each day, the segue from one period to another marked by a change in menu, a change in lighting, and a change in music. At 5:00 p.m., the stores began selling alcohol and began providing table service. The stores were open from 6:00 a.m. to 2:00 a.m., attracting customers 20 hours a day, a unique characteristic that turned Xando units into revenue-generating machines. The success of the first Hartford unit spurred Stenzler to open additional Xando units. A small chain was fashioned, offering an eclectic selection of coffee drinks, ranging from raspberry café au lait and caramel arctic mocha in the morning to alcoholic coffee beverages in the evening, when signature drinks such as Frangelicreamuccino and Chai Lullaby complemented the traditional offerings of a standard full bar.

As Stenzler was beginning to expand his novel Xando concept, brothers Jay and Shep Wainwright were making their debut in the restaurant industry to the south. The Wainwrights invested their futures in a concept reportedly popular in Paris, one that featured Pizza Romano—described as "crackly crust" flat bread—and exotic sandwiches. In February 1996, the brothers opened the first Cosi Sandwich Bar in New York City, establishing the unit on 52nd Street off Third Avenue. From the start, the Wainwrights focused on providing fast-service gourmet sandwiches, developing an in-store bakery that baked the store's bread. Like Stenzler, the Wainwrights enjoyed success from the start, prompting them to open additional units. As the brothers expanded, equipping each Cosi Sandwich Bar with its own bakery, they focused on bustling business districts in major metropolitan areas such as Washington, D.C., Boston, and Philadelphia.

1999 Merger

In 1999, the two award-winning concepts merged. (In 1998, Cosi Sandwich Bar was selected as a "Hot Concepts!" winner by *Nation's Restaurant News*). The merger resulted from a friendship formed among the principal partners of each concept. For several years before the merger, the Wainwrights had met with Stenzler and Marsh to discuss how they were dealing with particular business matters, sharing ideas related to training, operations, finance, and marketing. From these meetings, the idea of merging the two companies emerged. In an October 4, 1999 interview with *Nation's Restaurant News,* Jay Wainwright explained: "How the merger came about is, basically, in the last two months Andy [Stenzler] and I started talking about what it would be like if we put these two companies together, and every step of the way, the companies fit perfectly."

Before committing themselves to a merger, the two companies experimented with the idea. In Manhattan, they opened a

Xando and a Cosi next to each other, providing a shared eating space for the two concepts. The test marriage convinced all involved to push ahead with the corporate union. By September 1999, the two companies had agreed to merge, a proposal that promised to unite the 22-unit Xando concept with the 18-unit Cosi concept. At this point, Xando's units were located in Connecticut, Pennsylvania, New York, Virginia, Maryland, Washington, D.C., and Florida. Cosi's 18 upscale sandwich venues were located in Manhattan, Boston, Philadelphia, and Washington, D.C. The merger, completed in October 1999, created Xando Cosi, Inc., a company based in New York with Stenzler and Jay Wainright serving as co-chief executive officers and co-chairmen. Shep Wainright was appointed chief development officer, and Marsh and Kaufman were selected as president and chief operating officer, respectively.

Looking ahead to their new future together, the partners were optimistic about future growth. In addition to revamping the existing 40 units to the co-branded format, Stenzler and Wainwright announced that they would open 20 new units in 2000. The new stores were expected to range between 3,000 square feet and 5,000 square feet, slightly larger than the 2,500 square feet averaged by Xando and Cosi units. Revenues for 2000 were expected to reach $50 million. The company's marketing manager, Rammy Harwood, typified the buoyant mood prevalent at the time of the merger, expressing his feelings in a November 19, 1999 interview with the *Washington Business Journal.* "We're going to dazzle you," he said. "It's going to be like the universal living room."

One year after the merger was completed, executives at Xando Cosi had numerous reasons to celebrate. In September 2000, the company entered the Midwest market for the first time, establishing a restaurant in Chicago. Stenzler had received more than $60 million in funding to expand the chain, building on the 18 units opened in 2000. Penetration into Minneapolis and Detroit was expected soon, part of the company's plan to open 26 units in 2001 and reach a total of 198 units by 2003. Based on his expansion plans for 2001, Stenzler expected to generate $100 million in revenue in 2001, double the total collected in 2000. Once the company reached such stature, according to Stenzler, Xando Cosi would be ready to complete its initial public offering (IPO) of stock.

By the beginning of 2001, Xando Cosi operated a chain of 52 stores, with 20 of the units located in New York. Expansion plans were becoming increasingly ambitious. Stenzler was looking to transform the business into a national chain. As part of his plan to go national, Stenzler announced in February 2001 that the company would drop the word Xando from its corporate title and from the name of its stores. In the future, the company's stores would operate as Cosi, but retain the sun-and-moon logo formerly used by Xando. In a February 27, 2001 interview with the *New York Post,* Stenzler explained the company's new unified approach. "Here it is, a year and a half later, we've emerged as one company with one brand name, with one concept, with really one goal: To build a national brand known for excellence in bread and coffee throughout the day." In the months ahead, company units that enjoyed less traffic were to be sub-branded as "Cosi Downtown," restaurants that would not offer evening table service or alcohol.

Key Dates:

1994: Xando Incorporated is formed.
1996: Cosi Sandwich Bar Debuts in New York City.
1999: Xando and Cosi merge, forming Xando Cosi, Inc.
2001: The word Xando is dropped from company restaurants.
2002: Cosi, Inc. completes its initial public offering of stock.

When Stenzler announced his plan to expand nationally, he also revealed more specific plans regarding the company's IPO. The IPO was scheduled for either March or April 2002, at which point the company would gain a sizable amount of capital to fuel its ambitious expansion plans. Stenzler perceived great benefits to be gained from Cosi's IPO, as the company elevated itself from the realm of private placements to the world of public financing. "Our investors believe we're building a national lifestyle, a major national brand like Starbucks, McDonalds, or The Gap," he explained in a February 27, 2001 interview with the *New York Post.*

Red Ink and a 2002 IPO

The company failed to reach its goal of $100 million in sales in 2001, but the shortfall was far from its most pernicious weakness. The company generated $70 million in 2001, representing a nearly ninefold increase from the total recorded five years earlier. The company's operating costs, however, had increased at a more profligate rate, increasing at a 10 percent faster pace. Behind the accolades for innovation and behind the impressive physical expansion stood crippling financial losses, which was part of the reason April 2002 passed without the debut of Cosi on the stock market. In 1999, the company posted a net loss of $34.5 million. In 2000, the company posted a net loss of $23.2 million. In 2001, the company posted a net loss of $35.4 million. Stenzler's plans for an IPO stalled as the losses mounted, causing substantial alarm among management and potential investors alike.

Cosi's ability to reverse the trend of massive financial losses remained in doubt as it prepared for the future. The company was able to complete its IPO, however, making its debut on the NASDAQ Exchange in November 2002. The company raised $38.9 million from the offering, pricing its offering at $7 per share, below initial estimates that ranged between $8 per share and $10 per share. On the heels of its IPO, the company announced that it would strengthen its presence in Chicago and Columbus, Ohio. The company's hopes of becoming a national chain had yet to materialize, however. As it prepared for 2003 and the years beyond, the company's financial losses represented a serious concern.

Principal Subsidiaries

Cosi Sandwich Bar, Inc.; Xando Cosi Maryland, Inc.; Xando Florida, Inc.

Principal Competitors

AFC Enterprises, Inc.; Panera Bread Company; Starbucks Corporation.

Further Reading

Armstrong, David, "Mixed Drinks," *Forbes,* December 25, 2000, p. 62.

Chamis, Eleni, "Xando Gets Cosi: Merger Leads to New Look," *Washington Business Journal,* November 19, 1999, p. 31.

"Cosi," *Restaurants & Institutions,* November 15, 2001, p. 42.

"Cosi Sandwich Bar to Merge with Xando Inc.," *Nation's Restaurant News,* September 27, 1999, p. 126.

"Cosi Sandwich Chain Nets $38.9M in Cut-Rate IPO," *Nation's Restaurant News,* December 2, 2002, p. 63.

Kanter, Larry, "Andrew Stenzler, 31; Co-Chairman and CEO, Xando Cosi, Inc.," *Crain's New York Business,* January 31, 2000, p. 28.

Liddle, Alan J., "Xando's Outsourcing Is 'Cosi' But Not Carefree," *Nation's Restaurant News,* February 28, 2000, p. 46.

"Numbers to Chew On," *New York Post,* August 19, 2002, p. 35.

Rasmusson, Erika, "Raising the Coffee Bar," *Sales & Marketing Management,* October 2000, p. 28.

"66-Unit Cosi Sandwich Chain Eyes Possible IPO," *Nation's Restaurant News,* March 4, 2002, p. 82.

"Square Bagels and Plans to Cosi Up to an IPO," *New York Post,* February 27, 2001, p. 43.

Strauss, Karyn, "Xando-Cosi Merger Seen as Target for Larger Audiences," *Nation's Restaurant News,* October 4, 1999, p. 8.

—Jeffrey L. Covell

Cosmo Oil Co., Ltd.

1-1-1, Shibaura
Minato-ku, Tokyo 105-8528
Japan
Telephone: (03) 3798-3211
Fax: (03) 3798-3841
Web site: http://www.cosmo-oil.co.jp

Public Company
Incorporated: 1986
Employees: 1,892
Sales: ¥1.8 trillion ($13.6 billion) (2002)
Stock Exchanges: Tokyo Osaka Nagoya
Ticker Symbol: 5007
NAIC: 32411 Petroleum Refineries

Cosmo Oil Co., Ltd. operates as Japan's third-largest oil refiner and distributor with four refineries—Sakaide, Sakai, Chiba, and Yokkaichi—and a network of over 380 dealers and 5,300 gas stations. Competition brought on by deregulation in the 1990s has taken its toll on Cosmo's income, forcing the company to cut jobs, control costs, and pare back the number of its gas stations. In 1999, Cosmo Oil and Nippon Mitsubishi Oil Corp. began teaming up in various joint ventures. By 2003, the pair's distribution and refining venture controlled nearly 40 percent of the oil refining market in Japan.

Cosmo's Predecessors

Cosmo Oil was formed on April 1, 1986, with the merger of Maruzen Oil Co., Ltd. and Daikyo Oil Co., Ltd. Maruzen Oil began its operations as a producer of lubricating oil and in 1933 incorporated and underwent extensive reorganization to expand its existing refinery and to build a new one. Maruzen further increased in size in 1942 by amalgamating with several smaller companies, Toyo Oil Company, Toho Oil Company, Yamabun Oil Company, and Kyusha Refining Company. During World War II, Maruzen built a refinery and several storage facilities in China. Because Maruzen relied exclusively on crude oil imports during its early years, by the end of World War II its operations were curtailed.

Daikyo Oil was established in 1939 with the merger of eight refinery operators and a later merger with Edogawa Oil Company. Near the start of World War II, Daikyo began operation of a refinery in Yokkaichi that in 1943 processed crude oil brought in from the Netherlands East Indies. In 1946, it started operation of a refinery to process pine-root oil, a raw material readily available in Japan.

In the era immediately after World War II, the reconstruction of the Japanese economy required the establishment of an energy policy. At that time, coal was the primary source of energy in the country, and the importation of crude oil was viewed as a supplement to coal. In the 1950s, as new oil sources were discovered in the Middle East, Japan began importing more oil; the relatively close proximity of Japan to the Middle East oil fields, compared to that of the United States and much of Europe, gave the Middle East's oil a cost advantage in Japan. Firms in the Japanese oil industry built refineries along the coast to process this cheap oil.

By the 1970s, 99.8 percent of Japan's oil was imported, and oil was supplying 70 percent of the country's energy needs. A large portion of the oil imports was handled by international oil companies, Standard Oil Company (California), Texaco, Exxon, Mobil, and Shell, acting jointly with Japanese oil companies. Maruzen was not a partner with any of these large companies.

New Government Policies Affect Japanese Oil Industry

The shift to oil as the major energy source had an adverse impact on the coal industry. To lessen this impact, the Japanese government enacted the Petroleum Industry Law, which restricted the total amount of oil that could be imported. The Ministry of International Trade and Industry (MITI) set policies that had an impact on Maruzen and Daikyo. These laws came into play in the 1950s, when Maruzen had a contract with Union Oil Company of California to provide Maruzen's needs for crude oil. After the closing of the Suez Canal in 1956, Maruzen's president, Wada Kanji, negotiated shipping contracts for a fixed term and price. In the recession of 1962, however, these contracts became a financial burden. Wada contemplated a loan from Union Oil. Under the Foreign Capital Law, however, approval of the loan by

MITI was required. MITI at first refused approval but later agreed to it with the stipulation that MITI negotiate directly with Union Oil to secure the loan and that a new president be installed at Maruzen. While Maruzen was saved as a company by this action, members of the business community of Osaka, site of the company's home office, voiced disapproval of the treatment of Maruzen's president by MITI.

Despite this unfavorable reaction to its policies, MITI continued to play an important part in Japan's oil industry. When the first oil-supply shock was brought about in 1973 by the Organization of Petroleum Exporting Countries (OPEC), the energy situation in Japan became one of severe shortage. To offset this shortage, in December 1973 MITI placed limits on the use of oil in generating electricity. At the same time, the Japanese Diet passed the Petroleum Supply and Demand Normalization Law and the Emergency Measures Law for the Stabilization of the People's Livelihood to further reduce the need for oil. Investigations into price fixing by oil companies were undertaken by the Fair Trade Commission.

The Formation of Cosmo: Mid- to Late 1980s

As a result of these actions, the Japanese economy did not suffer as greatly from the 1979 oil crisis as it had from the one in 1973. At the same time, the oil industry had come under increased governmental regulation, which caused problems as oil supplies greatly increased during the 1980s. As world production of oil increased in the mid-1980s, and the value of the yen increased against the dollar, the price of oil fell rapidly in Japan, declining by more than half during 1986 alone. Despite this rapid decrease in cost, oil consumption in Japan in physical units fell by nearly 8 percent in 1985 and 2 percent in 1986. Oil companies faced high debt, poor cash flow, and decreased profit levels. To reduce these problems, in 1987 MITI began a five-year program of deregulation in the oil industry, with a goal of creating a stronger oil industry with fewer companies and less regulation. Previously, it had restricted imports of oil, placed controls on the refining of crude oil, and established quotas on the production of gasoline. These regulations began to be phased out, along with laws restricting the number of gas stations and where they could be located.

The formation of Cosmo Oil through the merger of Maruzen and Daikyo in 1986 and its subsequent growth through a merger in 1989 with Asia Oil Co., Ltd. was a part of the turbulence of the times. Asia Oil had been an affiliate of Daikyo Oil but operated independently after the formation of Cosmo Oil. Asia Oil's merger into Cosmo Oil was designed to reduce operating costs and improve operations at Cosmo, enabling the company to better withstand the competitive pressures being brought about by deregulation and decontrol.

At the start of 1990, Cosmo Oil had a network of more than 7,300 gasoline stations, about 14 percent of the 54,000 stations in Japan. It operated refineries in Chiba, with a capacity of 220,000 barrels per day; Yokkaichi, with a capacity of 175,000 barrels per day; Sakai, with a capacity of 110,000 barrels per day; and Sakaide, with a capacity of 140,000 barrels per day. Cosmo operated its own fleet of relatively new supertankers, including the Cosmo Galaxy, Cosmo Venus, Cosmo Jupiter, and Cosmo Neptune. An exploration subsidiary sought to develop oil fields throughout the world.

For the fiscal year ending March 31, 1990, Cosmo Oil produced approximately 132 million barrels of petroleum made up of 24 percent gasoline and naphtha, 34 percent kerosene and gas oil, 33 percent heavy fuel oil, and 9 percent lubricant and other products. Cosmo Oil purchased almost 69 million barrels of product from Japanese sources and imported about 60 million barrels.

During this time, Cosmo maintained a strategy of product innovation through research and development. In 1990, its research facility, Cosmo Research Institute, formulated a calcium phenate alkaline detergent additive that was awarded the Japan Petroleum Institute Prize. The additive was blended with engine oil used in automobiles or marine engines and improved the efficiency of that oil. To meet the higher demand for this product, which had been in development since 1971, Cosmo Oil planned to increase the capacity of its additive manufacturing facility.

Cosmo Oil's performance was tied to that of the world energy markets. After the 1979 energy crisis, the major international oil companies reduced their sales of oil to Japan, and other sources of supply were developed through direct purchase from oil-producing nations. Direct deals made by small Japanese oil companies, however, were often at prices higher than those gotten by the major oil companies. These higher prices were not a disadvantage during periods of tight supply, but during a worldwide glut, Japanese companies often canceled these direct deals temporarily, disrupting the relationship between buyer and seller.

Japan's Oil Industry Faces Problems: 1990s and Beyond

During 1990, as the price of crude oil increased and the yen fluctuated against the dollar, Cosmo struggled with a cost squeeze and a decline in profits. Rumors circulated that Cosmo Oil was a potential takeover target. By using contacts with the government, especially through the large number of former MITI officials among its employees, Cosmo Oil was been able to protect itself from some of the harsher features of deregulation. Along with others in the industry, Cosmo, however, was hampered by an excessive number of service stations. During the early 1990s, about 40 percent of all service stations in Japan operated at a loss—that number increased to nearly 70 percent by the late 1990s. Most oil companies, including Cosmo, were upgrading their service facilities by building newer, larger

Key Dates:

1933: Maruzen Oil Co. incorporates.
1939: Daikyo Oil Co. Ltd. is established with the merger of eight refinery operators.
1942: Maruzen expands by amalgamating with smaller companies.
1986: Cosmo Oil is formed by the merger of Maruzen Oil and Daikyo Oil.
1989: The company merges with Asian Oil Co. Ltd.
1996: Japan opens its market to competition by lifting its ban on the import of refined oil products.
1997: Company profits fall due to increased competition, a drop in prices, and overcapacity.
1999: Cosmo and Nippon Mitsubishi Oil Corp. begin forming joint ventures.
2002: The company reports a net loss for the first time in its history.

outlets. Cosmo was expanding its stations from sales outlets to full car-care centers. It was also offering higher-octane gasoline and better motor oil, both aimed at owners of high performance automobiles.

In 1996, Japan lifted its ban on the import of refined oil products, making way for increased competition. Cosmo and its domestic peers faced other problems as well. With 50 refineries and nearly 60,000 gas stations, Japan's overcapacity was a major issue. Industry analysts claimed that Japan's oil sector was producing 50 percent more than what it needed. Japanese oil concerns were also plagued by high operating costs and large amounts of debt. In 1997, Cosmo's profits fell by nearly 40 percent. In response, Cosmo launched a round of job cuts and began a cost reduction program.

Cosmo entered the new millennium determined to restore positive sales and earnings. In 2000, the company teamed up with Nippon Mitsubishi Oil Corp. to create Nippon Global Tanker Co. Ltd. That venture, along with other refining and distribution partnerships, left the pair in control of nearly 40 percent of Japan's oil refining market. Cosmo's restructuring and streamlining efforts appeared to pay off in 2000 and 2001, when net income began an upward climb. Sales also increasing during that time period, bolstered mainly by higher oil prices.

During 2001, the company published its first Environmental Report, signaling its focus on energy conservation and research and development related to environmentally-friendly fuel. Cosmo's Sakaide Refinery received the Director General's National Resources and Energy Award that year and the company also developed a Tropical Rainforest Project. In early 2002, the firm launched an Eco card that allowed its customers to participate in the company's environmental activities, it established solar powered generation systems in various gas stations, and it also set plans in motion to develop a hydrogen supply station that would act as a research center for fuel cell-powered vehicles. In May 2002, Cosmo was given a Green Reporting Award for its 2001 Environmental Report.

Meanwhile, conditions in the Japanese oil sector remained turbulent, due in part to over-supply and intense price competition. During 2002, crude oil prices began falling again and demand for petroleum products weakened. Sales fell and the company posted a net loss of $39 million, its first net loss since its creation in 1986. A November 2002 *Nikkei Weekly* article pointed to Cosmo's problems, claiming that "Cosmo Oil has actively pursued its cost reduction program, but has already gained nearly all of the benefits to be had through rationalization. It is currently engaged in various value-creation-targeted sales promotions. However, severe market deterioration outweighs the effect and the company's earnings potential is flagging." Indeed, it appeared that Cosmo Oil's future success hinged on a market turnaround along with its ability to overcome the industry's nagging pricing and capacity issues.

Principal Subsidiaries

Abu Dhabi Oil Co. Ltd.; Qatar Petroleum Development Co. Ltd.; Cosmo Oil Ashmore Ltd.; United Petroleum Development Co. Ltd.; Mubarraz Oil Co Ltd.; Toyo Oil Development Co. Ltd.; Cosmo Tanker Co. Ltd.; Cosmo Kaiun Co. Ltd.; Okinawa CTS Corp.; Shirashima Oil Storage Co. Ltd.; Ogijima Oil Terminal Co. Ltd.; Cosmo Petroleum Gas Co. Ltd.; Sakailpg Oil Terminal Co. Ltd.; Yokkaichi LPG Terminal Co. Ltd.; Hokuto Gas Service Co. Ltd.; Tozai Oil Terminal Co. Ltd.; Hokuto Kogyo Co. Ltd.; Sakaide Cosmo Kosan Co. Ltd.; Tokyo Cosmo Logistics Co. Ltd.; Kansai Cosmo Logistics Co.; Cosmo Oil Lubricants Co. Ltd.; Cosmo Matsuyama Oil Co. Ltd.; Kashima Oil Co. Ltd.; Maruzen Petrochemical Co. Ltd.; Cosmo Oil Service Co. Ltd.; Cosmo Asphalt Co. Ltd.; Cosmo Computer Center Co. Ltd.; Cosmo Research Institute; Cosmo Engineering Co. Ltd.; Cosmo Trade and Service Co. Ltd.; Cosmo Ventures Inc.; Cosmo Sea Farming Inc.; Cosmo Oil of U.S.A Inc.; Cosmo Oil UK Plc; Cosmo Oil International Pte Ltd. (Singapore); Cosmo Lubricants Taiwan Co. Ltd.

Principal Competitors

Idemitsu Kosan Co. Ltd.; Nippon Mining Holdings Inc.; Showa Shell Sekiyu K.K.

Further Reading

"Black Hole of Debt Gives Cosmo Oil Nebulous Outlook," *Nikkei Weekly*, November 18, 2002.
"Competition to Hit Japan Oil Profits," *Lloyd's List*, March 6, 1995, p. 2.
"Cosmo Oil Posts 1st-Ever Group Net Loss," *Jiji Press Ticker Service*, May 28, 2002.
Goto, Yasuhiro, "Cosmo Oil Wins Concession in Persian Gulf," *Nikkei Weekly*, June 6, 1994.
Flynn, Matthew, "Nippon Mitsubishi and Cosmo Tie-Up Could Fuel Drive for Petroleum Pacts," *Lloyd's List*, October 13, 1999, p. 4.
"Japan Struggles to Dismantle a Huge Petrol Time Bomb," *Financial Times London*, September 9, 1998, p. 36.
Rosario, Louise, "Business as Usual: Japanese Oil Industry Resists Shake-up," *Far Eastern Economic Review*, August 9, 1990.
"With Competition Fierce, Japanese Firms Pare Down," *Platt's Oilgram News*, January 11, 1999, p. 1.

—Donald R. Stabile
—update: Christina M. Stansell

Cree Inc.

4600 Silicon Drive
Durham, North Carolina 27703
U.S.A.
Telephone: (919) 313-5300
Fax: (919) 313-5452
Web site: http://www.cree.com

Public Company
Founded: 1987
Employees: 893
Sales: $155.4 million (2002)
Stock Exchanges: NASDAQ
Ticker Symbol: CREE
NAIC: 334413 Semiconductor and Related Device
   Manufacturing; 334419 Other Electronic Component
   Manufacturing; 327910 Abrasive Product
   Manufacturing; 421610 Electrical Apparatus and
   Equipment, Wiring Supplies, and Construction
   Material Wholesalers

Cree Inc. develops and produces semiconductors made from silicon carbide (SiC). Among the breakthroughs Cree's research on SiC made possible was the world's first blue light-emitting diode (LED), which, when used with existing types of LED's, made possible a variety of full-color electronic displays. Cree markets its LED's to various original equipment manufacturers in the United States, Malaysia, Japan, and Europe, including Osram Opto Semiconductors GmbH, Spectrian, and Sumitomo Corporation. The LED's are used in a broad variety of products, including indoor and outdoor arena video boards, billboards, traffic signals, interior automotive lighting, and liquid crystal displays in wireless devices. The company's subsidiary, Real Color Displays, produces full-color LED modules for large area video screens. Cree also manufactures SiC wafers, which it sells to the government, private industry, and universities for use in optoelectronic and microwave research, as well as silicon carbide crystals for use as gem stones in fine jewelry. Since the acquisition of its UltraRF subsidiary in 2000, Cree has produced components for power amplifiers used in base stations that transmit signals from wireless devices. Ongoing research at Cree is aimed at the development of LED's of ever-greater power and efficiency. Sixty-five percent of all Cree's sales in 2002 were made to international customers; the Malaysian market alone accounted for 23 percent in 2002, supplanting Japan as Cree's largest national market. Sixteen percent of Cree's 2002 revenue came from U.S. government agencies.

Beginnings and Breakthrough Products

The scientific work that eventually led to the founding of Cree Inc. was begun in the early 1980s at North Carolina State University (NCSU), where brothers Eric Hunter and Neal Hunter, along with Calvin Carter, began investigating the physical and electronic properties of silicon carbide (SiC), a rare, naturally occurring material. Their first work was funded by the Office of Naval Research (ONR), which hoped to develop processes for the production of microwave transistors from SiC that would supply the basis for higher power electronic systems for military aircraft. SiC's physical characteristics led researchers to believe that the material possessed significant advantages over the semiconductor materials being used at the time, such as silicon: SiC-based devices, it was thought, would be able to operate at much higher temperatures, much higher power and voltage levels, and much higher frequencies than those made from silicon. Furthermore, it was believed that LED's that emitted blue light could be produced from SiC. Unfortunately, the same properties that made SiC a good semiconductor material also made the material difficult to work with. It is extremely hard material, and its crystals have to be grown at very high temperatures, over 3,500 degrees Fahrenheit. In addition, crystals have to be grown very carefully because SiC can crystallize in more than 100 different atomic arrangements, many of which render the end product unusable. Once crystals have been grown, the hardness of the material makes it difficult to cut into wafers and etch with circuits.

The NCSU team found ways around many of these barriers; it developed proprietary processes for growing bulk SiC in single crystalline form, for applying SiC films, and for dry etching the material. In July 1987, armed with exclusive and perpetual licenses to ten NCSU patents they had developed, the core group of scientists left NCSU and formed Cree Research

Inc. Despite interest from California companies in seeing the company locate in the Silicon Valley area, Cree Research established its headquarters and laboratories in North Carolina's Research Triangle Park, a research community that included three major universities—NCSU in Raleigh, the University of North Carolina at Chapel Hill, and Duke University in Durham—various laboratories of the U.S. government, and a number of new high-tech corporations. There the firm continued its groundbreaking research, and soon had developed and patented a number of new discoveries. These included a process for reducing the levels of impurities in SiC thin films, equipment which was able to operate at the very high temperatures needed for the production of SiC materials, a process for the production of SiC wafers, a process for growing significantly larger SiC crystals, and a process for preparing the surface of SiC wafers.

In October 1989, Cree completed the development of its first products, the world's first blue light-emitting diode. Inventing a blue light LED was like finding the holy grail of electronics. Previously only red, green, yellow, and orange LED's were available. Combining these colors alone was not sufficient to produce the full spectrum of color. The addition of blue, the third primary color, made full-color billboard and arena-sized video and other displays possible for the first time. The new LED went into production in the summer of 1990, and by October Cree was shipping one million of them every month. Cree continued to work on new applications of the device. For example, the firm hoped to use a blue LED to develop a blue laser. With a much shorter wavelength than other lasers, a blue laser could be used could also be used for high-volume data storage media such as CD-ROMs and DVD's. Work on that particular application of the blue light LED would continued until into the 2000s.

Cree established a joint effort with the Microelectronics Center of North Carolina and the Office of Naval Research in May 1991 to develop another first: a high-power silicon carbide MESFET transistor that could function in the gigahertz range, an area significantly beyond the capability of conventional silicon and gallium arsenide transistors. The breakthrough was expected to lead to new transistors that could operate in power ranges up to 500 percent higher than older types. Cree's other research and develop programs in the early 1990s included work on new optoelectronic devices; larger, more homogeneous SiC wafers; and SiC semiconductors that could function at high temperatures.

By the early 1990s, Cree was also manufacturing SiC wafers, primarily for use in research; depending on the needs of Cree's customers, some wafers came with special epitaxial coatings. Such sales to researchers were part of a Cree strategy to increase future markets for its wafers by encouraging research that might result in the development of new SiC-based products. For its first five years, commercial interest in Cree's products was limited. Most of the company's revenues came from U.S. government contracts. In 1992, for example, federal government monies accounted for around 72 percent of the $595,000 Cree spent on research and development. Cree's government contractors included Defense Advanced Research Projects Agency (DARPA), the Office of Naval Research, the National Institute of Standards, and the U.S. Air Force. At the beginning of 1993, Cree also had research contracts with private industry, including Motorola and General Electric Corporation.

The Financial Side of Cree Research

During its first five years, Cree reported large operating losses. The first quarter of fiscal year 1993, in fall 1992, Cree announced its first profitable quarter. By 1993, the company revenues had increased to the point that about 40 percent came from sales, primarily SiC wafers, to researchers; the remainder of its revenues were from commercial product sales. In the first half of that year, 51 percent of Cree's commercial sales were in foreign markets, including Europe, Taiwan, and Korea. The lion's share of sales were to Japanese companies, however, primarily Shin-Etsu, a manufacturer of electronics materials, and Sumitomo Corporation, a distribution firm that served the Japanese optoelectronics market. Sales to Sumitomo alone accounted for 37 percent of Cree's total revenues in the first half of 1993.

In late 1992, Cree Research announced plans for a public stock offering. Wall Street skeptics discounted the company's chances, pointing out that Cree had lost money—lots of money—for most of its history. More significantly, they questioned whether or not it was healthy that Cree, a company whose production processes were extremely complex, was dependent on a small group of commercial customers, mainly General Electric and its Japanese distributors. Nonetheless, in February 1993 Cree floated what the *Portland Oregonian* called "the country's hottest initial public offering" of the early year. Opening at $8.25, the stock hit $25 a share before it finally came to settled in around $18. Within three months, it was selling at almost triple its opening price, while no other share launched in the early year had even managed to double its opening price. In all, Cree raised $13.28 million, most of which it planned to use to expand its production facilities in North Carolina.

Company Growth

Cree spent the middle 1990s refining its SiC technologies and expanding its international presence. In 1994, it acquired the Hong Kong-based Color Cells International and transformed it into a new Cree subsidiary, Real Color Displays. The following year, it signed a pact with Germany's Siemens AG for joint work to develop LED's that utilized Cree technology. Siemens also agreed to purchase LED chips and SiC wafers from Cree. Working under a new DARPA contract, Cree began intensifying its research into blue laser diodes for covert communication systems for the military, as well as for high-density

Key Dates:

1987: Cree Research Inc. is founded
1989: The company introduces world's first blue light-emitting diode (LED).
1993: Cree Research makes a public stock offering.
1994: Cree acquires Color Cells International of Hong Kong and establishes from it a new subsidiary, Real Color Displays.
1998: The conductive eye buffer LED is introduced; HB blue and Green LED's are launched.
1999: Cree demonstrates its four-inch silicon carbide (SiC) wafer.
2000: The company changes its name to Cree Inc.
2001: Cree introduces MegaBright blue and UV LED's and the Schottky diode.

optical recording and playback devices, such as CD-ROMs and DVD's—a market that was expected to be worth more than $2 billion by the middle of the 21st century. The company reported a milestone in its blue laser research in June 1997 when it successfully built an electrically pulsed gallium nitride-based blue light laser with a lifetime of more than an hour. It was but a small first step, however, since a commercially successful blue laser would have to have a lifetime of thousands of hours. If a blue laser still lay in the future, Cree's achievement at least showed that SiC was a viable material for its manufacture.

Cree opened up an entirely new market for its silicon carbide in October 1997 when it began selling the diamond-like SiC crystals as gem stones for jewelry. Cree's primary customer in this area was a firm called C3 led by Jeff Hunter, the brother of Cree's then-president and CEO, Neal Hunter. So enthusiastic was Wall Street for the venture that when C3 announced its intention to go public, Cree stock shot up to a 52-week high of $22.18. A year later, in November 1998, Cree was flying even higher. It reported a quarterly profit of $2.36 million, an increase of 100 percent over the same quarter a year earlier. Furthermore, its stock was selling for $27.50 a share, its production facilities were running at about 80 percent capacity, and the company had grown to approximately 275 employees and expected to add more in the 1999. Cree's success was due in part a new process that increased wafer size and quality. As if in recognition of its commercial successes, in February 2000 Cree Research changed its name to Cree Inc.

Challenges and Opportunities in the New Century

Taking advantage of its sterling reputation, Cree made a second stock offering in early 2000. Analysts continued to urge caution to investors. In their eyes, the fortunes of the company seemed precariously balanced on just a few sources of revenue. A mere five customers accounted for four-fifths of Cree's sales; 37 percent was from one company, Siemens AG. Because Cree had just forged a new contract with Siemens subsidiary, Osram GmbH, its future with Siemens looked secure. However, another large account, artificial gem stone firm C3—since renamed Charles & Colvard—was experiencing lower sales than expected and had delayed some shipments from Cree. As a result, Cree had to revise its projected revenues for 2001.

Although the firm was still heavily dependent on the U.S. government as well, these problems seemed to hurt Cree not at all. The offering raised $266 million. The latter half of 2000 had been one of the best half years in Cree's short history, with sales rising by 67 percent and net income doubling. In mid-February, Cree shares were selling for as high as $139. According to *Fortune* magazine, Cree was the 11th fastest growing company in the United States in 2000.

Cree began growing and expanding its semiconductor expertise in 2000. In May, it acquired acquisition of Nitres, Inc. for $233 million in stock. Based in California, Nitres developed nitride-based semiconductors, primarily for the U.S. Commerce Department and the military. Nitres became a wholly owned subsidiary, Cree Lighting Company. In November 2000, Cree made another important acquisition, UltraRF, the semiconductor division of linear power amplifier maker Spectrian Corp., for $95 million in stock. UltraRF later became Cree Microwave, a wholly owned subsidiary. As part of the same deal, Cree and Spectrian also agreed to conduct joint research into laterally diffused metal oxide semiconductors (LDMOS) and SiC MESFET components.

Cree continued to develop new products in 2000. In June, it introduced a line of low power LED's that operated at 50 percent of the power used by Cree's other LED's. At the end of the year, it announced a new lighting system for automobile dashboards that would never burn out. The system was slated for incorporation into Volkswagen and Audi models. The gallium nitride technology could also be used to boost the range and capacity of cell phone transmission towers.

Between 1999 and 2000 Cree's Japanese distributor, Sumitomo Corporation, was the target of a series of lawsuits in Japan brought by another Japanese firm, Nichia Corporation. Nichia claimed that Cree's LED's, which Sumitomo was selling in Japan, violated Nichia patents. Cree intervened in the suits, and by December 2001 Tokyo District Court had dismissed all charges ruling that no infringement had taken place. Nichia later appealed the ruling to the Tokyo High Court. Turning the tables on Nichia, Cree, together with NCSU, sued Nichia and its North American subsidiary Nichia America Corporation, for allegedly infringing patents for lateral epitaxial overgrowth technology. A round of countersuits ensued, including a claim by Nichia that Cree had misappropriated Nichia trade secrets—in essence committed industrial espionage—by means of a former Nichia employee who was employed by Cree lighting. The suit was still in litigation in summer 2002.

The U.S. government continued to be a major supporter of Cree Inc., in 2002. In February, it was the recipient of a $14.5 million contract to create LED's and laser diodes that could be used to detect biological agents such as anthrax. Later that summer the Navy awarded two contracts to Cree with a value of $14.4 million. The contracts were in conjunction with the so-called wide bandgap semiconductor initiative sponsored by DARPA. Cree's role was to develop semi-insulating substrates for microwave devices. It received $26.5 million more for work for the ONR and the Air Force Research Laboratories. Cree had a number of products under development in summer 2002. These included high efficiency LED's that might replace incandescent and fluorescent lighting in conventional lighting systems; high power, SiC-based devices for power transmission; and SiC-based transistors able to function at microwave frequencies.

Principal Subsidiaries

Cree Microwave, Inc.; Cree Lighting Company; Cree Research FSC, Inc.; Cree Funding, LLC; Cree Employee Services Corporation; Cree Technologies, Inc.; CI Holdings, Limited; Cree Asia-Pacific, Inc.; Cree Japan, Inc.

Principal Competitors

AXT Inc.; Agilent Technologies; Hitachi Ltd.; Philips Electronics N.V.; LG Electronics Inc.; Matsushita Kotobuki Electronics Industries Co., Ltd.; Mitsui & Co. Ltd.; Motorola Inc.; NEC Corporation; Nitronex Corporation; Planar Systems Inc.; Sony Corporation; Sumitomo Electric Industries Ltd.; Telefonaktiebolaget LM Ericsson; Three-Five Systems Inc.; Uniroyal Technology Corporation.

Further Reading

Bindra, Ashok, "Diode Operates At 350c, Switches At 7 Ns—SiC Promises Hot Diodes," *Electronic Engineering Times*, December 19, 1988.

Bindra, Ashok, "SiC Pushes Ahead," *Electronic Engineering Times*, May 27, 1991.

Colier, Joe Guy, "Columbia, S.C., University Lab Works on New Electronic Technology," *Knight-Ridder Tribune Business News*, December 7, 2000.

Kallender, Paul, and Yoshiko Hara, "Rohm Withdraws ITC Complaint Against Nichia But Continues State Action," *Electronic Engineering Times*, May 21, 2001, p. 31.

Klass, Philip J., "Silicon-Carbide Shows Promise for Avionic Use," *Aviation Week & Space Technology*, May 3, 1993, p. 50.

"LSI Logic Corp. Reorganizes Communications Product Group," *Electronic News*, November 27, 2000, p. 16.

Murphy, K. Maxwell, "Cree Shares Tumble After CNBC Raises Concerns About Gross Margins," *Dow Jones Business News*, October 13, 2000.

Naegele, Tobias, "Research Triangle Park, at 30, Reaches Maturity," *Electronics*, March 1, 1989.

Power, William, "Cree's Blue Light Has Bewitched IPO Investors, But It Isn't Clear if There's a Pot of Gold Ahead," *Wall Street Journal*, April 23, 1993.

Smith, Lisa F., "Durham, N.C., Chip Maker Sees Role in Many Fields," *Herald-Sun* (Durham, N.C.), November 4, 1998.

"Tech Investors See Cree's Light," *International Herald Tribune*, February 5, 2000, p. 16.

—Gerald E. Brennan

DeLorme

DeLorme Publishing Company, Inc.

Two DeLorme Drive
Yarmouth, Maine 04096
U.S.A.
Telephone: (207) 846-7000
Fax: (207) 846-7071
Web site: http://www.delorme.com

Private Company
Incorporated: 1976
Employees: 220
Sales: $35 million (2000 est.)
NAIC: 511210 Software Publishers; 511140 Database and
   Directory Publishers; 443120 Computer and Software
   Stores; 451211 Book Stores; 511130 Book Publishers

DeLorme Publishing Company, Inc. is a leading publisher of mapping software and paper maps and atlases for consumers and businesses. Known for producing detailed, color topographic maps, DeLorme publishes a paper map for each of the United States in the best-selling Atlas and Gazetteer series. DeLorme's Street Atlas USA, the first CD-ROM of detailed street maps offering complete coverage of the United States when it was released in 1991, continues to be a best-selling software product. Additional CD-ROM programs published by DeLorme include 3-D TopoQuads, XMap Business, Eartha Global Explorer, and DeLorme Topo USA. DeLorme is also a leader in Global Positioning System (GPS) software with a complete product line that is compatible with Earthmate, DeLorme's GPS receiver. DeLorme's headquarters in Yarmouth, Maine, houses Eartha, the largest rotating and revolving globe in the world.

1970s Entrepreneurial Roots

An enterprise that eventually would take on global scope began with one man at his kitchen table. According to company anecdote, David DeLorme, a Maine native and outdoorsman, was on a fishing trip at Moosehead Lake in the 1970s when he came to a fork in the road where his map indicated he should go straight. He realized then that he could make a better map, and

set about to do so. With a background in publishing as the editor of a compendium of Maine facts and tidbits called *The Maine Catalog,* DeLorme began work on piecing together a fully detailed map of the state of Maine. Gathering data from state highway, county, and town maps as well as federal surveys, DeLorme created a state map and had 10,000 copies printed in a large-format book. DeLorme himself then went town to town selling *The Maine Atlas and Gazetteer* out of his car. The mapbooks quickly caught on with hunters, fishermen, hikers, canoeists, campers, and salespeople because the maps detailed virtually every road, trail, river, stream, and body of water in the state. The maps initially featured and continue to include a gazetteer section that highlights a variety of sites to see and activities to do, including hiking and bicycle trails, canoeing and kayaking trips, and museum and historic sites.

By the early 1980s, DeLorme had a staff of eight employees who continued to revise the initial *Maine Atlas and Gazetteer* as well as create new maps. DeLorme and his staff began work on the most extensive and detailed map of Maine in an intermediate scale that allowed for a half-inch to equal a mile. This atlas was divided into 70 quadrangles depicting the longitudinal and latitudinal divisions into separate boxes that if pieced together would reach a height of 14 feet and a width of nine feet. To create this comprehensive detail, DeLorme and his staff utilized a variety of sources, ranging from pirated paper company maps to satellite photographs from NASA. In the end, the map took three years to plan and cost $100,000 to produce. DeLorme anticipated that the payoff for expending such resources could be great. At that time, he saw that the intermediate scale map could be used as a base upon which to expand future projects and ultimately place the map overlays into computer format that could be easily updated.

Mid-1980s Growth

The company had 75 employees by 1986 and had published atlases of other New England states, including New Hampshire, Vermont, and upstate New York. By 1988, the company had grown to over 100 employees in an overcrowded Freeport office and opened a distribution center in Portland. DeLorme published atlas and gazetteers for 11 states and had produced the

Company Perspectives:

At the forefront of the high-tech mapping industry, DeLorme is a leading publisher and producer of mapping software, GPS hardware, wireless and Internet mapping applications, as well as paper maps and atlases. Winning awards year after year, our products reflect the efforts of our dynamic, innovative, and talented workforce. We are headquartered in Yarmouth, Maine, just 15 miles north of Portland and 130 miles north of Boston. In our lobby, Eartha, a 3-story, 41-foot diameter rotating globe represents our vision to make the world and all its natural wonders immediately accessible to people of diverse backgrounds.

13th edition of the *Maine Atlas*. By the late 1980s, DeLorme sales had grown at least 50 percent since 1976, and, in 1987, the company posted a 200-percent sales growth, due in part to the growing popularity of its paper maps, but largely due to the addition of DeLorme Mapping Systems, a division devoted to computerized mapping technology. While paper maps constituted two-thirds of the company's business, sales were quickly shifting toward the computer technology market.

As DeLorme began to catalog and store data from paper maps onto computer databases, he quickly realized that there was no software program available to suit the needs of mapping. He hired several computer programmers and worked with them to develop the software and systems for mapping data. The task of computerizing data became the company's focus for three years, stalling further development and sales for other projects. Finally, in 1987, DeLorme produced a CD containing an atlas of the whole world. Areas of North America and Europe were visualized in a scale of ten miles to the inch, while other parts of the world were magnified at 20 miles to the inch. Other features included the ability to zoom out to satellite photo images of the world magnified at 420 feet to the inch. This initial software map provided the longitude and latitude for any global location within four decimal points.

As a result of the astounding detail of DeLorme's computer mapping technology, the company caught the eye of government officials. In the late 1980s, the company began work with defense contractors in Washington, D.C., providing expertise on government projects. However, an increasing number of customers who contracted with DeLorme with anywhere from $10,000 to $1 million were Fortune 500 companies who used DeLorme's XMap technology to integrate such information as site assessment into applications useful for their own industry. By 1989, DeLorme employed 15 computer programmers and company goals focused on continuing to attract technical personnel to increase their technology products.

The 1990s: Growing Gains and Pains

The push toward computer mapping technology brought DeLorme to the forefront in that market. In 1991 the company released Street Atlas USA, a CD-ROM detailing street maps across the entire United States. Upon its release, Street Atlas USA quickly became the top-selling mapping software program in the United States. Updated versions of that flagship program include more than four million sites of interest and businesses. Additionally, the XMap software suite, first introduced in the late 1980s, found a successful niche in the business sector and continued to help grow the company's business market.

By the mid-1990s DeLorme had established itself as the leading company in computer mapping software. In 1995 DeLorme held 44 percent of the market share, beating out such powerhouse firms as Rand McNally with 25 percent and Microsoft with 17.5 percent. In that same year, DeLorme partnered with the American Automobile Association (AAA) to produce AAA Map 'n Go, a CD-ROM travel planner that combined the extensive mapping data of DeLorme with AAA's huge database of lodgings, restaurants, and tourist attractions. In the late 1980s when the first network of global positioning satellites were placed in orbit, DeLorme was anticipating the need for the technology to link with the Global Positioning Satellite System (GPS). In 1996, DeLorme released the DeLorme GPS receiver, its initial hardware product created to integrate with DeLorme GPS software. Later, in 1998, the company released the Earthmate GPS receiver, which connected laptop and handheld computers to enable real-time navigation.

The company, dependent on government contracts in the 1980s, had by the mid-1990s shifted to a predominantly consumer and business oriented market. However, just two years after holding the premier market spot in computer mapping software, DeLorme slipped to a 28 percent share in 1997 behind the new market leader Rand McNally with 36 percent of the market. Company executives attributed the loss to increased competition in mapping software, the difficult retail environment, and a need for the company to develop new products more rapidly.

The company experienced some turbulent times in the 1990s. In 1995, DeLorme experienced an exodus of 53 employees out of a staff of 180 that some attribute to the unpredictable leadership of founder David DeLorme. DeLorme allegedly initiated a memo that was attributed to four top-level managers that notified employees they must reapply for their jobs or a newly created job. The four managers who were credited with the memo had received no warning the memo would be distributed, but then were placed in the position of mitigating damage control. David DeLorme maintained changes were necessary to secure a cutting edge spot in the rapidly shifting and competitive technical environment.

Some employees also questioned the ethical practices of the company. According to a report in the *Maine Times,* in 1996 Robert Crowder, a sales coordinator for DeLorme from 1990 to 1995, was "fired for expressing concern that company policies involved cheating the government." Crowder contended that DeLorme encouraged a practice of appropriating data from government sources and then using the data for DeLorme's commercial purposes. In 1999 the company was fined $780,000 after admitting in a plea agreement that the company claimed false ownership of proprietary government data of the Persian Gulf, Korea, and the former Soviet Union DeLorme had accessed between 1987 and 1991. According to a *Portland Press Herald* report, DeLorme had used the data for mapping materials sold to the Department of Defense but then claimed owner-

Key Dates:

1976: DeLorme is founded by David DeLorme; company publishes *The Maine Atlas and Gazetteer*, the first in the Atlas and Gazetteer series.
1987: Company creates first compact disc of world atlas.
1991: DeLorme produces the first consumer CD-ROM street atlas called Street Atlas USA.
1997: Company opens new headquarters in Yarmouth, Maine; company falls behind Rand McNally to hold second place in computer mapping software market.
1998: Eartha, the world's largest rotating and revolving globe, is unveiled at DeLorme headquarters, and company starts Eartha Education Alliance to educate children about the importance of geography.

ship on the information for subsequent CD-ROM products sold to other government agencies. While DeLorme admitted to the false claims, the company maintained that mistakes in attribution of ownership were unintentional.

In 1997 DeLorme relocated its company headquarters to Yarmouth in a $6 million, 100,000-square-foot building. In July 1998, the company unveiled Eartha, the biggest rotating and revolving globe in the world. Housed in the three-story glass atrium of the new company headquarters, Eartha was designed by David DeLorme and built by members of the DeLorme staff.

The impressive globe has a diameter of over 41 feet and a circumference of almost 130 feet. It took the staff over a year to compile the mapping data from satellite imagery, shaded relief, ocean-depth data, and road network and urban area information. The database was nearly 140 gigabytes, or 214 CD-ROMs. The surface of Eartha was comprised of 792 map sections mounted on panels that could be removed and updated. With an axis of 23.5 degrees, Eartha's rotation matched that of the Earth. The scale of Eartha was 1:1,000,000 of the actual Earth, which made one inch on Eartha equal to almost 16 miles on Earth. In 1999, Eartha was declared the "World's Largest Globe" by the *Guinness Book of World Records*. Listed among top tourist attractions in New England, Eartha was created to inspire and educate. David DeLorme stated, "Eartha is the largest image of Earth ever created. It will help us make even better maps and will help others envision how we on Earth are all connected. Eartha will instill a sense of wonder in people when they first see it and we hope they walk away from it with a better appreciation and knowledge of the world around them." To further its educational commitment, DeLorme launched the Eartha Education Alliance non-profit program in 1998. Available for groups of children from third to eighth grade, the program sought to offer hands-on experience to inspire and educate children about world and local geography.

Mapping a New Strategy for the 21st Century

Financial woes, prompted in part by economic recession, challenged the company in the late 1990s. DeLorme asked workers to take a two-week furlough in late December 2001. In early January 2002, the company laid off 52 of its 200 employees. The layoffs were part of the company's plan to restructure its workforce and focus on new product lines. Gordon Pow, DeLorme's president and chief operating officer, cited a drop from $30.2 million in net sales in November 2000 to $26.2 million in net sales in November 2001 as the prime reason for the "agonizing" cuts, which were targeted at employees in consumer products sales, marketing, and other functions. Hoping to revitalize sales, the company shifted from a consumer products market to focus on information systems for scientific and professional markets. At the beginning of 2002 DeLorme remained focused on its goal of leading the market in geographical satellite and aerial imagery.

Principal Competitors

Rand McNally & Co.; AAA; MapQuest.com, Inc.; Microsoft Corporation.

Further Reading

Canfield, Clarke, "DeLorme Fined for Lying to U.S.," *Portland Press Herald,* July 28, 1999, pp. 1A, 8A.
Clark, Jeff, "The Whole World in His Hand," *Down East,* September 1988, pp. 72–74; 88–89.
"DeLorme Publishing Co.," *Industry Standard,* October 22, 2002.
Halper, Evan, "Success at a Price," *Maine Times,* January 25, 1996, pp. 1–5.
Haskell, Meg, "U.S. Catches up to DeLorme; Mapmaker Fined $780,000," *Maine Times,* August 5, 1999, p. 9.
Liljeholm, Lyn, "Catalog Chronicles Maine Tidbits," *Portland Evening Express,* May 10, 1973, pp. 1, 12.
Long, Alan, "DeLorme Goes Global," *Mainebiz,* February 1998, pp. 26, 28.
Murphy, Edward D., "DeLorme Freezes Salaries, Seeks New Ways to Market," *Portland Press Herald,* February 3, 1998, pp. 1C, 7C.
——, "Most at DeLorme Told to Take Time off to Cut Costs," *Portland Press Herald,* December 4, 2001, p. 1C.
Smith, Jeff, "Charting New Territory," *Portland Press Herald,* July 4, 1989, pp. 9, 12.
——, "Finding His Way," *Portland Press Herald,* November 14, 1995, pp. 1C, 7C.
Turkel, Tux, "DeLorme Lays off 52, Maps out New Strategy," *Portland Press Herald,* January 8, 2002, pp. 1A, 7A.
——, "Maine's Master of Maps," *Maine Sunday Telegram,* August 30, 1981, pp. 13A-14A.
Vietze, Andrew, "A Whole New World," *Down East,* August 1998, pp. 84–85.

—Elizabeth Henry

Electrolux AB

St. Gorangsgatan
143, Stockholm
Sweden
Telephone: (08) 738-6000
Fax: (08) 656-4478
Web site: http://www.electrolux.com

Public Company
Incorporated: 1919 as Aktiebolaget Elektrolux
Employees: 87,139
Sales: SKr 135.8 billion ($12.9 billion) (2001)
Stock Exchanges: Stockholm London Paris Swiss
    NASDAQ
Ticker Symbol: ELUX
NAIC: 335221 Household Cooking Appliance
    Manufacturing; 335222 Household Refrigerator and
    Home Freezer Manufacturing; 335224 Household
    Laundry Equipment Manufacturing; 335212
    Household Vacuum Cleaner Manufacturing; 333112
    Lawn and Garden Tractor and Home Lawn and
    Garden Equipment Manufacturing

Electrolux AB operates as the largest appliance manufacturer in the world with customers in more than 150 countries. The company manufactures a variety of household appliances including refrigerators, washing machines, dishwashers, ovens, vacuum cleaners, lawn mowers, and chain saws. The firm also manufactures professional foodservice and laundry equipment used by hotels, restaurants, and laundromats. Electrolux's brand arsenal includes its namesake, along with Eureka, AEG, Frigidaire, Kelvinator, Zanussi, Flymo, Weed Eater, and Husqvarna. In 2001, the firm held the leading market position in North America, Europe, Latin America, and Australia. Electrolux completed a major restructuring effort in 1999, which left it positioned with two main business segments: Consumer Durables and Professional Products. In 2000, the company purchased the rights to market the Electrolux brand in the United States—the company had sold the brand along with its U.S. floor-care business in 1969.

Beginnings in Vacuum Cleaners

The Electrolux empire originated with the perspicacity and marketing flair of Axel Wenner-Gren, who spotted the potential of the mobile vacuum cleaner only a few years after its invention by Englishman H.C. Booth in 1901. In 1910 the young Wenner-Gren bought a part share in the European agent of a U.S. company producing one of the early vacuum cleaners, the clumsy Santo Staubsauger. After a couple of years as a Santo salesman for the German-based agent, Wenner-Gren sold his share of the company and returned to Sweden, where the building blocks for the future Electrolux, Lux and Elektromekaniska AB, were already in place.

Sven Carlstedt had formed Elektromekaniska in 1910 to manufacture motors for a vacuum cleaner based on the Santo, which was produced by Swedish engineer Eberhardt Seger. Since its founding in 1901, Lux had manufactured kerosene lamps. Now confronted with a shrinking market owing to the introduction of electric lighting, Lux head, C.G. Lindblom, proposed to Sven Carlstedt that the two companies form a joint venture for the production and marketing of a new vacuum cleaner.

In 1912 Wenner-Gren became the agent for the Lux 1 vacuum cleaner in Germany, subsequently taking on the United Kingdom and France. Over the next few years Wenner-Gren's role in the company grew, and the machine gradually became lighter and more ergonomic. Wenner-Gren foresaw a potential sales bonanza in Europe after the end of World War I. Initially unable to persuade his colleagues to step up production capacity, he overcame their reluctance by guaranteeing a minimum sales figure through his own sales company, Svenska Elektron (later known as Finans AB Svetro).

Lux and Elektromekaniska merged in 1919 as Aktiebolaget Elektrolux (the spelling was changed to Electrolux in 1957). Wenner-Gren became president and a major shareholder of the new company. In 1921 the Lux V was introduced. This new model resembled a modern cylindrical vacuum cleaner, but it glided along the floor on ski-like runners instead of wheels. The Lux V was to present serious competition to the upright Hoover machines in the 1920s.

Company Perspectives:

Our vision is for Electrolux to be the world leader in consumer durables for indoor and outdoor use, with a selected range of corresponding products for professional users. Through good growth and profitability, Electrolux shall create value for shareholders as well as for consumers, business partners, and employees. Value creation is our measure of operational performance within the Group, and is monitored for each sector, product line, and region.

The convenience and attractive styling of its product helped to get the new company off to a promising start, but the salesmanship of Electrolux's president probably played an even bigger part. Wenner-Gren was a great believer in the door-to-door sales techniques already espoused by competitors such as Hoover in the United States. Vacuum cleaners were demonstrated to potential customers in their own homes, and buyers were allowed to pay for their machines in installments. Wenner-Gren knew how to get the best out of his sales force.

To today's sales managers, sales training, competitions, and slogans like ''Every home an Electrolux home'' are familiar methods of boosting sales, but when Wenner-Gren introduced them they were revolutionary. He also believed in leading from the front. The story of how he sold a vacuum cleaner to the Vatican is part of company mythology. Four competitors demonstrated their machines first, each vacuuming their allocated area of carpet. When Wenner-Gren's turn came, instead of vacuuming the fifth area, he went over the first four again. The resultant bagful of dust persuaded the pope to add his palace to the growing number of Electrolux homes. Advertising, too, was imaginative. Not only did Electrolux make extensive use of the press, but in the late 1920s, citizens of Stockholm, Berlin, and London were liable to encounter bizarre vacuum cleaner-shaped cars in the streets.

Bizarre or not, the sales methods worked, and the company grew. Throughout the 1920s, new sales companies sprang up, not only all over Europe but also in the United States in 1924, Australia in 1925, and South America. Many of these were financed by Wenner-Gren himself rather than by Electrolux in Sweden. Vacuum cleaner manufacturing plants also started to open overseas, first in Berlin in 1926 and a year later in Luton, England, and Courbevoie, France.

By 1928 Electrolux had sales of SKr 70 million. It had five manufacturing plants, 350 worldwide offices, and 20 subsidiaries. In spite of this geographic expansion, the company was often short of funds, in part because of the system of payment by installments. It became clear that further growth would require increased capital, and it was decided to float the company on the London Stock Exchange and to issue more shares. Prior to flotation in 1928, Electrolux bought out many of the related companies owned by Wenner-Gren, though he retained his minority shareholding in the American Electrolux Corporation until 1949.

Flotation on the Stockholm stock exchange was postponed until 1930 owing to the stock market crash. When the shares did appear they were greeted with some mistrust, as it was thought that the company was overvalued and that sales would suffer during the anticipated recession. These doubts, however, were to prove unfounded.

Diversifying into Refrigerators in the Mid-1920s

During the 1920s Electrolux introduced a number of new products, including floor-polishers, a natural progression from vacuum cleaners, which were brought out in 1927. The main diversification of the 1920s, however, came through the acquisition in 1925 of Arctic, a company manufacturing a novel machine, the absorption refrigerator. This type of refrigerator has no moving parts, though early models required connection to a source of running water. Power can be provided by electricity, gas, or kerosene as opposed to the compression method of refrigeration, which relies on electric power. Early compressors were noisy and bulky, so the new Electrolux system had several advantages over its competitors' compression refrigerators.

A new air-cooled version of Electrolux's absorption refrigerators was introduced in 1931, and by 1936 more than one million had been sold. Demand for the machines grew as restrictions were placed on the use of food preservatives by legislation such as the United Kingdom Food Preservative Act of 1927. In the United States, Servel Inc. had acquired a license to manufacture Electrolux's refrigerators.

Electrolux's original vacuum cleaner factory on Lilla Essingen was devastated by fire in 1936. When it was rebuilt the following year, the opportunity was taken to fit it with the latest equipment and to install a central research laboratory.

In 1926 Wenner-Gren became chairman of the board, with Ernst Aurell taking over as president. During the 1930s Wenner-Gren remained chairman but reduced his involvement in the running of the company, prior to resigning from his post in 1939. Harry G. Faulkner, a British accountant who had been instrumental in the company's consolidation prior to the 1928 flotation, succeeded Aurell in 1930 and remained president throughout the 1930s.

With intensive marketing and continued investment in research and development, Electrolux rode out the Great Depression. By 1939 annual sales stood at SKr 80 million. In 1939 Gustaf Sahlin, former president of the United States Electrolux Corporation, took over the presidency of the parent company from Faulkner. Throughout World War II, despite the loss of some manufacturing plants, Electrolux managed to maintain many of its usual activities, opening operations in Australia, Venezuela, and Colombia. At home in Sweden, it acquired companies in the fields of commercial laundry equipment and outboard motors. Much energy, however, was diverted into the war effort, including the manufacture of munitions and of air cleaners for the Swedish forces.

After the war Electrolux resumed its normal operations, initially under Elon V. Ekman, who became president in 1951, and from 1963 to 1967 under his successor Harry Wennberg. The period was not without setbacks, however. Many subsidiaries that had been opened in Eastern European countries before the war disappeared from view behind the Iron Curtain. In addition, despite a British government contract to supply 50,000

Key Dates:

1919: Lux and Elektromekaniska merge to form Aktiebolaget Elektrolux.

1921: The Lux V vacuum cleaner is introduced.

1925: The company acquires Arctic, an absorption refrigerator manufacturer.

1956: Axel Wenner-Gren sells his stake in the firm to Wallenberg, a Swedish finance group.

1957: The company changes the spelling of its name to Electrolux.

1962: ElektroHelios, a Scandinavian market leader in compressor refrigerators and freezers, is acquired.

1967: Hans Werthén is named president.

1974: Electrolux purchases United States-based Eureka.

1984: Zanussi, an Italian household appliance manufacturer, is acquired.

1997: Michael Treschow is named president and CEO; a major restructuring effort is launched.

2000: The company buys the rights to the Electrolux brand in North America.

2002: Treschow leaves to head up Ericsson; Hans Straberg is named his successor.

---

built-in absorption refrigerators for prefabricated temporary houses, the company began to face problems in the refrigerator market. Compression technology had advanced and was proving more effective for the larger refrigerators that consumers were now demanding. Although at first the company concentrated on improving the design of the absorption refrigerator, Electrolux eventually was obliged to adopt compression technology.

Meanwhile, diversification continued. During the 1950s Electrolux started making household washing machines and dishwashers, and floor-cleaning equipment production was extended to an increasing number of countries, including Brazil and Norway. When, in 1956, Axel Wenner-Gren sold his remaining shares in Electrolux to Wallenberg, a Swedish finance group, annual turnover exceeded SKr 500 million. The association with Wallenberg has often stood Electrolux in good stead, helping, for example, to arrange overseas funding and to insulate the group from any hostile takeover bids.

In 1962, in an attempt to solve its refrigerator problems, Electrolux bought the Swedish firm of ElektroHelios. This firm, founded in 1919, had a major share of the Scandinavian market in compressor refrigerators and freezers, as well as making stoves. In the year following the acquisition, Electrolux launched a wide range of food-storage equipment, putting it in a strong position to benefit from the demands generated by the flourishing frozen food industry.

Major Acquisitions: Late 1960s–80s

Until the 1960s Electrolux had continued to operate along the lines conceived by Wenner-Gren in the early years. A new phase began in 1967, when Hans Werthén was recruited from Ericsson, another member of the Wallenberg group of compa-

nies. Werthén remained with Electrolux for more than 25 years, first as president, and from 1975 to 1991 as chairman, with Gösta Bystedt and then Anders Scharp succeeding him as president. Under this regime, a series of momentous acquisitions was to allow Electrolux to multiply its turnover by a factor of 60 in 20 years.

When Werthén took over management of the Electrolux group the company was in the doldrums; it had run into internal and external problems, and its technology was outmoded. Electrolux, an international company, had not been effectively integrated with its acquisition ElektroHelios, which still focused on the Scandinavian market. In many ways the merged companies had continued to behave as if they were still competitors, resulting in a net loss of market share in the refrigerator market. Only the vacuum cleaners were profitable: to use Werthén's own words, "they represented 125 percent of the profits."

Approaching the problem from a new perspective, Werthén managed to resolve the Electrolux-ElektroHelios conflict and get rid of the organizational overlap. His new head of production, Anders Scharp, set about updating production technology to challenge the much more advanced techniques he had seen in U.S. appliance factories. Werthén believed that Electrolux's problems could not be overcome simply by operational improvements. The company had a more fundamental problem: size.

As Werthén saw it, Electrolux was neither small enough to be a niche player, nor large enough to gain the economies of scale it needed to compete with such giants as Philips and AEG. Growth was the only way forward, and in the overcrowded market place for household goods, growth meant acquisitions.

The initial focus was on Scandinavia. One small competitor after another, many of them struggling for survival, was bought up by the growing company. The Norwegian stove manufacturer Elektra, the Danish white goods company Atlas, and the Finnish stove maker Slev were among the first acquisitions of the late 1960s. Soon Electrolux was shopping for competitors outside Scandinavia. The 1974 acquisition of Eureka, one of the longest established vacuum cleaner companies in the United States, gave Electrolux a large slice of a valuable market overnight.

At around this time there were glimmerings of hope for the reemergence of the absorption refrigerator. The quiet-running units were ideally suited to installation in smaller living spaces, such as mobile homes and hotel rooms. Electrolux managers soon sensed these new opportunities. After taking over competitors Kreft (of Luxembourg) and Siegas (of Germany) in 1972, the group became world leader in this sector.

In addition to expanding its share of the company's existing markets, Electrolux soon started to see acquisitions as a way of entering new areas, particularly those related to existing product lines. Electrolux acquired the British lawn mower manufacturer Flymo in 1968 because Werthén saw lawn mowing as an activity allied to floor cleaning. The provision of cleaning services seemed a logical extension to the production of cleaning equipment, prompting the purchase of a half share in the Swedish cleaning company ASAB.

Buying up the venerable Swedish firm of Husqvarna in 1978 gave Electrolux not only a new pool of expertise in commercial refrigeration, but also a flourishing chainsaw-manufacturing concern, which complemented its interests in outdoor equipment. Taking over a clutch of other chainsaw manufacturers over the following decade—including the U.S. firm Poulan/Weed Eater in 1986—enabled Electrolux to claim leadership of the worldwide chainsaw market. The outdoor products sector was further strengthened and broadened through the acquisitions of American Yard Products in 1988 and of Allegretti & Co., a U.S. maker of battery-driven garden tools, in 1990.

This program of acquisitions brought some more radical departures from existing product lines. In 1973 Electrolux bought Facit, a Swedish office equipment company. The deal also brought to Electrolux the production of Ballingslöv kitchen and bathroom cabinets. Initial doubts about whether Electrolux had the know-how to manage a high-tech company proved unfounded.

The purchase of Swedish metal producer Gränges was greeted with equal skepticism, since again the connection between the new and existing businesses appeared to be rather tenuous. Gränges was seen as a troubled company, but when Electrolux bought it in 1980, Werthén had already been chairman of its board for three years and had overseen a marked upturn in its fortunes. Gränges became part of Electrolux in 1980, and by the late 1980s Gränges' aluminum products and car seat belts represented a major aspect of Electrolux's business, although other parts of Gränges were sold off.

Under the presidency of Anders Scharp, which began in 1981, Electrolux's program of acquisitions began to focus on the consolidation and expansion of existing lines. Takeovers became increasingly ambitious as Electrolux saw within its reach the chance to become one of the world leaders in household appliances. Major steps toward this goal were the acquisitions of Zanussi in Italy, White Consolidated in the United States (the third largest white goods company in that country), and the white goods and catering equipment divisions of the United Kingdom's Thorn EMI, in 1984, 1986, and 1987, respectively.

Through the years, Electrolux gained a reputation for buying only when the price was right and for turning around sick companies, even at the cost of heavy staff cuts and management shake-ups. As the *Wall Street Journal* pointed out in 1986 in a piece about the acquisition of White Consolidated, the group balance sheet looked unhealthy immediately after some of the larger acquisitions, showing an equity-asset ratio as low as 21 percent.

Electrolux bounced back confidently, making divestments as well as acquisitions. One of Werthén's earliest acts as president had been the 1968 sale of AB Electrolux's minority shareholding in the United States Electrolux Corporation to Consolidated Foods, which raised SKr 300 million, although the subsequent Eureka purchase had placed the company in the curious position of competing against its own brand name. Management continued this policy of judicious divestment following acquisitions, when it was considered that all or part of the new member did not fit in with the group's strategy. Facit, for instance, was sold to Ericsson in 1983, and shortly after the purchase of White Consolidated, its machine-tool division, White Machine Tools, was sold off.

Another method of raising cash was through the sale of assets, although Electrolux acquisitions were not primarily motivated by a desire to strip assets. In the case of Husqvarna, the purchase price of SKr 120 million was more than covered within six months by the sale of its land and other property. A third way of recovering the costs of acquisition was the use of a troubled company's accumulated losses wherever possible to reduce the group's tax liability. This was a major incentive in the acquisition of Gränges.

Not every company was delighted to hear Electrolux knocking on its door. Many a takeover was resisted by the target company, although Electrolux was also sometimes called in to rescue a troubled company (as happened with Zanussi) or asked to act as a white knight (notably for the U.S. household appliance company Tappan in 1979).

Geographic Expansion and Restructurings in the 1990s

The 1990s brought major changes to Electrolux, spearheaded by a new management team. Werthén resigned as chairman in early 1991, Scharp became chairman and CEO, and Leif Johansson was named president of the firm, taking over as CEO himself in 1994. During Werthén's long reign, Electrolux had grown tremendously through acquisitions but had failed to effectively consolidate the acquired operations into existing ones. The result was an unwieldy array of brands, each of which needing the support of separate production and marketing operations. Electrolux was further hurt in the early 1990s by an economic downturn in its core European and North American operations and by the maturing of the white goods sectors in those same markets, which intensified competition. All told, profits for Electrolux from 1990 through 1994 were much lower than the heights reached during the late 1980s. The new management team responded by seeking out new markets for its core products, by gradually divesting its noncore industrial products operations, and by streamlining its remaining business units.

Electrolux targeted Eastern Europe, Asia, South America, the Middle East, and southern Africa in its 1990s push for global growth. The company had already, in 1989, arranged for Sharp Corporation to distribute some of Electrolux's products in Japan. Subsequent moves in Asia included the setting up of joint ventures in China for the manufacture of compressors, vacuum cleaners, and water purifiers, and the acquisition of majority stakes in refrigerator and washing machine factories in India. In January 1996 another Chinese joint venture was established for the production of refrigerators and freezers for commercial users. The newly opened markets of Eastern Europe were first targeted with the 1991 purchase of the Hungarian white goods company Lehel. A 1995 joint venture with Poland's Myszkow FNE Swiatowit began making washing machines under the Zanussi brand. In Latin America, where Whirlpool was dominant, Electrolux acquired 99 percent of Refrigeraçao Paraná S.A. (Refripar) in 1996. Refripar (soon renamed Electrolux do Brazil) held the number two position among Brazilian white goods companies. Also in 1996, Electrolux purchased a 20 percent stake in Atlas Eléctrica S.A. of Costa Rica, the leading producer of refrigerators and stoves in Central America. By 1994, about 10 percent of Electrolux's sales came from outside the European Union and North America. This figure more than doubled by 1996 to 20.4

percent, with non-EU Europe accounting for 7 percent, Latin America for 6.4 percent, Asia for 5.1 percent, Oceania for 1 percent, and Africa for 0.9 percent.

While undergoing this global expansion, Electrolux also moved gradually to concentrate solely on three core sectors: household appliances, commercial appliances, and outdoor products. Profits in the company's industrial products sector were falling and Scharp and Johansson determined that these noncore operations should be jettisoned. The culmination of this process came in 1996 and 1997, with the divestment of the Constructor group, producers of materials-handling equipment; the sale of the Swedish electronics operations of Electrolux Electronics, and a sewing machines unit; and the spinoff of Gränges to the public. The final divestment came in August 1997 when Electrolux's goods protection operation, which sold tarpaulins and storage halls, was sold to MVI, a privately owned investment fund.

Electrolux greatly reduced its acquisitions activity in the European Union and North America in the 1990s, although there was one major addition. In 1992 the company bought a 10 percent stake in AEG Hausgeräte, the household appliance division of Germany's Daimler-Benz. This stake was increased to 20 percent in 1993 and the following year Electrolux purchased the remaining 80 percent for about US$437 million. The purchase brought the company another strong European brand, which fit well into a renewed brand strategy for Electrolux. The company sought to position the Electrolux brand as a global brand and Electrolux, Zanussi, and AEG as pan-European brands, while continuing to maintain strong local brands such as Faure in France and Tricity Bendix in the United Kingdom.

Along with the new brand strategy, Electrolux began in 1996 to reduce its fragmented operations and become more efficient. A pan-European logistics function was set up for white goods and floor-care products. In late 1996 the company's North American white goods operation, Frigidaire Company, was combined with the two North American outdoor products companies, Poulan/Weed Eater and American Yard Products, to form Frigidaire Home Products. Merging these operations made strategic sense since the trend in retailing was toward single retailers selling both indoor and outdoor appliances. Similar consolidations were planned for Electrolux's operations elsewhere in the world.

In April 1997 Johansson left Electrolux to become the chief executive at Volvo AB. Replacing him as Electrolux president and CEO was Michael Treschow, who had been president and CEO at Atlas Copco AB, a maker of industrial equipment and, like Electrolux, part of the Wallenberg dynasty. It was left to Treschow to announce, in June 1997, a major restructuring plan, which had already been agreed upon before he took over. Over a two-year period, Electrolux would lay off more than 11,000 of its workers (11 percent of its workforce) and close 23 plants and 50 warehouses (half of its global total), with the reductions coming mainly in Europe and North America. A charge of SKr 2.5 billion (US$323 million) was incurred as the result of the restructuring in the second quarter of 1997.

Under the leadership of Treschow, Electrolux further streamlined its operations in 1998, divesting its recycling busi-

ness, its kitchen and bathroom cabinets interests, and various professional cleaning and heavy-duty laundry equipment units. The following year, the firm sold off its food and beverage vending machine businesses and its professional refrigeration equipment business. That year, Electrolux nixed a large portion of its direct sales force.

The company completed its restructuring efforts in 1999 and began to focus on maintaining its leadership position in the future. Treschow was confident that the firm's efforts would pay off, claiming in a 1999 *Appliance Manufacturer* article that the company was "ideally placed to meet the challenges of the new millennium." To back up that claim, the company began to develop new products that utilized cutting edge technology. In 1999, it teamed up with Ericsson to develop and market products for the "networked home." Managed under the joint venture, e2Home, these products would be connected via the Web to a variety of information and service providers. Another product line, the Live-In Kitchen, connected appliances to mobile phones, which among other features, allowed the owner to preheat their oven from their cell phone. As part of its foray into new technology, Electrolux also developed the Trilobite vacuum cleaner, a robotic product that used sensors to vacuum a room, and a Smart Fridge, a top-of-the-line refrigerator complete with built-in computer screen and Internet access.

Focusing on Brand Alignment in the New Millennium

By 2000, both sales and net income had increased steadily over the past three years. Sales had grown from SKr 113 billion to SKr 124.4 billion. Net income also had recovered, skyrocketing from SKr 352 million recorded in 1997, to SKr 4.4 billion secured in 2000. During that year, the company repurchased its rights to the Electrolux brand in North America, which it had sold in 1969 upon divesting its U.S. floor-care company. The purchase was part of its plan to align its brand names, especially in North America.

The company's operating environment became turbulent in 2001. Weakening demand and high costs related to upgrades at its refrigerator factories in North America forced the firm's operating income to fall by nearly 23 percent over the previous year. Despite these challenges, the company made two key acquisitions, including Email Ltd., Australia's largest household appliance manufacturer, and Italy-based Marazzini, a lawn mower manufacturer.

In April 2002, Hans Straberg took over as president and CEO as Treschow left the firm to head up Ericsson. Under new leadership, Electrolux shifted its focus from cost cutting to brand realignment. At the time, the company managed more than 50 different brands. The *Economist* reported in April 2002 that the company realized that "rationalizing the brands can be dangerous if done too quickly—so the rebranding will be more evolution than revolution. The Electrolux name will become the master brand, but the company will keep strong local brands, such as the Flymo lawnmower in Britain."

Facing strong competition and uncertain economic times, Straberg most definitely had his work cut out for him. Although the repositioning of the Electrolux brand name would no doubt face challenges, the company appeared to be well on its way to maintaining its leadership position in the appliance industry in the years to come.

Principal Subsidiaries

Electrolux Home Products Pty. Ltd. (Australia); Electrolux Hausgerate GmbH (Austria); Electrolux Home Products Corp. N.V. (Belgium); Electrolux do Brasil S.A. (99.9%); Electrolux Canada Corp.; Electrolux Home Appliances Co. Ltd. (China); Electrolux Holding A/S (Denmark); Oy Electrolux Ab (Finland); Electrolux France S.A.; Electrolux Deutschland GmbH (Germany); Electrolux Kelvinator Ltd. (India; 76%); Electrolux Zanussi S.p.A. (Italy); Electrolux de Mexico, S.A. de C.V.; Electrolux Associated Company B.V. (The Netherlands); Electrolux Norge AS (Norway); Electrolux Espana S.A. (Spain); Husqvarna AB; Electrolux Professional AB; Electrolux Holding AG (Switzerland); Electrolux UK Ltd.; Electrolux Home Products Inc. (U.S.A.); Electrolux North American Inc. (U.S.A.).

Principal Competitors

BSH Bosch und Siemens Hausgeräte GmbH; GE Consumer Products; Whirlpool Corporation.

Further Reading

"Brand Challenge; Electrolux," *Economist* (U.S.), April 6, 2002.
Brown-Humes, Christopher, "Electrolux to Plug into Households in Opening Markets," *Financial Times,* April 27, 1995, p. 25.
Burt, Tim, "Electrolux Set to Pull Out of Industrial Goods," *Financial Times,* October 30, 1996, p. 28.
Calian, Sara, "Electrolux to Cut Force by 11%, Mainly in North America, Europe," *Wall Street Journal,* June 13, 1997, p. A15.
Canedy, Dana, "Electrolux to Cut 12,000 Workers and Shut Plants," *New York Times,* June 13, 1997, p. D2.
"Can 'Mike the Knife' Give Electrolux a Net-Age Edge?," *Business Week,* September 13, 2000.
"Electrolux Expects to Be No. 1 Appliance Maker," *Appliance Manufacturer,* February 1994, p. 20.
"Electrolux News," *Appliance,* December 1999, p. 18.
"Electrolux News," *Appliance,* May 2002, p. 15.
"Electrolux Plots a New Strategy," *Housewares,* January 1, 1990, p. 78.
"Electrolux Sweeps into America," *Business Week,* September 23, 2002.
Electrolux: Two Epochs That Shaped a Worldwide Group, Stockholm: Electrolux, 1989.
Gordon, Bob, *Early Electrical Appliances,* Princes Risborough, United Kingdom: Shire Publications Ltd., 1984.
Holding, Robert L., "Globalization: The Second Decade," *Appliance Manufacturer,* May 1999, p. 34.
Jancsurak, Joe, "Big Plans for Europe's Big Three," *Appliance Manufacturer,* April 1995, pp. 26–30.
Kapstein, Jonathan, and Zachary Schiller, "The Fast-Spinning Machine That Blew a Gasket," *Business Week,* September 10, 1990, pp. 50, 52.
Lorenz, Christopher, "The Birth of a 'Transnational,'" *Financial Times,* June 19, 1989.
McGrath, Neal, "New Broom Sweeps into Asia," *Asian Business,* March 1996, p. 22.
McIvor, Greg, "Electrolux Comes Under the Scalpel," *Financial Times,* October 29, 1997, p. 19.
Moss, Nicholas, and Hale Richards, "Mike the Knife Cuts Deep," *European,* June 19, 1997, p. 17.
Racanelli, Vito, "Autumn Fall for Electrolux," *Barron's,* July 29, 2002.
"The Real Head of the Household," *Director,* November 1996, p. 17.
Reed, Stanley, "The Wallenbergs' New Blood," *Business Week,* October 20, 1997, pp. 98, 102.
Sparke, Penny, *Electrical Appliances: Twentieth-Century Design,* New York: E.P. Dutton, 1987.
"The Stars of Europe—Survivors," *Business Week,* June 11, 2001.
"Sweden's Electrolux Plans for Expansion into Southeast Asia," *Wall Street Journal,* January 4, 1995, p. B7.
Tully, Shawn, "Electrolux Wants a Clean Sweep," *Fortune,* August 18, 1986, p. 60.
Zweig, Jason, "Cleaning Up," *Forbes,* December 11, 1989, p. 302.

—Alison Classe
—updates: David E. Salamie and
Christina M. Stansell

Evergreen International Aviation, Inc.

3850 Three Mile Lane
McMinnville, Oregon 97128-9496
U.S.A.
Telephone: (503) 472-9361
Fax: (503) 472-1048
Web site: http://www.evergreenaviation.com

Private Company
Incorporated: 1960 as Evergreen Helicopters, Inc.
Employees: 4000
Sales: $700 million (2001)
NAIC: 111332 Grape Vineyards; 111335 Tree Nut
   Farming; 111998 All Other Miscellaneous Crop
   Farming; 111199 All Other Grain Farming; 111421
   Nursery and Tree Production; 311330 Confectionery
   Manufacturing from Purchased Chocolate; 311340
   Nonchocolate Confectionery Manufacturing; 311423
   Dried and Dehydrated Food Manufacturing; 311821
   Cookie and Cracker Manufacturing; 481112
   Scheduled Freight Air Transportation; 481211 Non-
   scheduled Chartered Passenger Air Transportation;
   481212 Nonscheduled Chartered Freight Air Trans-
   portation; 488119 Other Airport Operations; 488190
   Other Support Activities for Air Transportation;
   551112 Offices of Other Holding Companies

The "airline's airline," Evergreen International Airlines, Inc. is an air freight carrier that hauls cargo for a number of other passenger airlines and shipping companies. Its fleet includes 11 Boeing 747's and a few other types of planes. Evergreen also has several other ventures that handle freight on the ground, trade aircraft, and maintain planes. Helicopters were the company's original business, and it still has a large rotorcraft interest. In addition, the company runs a substantial farming operation on the land surrounding its base in Oregon's Willamette Valley. The company is not to be confused with the Evergreen Marine shipping empire of Taiwan or its airline, EVA Airways.

Origins

The Evergreen International Aviation group of companies was founded by Delford M. Smith. Smith, an orphan, was born in 1930. He went to work at an early age, first by delivering newspapers. Smith later worked at logging camps while attending the University of Washington. After graduating in 1953, he joined the Air Force. In 1957, Smith began flying helicopters and subsequently went on to work for agricultural, forestry, and oil concerns as well as on firefighting missions. Eventually, Smith set out on his own, buying his first choppers on credit. His company—Evergreen Helicopters, Inc.—was registered in Oregon on July 1, 1960. Early the next year, Evergreen Helicopters of Alaska was established. The company grew substantially during the Vietnam War. In fact, under contract from Royal Dutch/Shell to evacuate employees, it remained in Vietnam a few days longer than the U.S. military.

In 1974, Evergreen had bought the lease to a large air base in Marana, Arizona, from the Central Intelligence Agency, which was coming under congressional pressure to divest its holdings in airlines such as Air America. The Marana facility, which had the capability to work on any type of aircraft, became known as Evergreen Air Base and housed repair and overhaul operations.

By 1975, Smith had a fleet of 98 helicopters. He developed pioneering new uses for the rotorcraft, capitalizing on new opportunities as they arose. For example, Smith logged his own timber and flew it out of remote locations before lumber prices collapsed in the early 1980s. Also in 1975, Smith's company bought Johnson Flying Service, a small airline in Missoula, Montana, that had a license to fly anywhere in the United States as a "supplemental carrier." The growing company was relocated to McMinnville, Oregon, and renamed Evergreen International Airlines.

Evergreen Air, Inc., a holding company for the diversifying businesses, was registered in Oregon on August 3, 1978; the name of this entity changed to Evergreen International Aviation, Inc. (EAI) on December 15, 1980. Work soon began on a new 22,000-square-foot, two-level headquarters building. In 1978, the company bought 1,000 acres of land surrounding its base in tiny McMinnville and created Evergreen Farms.

Post-Deregulation Diversification

Soon, Evergreen was flying charters to Hawaii and the Caribbean. After deregulation of the airline industry, it ventured into scheduled operations to the Caribbean. Twice-weekly flights between Philadelphia and the Bahamas began in February 1979. The company also began offering tours from the Northwest to Hawaii and Las Vegas. However, deregulation allowed the major airlines to price Evergreen out of these markets. The company was more successful in setting up cargo routes on both sides of the country; however, it dropped its East Coast network in November 1979.

A new subsidiary, Evergreen Tours, was created in February 1980 to market tours and charters. The unit soon launched a joint venture with New York's Atlas Travel for travel to Israel.

Difficult and sensitive missions continued at the same time Evergreen was trying its hand in the pleasure flight market. The company transported the deposed Shah of Iran part of the way from Panama to Egypt via a DC-8 airliner. It had been referred by Executive Jet Aviation, Inc., whose planes did not have the required range or capacity.

The company began flying cargo to New York's John F. Kennedy International Airport in 1980. Evergreen had 228 aircraft on order at the time, from helicopters to DC-8s. The airline had 19 planes—some owned, some leased, and some being leased to others. The company was now building a 55,000-square-foot, three-level building to house its Evergreen International Airlines subsidiary. There were more than 1,200 employees in all. Total revenues for 1980 were estimated at $150 million. The airline and helicopter units were profitable in spite of the recession at that time. Nevertheless, a downturn in the construction industry led to less demand for Evergreen Helicopters' giant Sikorsky S-64E Skycrane. The company had two of this model, plus another 110 helicopters in its fleet. Evergreen was promoting the use of helicopters as high-speed ambulances in urban areas and was already operating them for hospitals in Houston, Phoenix, and San Diego.

In 1981, Evergreen set up overnight freight service for United Parcel Service (UPS). It continued to operate it for several years, until UPS took it over with its own aircraft. In 1982, the company entered into a more enduring contract, using helicopters to carry mail to remote outposts in northwestern Alaska.

In 1984, Evergreen acquired Airspur Helicopters, the Los Angeles area commuter helicopter service that Evergreen had previously been operating on behalf of Westland Inc., a subsidiary of the British helicopter manufacturer. This venture endured for only a short time. In May 1987, Evergreen established a regional hub in Terre Haute, Indiana, to sort and ship for the firm of Express Mail. When online, this unit, which employed 750 people, was processing 1.3 million pieces of overnight mail each week.

In December 1989, Evergreen supported the U.S. invasion of Panama, during which a dozen of its employees were captured by, then later escaped from, Manuel Noriega's troops. The Drug Enforcement Agency (DEA) hired Evergreen helicopters to defoliate drug fields in Latin America. The company was also spraying to eradicate blackfly-borne river blindness in West Africa on behalf of the World Health Organization.

In the late 1980s, Evergreen joined Aeroflot in opening an air cargo route between Alaska and Siberia. The company also participated in a heavy helicopter transport joint venture within the Soviet Union. In August 1989, Evergreen launched a scheduled freighter service between Hong Kong and New York via Columbus, Ohio. Flights for Qantas Airways Ltd. began at the same time. The company also flew cargo for Iberia and Air-India.

In the summer of 1989, Evergreen lost its Express Mail contract to Consolidated Freightways Corp.'s Air Train Inc. unit. The two-year contract, worth $173 million, went to Air Train (later Emery Worldwide Airlines Inc.) largely on the basis of lower cost.

Emery was suspended from its Postal Service contract during an over-billing probe in 1992. Evergreen did not win the subsequent ten-year, $1 billion "A-Net" contract to transport Express Mail traffic, but did win the $100 million "T-Deal" contract to operate an Express Mail hub in Indianapolis for ten years.

Thriving in the Early 1990s

Evergreen entered the 1990s with revenues of about $477 million a year and a staff of 2,300, including 450 pilots, and a fleet of 165 aircraft, including 16 Boeing 747's, worth approximately $1 billion. Its debt load was $600 million. Evergreen was co-owned by founder Del Smith and his two sons, Mark and Michael.

The company was again expanding its headquarters. In 1992, it increased its facilities fivefold at New York's John F. Kennedy International Airport. Scheduled JFK-Beijing freighter service was launched in May 1993. However, Evergreen suspended the service after two flights in the face of a reported anti-competitive "ambush" by Air China and China Eastern, as well as the threat of a boycott by Chinese freight forwarders and ground handlers. It was restarted in October after the U.S. Department of Transportation threatened sanctions. Federal Express Corp. bought Evergreen's China routes in 1995.

In addition to its cargo operations, which accounted for about three-quarters of the company's revenues, Evergreen had a number of sidelines, including a successful aircraft trading and leasing business, which helped the airline consistently maintain the correct size fleet. Its Evergreen Aviation Ground Logistics Enterprises, Inc. (EAGLE) subsidiary provided

Key Dates:

1960: Evergreen Helicopters is formed.
1974: The lease to the Central Intelligence Agency's Marana, Arizona, air maintenance facility is acquired.
1975: Evergreen buys Johnson Flying Service.
1978: A holding company and Evergreen Farms are formed.
1981: Evergreen sets up overnight freight service for United Parcel Service (UPS).
1987: Evergreen establishes an Express Mail hub in Indiana.
1989: Hong Kong-Columbus-New York freighter service begins.
1991: The company signs a major cargo contact with Japan Air Lines (JAL).
1993: The company enters the China market; JAL cancels its contract.
1995: FedEx buys the company's China routes.
2000: Evergreen Aviation Museum opens.

ground handling and other support services at nearly two dozen locations in the United States.

Uniquely, the company managed 7,300 acres of farmland in northwest Oregon. Originally bought in 1978 as a noise buffer for its helicopter testing, by the early 1990s diversified farming was one of Evergreen's fastest growing businesses.

The Gulf War was the cause for the worst year overall in the history of the aviation industry. However, Evergreen International Aviation was a dramatic exception. Airlifting supplies for the military build up added $150 million to its revenues. The company's helicopter crews remained after the war to support firefighting operations at Kuwaiti oil wells.

In May 1991, Evergreen began leasing Japan Air Lines four massive Boeing 747 freighters for the U.S. cargo service of Japan Airlines (JAL), which had recently grown to include Chicago. (These planes were furnished with Evergreen crews due to a pilot shortage in Japan.) Two years later, Evergreen won a Chinese government contract to establish scheduled flights between New York and Beijing.

In 1991, Evergreen began refueling Hong Kong-bound aircraft in Khabarovsk, Russia, to avoid high landing fees in Japan. However, a joint venture with Aeroflot's Far East division ran into a series of mishaps, including parts and fuel shortages and a managing director who absconded with the venture's corporate charter and checkbook. Evergreen was also involved in a helicopter services venture in the former Soviet republic of Georgia.

Mid-1990s Crisis

Revenues were more than $500 million in 1992. Evergreen sold $125 million in junk bonds to refurbish several badly worn Boeing 747's that had been leased by Pan Am Corp. before its demise. In late 1993, JAL, then in the midst of a recession at home, declined to renew its contract, which represented one-

third of Evergreen International Aviation's revenues. The air cargo industry as a whole was suffering from excess capacity.

The company took a $34.3 million loss on $401.2 million in revenues, down about $100 million, for the 1993–94 fiscal year. A $12.6 million deficit followed the next year, when sales were $366.1 million. Evergreen suspended payment on $454 million in debt in February 1994. In March 1994, creditors grounded one of the company's 13 Boeing 747's. On the positive side, Evergreen was able to lease five planes to UPS, including two 747's formerly used on the JAL contract.

Plans for a $15 million expansion of the Evergreen Air Center were deferred by debt and a $78 million lawsuit in 1996. The suit concerned junk bond notes held by Cargill Inc. With a number of creditors and rumors of hard-dealing "vultures," Chapter 11 may have seemed a natural solution. However, against the advice of his lawyers, Del Smith refused this course of action, aware that very few airlines had ever flown out of bankruptcy. Evergreen lost $10.3 million in 1996 but achieved a $21.2 million profit in 1997 following a new financing arrangement. Revenues at the airline rose 34.9 percent to $255.5 million.

In the spring of 1998, Evergreen added scheduled service from Indonesia to New York via Columbus, Ohio. Despite the Asian financial crisis, revenues rose 12 percent to $435 million in the fiscal year ending in February 1999. The airline accounted for about 65 percent of Evergreen International Aviation's total revenues.

Looking Back in 2000

Evergreen opened the Evergreen Aviation Museum in 2000. Its historic collection included the legendary "Spruce Goose" flying boat plus many other vintage civil and military aircraft, a number of them flyable.

Evergreen announced plans to open a scheduled route between Anchorage and Adak in the Russian Far East in early 2002 under a two-year subsidy from the U.S. Department of Transportation. The flights were intended to develop Alaska as a gateway from Russia. The company also based a Gulfstream 3 business jet in Anchorage to support cleanup of the military base on Amchitka Island and to provide other charter services. Evergreen was also expanding in Asia, adding the first direct air freight service between Columbus, Ohio, and Kuala Lumpur, Malaysia.

Principal Subsidiaries

Evergreen Agricultural Enterprises, Inc.; Evergreen Air Center, Inc.; Evergreen Aircraft Sales & Leasing Co.; Evergreen Aviation Ground Logistic Enterprises, Inc.; Evergreen Helicopters, Inc.; Evergreen International Airlines, Inc.; Quality Aviation Services, Inc.

Principal Competitors

Airborne, Inc.; Atlas Air Worldwide Holdings, Inc.; Cargolux Airlines International S.A.; Offshore Logistics, Inc.

Further Reading

Abruzzese, Leo, "Evergreen Forfeits Mexico All-Cargo Aviation Rights," *Journal of Commerce*, January 25, 1990, p. 2B.

Armbruster, William, "Evergreen Air Seeks to Boost US-China Service," *Journal of Commerce*, September 20, 1994, p. 2B.

——, "Evergreen International Halts Debt Payment; Carrier to Develop Restructuring Plan," *Journal of Commerce*, February 7, 1994, p. 1A.

——, "FedEx to Take Over Evergreen Air's All-Cargo Route Right to China," *Journal of Commerce*, February 27, 1995, p. 1A.

Barrett, Paul M., "Lesson of a Turnaround: Sometimes a Client Knows Best," *Wall Street Journal*, September 3, 1997, p. B1.

Brown, Craig, "Patriots' Work," *Oregon Business*, October 1991, pp. 60ff.

Cohn, Lisa, "Evergreen's Limelight Problem," *Oregon Business*, October 1988, p. 55.

Donnelly, Sally B., "Just Plane Dangerous?," *Time*, August 13, 2001, pp. 44–45.

Hong, Maria, "Evergreen Helps Fuel JAL's Growth," *Journal of Commerce*, December 30, 1991, p. 6.

McCafferty, Bob, "Evergreen Aviation Museum," *Air & Space Smithsonian*, August–September 2001, pp. 7ff.

MacPherson, James, "Adak Jet Service Thrown into Limbo," *Alaska Journal of Commerce*, November 4, 2001, p. 1.

——, "Evergreen Bases Gulfstream in Alaska," *Alaska Journal of Commerce*, September 2, 2001, p. 3.

——, "Evergreen to Fly Jets to Adak, Russia," *Alaska Journal of Commerce*, July 22, 2001, p. 5.

——, "In 40 Years, Evergreen Expands Around World," *Alaska Journal of Commerce,* November 4, 2001, p. 12.

Manning, Jeff, "Emery, Evergreen Exchange Fire Over Postal Service Job," *Business Journal-Portland*, February 1, 1993, pp. 1f.

——, "Evergreen International Lands UPS Deal, But Investors Cool," *Business Journal-Portland*, April 15, 1994, p. 4.

——, "Evergreen Reports Losses of $34.2 Million," *Oregonian*, September 30, 1994, p. B7.

Read, Richard, "JAL Hires Evergreen to Run Cargo Flights," *Oregonian*, May 14, 1991, p. C16.

——, "Playing Russian Roulette," *Oregonian*, November 11, 1993, p. F1.

Sanders, Lisa, "Flying Through Flak," *Forbes*, March 14, 1994, p. 14.

Sleeth, Peter, "Evergreen Creditors Take 747s," *Oregonian*, March 5, 1994, p. B6.

——, "Evergreen Tries to Avoid Chapter 11," *Oregonian*, February 11, 1994.

Stern, Richard L., "We're Opportunists," *Forbes*, December 10, 1990, pp. 56+.

—Frederick C. Ingram

Friedman, Billings, Ramsey Group, Inc.

1001 19th Street, North
Arlington, Virginia 22209
U.S.A.
Telephone: (703) 312-9500
Fax: (703) 312-9601
Web site: http://www.fbr.com

Public Company
Incorporated: 1996
Employees: 433
Sales: $178.9 million (2001)
Stock Exchanges: New York
Ticker Symbol: FBR
NAIC: 523120 Securities Brokerage

Friedman, Billings, Ramsey Group, Inc. (FBR) is an Arlington, Virginia financial holding company that through its subsidiaries concentrates on three businesses: investment banking and securities; specialized asset management products, including venture capital funds; and the online investment banking activities of FBR.com. Although a boutique operation located in the Washington, D.C. area, FBR has proven that in today's high-tech world, in which real-time market data is available outside of New York City, it can compete successfully against Wall Street firms much larger in size.

Establishing the Firm in 1989

The most prominent of the three partners who formed FBR in 1989 was Emanuel J. Friedman, the firm's chairman and co-CEO. According to press reports, Friedman, the son of a Wilmington, North Carolina, rabbi, used his bar mitzvah money to fund his first investment at the age of 13. He bought ten shares of tobacco company P. Lorillard Co. and after two months sold them, realizing a $60 profit. After attending Wilmington Junior College, he earned an undergraduate degree from the University of North Carolina-Chapel Hill. He moved to the Washington area and began taking night classes at Georgetown Law School, supporting himself by teaching junior high geography. In 1972 he tried to land a job with a stock

brokerage house but by his count was turned down by two dozen firms. Finally in 1973 he was hired as a retail broker by the Washington, D.C. firm of Legg Mason Wood Walker Inc., where he initially concentrated on the sale of gas, oil, and casino stocks. He did not fare particularly well during the early part of his career. Friedman told the *Baltimore Business Journal,* ''I had years of failure until I turned 37, when I met my partners.'' He turned his attention to following small savings and loan stock. In 1982 one of his future partners, Eric F. Billings, joined Legg Mason, then left two years later to work for Johnston, Lemon & Co., one of Washington's most prominent brokerage houses. Friedman joined Billings at Johnston, Lemon where both men served as senior vice-presidents in the institutional sales group and they met the man who would become the third, and youngest, partner of FBR, W. Russell Ramsey.

During his five years at Johnston, Lemon, Friedman became the firm's top revenue producer, selling to mutual funds, pension funds, bank trust departments, and other institutional customers, in the process gaining recognition in the Washington financial community. In some estimates, his institutional sales department accounted for as much as 40 percent of Johnston, Lemon's revenues. With the stock market crash in 1987 the firm began to encounter some difficulties, then was stunned in 1989 when Friedman decided to leave in order to form his own company, in the process taking Billings and Ramsey as partners, as well as a large portion of Johnston, Lemon's 25-person institutional sales department. Friedman maintained that it had been a longtime goal to start a firm and that he left Johnston, Lemon on friendly terms, despite hints in the press that internal differences led to his departure. Neither party, however, chose to publicly discuss any possible conflicts.

Opening for Business in 1989

Freidman, Billings, and Ramsey borrowed $1 million and set up shop as a research-based institutional brokerage boutique with $5,000 worth of used furniture in downtown Washington offices that had been abandoned by another brokerage. With Friedman serving as senior partner and holding the largest stake, FBR was focused at first on trading bank stocks and asset management, catering to large institutional investors and

Company Perspectives:

We believe that FBR occupies a unique position in the capital markets. From our roots as a research boutique, we have grown to a top 10 ranked national investment bank. Our research, institutional brokerage and investment banking services have placed us, with the Wall Street bulge bracket, among the top 10 lead-managed equity underwriters and among the leading research-driven national brokerages, in the United States. Yet, like a boutique, we achieve success through knowing our industries extremely well. This proprietary thought process enables us to provide independent research on small-cap to large-cap names, and to provide creative capital to issuers. We focus across research, brokerage, investment banking and asset management on six industry sectors: financial services, real estate, technology, energy, healthcare and diversified industries.

wealthy individuals. The firm quickly gained credibility in the eyes of investors when it was one of the first to warn of a collapse in the real estate market and urged customers to sell vulnerable bank and real estate stocks. According to a 1996 *Washington Post* profile, ''The banking crisis provided the opportunity for FBR to move from stock trading—where money is made at a rate of 6 cents a share—into investment banking—where fees can be earned by the millions of dollars. Convinced that some failing banks could be saved if investors would pour in some cash, FBR raised $30 million to bail out Ameribanc of Annandale in 1992. Ameribanc stock sold for only $2 a share, but investors got $3 a share when First Union Corp. bought the bank two years later.''

It was FBR's entry into the California market in late 1992, during the depths of a recession, that would solidify the firm's reputation. FBR proposed a bold recapitalization plan for Glendale Federal, a thrift on the edge of bankruptcy due to bad real estate loans. Although it managed $18 billion in assets, Glendale had a total market capitalization of just $30 million. FBR believed that Glendale could be saved and that investors were simply overreacting by retreating from the California market. It offered to raise $450 million in new funding for Glendale, a bid that was accepted by the thrift's management against the advice of the Wall Street firm of Goldman Sachs. The recapitalization plan worked, Glendale recovered, and FBR would go on to do many more lucrative bank deals. In addition to gaining the trust of investors, FBR generated the cash required for expansion and diversification.

In 1994 FBR formed a real estate group, bringing in veterans William R. Swanson and James D. Locke to head the operation. Despite never having raised money for a Real Estate Investment Trust, the firm soon undertook its first initial public offering (IPO), a solo effort that raised $350 million for Prime Retail Corp., a Baltimore shopping center owner. Because it elected not to follow the standard practice of spreading the risk over a syndicate of firms, FBR was able to retain the entire fee for the transaction. The real estate investment trust business, under the aegis of partner Billings, quickly became a major part of FBR's growing activities. From a handful of former Johnston, Lemon

employees in 1989, the firm grew to 200 strong by 1996, at which point the partnership evolved into a corporation, Friedman, Billings, Ramsey Group, Inc.

After the company started a mergers and acquisitions practice in 1995, Ramsey served as the point man for FBR's entry into the technology sector, a natural fit for a Washington-based company. The surrounding area was becoming a hotbed for information technology and communications. Not only was it home to America Online, the Virginia-Maryland corridor featured a number of universities that were developing emerging technologies. Moreover, the Department of Defense was shrinking, with the likely result that a number of military and space technology companies would spin off with former DOD personnel. FBR's first play in the technology arena was its 1996 underwriting of an initial stock offering for America's first Internet bank, Security First Network Bank of Pineville, Kentucky. With Wall Street lusting after Internet stocks, FBR's timing was perfect. Although the firm originally planned to sell 2.4 million shares for $15 to $17 a share, the interest was so intense that it elected to offer 2.8 million shares at $20 per share. Trading on the NASDAQ, the stock immediately doubled in price. With such a spectacular start, FBR was understandably enthusiastic about its technology business. Late in 1996 it launched Pegasus Venture Partners, a $25 million venture capital fund targeting Washington-area emerging high-technology companies.

With his partners staking out territory in real estate and high technology, Friedman focused on the company's push into specialized finance companies. The three men appeared to worked comfortably together. In fact, a major aspect of FBR's success was attributed to its corporate culture. Dress was extremely casual, generally jeans and shorts, and the three founding partners were known to everyone in the organization as Manny, Eric, and Russ. FBR provided daily breakfast, lunch, and dinner spreads in the company kitchen. It offered a company health club, complete with sauna and masseuse. Rather than raiding other companies, FBR preferred to hire young people who they could train and then promote through the ranks. As a result, the average age of employees was under 30, and the firm suffered almost no turnover. Overall, FBR was building a reputation as an innovative boutique operation that was proving that a company did not need to have a Wall Street address to become a significant investment player. Although that perception may have played well in the press, it sometimes complicated business. At times FBR was forced to manage an IPO on its own, and assume all the risk without broadening the range of potential investors, simply because it was unable to find a Wall Street firm willing to act in a secondary role. In addition, many Wall Street firms opted not to cover these stocks, resulting in depressed prices. As it became a major force in managing IPOs, FBR was also reluctant to act as a second fiddle to another firm.

Going Public in 1997

By 1997 FBR had emerged as a powerhouse in the Northeast, with additional offices in California, Boston, and London. In October 1997 it announced that after managing numerous IPOs, the firm itself would now go public. In addition, PNC Bank Corp. agreed in advance to acquire a 4.9 percent equity stake as well as to establish a strategic alliance with the firm. For PNC, the deal

---

Key Dates:

1989: The firm is formed as a partnership.
1992: FBR arranges the recapitalization of Glendale Federal.
1996: Friedman, Billings, Ramsey Group, Inc. is created.
1997: FBR goes public.
2001: Ramsey leaves the firm.

---

offered a number of benefits. Aside from realizing a gain if FBR should prosper, the Pittsburgh-based regional bank was now able to underwrite public offerings of stock and forward its goal of gaining a national presence. It was essentially a referral arrangement, with both parties steering business to each other. In December 1997 FBR completed its IPO, selling $220 million in stock at $20 per share, an event that caused concern in some quarters. The *Wall Street Journal* reported, "It may be a sign, some traders say, that the peak is near when an investment-banking firm that has made its fortune this year underwriting IPOs of financial-services and mortgage companies decides to sell its own stock." As much as 85 percent of the company's revenues came from IPO underwritings, prompting the *Journal* to further speculate as follows: "Friedman Billings has all its eggs in one basket. And lately the basket has been looking a little tattered. Indeed, aftermarket performance of its deal, especially the flood of mortgage-company deals it helped underwrite this year, has been slipping lately."

Despite concerns that 1998 would offer fewer IPO opportunities, especially among mortgage companies, FBR enjoyed a stellar start to the year. The $800.2 million the firm raised in four real estate investment trust deals bested all major Wall Street firms, making it the first time in a decade that one of the smaller investment firms earned top honors for an entire quarter. The success would be shortlived, however, as the stock market began to slide in June 1998, resulting in a scarcity of new issues. FBR managed just one IPO the entire summer, but of more importance, the firm chose to support some of the stocks the company had taken public, pumping almost $120 million into the market. In the end FBR was unable to maintain prices, resulting in a loss of $35 million by the time it was forced to back down and sell. In addition, the price of FBR stock suffered, losing close to 70 percent of its value, and for the first time in its brief history the company had to lay off staff, some 24 employees, or 7 percent of the workforce. After generating revenues of $256.1 million and net earnings of $34.3 million in 1997, FBR posted a loss of $16.2 million on revenues of just $122.9 million in 1998.

FBR regained some momentum in 1999 when it announced a new Internet venture, FBR.com, what the firm boasted would be the first publicly owned online investment bank. The web site offered customers access to FBR research and other investment banking services. After catering to institutional investors and wealthy individuals, FBR was now looking to appeal to small investors by setting aside 20 percent of stock in the IPOs it managed for sale to clients of FBR.com. Maintaining that the initiative had been under development since 1996, FBR denied that this was an attempt to provide a short-term solution to the firm's recent reversals. Nevertheless, investors responded en-

thusiastically, bidding up the price of FBR stock. By the end of 1999 the firm decided to make some structural changes to the organization. The founding partners turned over operational responsibilities to Robert S. Smith, a general counsel and executive vice-president, who was now named FBR's COO. As a result, the partners hoped to focus on the firm's future, in particular spreading its high-tech venture capital funds across the country and into Europe. To some observers FBR had become a technology shop, and others openly wondered whether this was the result of a strategy or simply trend chasing.

In January 2000, FBR announced a strategic alliance with Dawnay, Day Ladner, a United Kingdom venture capital firm, to invest in the Internet and associated technologies. Later in the year FBR teamed with Pacific Northwest-area entrepreneurs to create a venture capital fund to invest in technology companies in that region. On a different front in 2000, FBR initiated an acquisition of Money Management Associates, a Bethesda, Maryland, company that owned Rushmore Trust & Savings and controlled $920 million in assets. The $27.2 million deal was finalized in March 2001, and the assets were combined under the name of FBR National Bank, an FBR Group subsidiary. By acquiring a thrift, FBR had now grown from an investment boutique to becoming a diversified firm that offered broker-dealer services and investment banking with asset management, as well as retail banking.

While FBR was opening new offices in Cleveland, Dallas, and New York in 2001, one of its founding partners, Ramsey, stepped down from his position at the firm, although he retained his seat on the board and a 12 percent stake in the business. FBR also would invest in Ramsey's new venture capital fund, Capital Crossover Partners, which concentrated on Washington-area technology, media, and telecommunications companies. Ramsey's departure was the first step in FBR's move away from the tech sector, which had failed to be as lucrative as the firm had once hoped. FBR opted now to focus on sectors where it experienced previous success, such as financial services and real estate. In general, 2001 was a transitional year for the company, which instituted cost-cutting measures that reduced its staff by 15 percent by the end of the year. With the economy in recession, FBR positioned itself to take advantage of an eventual recovery. A merger between the company's real estate investment trust (FBR Asset Investment Corporation) and the FBR Group subsidiary, in a deal worth an estimated $750 million, was expected in 2003 to provide an infusion of capital for the firm. With no debt, a retail banking operation now in house, and its innovative spirit undiminished, the firm looked forward to a new era in its short but successful history.

Principal Subsidiaries

Friedman, Billings, Ramsey Capital Markets, Inc.; FBR Bancorp, Inc.; Friedman, Billings, Ramsey International, Ltd.; FBR Investment Services, Inc.; Friedman, Billings, Ramsey Investment Management, Inc.; FBR Venture Capital Managers, Inc.; Money Management Associates, Inc.

Principal Competitors

Robertson Stephens; SG Cowen Securities; Thomas Weisel Partners.

Further Reading

Andrejczak, Matt, "Trial and Error Pays Off for D.C. Investment Banker," *Baltimore Business Journal,* October 3, 1997, p. 17.

Block, Valerie, " 'Culture' Gets the Credit at Friedman Billings," *American Banker,* September 30, 1997, p. 29.

Hinden, Stan, "Top Analysts, 18 on His Staff Leave Johnston, Lemon & Co.," *Washington Post,* June 29, 1989, p. 1.

Knight, Jerry, "Investment Bankers Soar in Cyberspace," *Washington Post,* May 27, 1996, p. F10.

——, "Three Men with a Vision," *Washington Post,* October 28, 1996, p. F12.

Knight, Jerry, and Mark Leibovich, "Bulled Over by a Bad Market," *Washington Post,* October 5, 1998, p. F12.

McLean, Bethany, "An un-Wall Street IPO Upstart," *Fortune,* August 18, 1997, pp. 32–34.

Pulliam, Susan, and Anita Raghavan, "IPO for an IPO Firm May Be a Warning," *Wall Street Journal,* December 26, 1997, p. C1.

Winig, Eric, "With Tech Sector Waning, FBR Changes Direction," *Washington Business Journal,* May 4, 2001, p. 4.

Wirth, Gregg, "Friedman Billings Ramsey Becomes an Important Regional Player," *Investment Dealers' Digest,* May 26, 1997, p. 18.

—Ed Dinger

Friedrich Grohe AG & Co. KG

Hauptstrasse 137
D-58675 Hemer
Germany
Telephone: (49) (2372) 93-0
Fax: (49) (2372) 93-1322
Web site: http://www.grohe.com

Private Company
Incorporated: 1948 as Friedrich Grohe Armaturenfabrik
   GmbH & Co.
Employees: 5,898
Sales: EUR 900 million ($780 million) (2001)
NAIC: 332998 Enameled Iron and Metal Sanitary Ware
   Manufacturing; 332913 Plumbing Fixture Fitting and
   Trim Manufacturing

Friedrich Grohe AG & Co. KG is one of the world's leading manufacturers of bathroom fixtures and sanitary products and systems with a global market share of about 10 percent. Grohe produces faucets, shower heads, and plumbing fixtures, as well as flush toilet systems and thermostats. The company provides major international hotel chains with its bathroom fittings and equips public buildings with automatic faucets and concealed on-the-wall systems. Headquartered in Hemer, Germany, Grohe operates nine production plants in Germany and four abroad, in Portugal, Thailand, Canada, and China. Among Grohe's production facilities in Germany is Europe's largest brass foundry. Grohe still manufactures most of its products in Germany, but exports about 72 percent of the company's output. The company maintains 19 sales subsidiaries and sales offices in 140 countries. Investment firm BC Partners owns a 51-percent majority stake in Grohe.

Modest Beginnings and Postwar Construction Boom

Grohe's history began in the first half of the 20th century in Germany. Company founder Friedrich Grohe was the second son of German entrepreneur Hans Grohe. Hans Grohe, the sixth son of a weaver, grew up near Berlin and learned the weaving craft himself. However, in 1901 he started his own business in Schiltach, a small town in the Black Forest. At first he made metal casings for alarm clocks for the German firm Junghans, then the largest watchmaker in the world. Soon his business grew into a mini-factory for stovepipe rings, shower heads, spigots, faucets, and other bathroom fixtures, and employed about 100 people by 1928.

Friedrich Grohe joined his father's company for a time, but left in 1934 to strike out on his own. In 1936 he acquired Berkenhoff & Paschedag, a manufacturer of bathroom fixtures that had been in business since 1911 and was located in the small German town Hemer near Dortmund in Westphalia. Two years passed before Grohe's company received its first orders from abroad. World War II then interrupted the firm's development.

After the war, in 1948, the company was renamed after the owner: Friedrich Grohe Armaturenfabrik. Grohe greatly benefited from the postwar construction boom. The exploding demand for kitchen and bathroom fixtures put the company on the track to dynamic growth. In 1956 Grohe bought Carl Nestler, a manufacturer of thermostats which was located in the small town Lahr in the Black Forest. Grohe's first subsidiary was renamed Grohe Thermostat GmbH. In 1957, to help promote his products, Grohe started providing special training for retailers that carried Grohe's kitchen and bathroom fixtures and for the plumbers who installed them. Six years later, a brand-new manufacturing plant for thermostats was erected in Lahr.

New Ownership and Global Expansion after 1960

The 1960s brought a major change in the company's ownership. In 1961, Friedrich Grohe became CEO of his father's firm in Schiltach, which his brother Hans had been in charge of until his death. Although the two firms had coordinated their product lines to minimize direct competition—Hans Grohe focused on drains and shower heads, Friedrich Grohe on faucets and hot-and-cold-water mixers—and although they used the same distribution channels, the two families decided not to merge the two businesses. Instead, Friedrich Grohe sold a 51 percent majority stake in his company to the American telephone giant ITT (International Telephone & Telegraph) in 1968. In the same year Hans Grohe's third son, Friedrich's brother Klaus, entered the older Grohe family enterprise, while Friedrich Grohe kept a 27-percent stake in his brother's firm.

During the 1960s and 1970s Friedrich Grohe expanded internationally. In 1961 the company founded its first foreign subsidiary, in France. A second was established in Austria in 1965, followed by a third subsidiary abroad in Italy two years later. In 1973 Grohe set up its fourth European subsidiary, in the Netherlands. Five years later, the company expanded into Great Britain and Spain, and in 1979 into Belgium.

The death of company founder Friedrich Grohe in 1983 closed a chapter in the firm's history. The following year, Friedrich Grohe's heirs bought back ITT's majority stake in Friedrich Grohe and sold their 26-percent stake in Hansgrohe to the American Masco Corporation in Indianapolis. Due to growing competitive pressures, the two companies abandoned the idea of staying off each other's turf. To the contrary, over a period of several years they fought over the Grohe brand name rights. The conflict would not be settled until the early 1990s when it was decided that Friedrich Grohe would use the brand name Grohe while Hans Grohe would market its products under the Hansgrohe label.

Entering the U.S. Market in 1975

The establishment of Friedrich Grohe's first subsidiary in the United States in 1975 marked a new chapter in the company's history. A small office was opened in the outskirts of Chicago, and the first sales representative, Urell, Inc. in Massachusetts, started selling the European-style kitchen and bathroom fixtures to American builders, retailers, and plumbers. In 1976 the new venture was incorporated as Grohe America, Inc. and moved into a small warehouse-office complex. Two years later Al Corwin became Grohe America's CEO and successfully steered the young company through its initial growth phase, establishing Grohe as one of the leading brands in the top price segment for upscale bathroom design. Trying to catch up with the steadily rising demand, Grohe America kept moving to bigger facilities. In 1978 the company occupied one section of a larger warehouse facility; in 1986, it moved to a new 64,000 square foot warehouse in Wood Dale; and finally it settled into a

brand-new custom-built 90,000 square foot facility in Bloomingdale, Illinois, in 1993. Calvin retired in 1995 and was succeeded by Bob Atkins as CEO.

Although the faucets Grohe started selling in 1975 in the United States had a different look and functioned a little differently from the ones American consumers were used to, they increasingly gained acceptance. Grohe's single-hole fixtures were easy to use and install. Another factor that contributed to sales figures doubling every year was the constant stream of innovations in cutting-edge designs that Friedrich Grohe introduced to the market. In 1983 Grohe America launched Ladylux, the first pull-out spray kitchen faucet in the U.S. market. In 1989 Europlus, another pull-out spray kitchen faucet was introduced, which became a bestseller. While the first models had a plastic finish, they were replaced by the industry's first versions in solid stainless steel in the late 1990s. Another innovation, the Grohmix thermostat line, was launched in 1992. Equipped with a new kind of valve that automatically regulated water temperature as well as pressure, consumers could set the desired water temperature just as they would do for their heating or air conditioning systems. With an accuracy within one degree Fahrenheit, the Grohmix line allowed bath safety for households with small children, the physically disabled, or elderly persons. Depending on their budget, consumers could choose between a chrome, white, polished brass, or 23-karat gold finish. In the late 1980s Grohe became known for its innovative custom shower systems.

During this time Grohe America invested in a range of marketing efforts to increase the company's reach and boost sales. To promote the company's custom shower systems, Grohe began advertising directly to consumers. The print campaign featured the image of a naked couple taking a shower together in a large custom shower. In 1989 Grohe introduced a new product line for commercial customers. Five years later the company introduced its Select Showroom program for wholesalers. In 1996 Grohe America launched its first television ad campaign and introduced a limited lifetime warranty in 1997. By the mid-1990s Grohe America sold European-style fixtures worth $38 million, reaching a market share of approximately 1.7 percent.

Newly Positioned in the Changing Market of the 1990s

By the end of the 1980s Friedrich Grohe had become one of Europe's top manufacturers of kitchen and bathroom fixings. Sales had climbed to over DM 700 million and exports accounted for 70 percent of the total. Up until that time, the company's main concern had been on adjusting production capacity and logistics to meet an ever-growing demand. The situation changed fundamentally in the 1990s. After the unexpected construction boom brought about by the reunification of East and West Germany in 1990 began drying up, the German market stagnated. Moreover, the company was suffering significant losses from volatile exchange rates caused by weakening currencies in several countries around the world.

To secure further growth, Friedrich Grohe had to develop a new strategy. After a brief and ultimately unsuccessful attempt to venture into other bath-related products such as ceramics in

Key Dates:

1936: Friedrich Grohe acquires plumbing fixtures manufacturer Berkenhoff & Paschedag.
1948: The company is renamed Friedrich Grohe Armaturenfabrik.
1961: Grohe establishes its first foreign subsidiary in France.
1968: International Telephone & Telegraph (ITT) becomes majority shareholder.
1975: The company establishes a subsidiary in the United States.
1984: Friedrich Grohe's heirs buy ITT's majority stake back after the company founder's death.
1991: Company goes public.
1994: The company takes over the German DAL/Rost group.
1999: The Grohe and Rost families sell their holdings in Friedrich Grohe to investment firm BC Partners.
2000: Public trading is discontinued and the company is transformed into Friedrich Grohe AG & Co. KG.

the late 1970s, the company had stuck to its niche. This niche was nearing its growth limits. There were two types of enterprises competing in the international market—specialists and all-arounders. Although Grohe had become the leader among the specialists, the top players in the global league of bathroom outfitters offered the complete range of products from the shower divider to the floor tiles. Becoming an all-arounder would have required enormous investments. Friedrich Grohe decided to keep its focus on an expanded range of fixtures. The company grew through a number of acquisitions, continued to expand its international reach, and positioned itself as a world leader in water technology.

In 1991 Friedrich Grohe was transformed into a public stock company under the name Friedrich Grohe AG. The Grohe family retained a majority stake in the enterprise, while the IPO filled the company's bank account with cash to finance further growth. In the first half of the 1990s Friedrich Grohe acquired the German plumbing fixture makers H.D. Eichelberg & Co. GmbH, Herzberger Armaturen GmbH, and DAL-Georg Rost & Soehne GmbH Armaturenfabrik, including its subsidiaries Aqua Butzke AG and Eggemann GmbH. The acquisition of the privately owned DAL/Rost group catapulted Friedrich Grohe's sales over the DM 1 billion mark. DAL/Rost's line of bathroom installation and flushing systems and Aqua Butzke's automatic bathroom fixtures for public buildings complemented Grohe's product range. As part of the deal, the Grohe family—which owned all the company's common stock—gave up 26 percent to the Rost family.

In the mid-1990s increasing numbers of Asian competitors flooded the European markets with less expensive plumbing fixtures, putting established manufacturers, including Friedrich Grohe, under growing price pressure. At German building centers, do-it-yourself customers could buy a cheaper Asian fixture for around DM 50. Friedrich Grohe, by comparison, sold its high-quality fixtures through specialized retailers and directly to

plumbing firms, with prices starting at DM 200. As a countermeasure, Grohe started moving a part of its production abroad. A new factory in Thailand started putting out cheaper fixtures for the southern Asian mass market in 1996. Two years later Friedrich Grohe's second foreign production plant in Portugal started operations. In 1997 the company bought a 70-percent majority stake in Rotter GmbH & Co. KG, a supplier of sanitary equipment to businesses and public institutions.

To position Friedrich Grohe as a "world leader in water technology" the company invested over DM 50 million in a massive marketing campaign. Under the auspices of the Grohe name, the firm established four sub-brands: bathroom fixtures for consumers, such as faucets and hot-and-cold-water mixers, were sold under the label Groheart; thermostats, valves and other plumbing fixtures for kitchens and bathrooms were marketed under the Grohetec label; flush toilet fittings and tanks were labeled Grohedal; fixtures for professional water management in public buildings were sold under the brand name Groheaqua. The marketing campaign included ads in German plumbing trade magazines, as well as special interest and general interest consumer titles. The campaign not only raised Friedrich Grohe's public recognition but received a German marketing award in 1996. In addition to the ad campaign the company also initiated the Profi Club, which not only offered training to Germany's plumbing firms in how to use Grohe products and innovations, but also offered training in making their own enterprises more efficient. Up to 10,000 plumbers annually attended such training sessions and received the quarterly club magazine.

Going Private in 2000

In June 1999, to the surprise of the business community and shareholders, Charles R. Grohe, chair of Friedrich Grohe's advisory board and majority shareholder, announced that he and the Rost family were selling their stakes in the company. A few weeks later, the European investment firm BC Partners won out in the auction organized by Credit Suisse First Boston, over counterbidders including American equity house Kohlberg Kravis Roberts and U.S. plumbing supplier Kohler. BC Partners acquired all common shares from the two families, representing a 51 percent stake in Friedrich Grohe, and these shares were transferred to Grohe Holding GmbH. BC Partners went on to buy back all but 0.4 percent of the preferred stock that was publicly traded. On March 29, 2000, the public trading of Friedrich Grohe shares ceased. Ultimately, the company was transformed into a private entity—Friedrich Grohe AG & Co. KG.

During the next two years, measures were taken to strengthen Friedrich Grohe's position in the world market. The United States had become the company's most important market outside of Germany, generating DM 200 million—or about $160 million—in sales in 2000. The company also invested in new subsidiaries in Eastern Europe, specifically Poland and Russia, as well as in Asia, where Friedrich Grohe was planning to open a new production plant in Shanghai and to cooperate with a Chinese tile manufacturer. On the internal front the company reorganized its sales divisions and pushed its designer line of fixtures with higher profit margins. With a world market share of roughly 10 percent in 2001, Friedrich Grohe aimed at becoming the global leader in bathroom fixtures and sanitary installations.

Principal Subsidiaries

Friedrich Grohe AG & Co. KG; Grohe Deutschland Vertriebs GmbH; Grohe America Inc. (United States); Grohe Gesellschaft m.b.H. (Austria); ALPIGRO OÜ (Estonia); Grohe N.V. S.A. (Belgium); GROSAN ineniring d.o.o. (Slovenia); Giersch GmbH (Croatia); Alfred Hili & Co. Ltd. (Malta); Grome Marketing (Cyprus) Ltd.; Grohe Hungary Kft; Vertretung Friedrich GROHE AG & Co. KG (Bulgaria); EU RO International S.R.L. (Romania); Friedrich Grohe AG & Co. KG (Russia); TONGRO (Ukraine); Grohe A/S (Denmark); Grohe Nederland B.V. (Netherlands); Friedrich Grohe A.G. (Norway); Grohe S.A.R.L. (France); N. Sapountzis SA (Greece); Grome Ic ve Dis Ticaret Ltd. Sti. (Turkey); Grohe Limited (United Kingdom); Grohe Espana, S.A. (Spain); Friedrich Grohe Portugal, Lda.; Grohe Pacific Pte Ltd (Hong Kong); Grohe Pacific Pte. Ltd. (Singapore); Orgal A.L.F. Trade Ltd. (Israel); Grohe S.p.A. (Italy); Grohe Japan Ltd.; Grohe Canada; Grohe Polska Sp.zo.o. (Poland); Zastoupení Friedrich Grohe AG & Co. KG pro CR a SR (Czech Republic); GROHE Switzerland SA.

Principal Competitors

Hansa Metallwerke AG; Gerber Plumbing Fixtures Corporation; American Standard Companies Inc.; Kohler Co.; Moen Inc.; Masco Corporation; TOTO Ltd.

Further Reading

"Friedrich Grohe; Die Wanne ist voll," *Focus Magazin,* October 14, 1996, p. 320.

"Friedrich Grohe rollt auf Welle des Erfolgs," *HORIZONT*, December 8, 1995, p. 20.

"Grohe Promotes Family Safety With Grohmix," *Professional Builder and Remodeler,* January 15, 1992, p. 282.

Jury, Jennifer, "BC Partners Victorious In German Mega-Deal," *Buyouts, August 2, 1999.*

Spies, Felix, "Lifestyle für das Badezimmer," *Süddeutsche Zeitung,* March 1, 1997.

Wai, Cheong Suk, "Haute Water," *Straits Times (Singapore),* April 21, 2001.

—Evelyn Hauser

Frost & Sullivan, Inc.

7550 IH 10 West, Suite 400
San Antonio, Texas 78229
U.S.A.
Telephone: (210) 348-1000
Toll Free: (877) 463-7678
Fax: (210) 348-1003
Web site: http://www.frost.com

Private Company
Incorporated: 1961
Employees: 500
Sales: $45 million (2002 est.)
NAIC: 541611 Administrative Management and General
    Management Consulting Services; 541613 Marketing
    Consulting Services; 511140 Database and Directory
    Publishers; 611430 Professional and Management
    Development Training

Frost & Sullivan, Inc. is a leading market research, executive training, and consulting firm that operates around the world. The company produces hundreds of in-depth written reports each year on a wide variety of subjects, trains executives in management and marketing skills, and sponsors business conferences that help corporate leaders network while learning about the latest market trends.

Beginnings

Frost & Sullivan's roots date to 1961, when Daniel Sullivan founded a consulting firm in New York City to serve the high-tech and industrial markets. During the company's first decade it focused on researching new technologies, distribution channels, and business trends, along with performing strategic analyses of competing firms. Frost & Sullivan's focus on technology was reflected in its own operations, being the first firm of its type to offer data on tape, with a report on the world military equipment market that was delivered in 1962.

Following a successful first decade in business, the early 1970s saw expansion to Europe with the opening of an office in

London. In 1972 Frost & Sullivan established a Corporate Training division, which offered training in management and leadership, sales and marketing, and information technology. Another unit created during the 1970s was the Executive Summits division, which sponsored conferences for corporate executives to meet others in their industries and learn about market opportunities, technical trends, business strategies, and competitive threats. A new offering under development at the end of the decade was the World Political Risk Forecast Service, which would soon begin issuing reports and sponsoring conferences. At this time the growing company was increasing its analytical output, raising the average number of reports published from three per week to four.

During the 1980s Frost & Sullivan continued to develop new services, including the Market Engineering Consulting system, in which the company worked directly with clients to address industry challenges and problems. An offshoot of this system was a series of Executive Tutorial manuals that were written to help clients develop their own strategies for solving specific business problems.

In 1982 serious discussions were held with a foreign investor interested in acquiring the company, which was by now publicly traded, but talks broke down when a price could not be agreed upon. The firm had annual revenues of $9.1 million for the year, up from $6.8 million in 1980.

In 1987 Frost & Sullivan's political risk analysis service was offered online for the first time via the Data-Star system. The 5,000-page written report was initially offered electronically on a partial basis, with access to its full 85-country coverage added a few months later. The company's annual sales for 1987 were slightly less than $17.5 million, with net earnings of $290,000 reported.

During the mid-1980s Frost & Sullivan became the target of a friendly takeover attempt by New York publisher Theodore Cross. After he acquired 53 percent of the company's stock, much of it sold by executives of the firm, shareholders voted to accept $10 each for the outstanding shares. In January 1988 Frost & Sullivan was merged with a subsidiary of FAS Acquisition Co., which was owned by Cross and banking affiliates of

Company Perspectives:

Our value proposition to clients is to optimize their business performance by offering diverse strategic solutions that capitalize on growth opportunities within new and existing markets. We will sustain long-term client relationships by providing measurement-based, solutions-focused marketing consulting services leveraging our relevant industry expertise. We will increase long-term stakeholder value through sustained profitability, dynamic fiscal management and prudent use of corporate assets. We will create a positive work environment for our employees that: promotes personal growth and learning; rewards effort, initiative, and innovation; and, provides an opportunity to share in the prosperity of the company.

E.M. Warburg, Pincus & Co., making it a private firm. Founder Daniel Sullivan continued to serve as president and CEO after the merger.

Asian Expansion in the 1990s

Frost & Sullivan expanded to Asia during the 1990s, opening offices in China, Japan, India, and Singapore. During the early part of the decade the firm developed several Customer Engineering Centers, located at offices in the United States and abroad, which were designed to help clients develop customer surveys and do analyses of product launches and development concepts. The centers' offerings were available in many different languages.

Continuing to seek out new avenues for electronic data transmission, Frost & Sullivan became one the first market research firms to offer its reports online. By the mid-1990s the company's research was accessible via the Market Analysis and Information Database, I/PLUS Direct, and DIALOG, which was a major resource for librarians and other academic researchers. Users could search the company's reports and download, for a fee, those parts that were of interest, saving money over the cost of an entire report (which averaged $2,200 and 350 pages in length). As the company's clients were primarily large corporations, which bought the full reports, this new availability greatly increased their potential audience.

By this time Frost & Sullivan's primary areas of research included computers and electronics, healthcare, high-tech manufacturing, telecommunications, and pharmaceuticals. Other reports were compiled by the firm in the areas of chemicals, materials, biotechnology, energy, environment, entertainment/leisure, household goods, office equipment, packaging, and plastics. Markets covered were mostly in the United States and Europe, but also included some in Asia and Latin America. Frost & Sullivan often contracted with outside experts to write reports on specific subjects, though many were written in-house.

Included in the firm's detailed reports were information on products and services that gave descriptions, technical characteristics, and background information; profiles of companies that covered their history, market position, and outlook; analysis of the market with information such as distribution strategies and political factors; and five-year and interim forecasts for the market and the specific products and companies involved. Titles of Frost & Sullivan reports ranged from ''World Cancer Therapeutic Markets'' to ''Market Strategies for Board Games, Jigsaw Puzzles, and Playing Cards.''

In 1997 a joint venture was created by Frost & Sullivan and M.A.I.D. plc (which later was merged into Dialog Corp.). The new Delaware-based company, Frost & Sullivan Electronic Distribution, was jointly owned by both firms, and held electronic distribution rights to all present and future Frost & Sullivan material. Some new market reports also would be created for distribution solely through M.A.I.D.'s Profound business information service. As part of the deal, M.A.I.D. acquired a minority stake in Frost & Sullivan.

In 1998 the firm created another new division, called Stratecast Partners, which performed strategic analysis for telecommunications industry executives. The division offered consulting and market research on communications companies and the technology sector. The year also saw Frost & Sullivan move its headquarters from New York to San Antonio, Texas, though it continued to maintain an office in New York.

2001 Purchase of Technical Insights in Boosts Technology Research

In March of 2001 Frost & Sullivan purchased Technical Insights, which offered several subscription-based technology research services, as well as analytical reports on the fastest-growing technological developments. The spring of the year also saw the launch of several web sites that gave users access to Frost & Sullivan research. These included www.pharma.frost.com, www.biotech.frost.com, www.healthcare.frost.com, and www.medicaldevices.frost.com, which contained information on markets and products in the pharmaceutical, biotechnology, healthcare, and medical devices industries, respectively. The company's main web site, www.frost.com, was launched as well. A news-by-email service also was offered, which enabled users to receive instant updates on recent advances and market trends. The company now was producing as many as 500 full market reports per year on a variety of topics, and press releases about their findings reached the news media with increasing frequency, giving Frost & Sullivan a heightened public profile. Frost's conference division also was continuing to produce a number of meeting events, such as the annual Internet Marketing Strategies Conference held for five days in July in San Francisco.

The September 11, 2001 terrorist attacks on the Pentagon and the World Trade Center had a double impact on the company. The first came on that fateful morning when debris from the attack hit a 26-story building at 90 West Street, 100 yards from the twin towers, where Frost & Sullivan occupied a suite of offices on the 13th floor. The building was engulfed in flames, sustaining heavy damage, and was near collapse by the end of the day. The firm's 28 employees were all evacuated safely, though one sustained an injury from falling airplane parts—the cockpit of the doomed American Airlines Flight 11 had reportedly landed on the building's roof. The company had no choice but to close the office and relocate its staff to other area sites, also transferring its sales activities to San Antonio.

Key Dates:

1961: David L. Sullivan forms a market research and consulting firm in New York.
1972: A Corporate Training division is founded.
1988: Control of the company is acquired by Theodore Cross.
1997: A stake in the company is bought by M.A.I.D.; a joint electronic data venture is formed.
1998: The Stratecast Partners division is founded: the company moves to San Antonio, Texas.
2001: The acquisition of Technical Insights expands technology research capabilities; the New York office is destroyed in the 9/11 attacks and layoffs follow as the U.S. economy dips.

A second impact of the attacks, which had cast a pall on the U.S. economy, was a drop-off in business for the firm. In October Frost & Sullivan announced layoffs of 10 percent of its worldwide staff of 700. The restructuring also included a shift in focus as the company addressed new marketplace needs, with business units that were less affected by the post-9/11 economic downturn given a heightened emphasis.

Frost & Sullivan now had offices in China, India, Malaysia, Singapore, Australia, Japan, Canada, England, Germany, and France, in addition to San Antonio, New York, and San Jose, California in the United States. The firm began seeking investors to help partner in offering new e-learning and instructor-led training programs. Most of its training sessions at this time were offered in London and typically covered management techniques and the impact of technology in the marketplace. Outlining the company's response to the changing world situation, CEO David Frigstad emphasized Frost & Sullivan's global presence; the frost.com web site, with offerings including subscription-based information delivery, real-time updates, and analyst video conferences; and the firm's consulting services, which used its research capabilities to provide analysis and strategies to address client needs.

After four decades in business, Frost & Sullivan remained a leader in the fields of market research, executive training, and consulting. The company continued to produce hundreds of market research reports and dozens of informational conferences annually, in addition to offering training and advising major corporations on strategy and marketing decisions.

Principal Subsidiaries

Frost & Sullivan, North America; Frost & Sullivan, EMEA; Frost & Sullivan, Asia.

Principal Competitors

Datamonitor plc; Gartner, Inc.; International Data Group; The Yankee Group; Ziff Davis Media Inc.

Further Reading

Baatz, E.B., "Mediocrity Rules at High-Tech Market Research Firms," *Electronic Business Buyer,* September, 1993, p. 80.

"Dialog Expands Alliance with Frost & Sullivan," *Information Today,* May, 2002, p. 60.

"Frost & Sullivan Lost Office in NYC Attack," *San Antonio Business Journal,* September 17, 2001.

"Frost & Sullivan to Sell Controlling Interest to Princeton Publisher," *Wall Street Journal,* June 18, 1987.

"M.A.I.D. PLC in Distribution Venture with Frost & Sullivan," *Dow Jones News Service,* July 9, 1997.

O'Leary, Mick, "Frost & Sullivan Market Intelligence Completes 'Big Three' O," *Information Today,* May, 1995, p. 13.

Thomas, Mike W., "Frost & Sullivan Cutting Staff in the Wake of Terror Attacks," *San Antonio Business Journal,* October 5, 2001.

—Frank Uhle

Furr's Restaurant Group, Inc.

3001 East President George Bush Highway
Richardson, Texas 75082
U.S.A.
Telephone: (972) 808-2923
Fax: (972) 808-5713
Web site: http://www.furrs.net

Public Company
Incorporated: 1959 as Furr's Cafeterias, Inc.
Employees: 4,700
Sales: $184.9 million (2001)
Stock Exchanges: American
Ticker Symbol: FRG
NAIC: 722212 Cafeterias

Furr's Restaurant Group, Inc., based in the Dallas, Texas, suburb of Richardson, owns and operates 92 family-style cafeterias in 11 states under the names of Furr's Family Dining, Furr's Family Buffet, and Bishop's Buffet. The six Bishop's units are located in Iowa and Illinois, while the remaining Furr's restaurants are located mostly in the Southwest. In addition, the company operates Dynamic Foods, a Lubbock, Texas, food purchasing, processing, and distribution center that services all of the company's restaurants, providing as much as 85 percent of the food served system wide. To take advantage of excess capacity, Dynamic Foods also sells to a limited number of outside customers.

Postwar Boom for Cafeteria-Style Restaurants

Cafeterias originated in New York City and spread throughout the North, but due to a number of factors in the early decades of the 20th century they fell out of favor. The cost of city real estate as well as higher wages made them a unattractive investment. Moreover, cafeterias during the Depression were stigmatized as haunts for undesirables. While cafeterias faded from the scene in the North, they found fertile ground elsewhere, especially in growing Southern cities in the years following World War II. There was little difficulty in finding a large enough, inexpensive parcel of land that could accommo-

date a restaurant and parking lot, and low labor costs also contributed to making cafeterias a viable investment. Because few restaurant chains operated in the South, cafeterias were able to flourish in the region. While they offered a variety of inexpensive dishes, they also presented a décor that appealed to a family clientele. Cafeterias in the South were viewed as a place to eat after church on Sunday rather than as a hangout for petty thieves and bums. As a result, cafeteria chains formed and spread throughout the South in the postwar years.

The connection of the Furr's name to cafeterias dates to 1947 when forward-thinking Texas supermarket magnate, Roy Furr, began to combine dining with one of his grocery stores, a combination that was years ahead of its time. Furr was born in McKinney, Texas, in 1905 and gained business experience working for his father at the Kirkland Mercantile Company. After graduating from the University of Oklahoma, he taught school, then in 1923 moved to Amarillo, Texas, where he and his father established the Furr Food Store. He moved to Lubbock in 1929 and bought six grocery stores that formed the basis for a supermarket chain that expanded throughout West Texas and eventually into Colorado and New Mexico.

Furr's first cafeteria was built next door to one of his Odessa, Texas, grocery stores, opening in March 1947. The venture was successful, but the site only offered enough parking space for 25 cars. Furr decided to sell both businesses, but elected to only rebuild the supermarket. One of his employees, a baker named Cliff Andrews, boasted that if Furr would build a super cafeteria and let him manage it, it could "run circles around your supermarket." Furr agreed, and in April 1956 a Furr's Cafeteria, double the size of the original and offering five acres of parking, opened under Andrews's management. The operation proved so successful that Furr opened a second cafeteria in April 1956, and four more units by May 1959. The burgeoning chain to this point had been operated under Furr's Supermarkets. In June 1959, the business was spun off into a separate corporation christened Furr's Cafeterias, Inc. Roy Furr's son, Don Furr, who had been acting as director of the operation, was named president, and Andrews was named vice-president.

Furr's Cafeterias grew steadily, numbering 11 units by the end of 1962. To be certain of a consistent quality of food

Company Perspectives:

Since 1947, Furr's has placed home-cooked value and variety right around the corner. We are committed to providing quality food at reasonable prices. We offer a well-balanced menu with a variety of home-cooked favorites, including carved meats, baked fish and chicken-fried steak, fresh salads and vegetables, oven-baked breads and our famous desserts. Our wide selection of homestyle foods will please any group, large or small. Whether you choose from our ''by-the-item'' or ''all-you-can-eat'' pricing alternatives, you'll always receive great value at Furr's.

throughout the chain, the company in 1968 acquired the Lubbock-based Plains Meat Company, which it renamed Quality Control Kitchens, supplying meats, cooked foods, and bakery items to Furr's Cafeterias. This operation would ultimately become the Dynamic Foods subsidiary. On November 12, 1969, Furr's Cafeteria went public, issuing 260,000 shares of stock. Aside from cafeterias, the company also opened a pie shop in Lubbock in 1969, and another in Odessa in 1971. By the time of Roy Furr's death in 1975, Furr's Cafeterias owned and operated 57 units located in seven states.

Kmart Acquires Furr's Cafeterias in 1980

The Furr family business empire of restaurants, supermarkets, convenience stores, grocery warehouses, and realty company did not fare well during Roy Furr, Jr.'s tenure. By 1979 the company was forced to file for bankruptcy. The supermarket assets were acquired by West German investors, while Furr's Cafeterias was purchased for $70 million by Kmart Corporation in May 1980. For Kmart the move into the restaurant business was part of an aggressive diversification and expansion plan that included the acquisitions of Builders Square, Waldenbooks, and Pay Less Drug Stores. Kmart hoped to complement its department stores with the addition of Furr's Cafeterias on the same pad. In 1983 Kmart added a regional buffet chain when it paid $28 million for Iowa-based Bishop Buffets, founded in Waterloo, Iowa, in 1920 by Benjamin Franklin Bishop. Kmart opened new units under both the Furr's and Bishop's names but essentially allowed them to operate independently. By November 1986, however, Kmart, saddled with debt from its diversification efforts, was looking to focus on its core retailing business and decided to unload its restaurant assets, which had grown to 133 Furr's Cafeterias, spread from Texas to California, and 35 Bishop's Buffets located in the Midwest.

In January 1988 Kmart completed the sale of Furr's Cafeterias and Bishop Buffets to investor Michael Levenson's Cavalcade Holdings of Lubbock, Texas, for $237.5 million in a leveraged buyout. Levenson then packaged the assets in a limited master partnership, Furr's/Bishop's Cafeterias L.P. and sold 11 million units at $10 each, which were then listed on the New York Stock Exchange.

The 38-year-old Levenson never graduated from college, instead gaining business experience from a family-owned bank in New Mexico where he served as president. Fascinated by the

oil and gas industry, Levenson relocated to Texas in the late 1970s to buy and sell oil and gas leases. He then became interested in the takeover exploits of entrepreneur T. Boone Pickens and decided to make his own takeover attempts in order to gain control of a company to run. He bid unsuccessfully on Texas oil companies Tesoro Petroleum Corp. and Texas American Energy, as well as Hawaii's Aloha Airlines. In 1986 an investment banker introduced him to the cafeteria business when shares in the closely-held Wyatt chain became available. After some research into cafeteria-style restaurants, Levenson became convinced that the industry held untapped potential. He failed in his attempts to acquire Wyatt over the next two years, then learned that Kmart was interested in selling Furr's and Bishop's, and turned to Dean Witter Reynolds and other banks for the money to acquire the assets.

Levenson was extremely aggressive in his approach to the restaurant business. He quickly initiated a turnaround program that included cutting employee benefits and other overhead costs, and launched a marketing campaign with a budget that far exceeded that of his competitors, approximately 2.5 percent of revenues compared to 0.5 percent. Levenson brought other changes to the cafeteria concept as well. In remodeled units, the dessert and beverage sections were separated in order to avoid slowing down the entree and vegetable line. He introduced bakeries, take-out counters, and even separate rooms for children. He also launched all-you-can-eat promotions at many of his poorer-performing units. In short order he succeeded in boosting traffic to Furr's and Bishop's, causing some financial analysts to take notice and recommend the company as a good buy.

Levenson also began closing less productive units, especially Bishop's Buffets that were located in fading strip malls. Like owners of other southern cafeteria chains, Levenson harbored ambitions of expanding to the North, talking openly about his desire to explore such territories as Chicago, New York, and New Jersey. Nevertheless, he also rejected the Kmart strategy of building new units, maintaining instead that the cafeteria business was mature and that the better course was to grow by acquisitions. Operations would then be consolidated to realize increased efficiencies while at the same time gaining greater buying power and marketing clout. Levenson had also not forgotten about Wyatt Cafeterias. In 1986 he had signed a standstill agreement with the chain in order to take a look at the company's books, and now that the agreement had expired he began to renew his play for Wyatt, which if successful would have made Furr's/Bishop's the largest cafeteria chain. Once again, however, his acquisition hopes were dashed, and Wyatt was instead bought up by an employee stock ownership plan.

It was unlikely, however, that Levenson would have been able to take on the debt required to purchase Wyatt. He was already suffering under onerous interest payments that severely limited the possibility of growth. Moreover, Levenson acquired Furr's and Bishops at a time when the entire cafeteria segment was entering a slump. Chains, unable to successfully penetrate to other regions of the country, had overbuilt in the South. Increased cafeteria competition was also aggravated by the influx of fast food chains that lured away customers who no longer cared to wait in lines. For many, cafeterias were now seen as a bastion for senior citizens, leading to erosion in the young family business. In March 1991 Levenson converted the

Key Dates:

1920: Benjamin Franklin Bishop opens his first restaurant in Waterloo, Iowa.
1947: Roy Furr opens his first cafeteria in Odessa, Texas.
1959: Furr's Cafeterias, Inc., is established.
1968: Plains Meat Company, predecessor to Dynamic Foods, is acquired.
1969: Furr's goes public.
1980: Kmart acquires Furr's.
1983: Kmart acquires Bishop's
1988: Kmart sells Furr's and Bishop's to Michael Levenson's limited master partnership.
1991: The Furr's/Bishop's partnership is converted into a corporation.
2000: Company's name is changed to Furr's Restaurant Group, Inc.

partnership to a corporation but was subsequently unable to pay a dividend that he had promised shareholders. Not only was the company steadily losing money, it was charged with falsifying the registration statement when it was converted to a corporation. In December 1992, Levenson settled the matter by agreeing to pay a $50,000 fine to the Securities Exchange Commission without admitting or denying any allegations.

New Leadership in 1993

In June 1993 Levenson's reign at Furr's/Bishop's came to an end when shareholders enlisted 28-year-old investment banker Kevin E. Lewis to succeeded him as chairman and restructure the company's debt. Long-time fast food executive William Prather, former CEO at Hardees who had been brought in as a consultant, was then named the company's new chief executive. In a subsequent buyout, Lewis gained 60 percent of Levenson's outstanding stock and Prather 40 percent. Over the next four years most of Lewis's efforts would be devoted to restructuring the debt load incurred from Levenson's leveraged buyout, which continued to cripple the company, preventing it from performing necessary remodeling. In addition to the Furr's and Bishop's restaurants, Lewis and Prather also inherited several minor ventures, including some liquor stores and two El Paso Barbecue restaurants. In October 1994 Prather elected to resign as CEO in order to take the El Paso operation and strike out on his own. According to Prather, his decision resolved some internal issues at Furr's/Bishops. "With both Kevin and me there, we were top-heavy," he explained.

Now serving as both chair and CEO, Lewis finally succeeded in completing a recapitalization plan in January 1996. He stayed on as CEO for an additional year, as the business stabilized and the company posted net income of $8.4 million on revenues of $197.4 million for fiscal 1996. He then announced that he was stepping down as chief executive. Board member Kenneth Reimer, formerly of Tony Roma's, took over on an interim basis, and three months later Ted Papit was hired as president and chief executive. The former CEO of Black-Eyed Pea Restaurants expressed enthusiasm for the recent opening of a new unit that replaced one that had burned down.

Insurance money essentially funded a prototype restaurant that offered patio seating, a food-court-style serving arrangement, and a carry-out market. Papit also envisioned new marketing ideas. The situation at Furr's/Bishop's, however, was not as rosy as portrayed. In fiscal 1997, the company would again lose money, reporting a net loss of $5.4 million on revenues that had fallen to $193.5 million. Moreover, the company's stock, which traded around $2 per share in early 1996, began to steadily fall in value, eventually bottoming out at below 50 cents.

Papit's tenure at Furr's/Bishop's would be brief. After six months at the helm he announced he was resigning, then changed his mind only to become caught up in an unusual shakeup. In the spring of 1998 one of Furr's/Bishop's major shareholders, TIAA-CREF, the country's largest pension system, nominated its own slate of board members, which it then succeeded in installing. The unprecedented move was taken, according to a proxy statement, because "Teachers believes there is something fundamentally wrong at the company and the company has been operated for far too long for the benefit of a few rather than all the stockholders." The statement charged that the board approved "high consulting fees, executive compensation, and golden parachutes to certain members." Furthermore, the statement noted, "Notwithstanding the management's arguments that the company is on the verge of a turnaround, Kevin Lewis, as chairman of the board, recently completed selling all of the shares he owned in the company."

With Lewis ousted, Papit resigned and was replaced as chief executive on an interim basis by board member Suzann Hopgood, who had been on the previous board before resigning to join the TIAA slate. As it searched for a permanent CEO, the board approved a $20 million capital-improvement program intended to upgrade 20 restaurants. In October 1998 the company hired a new president and chief executive: Phillip Ratner, former head of both Spaghetti Warehouse and Acapulco Restaurants. Also within the first six months of taking control, the board decided to move the company's headquarters to Richardson, a suburb of Dallas, although Dynamic Foods would be left in place in Lubbock.

Under Ratner, Furr's continued to spend money on capital improvements, primarily to remodel existing units and to upgrade its computer and information system, as well as to improve the operations at Dynamic Foods. From the summer of 1998 through 1999, the company remodeled 30 of its restaurants, while closing down several that were underperforming. In February 2000 it opened a new unit under the Furr's Family Buffet banner that employed a "scatter-bar" concept that had proven popular with such restaurants as Golden Corral. Nevertheless, the company remained primarily committed to the straight-line cafeteria business. Also in that month the company changed its name to Furr's Restaurant Group. Although it was clearly making strides in turning around its financial condition at a time when other cafeteria chains faced serious problems, Furr's was unable to meet the $50 million market capitalization requirement of the New York Stock Exchange, and in August 2000 moved to the American Stock Exchange.

After posting two consecutive profitable years at Furr's, Ratner resigned in July 2001 to take over Marie Callender Pie Shops. In October he was replaced by Craig S. Miller, the former chief executive of Uno Restaurant Holdings Corp. With considerable experience in casual dining, Miller was charged with bringing a new perspective to the cafeteria business and building on a core base of loyal customers. Upon assuming his new job, he summarized the task ahead as one of finding "ways we can attract more guests to the restaurant and capture some of the growth in the foodservice industry that some of the cafeteria chains have not been able to keep pace with over the past several years." The challenges proved formidable, however, and amid falling revenues and net losses, Miller resigned a year later. As the cafeteria industry continued to struggle, and Furr's same-store sales continued to decline, the company filed for bankruptcy protection under Chapter 11 early in 2003. Whether new leadership could help restructure the cafeteria chain remained to be seen.

Principal Subsidiaries

Dynamic Foods; Furr's/Bishop's Cafeterias, L.P.; Cafeterias Operators, L.P.; Cavalcade Holdings, Inc.; Cavalcade Foods, Inc.

Principal Competitors

Buffets, Inc.; Luby's, Inc.; Piccadilly Cafeterias, Inc.; Shoney's, Inc.

Further Reading

Charlier, Marj, "Cafeteria Magnate Aims for Head of Line," *Wall Street Journal,* August 18, 1988, p. 1.

——, "Southern Cafeteria Chains Plot Expansion Into North," *Wall Street Journal,* June 17, 1988, p. 1.

Mayfield, Dan, "From Texas Roots, Furrs Grew into Giant," *Albuquerque Tribune,* July 30, 2001.

Opdyke, Jeff D., "At Furr's, Hopes for Revival Rest on Boss Who Knows Cash Flow, but Not Cafeterias," *Wall Street Journal,* May 18, 1994, T4.

Ruggless, Ron, "Cafeterias Struggle as Market Dwindles," *Nation's Restaurant News,* September 18, 1995, p. 1.

——, "Furr's/Bishop's Lewis Steps Down as CEO, Prexy," *Nation's Restaurant News,* January 1, 1997, p. 3.

——, "New Furr's Leader Miller Brings 'Casual' Approach to Cafeterias," *Nation's Restaurant News,* October 22, 2001, p. 4.

Schultz, Ellen E., and Susan Warren, "Pension System Ousts Company's Board in Big Victory for Institutional Investors," *Wall Street Journal,* May 29, 1998, p. A2.

Selz, Michael, "Cafeterias' Down-Home Cooking Stays Down South," *Wall Street Journal,* September 3, 1991, p. B2.

Yoshihara, Nancy, "Kmart Breaks Away from its Pattern of 1960s," *Los Angeles Times,* January 28, 1985, p. 2.

—Ed Dinger

Glotel plc

The Quadrangle
180 Wardour Street
London W1V 4AE
United Kingdom
Telephone: +44 (0) 20 7734 7722
Fax: +44 (0) 20 7734 9684
Web site: http://www.glotel.com

Public Company
Incorporated: 1989 as Comms People
Employees: 254
Sales: £98.35 million ($155.5 million) (2002)
Stock Exchanges: London
Ticker Symbol: GLO
NAIC: 561310 Employment Placement Agencies; 541512
   Computer Systems Design Services; 551112 Offices
   of Other Holding Companies

Glotel plc provides a full range of recruitment services, meeting temporary and permanent staffing requirements, as well as providing headhunting and executive placement services. The London, England-based company has long focused its efforts on the telecommunications and high-technology markets, becoming the leading U.K. recruitment company for those industries. At the same time, Glotel has expanded internationally—at the height of the 1990s high-technology boom, the company operated 24 offices throughout the world, nearly half of which were opened in the United States. Europe and Australia are also important markets for the company, and Glotel has been building a presence in the Asian markets as well. The United Kingdom accounts for slightly less than half of the company's total revenues, with the United States representing nearly one-third of Glotel's business. With the collapse of both the global telecommunications and high-technology markets at the turn of the century, the company has pared down its branch network to just 19 offices. Glotel also has responded to the shrinking demand in its core markets by expanding its range of services and by extending into other markets. Hit hard by the bankruptcy of two of its major U.S. clients which forced Glotel to write off more than £1 million in bad debt, sinking the company into losses, cofounders Les Clark, chairman, and Andy

Baker, CEO, took the unusual move of giving themselves and other executives temporary pay cuts. These moves have enabled the company to avoid reducing its own staff as it waits for the high-tech staffing market to rise again. Glotel is listed on the London Stock Exchange. At the end of its 2002 fiscal year (in March 2002) the company posted sales of £98.35 million ($155.5 million), down from a high of £165 million the year before.

Riding the High-Tech Boom in the 1990s

Les Clark had already built a career in the recruitment business when he joined with Andy Baker to launch what was to become Glotel. Clark had risen to become managing director at the recruitment arm of Hestair, a diversified U.K. company that was acquired by BET at the beginning of the 1990s. Working under Clark was Andy Baker, then still in his early 20s, who worked as a sales director at the Hestair recruiting subsidiary. When Clark was made redundant in the late 1980s, he and Baker decided to join together to create a new recruitment company, Comms People, in 1989.

From the outset, Comms People, as its name implied, targeted exclusively the telecommunications sector, which was just then becoming one of the most vibrant and fast-growing industries. Clark and Baker reasoned that the increasing specialization of the various branches of the high-technology market would step up the demand for growing numbers of qualified staff. At the same time, companies operating in the sector would require more assistance in locating temporary and permanent staff with the appropriate qualifications.

Clark risked his Hestair payoff package, as well as the mortgage on his home, to set up Comms People. The business operated as a partnership, however, with both Clark and Baker holding a 50 percent stake in the company. The two-man firm rented a small office, and with a single telephone began drumming for business. While Clark kept a tight rein on spending—the company car was a former pizza delivery van, complete with heated seats—the ambitious Baker began building up a pool of consultants for a growing number of telecommunications clients.

Comms People itself began hiring, and by the early 1990s the group boasted 20 employees of its own. The company's early specialization also had given it a leading share in the U.K.

market for recruitment in the telecommunications sector. Part of the group's success was its insistence on hiring staff with technical backgrounds; the company also provided intensive in-house training to keep its employees at the cutting edge of market developments. Before long, however, Comms People found its own focus had become too narrow, as the IT market in general began to boom during the decade. Comms People extended its reach into the broader IT sector, which led the group to adopt the new name, Comms & PC People.

The growing global nature of the IT business led Baker and Clark to begin to look beyond the United Kingdom. In 1992, the pair opened the group's first foreign office, in Amsterdam, which was to become the headquarters of a Europe-wide operation. The company also began expanding throughout the United Kingdom, opening offices in Manchester, Birmingham, Bristol, Edinburgh, and Newcastle through the mid-1990s. The company's telecommunications business in these markets was to gain steam with the roll-out of the next generation GSM mobile telephone network being developed across Europe.

Meanwhile Baker and Clark developed something of an expansion model—an existing employee with an interest in taking on a new challenge was sent to a new market, where the company replicated its own origins, renting a small office equipped with a telephone. The method provided a relatively low-risk and low-cost means of expansion. If after six months the office was to prove unprofitable, it could be closed easily with limited losses to Comms People.

In 1993, Comms People looked overseas to the United States, which had long been the motor for the IT industry. Baker and early employee Steve Moreschi, who also had worked with Baker and Clark at Hestair, traveled to the United States to scout locations. The pair settled on the fast-growing Atlanta market, seen as an important hub in the telecommunications sector. As Baker told the *Independent*: "Myself and Steve arrived on the Sunday, jet-lagged but excited, Delta Airlines economy," Baker says. "We asked people in a local bar where the good business district was and they said Buckhead. We found the tallest building there and set up an office, 10ft x 8ft with a desk and phone, only $700 a month, and we got a copy of the Atlanta Journal and took out a quarter-page ad in Communications Week."

The gamble quickly paid off—by the end of six months, the Atlanta office had hired its second employee. By the end of its first year, the U.S. operation had posted revenues of some $5 million. Moreschi was given the go-ahead to begin scouting

locations for new offices as the company prepared to expand across the United States. The timing was right—the United States was just entering an extended economic boom driven by the high-technology and telecommunications sectors—and Glotel found its services in high demand. By the middle of the decade, Comms & PC People had opened offices in Dallas, San Francisco, Boston, Los Angeles, Reston (Virginia), Philadelphia, Phoenix, New York, and Silicon Valley.

The opening up of the telecommunications markets in Europe—most of which had long been dominated by government-owned telephone monopolies—and a massive consolidation effort among the industry's major players, which saw the creation of a number of globally operating telecommunications operators, combined to boost demand for Glotel's services. The company's business quickly spread beyond the Dutch market into Belgium, then into Germany and France as well. By 1994, the group's sales had topped £8 million.

The high-tech boom soon spread to other markets, particularly the fast-growing markets in Asia. In 1995, Comms & PC People moved into Australia, setting up the first office in what was to become its Australasian division. The company opened offices in Melbourne and Sydney, directing its foray into the Asian markets from its Australian base as it prepared to expand with the opening of new local offices. The economic crisis that swept through the region in the late 1990s put a halt, however, to the group's Asian expansion.

Nonetheless, Comms & PC People continued to grow strongly into the late 1990s. By 1997, the group, which now numbered some 150 employees, had posted turnover of nearly £50 million, more than half of which came from outside the United Kingdom. By the end of its fiscal year in March 1999, turnover had topped £100 million. The company's staff also had expanded to more than 250—with a database of some 100,000 consultants on call worldwide. Interestingly, Comms & PC People itself seemed to inspire the loyalty of its own employees—17 of the company's first 20 employees remained with the company. Until then, Clark and Baker had financed their expansion through a combination of bank debt and the use of confidential invoice discounting, an accounting vehicle that allowed the company to raise financing based on its future income. Yet the company's fast growth and its continued ambitions required a larger capital base.

Surviving the High-Tech Bust at the Turn of the Century

Clark and Baker decided to take their company public in 1999. The offering was a relatively modest one—raising just the £13.5 million the company needed to wipe out its debt and fund its immediate growth plans. Clark and Baker reduced their own holdings to just 26 percent each in a successful public offering that placed much of the company's free-floating stock with institutional investors. As part of the public offering the company changed its name to Glotel plc.

Glotel's share price, which debuted at 140 pence, gained quickly as the high-technology boom went into overdrive at the end of the decade. By the end of 1999 the company's share price had topped 323 pence per share—and went on to near 830 pence at the height of the high-tech boom. The company continued to expand its office network, opening in Brussels and

Key Dates:

1989: Les Clark and Andy Baker found Comms People, a recruitment firm specializing in the telecommunications sector, in London.
1992: Comms People opens its first foreign subsidiary, in Amsterdam.
1993: The company launches its first U.S. office in Atlanta and changes its name to Comms & PC People as its focus expands to include broader high-technology markets.
1994: Revenues top £8 million.
1995: The company opens its first office in Australia.
1997: Revenues near £50 million.
1999: The company changes its name to Glotel and goes public on the London Stock Exchange.
2000: Revenues reach a high of £165 million (for the year ended March 2001) and the company's network expands to 24 offices.
2001: The company restructures, shutting down five offices and reducing staff as telecommunications and high-technology markets slump.
2002: Clark and Baker announce pay cuts and stock option incentives as a means to reduce costs.

Chicago and bringing its total to 24 offices by 2000, as its sales continued to soar, climbing from £132 million by the end of its fiscal year in March 2000 to £165 million by March 2001.

Yet by then Glotel had been caught in the turmoil of the high-technology market. The telecommunications industry had gone into a tailspin, marked by the spectacular collapse of a number of formerly high-flying players, such as Worldcom. The Internet-driven high-technology market followed quickly, and by the beginning of 2001 Glotel had already issued the first of what was to become a series of profit warnings.

Glotel's share price plunged as investors worried that the company had expanded too fast into the United States, leaving it vulnerable to the increasingly fragile market. Indeed, the company was hit especially hard when two of its major customers in the United States declared bankruptcy, leaving the company with more than £1 million in bad debt.

Glotel began fighting back and in 2001 began moving to reduce its reliance on the telecommunications sector—previously that sector alone had accounted for more than 60 percent of the company's activity—targeting other business markets, particularly the financial sector. The company was able to win business from such heavyweights as J.P. Morgan and the Bank of America. Yet the financial market was struggling as well—a situation exacerbated by the September 11 attacks of that year.

Glotel was forced into defensive mode. The company began cutting back on its staff, particularly by eliminating a layer of middle management and requiring directors to return to hands-on management. Glotel also began shutting a number of hardest hit offices, including its office in Los Angeles. By the beginning of 2002, Glotel had scaled back to just 19 offices. By then the company's sales reflected the difficult economic conditions as Glotel's revenues slipped back to just £98 million for the year.

In February of that year, Clark and Baker announced an unusual step in the company's effort to keep its head above water. The company instituted what it dubbed its "thin cat" solution, in reference to a series of so-called "fat cat" scandals that had swept the United Kingdom over the high salaries paid to executives by a number of money-losing companies. Instead, Clark and Baker announced their intention to take pay cuts. The founders also put into place an incentive scheme among other top executives, offering up options on their own stock—which had slumped to barely more than 30 pence—to executives who agreed to accept temporary pay cuts. The move was expected to help the company save more than £100,000 per month, enabling it to wipe out its bad debts.

While the European market had resisted the worst of the economic difficulties being experienced in the United States, Glotel continued to face into a slow hiring market at the end of 2002. As the company waited out a return to expansion in its core technology markets, it began expanding its range of services—to include headhunting and executive placement services—in order to provide a broader revenue base. After Clark and Baker had ridden high during the technology boom, the team showed their determination to guide Glotel through the high-tech bust as well.

Principal Subsidiaries

Global International Ltd.; Glotel, Inc. (United States); Glotel Managed Services Ltd.; Glotel Pty Ltd (Australia); Glotel Accounting Systems PLC; Glotel BV (Netherlands); Glotel GmbH (Germany); Glotel Holdings Plc; Contract Accountants PLC; Global Telecommunications Resource Ltd.; Glotel IT Ltd.; PC People Ltd. (Dormant); Comms & PC People Ltd. (Dormant).

Principal Competitors

Adecco SA; AdVal Group plc; CareerBuilder, Inc.; Corporate Services Group plc; Corporate Staffing Resources, Inc.; Fusion Staffing Services, LLC; Michael Page plc; HotJobs.com, Ltd.; jobpilot AG; Lorien plc; Manpower Inc.; Marlborough International PLC; Penna Consulting plc; Robert Walters plc; Select Appointments (Holdings) Limited; Spherion Corporation; Spring Group plc; Vedior NV; World Careers Network plc.

Further Reading

Curry, Lynne, "Big Business in a Nutshell: Start Small and Move Fast," *Independent,* September 23, 1997.
"Glotel Optimistic Despite Further Job Cuts," *Investors Chronicle,* May 25, 2001, p. 46.
"Glotel Shares Fall on Downbeat H1 Results," *FT Investor,* December 10, 2002.
Hanney, Brian, "Glotel Hit by Lay-offs in US," *Express,* July 3, 2001.
"Recruitment Agencies Hit Hard by Falling Markets," *Investors Chronicle,* July 6, 2001, p. 43.
Trapp, Roger, "Buoyant Glotel Tempted to Float," *Independent,* August 24, 1997.
——, "Floating into Uncharted Waters," *Independent,* June 27, 1999.
White, Dominic, "Glotel Resorts to a Whip-Round," *Daily Telegraph,* February 9, 2002, p. 30.

—M.L. Cohen

Guardian Media Group plc

75 Farringdon Road
London EC1M 3JY
United Kingdom
Telephone: +44 20 7278-2332
Fax: +44 20 7242-0679
Web site: http://www.gmgplc.co.uk

Private Company
Incorporated: 1821
Employees: 3,102
Sales: £440 million ($627.6 million) (2001)
NAIC: 511110 Newspaper Publishers; 511120 Periodical
  Publishers

Guardian Media Group plc (GMG) is an anomaly in the British media market. Wholly-owned by a private foundation, the Scott Trust, GMG remains protected from the pressures of commercial—and political—interests of its publicly listed rivals. GMG's not-for-profit basis enables the company to plow profits back into the company, which has in turn allowed the company to extend beyond its core newspaper publishing operations to embrace a variety of media, including radio, Internet, and television. GMG's National Newspaper Division publishes its flagship daily, the *Guardian,* as well the *Observer*—the world's oldest Sunday newspaper. The company also publishes a European edition of the *Guardian* and the *Money Observer*. GMG's Regional Newspaper Division publishes the *Manchester Evening Post* and is co-publisher for the Manchester edition of the free daily, *Metro*. GMG has stepped up its holdings in its Radio Division, which includes the Real Radio network of regional radio stations in South Wales, South and West Yorkshire, and Central Scotland; a 39.2 percent share of Radio Investments Ltd., which owns 24 local radio stations; and Jazz FM, which broadcasts in London and the northwest of England. GMG's 48 percent stake in Trader Media Group gives it a portfolio of magazine titles, including *Auto Trader, Top Marques, Bike Trader*, and *Truck Trader*. The company has also extended itself to the Internet, notably with the brand name and web site Guardian Unlimited, as well as with an 89.6 percent

holding in workthing.com, an employment recruitment and advertising site. Other holdings of GMG include an 86 percent share of M&G Media, which publishes the South African newspaper *Mail & Guardian*, and a 50 percent share in Trafford Park Printers, which prints the *Guardian,* the *Manchester Evening News,* and other newspapers. GMG posted sales of £456 million in 2001. The company is led by chief executive Bob Phillis.

Liberal Newspaper in the 1820s

GMG's history dates back to the 1820s, when John Edward Taylor launched a weekly newspaper in Manchester, England. The paper was to remain in the Taylor family's hands until the beginning of the 20th century. In 1855, after the repeal of the Stamp Duty, also known as the Tax on Knowledge, the newspaper became a daily, adopting a morning publishing schedule. In the 1870s, the Taylor family acquired an interest in another Manchester paper, the *Manchester Evening News,* which had been launched in the late 1860s.

The arrival of CP Scott as editor of the *Manchester Guardian* in 1872 marked a milestone in the company's history. Just 26 years old at the time of his appointment, Scott was to remain the newspaper's editor for 57 years. Over the course of Scott's tenure, the *Guardian* gained national and even international prominence. In 1907, Scott purchased the *Manchester Guardian* from the Taylor family, pledging to maintain the newspaper independence.

CP Scott's son, Edward Taylor Scott, took over as editor of the *Manchester Guardian* in 1929. Another son, John Russell, had purchased the *Manchester Evening News* in 1924, giving the Scott family control of both newspapers. In the 1930s, however, the Scott family's newspaper holdings were faced with crippling death taxes, which threatened to fold the company. Instead, the family created the Scott Trust in 1936, which took over ownership of the newspapers. The terms of the trust also guaranteed the *Guardian*'s editorial, commercial, and political interests. All profits made by the newspaper were plowed back into the company, buffering the group against potential downturns in its fortunes.

Company Perspectives:

Guardian Media Group plc is a U.K. media business with interests in national newspapers, regional and local newspapers, magazines and radio. The company is wholly-owned by the Scott Trust. The Scott Trust was created in 1936 to secure the financial and editorial independence of the Guardian in perpetuity.

In the 1940s and 1950s, the *Manchester Guardian* began its shift from regional newspaper to becoming on the United Kingdom's most prominent national newspapers. As part of this drive, the newspaper began printing news on its first page, which had traditionally held classified advertising. In 1959, the newspaper's name was changed to reflect its new national orientation, becoming known simply as the *Guardian*.

The *Guardian* gradually shifted its operations to London, which became the site of the paper's printing press in 1961. Yet the company maintained its ties with Manchester, and in 1961 it bought up rival evening newspaper *The Evening Chronicle*. This paper was merged into the *Manchester Evening News*, which added "Chronicle" to its name and claimed the number one spot among the United Kingdom's provincial newspapers.

Media Expansion in the 1970s

While the company remained committed to Manchester, the *Guardian* newspaper operations increasingly focused on London; when the paper's editorial staff moved to London, that city became the daily's headquarters. In 1967, the company, then called the Manchester Guardian and Evening News Ltd., reorganized its operations to reflect its dual focus. In that year the company created two subsidiaries, Guardian Newspapers Ltd. and Manchester Evening News Ltd.

The company then began to look beyond newspaper publishing for entry into other media categories. One of its first moves in this direction was a purchase of a minority stake in Anglia Television in 1968. In 1969, the company added radio, acquiring 10 percent of Piccadilly Radio owners Greater Manchester Independent Radio Ltd. By then, GMG had a new name, having christened itself the Guardian and Manchester Evening News (GMEN) Ltd.

GMEN added a number of new newspaper titles to its range, including the *Rochdale Observer* and other local newspapers in 1974, and then the *Stockport Advertiser* group of local papers in 1977. Two years later, the company added another group of local newspapers, published under the *Surrey Advertiser* name. Then, in 1981, GMEN bundled its *Stockport Advertiser* titles into a 50-50 joint-venture with the Stock Express newspaper group, forming Lancashire and Cheshire County Newspapers (LCCN) Ltd. GMEN acquired full control of the LCCN joint-venture in 1985.

With stakes in radio and television bolstering its growing newspaper holdings, GMEN turned to the magazine segment, acquiring, in 1982, the automobile sales magazine *Northwest Automart*. That magazine format was expanded in 1985 into a new magazine, *Northwest Jobs Mart*. In 1987, the group acquired two more titles in the *Automart* series, in Bristol and the North East, and launched a third for the Scottish market. The company then changed the name of the *Automart* series to *Auto Trader*. By the end of the decade, GMEN controlled nine *Auto Trader* publications.

The launch of a new rival, the Independent, in the mid-1980s forced the Guardian to respond by revamping its format in 1988. GMEN also prepared a European edition of its flagship newspaper, printed in Europe and available as a day-of-issue daily. In that year, GMEN reorganized its operations again, restructuring into four new divisions: Guardian, Greater Manchester, Surrey, and Auto Trader.

Independent Media Group for the 21st Century

GMEN's further media interests had remained relatively limited as it concentrated on building up its print operations in the 1980s. At the end of the decade, however, the group made a new stab at the television market, this time on the production side, acquiring a stake in Broadcast Communications in 1989. The following year, GMEN raised its position in Broadcast Communications to majority control. In that year, also, the company added a new newspaper title, the *Accrington Observer*, and bought into a 50-50 printing partnership, Trafford Park Printing, which printed the *Daily Telegraph*, and took over printing of the *Guardian*.

In 1991, GMEN stepped up its interests in television, joining the GMTV partnership and acquiring an independent television franchise. The company also stepped up its radio holdings, taking 20 percent of Trans World Communications plc.

A major purchase for the company came in 1993, when GMEN snapped up the *Observer*, the world's oldest Sunday newspaper, for £27 million in 1993. First published in 1791, the *Observer* had fallen on hard times since the mid-1980s, when its circulation had topped 800,000. As part of the Lonrho empire, led by Tiny Rowland, since 1981 the *Observer*—and its reputation—had suffered greatly during Rowland's efforts to gain control of the Harrod's department store group. With its readership slipping to a low of 500,000, the *Observer* had been faced with closure before GMEN stepped in to rescue the venerable newspaper. Added to GMEN's list of publications, the *Observer* nonetheless maintained its editorial independence.

GMEN changed its name to Guardian Media Group (GMG) to reflect its broadening media interests. In 1994, GMG acquired a number of new regional newspapers, including *the Reading Evening Post*, through its purchase of Thames Valley Newspapers, formerly part of the Thomson Corporation. In that year, the company sold off its radio station stakes to growing media group EMAP. The company also spun-off its *Auto Trader* publications into a new subsidiary called Auto Trader National Magazines, sparking rumors that the company might attempt to float this and other interests as part of a new public company. The following year, GMG purchased a small stake in Golden Rose Communications, which owned radio station Jazz FM. The company also bought a controlling share of South African group, M&G Media, which published the *Mail & Guardian* daily newspaper.

Key Dates:

1821: John Edward Taylor begins publishing the *Manchester Guardian* as a weekly newspaper.

1855: *Manchester Guardian* becomes a daily paper after repeal of the Stamp tax.

1872: CP Scott is named editor of *Manchester Guardian*, a position he holds for 57 years.

1907: Scott buys *Manchester Guardian*.

1924: Scott family acquires the *Manchester Evening News*, founded in 1868.

1936: Creation of the Scott Trust, which takes full ownership control of the *Manchester Guardian* and *Evening News*.

1959: *Manchester Guardian*'s name is shortened to the *Guardian* to reflect the newspaper's national scope.

1961: Printing of the *Guardian* is moved to London, followed by the editorial headquarters in 1964; company acquires the *Evening Chronicle* and combines it with the *Manchester Evening News*.

1968: Company acquires stake in Anglia Television as a first step into becoming a broader media group.

1972: Company changes its name to Guardian and Manchester Evening News Limited (GMEN).

1974: GMEN begins acquisitions of local and regional newspapers, beginning with purchase of the *Rochdale Observer*.

1982: GMEN acquires *Northwest Automart*, later renamed *Auto Trader*.

1989: GMEN acquires stake in Broadcast Communications, then majority control the following year.

1993: GMEN acquires the *Observer,* the oldest Sunday newspaper in the world; changes name to Guardian Media Group (GMG).

2000: GMG spins off Auto Trader division into Trader Media Group and sells its share in GMG Endemol to focus on radio station holdings.

2001: GMG acquires Scot FM and a regional radio license in Yorkshire.

In the mid-1990s, GMG took its first steps into the growing Internet media race, forming a new subsidiary, Guardian Unlimited, and launching web sites for both the *Guardian* and *Auto Trader*. These were joined the following year by a new site for the *Manchester Evening News*, Manchester Online. By 2000, Guardian Unlimited had launched more than ten web sites. By then, the company had launched a new daily, the free morning commuter paper *MetroNews*.

GMG sold off its stake in GMTV in 2000, turning instead toward boosting its radio interests—the company acquired Scot FM in 2001, then took control of Jazz FM in 2002. GMG also placed its *Auto Trader* subsidiary into a new joint-venture with BC Partners, an investment group which controlled, through Hurst Publishing, its own range of *Auto Trader* titles. The new company, owned at 52 percent by BC Partners and called Trader Media Group, now controlled more than 70 titles in the United Kingdom and elsewhere in Europe. GMG continued to shuffle its other assets, including combining its Broadcast Com-

munications television production subsidiary with the U.K. operations of fast-rising Endemol Productions to form GM Endemol in 1998. In 2000, however, Endemol paid GMG £26 million to acquire GM Endemol, as GMG decided to focus its spending on its radio, newspaper, and Internet holdings.

By then, GMG had a new radio success, with the launch of Real Radio in South Wales in 2000. The company acquired Scot FM in 2001, paying the Wireless Group more than £ 25 million, with the intention of renaming that station and placing it under the Real Radio banner. These moves fit in with GMG's strategy to build a nationwide network of regionally operating radio stations. In keeping with that ambition, GMG restructured its holdings again, forming the National Newspaper, Regional Newspaper, and Radio Divisions, in addition to the Trader Media divisions. The company was then awarded a new regional license, in Yorkshire, in 2001.

GMG launched a bid for a full takeover of Jazz FM in 2002. Although the bid initially met with resistance, Jazz FM's shareholders eventually agreed to a purchase price of £ 41 million. The move was seen as strong defensive ploy by GMG in the face of coming legislation that proposed to deregulate the U.K. media scene—enabling larger media groups and foreign media groups to gain ownership control of large parts of the U.K. media landscapes. While some observers cautioned that deregulation might lead to the U.K. media market falling into the hands of just a small number of large groups, GMG itself guaranteed its independence by the Scott Trust ownership foundation, was able to look forward to expanding its own media empire in the early years of the new century.

Principal Subsidiaries

Channel M Television Ltd.; GMG Radio Holdings Ltd.; Greater Manchester Newspapers Ltd.; M & G Media Ltd.; Guardian Newspapers Ltd.; Guardian Press Centre Ltd.; Real Radio Ltd.; Star Newspapers (Camberley) Ltd.; Surrey and Berkshire Newspapers Ltd.; Workthing Ltd. (89.6%); Trafford Park Printers (50%).

Principal Divisions

GMG Radio Holdings; Regional Newspaper Division; National Newspaper Division; Workthing.

Principal Competitors

Daily Mail and General Trust plc; Trinity Mirror plc; Associated Newspapers Ltd.; News International plc; Guardian Media Group plc; Independent News and Media UK Ltd.; Times Newspapers Ltd.; Telegraph Group Ltd.; Harmsworth Quays Ltd.; Johnston Press plc; SMG plc; Economist Newspaper Ltd.; Financial Times Ltd.; Express Newspapers PLC; Smurfit UK Ltd.; D C Thomson and Co Ltd.; West Ferry Printers Ltd.; Harcourt Publishers Ltd.; Greater Manchester Newspapers Ltd.; Guiton Group Ltd.

Further Reading

Darby, Ian, ''Will Phillis' Liberal Qualities Be Enough to Take GMG Forward?,'' *Campaign*, August 16, 2002, p. 12.

"A Guardian Fighting on Two Fronts," *Independent*, March 12, 1996, p. 14.

"GMG Profits Fall as It Invests in New Media," *Guardian*, September 6, 2001.

Hetherington, Alastair, *Guardian Years,* London: Chatto and Windus, 1981.

McNay, Michael, ed., *The Newsroom: The Guardian Past and Present,* Manchester: Guardian, 2002.

Potter, Mark, "Guardian Trumpets $60 Mln Bid for Jazz FM," *Reuters*, May 7, 2002.

Shah, Saeed, "Guardian Media Profits Collapse," *Independent*, August 3, 2002, p. 23.

Thurtle, Gary, "Jazz FM falls to Guardian Media Group," *Marketing Week,* June 6, 2002, p. 5.

Warner, Edmond, "Synergies, Strategies and All That Jazz," *Guardian*, May 11, 2002.

—M.L. Cohen

Gunnebo AB

P.O. Box 5181
Drakegatan 5
SE-402 26 Goteborg
Sweden
Telephone: (+46) 31 83 68 00
Fax: (+46) 31 83 68 10
Web site: http://www.gunnebo.se

Public Company
Incorporated: 1889 as Gunnebo Bruks Nya AB
Employees: 8,400
Sales: SEK 6.67 billion($703.4 million) (2001)
Stock Exchanges: Stockholm
Ticker Symbol: GUNN
NAIC: 561621 Security Systems Services

Acquisitive Gunnebo AB has quickly grown into one of the world's leading security groups. The Goteborg, Sweden-based holding company has focused its growth efforts on developing and manufacturing security equipment, devices, and systems. The company more than doubled in size between 1997 and 2001, nearing SEK 7 billion in sales (more than $700 million). Accordingly, Gunnebo AB has restructured itself into two division: Gunnebo Security, which accounts for more than 80 percent of sales, and Gunnebo Industrier, which includes much of the company's former operations. Gunnebo Security operates through three primary business units: Gunnebo Physical Security is the world's leading manufacturer of safes, bank vaults, vault doors, safety deposit boxes, and other security-related devices under such major brand names as Chubb Safes, Fichet-Bauche, Rosengrens, Garny, Tann, Haffner, and Lips; Gunnebo Integrated Security produces electronic security systems, including alarm systems, entrance control systems, close-circuit television systems, as well as alarm centers, adding brand names such as Gunnebo Mayor, Metro, Italdis, Hygiaphone, and Rizenthaler; and Gunnebo Physical Security, which produces perimeter control and security systems, including fences, gates, and alarms. Gunnebo Engineering includes the company's fastening systems, anti-skid and tire protection products, and heavy lifting machinery and equipment. That division, which produced SEK 1.2

billion in 2001, is slated to be sold off as Gunnebo completes its focus on its security products activity. Gunnebo is quoted on the Stockholm Stock Exchange and is led by Bjarn Holmqvist.

Swedish Manufacturing Force in the 19th Century

The Gunnebo entering the 21st century bore little resemblance to the Gunnebo founded in the late 18th century. Originally founded as a Swedish hammer mill by Hans Hultman in 1764, Gunnebo later came under German ownership in the 1850s. At that time, the mill was transformed into a foundry, Gunnebo Bruk, and went on to become one the largest manufacturers in its region by the 1870s. In 1889, the company was incorporated as Gunnebo Bruk Nya AB.

The Gunnebo site was modernized and outfitted with electricity in the late 1890s as Sweden underwent an extended economic boom period. The company's fortunes continued into the early years of the century, and Gunnebo continued to grow during World War I and the Depression. In the 1930s, the company became the first in Sweden to add electroplating facilities. Then, during World War II Swedish neutrality enabled the company to continue its growth.

The second half of the 20th century saw Gunnebo specialize in a number of product categories. The acquisition of Tage Wiberg in 1945 was a first step in this process as the company became the leading producer of nails for the Swedish market. Fastening technology—as the company called its expanding range of products—was to remain a core product line until the late 1990s. Other products were added, including high-grade chains in 1955, which led the company into a variety of automotive products, including snow chains and other tire protection products. The company also began manufacturing metals and metal products for the automotive industry through subsidiary Gnösjö-Gruppen.

In the early 1960s, Gunnebo recentered its production on four main sites: Gunnebo Bruk, Sya, Soraker, and Odeborg. In response to the poor economic climate brought on by the Arab oil embargo of the 1970s, Gunnebo restructured its operations into a group of decentralized businesses more reactive to their specific markets. This move led to an increasing internationalization of Gunnebo's sales. By the end of the 1980s, more than half of Gunnebo's sales came from outside of Sweden.

Focus on Security Products in the 1990s

The arrival of Bjarne Holmqvist as company CEO in 1995 signaled the start of Gunnebo's transition into a security products specialist. From the mid-1990s into the 2000s, Holmqvist led the company on a acquisition spree that transformed the company from a relatively minor Swedish manufacturer into a major player on the global security products field.

Holmqvist had been head of investment group HIDEF Kapital AB, which, in 1994, had acquired a security products company, EA Rosengrens AB. That company had been one of Sweden's most prominent safe manufacturers since the mid-1950s and was to form the foundation of Gunnebo. In 1995, HIDEF acquired Gunnebo and then changed its name to Gunnebo AB. Then, in 1996, the company listed on the Stockholm Stock Exchange's "A" list as it prepared for a new era of expansion.

With fresh financial backing, the new Gunnebo now set off on a buying spree. Among the first companies to be picked up were Mayor Ltd., based in England, a maker of turnstiles and other entrance control systems, and SCMD Sarl, a specialist in wire-mesh and sheet metal perimeter protection products, based in France.

In 1997, Gunnebo acquired Italdis Industria, based in Italy and that country's leading entrance control specialist. The acquisition not only extended Gunnebo's entrance control operations into southern Europe but also established the company as one of the continent's leaders in that market segment. While this and previous acquisitions had been of fairly small companies, in May 1997 Gunnebo made a more significant purchase when it acquired Germany's Wego System AG Sicherheitsanlagen, which had become a leading perimeter protection and entrance control company. The Wego acquisition boosted Gunnebo's perimeter protection business to more than SEK 900 million, giving the company the European lead in that market.

Gunnebo continued its acquisition program in 1997, buying Carl Seifet A/S, based in Denmark, adding that company's line of safes and vaults. Soon after, Gunnebo acquired Mauser Office GmbH, based in Germany, which added a line of bank vault, safety deposit boxes, and high-security safes to the Swedish company's growing security products offering. Meanwhile, Gunnebo was beginning to reorganize its other divisions, beginning a series of divestments of business no longer central to the company's strategy. Nonetheless, Gunnebo continued to invest in certain areas of its former operations, such as Gunnebo Industrier, which was to group the company's fasteners, heavy lifting, and automotive activities.

Yet security products had clearly become the thrust of the company's future. Gunnebo's acquisitions continued into 1998, with the creation of a French security products subsidiary, which then acquired small but well-known Hygiaphone SA, a maker of bank protection products, notably teller security windows. The company followed up that purchase with a move into Poland, acquiring Praediator Polska, a distributor of safes, alarms, and entrance control systems. That company was placed under Gunnebo's Rosengrens subsidiary, renamed Rosengrens Praediator, and gave Gunnebo a distribution network throughout Poland. The company then stepped up its presence in Finland, acquiring Polaraidat Oy, a manufacturer and distributor of perimeter protection products.

In mid-1998, Gunnebo signed a global cooperation agreement with the United Kingdom's De La Rue Plc.; as part of that agreement, Gunnebo acquired Garny Sicherheitstechnik, the leading German manufacturer of safes and security systems for financial institutions, for SEK 63 million. Gunnebo also took over De La Rue's Swedish safe manufacturing business. In addtion, De La Rue and Gunnebo agreed to cooperate on marketing each other's products in selected markets.

The addition of Garny gave Gunnebo the oldest safe manufacturing operation in Central Europe—the first Garny safes had appeared in 1813 and remained one of the leading brand names in the worldwide market. With Garny, Gunnebo's Security division was now able to claim the top European spot in security products, with sales of nearly SEK 1 billion. Garny, which focused on the banking sector, also strongly complemented Gunnebo's Rosengrens business, which targeted especially the commercial sector.

Global Leadership in the 21st Century

The year 1999 proved an important one for Gunnebo's new position as a security products specialist. By the end of that year, the company had sold off its automotive metals component, Gnosjo-Gruppen, to the Netherlands' Schuttersveld. As a result of that sale, more than 80 percent of Gunnebo's revenues now came from its security products.

By then, Gunnebo had completed another major acquisition—that of France's Fichet-Bauche. With a history dating back to the mid-1800s, including the development of the first fireproof safes, Fichet-Bauche had grown to become the leading manufacturer of safes, vaults, and other security products in southern Europe. Fichet-Bauche not only enabled Gunnebo to extend its position across most of Europe, it also added a new business area for the group, that of the fast-growing market for electronic security equipment and systems, including access control systems and closed-circuit television systems. The Fichet-Bauche acquisition, which cost more than SEK 400 million, added more than SEK 1.6 billion to Gunnebo's revenues. By the end of 1999, the company's sales had topped SEK 5 billion.

Gunnebo continued its acquisition drive through 1999 and into 2000. In June 1999, the company bought up full control John Tann Security Services Ltd., which had been a provider of post-sales services for the company's sales through its Rosen-

Key Dates:

1764: Gunnebo hammer mill is founded by Hans Hultman.

1850: Gunnebo mill is converted into a foundry and manufacturing plant and named Gunnebo Bruks.

1889: The company is incorporated as Gunnebo Bruks Nya AB.

1945: Gunnebo acquires Tage Wiberg and becomes the largest producer of nails in Sweden.

1980: The company adopts a decentralized organization and focuses on export sales.

1994: HIDEF Kapital AB, led by Bjarn Holmkvist, acquires Rosengrens, a maker of safes and other security products.

1995: HIDEF acquires Gunnebo, then changes its own name to Gunnebo AB and begins to specialize in security products.

1996: Gunnebo joins Stockholm exchange's A list and begins aggressive acquisition program.

1999: The purchase of Fichet-Bauche, of France, marks Gunnebo's largest acquisition to date as sales top SEK 5 billion for the year.

2000: Gunnebo acquires Chubb Safes, making the company a world-leader in the physical security products market.

2001: Gunnebo gains a foothold in U.S. entrance control systems market with purchase of Pinkerton subsidiary Omega Optical Turnstiles.

grens Tann subsidiary. The move was significant especially as it signaled Gunnebo's intention to boost its services activities, seen as an increasingly important segment of the security products market at the turn of the new century. Another small but significant acquisition came at the beginning of 2000, when the company purchased the Security Activity of Matra Nortel Communications in France, boosting Gunnebo's electronic security systems operations.

The year 2000 proved another turning point for Gunnebo. In August of that year, the company acquired Chubb Safes Plc, one of the world's leading brand names in safes and related physical security products. Chubb's history dated back to the early 19th century, when brothers Charles and Jeremiah Chubb patented the first secure locking mechanism, called the Detector Lock. In the 1830s, the Chubbs patented a new burglar-resistant safe, which helped the company become a household word. Chubb expanded throughout the rest of the century, not only within the British Empire but into the United States as well. By the end of the 20th century, Chubb had grown into a globally operating empire, employing more than 40,000, with sales topping £1.4 billion ($2.24 billion). In late 1997, Chubb was acquired by conglomerate Williams Plc, which bundled the company with another security products holding, Yale Intruder Security. Williams then sold Yale to Swedish group Assa Abloy, which in turn spun off Chubb Safes, selling it to Gunnebo.

The addition of Chubb not only boosted Gunnebo's position in its European base but also made it the world's leading manufacturer of physical security products, with control of four of the world's leading brand names. Gunnebo then began preparations to focus its operations entirely on security products,

restructuring its businesses under two primary divisions, Gunnebo Security and Gunnebo Industrier. The company began looking for a buyer for its profitable Gunnebo Industrier division at the end of 2000. Yet a downturn in market conditions forced the company to put the sale of that division on hold.

Gunnebo's acquisition drive continued into the new century, notably with the purchases of Garmann Clausen AB, based in Sweden, and Jorg Clausen A/S, based in Norway, which specialized in security products for cash handling systems. Both companies were then brought under Gunnebo's Rosengrens subsidiary. Another acquisition made in 2001 was that of France's CS Securité, formerly part of CS Communications & Systems, strengthening Gunnebo's electronic security systems operations. CS Securité was renamed Ritzenthaler shortly after its acquisition. Then, at the end of 2001, Gunnebo turned to the United States, buying Omega Optical Turnstiles from Pinkertons, by then part of the Securitas group. This acquisition gave Gunnebo a foothold into the U.S. entrance control market.

With sales topping SEK 6.8 billion at the end of 2001, Gunnebo had successfully transformed itself into one of the world's leading security products companies, its market share in certain product categories reaching 50 percent in Europe and up to 30 percent worldwide. Gunnebo showed no sign of slowing down its expansion, however. By mid-2002, the company had already made two more acquisitions, buying Germany's Leicher Group, a leader in automated cash handling products, and Riva Systems of Denmark, a specialist in point-of-sales equipment. Gunnebo appeared gung-ho to maintain its world-leading position into the new century.

Principal Subsidiaries

E A Rosengrens AB; Rosengrens Produktions AB; Gunnebo Perimeter Protection AB; Gunnebo Protection AB; Gunnebo Troax AB; Gunnebo Entrance Control AB; Gunnebo Wego AG; Fichet-Bauche SA.

Principal Divisions

Gunnebo Security; Gunnebo Industrier.

Principal Operating Units

Gunnebo Physical Security; Gunnebo Integrated Security; Gunnebo Physical Security.

Principal Competitors

ASSA ABLOY AB; The Eastern Company; Ingersoll-Rand Security and Safety; Masco Corporation; Master Lock Company; Napco Security Systems, Inc.

Further Reading

"Fichet-Bauche racheté par le suedois Gunnebo," *En Toute Securité*, no. 235, 1999.

"Gunnebo Acquires German Cash Handling Solutions Developer Leicher," *Nordic Business Report,* June 13, 2002.

"Gunnebo Acquires Germany's Leicher and Strengthens Its Position in Automated Cash Handling," *PrimeZone Media Network*, June 13, 2002.

"Gunnebo Acquires Riva Systems," *Nordic Business Report*, July 11, 2002.

—M.L. Cohen

VERSICHERUNGEN

HDI (Haftpflichtverband der Deutschen Industrie Versicherung auf Gegenseitigkeit V.a.G.)

Riethorst 2
D-30649 Hannover
Germany
Telephone: (49) 511 645-0
Fax: (49) 511 645-4545
Web site: http://www.hdi.de

Private Company
Incorporated: 1903 as Haftpflichtverband der Deutschen
    Eisen-und Stahlindustrie V.a.G.
Employees: 6,438
Total Assets: EUR 14.5 billion ($10.9 billion) (2001)
NAIC: 524126 Direct Property and Casualty Insurance
    Carriers; 52413 Reinsurance Carriers; 524128 Other
    Direct Insurance (Except Life, Health, and Medical)
    Carriers; 524113 Direct Life Insurance Carriers

HDI (Haftpflichtverband der Deutschen Industrie Versicherung auf Gegenseitigkeit V.a.G.) is Germany's third largest insurance group by premium income. Headquartered in Hannover, Germany, HDI is present around the world. The company's largest business division is reinsurance arm Hannover Re, one of the world's largest reinsurers. Most other of HDI's insurance operations, including life, accident, property and casualty, and auto insurance for private customers, as well as the management of its financial assets, are organized under the umbrella of Talanx AG. HDI's core business, liability and casualty insurance for corporate clients, is organized as a mutual insurer, a membership association which was founded at the beginning of the 20th century.

Origins in 1903

In December 1903, a group of German industrial entrepreneurs established a new organization to cover their liability insurance needs. Founded in Frankfurt am Main, Haftpflichtverband der Deutschen Eisen-und Stahlindustrie was not just

another insurance company. Under German insurance law, the Haftpflichtverband had the legal form of a nonprofit association, a "Versicherungsverein auf Gegenseitigkeit," in short V.a.G. This meant that its members were the insured as well as the insurers, cooperatively determining their insurance needs and the policies and conditions for their coverage. Such a new entity was unheard of in the world of business liability insurance, which was dominated by private insurance companies. The birth of the Haftpflichtverband, however, did not come out of the blue.

Business insurance cooperatives already existed in Germany around the turn of the 19th century. One of their domains was insuring workers against injury in case of work-related accidents. This was especially necessary in such industries as mining, steel and iron processing, and heavy machine building, which by their nature involved hazardous tasks. In 1900, a new law encouraged the "Berufsgenossenschaften," as those cooperatives were called, to establish their own organizations to offer business liability insurance for their corporate members. Shortly after the initiation of the new law, Hermann Blohm, co-owner of the Hamburg-based shipyard Blohm + Voss and representative of the northwestern chapter of the Berufsgenossenschaft for the iron and steel industry, proposed to undertake a survey among the organization's corporate members regarding to their liability insurance needs. Blohm's proposal was approved and the survey revealed that 237 out of 312 member firms had bought liability coverage from private insurers, leaving one quarter of all members uninsured. In the 68 cases in which firms that held liability policies were reimbursed for damage by their private insurers, the ratio of claims paid out to premiums paid was just 2 percent, hinting at the handsome profits the insurance companies must have made. The survey also showed that many of the participating companies were interested in a more affordable liability coverage that was tailored specifically to the needs of heavy industry.

Within the next two years, a commission consisting of members of the Berufsgenossenschaft in the cities Hannover, Saarbrücken, and Mainz worked out detailed proposals for a

Company Perspectives:

The Group operates in the following four corporate segments: primary property and casualty insurance, primary life insurance, reinsurance, financial services. The motto of each segment is sound solutions in insurance and financial services accompanied by good service. The top priority of HDI's income-oriented strategy is the long-term security and financial stability of the Group in the interest of its private and industrial policyholders. HDI's strategy for the future is to ensure that results remain stable; HDI Group is concentrating not only on developing the divisions but also on systematically expanding life insurance and old-age provision.

new liability insurance entity covering the German iron and steel industry. The commission also negotiated conditions with the German government agency for the insurance industry, the Reichsaufsichtsamt, and solicited letters of intent from its members to join the new organization. Designed to be independent from the Berufsgenossenschaft, the new association benefited from the organizational know-how gathered by its creator. The Haftpflichtverband's founding members especially emphasized being independence from private insurers. However, the Reichsaufsichtsamt requested that the Haftpflichtverband get reinsurance coverage. Since German insurers did not have an interest in backing up a new competitor, the Haftpflichtverband had to look abroad for a reinsurance partner and finally found one in Austrian insurer Erste Österreichische Allgemeine. After the new organization had been formally established at the founding meeting in late 1903, the Haftpflichtverband, consisting of 176 corporate members from six Berufsgenossenschaften of the iron and steel industry, started operations in April 1904.

Growth and Turmoil in the Early Years

In the 15 years following its foundation, the Haftpflichtverband's membership soared. At the end of its first year in business, the number of its members had climbed to 464. By 1920, the Haftpflichtverband counted 4,204 member firms. This expansion was only possible because the initially narrow definition of potential member candidates was broadened. One of the fundamental ideas at the time of the Haftpflichtverband's foundation was to limit membership to companies with very similar insurance needs in order to make risks comparable and more calculable, thereby keeping cost for liability coverage low. However, after the last of the eight German Berufsgenossenschaften in the iron and steel industry had joined the Haftpflichtverband in 1909, its bylaws were changed to allow member companies of the Berufsgenossenschaften in related industries to become part of the organization. The first new members admitted into the Haftpflichtverband were from the mining industry, who joined beginning in 1919, followed by the precision mechanics and electric appliances industries in 1920, the chemical industry in 1928, the southern German precious and non-precious metal processing industries in 1935, and the pottery, tobacco, leather, paper, and brewing industries in 1936. In addition to expanding its membership base, the Haftpflichtverband broadened its range of services. In 1928, its members were offered auto insurance; in 1932, accident insur-

ance was added. To reflect the broadened focus of the association in its name, the Haftpflichtverband's name was changed to Haftpflichtverband der Deutschen Industrie (HDI)—the liability association of German industry—in 1936.

While the Haftpflichtverband achieved remarkable growth in the first three decades of the 20th century, it was far from steady, being frequently interrupted by the major economic downturns resulting from Germany's political ambitions. The attempt of Germany to become a colonial power resulted in World War I. Consequently, Germany's heavy industry became engaged in building ships, tanks, and other goods for the military. Because of its solely domestic membership base, the Haftpflichtverband was not impacted directly by the beginning of World War I in 1914, and the association did not loose any of its customers, as many of Germany's export-oriented companies did. However, many of its member companies were crucial for Germany's war economy. With pressure to produce more war goods in less time using old machines and less qualified personnel, the risk of work-related accidents rose significantly—and so did the liability risk. The main threat, however, emerged slowly during the war years and accelerated after Germany's defeat in 1919, resulting in the most serious economic depression the country had known.

To finance the war and to pay off the enormous reparations demanded by the Allied countries, the German government freely used the easiest money machine at hand—the printing press. Thereafter, the value of German currency's rapidly declined, plummeting after World War I to half of its prewar value. To aggravate this state of affairs, the German government, by forcing domestic enterprises to buy war bonds that became worthless once the conflict had ended with Germany's defeat, made it impossible for companies to prevent the depreciation of their financial assets by investing abroad. This policy, together with accelerating inflation, posed a special threat to the insurance industry. Spiking inflation made risk calculation and the evaluation of occurred damages increasingly difficult and ultimately led to greater costs; concurrently, the value of premiums paid was diminished, thus draining financial reserves. In case of the Haftpflichtverband, its reserves almost entirely "evaporated" during the hyperinflation of 1923. On the other hand, the organization's policy of basing its premium charges on a member's payroll cost—which was also rising during the inflation years—averted total ruin. In 1923, the Haftpflichtverband abandoned its Austrian reinsurer, which had frequently tried to lure its members away with its own liability policies, and entered a partnership with the German industrial insurer Gerling Konzern. Together they founded the Eisen-und Stahl Versicherungsaktiengesellschaft, in which executive directors and board members of the Haftpflichtverband owned 75 percent of the shares.

A short period of economic stability in the 1920s was suddenly interrupted by the onset of the Great Depression in 1929, resulting in one-third of Germany's workers losing their jobs. Growing mass poverty provided the increasingly polarized and radical political climate that brought Adolf Hitler's National Socialist Party into power in 1933. By 1936, the country was preparing for another war. While the Nazis centralized economic politics initially provided some relief in the job market, it also contributed to setting the stage for World War II, which

Key Dates:

1903: Haftpflichtverband der Deutschen Eisen-und Stahlindustrie V.a.G. is founded.

1919: The company moves its headquarters from Saarbrücken to Hannover.

1936: The company is renamed Haftpflichtverband der Deutschen Industrie (HDI).

1953: HDI opens membership to individuals.

1970: HDI merges with Feuerschadenverband rheinisch-westfälischer Zechen.

1987: Security consulting subsidiary HAST Hannover Sicherheitstechnik GmbH is founded.

1991: Life insurance subsidiary HDI Leben AG is established.

1994: Initial public offering of Hannover Re's stock is made.

1996: HDI acquires Transatlantische Lebensversicherung AG and Citibank's German insurance operations.

1996: Holding company HDI Beteiligung AG is established.

1998: The company enters two joint ventures with Deutsche Postbank AG.

2001: HDI's private insurance business is transferred to HDI Privat Versicherungs AG.

was even more devastating for the country's economy. Centrally administered insurance premiums, artificial restrictions in the insurance market, and the replacement of elected delegates to the Haftpflichtverband's governing bodies by Nazi-friendly managers characterized the years of the Nazi rule, which ended with Germany's unconditional defeat in May 1945.

Becoming a Full-Service Insurer in the 1950s

After the country had been rebuilt, the German economy not only recovered but subsequently entered two decades of strong growth. Industrial output more than doubled between 1950 and 1960. During this time, HDI again expanded its membership base, began offering a broader range of insurance coverage, and revamped its organization, setting off on the path to becoming an all-round insurer.

Prosperity for All, a book written in the 1950s by the country's new economic minister Ludwig Erhard, became the vision of the postwar generation. For HDI, the year 1953 became a historical stepping stone as the company took a strategic step forward. In that year, HDI, which formerly had limited its clientele to corporate members of the Berufsgenossenschaften, changed its bylaws to offer insurance coverage to individuals. Also in 1953, HDI's organizational structure changed. The split of Germany into two states after World War II had left the association with a geographically unbalanced network of branch offices—some of which had been dissolved—with four of them located in Hannover. The 14 different divisions covering certain industries were replaced by nine regional branch offices. The new bylaws also cut back the number of directors. However, HDI stuck with its concept of being an insurer without a sales organization. This strategy enabled the company to

keep administrative costs extremely low—at about 12 percent of premium income—making it possible to attract new customers by offering affordable premiums.

HDI's fastest growing business segment in the 1950s and 1960s was auto insurance. Between 1958 and 1967, premium income from auto insurance rose an average of 20 percent per year. However, cost for damage payments also increased significantly, sometimes even faster than premium income. Since auto insurance accounted for at least two-thirds of HDI's total business, the company took steps to expand its product range in order to better balance risks. Beginning in 1959, HDI offered fire, theft, and water damage insurance, followed by broken glass and storm insurance in 1962.

In the area of fire insurance, HDI had been cooperating with the Feuerschadenverband Rheinisch-Westfälischer Zechen, another cooperative insurer specializing in fire insurance. HDI had helped launch the Feuerschadenverband in 1920, and part of its membership overlapped with HDI's. When HDI itself started offering fire insurance, the relationship between the two grew somewhat tense. However, in 1968 HDI and Feuerschadenverband started negotiations which resulted in the merger of the two, effective January 1, 1970. Since the proposed name for the new entity, Versicherungsverband der Deutschen Industrie V.a.G., was not approved by the German authorities, it was called Haftpflicht- und Feuerschadenverband der Deutschen Industrie V.a.G. Six years later the company's name was changed back to Haftpflichtverband der Deutschen Industrie V.a.G.

The merger had brought HDI closer to the leading group of German insurers. In the 1970s and early 1980s, the company intensified its cooperation with Hannoversche Leben, a Hannover-based life insurer with the same legal form as HDI's. The reinsurer of the Feuerschadenverband, Aktiengesellschaft für Transport- und Rückversicherung, was renamed Hannover Rückversicherung (Hannover Re) in 1976. One year later, HDI, together with Hannoversche Leben, established Hannover Rechtsschutz-Versicherungs-AG, a new subsidiary offering legal insurance, which was taken over by HDI in 1981. In 1980, Hannover Allgemeine Versicherungs-AG, a subsidiary of Hannover Re, started operations.

While HDI's domestic organization was growing, the business climate in Germany turned around completely after the oil price shock of October 1973, when oil prices skyrocketed after Arabian oil-producing countries greatly reduced their output. It took a decade for the German economy to recover, putting the market for industrial insurance, especially fire insurance, under high pressure. With environmental protection and conservation of natural resources becoming a new paradigm, the risks of technological progress were looked upon more critically. The insurance industry was also faced with calculating previously unknown risks, such as those associated with nuclear power stations. These new risks had to be calculated and translated into new insurance policies. Another new wrinkle in the area of liability insurance was the manufacturer's liability for the quality and performance of its products, which was introduced in 1976. In the 1980s, disaster prevention became more and more important. HDI also established several consulting subsidiaries that advised clients in security issues regarding fire safety, auto fleet safety, and the prevention of environmental pollution.

Altogether, the number of HDI subsidiaries rose from four at the end of the 1970s to 22 by 1989.

Expansion and Refocusing: The 1990s and Beyond

The 1980s and 1990s were characterized by the rapid globalization and consolidation of the world's financial markets. In summer 1990, the European Union liberalized the insurance market for industrial risks, allowing insurers to offer their products and services in any of its member countries. Four years later, the rest of the insurance market followed suit. HDI followed its industrial clients abroad, setting up foreign subsidiaries in Austria, the Netherlands, Belgium, France, the United Kingdom, Brazil, Argentina, and the United States between 1978 and 1987. By 1992, the number of HDI's foreign subsidiaries reached 19, bringing in almost one-third of the company's premium income from outside of Germany. In 1994, HDI entered a strategic partnership with Britain's third largest insurer, Royal Insurance (Global) Ltd. This partnership opened Royal's network of branch offices in over 80 countries to HDI, making it possible for the company to insure its industrial clients anywhere in the world.

While the reunification of East and West Germany in October 1990 brought about a new boost for business, it also led to a dramatic increase in claims, mainly in auto insurance, which still accounted for a considerable part of HDI's revenues. After the company slipped into the red in 1990, HDI's management decided to venture into life insurance, a less risky insurance segment. However, a newcomer in this market, HDI had a sluggish start. To lower cost, the company started reorganizing its operations in 1993, cutting back on staff and reducing the number of main branch offices from 19 to 11. One year later, Hannover Re went public on the German Stock Exchange, and a holding company was set up for HDI's foreign subsidiaries. A cautious approach to taking on new risks and raising auto insurance premiums, together with the cash from Hannover Re's initial public offering led the company's insurance operations back to profitability in 1994.

Beginning in the mid-1990s, HDI expanded significantly, focusing on new business in direct life insurance and on international growth. In 1996, the company acquired Citibank's German insurance subsidiaries, including a direct life and an accident insurer. These were organized into a new subsidiary, CiV Versicherung AG, and continued selling their policies at Citibank branch offices. In the same year, HDI took over life insurer Transatlantische Lebensversicherung AG from British Lloyds Abbey Life, which was renamed Aspecta Lebensversicherung AG. Other acquisitions included Italian insurer BNC Assicurazioni S.p.A., Brazilian Hannover Paulista Seguros S.A., and Swedish insurer Skandia in 1997, followed by special insurer Claredon Insurance Group in the United States in 1998. In that year, HDI also signed an agreement with one of Germany's leading banks for private customers, the banking division of Germany's privatized post office Deutsche Postbank AG, to partner up and sell life and accident insurance at Postbank's large network of branches at German post offices. The two joint ventures, PB Lebensversicherung and PB Versicherung AG, started operations in 1999. Also in that year, the planned merger of HDI with HUK-Coburg, Germany's second

largest auto insurer with the same legal form as HDI, was vetoed by HUK's member representatives.

As a result of its expansion, HDI doubled its premium income between 1993 and 1999. However, a large number of claims and the high investment in the company's new ventures resulted in a loss in 2000 and 2001. Although HDI held on to the legal form of a mutual insurance association, the company made significant changes at lower levels of its organization. In 1996, a new holding company, HDI Beteiligung AG, was founded as a management holding for most of HDI's operations. This enabled the company to raise funds in the world's capital markets to finance its rapid expansion. In 2000, HDI announced that it was planning to take the sub-holding, which in the meantime had been renamed Talanx AG, public by 2004 or 2005. In 2001, the company spun off its insurance business for private customers, which was transferred to newly formed HDI Privat Versicherung AG, a Talanx subsidiary. HDI, the mutual insurer, refocused on its core business with industrial clients. In mid-2002, HDI's management saw possibilities for further growth in corporate pension plans, international life insurance, financial services, and possibly a takeover of Gerling Globale Rück, the reinsurance arm of one of HDI's main competitors which was put up for sale in summer 2002. To strengthen the company's financial basis, HDI was also planning to offer another 20 percent of Hannover Re's stock for sale under favorable stock market conditions.

Principal Subsidiaries

Talanx AG; ASPECTA Global Group AG; HDI International Holding N.V. (Netherlands); HDI Pension Strategy & Management GmbH; HDI Rechtsschutz Versicherung AG; HDI Privat Versicherung AG; HDI Pensionsfonds AG; HDI Pensionskasse AG; HANNOVER International AG für Industrieversicherungen (Austria; 99.76%); HANNOVER International (Belgie) N.V. (Belgium); HANNOVER International Insurance (Nederland) N.V. (Netherlands); HANNOVER International (France) S.A. (99.99%); HANNOVER International España Cía de Seguros y Reaseguros S.A. (Spain); International Insurance Company of Hannover Ltd. (United States; 75%); HANNOVER International Seguros S.A. (Brazil); HDI Assicurazioni S.p.A. (Italy; 66.08%); CiV Versicherung AG; PB Versicherung AG (50%); ASPECTA Versicherung AG; Hannover Finance, Inc. (United States; 70.32%); Insurance Corporation of Hannover (United States; 75%); Clarendon Insurance Group, Inc. (United States); Magyar Posta Biztositá Rt. (Hungary); Hannover COOP Bulgaria Insurance Company A.D. (Bulgaria; 95.01%); Hannover Rückversicherungs-AG (75%); Euro International Reinsurance S.A. (Luxembourg); E+S Rückversicherungs-AG (51.57%); Hannover Life Reassurance Company of America (United States; 75%); Hannover Life Reassurance (UK) Ltd. (75%); Hannover Life Re of Australasia Ltd. (Australia; 63.29%); Caisse Générale de Réassurance S.A. (Luxembourg); E+S Reinsurance (Ireland) Ltd. (51.57%); HDI Reinsurance (Ireland) Ltd.; Hannover Life Reassurance (Ireland) Ltd. (75%); Hannover Reinsurance (Ireland) Ltd. (75%); Hannover Reinsurance Group Africa (Pty.) Ltd. (South Africa; 72.64%); Hannover Re (Bermuda) Ltd. (75%); Hannover Re Sweden Insurance Company Ltd. (75%); CiV Lebensversicherung AG; ASPECTA Lebensversicherung

AG (Germany); HDI Lebensversicherung AG; PB Lebensversicherung AG (50%); HANNOVER International Seguros S.A. (Brazil); HDI Assicurazioni S.p.A. (Italy); ASPECTA Assurance International Luxembourg S.A.; ASPECTA Assurance International AG Liechtenstein; ASPECTA Japan KK; Magyar Posta Életbiztositá Rt. (Hungary); HDI Asset Management GmbH; Ampega Investment AG (90%); Ampega Immobilien Management GmbH.

Principal Competitors

Munich Re; Allianz AG; Gerling-Konzern Versicherungs-Beteiligungs-AG; AMB Generali Holding AG; AXA Konzern AG; ERGO Versicherungsgruppe AG; GeneralCologne Re.

Further Reading

"Citibank verkauft Versicherungsgeschäft and den HDI," *Frankfurter Allgemeine Zeitung*, December 21, 1995, p. 19.

Der HDI und seine Mitglieder. Eine Unternehmensgeschichte, Hannover, Germany: HDI Haftpflichtverband der Deutschen Industrie Versicherung auf Gegenseitigkeit V.a.G., 2001, 75 p.

"HDI will mit Lebensversicherung weiter wachsen," *Süddeutsche Zeitung*, June 25, 1991.

"Postbank und HDI gründen Versicherungen," *Frankfurter Allgemeine Zeitung*, August 13, 1998, p. 16.

"Versicherungsgruppe HDI investiert stark in der Sparte Leben," *Frankfurter Allgemeine Zeitung*, July 26, 2000, p. 20.

"Versicherungsgruppe HDI strebt Partnerschaft mit Postbank an," *Frankfurter Allgemeine Zeitung*, August 27, 1997, p. 16.

"Versicherungsgruppe HDI will Kasko-Versicherung sanieren," *Frankfurter Allgemeine Zeitung*, August 30, 1993, p. 14.

—Evelyn Hauser

The Heat Group

601 Biscayne Boulevard
Miami, Florida 33132-1801
U.S.A.
Telephone: (786) 777-4328
Fax: (786) 777-1615
Web site: http://www.nba.com/heat

Private Company
Incorporated: 1987
Employees: 80
Sales: $99 million (2001)
NAIC: 711310 Promoters of Performing Arts, Sports, and
Similar Events with Facilities

Originally formed to bring a National Basketball Association franchise to Miami, Florida, The Heat Group has evolved into a multifaceted sports and entertainment company and is owned by Carnival cruise ship mogul Micky Arison. The cornerstone of the Heat Group remains its NBA team, the Miami Heat, but after building 20,000-seat American Airlines Arena for the franchise, the parent corporation has focused on taking full advantage of its state-of-the-art facility by booking the arena as much as possible. In addition to the Miami Heat, The Heat Group owns the Miami Sol, a Women's National Basketball Association (WNBA) team, which plays during the NBA's off season. The company also has a stake in a New York business that produces stage shows and is involved in real estate ventures.

Florida Cities Vie for NBA Franchise in the Mid-1980s

At the start of the 1980s, the National Basketball Association was a troubled enterprise. A majority of its clubs were losing money, and a few were in actual danger of folding. With the emergence of star players Larry Bird and Magic Johnson, interest in the game began to pick up, and the institution of a salary cap in 1983 greatly improved the financial picture for owners. However, it was the 1984 hiring of David Stern as NBA commissioner that was the key to launching the league on an extended period of strong growth. He marketed the NBA's stars

to great effect, boosting the gate as well as broadcast revenues. He was also fortunate, of course, that in the same year he was hired, just as the careers of Bird and Johnson were peaking, the most marketable athlete in the world was taking the stage: Michael Jordan. Instead of shrinking the league, the NBA in the mid-1980s began to consider expansion, and a number of cities lobbied the league for a franchise. In Florida, three cities had groups vying for teams: St. Petersburg, Orlando, and Miami.

The Miami Sports and Exhibition Authority, formed to bring professional sports to Miami, originally supported the NBA application of car dealer Alan Potakmin and real-estate investor Seth Werner, but eventually decided to back the efforts of a new group that featured long-time friends, former NBA star and coach Billy Cunningham and ex-NBA player agent Lewis Schaffel. They recruited two other partners, theatrical producer Zev Bufman and Carnival Cruise Lines founder Ted Arison, who had turned over control of Carnival to his son Mickey and was looking to diversify his holdings. Cunningham and Bufman then assumed the lead roles in the group's efforts to land an NBA team in Miami, which they originally intended to call the Florida Heat. Not only did the investors have to pay a $100,000 non-returnable deposit to the NBA, it was imperative that the city of Miami demonstrate that it had a new arena under construction. As a result, the Heat Group announced that unless construction on a proposed 16,000-seat facility had begun by August 1986, which would allow a new team to begin play for the 1987–88 season, it would withdraw its bid. When construction was delayed by several months, the group continued on, believing that Miami would still be successful in winning an NBA team. It was widely believed that the league would expand to just one of the three contending Florida cities, and those in Miami who were concerned with this matter had little doubt that their community would be the clear-cut winner.

The NBA expansion committee announced their recommendations to club owners on April 2, 1987, calling for new teams in Charlotte and Minnesota. While applications from Anaheim, St. Petersburg, and Toronto were turned down, the committee also decided that a third franchise should be awarded but had been unable to choose between the Florida Heat group and the Orlando Magic group, opting to table the decision until the league's annual meeting to be held in six months time. According to press accounts, the selection committee was concerned about the Heat's new arena, located in an area of Miami known as a hangout for drug dealers and prostitutes. By failing to choose between Orlando or Miami, however, the expansion committee unwittingly reignited a longstanding feud between the two cities. With the opening of Disney World in 1971, Orlando began to compete with Miami for tourist dollars, and now Orlando's college football Citrus Bowl game was scheduled to be played New Year's Day, in direct competition with Miami's more established Orange Bowl. Local media personalities began making stinging comments about each other's city, and the situation threatened to become a public relations nightmare for the NBA. Clearly the league could not wait until its October meeting to settle the matter, and by failing to choose between the Florida cities the NBA had merely insured that the community that lost was going to be extremely angry and bitter. Only days after the expansion committee made its recommendations, the media-savvy league defused the situation by awarding franchises to both Orlando and Miami. The two cities could now take their rivalry to the basketball court, much to the financial benefit of both franchises and the NBA.

Even as the Heat Group geared up for NBA play, its entry into the league remained contingent upon selling 10,000 season tickets by a December 1, 1987 deadline. Although some 14,000 fans had placed $95 deposits on season tickets, by early November the team had received only 7,500 completed applications and half-payments on tickets. A last minute purchase of 200 tickets by the Latin Builders Association put the Heat over the 10,000 threshold and put to rest any fears that the NBA would rescind the franchise. In addition to setting up a sales staff to handle season tickets, the Heat Group was also busy assembling a front office to hire coaches and evaluate college players and current NBA players who might become available in the expansion draft. Moreover, there were team colors, a logo, and uniforms to select, as well as radio and cable television contracts to negotiate.

The city of Miami had been interested in building a first-class arena since the 1950s, and finally, in order to accommodate the new NBA team, the dream came true when in July 1988 the $52 million facility opened. It was able to seat 15,500 for NBA games and featured 16 skyboxes. At the time, Miami Arena was the largest facility of its kind in Southeast and considered to be one of the finest in all of the country, but within a few years it became obvious that the Miami Arena was the last of a generation of arenas that would now be superceded by a wave of new buildings offering far better accommodations,

including the luxury suites and premium seating sections that became all-important to the financial health of contemporary basketball and hockey franchises. The 16 skyboxes at Miami Arena, once lauded, were now regarded as too few and hardly luxurious, their view from the rafters being one of the worst in the building. Moreover, the building's concessions were substandard and the Heat received none of the parking revenues. As early as 1991, the press reported rumors that the Heat was interested in building its own arena, mostly likely in Broward county. The fact that Bufman and businessman Wayne Huizenga had recently formed a partnership to develop arenas only added to the intrigue. Throughout most of the 1990s, the Heat was the constant subject of speculation, as the team bickered with the Miami Sports and Exhibition Authority over the Miami Arena. Relocating the franchise to Broward or some other community was very much a real possibility.

Pat Riley Hired in 1995

The basketball team, in the meantime, proved more successful off the court than on. Despite winning only 15 games in its first NBA season and just 18 games the next, the Heat played before consistent sellout crowds. The team made the playoffs in 1991–92, despite having a losing record, but were quickly dispatched in three games by Michael Jordon and the Chicago Bulls. The Heat fared better in the playoffs two years later but still lost in the opening round. The following season saw the team regress and miss the playoffs, but it marked the beginning of a number of positive changes in the franchise. In February 1995, the Arison family bought out Cunningham and Schaffel, giving Ted Arison's wife, Marilyn, 88 percent of the club. Son Micky was subsequently named managing general partner. Coach Kevin Loughery was offered a front office job and eased out of the organization. In September 1995, the Heat hired Pat Riley, the well regarded former coach of the Los Angeles Lakers and New York Knicks to serve as coach and team president. Riley quickly restructured the Heat's roster and within two years built a contending team that in 1996–97 surprised most experts by winning the Atlantic Division.

With Micky Arison now at the head, the Heat Group intensified its efforts to secure a new arena while at the same time hinting that it might simply sell the franchise. Both the Heat and the Florida Panthers National Hockey League team signed a letter of intent to negotiate with Broward County, which is just north of Miami, on a proposed arena they would share, but the matter was complicated by the looming sale of the Panthers. When a deadline imposed by owner Wayne Huizenga expired with no further movement, the Heat Group decided in April 1996 to abandon the effort to move to Broward and instead began to negotiate in earnest with Dade County, in which Miami is located. In June, a deal was reached with the county to build a $165 million, 20,000-seat arena as part of a retail and office complex expected to revitalize the downtown area near the Port of Miami. The $165 million was to come from tax exempt revenue bonds issued by Dade and backed by hotel taxes and a sales tax rebate. The plan was contingent, however, on the acceptance of two ballot initiatives put before the voters in the fall elections. One approved the use of a site on Biscayne Bay and the second approved the use of public funds to finance the arena. There was strong political opposition to the proposal, and a political action group, the Stop the New Arena Committee, maintained that the use of tax dollars and public land for the arena violated the county's charter and state law. The Heat went to court to block the group's attempt to place its own initiative on the ballot, but according to polling data the arena-funding question was sure to be defeated. At the eleventh hour, a compromise was reached between Arison and Dade County Mayor Alex Penelas, who had long opposed the public debt aspect of the proposal. Instead, the Heat now agreed to privately place the $165 million in bonds as well as pay the debt service. The privately placed bonds would be insured by MIBA Insurance Corp., backed by arena revenues and using the team as collateral. For its part, the county agreed to pay as much as $6.5 million a year to help operate the facility, offset by a $2 parking surcharge. The county also shared in annual net profits, but in effect the Heat Group would be the owners, moving the company beyond basketball and into the arena business.

New Arena Opens on Eve of 2000

With naming rights sold to American Airlines, the Heat's new arena opened on December 31, 1999, not with a basketball game but with music, the Millennium Concert Spectacular of Gloria Estfan, a Miami favorite. After playing the first 13 games of the 1999–2000 NBA season in Miami Arena, the Heat played its first game in its new home on January 2, 2000. The facility seated 19,600 for basketball and could be set up in five different configurations for other events, with seating that ranged from 5,000 to 20,000 patrons. Some 140, 12-seat luxury suites were also available, featuring private balconies overlooking the water. ''Starbox'' holders enjoyed courtside lounges with private dining beneath the court. A number of six-seat loge boxes also offered exceptional views of the game from perches overlooking the court. The impact on the balance sheet for the Heat was immediate and dramatic. The year before moving into the new arena, the team lost close to $15 million, albeit due in large part to a shortened season caused by the NBA locking out players during the negotiation of a new collective bargaining agreement. Basketball games in American Airlines Arena produced 40 to 50 percent more revenues as a result of the increase in premium seating options, greater sponsorship opportunities, vastly improved concessions, parking fees, and other ancillary income. Aside from the arena itself, the Heat Group hoped to take advantage of the nearby marina in order to host boat shows, regattas, and other events. It also formed a real estate venture called Calor to help in developing the area surrounding the arena into a thriving retail and entertainment locale.

American Airlines Arena, like similar venues around the country, booked major concerts, the circus, and ice shows, but unlike many it lacked a hockey co-tenant to help keep the building in constant use. The Panthers ultimately found a home in Broward County, moving into their own state-of-the art arena. To help fill the schedule during the summer months, The Heat Group pursued a team in the WNBA, the women's professional basketball league formed by the NBA in 1996, with the individual teams operated by NBA franchises. In 1999, the Heat Group was awarded a WNBA franchise to begin play in the summer of 2000. Rather than involving the fans in coining a name for the new team, the Heat Group and WNBA decided to call the team the Miami Sol, the Spanish word for sun and an allusion to the sun and fun reputation of South Florida.

With Heat and Sol games accounting for 125 days a year and concerts another 50 to 60, the American Airlines Arena still had many available dates in the year. To help fill this gap, the Heat Group in 2002 bought a minority interest in a New York company, Creative Battery, which produced stage shows. Although Creative Battery was focused on launching Broadway shows that could then be taken on the road and possibly translated to film or television, the Heat Group's primary objective was to bring in shows to the arena and lessen its reliance on rentals, thereby cutting down on the high cost of license fees. The move would also likely help American Airlines Arena when a new performing arts center opened close by in 2004. Although the Heat basketball team remained its signature enterprise, the Heat Group was now a company with ever-widening aspirations for the future.

Principal Subsidiaries

Basketball Properties Ltd; Calor.

Principal Competitors

The Miami Arena; Office Depot Center.

Further Reading

Buckley, Cara, ''Miami Arena Operator Teams Up with New York Theater Outfit,'' *Miami Herald*, April 17, 2002, p. 1.

Chastain, Bill, ''The Heat Is On,'' *Sport*, February 1993, p. 76.

''Cross: Arena Just the Beginning of Complex,'' *Amusement Business*, January 17, 2000, p. 23.

Lowenstein, Roger, ''Once Ailing NBA Grows Selective As Expansion Plans Draw Investors,'' *Wall Street Journal*, January 15, 1996.

Mullins, Betsy, ''Is the Heat Hot to Trot?,'' *South Florida Business Journal*, October 28, 1991, p. 1.

Waddell, Ray, ''Miamian's OK New Arena at Heat's Expense,'' *Amusement Business*, November 18, 1996, p. 1.

—Ed Dinger

Hilti AG

Feldkircherstrasse 100
Postfach 333
FL-9494 Schaan
Liechtenstein
Telephone: + 423 234 2111
Fax + 423 234 2965
Web site: http://www.hilti.com

Public Company
Incorporated: 1941 as Maschinenbau Hilti OHG
Employees: 14,390
Sales: SFr 2.99 billion ($2.02 billion)(2002)
Stock Exchanges: Swiss
Ticker Symbol: HILTI
NAIC: 332722 Bolt, Nut, Screw, Rivet, and Washer
   Manufacturing; 325211 Plastics Material and Resin
   Manufacturing; 332510 Hardware Manufacturing

Hilti AG is the largest industrial corporation in tiny Liechtenstein and one of the world's leading manufacturers of power tools for the professional construction and building maintenance markets. Hilti's trademark red-and-white cases enclose a full range of power tools including direct fastening systems, anchors and screw technologies, positioning systems, drilling and demolition equipment and technology, diamond coring systems, installation systems, and fire-stop and foam systems. The company has also been developing a laser measuring unit since the early 2000s, including a joint-venture with Germany's Jenoptik, concluded in January 2003. In addition to manufacturing, Hilti also runs a strong service operation, providing consulting and technical assistance on major construction projects worldwide. Hilti has long been an internationally operating company, with production plants in Austria, Germany, the United States, Mexico, Hungary, China and in its home base of Schaan, Switzerland. Hilti also operates its own sales and marketing network, extending its reach into more than 120 country markets. Europe is the group's largest market, accounting for 63 percent of the group's sales of nearly SFr 3 billion in 2002. (Like most Liechtenstein companies, Hilti uses the Swiss currency.) North America is also an important market for the company, at 25 percent of sales, while the Asia/Pacific region accounts for 10 percent of sales. While Hilti is a public company, all voting rights are held by the family-controlled Martin Hilti Foundation, and only participatory shares are listed on the Swiss stock exchange. In February 2003, Hilti announced plans to buy back all participatory shares in order to take the company private. The company is led by chairman and son of company founder Michael Hilti and CEO Pius Baschera.

Garage Origins During World War II

Martin Hilti and older brother Eugene set up a mechanical workshop in their garage in the town of Schaan, in Liechtenstein, in 1941. Then just 26, Martin Hilti's background included studies in mechanical engineering and automotive design at the Wismar Engineering College in Germany and the brothers began producing equipment and components on contract for the German automotive industry. If tiny Liechtenstein adopted a neutral status during World War II, Martin Hilti did not. In fact, he edited a Nazi-sympathizing newspaper during the war and was later suspected of having helped Nazi leaders launder assets. (At the end of his life, Hilti admitted to having served what he called an ''inhuman regime.'')

Hilti's support for the Nazi government helped the company win contracts in Germany, and the company, Maschinenbau Hilti OHG, quickly grew to more than 100 employees. While at first the company manufactured products based on other designs, the Hiltis became interested in developing their own product designs. With the collapse of the Nazi government, the Hiltis were forced to find new markets. The company turned to Switzerland, and began contract manufacturing of equipment for that country's textile industry.

The Hilti business grew strongly over the next decade, leading the company to begin extending its sales into other countries. The importance of the Italian textile market made that country a natural choice for the company's first new international market, and in 1952, Hilti opened a representative office there. The following year, Hilti turned to Belgium, turning to a third party, Pastiels SA, to handle its sales and distribution. Meanwhile, Hilti continued to search for a new line of products that the company would be able to develop itself.

At the end of the 1940s, Martin Hilti discovered power tools—or more specifically, a new type of tool for fastening nails using a piston device to drive the nails in a variety of surfaces, including concrete and steel. Hilti was so enthusiastic about the machine's potential that he bought up the original design and patent rights. Hilti then set to work refining the device, and, especially, developing a safer design. In 1952, Hilti released its first hand-tool for driving threaded studs. That design was followed in 1953 with the group's first high-velocity fastener, at first sold under the Perfix brand name. By 1954, the company had adopted its own name as the brand name for its growing tool line. In 1956, the company improved on the design, adding a trigger-firing mechanism.

Hilti focused more and more of its attention on developing its fastener tool range, and especially its piston-driven fastener device. By the mid-1950s, the company had settled on gunpowder as a means of delivering thrust to the fastener piston and by 1957, Hilti had perfected his design. In that year, the company launched the DX 100 power-actuated fastening tool. That product was to put Hilti on the map among the world's professional hand tool manufacturers.

The success of the DX 100 led Hilti to expand its international presence, extending its sales network into Sweden, Ireland, England, South Africa, the United States, and Peru before the end of the decade. In 1960 the company converted to a limited liability company, changing its name to Hilti Corporation. In that year, the company founded two new international subsidiaries, Hilt France SA and Hilti Australia Pty. Ltd., as its sales continued to enjoy international growth.

The success of the DX 100 encouraged the company to exit its textile equipment production and to focus entirely on the professional power tool market. In the 1960s, Hilti began adding new product lines, such as a range of drilling and anchoring tools and systems in 1964. While a number of its products remained based on third-party designs, Hilti introduced its first in-house designed rotary hammer drill in 1967. Much of the company's later success came as a result of its growing commitment to research and development, which took on steam with the building of a technical center in 1964. Meanwhile the company's expanding product line led it to construct a new factory in Liechtenstein, which took over it powder-actuated tool production.

As Hilti moved to take control of its own product designs, it also took more and more control of its distribution network, acquiring a number of formerly independent distributors. The company also set up a number of new foreign subsidiaries including in Canada in 1961, Greece and Japan in 1963, and Mexico in 1964. The following year, the company set up sales agencies in Chile, Ecuador and Spain, and established the Hilti Charter, created a unified international marketing and sales program.

Global Power Tool Powerhouse in the 1980s

Eugene Hilti had died in 1964 and Martin Hilti had assumed full control of the company. Over the next decade, Hilti built the company into one of the world's professional power tool leaders. In 1970, the company added its first international production site, in Austria, which was followed by two more foreign plants, in Germany and in the United States, in 1971. By then, too, Hilti had begun taking control of its US sales representative, a move completed in 1972. Hilti had meanwhile been redeveloping its corporate structure, adopting a board of directors in 1969 and establishing three corporate areas, finance, engineering and marketing, in 1973. In that year, the company established a second research and development facility, in Germany.

Hilti added two more production plants at the end of the 1970s, a plastics manufacturing operation in Germany, acquired in 1975, and a factory for anchor production in England, acquired in 1978. The following year, the company transferred its US production operations to Tulsa, Oklahoma, which also became its headquarters for its North and South American operations. Hilti's growth proved especially strong in the United States, and North America quickly became the company's single most important country market.

In 1980, the Hilti family created the Hilti Family Trust (later renamed the Martin Hilti Family Trust), which held all of the company's family-held shares in the company, a move designed to keep the company under the Hilti family's control. This move was a build-up to the company's public offering in 1986, with a listing on the Swiss stock exchange through the issuing of non-voting participation certificates. The company also issued a limited number of registered shares. By then, the company had added a new product range, that of diamond coring tools. In 1985, Hilti reorganized its production into three divisions: drilling and demolition; powder-actuated fastening; and anchor technology. In 1986, Hilti added another new product line, that of construction chemicals.

Through the 1980s, Hilti entered a number of new markets, including China in 1981, while continuing to integrate its international sales and marketing network. In 1986 the company established a subsidiary in Korea to take over its operations in that country. The following year, the company created a new subsidiary in Chile as well. In 1989, Hilti strengthened its presence in Central Europe—the company had been operating in Poland and Czechoslovakia since the late 1960s—with the establishment of a chisel manufacturing plant in Hungary.

Hilti's growth remained strong throughout the 1980s, with sales jumping from SFr 1 billion at the beginning of the decade to more than SFr 2 billion by decade's end. By then, Martin Hilti was approaching retirement, and in 1990 son Michael Hilti was placed at the head of day-to-day operations. Martin Hilti remained on as chairman of the board of directors until 1994, at which time Michael Hilti assumed that role as well. Martin Hilti died in 1997.

3Cs for the New Millennium

In the late 1990s, Hilti shifted its target to the fast-growing Asian markets—site of the many of the world's largest construction projects. In 1994, the company established a new

Key Dates:

1941: Martin and Eugene Hilti set up a machine shop in the garage in Schaan, Lichtenstein.

1948: Hilti acquires patents to piston-driven nail fastener.

1952: Company establishes sales subsidiary in Italy, beginning company's internationalization.

1957: The DX 100 powder-actuated nail fastener debuts.

1960: Company converts to limited liability status and adopts Hilti Corporation name.

1964: Eugene Hilti dies, and Martin Hilti takes full control of company's direction

1970: Company opens first foreign production site, in Austria, followed by plants in Germany and in the United States in 1971.

1980: Hilti family places all shares in company in Hilti Family Trust.

1986: Hilti goes public, placing participatory shares on Swiss stock exchange.

1990: Michael Hilti, son of Martin Hilton, becomes company chairman.

1995: A production facility in China is set up.

2003: Jenoptik and Hilti form the Hillos joint-venture; company announces intention to be delisted from the Swiss exchange and go private.

hostile takeover. The company remained public however, leaving its non-voting participatory shares on the market.

Hilti topped SFr 3 billion in sales at the turn of the century. The company continued to expand its operations with the new decade, and particularly by targeting growth in its laser positioning segment. In 2001, the company acquired Ammann Holding AG, a Swiss company specialized in rotating lasers and laser tools for construction of sewers. The following year, Hilti began a cooperation with Germany's Jenoptik to produce laser-based distance measurement devices. In January 2003, the two companies expanded their partnership, setting up the joint-venture company Hillos GmbH, to expand their collaboration into other laser-based positioning tools and equipment. The next month, citing an uncertain global financial climate, Hilti management announced that it intended to buy back all outstanding Hilti shares traded on the Swiss stock exchange and take the company private. Management stressed that in doing so, Hilti would remain committed to its growth strategy and core industrial businesses.

Principal Divisions

Positioning Systems; Cutting and Sanding; Screw Fastening Systems; Diamond Systems; Drilling and Demolition; Direct Fastening; Anchoring Systems; Installation Systems; Firestop Systems; Foam Systems.

Principal Competitors

Adolf Wurth GmbH und Co. KG; Cooper Industries Ltd.; Danaher Corp.; Nursery Supplies Inc.; Stanley Works; Snap-On Inc.; Industria e Comercio Metalac S.A.; United Southern Industries; Fimalac S.A.; Toro Co.; Fiskars Oy Ab; Grupo Ficosa International; Facom S.A.; Sandvik S.A.

Further Reading

Hall, William, ''Selling Power,'' *Financial Times*, June 23, 1997, p. 3.

——, ''Strong US Sales Help Lift Hilti,'' *Financial Times*, April 20, 2000, p. 24.

''Hilti Doing Everything to Retain Independence,'' *AFX Europe*, September 29, 1999.

''Hilti Tools Measure Up to Tough Demands,'' *Gulf Construction*, May 1, 2002.

''Jenoptik und Hilti bilden Gemeinschaftsunternehmen, *Frankfurter Allgemeine Zeitung*, January 18, 2003, p. 16.

''Liechtenstein Businessman Linked to Nazis,'' *Jewish Bulletin News*, September 8, 2000.

''Stagnation des Hilti-Konzernumsatzes,'' *Neue Zurcher Zeitung*, January 11, 2002

—M.L. Cohen

office in Hong Kong, which took over direction of Hilti's Asian operations, until then conducted from the company's Schaan, Liechtenstein headquarters. The following year, Hilti inaugurated a new production plant in China; the increased production capacity led the company to expand its sales and marketing networks into Thailand, Vietnam, Indonesia, India, and the Philippines between 1995 and 2000.

Hilti added two new product lines in 1998, those of laser positioning equipment and cutting and sanding tools. The company had also become an industry leader in fire-stopping equipment and systems, adding to a long list of company-held patents. By then, the company had rolled out a new corporate strategy, that had been in the works since 1966, launching what it called its Champion 3C Strategy, which stood for customer focus, remaining competitive, and concentrating on its core markets.

The 3C strategy helped Hilti remain a champion, as the company continued to build on its global industry leadership position at the turn of the century. Hilti had also moved to tighten its shareholding—at the end of 1999, the company bought up the 12 percent of registered voting rights not already held by the company, effectively eliminating any attempt at a

Hitachi Zosen Corporation

7-89, Nanko-kita 1-chome
Suminoe-ku, Osaka 559-8559
Japan
Telephone: (06) 6569-0001
Fax: (06) 6569-0002
Web site: http://www.hitachizosen.co.jp

Public Company
Incorporated: 1934 as Hitachi Shipbuilding
Employees: 10,403
Sales: ¥439.1 billion ($3.29 billion) (2002)
Stock Exchanges: Tokyo Osaka Nagoya
Ticker Symbol: 7004
NAIC: 33312 Construction Machinery Manufacturing;
    333298 All Other Industrial Machinery
    Manufacturing; 333999 All Other Miscellaneous
    General Purpose Machinery Manufacturing

Hitachi Zosen Corporation operates as one of Japan's largest heavy industrial machinery firms. The company got its start as a shipbuilder during the 1880s in Japan. A devastating industry slump during the 1970s and 1980s forced Hitachi to diversify—its key business segments are now related to environmental equipment, energy, industrial, and precision machinery, electronics and information systems, steel construction, and marine and disaster prevention systems. In 2002, the company and NKK Corporation merged their shipbuilding businesses together and spun off the venture as Universal Shipbuilding Corp. During that year Hitachi Zosen created a new corporate brand image under the name Hitz. The firm plans to eventually adopt this as a corporate name once recognition is established.

Early History: 1880s–1920s

Hitachi Zosen's predecessor, the Osaka Iron Works, was founded by British entrepreneur Edward H. Hunter on April 1, 1881. Hunter had come to Japan in 1865 and had worked in the Onohama Shipyard in Kobe before moving to Osaka. He built a modern shipyard at the junction of the Aji and Nakatsu rivers where his first vessel, the *Hatsumaru,* was completed in 1882. At the time Japan was in the midst of a 50-year transformation from a semi-feudal to an industrial nation initiated by the restored Meiji emperor to catch up with Western technology. The Osaka Iron Works, producing ships and other heavy equipment, was crucial to Japan's modernization. Hunter said the company should "conceive and construct everything ourselves." This philosophy has guided the Hitachi Zosen Corporation through much of its history.

The Osaka Iron Works' first yard, a six-acre facility with a dock 72 meters long and 11.5 meters wide, could construct wooden and iron ships weighing up to 1,000 tons. The company also produced compound engines and boilers, irrigation pumps, bridges, and other equipment for the rapidly developing Japanese industrial sector there.

In 1900, Osaka Iron Works began operating a second yard, the Sakurajima works, at the mouth of the Aji River to build ships weighing over 1,000 tons. A passenger-cargo ship, the 1,568-gross-ton *Taigi Maru,* was the first ship launched from the new yard and the first ship weighing over 1,000 tons built by the company. In 1908, Osaka Iron Works launched the first tanker built in Japan; its 531-gross-ton *Tora Maru* joined the Standard Oil fleet.

Hunter married a Japanese woman and changed his name to Hanta. In 1915, his son and successor Ryutaro Hanta successfully completed a licensing agreement to use the Isherwood method to build ships. The technique, which originated in Great Britain, significantly reduced both costs and construction time.

As Japan's industrial capacity developed, its shipping needs expanded. The Osaka Iron Works acquired other facilities to meet the demand, including the Innoshima Shipyard in 1911, the Bingo Dockyard in 1919, Harada Shipbuilding Works in 1920, and the Hikojima Dockyard in 1924.

The Osaka Iron Works also produced a number of notable engineering works outside of shipbuilding during the early decades of the 20th century. The company began providing equipment to the hydroelectric industry in 1924, when it received its first order for water gates for a dam. In 1926 the Otabashi

Bridge, which is still in use, was built in Gifu Prefecture using a new cable erection method pioneered by the company.

The War Years

In the 1930s, militant nationalists who encouraged aggression in Asia increasingly influenced the government. Japan secretly began augmenting its navy in violation of treaties it held with Britain and the United States. In 1931, Japan invaded Manchuria, setting up a puppet regime called Manchukuo, and by 1937 Japan was at war with China. In 1941, Japan attacked the United States, precipitating U.S. entry into World War II.

Much of Japan's military success came as a result of its powerful modern navy. A number of old merchant ships built by Osaka Iron Works, known as Hitachi Shipbuilding after 1934, were converted to naval use. While most of the large ships were built by Hitachi's competitors like Mitsubishi, Ishikawajima, Kawasaki, Mitsui, and Harima, the company did produce smaller vessels designed for military use including minesweepers, large landing craft, and *Maru-Yu* series transport submarines. Hitachi also built at least one aircraft transport ship with a flight deck for the army, the *Kumano Maru*. The 465-foot vessel was launched at Innoshima in January 1945.

In 1943, Hitachi opened the Kanagawa works and acquired Mukaishima Shipyard. The company changed its name to Hitachi Zosen Corporation that year. After the war, the U.S. occupation forces reorganized defense-related industries. Despite serious bomb damage at its shipyards during the war, Hitachi began building fishing and coastal transport ships almost immediately.

Postwar Growth

While other industries received government assistance to rebuild in the 1950s, the shipbuilding industry was left on its own. Japanese shipbuilders like Hitachi had to be flexible to survive—management sometimes put high-level engineers to work on the assembly line to fill orders on time. The industry developed extremely efficient methods to compete with European shipyards, and Japanese rock-bottom prices and top quality increased foreign orders. By 1955, Japan was the greatest shipbuilding nation in the world, and Hitachi was one of the busiest shipbuilders in Japan. Political uncertainties in the Middle East after the Suez Canal was closed temporarily in 1956 forced oil producers to seek economical means of bypassing the canal. Japanese shipbuilders were ready to meet the demand for larger oil tankers.

Meanwhile, Hitachi also entered other areas. In 1957, the company built the world's largest diesel engine with B&W Diesel of Denmark. In 1964, the company built its first full-scale turnkey plant, a chemical-fertilizer plant for the Gujarat State Fertilizer Company of India, in a record 33 months.

The Japanese shipbuilding boom continued into the 1960s. New technology allowed the construction of bigger ships. By 1966, Hitachi was capable of building ships weighing 250,000 tons, a feat unthinkable only a few years earlier. Technological developments revolutionized the shipbuilder's methods. By the early 1970s, Hitachi designed huge 250,000-ton tankers entirely by computer. Ships assembled at the company's Sakai Works used automated machinery to piece together various sections.

Hitachi opened several overseas offices during this period— in New York and London in 1956, Hong Kong in 1960, and Düsseldorf in 1961. With many of its orders for new ships and equipment coming from foreign countries, the Japanese shipbuilding industry was caught by surprise by the 16.9 percent revaluation of the yen in 1971. Prices for Japanese ships had gone up substantially in recent months, however, and the industry remained optimistic.

Hitachi Zosen acquired Maizuru Heavy Industries in 1971, and the Maizuru works became Hitachi's principal naval vessel and equipment production site. A year later, Hitachi opened a branch office in Singapore. In 1973, Hitachi began production at its new Ariake works in Kyushu. The Ariake works had two docks, 630 meters and 360 meters, respectively, and was equipped with state-of-the-art shipbuilding machinery. The facility was capable of producing ships weighing up to 600,000 tons.

Problems Arise: 1970s

The oil crunch of 1973 to 1974 soon crimped Hitachi's growth plans. Reduction in oil shipments eliminated demand for new supertankers and put many ships in mothballs. The glut in shipping capacity precipitated a depression in the industry that would last almost 15 years. Although the new Ariake works had enough large ships on order to keep it active through 1977, new supertanker orders dropped off and Hitachi had to realign its production capabilities. The Ariake works accepted orders to build oil rigs, oil storage tanks, and natural gas storage tanks, and in 1974 the Mukaishima works began specializing in steel structures like bridges, water gates, steel stacks, and pipes.

With about 50 percent of its turnover continuing to come from shipbuilding, Hitachi was hit hard by declining orders and canceled orders for supertankers as the 1970s went on. Further trouble came when rising material costs reduced the company's profit margin. Hitachi had continued to enter into fixed-price contracts long after European shipbuilders had gone over to flexible contracts. The company recorded a 25 percent decrease in earnings despite a 28 percent increase in turnover in 1975. In 1979, the company lost almost ¥11 billion. The industry as a whole addressed declining profits by petitioning the Ministry of Transport (MOT) to subsidize scrapping of redundant facilities. The MOT authorized scrapping 35 percent of the industry's capacity. In addition, the 39 largest Japanese shipbuilders formed a cartel to voluntarily limit production. Demand hovered under even this limit, and cartel members accepted orders at about ten percent below cost in 1980, an improvement over quotes 40 percent below cost that shipbuilders made to keep the docks from falling idle in preceding years.

Hitachi continued to slim down its work force in the 1980s and to increase non-shipbuilding activities. In 1982, Hitachi's

Key Dates:

1881: Osaka Iron Works is founded by Edward H. Hunter.
1900: The Sakurajima Works is established to build ships weighing over 1,000 tons.
1943: The company adopts the Hitachi Zosen Corporation name.
1957: Hitachi and B&W Diesel of Denmark build the world's largest diesel engine.
1964: The firm builds a full-scale turnkey plant for India's Gujarat State Fertilizer Company.
1971: Maizuru Heavy Industries is acquired.
1974: An oil crisis forces the company to realign production capabilities.
1986: The firm launches a major restructuring effort.
1991: Diversification efforts begin in four major business areas.
2002: Hitachi and NKK Corp. merge their shipbuilding operations together to form Universal Shipbuilding Corp.

plants and machinery and offshore structures groups accounted for more than half of the company's turnover for the first time. The company also opened a branch office in Beijing that year.

In 1986, Hitachi Zosen purchased the Chicago-based Clearing Inc., a company it had licensing agreements with since 1955, for $64 million. Hitachi Clearing produced automotive stamping presses at its facility in Chicago.

Restructuring Begins: 1986

Hitachi Zosen undertook a major restructuring in 1986, organizing its units along product lines. At the same time, new pressures on Hitachi Zosen came from the lower prices developing nations offered on heavy equipment and ships. Manufacturers in Korea and Taiwan, paying their workers less, could drastically undercut Hitachi Zosen's bids. The appreciation of the yen against the dollar also hindered growth.

The Japanese Ministry of Transport called for another 20 percent reduction in excess industry capacity in addition to the 35 percent cut of 1979, and after reporting a loss of ¥70 billion in 1986, Hitachi Zosen announced plans to eliminate more jobs over the next two years. By 1988, the company employed only 5,596 workers, down from 24,660 ten years earlier. The shipbuilding industry received governmental permission once again to organize a "depression cartel" to set production ceilings and force prices up.

In 1989, the shipbuilding industry finally began to show signs of a real recovery in demand. As a result of increased oil imports to industrialized countries and the gradual aging of the world's oil tankers in general, orders for new ships increased 54 percent industry-wide, and Hitachi Zosen's leaner shipyards were booked solid for two years. The company actually turned some orders away. Even better, analysts expected the demand to remain strong throughout the 1990s.

Historically more marine-dependent than its Japanese competitors, Hitachi Zosen Corporation increased its non-shipbuilding activities in the late 1980s, placing greater emphasis on lines such as steel structures, construction machinery, environmental protection facilities, nuclear power equipment, industrial machinery, prime movers, and plants. Management hoped that this diversity, combined with greater global demand for ships, would provide opportunities for growth in the 1990s.

Opportunities for Growth: 1990s and Beyond

Diversification, in fact, played a huge role in Hitachi's strategy throughout the 1990s. During 1991, the company began to focus on four major business areas: production and transport systems; environmental protection; resources and energy; and infrastructure and information services. As the firm continued to cut its reliance on shipbuilding, profits began an upward climb. That year unconsolidated net profits grew by 98.5 percent over the previous year. In 1992, the company's shipbuilding subsidiary in Singapore went public. It also sold Hitachi Zosen Clearing—the U.S. subsidiary it had purchased in the 1980s—due to faltering sales.

Hitachi's profits continued to show promise, signaling that the firm's strategy was paying off. As a November 1993 *Nikkei Weekly* article claimed, "That Hitachi Zosen managed to stay afloat and prosper during the worst business conditions to hit Japan's shipbuilders since the end of World War II is largely due to the decision to turn the company into an 'all weather' entity by diversifying." Part of this diversification that bode particularly well for Hitachi was its involvement with household and industrial waste disposal. In 1996, the company opened a refuse incinerator in the eastern district of Saitama Prefecture and established Japan's first super refuse-fired power generation facility. The firm also entered the electric power supply business.

Hitachi's financial position began to falter during the late 1990s as management continued to revamp business operations. Unprofitable businesses were sold and the firm launched a series of job cuts. Hitachi's boldest move, however, came in 2002 as it merged its shipbuilding operations with those of NKK Corp. The joint venture, Universal Shipbuilding Corp. operated as Japan's second-largest shipbuilding concern and was spun off in October 2002.

The company also launched a new five-year management plan in April of that year. Entitled Hitz-Advance, the new initiative called for a major restructuring with a new focus on environmental systems, industrial and precision machinery, energy, electronics and information systems, and marine and disaster prevention. Hitz, a new corporate brand launched during 2002, was expected to eventually become the official corporate name of the company once it became more well known in Hitachi's markets.

This five-year plan pointed to the company's ultimate goal—to transform from a heavy-industrial concern to a value-added integrated products and services firm. As Hitachi worked to realign its businesses, global economies remained weak and the company battled intense competition, fluctuating prices, and lackluster demand caused by a fall in capital spending. Nevertheless, management remained hopeful that its efforts would pay off in the years to come. Whether or not Hitachi Zosen would excel along its new path, however, remained to be seen.

Principal Subsidiaries

Hitachi Zosen Singapore Pte. Ltd.; Hitachi Zosen Services Sdn Bhd. (Malaysia); Hitachi Zosen Europe Ltd. (UK); Hitachi Zosen U.S.A. Ltd.; Hitachi Zosen Engineering U.S.A. Ltd.; Dalian Dali Steel Works Co. Ltd. (China); Zhenjiang Zhengmao Hitachi Zosen Machinery Co. Ltd. (China).

Principal Divisions

Environmental Systems; Industrial and Precision Machinery; Energy; Electronics and Information Systems; Marine and Disaster Prevention.

Principal Competitors

Chiyoda Corporation; Kawasaki Heavy Industries Ltd.; Mitsubishi Heavy Industries Ltd.

Further Reading

De Silva, Gary, "Hitachi Zosen to Go Ahead with Long-Awaited Public Share Offer," *Straits Times*, September 19, 1992.

Furukawa, Tsukasa, "NKK, Hitachi Zosen to Become Shipmates in Shipbuilding Tie," *American Metal Market*, February 27, 2001, p. 3.

"Hitachi Zosen Aims to Become 800 Bil. Yen Firm," *Japan Economic Newswire*, December 25, 1990.

"Hitachi Zosen Cuts Costs, Raises Profits," *Nikkei Weekly*, May 3, 1993, p. 12.

"Hitachi Zosen to Move Away from Shipbuilding," *Japan Economic Journal*, January 12, 1991.

"Hitachi Zosen Reaps Rewards of 'All-Weather' Restructuring," *Nikkei Weekly*, November 8, 1993, p. 12.

Shimizu, Shogo, "Shipbuilder Swabs Up Profits by Burning Up Trash," *Nikkei Weekly*, September 19, 1994, p. 10.

"Those Rich, Polluted, Soon-to-Be-Automated Japanese," *Economist*, December 18, 1971.

Tanzer, Andrew, "The Japanese Do It Again," *Forbes*, October 16, 1989.

—Thomas M. Tucker
—update: Christina M. Stansell

Internacional de Ceramica, S.A. de C.V.

Avenida Carlos Pacheco 7200
Chihuahua, Chihuahua 31060
Mexico
Telephone: (614) 429-1111
Fax: (614) 429-1166
Web site: http://www.interceramic.com

Public Company
Founded: 1978
Employees: 3,178
Sales: $300 million (2002)
Stock Exchanges: Mexico City New York (for American
    Depositary Receipts)
Ticker Symbols: CERAMIC UB; ICM
NAIC: 325520 Adhesive and Sealant Manufacturing;
    327122 Ceramic Wall and Floor Tile Manufacturing;
    421320 Brick, Stone and Related Construction
    Material Wholesalers; 444110 Home Centers; 551112
    Offices of Other Holding Companies, Not Elsewhere
    Classified

Internacional de Ceramica, S.A. de C.V. (Interceramic), a Mexican holding company, is the largest manufacturer of ceramic glazed floor tiles in North America and is also a leading manufacturer of ceramic glazed wall tiles, with some 80 different product lines in all. The company also make grouts and adhesive materials to complement its tile product lines and has a tile factory in the United States. Internacional de Ceramica also imports and distributes ceramic glazed floor and wall tiles, distributing them in Mexico through a network of franchised and company-owned stores and, in the United States, through independent distributors and a network of wholesale/retail stores owned and operated by a U.S. subsidiary. Sales in the United States, where the company is known as Interceramic, account for about half the total.

Making Floor Tiles in the 1980s

A member of an important landowning family in the northern Mexican state of Chihuahua, Esteban Almeida was a cattle rancher who established links north of the border when he fled to Texas during the revolution that convulsed Mexico in the second decade of the 20th century. The business prospered after his return, so the Almeida family borrowed money from Texas bankers and also went into the automotive business as a franchised distributor for Chrysler Corp. Because the Mexican government began seizing land and setting cattle prices during the 1970s, the Almeidas shifted their resources from ranching to banking. In 1982, however, the value of the peso dropped precipitously, and the government nationalized the nation's banks in order to restructure the financial system.

The Almeidas, although now virtually bankrupt, had, in the early 1960s, established a small brick-making company in order to erect buildings on their properties. This company was converted into a tilemaker in 1978, becoming the first tile producer in North America to adopt the Italian single-fired production process, which resulted in lower firing times and energy usage, thereby allowing the manufacture of high-quality products at relative low cost. A related, family-owned business extracted the clay from the Almeidas' own mines. The machinery came from Italy and Spain. Esteban's son Oscar stepped aside to allow his son, Victor, to run the firm's day-to-day operations. Like most Mexican companies, Interceramic was a traditional family business, with Victor Almeida in charge and the second-in-command his brother-in-law. Most of the other high executives were sons of men who had worked for Victor's grandfather or father. By the mid-1990s, however, Victor had brought in new blood in the form of top managers who were mostly under 40. The firm's organizational structure was more open and informal and less hierarchical than the traditional Mexican practice.

The construction business was among the Mexican sectors hardest hit by the peso crisis. The company produced three million square meters of tile in 1982 but then had to close two of its four furnaces for a time. By the end of 1986, however, Interceramic had raised its production capacity by 50 percent without being able to fully satisfy the demands of the market. Additional firing capacity was put into operation in late 1986, raising production to 4.5 million square meters in 1987, but this still did not meet market demand. An unexpected amount of business was coming not from building contractors but from homeowners who found it cheaper and more durable to cover their floors with tiles than rugs. Sales rose from 9.49 billion pesos

Key Dates:

1978: Internacional de Ceramica (Interceramic) is founded.
1987: Interceramic makes its initial public offering of stock.
1988: Interceramic establishes U.S. headquarters in Texas.
1989: The company forms a joint venture to market tiles in the United States.
1992: Interceramic has become the leading producer of tiles in Mexico.
1995: The company begins making wall tiles, both in Chihuahua and Texas.
2000: Interceramic forms a strategic alliance with U.S.-based Kohler Co.

(about $15.5 million) in 1986 to 40.37 billion pesos (about $28.71 million) in 1987. Because of the scarcity of funds available from the banks and their high interest rates, Interceramic decided to became a public company in 1987, when its shares were first offered on Mexico City's stock exchange. Some 45 percent of the 12.97 billion pesos (about $9.22 million) raised from the sale of shares was earmarked to repay debts.

From Interceramic's inception, the Almeidas saw as vital to the company's future an expansion of sales into the United States, and for this reason chose Interceramic as the brand name for its products. It was unknown north of the border, however, and had to go through a trial-and-error process of finding good managers to help the company develop a distribution network. In Mexico, homeowners typically bought their tiles directly from the manufacturer, but in the United States a contractor almost always served as an intermediary. Moreover, Interceramic soon learned that American customers demanded much better service. "The Mexican customer would take just about any beating you gave him," Victor Almeida told Paul B. Carroll of the *Wall Street Journal* in 1994. Another barrier to sales were tariffs as high as 60 percent, since Washington claimed that, among other factors, Mexico was subsidizing Interceramic's exports by providing cheap fuel through the government-controlled oil monopoly.

Interceramic's exports still came to less than 10 percent of company revenue when, in 1988, the company established U.S. headquarters and a distribution center in El Paso, Texas, a three-hour drive north of Chihuahua. This office moved the following year to Carrollton, Texas, where another distribution center was opened. Prompted by its American managers, the company began producing the smaller (and more subdued) 4¼-inch-square tiles used in the United States rather than the more flamboyant 6-by-6-inch tiles typical of the Mexican market. Although initial sales north of the border were through independent distribution, Interceramic eventually established a network of company-owned wholesale/retail stores in the southern United States. In 1989 Interceramic formed a joint venture with Armstrong World Industries, Inc., which invested 44 billion pesos (about $177 million) to market Interceramic's products in the United States. The joint venture, Recubrimientos Interceramic, S.A. de C.V., became the owner of a recently estab-

lished second Interceramic tile plant in Chihuahua, with the right to purchase up to 50 percent of the first-quality glazed ceramic floor tiles made at this plant for sale in the United States. Dal-Tile, Inc. later became the successor to Armstrong's interest in this venture.

In order to respond quickly to changes in consumer fashions, Interceramic established a large research-and-development unit, with its own kiln and computerized design tools next to a pilot production line. When a competitor introduced a tile pattern simulating a parquet floor, Interceramic rushed large shipments of similar tiles to its distributors in only 35 days. The company, to reduce costs, invested heavily in new equipment that stamped, glazed, silk-screened, and baked the tiles with almost no resort to human hands. By 1994 the percentage of the production run considered to be first quality had risen from 70 percent to 81 percent, while the percentage of scrap had fallen from 11 to 9 percent.

Expansion in the 1990s

In 1990 Interceramic raised its production to 5.93 million square meters of ceramic tile, some 32 percent of the Mexican market for this floor and wall product. At the beginning of 1991, the company raised $7.6 million by selling American Depositary Receipts, the equivalent of shares, on the New York Stock Exchange. Interceramic had net sales of $71.7 million and operating income of $7.4 million in 1991. It held 80 percent of the luxury end of the Mexican floor tile market in 1992 and also was marketing a Vision brand of medium-priced tiles there. Its share of the wall tile market in Mexico was 8 percent, although it was not yet manufacturing this product. The company had 85 independent distributors in Mexico and 77 in the United States. A third U.S. distribution center had opened in San Antonio. Speaking of Interceramic, a Mexico City investment analyst told Norman Peagam and Michael Marray of *Euromoney,* "They have the best technology they can get, they are continuously improving their equipment, and they invest money in market research. They do their homework and they know exactly where they want to go." A New York analyst agreed, adding, "From the CEO of the company to the worker on the assembly line, they know exactly what they are doing. It is a very lean operation and very efficiently run—on the financial side they are very knowledgeable and sophisticated."

Although Interceramic held only a 2 percent share of the $1 billion U.S. tile market in 1992, U.S. sales had risen to more than 20 percent of company revenue. The export pace gained impetus when the North American Free Trade Agreement came into force in 1994, resulting in a gradual reduction of the 20 percent U.S. duty on Interceramic's products. By late that year the company held 7 percent of the U.S. floor tile market as well as 20 percent of the total Mexican tile market, which made it the leading tile producer in Mexico. Its system of selling through independent distribution in Mexico was giving way to a mixed network of company-owned distribution and an extensive, exclusive franchise web throughout the country, operating under the Interceramic name. In 1995 the company added a third manufacturing facility in Chihuahua and opened another in Garland, Texas, which also became the new site of U.S. headquarters. Both the new Chihuahua plant and the Garland one were for the production of glazed ceramic wall tile.

Following the December 1994 peso devaluation, Interceramic's 1995 net sales fell by 20 percent. The next year, however, they rose by 42.5 percent. Interceramic's net sales grew 29 percent between 1996 and 2000, and its operating income increased by 96 percent over this period. In 1998 the company organized a subsidiary to open and operate wholesale/retail locations throughout the Mexico City metropolitan area. The following year it organized another subsidiary to acquire the operations of the company's franchisee in the Guadalajara metropolitan area. Interceramic formed a strategic association in 2000 with the U.S.-based Kohler Co., a leader in kitchen and bathroom fixtures. Kohler took an 11 percent stake in Interceramic's common stock, and the Interceramic franchise network began distributing Kohler products throughout Mexico. A new Interceramic facility for the production of grouts and adhesives in central Mexico was completed in 2001.

Interceramic in 2000–01

Interceramic was producing glazed ceramic floor tile at two Chihuahua facilities: the ICSA and RISA plants. The latter was owned by the joint venture with Dal-Tile, which retained Armstrong's right to purchase up to half of the plant's first-quality production for sale in the United States. A third Chihuahua facility, the Azulejos plant, located adjacent to the RISA plant, was devoted to the manufacture of large-format wall tile and also was producing trim pieces. The Garland plant was engaged in the manufacture and production of both small and larger-format glazed ceramic wall tile and related trim pieces, all for the U.S. market. These four plants accounted for 47, 25, 15, and 13 percent, respectively, of Interceramic's installed capacity of 264 million square feet (24.5 million square meters) in 2000, all of which was being utilized. In addition, a joint venture with Custom Building Products of California, Inc., established in 1993, owned and operated a plant, adjacent to the ICSA facility, for the development and manufacture of grouts and adhesive materials used in the installation of ceramic tile. This joint venture subsidiary opened a second grout and adhesive plant in the central Mexican town of Huichapan, Hidalgo, in 2001. Another Interceramic subsidiary owned several Mexican mining properties from which substantially all the clay used in the company's Mexican production facilities was derived.

The products manufactured by Interceramic in Mexico were being marketed by a national network of exclusive franchise stores as well as a number of company-owned stores in the Mexico City and Guadalajara markets. In the United States, a subsidiary was selling Interceramic's products through independent distributors and a network of wholesale/retail stores owned and operated by Ceramic Tile International, Inc., a subsidiary of Interceramic USA. Current Ceramic Tile International locations were in Austin, Dallas, El Paso, Fort Worth, Houston, Plano, and San Antonio, Texas; the Atlanta metropolitan area; Albuquerque, New Mexico; Las Vegas, Nevada; Phoenix and Scottsdale, Arizona; and Tulsa, Oklahoma. Some of the

ICSA plant's production was being sold to Dal-Tile for resale in the United States under Dal-Tile brand names. Canadian sales were mostly through a Toronto distributor. In addition, Interceramic was importing ceramic floor and wall tile, primarily from Italian and Spanish manufacturers, for distribution and sale in the United States. These imported tiles, and similar products by U.S. manufacturers, were being stocked by Ceramic Tile International along with Interceramic's own output.

Interceramic's net sales in 2000 came to 2.55 billion pesos ($264.91 million). Its operating income was 264.42 million pesos ($27.52 million) and its consolidated net income was 132.65 million pesos ($13.8 million). Mexico accounted for 57 percent of consolidated sales and the United States for 43 percent. The long-term debt of 1.11 billion pesos ($115.69 million) at the end of the year was 25 percent lower than the total at the end of 1998. Interceramic's net sales in 2001 reached 2.71 billion pesos ($294.42 million), of which Mexico accounted for 59 percent. Net consolidated income was 174.04 million pesos ($18.94 million). Company debt had fallen to $103.6 million at the end of 2001.

Oscar Almeida and his immediate family members owned nearly 49 percent of Interceramic's common stock in 2001; he owned 44 percent directly. Banamex Trust owned 10.7 percent and Banco Accival, an affiliate of Banamex, owned 13.6 percent. Kohler owned 11 percent.

Principal Subsidiaries

Adhesivos y Boquillas Interceramic, S. de R.L. de C.V. (51%); Distribucion Interceramic, S.A. de C.V.; Intercabados del Noroeste, S.A. de C.V.; Intercabados del Occidente, S.A. de C.V.; Interceramic, Inc. (U.S.A.); Interceramic de Occidente, S.A. de C.V.; Interceramic Trading Company (U.S.A.); Operadora Interceramic de Mexico, S.A. de C.V.; Procesadora de Materiales Cerro Grande, S.A. de C.V.; Recubrimientos Interceramic, S.A. de C.V. (50.01%).

Principal Competitors

Lomosa; Porcelanite, S.A. de C.V.; Vitromex.

Further Reading

Carroll, Paul B., ''The Brass Ring,'' *Wall Street Journal*, October 28, 1994, p. R8.
Fierro, Leticia, ''Con los pies bien puestos en el piso,'' *Expansion*, October 14, 1987, pp. 89–93.
Peagam, Norman, and Michael Marray, ''Interceramic: No Ceiling for the Tile Market,'' *Euromoney*, May 1993, pp. 134, 136.
Reygadas Anfossi, Armando, ''Mas cerca del norte,'' *Expansion*, February 19, 1992, pp. 56–57, 59.

—Robert Halasz

Julius Meinl International AG

Julius Meinl Gasse 3-7
1160 Vienna
Austria
Telephone: +43 1 48860
Fax: +43 1 485 85 95
Web site: http://www.meinl.com

Public Company
Incorporated: 1862
Employees: 2,905
Sales: EUR 209.15 million ($200 million) (2001)
Stock Exchanges: Vienna
Ticker Symbol: JMI.EAV
NAIC: 311920 Coffee and Tea Manufacturing; 551112
    Offices of Other Holding Companies

With a history spanning nearly 150 years, Julius Meinl International AG has pulled an about-face for the new century. Once renowned as one of the leading supermarket and retail groups in Central Europe, the Vienna, Austria-based holding company has all but exited retailing, returning instead to its earliest roots as a coffee roaster—the company's Meinl brands are leaders in Central Europe—and producer of gourmet teas, jams, jellies, and other fine foods. Meinl has nonetheless held on to its prestigious flagship store in Vienna's city center, which trades under the Gourmet banner. The company also has retained its retail networks in the Czech Republic and Poland, which total more than 100 stores, although Meinl has suggested that it is interested in selling these outlets as well. On the production side, Meinl operates coffee roasters in Austria, Italy, Slovenia, and Slovakia and a jam and preserve processing facility in Vienna. Meinl, which, although listed on the Vienna stock exchange, is controlled by the founding Meinl family, also operates its own bank, Meinl bank, which specializes in investment and private banking. Another Meinl operation is a successful online commerce site, selling the company's branded products around the world. To support sales of its roasted coffees, Meinl, which many consider as a primary player in the creation of the famed Viennese café culture, has begun an attempt to export the European coffeehouse; in 2002, the company opened its first coffee café in Chicago. The company expects to open similar cafés in other major cities in the early years of the new century. The company is led by Julius Meinl IV and Thomas Meinl, representing the fourth generation, and by Julius Mcinl V, the fifth generation of the Meinl family to lead the business. Despite its narrowed focus, the company produced revenues of more than EUR 209 million ($200 million) in 2001.

Roasting Success in the Mid-19th Century

Vienna had long played a central role in the European coffee market. After the Austrian army broke through the Turkish siege of the city in 1683, the routed invaders left behind bags of green coffee beans—considered as camel fodder by the Turks. The first Viennese "Kaffiehaus" opened soon after. For the most part, however, Viennese coffee drinkers purchased the raw beans for roasting at home. Into this market came Julius Meinl, who opened his own small store in 1862. Meinl became noted for his blends of raw beans, imported from all over the world.

Yet coffee remained expensive, and the roasting process a delicate one—customers often burned the precious coffee beans. This situation led Meinl to the innovation that was to provide the basis for an empire that came to span much of the Austria-Hungarian empire: Meinl began roasting coffee in his own shop and selling the roasted coffee to his customers. The idea met with instant success, and before long Meinl had begun opening a chain of coffee shops throughout the city.

Customers did not come to Meinl's shop only to buy coffee. They also came to drink it, which led Meinl to begin converting his shops into coffeehouses. Before long, the coffeehouse culture caught on, becoming a hallmark of the Austrian capital city before the concept spread throughout Europe. Meanwhile, Meinl capitalized on the growing popularity of his retail chain to introduce other goods and commodities, with an emphasis on fresh foods and delicatessen items, and the shops began to evolve into full-scale groceries.

In 1891, Meinl built a new, dedicated roasting facility to meet the growing demand for his company's coffee, as the

Company Perspectives:

Corporate Strategy: Julius Meinl International AG is an investment holding company which is based in Vienna and whose activities are concentrated mainly in Central and Eastern Europe, thus continuing a long Julius Meinl tradition of playing a leading role in the heart of Europe since 1862.

For almost 140 years the name ''Julius Meinl'' has stood for the highest quality in goods and services and in the retail trade, with a brand name which is known far beyond the borders of Austria itself. The many years' experience which Julius Meinl International has gained in the markets of Central and Eastern Europe means that it is well placed to determine what local requirements are. It is on this local market knowledge that investment decisions are based. The current investment portfolio of Julius Meinl International covers the areas of retail trading, coffee and real estate. With its commitment to the principle of ''shareholder value,'' the company will base its evaluation of every investment on how, and to what extent, value growth can be achieved. This is the only criterion on which investment and disinvestment decisions are based. However, the ''Julius Meinl'' brand name will continue to be the common factor in all management decisions, the company's tradition making it essential to maintain the highest standards in quality and service. This is where the future of Julius Meinl lies.

brand gained an international reputation for its distinctive blends. For its new facility, the company chose the spot on which the Turkish army had abandoned the original sacks of coffee beans. That location was to remain the company's headquarters into the 21st century.

The end of World War I and the breakup of the Austria-Hungarian empire spelled new opportunity for the Meinl company as trade restrictions were lifted in the Central European region. During the postwar era the company rapidly expanded its empire into the newly created independent countries of Central Europe. By the 1930s, the Meinl retail empire had grown to more than 600 company-owned stores, and some 400 franchised stores, making the leading retailer in all of Europe and a mainstay of daily life throughout most of Central Europe. The company also had built a strong string of food processing plants, enabling it to produce foods and other items under the Meinl brand.

The Meinl family, now one of Vienna's wealthiest, also had expanded their interests beyond retailing. In 1923, Julius Meinl II, now head of the family company, established the Spar- und Kreditverein der Freunde & Angestellten der Julius Meinl AG, a savings and loan operation that later grew into the private Meinl Bank.

The outbreak of World War II, however, brought an end to the Meinl family's expansion. The company's bank was shut down in 1943; meanwhile, the country's Central European holdings were ravaged by the war. With the end of hostilities, most of Meinl's former retail empire had fallen within the sphere of influence of the Soviet Union.

Rebuilding in the Post-Cold War Era

Forced back within its Austrian market, Meinl nonetheless maintained its stature as a leading domestic retailer, while building an international reputation for its fine-quality roasted coffees. In 1956, the company, then led by Julius Meinl III, returned to the banking sphere with the reopening of the Spar- und Kreditvereines. That business grew again in the 1960s when the company acquired Bankhauses Brunner & Co. KG in 1969. The two banks maintained separate operations until they were merged under a single name, Meinl Bank, in 1979.

The early 1980s saw the first signs of a thaw in the Soviet Union-dominated countries of Central Europe. Meinl, which continued to enjoy strong name recognition in those countries, was among the first to stake a foothold in these markets. Hungary became the first country to relax its trade laws, allowing joint ventures with foreign companies as early as 1980. Meinl entered an agreement with the supermarket group Csemege, then Hungary's largest. As Thomas Meinl told *Supermarket News:* ''The stores were shabby, dirty and desperately old-fashioned. There was not much choice of products, and those that were available were of poor quality.'' Meinl nonetheless entered the shops, setting up its own ''Meinl Corners'' to sell its branded coffees, teas, jams, and other products. In this way, the Meinl brand reappeared on the shelves in Hungary's kitchens. Elsewhere in the Eastern Bloc, Meinl reached distribution agreements with local partners to introduce its products to such markets as Czechoslovakia, Poland, and elsewhere.

The end of the 1980s brought the end of the Cold War era, reopening the Central European economy to outside interests. Meinl quickly prepared a new expansion drive into its former territories. In 1989 the company sold off one of its domestic subsidiaries, which had been operating a chain of discount stores in Austria, and used that capital to set up a new holding company, Julius Meinl International, to guide its expansion.

In 1990, the company moved to acquire a 51 percent controlling interest in former partner Csemege, using that company's 104 retail stores as a basis for its Central European relaunch. The company promptly renamed the stores as Csemege-Julius Meinl and began an extensive renovation program designed to bring the supermarket chain up to Western standards.

By 1992, Meinl had reentered a number of new markets, setting up four franchise stores in Poland, and beginning exports of its branded products to Romania and Bulgaria. The company, which took its Julius Meinl International holding company public with a listing on the Vienna stock exchange that year, also set up two new subsidiaries to prepare its reentry into the newly separated Czech Republic and Slovakia markets. The company made its first acquisition in Slovakia in 1992, acquiring the Baliarne coffee roasting plant. Meinl also continued adding to its Hungarian holdings, including buying up a 30-store chain in the western part of the country in 1992.

Meinl entered the Czech Republic in 1994 with the opening of its first store in Prague. That same year, the company expanded its Czech interests with the acquisition of the Pramen Brno supermarket chain, which operated 27 stores. The company continued building its holdings in the Czech Republic, expanding to 70 stores by 1996. Nearly all of these locations were owned outright by the country. Meanwhile, Meinl had been growing strongly in Hungary as well, nearing 150 Csemege-Julius Meinl stores at mid-decade. The company also had developed two other store formats, the 42-store chain of Jeee discount stores, and the eight-store chain of Jeee Cash se Carry stores.

Returning to Roots for the New Century

Poland became the company's next target in 1996, when the company acquired a 51 percent stake in small retail group Major SA, which then operated five stores. Meinl immediately began plans to add five new stores, with plans to increase its Polish presence to as many as 20 stores by the end of the decade. Meanwhile, in Austria, Meinl attempted to take a share of the supermarket sector, opening some 39 PAM PAM supermarkets in that country.

The year 1996 was to mark a new turning point in Julius Meinl's history, however. In that year, Austria joined the European Common Market, eliminating the trade barriers that had previously protected Austrian businesses. Meinl soon found itself faced with head-to-head competition with a number of Western Europe's retailing giants as they prepared to enter the Austrian market.

In the late 1990s, Meinl's Austrian stores, which numbered some 340, were struggling, slipping into losses. In 1997, the company split its Austrian operation into separate production and retail subsidiaries, then sold off most of its industrial wing to a Swiss investment group. Part of the company's reasoning behind this move was its interest in focusing its own production interests on a more limited number of high-quality, Meinl-branded items. This interest was quickly revealed to include an exit from retailing, at least in the Austrian market. By 1998, the company was rumored to be looking for buyers.

Meinl appeared to have found its buyer at mid-1998 when German retail group Rewe agreed to buy up its Austrian retail holdings. That deal quickly foundered on the Austrian monopolies commission's objections that the deal would give Rewe too great a share of the Austrian retail market. The purchase finally went through, but in a far limited form, when Rewe made a new offer to acquire just half of Meinl's Austrian stores.

Meinl nonetheless remained committed to selling off its Austrian grocery holdings, and by mid-summer had announced its intention to convert some 100 of its remaining stores into a new "Gourmet" concept, featuring an emphasis on fresh foods and delicatessen items, while putting up another 77 stores, including 21 supermarkets, for sale. By 2000, with profits under pressure, Meinl had abandoned the smaller store format as well, selling out almost all of its remaining properties to the Spar supermarket group. The company kept, however, its historic Graben city center store, which continued to operate under the Gourmet fascia.

Meinl had in the meantime continued to expand in its more successful Central European operations, buying up Czech store chain Pronto Plus in 1998, adding 20 stores to bring its total to some 120 in that country. Yet the slump in the Eastern European economies at the end of the decade, as well as ferocious competition from Europe's major supermarket groups, which were battling for dominance of these markets, thwarted the modestly sized Meinl's expansion plans. By 1999, the company had sold off its Hungarian holdings to Belgium's Delhaize supermarket group. At the same time, Meinl announced its intention to end further investment through its international subsidiary. While the company held onto its Czech and Polish stores, these were slated for restructuring, reducing the number of outlets, while the company looked for buyers in the early 2000s.

Instead, Meinl decided to concentrate its efforts on boosting worldwide sales of its roasted coffees, which included such famous labels as Jubiläum, Der Mocca, Präsident, Der Schonende, Kaiser Melange, King Hadhramaut, and others. To these the company added its own branded teas, as well as jams, jellies, and other gourmet food items. Initially targeted at the Western European markets, Meinl's sales quickly took off worldwide, particularly through the development of its own e-commerce site. At the same time, the company began to look for other investment opportunities, with a particular interest in online businesses.

Central Europe remained, however, a privileged market for the company, where its brand retained continued strong recognition. By 2002, the company moved to reenter these markets in its new, more specialized form. The company began selling its coffee in Hungary at the beginning of that year, launching the brand first through retail channels before adding sales to the restaurant and café sector as well. Meanwhile, Meinl sought to boost its brand recognition in farther-flung markets.

In 2002, the company opened its first international coffee-house, choosing the city of Chicago for this new move. Featuring a "European" design (the company flew in the café's décor from Austria), the new coffee shop offered table service and free newspapers, as well as American-style takeout service. The shop proved a ready success, and the company made plans to roll out more shops in Chicago and in other major cities. Expansion of the café concept was to remain limited, however, as Meinl viewed this new activity primarily as a means of stimulating sales of its coffee and other branded products. Meinl had successfully negotiated a return to its roots as one of the world's most respected coffee brands.

Principal Subsidiaries

Alfa Piac Kft (Hungary); Incab SpA (Italy); Julius Meinl AS (Czech Republic); Julius Meinl d.o.o. (Slovenia); Julius Meinl Kava Sro (Czech Republic); Julius Meinl Morava AS (Czech Republic); Julius Meinl Pramen AS (Czech Republic); Julius Meinl SA (Poland); MT Property Srl (Romania; 35%); Meinl Bank; The Drogerie SA (Czech Republic).

Principal Competitors

Philip Morris Companies Inc.; Procter and Gamble Co.; Japan Tobacco Inc.; Astor Products Inc.; Sara Lee Corporation; Great Atlantic and Pacific Tea Company Inc.; Sara Lee/DE NV; Tomkins PLC; Morinaga Milk Industry Company Ltd.; Starbucks Corporation; Nestle Holdings UK PLC; Tchibo; Frisch-Rost-Kaffee GmbH; Joh Johannson A/S; Asahi Soft Drinks Company Ltd.; Scottie MacBean Inc.; Volcafe Holding Ltd.; Melitta Unternehmensgruppe Bentz KG; Kraft Foods UK Ltd.; Strauss-Elite Group; Daesang Corporation; Montana Coffee Traders Inc.; Pokka Corporation; Luigi Lavazza SpA; S and D Coffee Inc.; Elite Industries Ltd.; Chock Full O'Nuts Corporation; Key Coffee Inc.; Karl Struppe Ges mbH; Autobar Group Ltd.; Wedl und Dick Ges mbH; McCormick UK Ltd.; Linton Park PLC; Tetley USA Inc.; Douwe Egberts France SNC.

Further Reading

Amato-McCoy, Deena, "Vienna Retailer to Expand Its Home-Shopping Service," *Supermarket News,* March 17, 1997, p. 63.

"Der Meinl-Mohr geht mit Tee und Kaffee nach Westeuropam," *Der Standard,* January 27, 2000, p. 26.

Dowdell, Stephen, "Meinl Feels at Home Moving East," *Supermarket News,* June 15, 1992, p. 20.

"Julius Meinl Ups Czech Investment," *Eurofood,* July 4, 2002, p. 16.

"Meinl Store Sale Upset," *Eurofood,* October 7, 1999, p. 5.

"Rewe/Meinl Merger Approved in Slimline Form," *Eurofood,* February 11, 1999, p. 7.

Rostan, Tim, "Vienna's Julius Meinl Waltzes into US," *CBS Marketwarch.com,* August 16, 2002.

—M.L. Cohen

JUVENTUS

Juventus F.C. S.p.A

Piazza Crimea 7
10131 Turin
Italy
Telephone: (39) 011-65631
Fax: (39) 011-66054550
Web site: http://www.juventus.it

Public Company
Founded: 1897
Employees: 90
Sales: $133 million (2000)
Stock Exchanges: Italian
Ticker Symbol: JUVE
NAIC: 711211 Sports Teams and Clubs

One of the premier professional soccer clubs in the world, Juventus F.C. S.p.A., with its home field in the 71,000-seat Delle Alpi stadium in Turin, Italy, is one of the dominate teams in its league. Since its founding in 1897, it has garnered 25 Serie A league championships, more than any of its competitors. Also, in international competition, it has won three UEFA European Champions Cups. The club has fielded some of the best, world-class players in the sport, including, recently, Zinedine Zidane, who some consider the best of the best. The extremely popular team boasts a following throughout Europe of 17 million fans, with 11 million (over a third of the country's fans) in Italy alone. A private company until 2001, when it made its initial public offering (IPO), Juventus F.C. is still under the control of the Agnelli family, which has owned a majority share of the Juventus since 1923.

From Local Sports Club to National Competitor

In need of a change of pace, a group of young students took time out from their rigorous schooling at the Liceo D'Azeglio in Turin, to form Juventus F.C. as a sports club. The year was 1897. The young men were looking for some fun, and they banded together from a common interest in a relatively new craze: football (or soccer, as it is called in the United States), which, originating in Great Britain, was then quickly spreading

throughout Europe. It was not until 1900 that the club fielded its first team, decked out pink shirts.

Initially, under the club's president Enrico Canfari, the fledgling team played against more experienced teams in the city before branching out and playing clubs in other cities. It soon became a highly competitive team, and in 1905, two years after adopting its familiar black and white colors, it won its first league championship. In that season, it had some tough contests against teams from Milan and Genoa, making it a very exciting time for the team and its fans.

Juventus first started playing at D'Armi Square, an arena still used for sporting events at the end of the 20th century. The team did well in its early history there, but, despite some of its achievements, through the first few years of the 20th century the club never achieved the success of such stronger competitors as Provercelli and Casale, not, at least, until the end of World War I.

After the armistice, Juventus began a rapid rise to some preeminence. A major reason for this development was the fact that it obtained the talents of a group of major players, notably the goalkeeper Giovanni Giacone and two full backs, Osvaldo Novo and Sesia Bruno, the first Juventus players to play on the national team. Also an important figure was the club's president, Corrado Corradini, a belletrist who both guided the team's fortunes and wrote its anthem.

1920s–30s: The Rise of Juventus in Italian Football

In 1923, the same year in which Giampiero Combi, one of the sport's most distinguished goalkeepers, made his playing debut for Juventus, Edoardo Agnelli became the new president of the club. Agnelli, son of Fiat founder Giovanni Agnelli, was quickly convinced of the need for a larger stadium to accommodate his team's growing number of fans. The club soon moved into a bigger, stone-walled facility in Corso Marsiglia.

The team also began attracting major players. Joining the club under Agnelli were its first real coach, Jeno Karoly, and inside left Ferenc Hirzer, both Hungarians. They augmented the talents of a handful of major players, including Combi and Virginio Rosetta, who, joining the team from Pro Vercelli,

Company Perspectives:

The Company plans to increase and diversify its revenue streams and to enhance its profitability, while making it less sensitive to sports performance, by pursuing strategies intended to reinforce its core business and to develop new side-operations in connection with the exploitation of sports events. More specifically, the Company is focused on the following, closely interconnected strategic goals: to maintain the Team up to its standard of excellence in order to score a number of victories or otherwise resounding results in both domestic and international football matches; to add value to Juventus's brand name with a view to establishing and improving its image as a testimonial in the eyes of the business community to develop further its own commercial operations, partly by expanding its supporter base in countries which have recently shown to be greatly interested in the "football world"; and to work out and implement income-diversification projects, with a special emphasis on less volatile and steadier sources of revenues, partly by investing in side-activities, along with, yet closely related to, its core business in the entertainment, leisure, and trade areas, then by ensuring increased visibility to the Team's weekday activities in addition to officially scheduled sports events.

became the first players ever transferred for money in European football history. Others on the team included Carlo Bigatto, Giuseppe Grabbi, and Frederico Munerati. Karoly coached the team to its second league title in 1925. By that time, Juventus had become a major power in Italian sports.

Juventus became a dominant team in the early 1930s, winning five league championships between 1930 and 1935 and providing several of the players who won the World Cup in 1934. Juventus simply had a talent-rich team, and under coach Carlo Carcano the club had its first golden era. It was spearheaded by the "Trio della Legenda" (legendary trio) made up of Combi, Rosetta, and another fullback, Umberto Caligaris, but it also had other star players, including Luigi Bertolini, Felipe Borel, Renato Cesarini, Giovanni Ferrari, Luis Monti, Raimundo Orsi, and Mario Varglien. It was also during this period, in 1933, that the team began playing in a new stadium that had been built by the city to accommodate the World University Games. It would remain the home of Juventus for the next 57 years.

Dominance Lost and Regained

In 1935, two years after Juventus began using its new facility, Edoardo Agnelli died in a plane crash in Genoa, Italy. Although his death stunned the club, it continued to hold a dominant place in Italian football right up until World War II, and by 1937 it had won its first Italian Cup. The war then put European football on hold, and though it came back strong with the restoration of peace, in the first few postwar years Juventus lost its primacy in Italian football to Torino, which won repeated national championships from 1945 to 1949.

During that period, in 1947, Gianni Agnelli assumed control of the team. He led it to another championship season in 1950.

Although its success was partly the result of the 1949 loss of Torino's first team in another air disaster, Juventus served notice that it was once again a major competitor. Still, it had to rebuild, which it proceeded to do during the 1950s under the leadership of Gianni's younger brother Umberto Agnelli, who took over the presidency in 1955. With Umberto in that post, the team once again reached Italian football dominance. It won championships in 1958, 1960, and 1961.

Although Juventus again had to rebuild in the early part of the 1960s, in 1967, under the presidency of Vittore Catella, it again won its league championship. Then, starting four years later, in 1971, with Giampiero Boniperti as president, the team began a long period of successful seasons. Between 1972 and 1986, it won nine championships and earned victories in all the European and international tournaments in which it played. Its world class players during that period included Pietro Anastasi, Roberto Bettega, Antonio Cabrini, Franco Causio, Giuseppe Furino, Claudio Gentile, Michel Platini, Gaetano Scirea, Marco Tardelli, and Dino Zoff.

Juventus performed particularly well during the 1983–84 and 1984–85 seasons. In the former season, Juventus won both the Cup Winners' Cup and the Super Cup, and in the latter, the team claimed the European Cup and the Intercontinental Cup. Unfortunately, Juventus's achievement in winning its first European Cup was marred by events that occurred at the Heysel Stadium in Brussels, Belgium, where, in the championship match, the team was pitted against UK's Liverpool club. Poor placement of spectators in the stands led to fighting between rival fan groups, then to the collapse of a wall and the death of 39 Italian fans. Juventus beat Liverpool 1–0 in the tragic game. Michel Platini, the great French player, scored the game-winning goal. Giovanni Trapattoni, who later became the Italian national team's coach, was the club's trainer. Much of the team's success came from the play of defensive stand outs Stefani Tacconi and Marco Tardelli.

The 1990s: A Major Peak and Subsequent Decline

In 1990, with Dino Zoff serving as coach and Vittorio Chiusano as president, Juventus won both the Italian and the United European Football Association (UEFA) cups, and three years later again won the UEFA Cup. In the next year, 1994, new managers took over the operational control of Juventus. The new leaders, known as "the triad," were Roberto Bettega, Antonio Giraudo, and Luciano Moggi. They installed Marcello Lippi as chief trainer or coach, and he immediately guided the club to a championship and the Italian Cup in the 1994–95 season. However, the team lost in the finals of the UEFA Cup tournament.

The following season, 1995–96, proved to be the best of decade for Juventus. It won the Intercontinental Cup in Tokyo, the European Cup, Super Cup, and the team's 24th Scudetto (Italian Championship). Also, it just lost the championship in the Champions League to Borussia Dortmund of Germany in the final game of that competition. Furthermore, although it would not reach such a peak for the rest of the decade, the team remained highly competitive. It did fare well in Italian competition, playing to the wire for a championship in 1997 and 1998, but it won no more cups in international competition, which was then dominated by Barcelona, Dortmund, Real Madrid, Chelsea, and Bayern Munich.

Key Dates:

1897: Students in Turin, Italy, organize Juventus F.C. under the presidency of Enrico Canfari.
1905: Juventus wins its first league championship.
1923: Edoardo Agnelli assumes financial and operational control of team.
1935: Edoardo Agnelli dies in an airplane accident.
1937: Juventus wins its first Italian Cup.
1950: The team wins its eighth league championship.
1984: Juventus wins Cup Winners and Super Cups.
1985: The team wins European and IC Cups.
1990: Juventus wins the UEFA Cup for the first time.
1997: The team wins the Italian championship and repeats this triumph in 1998.
2001: The team goes public.

Still, the 1995 to 1998 team, fielding the same players in that period, was one of two Juventus teams to be placed by *Soccer Digest* among the top 25 professional teams of all time (the other was the 1984–85 Juventus squad). The club, led by Didier Deschamps, Pietro Vierchowod, Gianluca Vialli, Fabrizio Ravellini, and an up-and-coming Alessandro Del Piero, had great talent at every position. Starting in 1996, Juventus also fielded a player who would become one of the game's all-time greats— Zinedine Zidane. Although he already had a reputation as a talented player, until he moved to Italy's Serie A league with Juventus, he had very little international experience. Thanks to Zidane, Juventus rallied from Champions League disappointment to finish second in Serie A. He was of tremendous help keeping Juventus competitive through the next few years, when the team's fortunes generally waned. Among other accolades he received, Zidane was named *Soccer Digest*'s Player of the Year in both 2000, when he was still playing for Juventus, and 2001, when he left Juventus to play for Real Madrid.

Towards the end of the decade, even with Zidane's great play, Juventus was struggling. Among other disruptive turns, Marcello Lippi resigned in the 1998–99 season. The job of trainer or coach fell to Carlo Ancelotti, who came over from Parma, a team that during Ancelotti's first of two seasons as trainer had the best year in its history. He was able to guide Juventus into two Italian championship playoffs but not to the cup.

2000 and Beyond: Rebuilding the Club into a Global Business

Despite the team's declining fortunes, Juventus was initially supportive of Ancelotti. It even rebuffed an effort by Milan to acquire Anecelotti after Milan dismissed its head trainer Alberto Zaccheroni. Despite the the team's fading glory, Juventus inked a two-year renewal of Ancelotti's contract in March 2000, but by the end of the season decided to buy out the contract and dismiss him. Ancelotti then went to Milan after all, and, in June of 2001, Marcello Lippi again returned to the helm of Juventus.

With the advent of the new century, Juventus undertook a strategic move to refashion itself into a global business. It set out to find international sponsors to help it become such a business, something European arch rivals like Manchester United had already accomplished. Between 2000 and 2001, it hoped to double its international sponsorship revenue from about 25 percent to 50 percent. With one of its major sponsors, Pepsi Cola International, it launched a "Dream Prize" campaign, offering club fans across the globe a chance to watch the team in live action and meet its star players.

The club also decided to sell 32 percent of its stock, and in 2001 made its initial public offering (IPO) on the Italian stock exchange. Until that time, although it had been a limited company since 1996, 99 percent of its shares belonged to IFI, a company owned by the Agnelli family. However, like the stock of AS Roma and Lazio, two other Italian football clubs, that of Juventus underperformed. Also, it had other problems shared by rival teams, including the failure of pay-per-view television to catch hold. The club still believed it would benefit from its public sale of stock, thanks to some planned capital projects, including Mondo Juve (a large leisure facility open to the public) and the purchase of the Stadio Della Alpi, which would be transformed into a smaller venue with premium seating.

Principal Competitors

F.C. Internazionale Milano S.p.A.; Arsenal Football Club; Milan A.C. S.p.A.; Leeds United plc; Manchester United plc; S.S. Lazio.

Further Reading

Farber, Michael, "Soccer Chic," *Sports Illustrated*, May 16, 1994, p. 64.
Israely, Jeff, "Whose Ball Is It Anyway?," *Time Atlantic*, April 22, 2002, p. 53.
"Italian Clubs Are a Little Offside," *Business and Finance*, August 15, 2002, p. 60.
"Juventus Eyes Success off the Pitch," *Nation* (Thailand), November 20, 2000.
Saporito, Bill, "Zidane Makes the French Connection," *Time Atlantic*, May 27, 2002, p. 61.
"ZZ Is Back on Top," *Soccer Digest*, November, 2001.

—John W. Fiero

KAISER PERMANENTE®

Kaiser Foundation Health Plan, Inc.

1 Kaiser Plaza
Oakland, California 94612
U.S.A.
Telephone: (510) 271-5800
Fax: (510) 271-6493
Web site: http://www.kaiserpermanente.org

Not-for-Profit Company
Incorporated: 1945
Employees: 90,000
Total Assets: $17 billion (2001)
NAIC: 524114 Direct Health and Medical Insurance
    Carriers; 621999 All Other Miscellaneous Ambulatory
    Health Care Services

Kaiser Foundation Health Plan, Inc., providing its services under the Kaiser Permanente name, is the largest not-for-profit HMO in the United States. It now serves about 8.2 million members in 9 states and Washington, D.C. The Oakland, California-based organization underwrites the Permanente Medical Groups, which, through the care of over 11,000 physicians, furnish medical care to Kaiser Permanente subscribers. Describing itself as ''an integrated health delivery system,'' Kaiser Permanente provides an array of services to its membership: it organizes and coordinates or provides its subscribers' health care (including preventive medicine), and it also provides other medical and pharmacy services through its network of Kaiser Foundation Hospitals and their subsidiaries.

1933–40: First Prepaid Health
Insurance Plan Is Developed

What would eventually evolve into Kaiser Permanente initially began with no affiliation with the Kaiser Foundation. It was the creation of Dr. Sidney R. Garfield, a young surgeon who, during the Great Depression, saw a way to help the thousands then at work constructing the Los Angeles Aqueduct. To help accommodate the health-care needs of the workers, Garfield set out to build a small hospital in the Mojave desert. The result was Contractors General Hospital, an unassuming 12-bed facility located six miles from a small town called Desert Center.

Garfield faced problems, however, including insufficient funds to keep the hospital solvent. Among other things, insurance companies were slow to pay his patients' bills. Furthermore, some of the workers had no insurance at all, so the good doctor was often obliged to treat patients without any payment at all. He was helped out of his dilemma by Harold Hatch, a former engineer who became an insurance agent in the financial vicissitudes of the times. Hatch conceived of a plan whereby insurance companies would pay Garfield a fixed per diem up front based on the number of patients covered by their policies. That arrangement, the first prepayment plan, allowed Garfield to fund sufficiently the hospital's operation and focus much of his attention on preventive medicine. Thousands of workers entered the program at a great bargain price of just five cents a day, or ten cents if the workers elected to also gain coverage for medical problems arising from non-job related causes. The plan proved a tremendous success. However, when the aqueduct project neared completion, Garfield began making preparations for returning to private practice.

Enter Henry Kaiser, the founder of Kaiser Aluminum and one of the nation's last, self-made, old-school captains of industry. Kaiser had undertaken the responsibility of finding adequate health care for the 6,500 workers then building the Grand Coulee Dam, a major construction project that would take several years to complete. Contacted by Kaiser, Garfield took up the challenge of adopting his prepayment plan approach to the needs of the Grand Coulee Dam workers. He recruited doctors to work under the plan and saw to the renovation and modernization of an old hospital that could serve the construction workers.

1940s–50s: Garfield's Health Plan
Is Made Available to the Public

Like the Los Angeles Aqueduct project health-care plan, that undertaken at the Grand Coulee Dam was a major success. But when this construction project neared completion in 1941, it looked as if Garfield's innovative system of funding medical care was again going to be terminated. The events of December 7, 1941 soon changed the plan's prospects, however. World War II turned the United States into the ''arsenal of democracy,'' and it gave Henry Kaiser another important role to play. Thousands of workers migrated to the Kaiser Shipyards in

Richmond, California, where they were building everything from Liberty Ships to aircraft carriers. Kaiser again called on Garfield, this time to fill the healthcare needs of 30,000 workers and their families. Garfield, whose military obligation was deferred for the purpose, met those needs and in the process entered into a formal association with Kaiser that became the cornerstone of Kaiser Permanente.

At the war's industrial peak, with prepayment health-care plans in effect at Richmond and other Kaiser-run yards and factories in California, the plans served about 200,000 members. Membership quickly dropped, though, when the war ended. In order to keep the plans viable, in 1945 they were opened to the general public. Yet membership still fell to 25,000.

1960s: Kaiser Permanente Is Restructured and Expands

It would take a few years before the membership reached levels held during the peak of the war, but, by 1952, it had grown to over 250,000, thanks in part to major help from Los Angeles-region management and labor groups, including support from the International Longshoreman's and Warehousemen's Union and the Retail Clerks Union. Membership in the health plan doubled over the next three years, reaching the 500,000 mark in 1955. That year, Kaiser Permanente was reorganized. Its goal was to become more effective in facilitating partnerships with medical professionals and to provide physicians with a financial stake in its program. In its restructuring, the organization laid the foundation for what would be its mode of operation into the next century.

At the time of its restructuring, Kaiser Permanente had just its three west coast regions: northern California, southern California, and Oregon. In 1958, it establish a fourth region in Hawaii. It also continued to increase its membership at a steady pace. By 1963, it had enrolled over one million members, and, by 1968, two million members. In the next year, 1969, it also added two more regions: Colorado and Ohio.

1970–96: Steady Growth Despite Stiffening Competition

Kaiser Permanente's growth continued throughout the 1970s. By 1976, it membership climbed over the three million mark. Also, in the following year, all six of its regions gained federal qualification as HMOs, and three years later the organization again began expanding its geographic coverage when, in a joint venture with the Prudential Insurance Company of America, it established a group-practice prepayment plan in Dallas. The plan would later become Kaiser Permanente's seventh region.

In 1980, the organization established its first region in the eastern United States, in the Washington, D.C., area. At that time, it acquired a nonprofit practice prepayment plan that, in addition to the nation's capital, covered parts of Maryland and Virginia. The new region brought the organization's total number to eight. Two years later, after reaching an enrollment of four million members, Kaiser Permanente established a ninth region in the greater Hartford area in Connecticut. That region would later expand to include Fairfield County in Connecticut, Westchester County in New York, and the I-91 corridor area of Massachusetts.

The organization expanded again in 1985, when it added three more geographic regions to its total: Georgia, Kansas City, and North Carolina. Altogether, at that time, Kaiser Permanente had plans in 12 regions. The expansion into new geographic areas resulted in additional memberships, which, in 1987, reached five million, and by 1990, 6.5 million.

Although Kaiser continued to grow its membership at a steady rate, competition from smaller HMOs began taking its toll by the early 1990s, and between 1991 and 1993 its total number of annual subscribers dropped slightly, from 6.72 million to 6.59 million in 1993, and it did not climb above the 1991 enrollment again until 1995. Moreover, its net income fell off, from $848 million in 1993 to $550 million in 1995. Led by CEO Dr. David Lawrence and COO Richard Barnaby, Kaiser's management decided that the giant needed to pursue more aggressive growth. Accordingly, the company began seeking new acquisitions.

In 1996, the year following its 50th anniversary, Kaiser Permanente enrolled health plan membership reached 7.4 million. The company also established an affiliation with Community Health Plan of Albany, New York, adding 398,000 more members. In the next year, it also entered an affiliation arrangement with Group Health Cooperative of Puget Sound, adding its 670,000 members to its roll. In addition, it purchased part of the assets of Humana Group Health, Inc., in Washington, D.C., and acquired another 117,000 members. These additions brought Kaiser's total membership close to nine million.

Late 1990s and Beyond: Meeting Financial Challenges

It was also in 1997 that the organization took a groundbreaking step when it established a partnership with the AFL-CIO, becoming the first health-care management program to partner management with labor. The partnership was created to improve health-care quality for the plan's members and the communities it served while, at the same time, provide employees with the best possible employment and income security as well as afford them and their unions the opportunity to participate in policy planing and decision making.

However, despite its membership growth, Kaiser Permanente faced some tough problems in 1997. One year after posting a $265 million profit, for the first time in its history it went into the red, recording a loss of $266 million. Its deficits continued in 1998, causing Kaiser, still under the leadership of Dr. Lawrence, to take remedial action. Among other measures, the company sold off its stagnant Texas division to Sierra Health Services, sought projects to cut back in marginal areas or expand in profitable ones, and encouraged belt-tightening efforts throughout its staff. It also hired Dale Crandall from APL Ltd. as its CFO, hoping to tap into his private sector experience as a means to improving operations and profits. In the search for more profitable markets to enter, in 1998 the company also undertook a partnership alliance with Miami-based AvMed Health Plan, thereby gaining a foothold in Florida.

Analysts attributed Kaiser's woes partly to its inexperience in adapting to major changes as well as its rates, which, historically, had been lower than those of its competitors—rates which were no longer covering ballooning healthcare costs. Also, Kaiser had begun a five-year, $2 billion investment in technology, discovering along the way that it was proving far more costly than anticipated. These factors soon forced Kaiser to seek rate increases with some of its large-contract membership groups. In 1998, for example, it sought a 12 percent premium hike for members in CalPERS (California Public Employees' Retirement System), but its request was rejected. Elsewhere, when it did succeed in getting premium increases, the company found that it risked losing contracts to stiffening competition.

In its ongoing assessment of its fiscal condition, Kaiser decided to sell off its North Carolina operations. It announced its attention to do so in 1999 and followed through with its sale in 2000. That same year, the company opted to seek rate increases for its Medicare HMO, Medicare + Choice, to compensate for reductions in federal reimbursements. By 2001,

these measures had helped improve Kaiser's financial condition. In February 2002, the company announced that the Kaiser Foundation Health Plan Inc. and Kaiser Foundation Hospitals and their subsidiaries, for calendar 2001, garnered a net income of $681 million. Membership had also grown to 8.2 million, up 122,000 from the previous year.

In March 2002, Kaiser Permanente announced that it was naming George C. Halvorson as its new chairman and CEO. At the time of his selection, Halvorson was president and CEO of HealthPartners of Minneapolis. He took his post in May. To help in the transition, Lawrence agreed to serve as chairman emeritus and act in an a close advisory relationship with Halvorson through the close of the year.

Principal Subsidiaries

Kaiser Foundation Health Plan (Oakland, California); Kaiser Foundation Health Plan (Denver, Colorado); Kaiser Foundation Health Plan (Atlanta, Georgia); Kaiser Foundation Health Plan (Honolulu, Hawaii); Kaiser Foundation Health Plan (Rockville, Maryland); Kaiser Foundation Health Plan (Cleveland); Kaiser Foundation Health Plan (Portland, Oregon).

Principal Competitors

Aetna; PacifiCare; WellPoint Health Networks.

Further Reading

Bole, Kristen, "Kaiser Expects 'Significant' Losses in '98 Despite Efforts," *Business Journal*, October 26, 1998.

Cole, Benjamin M., "Kaiser Takes a Giant Step Toward Improvement," *Los Angeles Business Journal*, February 10, 1992, p. 30.

"Kaiser Permanente: Its Past, Present, and Future," *Medical Economics*, January 23, 1995, p. 94.

"Kaiser Permanente Names New Health Plan and Hospitals Chairman and CEO; Retiring Chairman and CEO Dr. David M. Lawrence to Stay on through the End of Year," *PR Newswire*, March 7, 2002.

Kirchheimer, Barbara, "Kaiser to Sell Ailing N.C. Health Plan," *Modern Healthcare*, August 23, 1999, p. 20.

Kyle, Lori, "Managed Care Pioneer Kaiser Turns 50," *Business Journal*, October 9, 1995, p. 30.

Rauber, Chris, "Giant HMO Prowling for Acquisitions," *San Francisco Business Times*, September 13, 1996, p. 1.

——, "Kaiser Dumping Five Plans to Cut Costs," *Modern Healthcare*, June 28, 1999, p. 18.

——, "Kaiser Expects Another Growth Spurt," *Business Journal-Portland*, January 30, 1998, p. 3.

——, "Kaiser Introduces New Plan to Boost Growth; HMO Giant Wants to Alter Stodgy Image," *San Francisco Business Times*, October 8, 1993, p. 1.

Robertson, Kathy, "Kaiser Scrambles to Keep up with Whirlwind of Change," *Sacramento Business Journal*, July 7, 1997, p. 3.

Smillie, John G., *Can Physicians Manage the Quality and Costs of Health Care?: The Story of The Permanente Medical Group*, Oakland, Calif.: Permanente Federation, Inc, 2000.

Speizer, Irwin, "(IM) Permanente," *Business North Carolina*, June 1999, p. 36.

"United Health Not First to Put Medical Decision-Making in Hands of Doctors; Kaiser Permanente Did It 50 Years Ago," *Business Wire*, November 9, 1999.

—John W. Fiero

The Lifestyle Company *Kanebo*

Kanebo, Ltd.

20-20 Kaigan 3-chome, Minato-ku
Tokyo 108-8080
Japan
Telephone: (+81) 3-5446-3002
Fax: (+81) 3-5446-3027
Web site: http://www.kanebo.co.jp

Public Company
Founded: 1887
Employees: 14,718
Sales: $4.4 billion (2001)
Stock Exchanges: Nikkei
NAIC: 215620 Toilet Preparation Manufacturing; 313111
    Yarn Spinning Mills; 313210 Broadwoven Fabric
    Mills; 313221 Narrow Fabric Mills; 422210 Drugs
    and Druggist Sundries Wholesalers; 312111 Soft
    Drink Manufacturing; 311330 Confectionary
    Manufacturing from Purchased Chocolate; 311423
    Dried and Dehydrated Food Manufacturing; 311520
    Ice Cream and Frozen Dessert Manufacturing

Kanebo, Ltd. is a conglomeration of businesses dedicated to bringing beauty to daily life through the application of new technologies to cultural and lifestyle preferences. The company produces and distributes premium cosmetics, toiletries, textiles, men's and women's fashion merchandise, and food products. The company distributes prescription and over-the-counter drugs and Chinese medicines. Cosmetics comprise more than one-third of the company's revenue base, with broad distribution throughout Asia and Europe and exclusive sales outlets in the United States. Kanebo offers cosmetics and toiletries under a variety of brands, in accordance with different markets. Kanebo's textiles operations produce threads, filaments, yarns, and fabrics in cotton, silk, wool, nylon, acrylic, and other materials. Fibers include absorbents and nonwovens for commercial uses. Fashion merchandise is produced and distributed for Christian Dior, Jean Lanvin, and other clothing designers. The Foods Division manufactures frozen desserts, nutritional beverages, chewing gum, and instant foods. Kanebo's produc-

tion facilities are located in North and South America, Europe, and along the Pacific Rim, as well as in Japan.

Tokyo Company Grows into International Textiles Concern

Kanebo formed in 1887 as the Tokyo Cotton Trading Company, based in Kanegafuchi, Tokyo. Actual operations, spinning raw cotton into thread, began in 1889. The company adopted an emblem taken from a cross-section drawing of a thread spindle, found in a British report about spinning machinery. The company changed its name in 1893 to Kanegafuchi Spinning Company and instituted a trademark bearing a temple bell and the Kanegafuchi name.

The important milestones of Kanebo's early years included the launch of new operations, such as the weaving of cotton textiles, begun with the completion of the Hyogo plant in 1905. The company then turned to the spinning and marketing of silk, opening a spinning plant in Kyoto in 1908 and a raw silk reeling factory in 1921. The company provided for its employees by establishing the Kanebo Mutual Aid Association in 1905 (now Health Insurance Association) and opening a free medical clinic in Hyogo in 1923. After the 1923 Kanto earthquake destroyed the original plant in Kanegafuchi, the company did not rebuild it.

Kanebo expanded distribution and launched new business ventures during the 1920s and 1930s. International trade began with the establishment of the South American Colonial Company in 1928 and extended to the United States in 1935. Within Japan, the Kanebo Service Company formed in 1931 to manage retail stores throughout the country. In 1934, the company initiated production of woolen yarn, chemical fiber, and flax fiber. Kanebo chemists invented the first Japanese-made synthetic fiber, Kanebian, in 1939. In 1936, the company introduced Kanebo Silk Soap, a premium quality soap containing oils extracted from the chrysalis of the silkworm; Kanebo distributed the product worldwide. The Kanegafuchi Industrial Company formed in 1938 to continue the development of new businesses.

World War II interrupted operations at Kanebo when almost all facilities were destroyed within Japan and overseas in 1945. Kanebo started fresh in 1947 with the institution of a modified

Key Dates:

1889: Cotton thread spinning operations begin at Kanegafuchi.
1905: Kanebo begins to weave cotton fabric.
1908: The company begins to spin silk thread.
1928: South American Colonial Company is formed.
1934: Production of woolen yarn, chemical fiber, and flax fiber begins.
1947: Recovery from the destruction of World War II begins with ''Speed, Service, Saving'' campaign.
1961: Kanebo enters the cosmetics industry.
1964: Kanebo diversifies into the manufacture of fashion merchandise and confectioneries.
1971: The company name is changed to Kanebo, Ltd.
1980: Kanebo Cosmetics Europe joint venture is formed.
1988: Ten Year Management Program to expand the company and its improve operations commences.
1995: Kanebo restructures its operations to adapt to a decline in sales as Japanese economy stagnates.
2000: Kanebo Cosmetics enters the mainland United States market with a store in New York City.
2002: Kanebo Foods Division introduces several beverages for nutrition and weight loss.

company emblem, a new flag, and a company song. Kanebo reestablished operations under the 1949 campaign for ''Speed, Service, Saving,'' which reflected the company's goals as it rebuilt. An employee badge carried three ''S's'' in red, white, and blue along with the company emblem. In 1955, Kanebo restored operations in South America with the formation of Kanebo do Brasil S.A. The Kanebo Comprehensive Research Center, founded in 1958, generated new ideas for business ventures.

Postwar Diversification and Expansion

During the 1960s and 1970s, Kanebo diversified into new areas of business, including cosmetics, clothing, prepared foods, and pharmaceuticals, and expanded into new fields within the textiles industry. In 1961, Kanebo acquired cosmetics manufacturing operations from Kanegafuchi Chemical Industries Company. Kanebo established 14 sales organizations throughout Japan to distribute the premium quality cosmetics. Kanebo established a laboratory in Paris in 1965 and opened a new cosmetics plant in Odawara in 1969. Kanebo began clothing manufacturing activities in 1964 when the company signed a licensing agreement with French fashion designer Christian Dior to produce and distribute men's and women's couture and ready-to-wear apparel in Japan. For Warnaco, Inc., Kanebo began to manufacture and market men's shirts under the Hathaway brand.

Kanebo Haris, Inc., formed in 1964 as a confectionary maker when Kanebo acquired Tachibana Confectionary Company, producer of frozen desserts. Kanebo created new products, such as the popular Chewing Bon gum, and began to produce chocolate. In 1971, Kanebo purchased another frozen dessert maker, Izumi Confectionary, and combined frozen dessert manufacturing into one facility. The acquisition of Watanabe Confectionary Com-

pany expanded Kanebo's product line to instant beans, soups, and rice cakes. The company began to sell the Belmie canned brand of coffee in 1973 and non-fry noodles in 1976. A new chewing gum, Play Gum, was introduced in 1978.

Kanebo expanded operations to accommodate demand for synthetic fibers and chemical materials. A new plant in Hofu began production of nylon in 1963 and polyester filament in 1969. Kanebo produced synthetic leather and acrylic fibers beginning in 1969 and 1970, respectively. Production of polyester expanded to a plant in Hokurika in 1972. New subsidiary companies supported Kanebo's interest in synthetic materials. A 1978 joint venture with Asahi Kasei, the Japan Synthetic Textile Company, addressed rising demand for synthetic materials for absorbents, nonwovens, and other uses. A 1975 joint venture with National Starch Company developed and distributed chemical products with industrial applications, such as adhesives, resins, and specialty chemicals.

With the acquisition of Yamashiro Pharmaceuticals Company in 1966, Kanebo entered into yet another new field of business. The division expanded into traditional herbal medicines with the establishment of a laboratory for product research and development in 1976. Two years later, Kanebo introduced Herbal Extract Tablets, a line of Chinese herbal medicines.

The final area of business diversification transpired in 1977 with the formation of Information Systems. The subsidiary marketed IBM-compatible software for business uses. Sold internationally, the software included applications for accounting, banking, securities, manufacturing, and distribution.

Cosmetics proved to be the most enduring and profitable venture as Kanebo expanded the business internationally in the 1970s. Asian distribution included Thailand, Taiwan, Indonesia, the Philippines, Singapore, and Hong Kong. Kanebo Cosmetics of Hawaii was established in 1975. The company entered the European retail market in 1979 with the introduction of its Lady '80s brand of cosmetics at Harrods of London. Kanebo formed a joint venture, Kanebo Cosmetics Europe, Ltd., with UTC International, establishing marketing operations in Zurich. UTC International, a warehouse group, distributed the cosmetics to 1000 distribution outlets in nine countries: Switzerland, Germany, France, Austria, Finland, Norway, Sweden, Spain, and England. UTC also operated Jelmoli, an upscale department store and natural market for Kanebo cosmetics.

Entering the 1990s with Strong Financial Standing

Kanebo celebrated its centennial anniversary in 1987 amidst economic prosperity in Japan, with strong consumer spending and capital investment. In fiscal year ended March 30, 1989, Kanebo recorded revenues of ¥481.6 billion ($3.6 billion) and net earnings of ¥2.9 billion ($21.5 million). These represented an increase over fiscal 1987–88 of 26.1 percent and 22.7 percent, respectively. Approximately 40 percent of sales originated from the company's fibers operations and approximately 25 percent came from cosmetics. In order of highest sales, fashion, foods, chemicals/materials, and pharmaceuticals comprised the balance.

In order to maintain steady growth, Kanebo developed a long-term strategy to improve operations and increase revenues.

The Ten Year Management Program involved four goals: to develop the fashion and non-textile divisions, particularly the cosmetics division; to continue to generate steady growth in the textiles; to create overall solidity of the organization; and to explore opportunities in new fields of business. The company reorganized its operating divisions to place emphasis on competitiveness in the marketplace based on merchandise, quality, and customer service. The company adopted a new philosophy at this time. ''Art Through Technology'' reflected Kanebo's emphasis on beauty and lifestyle. Kanebo sought to use technology to enhance the beauty of daily living and launched the LIFE Institute to study culture and lifestyle.

In the fashion sector, Kanebo implemented a variety of strategies to increase business activities. The company began to manufacture and distribute footwear and apparel for Fila Holding S.p.A., an Italian fashion house, in 1986. A joint venture with China, established in 1987, initiated operations in Shanghai for the production of hosiery. The facility produced eight million pairs of nylon stockings, about half for the Chinese market and the balance being exported to the United States, Japan, and southeast Asia. Kanebo and Warnaco expanded its licensing agreement to include men's clothing and accessories in traditional American styles, such as suits, sport coats, jackets, sweaters, and belts. Made in Italy for the Japanese market, suits priced at ¥120,000 or $920. The two companies changed the brand name to ''Charles F. Hathaway.'' Also, in 1989 Kanebo purchased 20 percent of Jacqueline de Ribes, a ready-to-war fashion house in Paris.

The company's attention to the cosmetics market involved improvements to customer service and the ability to respond to local trends more quickly. The Chain Store Distinctive Design Plan reorganized the cosmetic sales space and developed sales techniques to correspond with local patterns of consumption at more than 1,600 chain store locations.

Kanebo also addressed increased competition from self-help cosmetic counters. The company identified three kinds of sales outlets: self-selection, recommendation, and ''beauty related.'' New brand development for the self-selection market included the men's NFL line. The recommendation market engaged consultants to assist customers in choosing the right products for their skin. Blush Up Salons sold the Lissage brand at chain stores and charged for beauty services. The beauty related market involved fitness and professional salons where cosmetics were made part of overall appearance.

New products for the European market included Device cosmetics for men, the Tiffa Alga skin care line, and Affinique CN Essence FX Cream, or ''La Crème,'' introduced in 1989. A result of several years of research, the La Crème skin moisturizer incorporated key new ingredients, such as kanzou, a rare Chinese herb used for over 4,000 years, and a new Silk Fibroin Derivative. Marketed at ''the world's most expensive cream,'' the product retailed at £250 in the United Kingdom and FFr2,500 in France for a 40 gram jar. Despite the high price, Kanebo sold 160,000 units immediately and 9,000 units per month afterward.

International expansion of cosmetics distribution involved new markets and expansion within existing markets. Kanebo

Cosmetics Europe established a new plant in 1991. The company focused on West Germany and the United Kingdom for 50 percent sales growth. Kanebo entered the South Korean cosmetics market in 1992. Kanebo's popular fade resistant lipstick, T'Estimo Rouge II, launched in Japan in 1992 with great success, was introduced to Europe, Taiwan, and Thailand in spring 1993.

A third area of capital investment involved the pharmaceuticals division. A ¥1 billion production facility opened in 1989 as the company prepared for expansion in the pharmaceuticals industry. The company reorganized its research and development for prescription drugs into three categories: cardiovascular, dermatological, and immunological. Biomedical research with University of Pittsburgh Medical Center focused on cancer immunology, while Product Design Labs, Inc., a U.S. subsidiary, began clinical tests on an antibody for leukemia. New products in the early 1990s involved drugs developed by other companies. Kanebo acquired rights to distribute Hexalen, an oral anti-cancer agent for advanced ovarian cancer, and for Reslin Tablet, an antidepressant.

The Textiles and Fibers Division expanded through new distribution, increased production, and the introduction of new products. Kanebo began to produce a biodegradable pineapple leaf fiber. The company established a cotton spinning operation with Kanematsu-Gosho Trading Company in Tifton, Georgia, close to raw material and the American consumer market. Kanebo Spinning Company built a new facility which housed machinery with 20,000 spindles. Eastman Chemical Products Company signed an agreement with Kanebo to distribute throughout North America a special kind of colored polyester staple fibers. Kanebo exported its nonwoven Belima X fiber, made of polyester and nylon, for use in production of wipes for polishing eyeglasses.

Activities at the company's other divisions included new products, licensing agreements, and technological collaboration. In 1992, the Toiletries Division obtained exclusive import and sales rights for Claude Montana fragrance and bath line. Limited distribution involved 450 premium cosmetics outlets in Japan. The Foods Division introduced new ice cream products and began to produce and sell Samontana brand ice cream under an agreement with the Italian licensor. The Electronics Division, established in 1985, began to manufacture megabit DRAM (dynamic random access) chips in 1988. In 1991, the division opened an office in Indonesia to market software through a joint venture with Perkom Indah Muni. New technologies and products in the early 1990s included a rechargeable lithium battery developed with Seiko Instruments, a textile printing technology developed with Cannon, a self-crimping hosiery yarn, and a new pigment for cosmetics made of silk coated grains of gold.

After several years of steady growth, executives at Kanebo thought the company was well positioned for sustained growth. The Asian economic crisis unexpectedly changed the situation in Japan, leading the company into losses in fiscal 1992, at ¥6 billion on revenues of ¥681.4 billion. While cosmetics and toiletries sales increased, due to the company's customer service programs, other areas of business reported slower sales. In fiscal 1993–94, revenues declined in all areas of operation.

Kanebo reported sales of ¥418.9 billion and a net loss of ¥3.7 billion. Revenues from cosmetics declined 4.9 percent, while clothing manufacturing declined 19 percent. Synthetic fibers sales declined 19.7 percent and natural fibers declined 29.5 percent. Kanebo reduced its wool production by one-third, nylon filament by 40 percent, and polyester filament by 20 percent. The company reduced its workforce by 2,000 over three years through attrition and limited hiring. Natural and acrylic fiber production operated profitably in 1995, but the depreciated value of the yen required the company to reduce its volume of exports. The devastating Kobe earthquake in January 1995 negatively affected consumer spending in Japan.

Kanebo took several actions to restructure operations for profitability and efficiency. The company terminated its joint venture with National Starch and Chemical Company in 1994 and separated the textiles and fibers division into subsidiary companies in 1996. Kanebo withdrew from the polyester staple business and converted the plant to the production of resins, establishing a new subsidiary. Overseas production lowered overhead, prompting Kanebo to modernize and increase production at its Indonesian spinning and weaving facilities. Through a transfer of stock from UTC, Kanebo took complete control of Kanebo Cosmetics Europe in 1998 to take advantage of its annual 10 percent sales growth. Kanebo sold its pharmaceutical development operations to former collaborator Nippon Organon in 1999 but retained drug distribution operations.

Unrelated to the company's financial challenges, in 1997 Christian Dior discontinued its licensing agreement with Kanebo for the production and distribution of men's apparel, preferring to handle those operations itself. Kanebo continued to manufacture and distribute women's and children's clothing for Christian Dior. The company compensated for the loss when it signed an exclusive agreement to manufacture and distribute a new collection of women's ready-to-wear by Jean Lanvin beginning in spring 1998. The agreement involved importing to Japan a collection by designer Ocimar Versolato, establishing Lanvin collections in Japanese department stores, and opening 13 boutiques specifically for Lanvin fashions.

Recovery in the Late 1990s and 2000s

As Kanebo recovered from financial difficulties, the company renewed its emphasis on cosmetics as a source of revenues, particularly in foreign markets. Kanebo entered the mainland United States cosmetics market for the first time in February 2000. The company opened a store in New York City, selling the Sensai Cellular Performance and Sensai Ex-Bio brands of skin care products as well as Kanebo make-up. Bergdorf Goodman in New York began to sell Kanebo cosmetics the following May. During the first month, the staff sold 35 jars of Sensai Ex La Crème, billed as "a facelift in a jar," at $500 per jar.

Kanebo's Cosmetics Division continuously launched products attuned to the latest trends, applying new cosmetic technology. Almost all of the products in the Make-up Collection contained a silk derivative to prevent the colored pigments from drying the skin. Kanebo Cosmetics sought to attract young career women with medium-priced merchandise; the Aqua brand was set to compete with Shiseido's Aupres line. The Inner Balance line of skin care products for young women used natural ingredients and applied the principles of aromatherapy; Kanebo introduced the line to European outlets in July.

Kanebo sought to increase its market presence in Asian countries, particularly China, Taiwan, and Thailand. Finding women in Thailand to be more concerned with cosmetics than in other places, Kanebo formed a joint venture with Tasin Industrial in Thailand in early 2001 and launched four lines of cosmetics. The Kate line was priced inexpensively to appeal to young women, while It Be Switch was priced higher and displayed behind the sales counter. The company introduced two high end lines, RMK Ramiko and Shic Shoc. Hair-care and body-care products were offered for both men and women.

Kanebo's textiles and fibers subsidiaries applied new technologies to develop products. These included a biodegradable fiber derived from cornstarch and an antibacterial yarn, LivefreshN. In June 1999, Kanebo launched New Supreino, a high-luster cotton fabric which maintained its smooth texture after several washes. Kanebo increased production of the highly water-absorbent Bell Oasis fiber made from a proprietary acrylic polymer. In early 2000, Kanebo Goshen launched a new polyeurethane fabric useful for laminating other fabrics as a moisture-proof film.

Kanebo streamlined operations by selling it chemical and information systems subsidiaries in 2000 and focusing on development of health products. The company purchased over-the-counter and prescription drugs for sale in convenience stores and volume retailers where Kanebo brand cosmetics and toiletries were sold. Kanebo's Foods Division developed nutritional beverages supporting children's growth, eye health, blood pressure control, and weight control. In early 2002, Kanebo launched "diet cosmetics" products after clinical research found that the aroma of raspberry helped the body burn fat and assisted with weight loss. The products included diet supplements and a lotion and competed with Shiseido's grapefruit-based products.

Kanebo expanded distribution of cosmetics in the United States. When Barneys New York unveiled a new cosmetics department in spring 2002, a Kanebo cosmetics counter was included. Under the agreement, Kanebo product sales were to be exclusive for six months before Kanebo sought new outlets on the West Coast and in the Midwest. In addition to the two Sensai brand products, Kanebo introduced a mid-priced line of cosmetics under the brand name Cynthia Rowley. The company planned to launch a new premium cosmetics line by 2005.

Principal Subsidiaries

Kanebo Cosmetics; Kanebo Cosmetics Europe, Ltd.; Kanebo COSMILLION, Ltd.; Kanebo Goshen Spinning Corporation; Kanebo Home Products Company, Ltd.; Kanebo Textiles Company, Ltd.

Principal Divisions

Cosmetics; Fashion; Foods; New Materials; Pharmaceuticals; Textiles.

Principal Competitors

Kao Corporation; Lion Corporation; Shiseido Company, Ltd.

Further Reading

"A Yen for the UK?," *Soap Perfumery & Cosmetics*, November 1991, p. 26.

Aktar, Alev, "Costly Kanebo Makes U.S. Debut," *SalonNews*, August 2000, p. S18.

"Eastman, Kanebo OK pact for Polyester," *WWD*, May 27, 1988, p. 11.

Ergenc, Nadi, "Ciba Signs Inorganic Antimicrobial Deal," *Specialty Chemicals*, June 2001, p. 14.

Furukawa, Tsukasa, "Kanebo Institutes Major Restructuring, Will Cut Nylon, Poly Filament Production," *WWD*, July 26, 1995, p. 12.

——, "Kanebo, Kanematsu-Gosho in Cotton-spinning Venture," *Daily News Record*, January 28, 1988, p. 2.

——, "Kanebo to Open New York Store," *WWD*, February 4, 2000, p. 15.

——, "Warnaco, Japan's Kanebo to Expand License Deal," *Daily News Record*, November 10, 1988, p. 5.

Isaacs III, McAllister, "How Kanebo Spinning Makes Top Quality Yarn," *Textile World*, November 1992, p. 62.

"Jean Lanvin, Kanebo in Japanese venture," *WWD*, February 14, 1997, p. 9.

Larson, Mark, "Small Software Firm Inks Pact with Japanese Outfit; Retail Interact Pursues International Markets," *Business Journal Serving Greater Sacramento*, June 2, 1990, p. 17.

Pagoda, Dianne M., "Two-Day Show Tops off Kanebo's Centennial," *WWD*, July 13, 1987, p. 6.

—Mary Tradii

Klaus Steilmann GmbH & Co. KG

Feldstrasse 4
D-44867 Bochum-Wattenscheid
Germany
Telephone: (49) (2327) 940-0
Fax: (49) (2327) 940-116091
Web site: http://www.steilmann.de

Private Company
Incorporated: 1958
Employees: 12,800
Sales: EUR 550 million ($415 million) (2001)
NAIC: 315234 Women's and Girls' Cut and Sew Suit, Coat, Tailored Jacket, and Skirt Manufacturing; 315212 Women's, Girls', and Infants' Cut and Sew Apparel Contractors; 315222 Men's and Boys' Cut and Sew Suit, Coat, and Overcoat Manufacturing; 315224 Men's and Boys' Cut and Sew Trouser, Slack, and Jean Manufacturing; 315993 Men's and Boys' Neckwear Manufacturing; 315223 Men's and Boys' Cut and Sew Shirt (Except Work Shirt) Manufacturing; 315211 Men's and Boys' Cut and Sew Apparel Contractors; 315999 Other Apparel Accessories and Other Apparel Manufacturing; 448120 Women's Clothing Stores

Klaus Steilmann GmbH & Co. KG is Germany's third largest apparel maker and ranks among the top five in Europe. Steilmann designs and manufactures women's and men's wear under private labels, mainly for leading German clothing wholesalers and retailers. The group's women's wear division, which contributes three-quarters of total sales, includes subsidiaries Apanage, A. Hölscher, Kirsten Modedesign, and Nienhaus & Lotz. Steilmann's menswear is designed and managed by subsidiaries Dressmaster and Cruse Bekleidung. In addition to private label production, Steilmann markets about 20 percent of its products under its own labels, such as KS, Apanage, Swept, Emozioni, and Stones. About one-third of Steilmann's output is manufactured in the company's 52 factories around the world,

mainly in Romania and other eastern European countries. About 45 percent of Steilmann's clothing is sold outside of Germany, mainly in Western and Eastern Europe, but also in North America, Mexico, Japan, and other countries. The Steilmann group operates its own shops and shop-in-shops: 30 Apanage shops in Germany; 75 Julie Guerlande shops in France; and 100 Steilmann shops in eastern Europe. The Steilmann group is owned and managed by the founder's family.

A Leading Apparel Maker in Postwar Germany

Klaus Steilmann, the company founder, was a child of the Great Depression. Born in 1929 into a farmer's family in the small town of Neustrelitz in northeastern Germany, Steilmann dreamed of becoming a lawyer but had to serve in the German army as a young man during World War II and was taken a prisoner of war. A few years after the war, in 1950, he made his entrance into the fashion industry when he met a director of C&A Brenninkmeyer, one of Germany's leading apparel makers, in Berlin, where he started an apprenticeship at the company. In the evening, Steilmann went to school and got his high school diploma in 1951. For the next three years, Klaus Steilmann worked at C&A's purchasing department for women's coats and dress-suits at different locations. In 1955, he moved to the Ruhr where he took a position as assistant director of Josef Meyer, a women's coat manufacturer. However, after working as the boss's right hand for two years, Steilmann decided to strike out on his own. In 1958, he placed a newspaper ad stating that he was looking to buy a small sewing workshop. He finally found what he wanted: a small factory for men's suits with 40 seamstresses in Wattenscheid, near Bochum. In November 1958, Steilmann founded his own company, Klaus Steilmann GmbH & Co. KG, with a start-up capital of DM40,000, and began making coats for women.

Steilmann entered the women's fashion industry at a favorable time. The postwar economic boom in Germany had boosted the purchasing power of German women, whose hunger for coats and dress-suits seemed endless. In its first business year, Steilmann's business generated DM 7.8 million in sales, which placed him among Germany's large coat manufacturers. The company soon expanded its product range to include

Company Perspectives:

We have been the retailer's innovative partner since 1958 and today we are among the top four apparel makers in Europe. Over 22,000 retailers worldwide trust in us. Steilmann stands for an excellent price-performance ratio and for convincing product lines and individual products. The Steilmann group has a leading position in its segment of private label apparel manufacturers. In line with the group's new orientation, we evolved from a product-oriented manufacturer to a marketing-oriented purchasing and service partner. Our new focus extends from the development of strategic partnerships to area management. With our double strategy we, together with our retail partners, are able to quickly and flexibly react to market demands. On one hand, we gather detailed knowledge of our target groups and develop guiding principles around which all company divisions are focused. On the other hand, we trust in the novelty of our creations. We constantly offer new collections and focus on cutting down the time gap between order and delivery. Thirty percent of our products are manufactured in our own plants which—like the plants of our contractors—are operated under the high environmental and social standards specified by Steilmann. Decisive, innovative, and sustainable management is the basis of the group.

women's dress-suits. By 1960, Steilmann's sales had already doubled. Three years later, the company competed with Germany's market leaders in women's wear.

Right from the beginning, Klaus Steilmann worked on distinguishing himself from other competitors. His company created fashion with a mass appeal that attracted large customers such as fashion retailers C&A and Peek & Cloppenburg, as well as Germany's leading department stores. The company's attitude was summed up by Steilmann's slogan "fashion for millions—not just for millionaires." In addition, Steilmann offered his clients another special service. The way the fashion industry used to work was that, at certain predetermined times of the year, fashion retailers were able to order the textile manufacturers' latest collections for the upcoming season at fashion tradeshows. This system was somewhat stiff and clearly favored the manufacturers. If consumer demand was weaker or stronger than expected, or if the weather did not cooperate, fashion stores did not usually have a way to adjust to such circumstances. Steilmann customers, by contrast, were able to place additional orders and receive their merchandise shortly thereafter.

Continued Growth in the 1970s–80s

The 1970s marked the end of the postwar era in Germany and brought major changes for the fashion industry. On one hand, cars and new household appliances, such as washing machines and TV sets, started competing for consumer cash. Despite the fact that those goods were significant expenses for German households, their popularity was on the rise. As a side effect of this new pattern of consumer spending, people started cutting back on expensive clothing, including coats and dress-suits. On the other hand, people's lifestyles became somewhat less formal in everyday life, compared with the previous era,

which showed in a growing demand for more casual clothing. Skirts, pants, and blouses replaced the dress-suit; jackets replaced the coat.

Steilmann expanded its product range to include these new items and ventured into men's wear through a series of acquisitions. In 1970, Steilmann acquired Herne-based men's wear maker Dressmaster, a company that offered a whole range of men's fashions from casual to formal, and operated the company both as a contractor and as a producer of its established Stones clothing line. Two years later, Steilmann added Gelsenkirchen-based firm Nienhaus & Luig belchic GmbH & Co. KG, a manufacturer specializing in trendy dresses and combinations for young women, to its women's wear division. The new subsidiary, which marketed its products under the labels Lisa Marlén and Emozioni, was later renamed Nienhaus & Lotz GmbH. With the acquisition of men's fashion manufacturer Cruse Bekleidung GmbH & Co. KG in 1981, Steilmann further strengthened its men's wear arm. In 1988, the company entered a joint venture with German Chanél couturist Karl Lagerfeld to create and market the designer collection KL by Karl Lagerfeld, a high-fashion line with a broader appeal.

Klaus Steilmann's enterprise became one of Germany's largest apparel manufacturers. The company's creations were in such high demand at the regular fashion trade shows that Steilmann's sales representatives had to set up more and more ordering tables; they even took orders standing when there were not enough tables to seat all the eager-to-order visitors. In addition to the company's strong domestic growth, Steilmann expanded internationally, tackling new markets in western and eastern Europe. By the end of the 1980s, the company was present in the world's major markets, including the United States and Canada, Japan, Australia and Mexico.

Struggling Against New Market Forces in the 1990s

Up until the 1990s, Steilmann had not encountered any major setbacks on its way to becoming Germany's largest women's wear manufacturer and a major player in the European apparel industry. However, beginning in the 1970s and continuing into the 1980s, the progressive movement toward globalization changed the fashion industry forever. Large clothing retailers—looking for ways to cut cost—started ordering their merchandise from the sewing factories sprouting up all over eastern Asia. This move was made possible by the changing taste of consumers who preferred more and more casual wear. While women's dresses, dress-suits, and coats required sophisticated manufacturing techniques, the more casual skirts, blouses, and pants could be made with less know-how—and for much less money. Consequently, Germany's clothing retailers started bypassing their own garment makers, and their Asian contractors copied the latest European fashion styles.

Steilmann was not among the many German clothing manufacturers going out of business during that time. However, the company's profit margins began to shrink and its market position in relation to its customers began to weaken. The big department stores and clothing retailers were not willing anymore to pay premium prices for fashions "Made in Germany," while the average German consumer preferred a more varied wardrobe of a lesser quality over only a few very expensive

---

Key Dates:

1958: Klaus Steilmann sets up his own women's coat manufacturing company.
1970: Steilmann acquires Herne-based men's wear manufacturer Dressmaster.
1972: The company buys women's fashion maker Nienhaus & Luig belchic.
1981: Steilmann takes over men's wear producer Cruse Bekleidung.
1999: Former Hugo Boss executive Joachim Vogt becomes Steilmann's CEO.
2001: Britta Steilmann returns and takes over the leadership of the family business.

---

pieces of exceptional quality. Some German apparel makers began early on to move their production abroad. Convinced that moving production facilities outside the country would weaken the purchasing power of Germany's consumers and therefore the country's economy in the long run, Klaus Steilmann waited a long time before following suit. However, at the beginning of the 1990s market pressures became so severe that his company had to quickly adjust its business policy in order to survive.

By that time, Steilmann consisted of more than 30 subsidiaries. In 1992, the firm closed four of its German production sites and cut its domestic workforce by 17 percent. In 1992, for the first time in the company's history, Steilmann reported shrinking sales and shrinking profits. Despite measures to keep down cost, industry overcapacities, unfavorable exchange rates, and the weakening domestic demand contributed to the recessive market environment in which Steilmann found itself in the mid-1990s. Unlike many competitors that moved their manufacturing to Asia, Steilmann focused its international activities on eastern Europe after the breakup of the Soviet Union had opened the Iron Curtain. Klaus Steilmann explored the countries east of Germany and found a sophisticated fashion industry and skilled workforce in Russia, where he could employ three dozen Russian workers for the cost of one of his German workers. By 1995, the number of domestic Steilmann subsidiaries had been cut almost by half, from 40 down to 22. The company invested in three new production sites in Romania and used a number of other foreign sub-contractors. In 1970, 70 percent of Steilmann's output was manufactured in Germany. Twenty-five years later this percentage had gone down to 18 percent. By the end of the 1990s, only two production plants remained in Germany, and these contributed less than 2 percent to Steilmann's total output.

Shakeups and Strategies in the 1990s and Beyond

In June 1994, company founder Klaus Steilmann turned 65. Although his two eldest daughters, Britta and Ute, as well as his wife Ingrid, worked at the company in leading positions, he had not yet decided yet who would become his successor. A possible candidate, the long-time chair of Steilmann's advisory board Lothar Wackerbeck, who worked for Deutsche Bank, had switched to Steilmann in January 1993 to learn the nuts and bolts of apparel manufacturing. But before his retirement, Klaus

Steilmann wanted to resolve the problems with which his company was struggling. After sales had dropped by another 8 percent in 1994, Steilmann merged the management of several divisions and organized them under the group holding company Britta GmbH as independent profit centers. Wackerbeck left the firm—Steilmann obviously needed an industry expert and experienced salesman more than it did a banker—and Franz Konrad, a long-time Steilmann manager who had left the company in 1984, joined Klaus Steilmann at the top of the firm's management.

In the following years, Steilmann enacted several cost-cutting measures. It closed down more of its domestic production facilities, including women's coat and suit maker Heitmann; discontinued unprofitable activities, such as the company's cooperation with top designer Karl Lagerfeld; and focused on listening more to its customers. The company started setting up a number of its own outlets around the world and launched men's wear under the Stones label in the United States. Steilmann also invested in the eco-collection "It's One World"—an initiative of Klaus Steilmann's oldest daughter Britta to introduce environmentally sustainable technologies and products. In addition, the company ventured into corporate uniform manufacturing, which was added as a new profit center, and launched the business collection Klaus Steilmann Men.

After Steilmann's 40th anniversary in 1998, the company reported that sales were going up again. Klaus Steilmann's three daughters and his wife were now more actively involved in the family business. His oldest daughter, Britta, managed the group's export and retail business, while his second oldest daughter, Ute, was responsible for the company's skirt division. At the same time, his wife Ingrid led the advertising, marketing, and personnel departments, and his youngest daughter Cornelia worked as an executive assistant. It seemed to be just a matter of time until Klaus Steilmann would hand over the reins to his daughters, who were also members of the company's advisory board. However, the rest of the family was not willing to back Britta Steilmann's strategic vision to shift the company's main focus from inexpensive private label mass production to a marketing and design oriented manufacturer of higher-priced brand name collections. In January 1999, Britta Steilmann left the family business and set up her own consulting firm.

After Britta Steilmann's departure, Klaus Steilmann started looking for an alternative way to secure the future of his enterprise. In September 1999, about three months after Klaus Steilmann had turned 70, the company announced the appointment of Joachim Vogt, the former CEO of Germany's leading men's wear manufacturer Hugo Boss AG, as Steilmann's successor. Vogt's job was to reorganize the company under a management holding run by managers from outside the family and to boost Steilmann's revenues and profits to make the company fit for a possible initial public offering within five years. Vogt closed down five German production facilities, reducing Steilman's domestic workforce by one-fifth. He also reduced the company's workforce abroad by almost one-third and cut down the number of contractors. During Vogt's two-year tenure, sales dropped by roughly 20 percent. While Vogt maintained that profits had gone up at the same time, the Steilmann family was not happy with his work and with the fact that profits were down to less than 1 percent of sales.

To everyone's surprise, Steilmann announced in mid-2001 that Britta Steilmann would take over as the company's new CEO. After studying fashion, design, and marketing in New York, Paris, and Montreal, Britta Steilmann had joined the family business in her early twenties. Starting out as a marketing and product manager, she soon developed a special interest in environmentally sustainable fashion design, resulting in the launch of her first eco-collection in 1992, which brought her into the public eye. She then became responsible for Steilmann's environmental department, and in the second half of the 1990s joined the company's top management, heading Steilmann's foreign subsidiaries as well as its retail and public relations activities. Joining the ranks of her father's enterprise again after her short stint as a strategic consultant for Internet start-ups, she seemed to be well suited to lead the Steilmann group into a new era. In fall 2001, the company introduced Steilmann's new executive management team: Britta Steilmann, responsible for group strategy; her sister Ute, responsible for design and production; former Nike-manager Jürgen Schlebrowski, responsible for distribution; and CFO Julian Deutz, a former Bertelsmann manager. In 2001, the 36-year-old Britta Steilmann said that her plans to sell more Steilmann fashion in Steilmann shops under Steilmann labels had to wait until the company's profits returned to a satisfactory level. For the next few years, Steilmann would continue making "fashion for millions—not just for millionaires."

Principal Subsidiaries

Apanage GmbH & Co. KG; A. Hölscher GmbH; Kirsten Modedesign GmbH & Co. KG; Nienhaus & Lotz GmbH; Dressmaster GmbH; Cruse Bekleidung GmbH & Co. KG; Steilmann Osteuropa GmbH & Co. KG; Steilmann Bukarest SRL (Romania).

Principal Competitors

Hugo Boss AG; H&M Hennes & Mauritz AB; Escada AG; Benetton SpA; Gardeur AG; Esprit Europe GmbH.

Further Reading

"Britta Steilmann geht," *Frankfurter Allgemeine Zeitung*, January 20, 1999, p. 16.

"Britta Steilmann kehrt ins Familienunternehmen zurück," *Frankfurter Allgemeine Zeitung*, August 21, 2001, p. 19.

"Britta Steilmann verlässt das Unternehmen," *TextilWirtschaft*, January 19, 1999, p. 10.

Buchhorn, Eva, "Was macht eigentlich Britta Steilmann?," *manager magazin*, December 1, 2000.

"Cruse startet mit Klaus Steilmann Men," December 3, 1998, p. 10.

"Der Export wächst wieder," *TextilWirtschaft*, July 16, 1996, p. 148.

Garding, Christoph, "Karriereknick," *Focus Magazin*, October 30, 1993, p. 202.

Jaspert, Werner, "Die Rückkehr der Britta Steilmann," *Süddeutsche Zeitung*, August 21, 2001, p. 25.

Kehrl, Helmut, "Verschobene Gewichte," *TextilWirtschaft*, October 10, 1996, p. 262.

"Klaus Steilmann, Konzernchef der Steilmann-Gruppe," *HORIZONT*, July 1, 1994, p. 50.

"Klaus Steilmann wird 70 Jahre," *TextilWirtschaft*, June 10, 1999, p. 65.

Koch, Brigitte, "Bei Steilmann treten die Töchter in die Fusstapfen des Vaters," *Frankfurter Allgemeine Zeitung*, April 18, 1995, p. 19.

Meck, Georg, "In Porträt: Britta Steilmann," *Frankfurter Allgemeine Sonntagszeitung*, January 13, 2002, p. 42.

"New Chief for Steilmann," *WWD*, August 28, 2001, p. 4.

Ott, Martin, "Britta Steilmann löst Joachim Voigt ab," *TextilWirtschaft*, August 23, 2001, p. 6.

——, "Britta Steilmann hat Führung neu formiert," *TextilWirtschaft*, September 6, 2001, p. 6.

——, "Steilmann: 'Wende erst im nächsten Jahr'," *TextilWirtschaft*, November 1, 2001, p. 6.

"Steilmann Group Reports Sales Down 2.8% for 1996," *WWD*, March 12, 1997, p. 24.

"Steilmann to End KL License Pact with Lagerfeld," *WWD*, November 9, 1995, p. 2.

Weber, Stefan, "Klaus Steilmann geht Joachim Vogt kommt," *Süddeutsche Zeitung*, September 24, 1999, p. 25.

——, "Britta Steilmann steckt nach ihrer Rückkehr hohe Ziele," *Süddeutsche Zeitung*, November 8, 2001, p. 28.

—Evelyn Hauser

Kleiner, Perkins, Caufield & Byers

2750 Sand Hill Road
Menlo Park, California 94025
U.S.A.
Telephone: (650) 233-2750
Fax: (650) 233-0300
Web site: http://www.kpcb.com

Private Company
Incorporated: 1972
Employees: 60
Total Assets: $37 million (2001 est.)
NAIC: 52391 Miscellaneous Intermediation

Kleiner, Perkins, Caufield & Byers is a leading Silicon Valley venture capital (VC) firm. Partner John Doerr told the *Washington Post* in 1990, "We don't just try to launch successful companies. We try to launch successful industries." The firm reckons that the hundreds of companies it has backed—including such household names as Sun Microsystems, Compaq Computer Corp., Lotus, Netscape Communications Corp., America Online Inc., and amazon.com—have a combined market cap of about $650 billion and have created 250,000 new jobs. KPCB's involvement with companies goes further than writing checks. The firm's partners assemble management teams and often sit on boards of the companies they sponsor. An informal version of the Japanese "keiretsu" system encourages resource sharing and deal making among KP-backed companies.

Origins

Thomas J. Perkins studied engineering at MIT and picked up an MBA at Harvard. He began his career at Hewlett-Packard Co., eventually being picked to lead its new computer division in 1965. At the same time, he was starting a small company to build a low-cost laser he designed. It eventually merged with Spectra-Physics. This deal inspired his career in venture capital.

Perkins called on San Francisco investment banker Sanford R. Robertson for advice. Through Robertson, Perkins met his first partner, Eugene Kleiner, one of the founders of Fairchild Semiconductor, the hugely successful Silicon Valley chipmaker.

Kleiner Perkins, as the firm was called, raised $8 million for the first fund. It would average a 41.5 percent return over ten years. The $1.6 million the firm invested in Tandem Computers Inc. in 1975 was worth $203.4 million in 1982. Genentech was an even better investment, with a return of 200 to 1 in two years.

However, eight of the 18 investments were considered losers. One of these, Advanced Recreation Equipment Corp., was launching a combination snowmobile-motorcycle in time for the Arab oil embargo, which crushed the off-road market. Losses in a tennis shoe resoling company and a waste treatment company proved the company's expertise lay in high tech.

The second fund, set up in 1978 with $15 million, would grow at a compound rate of 99.3 percent in its first five years. A subsequent $55 million fund launched in 1980 grew at a compound rate of 62.3 percent in its first three years.

To achieve these kinds of returns, Kleiner Perkins got involved in ventures at their earliest stages. The firm worked closely with the scientists, engineers, and entrepreneurs who founded them. Perkins later told the *New York Times* his two criteria for investment. One was insight into an emerging new market. The other was a competitive advantage through technology.

Next, KP methodically tried to eliminate risk in all areas of the venture: technological risk, financial risk, operating risk, and market risk. In its first decade, Kleiner Perkins invested in about 50 companies, mostly high-tech Silicon Valley start-ups, through three funds totaling $78 million. These funds were reportedly averaging annual returns of 50 percent.

Setting a Record in 1982

In 1982, Morgan Stanley & Co. teamed with KP to raise $150 million for what was then the largest venture fund ever assembled, according to *Business Week*. The deal broadened KP's already considerable fund-raising ability, while allowing Morgan Stanley an inside track on high tech companies as they matured into sizeable enterprises.

Company Perspectives:

Kleiner, Perkins, Caufield & Byers is committed to helping entrepreneurs build sustainable technology businesses. For nearly 30 years, we have invested in hundreds of market-defining ventures that have resulted in the creation of over 250,000 new jobs, over $100 billion in new revenue, and over $650 billion in market capitalization. We're constantly on the look out for ideas with the promise to invent new business categories or radically alter existing ones. Our focus is on new technologies and new applications of technology that will drive high-impact change. Along with technology, the greatest assets businesses have are talented people That's why our partners put all of our efforts behind strong entrepreneurs who turn concepts into companies. We help make things happen. We know that it takes more than solid financial support to getting a company off the ground. We've long recognized that collective strength and experience are essential to building a business. We pioneered the idea 20 years ago of bringing the businesses we work with into an informal network, which we call a Keiretsu. Entrepreneurs gain access to our unmatched portfolio of companies and associations with global business leaders. These relationships are the foundations for strategic alliances, partnership opportunities, and the sharing of insights to help build new ventures faster, broader, and with less risk.

Kleiner stepped down from an active role in the firm in 1982. By the early 1980s, Kleiner, Perkins, Caufield & Byers, as the firm was then called, had expanded to five partners, including Frank J. Caufield, a former U.S. Army intelligence officer, and Brook H. Byers, an expert in electronic and medical technology with a degree from Georgia Tech. Two other former partners, James G. Treybig and Robert A. Swanson, left to lead the companies they founded, Tandem and Genentech, respectively.

L. John Doerr and James P. Lally joined the firm from Intel Corp. Doerr, who had been a top sales rep at Intel, would back some of KPCB's biggest deals, including Sun Microsystems, Cypress Semiconductor, Compaq, and Lotus Development. Investments could only be made through a consensus of all of the partners.

The venture capital business had changed in the 1980s. Money had flooded into Silicon Valley, hoping to cash in on the new technology of computers. Young MBA's earning colossal starting salaries at investment banks would become a symbol of the decade's lust for deal making.

One of KPCB's more notorious investments of the decade was in Go Corporation, whose purpose was developing a pen-operated computer. The company collapsed after spending six years and $75 million on the project. This did not slow down KPCB. KPCB VI, the firm's sixth fund, raised $173 million in 1992; it would return $878 million in the next ten years.

KPCB started a ''CEO-in-residence'' program in 1993 with William Campbell, formerly head of Go, which had just been sold off to AT&T. He was later picked to lead Intuit, the maker of Quicken accounting software.

1995: Year of the IPO

Investors of all stripes had a good year in 1995, and Kleiner Perkins was on top of the VC pile as numerous tech companies had their initial public offerings. Kleiner Perkins had stakes in 13 companies that went public in 1995; these holdings were valued at $1.1 billion at the end of the year. KP's 13.3 percent share of Netscape Communications, acquired for $5 million, was worth $455 million by the end of the year.

KPCB had added an office in Palo Alto, California, a couple of years earlier, and in 1996 moved to a ski lodge-styled building on Sand Hill Road in the pricey San Jose suburb of Menlo Park. This neighborhood was ground zero for Silicon Valley venture capital.

By this time, Kleiner Perkins was considered the blue chip among its peers in the valley and John Doerr, the grandmaster of the game. The firm was reviewing 2,000 business plans every year, though it only funded 1 percent of them. The percentage of profits its general partners pulled from its funds, 30 percent, was the highest carry charge in the business. KPCB still had a reputation for being very selective of its clients, or limited partners, who were mostly large foundations and wealthy individuals. The firm could afford to be. KPCB invested $8 million in amazon.com in 1996; this stake was worth $60 million at the time of the company's 1997 initial public offering and peaked at $113 a share in 1999.

A number of outstanding optical networking deals were made in 1999, most backed by Vinod Khosla, the Indian-born co-founder and former CEO of Sun Microsystems Inc. who had joined Kleiner Perkins in 1986. Cisco Systems acquired Cerent Corporation for $7.3 billion in stock, the highest price ever fetched by a privately owned technology company. Redback Networks acquired Siara Systems for $4.3 billion in stock. Juniper Networks, a maker of routers for fiber optic networks, went public in June 1999; its shares rose 900 percent in the next six months.

The Bubble Bursts in 2000

After a couple of years of enormous, some would say irrational, valuations for Internet companies, the dot-com bubble burst in the spring of 2000. In June 2000, Webvan Group Inc. acquired KP company Homegrocer.com for $1.2 billion—all of it in soon-to-be worthless stock. There were also companies in the portfolio that, though their share prices crashed precipitously when the Internet bubble burst, were still profitable for KPCB due to the very low prices it was able to obtain by getting in during the very earliest stages. These included Handspring and WebMD.

Though it was becoming more difficult to lure top executive talent into start-ups, KPCL was able to attract Ray Lane, former president of software giant Oracle, who became a general partner at Kleiner Perkins in August 2000.

Venture Capital Journal reported that the number of U.S. venture-backed IPO's fell from 229 to 37 between 2000 and 2001. It was becoming more difficult for firms to find promising investments. In 2002, KPCB reduced the size of its tenth fund from $627.5 million to about $471 million. There was too much money chasing and not enough deals, reported industry journals.

Key Dates:

1972: Thomas Perkins and Eugene Kleiner start first fund for their venture capital firm.
1982: Morgan Stanley & Co. joins Kleiner Perkins in creating a record-setting $150 million fund.
1995: Public trading of several KP companies values its holdings at $1 billion.
1999: Optical networking IPO's fetch billions.
2000: KPCB partners in starting a short-lived London office.
2002: KP Keiretsu-generated Excite@Home broadband provider files for bankruptcy.

KPCB appeared to be taking a beating in the communications sector. "Never before has the firm had such a spectacular string of flameouts," wrote *Venture Capital Journal* of KPCB's broadband investments in 2002. Excite@Home was one of KPCB's biggest flops. It was formed from two KPCB portfolio companies, the Internet portal Excite and broadband access provider @Home. Once valued in the billions, the company was bankrupt by 2002. Its chairman, Tom Jermoluk, had joined KPCB as a general partner in May 2000.

The start-up of a London office in 2000 was also something of a misadventure. Launched in conjunction with management consultants Bain & Co. and private equity firm Texas Pacific Partners, Evolution Global Partners was to develop e-commerce companies in partnership with multinational corporations; however, by November 2001 it had terminated most of its employees and relocated to Silicon Valley.

In 2002, Kleiner Perkins was named as a defendant in a class action lawsuit related to the Martha Stewart Living Omnimedia (MSLO)/ImClone affair. The suit alleged Kleiner Perkins and others dumped MSLO stock just before news broke of insider-trading allegations against Martha Stewart.

Principal Competitors

Accel Partners; Benchmark Capital; Hummer Winblad Venture Partners; Menlo Ventures; Redpoint Venture Parters; Sequoia Capital.

Further Reading

Akin, David, "The Shoguns Who Are Set to Shape the New Wired World: Enter the Keiretsu," *National Post,* January 12, 2000, p. C2.

Aragon, Lawrence, and Dan Primack, "Kleiner Perkins Joins Growing Movement to Trim Fund Size," *Private Equity Week,* March 25, 2002.

——, "Downsizing Hits Kleiner Perkins: Famed VC Tells LPs It Will Call Down 20% to 25% Less Cash in Latest Fund," *Investment Dealers' Digest,* March 25, 2002, pp. 10–11.

Bransten, Lisa, "Search for Talent Pits Recruiter Against a Venture-Capital Firm," *Wall Street Journal,* August 14, 2000, p. B8.

Calvey, Mark, and Jim Gardner, "Doerr's Venture Outlook," *Business Journal-Portland,* January 12, 2001, p. 7.

Campbell, Katherine, "Entry Is by Invitation Only: This Small and Tightly Knit Partnership Remains Committed to the Valley," *Financial Times* (London), September 13, 2000, p. 3.

Chinwala, Yasmine, "US Venture Capital Firm Named in Martha Stewart Suit," *efinancialnews.com,* August 22, 2002.

Chira, Susan, "Talking Business with Perkins of Kleiner Perkins," *New York Times,* August 28, 1984, p. D2.

Edwards, Owen, "ASAP Legends: Thomas Perkins," *Forbes,* ASAP Supp., August 26, 1996, p. 82.

Foremski, Tom, "Lane Joins Kleiner Perkins," *Financial Times* (London), Companies & Finance: The Americas, August 24, 2000, p. 15.

"The Godfather of Broadband," *Fortune,* January 24, 2000, p. 108.

Holson, Laura M., "A Capitalist Venturing in the World of Computers and Religion," *New York Times,* January 3, 2000, p. C1.

Moukhieber, Zina, "Kleiner's Web," *Forbes,* March 25, 1996, p. 40.

Peltz, Michael, "High Tech's Premier Venture Capitalist," *Institutional Investor,* June 1996, p. 89.

Pham, Alex, "Technology & Innovation from the Valley: They're Ahead of Their Time on Funding," *Boston Globe,* March 27, 2000, p. C2.

Primack, Dan, and Lawrence Aragon, "The Big Squeeze: After Expanding for Seven Years, the Venture Industry Had to Contract. But the Pain Is More Intense Than Even Veteran VCs Expected," *Venture Capital Journal,* May 1, 2002.

Privett, Cyndi, "Kleiner Raises $150 Million," *The Business Journal,* May 19, 1986, p. 6.

Rutter, Nancy, "Fastest VC in the West," *Forbes,* October 25, 1993, p. 105.

Schrage, Michael, "US Company Encourages Firm Relationships, Japanese-Style," *Washington Post,* March 9, 1990, p. G3.

Sinton, Peter, "Venture Capital Firms Hit Pay Dirt with Stock Offerings," *San Francisco Chronicle,* Bus. Sec., March 18, 1996, p. B3.

Stein, Tom, "Keiretsu Comedown: Kleiner Perkins Learns That Not Everything from Japan Works Right Out of the Box," *Venture Capital Journal,* April 1, 2002, pp. 32–7.

Taylor, Roger, "Silicon Valley's Idea Man," *National Post,* July 26, 1999, p. C12.

Tully, Shawn, "How to Make $400,000,000 in Just One Minute . . ." *Fortune,* May 27, 1996, p. 84.

Veverka, Mark, "Pied Piper of the 'Net'," *Barron's,* June 10, 2002, pp. 19–22.

Wilson, Jack, *The New Venturers: Inside the High-Stakes World of Venture Capital,* Reading, Mass.: Addison Wesley, 1985.

—Frederick C. Ingram

Kuehne & Nagel International AG

P.O. Box 67
CH-8834 Schindellegi
Switzerland
Telephone: (01) 786 9511
Fax: (01) 786 9595
Web site: http://www.kuehne-nagel.com

Public Company
Incorporated: 1890 as Kühne & Nagel, Bremen
Employees: 17,500
Sales: SFr 8.4 billion ($6.1 billion) (2001)
Stock Exchanges: Swiss
Ticker Symbol: KNIN
NAIC: 493110 General Warehousing and Storage;
484121 General Freight Trucking, Long-Distance,
Truckload; 483211 Inland Water Freight
Transportation; 481112 Scheduled Freight Air
Transportation; 541614 Process, Physical Distribution,
and Logistics Consulting Services

Kuehne & Nagel International AG (KN) operates as a leading transport and logistics concern with more than 600 locations in 94 countries. The company's international forwarding unit includes sea and airfreight, international overland, and rail business segments. KN also acts as a major contract logistics firm offering a wide range of warehousing and distribution services, as well as specialized defense and airport logistic services. Third-generation family member Klaus-Michael Kuehne owns 55.75 percent of KN and acts as president and delegate of the firm's board of directors. In 2000, KN entered an alliance with Singapore-based SembCorp Logistics Ltd., gaining a foothold in the Asia-Pacific region. As a result of the deal, SembCorp took a 20 percent stake in KN. The group is known as both Kühne & Nagel and Kuehne & Nagel, depending on language and country. In German-speaking countries, France, and Turkey, the company is referred to as Kühne & Nagel. In all other languages, however, the ü has been replace with ue.

Early History: Late 1800s–Early 1900s

August Kühne, the son of a forester, was born in 1855. He had intended to study law, but when his father could not afford to fund his studies, he began an apprenticeship with L.G. Dyes & Co., a Bremen import and export company. He completed his apprenticeship but was laid off during the economic slump of the mid-1870s. After a while he began work as a shipping clerk with Fr. Naumann, a forwarding company in Bremen. He rose to be a partner in the firm and became engaged to Naumann's daughter. She died before the wedding and August later fell out with Naumann. In 1890 he left Naumann's company to set up his own business.

Friedrich Nagel, who was born in 1864, was a shipping agent at Fr. Naumann. August Kühne persuaded Nagel to join him as a business partner. They scraped together their working capital of just 30,000 marks, and placed an advertisement in the *Bremen Nachrichten,* the local newspaper, on July 1, 1890. The advertisement announced that "a forwarding and commissioning agency under the name of Kühne & Nagel has been established here and in Bremerhaven."

Initially KN went into business as a forwarder of glassware and cotton. An essential part of the activities of a forwarding agent is pooling services, the grouping together of consignments from several customers to form one full load, to be transported to the same destination. The risk is that railway cars must sometimes travel half full to meet deadlines. KN kept to schedules, absorbing extra costs itself, and the clients' confidence was won. At the same time, the firm established warehouses for brand-name merchandise.

During the final years of the 19th century, sugar was a main German export commodity. When the Weser River, along which much sugar was shipped to England, froze up, August Kühne sensed an opportunity for more business. He convinced the managers of large sugar refineries in Hamburg that the problem could be solved by his forwarding firm. KN routed the sugar during the winter months by rail to Bremen, where it was transferred to ocean-going ships.

Before long the firm's activities included general export and import shipping, and specialization in expert handling, sam-

Company Perspectives:

The Kuehne & Nagel Group's strategy of providing high value integrated logistics services will be of decisive importance to the future development of the company. The trend towards outsourcing logistics services continues. Intensified cost pressure in international competition is forcing companies in trade and industry to concentrate on their core competence. The demand for logistics services from a single source and a "Lead Logistics Provider," able to generate savings potential and increased efficiency by management, coordination and optimization of the global supply chain is growing. For Kuehne & Nagel this represents a new and highly promising business potential.

pling and testing of cotton, grain, lumber, feedstuff, and sugar. Added to this were pooling services or consolidations, general warehousing, and distribution warehouses for the ever-increasing volume of brand-name merchandise.

When it became apparent the firm needed a branch in Hamburg, its foundation was entrusted to Adolf Maass, a former apprentice with the firm who had become manager of the glass transport department. Maass founded the Hamburg office at Groningerstrasse in February 1902. The branch developed rapidly, and transport by water along the Elbe River began to flourish. In 1910 Adolf Maass became a partner in KN.

In 1907 Friedrich Nagel died, and August Kühne took over his shares in the business. Although no member of the Nagel family has been involved with the firm since Friedrich's death, Kühne & Nagel had already become an established name among freight forwarders, and so Nagel's name has been retained in the company's title.

August Kühne's thoughts turned to a successor. His eldest son had died, and two other sons had expressed no interest in joining the business. One son, Alfred, however, decided to forego training as an artist, and in 1910 began an apprenticeship in the Hamburg branch. After two years, Alfred Kühne continued his apprenticeship in Bremen, working in all the main departments, under the supervision of his father.

In 1909 August Kühne acquired the von Kapff Mansion near the Weser Bridge in Bremen, where he had worked as an apprentice. He converted the building into his company's headquarters, and it was still the site of KN's German head office in the early 1990s.

In the years before World War I the business flourished. Both the Bremen and Hamburg branches were efficient and profitable, employing 50 people between them. Bremerhaven had warehousing facilities, just like Bremen; there were representatives of the firm in Lübeck and Leipzig, and in 1913 an office was opened in Berlin, the capital of imperial Germany.

Finding Opportunity in the 1920s

The outbreak of World War I in August 1914 brought business to a near-standstill, however. Most overseas connec-

tions were cut immediately. Many employees were called up for military service, while others volunteered, including Alfred Kühne, his younger brother Werner, and Adolf Maass. August Kühne tried to keep the business going, but the total naval blockage of 1915 put an end to the last ocean connections that had been sustained with a few neutral states. By the end of the war in 1918, German merchant ships had all but disappeared from the seas. All cargo ships had to be surrendered to the victorious powers and operated under foreign flags. German offices, warehouses, and seaports were undamaged, however. Whereas before the war KN had engaged mainly in transporting imported merchandise, now the firm handled increasing amounts of exports.

Alfred Kühne, who had spent some time arranging sea freight forwarding in Rotterdam, returned to his father's company in 1921. At the same time, his brother Werner also joined the Bremen office. In the autumn of 1921 they both moved to Hamburg.

In the early 1920s KN took over another company, Johs. Weber & Freund, which brought in more business in the field of imports as well as in the pooling service. A joint venture with a Prague forwarding agent, the Europäische Transport-gesellschaft, increased dealings with Czechoslovakia.

The rapid devaluation of the German mark in 1923 brought havoc to German businesses. The Hamburg branch of KN was weakened by the departure of five head clerks who set up in business on their own and persuaded other clerks to join them. Even Adolf Maass, manager of the Hamburg branch, thought of leaving. Alfred and Werner Kühne, aged 28 and 25, respectively, persuaded their father to let them run the Hamburg office. Alfred took over the import department, Werner the export department, and Adolf Maass remained, running the bulk cargo and grain departments as well as the business with Czechoslovakia.

Alfred Kühne wanted to extend the existing special services handling raw materials. He established services for cocoa and leather products and developed the firm's business with Switzerland and Austria, also venturing into the Balkan countries. Werner Kühne expanded the export department, setting up services to England, South America, the United States, and Canada. He traveled abroad a great deal, creating a network of foreign representatives.

In 1924 a branch was opened in Lübeck to handle traffic in the Baltic sea. Additional domestic representative offices were opened in Cottbus, Magdeburg, Gera, Erfurt, Frankfurt, Braunschweig, Hanover, and Stuttgart. In 1928 August Kühne made both sons his partners.

The later 1920s were a time of rampant inflation and mass unemployment in Germany. Like nearly all German firms, KN was struck by a serious downturn in business.

On May 20, 1932, the founder and senior partner, August Kühne, died at the age of 77. Alfred and Werner Kühne became joint partners, with Werner in Bremen and Alfred in Hamburg, the main offices in the two most important German seaports. When Adolf Maass left in April 1933 to become a partner with

Key Dates:

1890:	August Kühne and Friedrich Nagel establish Kühne & Nagel, a forwarding commission agency.
1902:	Adolf Maass heads up the Hamburg branch office.
1907:	Nagel dies; Kühne takes over his shares.
1914:	The outbreak of World War I brings business to a near-standstill.
1932:	August Kühne dies; sons Alfred and Werner become joint partners.
1946:	KN focuses on providing transport in the three remaining German occupation zones.
1950:	The company opens a modern warehousing and cargo-handling facility in Hamburg Free Port.
1959:	Kühne & Nagel AG is formed in Switzerland.
1981:	British conglomerate Lonrho Plc acquires 50 percent of KN's shares.
1992:	KN repurchases Lonrho's shares.
1994:	KN goes public.
2001:	The company acquires USCO Logistics Inc.

his relatives in another business, Alfred and Werner Kühne were left as sole owners.

Cartage and barge operations were added to the Hamburg business, while Bremen expanded the pooling service, lumber shipments, and dealings with England, and had great success handling cotton. In 1932 a bonded warehouse was set up in Leipzig, and in 1934 a KN branch was opened in Stettin, which specialized in handling fibers.

The outbreak of World War II in September 1939 brought overseas traffic to a standstill. A restricted pooling service within Germany operated throughout the war. Highway and traffic routes were opened up, establishing a link to both the Middle East and the Far East, via Russia.

Alfred Kühne suffered from a foot disability, which meant he could not serve in the army. He continued to run the company, helped by Ludwig Rössinger who had joined KN in 1924 as representative in Frankfurt. KN was reorganized in 1942 and was run from the central office in Berlin. In the same year, a branch was established at Königsberg and another at Regensburg in 1943.

The war left much of Germany's industry in ruins, and its seaports had been destroyed by bombing. KN's headquarters in Bremen, including the archives, were completely destroyed during an air raid in 1944. By 1945 there were few docks left in Germany, and large areas of industrial hinterland had been lost. Germany was divided into four occupation zones, while the Allies decided the shape of the future Germany.

Postwar Growth

When the first oceangoing vessels, mostly carrying food parcels from the United States, tied up in Germany, KN established emergency offices and converted its damaged facilities into makeshift work places. Without hope for the resumption of worldwide shipping activities, KN concentrated its efforts on providing transport in the three remaining German occupation zones. In 1946 a branch was established in Düsseldorf, followed by one in Braunschweig in 1947.

Gradually the German economy recovered, helped by a massive amount of aid from the United States, known as the Marshall Plan. Sugar, cocoa, coffee, and cotton imports increased. Ruined quays were rebuilt. Alfred Kühne took the opportunity to erect a modern warehousing and cargo-handling facility in Hamburg Free Port. It was opened in September 1950, and had a storage capacity initially of 6,000 square meters, which was later expanded to 25,000 square meters.

During the period of postwar reconstruction, political leaders and industrialists came increasingly to realize that the future lay in a tightly interlinked Europe. With this in mind, KN swiftly expanded its German organization, linking the seaports by means of rail and trucks. Branches were opened in Frankfurt in 1949; Bonn—the new capital, Passau, and Hanover in 1950; Mannheim in 1953; Cologne in 1954; Munich and Stuttgart in 1955; Bielefeld in 1960; Wuppertal in 1961; and Hagen and Nuremberg in 1963. Altogether the 19 German branches had 1.6 million square feet of storage area.

Changes took place in top management. Werner Kühne emigrated to South Africa at the end of 1951, and Dieter Liesenfeld, junior partner since 1945, left the company at the end of 1953. Ludwig Rössinger became Alfred Kühne's partner on January 1, 1954.

In the postwar economic boom of the 1950s and 1960s, worldwide cargo traffic assumed great proportions. KN realized that to benefit from the new trade routes it was necessary to have employees on the spot and thus began to establish a worldwide network of operating bases. As well as road, rail, and sea freighting, the air freighting business began to grow in importance.

The formation of the European Economic Community (EEC) produced an increase in traffic; in response KN instituted an express service by rail to and from all EEC countries. KN needed to find suitable forwarding agents in European countries; where this was not possible, KN set up subsidiaries. Consequently, in 1954 establishments were set up in Antwerp and Rotterdam, followed by the foundation of Kühne & Nagel AG, Switzerland, with offices in Basel and Zürich in 1959. In 1963 KN became the majority shareholder in Proodos S.A., of Athens. Special pooling services from Italy were incorporated in 1964, and the Kühne & Nagel S.a.r.l., Milan, was founded. This completed the European organization for the time being.

Canadian Expansion: 1950s

In 1953 a KN subsidiary was founded in Canada, with branches in Toronto and Montreal. At the time Alfred Kühne said, "We want to create an organization paralleling that in Germany and Western Europe. We have chosen Canada because we consider her a country of great potential, and because she is a nation of dynamic progress." The basis of the Canadian expansion was the tremendous growth in German imports. A licensed customs house broker, J.W. Mills & Son, Ltd., of Montreal and Toronto, was incorporated into KN, thus making it possible to combine shipping operations with customs clearance.

In the winter, when Montreal and Toronto were cut off from the Atlantic by the freezing up of the St. Lawrence River, KN used the ice-free ports of Halifax and St. John. Consignments from Europe were loaded into boxcars and sent by rail to Montreal and Toronto. KN also established bonded warehouses and eventually built up a total storage area of 329,000 square meters in Canada.

A branch was opened in Vancouver in 1957 to handle incoming goods from Japan and Hong Kong, and to reship them to eastern Canada. To complete the chain, additional branches were opened in Quebec City, Hamilton, Ontario, and Winnipeg. KN is the biggest freight forwarder in Canada.

By the late 1960s, KN was run by a third-generation member of the Kühne family, Klaus-Michael Kühne, Alfred Kühne's son. Klaus-Michael Kühne joined his father and Ludwig Rössinger as a junior partner in 1963, having completed an apprenticeship in banking. In 1966, at the age of 30, he joined the top management as chairman of the executive board. He initiated the further growth of KN's activities with particular emphasis on Europe and the Far East. The KN organization had 400 offices in 60 countries around the world.

Alfred Kühne died in 1981. In July of that year, the British conglomerate Lonrho Plc acquired 50 percent of KN's shares at a cost of DM 90 million. After the purchase, Klaus-Michael Kühne and Lonrho's head, Roland W. (Tiny) Rowland acted as joint chief executives of the entire organization. The main reason for the sale of half of KN to Lonrho was losses sustained by the Kühne family in attempting to expand its shipping fleet.

Expansion: 1980s and Early 1990s

During the 1980s KN Germany operated as the biggest KN company worldwide, even though its senior management was based in Switzerland at Pfäffikon. In 1989 the prestigious German business publication *Manager Magazin* voted Klaus-Michael Kühne "Mr. Europe," reflecting the farsighted approach KN took in the increasing economic integration of Europe and the removal of internal trading barriers, scheduled for 1993.

In 1985 KN's management devised a pan-European strategy to prepare the company for the single European market. The company's top priority was to expand its transport, warehousing, and distribution network in Europe. This concept was called "KN Euro Logistics."

To prepare for the single market, KN bought into leading freight companies in Italy (Domenichelli SpA), The Netherlands (Van Vliet BV), the United Kingdom (Hollis Transport Group Ltd.), and Spain (Transportes TresH). Further capacity was acquired in Denmark, Norway, and Sweden. KN also looked to acquire a stake in a suitable company in France. These acquisitions were masterminded by a special corporate development department.

Without doubt, German reunification was the outstanding event of the 1990 business year. In May 1990 KN founded, via a joint venture contract with the former state-owned forwarder VEB Deutrans, the KN Speditions-GmbH in East Berlin. Later, after KN bought out the Deutrans share, it became a wholly owned KN company. It consisted of a network of a dozen branches, field offices, logistics depots, and air freight stations in the five states of the former German Democratic Republic.

By the early 1990s, KN was the second largest freight forwarding firm in Germany, behind Schenker-Rhenus, but reunification provided the impetus to KN to expand its "KN Euro Logistics" service across Germany. KN held the contract to distribute branded goods across Germany for three major manufacturers—Philip Morris, maker of Marlboro cigarettes; Tchibo coffee; and Thomson Consumer Electronics Group.

The 1990 annual report stated that the company's future strategy would "continue to center on the consolidation and integration of KN's activities in Europe." KN's involvement in Eastern Europe began in the 1950s, when imports of timber, paper, and furniture were forwarded from Romania, Poland, and Hungary. Political and economic liberalization in the former communist-bloc countries presented many business opportunities for KN. KN formed joint ventures or signed contracts of cooperation with local freight forwarders in Soviet Russia, Romania, Bulgaria, Albania, Hungary, Poland, Czechoslovakia, and Yugoslavia. KN aimed to provide the full range of freight forwarding services, as well as special container, trade fair, seaworthy packaging, and distribution services. The company also adopted a new management structure that year, which was designed to aid in European expansion.

The year 1990 saw a reduction in KN's net operating profits to SFr 34.2 million from SFr 37.5 million in 1989. The decline was in part due to the general economic downturn and to unavoidable losses in connection with the development of new products ("KN Euro Logistics"). The weakening of the U.S. dollar, high interest rates, the Persian Gulf War, and overdemand in some European countries leading to higher costs all contributed to the decline in profitability. Substantial additional costs for freight purchasing were necessary—KN's own transport capacities were limited at the time. Therefore, KN planned to acquire additional vehicles to fulfill this demand, particularly in Germany. Canada, the Far East, and several European countries were the main contributors to net profits.

Becoming a Major Global Logistics Company: 1990s and Beyond

KN spent the remaining years of the 1990s focused on positioning itself as a major player in the logistics industry. The company's first step in its game plan included the purchase of Lonrho's 50 percent stake in the firm. Then in 1992, after securing a record net profit of $26.6 million, KN announced its intention to go public. In May 1994, the company listed on the Zurich and Frankfurt exchanges. The company also established a Russian subsidiary that year and purchased a majority stake in a forwarding concern that had locations in Norway, Sweden, and Denmark. During 1994 KN posted record sales and income.

KN's strategy, including its focus on its logistics operations, continued to pay off for the company. Sales and income soared as the firm landed lucrative logistics-related contracts, including one with E.I. de Pont de Nemours & Co. in which KN would operate the chemical giant's leveraged distribution activities in Europe, the Middle East, and Africa. Klaus-Michael Kühne summed up the company's direction in a 1998 *Journal of Commerce* article claiming, "Logistics operations are of crucial significance for the further evolution of the Kuehne & Nagel group." Kühne stepped down from his CEO post in July 1999 but remained president and delegate of the company's board of directors.

Klaus Herms, KN's new CEO and longtime company executive, continued in his predecessor's footsteps in the early years of the new millennium. In November 2000, KN forged a strategic alliance with Singapore-based SembCorp Logistics Ltd., giving the firm a foothold in the Asia Pacific contract logistics market. One year later, the company pushed ahead in the North American market with the $300 million acquisition of USCO Logistics Inc., a warehouse-based logistics service provider based in Hamden, Connecticut. During 2002, Nortel Networks divested its global outbound logistics operations management business to KN, which further strengthened the company's global reach. KN also was selected by department store chain JCPenney Company Inc. to operate four regional distribution warehouses.

KN's financial performance continued to move in a positive direction, as it had since the mid-1990s. Both revenue and profits increased during 2001. The faltering North American economy forced KN to restructure certain operations at its new USCO Logistics subsidiary. The company's other regions, however, proved to be on track for future gains. Europe continued to be the company's most lucrative market, but its North, Central, and South America; Asian Pacific; and Middle East and Africa businesses continued to strengthen. KN's international forwarding business was its largest contributor to revenues and contract logistics remained a close second. With a strong global strategy in place and a longstanding history of success behind it, Kuehne & Nagel appeared to be well positioned for growth in the years to come.

Principal Subsidiaries

Kuehne & Nagel Management AG; Kuehne & Nagel Internationale Transporte AG; Kuehne & Nagel Liegenschaften AG; Kuehne & Nagel Treasury AG; Nacora Holding AG; Nacora Agencies AG; Nakurail AG; Ferroviasped Holding AG; Kuehne & Nagel Asia Pacific Holding AG.

Principal Competitors

Danzas Group; Panalpina World Transport Holding Ltd.; Stinnes AG.

Further Reading

"Connecting the Missing Link," *Journal of Commerce,* July 30, 2001, p. 26.

Elias, Rahita, "Swiss Giant Kuehne & Nagel Posts Best Results Ever," *Business Times London,* May 4, 1995, p. 1.

Koenig, Robert, "Kuehne & Nagel Plans to Expand Logistics Facilities," *Journal of Commerce,* April 16, 1998, p. 11A.

"Kuehne Confirms Lonrho's 280 MLN DM Sale of Kuehne & Nagel Stake," *AFX News,* January 23, 1992.

"Kuehne & Nagel Appoints Herms CEO," *AFX News,* July 8, 1999.

"Kuehne & Nagel Poised to Go Public," *Lloyd's List,* June 19, 1993, p. 2.

Kühne & Nagel, *75 Years Kühne & Nagel,* Bremen: Carl Schünemann, 1965.

"Transforming Kuehne & Nagel," *Journal of Commerce,* November 6, 2000.

Widman, Miriam, "Kuehne & Nagel Unveils Management Structure Hopes to Serve Europe Better," *Journal of Commerce,* January 3, 1990, p. 5B.

—Caroline Hinton
—update: Christina M. Stansell

LDB Corporation

444 Sidney Baker Street South
Kerrville, Texas 78028
U.S.A.
Telephone: (830) 257-2000
Fax: (830) 257-2003
Web site: http://www.mrgattis.com

Private Company
Incorporated: 1970
Employees: 1,200
Sales: $118 million (2001)
NAIC: 422490 Other Grocery and Related Products
Wholesalers

LDB Corporation, operating out of Kerrville, Texas, is a privately held company that operates through its Mr. Gatti's subsidiary, a family-oriented pizza restaurant chain. Mr. Gatti's is a major regional player in the pizza industry, with more than 200 units located primarily in the Southwest and Southeast, most of which are franchised. In addition to pizza, Mr. Gatti's features a selection of Italian dishes. In recent years the company has concentrated its efforts on its GattiTown concept, pizza superstores that offer a variety of eating and entertainment features, including bumper cars, a carousel, and other rides; Italian-style buffet and salad bars; and individual party rooms.

L.D. Brinkman Founding the Business in 1970

LDB Corporation took its name from the initials of its founder, and current chairman, president, and CEO, Texas entrepreneur Lloyd D. Brinkman. The grandson of Danish immigrants, Brinkman started his business career raising Brangus cattle in the Dallas area, as well as running a successful carpet distribution business. In 1970 he traded a 1.8 percent stake in his distributorship to acquire Miami-based Giffen Industries, which he renamed LDB Corporation. In 1971 he moved its headquarters to Dallas, and then in 1975 relocated to Kerrville in central Texas, some 100 miles west of Austin and close to the cattle ranches where he raised his purebred Brangus cattle. Originally a roofing company, Giffen in the late 1960s evolved

into a freewheeling conglomerate, with scores of unrelated and generally unprofitable companies cobbled together, involving such products as snowmobiles, boats, and lawn furniture. Brinkman was immediately besieged by creditors, and only a $15 million consolidation loan from the Banque Canadienne Nationale allowed him to avoid bankruptcy court. For the next eight years Brinkman unloaded or liquidated the unprofitable businesses, while retaining some of the floor-covering assets to complement his previous holdings, and rearranged debt. By 1978 LDB was once again liquid, although it consisted of little more than Brinkman's original carpet business. He now began to rediversify, in the process gaining minor stakes in two trucking companies, as well as buying into a mobile and modular home business, which he renamed Brinkcraft. He also spent some of his cash to acquire the Mr. Gatti's pizza chain.

Mr. Gatti's was founded in 1964 by a retired Air Force Lieutenant Colonel named James Eure. Although pizza had been sold since the early decades of the 20th century, mostly in the major East Coast cities with large concentrations of Italian Americans, a major pizza craze swept the country after World War II, resulting in a large number of mom-and-pop operations and, eventually, companies with bigger plans. In 1958, Frank and Dan Carney opened the first Pizza Hut in Wichita, Kansas, and a year later they incorporated and opened their first franchise unit in Topkea, Kansas. Whereas Pizza Hut was devoted to a table and chairs concept, Detroit native Tom Monaghan founded Domino's Pizza in 1960 and pioneered the pizza delivery chain. A short time later Michael Ilitch, also from Detroit, founded Little Caesars, which focused on the carry-out of inexpensive pizza. Each of the three future pizza magnates unknowingly carved out a unique share of the market and for many years were dominant in the industry.

Second-tier players, such as Dallas-based Pizza Inn and Mr. Gatti's, got their start in the early 1960s. Because he traveled widely while in the Air Force, Eure was able to collect pizza recipes, settle on a favorite, and make plans for opening a pizza restaurant when he retired from the service. His approach to the business was to concentrate on high-quality ingredients, offering fresh meats and dairy products. Sauce and pizza dough were to be made according to his recipe and the dough was required to be rolled by hand. In 1964 he opened his first restaurant, called "The Pizza Place," in a former Austin, Texas convenience store.

LDB's Acquisition of Mr. Gatti's in 1978

Eure did just $71,000 in sales during his first year in operation, but as business improved steadily he began opening more stores and initiated a franchising program. By 1969 the aspiring chain had grown to 18 stores. In 1973 Eure drew upon his wife's maiden name, Gatti, to provide the operation with a new name: Mr. Gatti's. A year later, however, Eure sold the chain to a group of investors headed by George Baker, a former president of Kentucky Fried Chicken. Under Baker's leadership Mr. Gatti's enjoyed even greater growth, expanding to 88 restaurants by 1978 when Brinkman and his LDB Corporation bought the Austin-based operation. The terms of the deal called for an initial payment of $3 million, followed by a number of deferred payments based on earnings. In the end Brinkman paid $10.5 million for Mr. Gatti's.

As a part of LDB, Mr. Gatti's enjoyed explosive growth over the next three years. In June 1982 the number of Mr. Gatti's restaurants totaled 258, about a third owned by LDB. By the mid-1980s the chain grew to more than 300 and cracked the top five pizza chains in total units. In fiscal 1986 chainwide sales totaled $130 million. The franchise fee stood at $10,000 per unit, with a royalty of 4 percent of gross sales. Mr. Gatti's also grew via acquisitions, buying existing operations to expand into such markets as Tennessee and Arkansas.

Mr. Gatti's also was displaying an innovative spirit. In 1982, to take advantage of the big-screen televisions its stores offered, the chain began experimenting in a few of its restaurants with a free videotaping service, The Instant Replay Program, which concentrated on sporting events such as little league games, children's soccer games, and adult softball games, as well as high school plays. Customers called in with the date and location of the event, the store arranged for someone to do the filming, and by the time people arrived at their local Mr. Gatti's restaurant the videotape was ready to air and tables set up. No minimum charge was required. Patrons ordered off the regular menu and received a 10 percent discount. For parties of 30 or more, buffets were made available. Copies of the videotaped event also were available for sale. Recording equipment required about a $4,000 investment from each store, the taping cost the restaurant around $50, and overall the initiative was just a break-even offer. Nevertheless, it resulted in excellent community relations and served to stimulate business in general. Within a couple of years all of the LDB-

owned stores offered the taping service and about 90 percent of the franchised operations.

In 1984 Mr. Gatti's launched an advanced computerized ordering system for pizza delivery in Austin dubbed Call 1. It relied on a single telephone number suffix, 2222, and was easily remembered by customers. All calls were received at a central location and the order was routed electronically to the closest Mr. Gatti's unit. Because of the efficiency of the system Mr. Gatti's was able to offer a 30-minute delivery guarantee in keeping with the standard set by Domino's. Moreover, the system used order-takers who were trained to encourage the sale of extra toppings and drinks. As a result, the average delivery check grew to $11 while in-store checks totaled $8. Call 1 also quickly provided the order-taker with information on the customer's previous transactions, which not only helped in the selling but insured that delivery information was accurate. The system, using the 2222 suffix, was rolled out successfully to the Louisville, Kentucky market in 1985, followed by Nashville, Tennessee, and other larger cities. In some markets Mr. Gatti's implemented what it called "Hot Zones," limited areas where traffic conditions permitted a 30-minute delivery guarantee.

Although Mr. Gatti's opened a number of delivery-only units, the emphasis of the chain remained on its full-service restaurants. A major facet of this strategy was the three-room arrangement of its restaurants, offering different atmospheres for different customers. The main dining room, with its big-screen television, provided entertainment as a complement to the dining experience. A quieter area could be found in the "Garden Room," where diners were provided with a more adult décor. The third room, the "good times room," was set up theater-style and was where the videotaped sporting and other events were replayed for private parties. In general usage it was geared toward children, entertaining them with cartoons and movies. In the late 1980s the Mr. Gatti's chain made a concerted effort to upgrade its older one-room stores to the three-room format. Although the conversion did not result in an increased number of seats, it generally boosted revenues by some 20 percent. The chain also expanded a lunchtime all-you-can-eat buffet to the evenings, Monday through Thursday. Instead of being limited to doing the bulk of its business on Friday and Saturday evenings, Mr. Gatti's was now able to make inroads on other nights of the week.

Selling the Carpet and Flooring Assets in 1987

In 1987 Brinkman elected to sell his carpet and flooring business for $57 million to John Crowther Group PLC, a British manufacturing and distribution company. At the time, it was reported that Brink planned to use the proceeds to accelerate the growth of Mr. Gatti's. Rather than focus solely on his pizza business, however, Brinkman and LDB invested in more than a dozen publicly held companies over the next several years, many of which proved to be poor choices that resulted in LDB losing $64 million from 1988 to 1992. Mr. Gatti's, in the meantime, also endured a difficult stretch. Early in 1990 Brinkman assumed the presidency and initiated cost-cutting measures that included reduced pay for senior officers and relocating the pizza chain's headquarters from Austin to Brinkman's offices in Kerrville. By eliminating duplicate administrative functions, LDB saved about $1 million in annual payroll. In addition, the business was reorganized, split into two divisions, Northern and Southern, each headed by a division president who reported directly to Brinkman.

In October 1991 Mr. Gatti's filed for bankruptcy, although LDB was not affected. Brinkman maintained that the subsidiary was a profitable business with considerable assets but that it sought court protection because of a problem with a real estate loan with NCNB Texas National Bank. In fact, Mr. Gatti's listed assets of $51.6 million and liabilities of just $13.2 million. The roots of the problem reached back six years when Mr. Gatti's took out a $10 million loan with RepublicBank Dallas, which subsequently merged with Interfirst, becoming First RepublicBank. When NCNB acquired the assets of First RepublicBank in 1988, Mr. Gatti's loan was included. Although, according to Brinkman, Mr. Gatti's was current on its payments, the bank began to treat the loan as a bad debt. It charged that a provision of the loan had been breached because Mr. Gatti's had advanced funds to LDB. Brinkman claimed that he attempted to provide more collateral to back the loan, but NCNB not only insisted on regular note payments but also wanted a percentage of the company's profits to pay off the debt, a move that would have hampered the chain's ability to remodel older stores and grow the business. When negotiations broke down, NCNB filed suit seeking immediate repayment of the loan, prompting Brinkman to file for Chapter 11 reorganization.

Little more than a year after it filed for protection Mr. Gatti's emerged from bankruptcy a significantly smaller chain. Although the number of franchised stores remained around 170, company-owned units dropped to 59 from 156 just four years earlier, as less productive stores were sold off or closed. As a result, LDB rebounded, returning to profitability in 1993, earning $131,000. The company's stock, which at one point dipped below $1, also began to show improvement. Nevertheless, the business, by the estimation of many, was undervalued. In September 1994 Brinkman decided to take LDB private, offering to buy outstanding shares at $5.50 each, which placed a $10.2 million value on the company, less than 25 percent of the $41.8 million in sales LDB posted the previous year. Moreover, the corporation boasted cash and securities worth $5.2 million, which offset $2.80 per share of Brinkman's offer. Despite questions in the press about the deal, there was never a chance that the offer would be rejected because Brinkman and his partner in the deal, Tom Thomas, together owned 69 percent of the stock.

Also not included in the financials of Mr. Gatti's, which had a bearing on the future worth of LDB, was the chain's success with a new type of store it called GattiLand, which was set to rival the pizza-game room operations of Showbiz Pizza Time and Chuck E. Cheese. GattiLand offered what Brinkman termed "eatertainment" and moved the chain away from the fast-food arena. Mr. Gatti's began experimenting with the GattiLand concept around 1987, and for the next several years sought to determine the ideal size and the proper mix of entertainment and food. Unlike some of his competition, Brinkman did not want GattiLand to be exclusively a children's operation. Instead he wanted to attract the entire family, from toddlers to grandparents. To maintain the proper image and avoid becoming a teen arcade hangout it banned anyone wearing cutoffs or tank tops. Moreover, smoking was prohibited and no alcoholic beverages were sold. Patrons were charged a flat fee, based on age, that entitled them entry to GattiTown's midway and other entertainment areas, as well as all the food and drink they wished from an extensive menu of items, available from a buffet and custom-prepared in front of customers on stoves. The midway offered games and rides, such as bumper cars and a carousel. Moreover, a GattiGear shop sold T-shirts and other memorabilia.

With LDB taken private, the financial picture of Mr. Gatti's became closely guarded, making it difficult to determine how effective the GattiLand concept was in helping the chain to keep pace in the highly competitive pizza industry.

Principal Subsidiaries

LDB Food SVC Inc.; Mr. Gatti's Inc.

Principal Competitors

Domino's Pizza, Inc.; Papa John's International, Inc.; Pizza Hut Inc.

Further Reading

Curtis, Janice, "Pepperoni and Videotaping Are a Big Draw at Mr. Gatti's Pizza," *Dallas Business Courier,* June 3, 1985, p. 23.

Mack, Toni, "Brinkmanship," *Forbes,* June 7, 1982, p. 73.

Opdyke, Jeff D., "Some Critics Question the Fairness of LDB Corp.'s Plan to Go Private," *Wall Street Journal,* September 21, 1994, p. T2.

Strenk, Tom, "Gatti's Gets the Call," *Restaurant Business,* June 10, 1987, p. 148.

Tyson, Kim, "Mr. Gatti's Files for Chapter 11," *Austin American-Statesman,* October 11, 1991, p. C1.

——, "New Mix of Pizza and Play," *Austin American-Statesman,* December 13, 1997, p. D1.

—Ed Dinger

Lifeline Systems, Inc.

111 Lawrence Street
Framington, Massachusetts 01701-8156
U.S.A.
Telephone: (508) 988-1000
Toll Free: (800) 451-0525
Fax: (508) 988-1384
Web site: http://www.lifelinesys.com

Public Company
Incorporated: 1974
Employees: 840
Sales: $96.6 million (2001)
Stock Exchanges: NASDAQ
Ticker Symbol: LIFE
NAIC: 334290 Other Communications Equipment
  Manufacturing

Lifeline Systems, Inc. is the dominant market leader in personal emergency response monitoring systems (PRS) and related services geared towards the elderly or disabled individuals. The Framington, Massachusetts, company markets its products and services to hospitals, nursing homes, and other health care providers. It has approximately two-thirds of the 600,000 subscribers that make up the North American PRS market, comprised mostly of women in their 70s and 80s who live alone. Subscribers in distress contact Lifeline's central monitoring facility located in Framington, which processes more than 21,000 call per day and dispatches appropriate assistance.

Personal response systems such as those sold by Lifeline provide two essential services—monitoring their subscribers and acting to dispatch appropriate assistance to them if necessary. A control console located in the subscriber's home connects to portable and installed sensors strategically placed throughout the residence. Like home protection systems, the PRS includes smoke sensors as well as motion detectors but also offers more advanced features. In addition to checking or changing the system through the console, users have access to a hand-held wireless touch pad with the same controls. In case of dire emergency they can use a pendant sensor and by pressing a single button call for help. When the console receives an emergency signal, it is programmed to alert appropriate parties—which may be emergency medical services, police, or fire—then transmit pertinent information about the user. The console immediately commandeers the telephone line in the home, reserving it for emergency communication. In more advanced systems, a speakerphone can communicate with the user from anywhere in the home. Moreover, users do not have to consciously seek assistance. A timer will call for help if the user has not used the telephone or checked in by pushing a special button on the console after a specified period of time has elapsed. The second component of a monitoring system is the emergency response center, which may be located in an area hospital, local social service agency, or Lifeline's Framington facility. Because PRS helps to reduce the time a subscriber spends in the hospital or a nursing home, Lifeline and similar services are an effective way for health organizations to help contain costs and have become increasingly added to the care plans of elderly patients. Beyond the prospect of saving the lives of its users, PRS provides a psychological benefit—a sense of security for both subscribers and their families.

Lifeline Origins in 1974

Lifeline was founded by Dr. Andrew S. Dibner and his wife Susan in 1974. Born in New York City in 1926, Dibner had firsthand knowledge about the frailty of older people. At the age of 12, he was awakened by his grandmother in the throes of a heart attack in the hallway of the family home. Years later, an elderly family friend suffered a stroke while staying alone in a summer cottage, and four days passed before a neighbor discovered her. By then it was far too late to provide successful treatment, and she died six months later in a nursing home. As an adult, Dibner became a psychologist, earning a doctorate at the University of Michigan, and began working with older people as chief counselor and chief clinical psychologist at a Veterans Administration mental health clinic in Boston. He was also involved with the Age Center of New England. In 1964, he began teaching psychology at Boston University and became a founding member of its Gerontology Center. It was during 1972, when he was spending a year studying personality changes in advanced age at Duke University's Center for the Study of Aging and Human Development, that Dibner experienced a moment of inspiration that changed his life and led to the creation of Lifeline. He was shaving one morning, listening to a radio broadcast from astronauts on the moon. While musing about the technological feat that made such communications possible, he reflected on the plight of frail individuals, living alone, who perhaps had fallen and were unable to summon help. If we could talk to men on the moon, he reasoned, surely there must be a way to communicate with elderly persons who lived alone in a house or apartment. As he pondered the problem, he conceived of a timer-and-alert mechanism that would automatically tap into the telephone line and call for help if it was not reset by a person's normal household routines, such as turning off lights or opening a refrigerator.

Dibner believed in his vision of a personal monitoring device but was unable to convince manufacturers to develop a marketable product that could be used in a viable response system. He and his wife Susan, who had a doctorate in sociology and was a consultant for the Center for the Study of Aging and Human Development, refused to give up, becoming virtually obsessed by the PRS concept. Reflecting years later on that period, he recalled, "We nearly went broke. Almost lost our house. We had young children. It was Awful! My wife and I were both academics and we despised business at the time. But, we believed it was so important that we were determined to make it happen." Despite the daunting challenges, this unlikely pair of entrepreneurs co-founded Lifeline Systems in 1974, headquartered at first in Watertown, Massachusetts. They spent the first two years attempting to develop a prototype with next to no money. According to Dibner, "I found an unemployed engineer who built the first model, then a small manufacturer who made burglar alarm equipment. It was hard to get venture capital. At first, even the company's accountant and lawyer worked on the cuff." Two more years passed before Lifeline was able to make its first sale to a Veterans Administration research center. It was a major government research grant, however, that stabilized the company's finances and helped Lifeline begin to establish itself. Moreover, the two-year study funded by the grant confirmed Dibner's belief in the value of a personal monitoring system. The project involved 200 elderly people using the Lifeline system and 200 without it. Those connected to Lifeline spent less time in the hospital or in nursing homes, resulting in appreciable cost savings and invaluable peace of mind.

During its first few years in existence, Lifeline unsuccessfully attempted to market its product directly to consumers. Dibner believed that physicians would be key allies in endorsing Lifeline to their patients but, as he noted years later, "Unfortunately, many of them have failed to place much emphasis on help beyond what they themselves do for the patient. Dibner and his wife began to step back from active management of the company. For a number of years, Dibner served as a vice-president of marketing, but eventually he and his wife sold their interest in the business. Lifeline's current chairman, L. Dennis Shapiro, took over as chairman and CEO in July 1978. Several months later, the

company changed its marketing strategy, opting to target hospitals and nursing homes rather than the patients directly. The institutions would purchase or lease Lifeline equipment, then rent it to their patients at reasonable rates. In this way, social workers and discharge people were the ones who sold Lifeline to patients and their families. Revenues began to grow steadily for Lifeline in the early 1980s, despite the fact that Medicare, Medicaid, and most private insurers did not yet consider the Lifeline service to be essential, choosing to categorize it as a preventive measure that did not warrant reimbursement.

Going Public in 1983

Annual revenues reached $6.4 million in 1982 and the company turned profitable. In 1983, Lifeline went public at $13 a share, with the proceeds earmarked for the development of new products, plant expansion, and the implementation of a new equipment leasing program. It was an attractive offering because the number of Lifeline programs had grown from 500 in 1982 to more than a 1,000 a year later. With the United States having some 5,000 acute-care hospitals, Lifeline's primary market, which cared for an estimated three million patients, there was considerable room for growth. Telephone answering machines and burglar alarms were becoming commonplace in American households, making people more comfortable with the idea of an electronic home monitoring system. Moreover, despite the reluctance of insurers to accept PRS, the demographics of America's aging population favored Lifeline, with an ever-increasing number of potential users able to afford the service. When the cost-savings of using personal response systems became apparent to these organizations and patients were actively encouraged by insurers to rely on them, Lifeline could expect its prospects to improve considerably in the future.

Lifeline's annual revenues totaled $9.6 million in 1983 and reached $17.4 million in 1985, with $1.2 million in profits. By now, the company was well established and had carved out the lion's share of the emerging PRS market with about 70 percent of the business. Along the way, however, Lifeline developed some problems. It made ill-fated attempts to develop and launch new types of monitoring products. In February 1984, it introduced a bedside arrhythmia monitor to check the electrical activity of a patient's heart. Money was also spent on developing a pulse monitor as well as a dietary management system for hospitals. These attempts to expand Lifeline's product line was partially responsible for the company losing its focus. According to a 1991 *Boston Business Journal* profile of Lifeline, by 1987 the company's business "was well established but sluggish. Chronic problems with customer service and employee morale were holding the company back from fully taking advantage of its growing market." Product quality was also inconsistent, and the units were difficult to install. As a result, revenues leveled off at the $17 million level and the company began to lose market share to its competitors. To reverse this trend, new upper management was recruited, in particular a former Xerox executive named Arthur Phipps.

Having earned an engineering degree from West Point and served four years in the Air Force, Phipps was well versed on the virtues of discipline, a quality much needed at Lifeline. Moreover, he held a master of science degree in Electrical Engineering from the University of Rochester as well as a degree from the Harvard Graduate School of Business in Program Management

Key Dates:

1974: Lifeline Systems is founded by Andrew and Susan Dibner.
1979: The company's marketing focus shifts from individuals to institutions.
1983: The company goes public.
1996: CareTel Inc. is acquired.
1999: The company's headquarters are moved to Framington, Massachusetts.
2002: SOS Industries is acquired.

Development. He went on to work for Eastman Kodak and General Dynamics Corporation, and during his more than 20 years at Xerox held a number of executive positions. He joined Lifeline in 1987 as chief operating officer and subsequently took on the additional role of president of the company. By the start of 1989, he became chief executive officer. During his first few months with Lifeline, he focused on smoothing over problems with its customers, spending a lot of time simply listening to them. He then began tackling internal problems, turning to cross-functional committees to study such matters as why customers were often shipped the wrong item, resulting in an inordinate number of credit memos being issued. It soon became apparent that customers were simply confused about which item to order. Not only were order-entry clerks not properly trained about the Lifeline products, they were further hampered by the salespeople's lack of a formal order form to complete. Communications were breaking down between the customer and sales, as well as between sales and manufacturing. Because of these findings, the catalog was redesigned, order clerks were better trained about Lifeline products, and visibility charts were posted to keep track of ongoing errors in order to take further steps to eliminate them. As a result, the amount of credit memos was drastically reduced, and the number of order clerks could be cut from six to just two. Phipps had brought the visibility charts from Xerox and used them throughout the company to not only isolate the source of problems but, by posting them, to also involve employees in solving problems. Lifeline's success in improving its operations was recognized in 1991 when the company won the Shingo Prize for manufacturing excellence.

Growth in the 1990s and Beyond

Under Phipps, revenues began to grow once more, and Lifeline was able to begin spending money on advertising. In 1990, the company budgeted virtually no money for promotion. The following year, Lifeline budgeted about $1 million, an amount it doubled in 1992. It also established an in-house telemarketing operation. In addition to targeting the elderly, Lifeline attempted to expand its focus to include a wide range of people who might benefit from a personal monitoring systems, including "latchkey" children and single women, but its primary customers remained the elderly or physically-challenged individual. Phipps was replaced as president and CEO in January 1993, but he left the company well positioned for ongoing growth throughout the decade. His replacement, Ronald Feinstein, had been a director of Lifeline since 1985 and in the previous two years had been president and CEO of International Business Interiors.

In the mid-1990s, Lifeline continued to be the PRS market leader, a position it maintained in large part by continuing to roll out improved equipment. The CommuniCator Plus, a premium model introduced in 1994, incorporated a full-function telephone into the system with special features to accommodate users with visual or hearing limitations. CarePartner, launched in 1995, employed digital speech technology to clarify alarm messages sent by users.

Lifeline also grew its business through acquisitions. In 1995, it paid $1 million for Tele-Response and Support Services, Inc. of Raynham, Massachusetts, a distributor of Lifeline products and service. The following year Lifeline, through a Canadian subsidiary, acquired CareTel, Inc., a Toronto company that had 3,000 subscribers to its personal response service, ProtectAlert. For a period of time in the late 1990s, Lifeline was on the verge of being purchased itself. A tentative agreement was actually signed in October 1988 with Protection One, Inc., a leading residential security-alarm company with more than 1.5 million subscribers worldwide. By September 1999, however, with delays in the regulatory process, the parties agreed to terminate the merger.

Lifeline continued to maintain market share and improve its business in the late 1990s. Annual revenues that totaled $57.4 million in 1997 grew to nearly $71 million in 1999. To accommodate growth, the company moved its corporate headquarters into a 84,000-square-foot facility located in Framington, Massachusetts. As it entered the 21st century, Lifeline continued its push for external expansion. In February 2001, it acquired SOS Industries, a Florida-based PRS provider with more than 10,000 subscribers in 37 states. The Canadian operation also expanded by acquiring the Argus Emergency Medical division of Microtec Enterprises. By the end of 2001, Lifeline had over 400,000 subscribers and annual revenues stood at $96.6 million. Firmly entrenched in the marketplace, the company appeared well positioned to remain the dominant PRS provider in North America.

Principal Subsidiaries

Lifeline Systems Canada, Inc.; Lifeline Systems Export, Inc.

Principal Competitors

American Medical Alert Corporation; Napco Security Systems, Inc.; Response USA Inc.

Further Reading

Dietz, Jean, "Medical Care at the Push of a Button," *Boston Globe*, October 30, 1988, p. B15.

Glass, John, "Four Object Lessons from the Brink of Ruin," *Boston Business Journal*, May 27, 1991, p. 9.

Kleinfield, N.R., "Home Medical Alert System," *New York Times*, June 25, 1984, p. D1.

Lammers, Teri, "The Troubleshooter's Guide," *Inc.*, January 1992, p. 65.

"Lifeline Systems: Chief Executive Mobilizes Rank and File to Take Action," *Boston Globe*, June 9, 1992, p. 59.

—Ed Dinger

Massachusetts Mutual Life Insurance Company

1295 State Street
Springfield, Massachusetts 01111-0001
U.S.A.
Telephone: (413) 788-8411
Fax: (413) 744-6005
Web site: http://www.massmutual.com

Mutual Company
Incorporated: 1851
Employees: 9,000
Total Assets: $234 billion (2001)
NAIC: 524113 Direct Life Insurance Carriers

Massachusetts Mutual Life Insurance Company (Mass-Mutual) has changed slowly over a long period of time, and by doing so has undergone a complete metamorphosis: from personal insurer to financial giant with $234 billion in assets. MassMutual serves over ten million clients and provides them with mutual funds, money management, trust services, retirement planning products, life insurance, annuities, disability income insurance, and long-term care insurance. The MassMutual Financial Group—the marketing designation under which Massachusetts Mutual and its subsidiaries operate—has over 1,200 offices in the United States, Hong Kong, Japan, Taiwan, China, Macao, Argentina, Chile, Bermuda, and Luxembourg.

Origins

MassMutual began operating in 1851 in Springfield, Massachusetts, in a room with three chairs, a table, and a city map on the wall. George W. Rice, a young insurance agent who was selling policies for Connecticut Mutual Life in Hartford, Connecticut, had wanted to open a business in neighboring Massachusetts. Like Connecticut Mutual, the new agency was a mutual company—a company owned by its policyholders.

Rice's Massachusetts Mutual was one of about a dozen mutual companies that had sprung into existence between 1843 and 1851. Mutual companies became attractive vehicles in the nascent insurance industry because they required little working capital, but a Massachusetts state law required an initial stock subscription of $100,000 for insurance companies, so Rice encouraged 31 investors to purchase stock in the new venture. In 1867, MassMutual retired the stock and became the mutual company it was intended to be.

Caleb Rice, a relative of George W. Rice, was the company's first president. He steered MassMutual's growth for its first 22 years, making him the longest-serving president in the company's history. Rice wore many hats. A former lawyer, state legislator, and county sheriff before coming to MassMutual, Rice was elected the first mayor of Springfield in 1852. MassMutual sold its first policy on August 2, 1851, to Harvey Danks, a MassMutual agent. Soon after, roaming agents like Danks sold policies to New England homeowners and workers. At higher premiums, MassMutual also insured railway and steamship workers, gold-rush adventurers, and people traveling south of the Mason-Dixon Line.

For the next several decades, MassMutual's expansion mirrored that of the United States. In the 1850s, the country was expanding westward. The company followed suit. By 1855, agencies were functioning in New York City, Cleveland, Chicago, and Detroit. In 1868, MassMutual reached the West Coast—before the transcontinental railroad was completed—and established an office in San Francisco.

Between 1850 and 1900, the volume of life insurance in force in the United States rose from $96 million to nearly $7.6 billion. Expansion and aggressive marketing were largely responsible for the growth. The late 19th century was an age of great technological advancement and ushered in a new era for life insurance companies. In 1885, MassMutual bought its first typewriter. Soon after, telephones were installed, which facilitated better communication between agents and the home office.

In 1886, Colonel Martin Van Buren Edgerly was named president. Edgerly had joined MassMutual in 1859 and spent his entire career with the company. He was the first of many career men to take the helm of MassMutual, which tends to look inward for leadership.

Company Perspectives:

We strive to serve our clients not just at one moment in time, but over the lifetime of their relationship with us. We help individuals, families, and institutions assess and plan for the future.

Regulated Growth: Late 1800s–Early 1900s

Edgerly oversaw a decade of carefully regulated growth and was replaced in 1895 by John Hall. Hall steered the company through the late 19th century, including the Spanish-American War of 1898—during which the company took minimal losses—and through the numerous business scandals of the early 20th century.

In these years of the robber barons, many insurance companies played fast and loose with laws governing their conduct. To encourage agents to sell more, firms paid excessive commissions. Dishonest executives used the sizable assets of their companies to control other corporations as well as for private purposes. MassMutual, however, kept clean and continued its regulated growth: the home-office staff grew from 16 in 1884 to 100 in 1907. MassMutual also continued, without change, its practice of selling only life insurance policies payable in a lump sum at death or maturity. The company's first innovation came in 1901, when it began offering policies under which proceeds would be paid over a fixed period or for life.

The company was not a target of the 1906 Armstrong Committee investigation, which uncovered many abuses by New York life insurance companies. The commission had been appointed by the New York state legislature, and its findings affected life insurers throughout the United States. Henceforth, companies were required to distribute dividends annually, to restrict the size of agents' commissions, and to regulate the nature of their investments. The investigation constituted a purge of sorts and signified the industry's maturation.

In the wake of the Armstrong investigation, insurance companies offered more services and products to attract customers who had been disenchanted by the exposed corruption. In 1914, MassMutual instituted a premium waiver in the event of disability, and in 1918 the company designed policies with clauses that provided income in the event of disability. Few significant losses were posted during World War I, although the influenza epidemic of 1918 hit the company hard. By 1924, there were 400 home-office employees, and the amount of insurance in force passed $1 billion.

The stock market crash of 1929 and the ensuing Great Depression hit MassMutual hard. Death claims and policy lapses increased greatly due to an unusual number of suicides and general economic hardship. So pervasive were policy terminations that the company's insurance in force on July 1, 1932 was less than it had been at the beginning of the year. MassMutual, aside from being an insurer, became a last resort for desperate people seeking financial help. The company doled out millions of dollars in low-interest policy and premium loans. In 1932 alone, the company made $26 million in new policy loans, and from 1929 to 1937 the company made $129 million in policy loans and another $63 million in premium loans. The Depression also saw the introduction of new products. In 1930, MassMutual introduced its first family-income policy. Seven years later, the firm issued its first substandard risk product, and in 1938 the first pension trust policy was issued. Under the leadership of President William H. Sargeant and Bertrand Perry, who succeeded Sargeant in 1936, MassMutual stumbled, but emerged from the Depression and World War II virtually unscathed.

Finding Postwar Opportunities

When Alexander MacLean assumed the presidency in 1945, he became the first actuary to take the reins of the company. Consequently, many new products and services were introduced during his tenure. As unions and collective-bargaining units grew in strength, the atmosphere became more conducive to the development of group coverage. In 1946, MassMutual first entered the growing group business, offering group policies and managing group pensions. MassMutual's first group product was a combination pension and insurance policy for Brown-Forman Distillers, the Louisville, Kentucky-based company that produced Jack Daniels whiskey. By 1950, the group department had grown exponentially, employing 200 people in the home office and in the field.

As the postwar economy boomed, MassMutual continued its steady growth. By 1951, assets totaled $1.4 billion and the company had more than $3 billion of insurance in force. The home-office staff numbered 1,350, serving a client base of more than 700,000. There were 87 general agencies and 110 district agencies in 44 states. This decentralization was key to the company's success. The company hired general agents who in turn hired and trained local groups of agents. Successful general agents were often promoted to the Springfield home office. To further develop the strength of field agents, MassMutual instituted a training program for field representatives and encouraged its workers to complete the American College's Chartered Life Underwriter designation. The system worked. Between 1948 and 1957, the total life insurance in force doubled, from $2.7 billion to $5.4 billion.

In the increasingly complex postwar world, investing became a thorny problem. Bonds and mortgages were traditionally the investments of choice, because they were low-risk, high-security outlets, but in the 1950s, when insurance companies began to purchase more lucrative, riskier stocks, MassMutual followed suit. Still, the firm's original purpose—selling whole-life policies—remained constant.

During the late 1960s, James Martin, who was named president in 1968, involved the company in several public-oriented initiatives, investing $75 million in a Springfield office, retail enterprise, and a hotel complex, as well as supporting downtown mortgage-financing pools to rejuvenate urban development in medium-sized cities like Springfield. In 1969, assets topped $4 billion.

Key Dates:

1851: George W. Rice establishes MassMutual.
1868: The company expands and establishes its first office on the West Coast.
1901: The firm begins offering policies under which proceeds will be paid over a fixed period or for life.
1930: MassMutual introduces its first family-income policy.
1946: The company offers its first group coverage policy to Brown-Forman Distillers.
1969: The company's assets exceed $4 billion.
1981: The firm offers universal life policies.
1983: The company is reorganized into four divisions.
1990: The firm diversifies into mutual funds management by acquiring Oppenheimer Management.
1995: MassMutual announces its merger with Connecticut Mutual Life Insurance Co.
2000: MassMutual Trust Co. F.S.B. is formed to operate as a federal savings bank; CRC Protective Life of Hong Kong is acquired.

Fighting Economic Downturn: 1970s–Early 1980s

MassMutual surged ahead during the economic downturn of the early 1970s, installing new computer technology and liberalizing the work place. In 1974, MassMutual became the first major life insurance company to institute flextime. Soon after came the installation of a new database linking the home office with general agencies, allowing field agents to obtain information on policies more quickly.

During the late 1970s, inflation and the ensuing recession caused interest rates to soar. Individual investors began investing in high-yield money market accounts. Many life insurers, MassMutual included, experienced a rash of policy loans and had to borrow money at expensive rates to cover the loans since the bulk of their assets were tied up in long-term, low-yield securities. In this environment, many insurance companies turned toward the design and sale of new financial products for relief. MassMutual largely resisted the temptation, sticking to life and health insurance and pension-related products.

It became apparent that changes were in order when MassMutual began to lag behind other, more innovative insurance companies. In 1981, when insurance in force grew by an average of 16 percent for the top 50 insurance firms, MassMutual's insurance in force rose only 9.9 percent. William Clark, who had taken over as president in 1980, saw that it was time to shift gears, and in the next seven years MassMutual introduced several new products and changed investment policies. Clark also reorganized the company.

In 1981, MassMutual introduced universal life policies—two years after they first appeared on the insurance scene. The policies offered flexibility in paying premiums and allowed money collected from premiums to go into an account that could be invested in high-yield money market funds. Universal life, along with other new products, proved a big seller.

To discourage policy loans, MassMutual introduced a program through which 750,000 whole life holders accepted a much higher schedule of dividends in return for an adjustable rate of interest on future policy loans. In 1985, a large dividend-scale increase was implemented for life and health policies, and $440 million in dividends were distributed that year.

MassMutual Reorganizes in 1983

The firm was reorganized in 1983 into four divisions: individual products, group life and health, group pensions, and investments. Each was accountable for its own business. At roughly the same time, a new subsidiary was created—MML Investors Services—that served as an outlet selling noninsurance financial products. Its chief product is a line of mutual funds.

During the 1980s, group pensions became increasingly important. In anticipation of this, the unit was upgraded to a division in 1981. By 1984, the group-pension division's assets had reached $5 billion, making MassMutual one of the biggest managers in the country. In 1989, pension sales reached $1.5 billion. The division offered a variety of products, ranging from interest-guarantee contracts to annuity contracts.

As assets grew, due in part to the growth of pensions, MassMutual devised new strategies for its investment-management group. In 1985, assets stood at $15.7 billion. By 1989, they had risen to $25.1 billion. Traditionally, MassMutual had specialized in long-term investments, but after reorganization the firm diversified its holdings. With more assets behind it, MassMutual became increasingly involved in mortgage lending. In 1985, for example, the investment-management group issued $693 million in commercial mortgage pass-through certificates—the largest commercial loan issue ever. The amount of invested assets under investment management's control grew from $12.4 billion in 1985 to $21.8 billion in 1989. Individual life insurance in force was $81.5 billion in 1989, up from $54.1 billion in 1985, and new sales tripled over the same time period for life and health benefits.

While Massachusetts Mutual's methods and products had changed greatly since 1851, its philosophy—pragmatic and agent oriented—had not. Even though the firm had come to rely on products other than life insurance, it continued to view serving policyholders and employee-benefit clients as its primary reason for being. Despite the huge growth of the group pension and financial products divisions, MassMutual was still seen essentially as an insurance company.

Diversification Brings a New Image: 1990s and Beyond

The insurance company, however, began to take on a different appearance during the 1990s. In 1990, it acquired Oppenheimer Management as part of its strategy to diversify into mutual funds management. Then, in 1993, it created subsidiary Concert Capital Management to oversee $52 million in retirement fund and endowment assets. By this time, the industry had become highly competitive and MassMutual was positioned as the 12th-largest insurance concern in the United States based on total assets.

In a move to solidify its position in the industry, MassMutual agreed to merge with Connecticut Mutual Life

Insurance Co. in 1995. The deal was completed the following year and created the fifth-largest mutual life insurance company in the United States. MassMutual continued its diversification efforts in 1996 by creating Antares Leveraged Capital Corporation, a commercial finance unit providing lending services. By this time, assets had surpassed $100 billion.

Even as staunch competition in the insurance and financial sector continued, MassMutual achieved remarkable financial success during the late 1990s and into the new millennium. In 1998, the company posted a record year with net income increasing by 37 percent over the previous year to $359.2 million. The firm's positive results brought pressure to go public; however, company management believed that MassMutual's customers would be better served by maintaining its mutual company status.

Net income and sales continued to rise in 1999. That year, the company announced a new marketing name, MassMutual Financial Group, in an attempt to strengthen its image as a diversified financial services company. Chairman and CEO Robert O'Connell commented on the company's direction in a November 1999 *South Florida Business Journal* article, claiming that "you have to continue to offer new products and services and find new ways to grow your customer base, or you tend to wither away. The days when a company in our industry or elsewhere (in finance) could keep selling the same products without constant innovation are gone." Indeed, between 1999 and 2001, MassMutual and its domestic insurance subsidiaries launched 40 new products. By 2001, nearly 70 percent of revenues stemmed from these products.

MassMutual's financial success continued in 2000, which proved to be another record-setting year for the company. Total sales increased by 31 percent, revenues by 23 percent, and total assets under management grew from $206.6 billion secured in 1999 to $213.1 billion. That year, the firm stepped up its Asian operations and completed its purchase of CRC Protective Life of Hong Kong, which it renamed MassMutual Asia. MassMutual also took advantage of new laws that allowed insurance companies to enter the banking sector by creating MassMutual Trust Co. FSB, a federally chartered savings bank that offered investment services and estate planning.

In September 2001, the company's OppenheimerFunds subsidiary offices—residing in Two World Trade Center—were destroyed as a result of the terrorists attacks made against the United States. The subsidiary did not lose a single employee and recovered quite well, posting strong results along with its parent company for the year. Believing that diversification played a key role in its success during difficult economic times, MassMutual continued to move on that front. Its strategy for the future was centered around innovation and new product development, global expansion, and customer satisfaction.

Principal Subsidiaries

Antares Capital Corp.; C.M. Life Insurance Company; Cornerstone Real Estate Advisors Inc.; David L. Babson & Company Inc.; MassMutual International Inc.; MML Bay State Life Insurance Company; MML Investors Services Inc.; OppenheimerFunds Inc.; The MassMutual Trust Company, FSB.

Principal Competitors

New York Life Insurance Company; Northwestern Mutual; Prudential Financial Inc.

Further Reading

Freer, Jim, "MassMutual 'Must Offer New Products'," *South Florida Business Journal*, November 12, 1999, p. 31.

Massachusetts Mutual Life Insurance Company: A Commitment to Service, 1851–1987, Springfield, Mass.: Massachusetts Mutual Life Insurance Co., 1987.

"MassMutual Financial Group 2000 Results Soar, Marking Year of Dramatic Growth," *PR Newswire*, February 20, 2001.

"MassMutual Launches $10 Million Ad Campaign," *A.M. Best Newswire*, August 28 2001.

"MassMutual Reports Increase in Net Income," *A.M. Best Newswire*, March 11, 2002.

"MassMutual Starts New Year With New Name," *A.M. Best Newswire*, December 29 1999.

Reich-Hale, David, "Exec Departs; MassMutual in Bank Retreat?," *American Banker*, July 2, 2002, p.1.

—Daniel Gross
—updated by Christina M. Stansell

Matth. Hohner AG

Andreas-Koch-Strasse 9
D-78647 Trossingen
Germany
Telephone: (49) 07425-20-0
Fax: (49) 07425-24-249
Web site: http://www.matth-hohner-ag.de

Public Company
Incorporated: 1857
Employees: 426
Sales: $68.2 million (2001)
Stock Exchanges: Stuttgart
Ticker Symbol: HOH
NAIC: 339992 Musical Instrument Manufacturing

Matth. Hohner AG is the oldest and largest producer of harmonicas in the world. The German firm also makes accordions, percussion, and woodwind instruments and distributes musical goods made by other firms. Hohner products are available worldwide, with the United States accounting for almost half of sales. K.H.S. Musical Instrument Co. Ltd. of Taiwan owns controlling interest in the firm, while the descendants of founder Matthias Hohner hold 9 percent.

19th-Century Beginnings

Hohner's founder and namesake, Matthias Hohner, was born in 1833 in Trossingen, Germany, on the edge of the Black Forest. Trained as a watchmaker, Hohner became interested in the musical instrument known as the mouth organ, which had been developed in Germany beginning in the 1820s, and began making experimental versions. The mouth organ (later known as the harmonica) was a handheld instrument that had a series of parallel holes which contained small reeds. When air was blown through, they vibrated to produce different tones. The reeds were tuned to a musical scale, and the instrument had two sets, which allowed a tone to be made when inhaling as well as exhaling.

In 1857, after months of experimentation, Hohner began producing mouth organs for sale, and, with the help of an assistant, he built 650 during the year. Hohner proved to have a knack for

marketing, and demand soon outpaced production, which led to the hiring of more employees. In 1862 the rapidly growing company began exporting to the United States, one of a growing list of countries in which the firm's instruments were becoming available.

Part of Hohner's success was due to the nature of the instrument. The mouth organ offered a distinctive sound, was highly portable, and was inexpensive to purchase, which made it attractive to consumers. At the same time, music stores could easily stock them on a small upright display at the front counter, which yielded high visibility while utilizing only a small amount of retail space. Hohner's instruments were emblazoned with an elaborate, engraved emblem which instantly identified his products and made them stand out from their competitors. He also realized consumers' need for diversity, and his mouth organs were made in a wide variety of different musical keys and styles. The company's offerings began to gain a reputation for quality, and in 1873 at the Vienna world exhibition the firm received the first of many honors for its harmonicas.

By 1877 Hohner was employing 86 workers at his factory in Trossingen who were making more than 85,000 instruments a year by hand. In 1880 the first machines were purchased to automate some aspects of production, which increased output. The company's growth continued to be strong, helped in part by the many immigrants to the United States from Germany, who took with them an interest in the harmonica. In 1887 several additional Hohner workshops were opened in other villages around the area to meet the rising demand. During these years Hohner established a paternalistic relationship with his employees, which paid off with strong loyalty and minimal labor strife.

In 1896 Hohner created the Marine Band harmonica, named after John Philip Sousa's famous musical group. The new model would become an enduring classic, favored by a wide range of musicians, especially in the folk and blues fields. Sousa himself was engaged to assist in the instrument's promotion, and his endorsement was featured in ads and on the harmonica box itself.

Early 1900s: New Leadership, Continued Growth

In 1900, two years before his death, Matthias Hohner transferred ownership of the company to his five sons. By this time the firm was selling 96 percent of the 3 million harmonicas it made each year in the United States, and the turn of the century saw the company open an office in New York City. In 1906 and 1907 competitors Hotz and Pohl of Knittlingen were purchased, and in 1909 the company became known as Matth. Hohner AG. By 1913 the company's 3,000 employees were producing 10 million harmonicas a year.

Popularity of the instrument remained high during World War I, and Hohner supplied instruments to armies on both sides of the conflict through its neutral Swiss branch as well as by using cover addresses and other tactics. By 1920 the company was employing 4,000 workers and producing 20 million harmonicas a year. At this time Matthias Hohner's grandson, Ernst Hohner, was named chief executive.

The 1920s were a golden age for the harmonica, and Hohner was the leading brand name in North America, supplying the majority of instruments sold there. At the end of the decade the firm acquired rival harmonica makers Christian Weiss and Andi's AG. In 1931 Hohner branched out into music publishing and also founded a musical conservatory and the German Harmonica Association.

The company continued to place a strong emphasis on marketing, which included encouraging schoolteachers to get their students to take up the instrument, as well as the creation of harmonica orchestras, schools, and clubs. Attempts were also made to develop the instrument's appeal to classical musicians, though this did not succeed. Numerous popular musicians took up the harmonica, however, and many folk, blues, western, and hillbilly recordings of the era featured its familiar warbling sound. This exposure in turn helped increase sales, as did its use by celebrities (such as silent film comic Buster Keaton and boxer Max Schmeling), many of whom happened to have been given their harmonicas by Hohner.

1930s–40s: Accordions and the German War Machine

The 1930s saw the company making great numbers of accordions, keyed instruments that used air pressure created by squeezing to vibrate tuned reeds. The market for accordions was especially strong in Germany, where they were used as a solo instrument and in small ensembles. By 1939 the company had 5,000 employees.

With the rise of the Nazi party and the subsequent war in Europe, Hohner was enlisted to produce detonators for the German government. The company installed its first mechanical

conveyor systems to facilitate this work, which was mostly done by women. Hohner had earlier made harmonicas imprinted with swastikas, though the Nazi party took issue with the practice, considering the symbol's use on Hohner's product a trivialization. The harmonica was dismissed by many Germans, due to its association with "degenerate" American jazz and blues music as well as its relatively primitive nature.

Still, production of harmonicas continued during the war years, and following Germany's surrender the company again turned its full attention to instrument making. The partition of the country by the Allies was relatively painless for Hohner, as Trossingen was located in democratic West Germany, which recovered from the ravages of war more quickly than did the Communist-ruled East. The company did face a number of obstacles, however, including the consolidation of Hohner's main competitors in East Germany and the subsequent closure of markets behind the iron curtain, as well as the expropriation of the firm's Shanghai office by the Chinese. The Japanese also began to market harmonicas to other Asian countries, cutting into Hohner's presence in that region.

Despite these challenges, by the early 1950s Hohner was again producing great numbers of its instruments for worldwide consumption.

Stagnation in the 1960s

The rise of rock and roll music in the latter half of the decade coincided with a precipitous drop in sales of harmonicas and accordions, however, and the company failed to adapt to the situation, resulting in a prolonged period of decline. Some attributed this to the leadership of Ernst Hohner, who after many years at the helm had difficulty seeing that the changes in popular music constituted a long-term trend, rather than just a fad that would soon die out.

In 1960 Hohner's New York City office was moved to Hicksville, New York, where the cost of doing business was much lower. In 1962 Hohner began producing recorders, tube-shaped wooden instruments that users blew into while fingering a series of holes to make different tones.

Though there was a resurgence of interest in harmonicas during the early 1960s (both Bob Dylan and Beatle John Lennon played Hohners), the company's response to the opportunity was muted. As a sign of its inability to connect with the teenage market, Hohner's Beatle harmonica misidentified Paul McCartney and George Harrison on the instrument. In 1965 longtime CEO Ernst Hohner retired after 45 years in charge of the firm.

The continuing depressed state of harmonica sales led the company to pursue other areas of production, and in the mid-1970s it began serious work on developing electronic instruments. Hohner also began to make some harmonicas in the United States at this time, the first being a 64-reed model designed by virtuoso performer Cham-Ber Huang.

1980s Challenges

The year 1982 saw Hohner's U.S. base of operations move to Richmond, Virginia, from Hicksville, closer to incoming shipments of German instruments. In 1986 the U.S. division formed

Key Dates:

1857: Matthais Hohner begins making mouth organs in Trossingen, Germany.
1862: First Hohners are exported to the United States.
1880: New machinery boosts manufacturing efficiency.
1887: Annual production tops one million.
1900: Matthais Hohner passes control of firm to his sons; the first office opened in the United States.
1907: Company acquires competitors Hotz and Pohl.
1920: Ernst Hohner takes over as CEO; production of harmonicas hits 20 million.
1930s: Growing numbers of accordions made, largely for the German market.
1940s: Hohner produces detonators for German military during World War II.
1950s: After a postwar recovery, market for harmonicas enters long decline.
1965: Ernst Hohner steps down as CEO.
1980s: Company focuses on production of electronic instruments.
1986: Hohner's U.S. subsidiary forms distribution arm HSS Inc. with Sonor and Sabian.
1987: Company cuts work force to 1,000.
1989: Kunz-Holding GmbH purchases two-thirds of Hohner stock.
1997: K.H.S. Musical Instruments acquires majority ownership and restructuring begins.
2001: Hohner reports first profits in two decades.

Hohner/HSS with instrument makers Sonor and Sabian to distribute musical instruments such as guitars and cymbals. Hohner/HSS also later began selling guitars under its own name.

With revenues shrinking and losses piling up, the company reached a crisis point during 1986 and 1987. Hohner was forced to make sizable layoffs, and the total number of workers dropped to 1,000. In 1989 controlling interest in the company was acquired by Kunz-Holding GmbH & Co., a wood products manufacturer with sales of approximately $1 billion. Kunz obtained 67 percent of the public firm, with the Hohner family retaining an 8 percent stake.

Despite this turmoil, Hohner was having some success with educational musical instruments, marketing items like the Rainbow Harmonica, introduced in 1994. This product featured four color-coded holes and was designed to enable elementary school students to quickly learn simple tunes. Other rhythm instruments for schools were marketed under the Play & Learn name.

Late 1990s and Beyond

In 1997 Kunz-Holding sold most of its stake in Hohner to HS Investment Group, Inc., a Virgin Islands-based arm of K.H.S. Musical Instrument Co. Ltd. of Taipei, Taiwan. K.H.S., which had been founded in 1930, had factories in Japan, Taiwan, China, and the United States, and employed 1,000. The firm had annual revenues of $90 million. Hohner had experienced two consecutive decades of annual losses at this point,

with red ink totaling DM 4.5 million on revenues of DM 177.2 million during its most recent fiscal year.

Though the company still produced the majority of harmonicas made worldwide, it was feeling the heat of competition from Japan and China, and it soon began looking to those countries for cheaper sources of parts. Following the K.H.S. takeover, the company's board had been stocked with its appointees, and in late 1997 they voted to transfer some production to K.H.S. plants overseas. The company's less expensive, "entry-level" harmonicas would be made there, with the professional grade models continuing to be assembled in Trossingen. Other efforts to bring Hohner back to profitability saw the work force slashed from 858 to 598 during 1997, with the staff at Trossingen cut from 493 to 200.

More job cuts were made the following year as the struggle to get back on track continued. Other restructuring moves included streamlining the organizational hierarchy, combining production and administrative operations in Germany at a single site, and revising product offerings to bring them into line with consumer demands. Units that sold electronic products and pianos in Europe were divested, and an infusion of cash from both K.H.S. and Kunz-Holding helped the company pay down loans of DM 20.5 million. The restructuring also saw Hohner experiencing turnover at the top, with several changes in board members and executives.

In early 2000 Hohner moved its U.S. subsidiary into a new headquarters in Glen Allen, Virginia, just north of Richmond. The U.S. division subsequently announced a joint venture with Playful Harmonies, a six-year old company specializing in musical products for children, to produce a combined line of instruments and activity materials. The company's fortunes were starting to improve, with sales in both France and the United States picking up. At this time percussion instruments accounted for nearly half of revenues, with wind instruments 37 percent and other types 17 percent. For its fiscal year ending March 31, 2001, Hohner posted its first profit in more than 20 years, making DM 4.76 million on sales of DM 151.7 million.

Recovering at last from a long period of decline, Hohner was nearing its 150th birthday in better shape than it had been in decades. Though the world market for harmonicas would likely never again approach the heights of the early 20th century, the Hohner name and reputation for quality were still strong, and the reconstituted company faced the future with good prospects for continuing profitability.

Principal Subsidiaries

Sonor GmbH; Hohner, Inc. (United States); Hohner/HSS Inc. (United States); Hohner U.K.

Principal Competitors

Boosey & Hawkes plc; Roland Europe SpA.

Further Reading

Berghoff, Hartmut, *Zwischen Kleinstadt und Weltmarkt: Hohner und die Harmonika: 1857–1961,* Paderborn: Schoningh, 1997.

Fear, Jeffrey, ''Zwischen Kleinstadt und Weltmarkt: Hohner und die Harmonika 1857–1961: Unternehmensgeschichte als Gesell-schaftsgeschichte (Review),'' *Business History Review*, December 22, 1998.

Gerring, Jane, ''Hohner Looks Toward Instruments of Change,'' *Richmond Times-Dispatch*, May 3, 1999, p. D7.

''Hohner Enhances Service With New Showplace Warehouse,'' *Music Trades*, December 1, 2000, p. 68.

''Hohner Expands With New U.S. Headquarters,'' *Music Trades*, February 1, 2000, p. 48.

''The Hohner Money Machine,'' *Music Trades*, June 1, 1999, p. 74.

McNatt, Glenn, ''Humble Harmonica Turns 100,'' *Baltimore Sun*, April 7, 1996, p. 1J.

''New Structure at Hohner Promises Strong Future,'' *Music Trades*, March 1, 1999, p. 28.

Pearson, Robin, ''Zwischen Kleinstadt und Weltmarkt: Hohner und die Harmonika: 1857–1961. Unternehmensgeschichte als Gesell-schaftsgeschichte. (Review),'' *Business History*, April 1, 1999.

Schmid, John, ''Harmonica Maker Battles the Blues,'' *International Herald Tribune*, October 27, 1997, p. 1.

''Taiwan Musical-Instrument Company Takes Over German Icon,'' *Deutsche Presse-Agentur*, November 17, 1997.

—Frank Uhle

Melitta Unternehmensgruppe Bentz KG

Marienstrasse 88
D-32425 Minden
Germany
Telephone: (49) 571 4046-0
Fax: (49) 571 4046-499
Web site: http://www.melitta.de

Private Company
Incorporated: 1923 Bentz & Sohn
Employees: 3,827
Sales: EUR 1.4 billion ($1.4 billion) (2001)
NAIC: 311920 Coffee and Tea Manufacturing; 326199
All Other Plastics Product Manufacturing; 322299 All
Other Converted Paper Product Manufacturing;
322224 Uncoated Paper and Multiwall Bag
Manufacturing; 335211 Electric Housewares and
Household Fan Manufacturing

Melitta Unternehmensgruppe Bentz KG is the holding company of the Germany-based Melitta group of companies, a leading European manufacturer of roasted coffee, coffee filters, and coffee makers marketed under the "Melitta" brand. Melitta's SystemService division sells professional coffee makers and related equipment to the catering and hospitality industries. Besides its coffee-related products and services, Melitta makes food wrapping products under the "Toppits," "Albal," "Glad," and "Handy Bag" labels and household cleaning products under the "Swirl" and "gameo" brands. Melitta also produces tea-related products and specialty papers and owns a 25 percent share in German beverage manufacturer Eckes-Granini GmbH & Co. KG. Three-fifths of the company's revenues come from Germany, another quarter from Europe, and about 15 percent stem from sales in North and South America. Melitta's network of about 50 production plants and sales offices spans the globe, including Russia and China. Three grandsons of the company founder own and manage the family business.

A New Kind of Coffee Filter in 1908

Not very often does a housewife lay the groundwork for a commercial empire, but that was exactly what happened in the case of Melitta. Melitta was the name of company founder Amalie Auguste Melitta Bentz, the daughter of a bookstore owner in Dresden, Germany, who had married Johannes Emil Hugo Bentz, the son of a school director. Melitta raised their two boys—Willy and Horst—as a homemaker, while Hugo Bentz provided for the family, working as a manager at a Dresden department store. Melitta Benz enjoyed drinking a cup of coffee once in a while, but was unsatisfied with the bitter coffee ground found in the beverage, which the brewing methods of the time were not able to filter out. The metal or porcelain sieves used to do the job either let too much coffee ground into the cup, or they were so narrow that the coffee was cold by the time all the water had passed through. One day, Melitta Benz had an idea: She took an old brass pot, cut a few holes into the bottom with a nail and a hammer, took a sheet of blotting paper out of her eldest son's writing book and put it into the pot. The first Melitta coffee filter was born. To make sure that nobody could steal her idea, Melitta Benz took her invention to the Royal Patent office in Berlin. On June 20, 1908, the authority granted her legal protection for the "coffee filter with filtration paper" as a registered utility good. Six months later, Melitta and Hugo Bentz registered a home-based business with a capital of less than DM1. They transformed a small room in their four-bedroom apartment in Dresden into a "coffee filter workshop" and got to work.

To get the endeavor off the ground, the Bentz family had to be energetic and creative. Hugo Bentz gave up his position at the department store, and he and Melitta worked full time at their small family business operation, joined by their two sons after school. They bought the metal filters and filter paper from local suppliers, assembled the coffee filters and packaged them for sale. Their sons delivered cartons with coffee filter paper using a small trailer. Hugo Bentz demonstrated the use of the new coffee filters in shopping windows, a task that was later delegated to sales-savvy women hired for the job. Melitta Bentz invited a group of female friends to have coffee in her home,

Company Perspectives:

The difference between a branded and a ''no-name'' product is the consistent and reliable information which only a brand can provide. In fast-changing consumer environments, the brand offers information and orientation amid the confusing variety of goods on offer. Consumers have the possibility to find out about branded products via a global network of information. This mass of globally available information, however, also represents a changed paradigm for the manufacturers themselves. Competition, trends, and consumer behavior are changing at an ever faster pace. This requires greater flexibility of both companies and their employees, as well as an ability to adapt more rapidly to changing market conditions. In order to succeed in fast-moving markets, companies need new products, lean business processes, and tailored distribution systems. We regard the fulfillment of these requirements as a central strategic objective. Skilled and highly-trained employees are the guarantee that a culture of change can establish itself in our operating divisions and become everyday practice.

where she demonstrated her new invention. In 1911, the Melitta coffee filter received gold and silver medals at the renowned international Dresden Hygiene Exhibition. In the same year, Melitta Bentz gave birth to their daughter Hertha. Soon the business operation had to be moved to a bigger room in the Bentz family's residence and, not long after, even that room became too small.

Moving to New Headquarters in 1929

Just when business started taking off in earnest, it came to a sudden halt. In 1914, World War I broke out. The German government rationed paper and stopped coffee imports. Hugo Bentz was drafted into the German army. In that situation, continuing the coffee filter production had become impossible. Melitta Bentz kept the business running by selling cartons. In 1915, the business was moved into an old locksmith workshop in Dresden's Wildermannstrasse. After the war had ended in 1919, the coffee filter business took off again. In 1922, the Bentz family began exporting their coffee filters to Czechoslovakia and Switzerland. One year later, they officially registered their company under ''Bentz & Sohn.'' By 1925, a number of competitors had emerged that imitated ''Melitta'' coffee filters. To make the original distinguishable from the ''fakes,'' Melitta launched a distinct package design characterized by bright red and green colors. This design principle prevailed into the next century. In 1926, the company started a new promotional campaign, sending ''coffee filter demonstrators'' on a national tour of major household appliance stores.

By the end of the 1920s, Melitta's business had once more outgrown its location. However, a bigger one could not be found in Dresden at that time. In a stroke of luck, while traveling in Westphalia, Melitta and Hugo Bentz spotted an old chocolate factory in the small town of Minden. They bought the factory and moved their business with 55 employees to Minden

in spring 1929, registering their firm at that time as Melitta Bentz. Later the name was changed again to Bentz & Sohn. The city of Minden gave the business a head-start by waiving taxes on profits for the first five years. That came just at the right time, since Germany had entered a severe economic downturn. In February 1932, Melitta and Hugo Bentz retired from active participation in the family business and transferred the company to their two sons. The company was transformed into Melitta-Werke AG and a new logo launched for the ''Melitta'' brand.

Willy and Horst Bentz expanded the business during the 1930s. Besides selling coffee filters and filter paper to consumers, they also ventured into the hospitality industry. At the same time, the company's product range broadened, including aluminum and ceramic filters besides the original brass version. In addition, the shape of the filters and filter papers was constantly improved. The year 1932 saw the introduction of so-called ''fast-drip-filters,'' square filter paper that was pushed into the filter with the help of plungers. Five years later the company introduced a coffee filter with a conical shape and inner-wall grooves with matching filter bags, for which the company received a patent in 1937. In the same year, the company included waxed paper for wrapping sandwiches into its range of products. In 1938, the first Melitta commercial for a new fast-drip filter was shown at German movie theaters.

Expansion Follows World War II

The onset of World War II, in September 1939, once again interrupted Melitta's development. The company had just acquired a paper factory in Kreuznau near Düren to meet the rising demand for coffee filter paper. However, the production of civil goods was restricted by the German government, and the company had to produce war goods such as ammunition belts and cookware for the army. The company's production plants and office buildings were left untouched by the war, but immediately after it ended they were confiscated and occupied by the Allied Forces. For the twelve years that this situation lasted, the company used temporary sites to keep their operation up and running, sometimes using the back-rooms of restaurants. Hugo Bentz died in January 1946, only a few months after the war had ended. Melitta Bentz witnessed the postwar reconstruction and the beginning of a dynamic upswing for the business operation she had started. In 1950, the year of her death, her company was grossing DM4.7 million.

The economic boom that followed World War II lasted for more than two decades. During these times of dynamic growth, Melitta tried hard to keep up with demand in a seller's market where orders had to be restricted to serve as many customers as possible. The constant cash flowing from sales that grew at two-digit rates enabled the company to make major investments in its production infrastructure, to expand its product range and to conquer new markets abroad. In the late 1950s, Melitta built a brand-new paper factory for its filter papers. In the early 1960s, the company began manufacturing food wrapping paper, lunch bags, plastic and aluminum wrapping foil, and cleaning cloths. A decade later, Melitta added vacuum cleaner bags to its range of products. However, the imagination of CEO Horst Bentz did not stop there. He envisioned a company that could supply anything that goes on a set table, including porcelain dishes,

Key Dates:

1908: Melitta Bentz receives legal protection for the coffee filters she invented and starts her own business.
1923: The company Bentz & Sohn is officially registered.
1925: Melitta introduces the red-green packaging design.
1929: The business is moved from Dresden to Minden.
1937: The company receives a patent for its conical coffee filter and filter paper.
1960: Melitta's first subsidiary abroad is established in Canada.
1962: The company launches ground coffee in a vacuum pack.
1963: Melitta introduces its own line of food wrapping products.
1968: Melitta enters the Brazilian market.
1971: The company starts selling vacuum cleaner bags.
1990: The company reorganizes, and a management holding company is established.
1992: The company acquires specialty paper manufacturer Neu Kaliss Spezialpapierwerke.
1996: The food wrapping products division Cofresco Frischhalteprodukte GmbH & Co. KG is formed.
2001: IT-service firm is established as a joint venture with software firm Syskoplan AG.

juices, candy, and cigars. According to this vision, Melitta acquired a number of smaller companies and shareholdings.

While extending its product range, the company also extended its reach, at first into Western Europe. In 1960, Melitta established its first subsidiary overseas in Canada. During the 1960s and 1970s, paper factories and coffee roasting facilities were set up in the United States and Brazil. While expanding its business, the company kept refining its coffee filters and the ways to market them. In the 1950s, Melitta changed the filter design which—according to the latest trends—were made of stoneware with a pastel finish. German customers were encouraged to try out the new fast-drip filters at home for four weeks before they had to pay for them. During the 1960s, Melitta demonstrated its filters at trade shows attended by the general public, serving over two million cups of coffee. In 1962, the company launched ground coffee in a vacuum pack for the first time. Later in the decade, new filters in different sizes were introduced that made it possible to brew a certain number of cups when filling the filter up to the rim. After heat-resistant plastics had been invented, Melitta filters made from that new material were introduced. In 1965, Melitta launched its first coffee maker, the machines that began replacing the hand filter. The company also began manufacturing coffee makers for professional caterers, including a new pyramid-shaped filter. By the end of the 1970s the Melitta group of companies employed 10,000 people. Annual sales had grown to DM 1.6 billion—three hundred and fifty times as much as in 1950.

Consolidating in the 1980s–90s

The expansion of the 1950s, 1960s, and 1970s came with a price tag. While sales had exploded, cost followed suit. By the late 1980s, the company was in the red. In 1988, Melitta redefined its strategic positioning in five core markets, and each of them got its own brand. ''Melitta'' remained the main brand for coffee and coffee related products; ''Toppits'' was the brand for wrapping products to keep food fresh and tasty; ''Swirl'' was the label for cleaning-related products such as vacuum cleaner bags; ''Cilia'' was the brand name for tea and related products; and ''Aclimat'' the label for products in the area of home furnishings.

On the other hand, the company disengaged from many other activities that did not fit into one of these core areas, including porcelain, candy, fruit juices, and cigars. In 1990, a management holding was established, and the operative business split into legally independent firms. One area that was strengthened was paper production. In 1992, Melitta acquired German specialty paper manufacturer Neu Kaliss Spezialpapierwerke. To cut cost, the company's coffee maker production was moved to Portugal. In 1996, the food wrapping products division was brought into a joint venture with Dow Brands Europe, a subsidiary of Dow Chemical, and renamed Cofresco Frischhalteprodukte GmbH & Co. KG, with Melitta owning a 65-percent share. German electric appliances manufacturer Miele & Cie. acquired half of Melitta's coffee maker production subsidiary in China to include vacuum cleaners in its product range, while the North American coffeemaker production was sold off to small appliances maker Regal Ware. Melitta's French subsidiary acquired the Codiac group, a supplier of parts for electric household appliances, to break into the French market for vacuum cleaner bags. Another new venture, the production of biodegradable foil, was abandoned and sold.

Besides coffee filters and coffee makers, selling roasted coffee became an ever growing part of Melitta's business. At first the raw coffee was roasted in Minden, until, in 1966, the company acquired Bremen-based coffee roaster Carl Ronning. While Germany was the company's major market for coffee, Melitta also started roasting and selling it in Brazil and the United States. Up until 1991, the company's Brazilian subsidiary produced losses. However, by 1995 the Melitta brand had a four percent market share—the second largest among the many competing coffee roasters. In 1995, the company even opened several dozen coffee shops on the East Coast of the United States and in Florida under the name ''Coffee World.'' Rather than competing with the country's leading specialty coffee chains, Melitta was hoping that these stores would raise American consumers' awareness for the brand which would then—hopefully—translate into higher supermarket sales. Meanwhile the coffee market in Germany reached a saturation point with the beginning of the 1990s. Competition became fierce and prices declined, but Melitta was able to compete with the German market leader. In 1999, the company launched a new advertising campaign which had been developed for over a year behind closed doors. In 2002, Melitta was Germany's second largest vendor of roasted coffee to the country's grocery stores. Melitta also succeeded in marketing its vacuum cleaner bags to grocery store chains. In addition, the company made private-label coffee paper filters for retail chains to utilize its production capacity. By 2001, private-label production accounted for one quarter of Melitta's total paper filter production.

At the beginning of a new century, Melitta's position in its core markets was strong. However, the markets themselves were saturated. The company's search for new markets with high growth potential had largely failed. Horst Bentz' sons Jörg, Stephan, and Thomas owned and managed the company by taking turns in their respective areas of responsibility in order to foster among them a better understanding of the whole operation. Looking ahead, the three grandsons of company founder Melitta Bentz saw the business expand its core activities mainly into other European countries, especially France, the United Kingdom, Spain, Poland and Russia. Other impulses were expected to come from product innovations, such as non-stick-aluminum baking foil, new kinds of coffee filters and coffee makers, and new coffee specialties. Whether or not their children would carry on the family leadership for another generation had yet to be determined.

Principal Subsidiaries

Melitta Bentz KG; Melitta Haushaltsprodukte GmbH & Co. KG; Melitta Kaffee GmbH; Melitta Ges.mbH (Austria); Melitta GmbH (Switzerland); Melitta France S.A.S.; Melitta N.V. (Belgium); Melitta Nederland (Netherlands); Melitta Scandinavia A/S (Denmark); Melitta Scandinavia AB (Sweden); Delphy Industries S.A.S. (France); Codiac France S.A.S. (France, 49%); Vriesco Plastics B.V. (Netherlands); Primafilter B.V. (Netherlands); West-Clean AB (Sweden); Gameo AB (Sweden); Coffee Club Franchise B.V. (Netherlands, 75%); Melitta Emballages Ménagers Distribution S.A.S. (France); Melitta Russland AG (Russia); Melitta Chicago Review s.r.o. (Czech Republic); Melitta do Brasil Industria e Commercio Ltda. (Brazil); Melitta North America Inc. (United States); Melitta SystemService GmbH & Co. KG; Cofresco Frischhalteprodukte GmbH & Co. KG (65%); Melitta Beratungs- und Verwaltungs GmbH & Co. KG; Melitta Pacific Ltd. (China).

Principal Competitors

Tchibo Holding AG; Jacobs Kraft Foods International, Inc.; Alois Dallmayr KG; Nestlé Beverages; Starbucks Corporation; Luigi Lavazza S.p.A.; Sara Lee Beverage; Whitbread PLC; Miele & Cie. GmbH & Co. KG; WMF Württembergische Metallwarenfabrik AG; Moulinex S.A.

Further Reading

Drohner, Klaus, "Kaffeeröstern droht Preiskrieg," *Lebensmittel Zeitung*, October 20, 2000, p. 1.

Helmer, Wolfgang, "In der Unternehmensgruppe Melitta schwört man auf die Rotation," *Frankfurter Allgemeine Zeitung*, October 18, 1995, p. 29.

Hollreiser, Eric, "Melitta Plans Chain of Coffee Shops," *Philadelphia Business Journal*, June 2, 1995, p. 3.

Kapner, Suzanne, "Melitta Brews Brand Recognition at Coffee World," *Nation's Restaurant News*, October 9, 1995, p. 16.

"Licht und Schatten bei Melitta," *Lebensmittel Zeitung*, May 23, 1997, p. 18.

Mayr, Michael J., "Melitta verdoppelt seinen Exportmarkt," *Wirtschaftsblatt*, January 23, 2003, p. 20.

"Melitta do Brasil ist inzwischen eine Ertragsperle der Gruppe," *Frankfurter Allgemeine Zeitung*, July, 29, 1997, p. 16.

"Melitta ist kein potentieller Übernahmekandidat," *Lebensmittel Zeitung*, January 18, 2002.

"Melitta kooperiert mit Dow Chemical," *Frankfurter Allgemeine Zeitung*, September 13, 1996, p. 23.

Queck, Matthias, "Melitta-Gruppe sucht neue Wege," *Lebensmittel Zeitung*, June 9, 2000, p. 14.

"Rote Zahlen im Melitta-Filter," *Süddeutsche Zeitung*, September 10, 1992.

Rottenberger-Murtha, Kerry, and Richard P. Kern, "Profiles in Marketing: H.-Helmut Radtke," *Sales & Marketing Management*, February 1993, p. 161.

Vongehr, Ulrike, "Männertrio löst Melitta-Mann ab," *HORIZONT*, September 16, 1999, p. 24.

Zimmermann, Tassilo, "Gründlicher Hausputz bei Melitta," *Lebensmittel Zeitung*, July 20, 2001, p. 12.

——, "Melitta setzt auf internes Wachstum," *Lebensmittel Zeitung*, June 7, 2002, p. 14.

——, "Melitta sucht neue Wege," *Lebensmittel Zeitung*, February 22, 2002, p. 14.

—Evelyn Hauser

The Middleton Doll Company

West 239 North 1700 Busse Road
Waukesha, Wisconsin 53188-1160
U.S.A.
Telephone: (262) 523-4300
Toll Free: (800) 242-3285
Fax: (262) 523-4193
Web site: http://www.leemiddleton.com

Public Company
Founded: 1978
Employees: 2
Sales: $27.2 million (2001)
Stock Exchanges: NASDAQ
Ticker Symbol: DOLL
NAIC: 525930 Real Estate Investment Trusts

Formerly Bando McGlocklin Capital Corporation, The Middleton Doll Company is primarily involved in the doll business through its Ohio subsidiary Lee Middleton Original Dolls, Inc., although technically the Wisconsin firm remains a real estate investment trust. Lee Middleton Original Dolls, founded by the late doll designer Lee Middleton Urick, is a leading maker of realistic, hand-sculpted, collectible dolls. Since acquiring the operation in 1993 because of a bad real estate loan, the parent corporation has become so focused on dolls that it adopted the Middleton name in 2001 in order to help investors better evaluate its business. It even chose DOLL as its ticker symbol on the NASDAQ. Middleton Doll continues to operate Bando McGlocklin Small Business Lending Corporation, an REIT, as well as timepiece maker License Products, Inc., which Bando McGlocklin also picked up because of a bad loan. In addition, management runs a separate, publicly traded company, InvestorsBancorp, which was spun off in 1993.

Lee Middleton Starting Business in Her Kitchen in 1979

Lee Middleton grew up in Springfield, Ohio, interested in a variety of arts and crafts. Because her high school lacked formal art studies she had to settle on a mechanical drawing class to satisfy her aspirations in the graphic arts. Other than taking a few courses at an artist's school in Arizona, she was essentially self-taught, forging her own unique path. Middleton was deeply devoted to Christianity, yet fascinated by the workings of crime and police laboratories. She also had a keen interest in anatomy. All of these influences and skills would eventually come together in her doll creations. Lee Middleton knew some success as a painter and writer, selling verses to major greeting card companies, but it was not until 1978, when she and her family were living in Coolville, Ohio, that she decided to try sculpting porcelain dolls at her kitchen table. Her interest in anatomy led her to depict her baby dolls as realistically as possible, even down to the proper weight, and her religious faith infused them with a spirit that struck a cord with collectors. Eventually she would include a small Bible with each doll she sold. After she had completed several pieces that she thought were ready to show, she entered them in competition at a doll show in Columbus, Ohio. When she returned home that night her husband Lloyd was surprised to learn that not only did she win best of show she sold every doll she brought.

Encouraged by her initial success, Lee and her husband started up a business they called Kingdom Doll Originals and began to travel the doll shows, paying for a table to sell her creations to individual collectors. Her ambition at this point was simply to sell as many dolls as she could produce at home, but soon gift shops and doll shops began pressing her with wholesale orders and in order to accommodate these customers she began enlisting family members, friends, and others to make the dolls out of their own homes. In 1980 demand for Lee's work outstripped the capacity of this makeshift kitchen table assembly line, and her husband found accommodations in the basement of an old bank building in Coolville at $50 a month. Kingdom Doll outgrew that space in four months and annexed the ground floor of the bank for $50; in another six months, the company took over the second floor for $75.

Introducing Vinyl Dolls in 1984

Although the business, which now became known as the Middleton Doll Company, was growing at a steady clip, the porcelain medium was problematic. The process was time-consuming, requiring that each part be molded and hand-cleaned before it could be fired and decorated. Because so few could be produced, the dolls had to be priced between $500 and $700. Lee Middleton decided to replicate her porcelain designs in vinyl, which would speed the production process, lower the price on the dolls to the $100 to $200 range, and as a result allow more people to own her work. The only drawback was that vinyl dolls were not considered collectibles. Lee Middleton's artistry and innovative spirit, however, soon broke down that barrier. She pioneered the porcelain look in vinyl with her "Baby Skin" dolls. They were renowned for their lifelike qualities and became the first vinyl dolls to be numbered and signed and to achieve collectible status.

With the introduction of vinyl, sales for Kingdom Doll improved significantly, reaching $350,000 in 1984 and setting the stage for even greater growth. By 1988 employment at the company increased to 50 and sales reached $4.8 million. To accommodate the increased business, a former Coolville hardware store and the first floor of the Oddfellows Lodge were leased for dollmaking. Plans were made to build a 34,000-square-foot state-of-the-art manufacturing facility in Belpre, Ohio, housed in a structure with a gingerbread façade to make it look like a giant dollhouse. As an inducement to locate in Belpre, the city provided ten acres of land for the plant, and the $800,000 in construction costs were raised from lenders, including Bando McGlocklin, which in 1987 invested $2.4 million in Middleton Doll. To this point the dollmaker had no investors, and its financial backing was limited to a $400,000 line of bank credit.

As the business grew so too did the need for managerial assistance. For a while the Middletons had a friend named Bob McCloy, an attorney and accountant, come in once a week to help them, but soon they asked him to devote himself to the business on a full-time basis, hiring him as a vice-president in charge of administration and finance. Lloyd continued to serve as president, with Lee the chairman of the company. Even as they were named Ohio Small Business Persons of the year for 1989, however, their lack of business expertise was beginning to show. The new plant came in well over budget, due to add-ons and other changes, and in the end cost $1.25 million.

Moreover, their marriage splintered and the Middletons filed for divorce. In 1990 they reached a settlement that gave ownership of the business to Lee while Lloyd received $124,000 over four years in alimony. Before his departure Lloyd hired a new plant manager, Michael Dugay, who initiated an ill-advised marketing strategy during his brief tenure. Believing that the dolls held great potential at major urban department stores, he spent heavily on advertising, but with little effect. Early in 1991 the company, now called Lee Middleton Original Dolls, Inc., failed to keep up with the payments on its development loans. By the end of the year Dugay was gone and the company filed for Chapter 11 bankruptcy protection, which revealed that the company had liabilities of more than $4 million and assets of $2.8 million. Rather than allow the doll company to be auctioned off, Bando McGlocklin decided that its interests were best served by assuming control and attempting to turn around the business. In 1993 it purchased Lee Middleton Original Dolls for $1, gaining a 51 percent stake, with Lee Middleton owning the rest and continuing to provide the artistic talent behind the business.

The names behind Bando McGlocklin were former professional athletes Sal Bando, who played major league baseball for many years in Oakland before finishing his career with the Milwaukee Brewers, and Jon McGlocklin, who played for the Milwaukee Bucks professional basketball team. The two met and became friends at a charity golf tournament in 1977, the same year that Bando signed with the Brewers. McGlocklin was already retired and making the transition to a career after athletics, and because Bando was at the tail end of his playing days, the two agreed to pursue opportunities together. In 1980 they were approached by George Schonath about starting a venture capital firm geared toward small businesses. A business school graduate of the University of Wisconsin-Madison, the 39-year-old Schonath had extensive experience in lending, including a stint with a Wall Street investment banking firm. From 1970 to 1975 he also ran his own venture capital firm in Milwaukee. He became acquainted with Bando and McGlocklin while working with a financial planner hired by the athletes. The three men agreed to go into business, formed Bando McGlocklin Small Business Lending Corporation, and recruited some 35 investors, altogether raising $3 million in equity capital.

Although the Bando and McGlocklin names proved to be a useful calling card, the perception that the firm was nothing more than a scheme by a pair of ex-jocks was also a drawback. In fact, Bando gained experience working in the credit card marketing department for BankAmerica Corp. during his years in Oakland. Nevertheless, both he and McGlocklin had much to learn from Schonath, who served as chairman and chief executive officer in the new company and gave them a thorough education in commercial lending. The firm specialized in long-term loans of $1 million and less, which banks and insurance companies generally avoided. Licensed by the U.S. Small Business Administration as a small-business investment company (SBIC), Bando McGlocklin was able to borrow $3 from the SBA for every dollar it received in investor capital. The company's strategy from the outset was to concentrate on making a large number of small loans for the sake of diversification rather than risking a lot of money on just a few companies. The returns might not be as spectacular, but they were more reliable. Ironically, Bando McGlocklin was uninterested in taking a stake in the companies in which it invested, unlike most other venture capital funds. Instead, it preferred to make loans and let entrepreneurs remain independent, a stance that attracted business from small business owners who, fearing interference, were reluctant to turn to venture capitalists for funding. Because it had no say in the running of the companies, it placed a great deal of emphasis on funding entrepreneurs in which it believed, one of which proved to be Lee Middleton.

Bando McGlocklin Going Public in 1987

The vast majority of Bando McGlocklin loans were backed by real estate, so that it was not surprising that in 1986 the three partners decided to start a real estate investment trust (REIT), Bishops Woods I. In May 1987 the firm went public as Bando McGlocklin Capital Corp., raising $4.2 million. Following a restructuring of the business in 1993, the SBIC was transferred to a subsidiary, InvestorsBancorp, leaving the parent company to begin converting to a REIT, a process not completed until 1997 when InvestorBancorp was created as a separate corporation to make small business loans. Bando McGlocklin now began to lease warehouse and light industrial space to businesses. By now the company also found itself inadvertently taking over some of the small businesses to which it had previously loaned money. In addition to Middleton Dolls, it also gained control of License Products Inc. The recipient of a loan in 1988, the company by 1993 was in default to Bando McGlocklin, which instead of selling off the business decided to try turning it around.

Increasingly during the 1990s the doll business became the focus of Bando McGlocklin. After losing $350,000 during the first year after emerging from bankruptcy, Lee Middleton Original Dolls began to show a profit, growing to $1.8 million in 1996. Much of that improvement was attributed to Lee Middleton's introduction of her newborn babies line in 1994 and the 1996 expansion of her Artist Studio Collection, a line of expensive, limited-edition collectible dolls. She remained the company's only artist, but as demand for Middleton's infant dolls grew, it became clear that other designers would have to be hired. Lee Middleton's health also was becoming a factor. She was forced to undergo heart bypass surgery in 1996, and then on the evening of January 30, 1997, while working at her studio, she was struck by a fatal heart attack. Finding an artist to replace her was now a daunting but imperative task.

Riva Schick, the first doll designer to have her work produced under the Middleton banner, was similar to Lee Middleton in many ways, especially her talent for realistically sculpting infants, yet she was not even familiar with her predecessor's name. Growing up in British Columbia, Canada, Schick had to make her paper dolls because her family could not afford to buy dolls for her. Religious and self-taught like Lee Middleton, she worked as a postal clerk for 17 years before quitting to see if she could forge a career in dollmaking, which she had only taken up in 1990. Working at her kitchen table, like Lee Middleton, she produced one-of-a-kind, hand-sculpted dolls, which she sold at shows. She did not even read her first collectors magazine until 1997, from which she learned about International Toy Fair 1997. She was determined to show her work at the fair, but just as she was set to leave, her father died and she had to send her sisters-in-law to submit her work. Nevertheless, her dolls generated enough interest that several companies asked her to contact them. Nothing worked out and she was about to give up on signing with a dollmaking company when she finally called Lee Middleton Original Dolls and was asked to submit some pictures of her work. In a matter of days she was visiting the factory and was signed to sculpt for the company. Her rise to stardom in the doll world was rapid. Within months she won "Best New Doll" and "Best New Doll Artist" at the International Collectibles Exposition.

Other doll artists would soon join Schick at Lee Middleton Original Dolls, including Eva Helland, Linda Henry Boving, and Mavis Snyder. The business was trending upward, clearly outperforming Bando McGlocklin's other investments. In 1998, following Lee Middleton's death, the firm acquired the rest of the doll company from her estate for $5 million in cash. Lee Middleton Original Dolls became increasingly involved in the design of licensed dolls. In 2000 it worked with the Walt Disney Internet Group to create two new dolls based on Cinderella and Belle from "Beauty and the Beast." A year later it brought out three Little League dolls based on the three words in the group's insignia: Loyalty, Courage, and Character. Lee Middleton Original Dolls worked with Procter and Gamble to produce Gentle Touch Baby for Pampers. It also introduced Small Wonder, its first dolls that were intended for play. With such increased activity the company outgrew its Belpre facility and in 2000 moved its corporate headquarters to Columbus, Ohio.

Bando McGlocklin remained based in Wisconsin, but decided in 2001 to more closely align itself with the doll company in an effort to alleviate investor confusion on Wall Street and transfer the success of its doll business to the price of its stock. To achieve this end the parent corporation changed its name to The Middleton Doll Company. Although their names were removed, both Bando and McGlocklin maintained their roles in the organization, with Bando on the board of directors and McGlocklin serving as senior vice-president. The operating subsidiary, however, retained the name Lee Middleton Original Dolls, easing the concern of her devoted fans. It also continued to look for new opportunities. In 2001 the company opened Newborn Nursery Adoptions centers at 40 participating retailers around the country, expanding on a concept that had begun years earlier at the Belpre factory and company stores. Customers did not just purchase a Middleton doll, they adopted it, a process in which adoption papers listing the doll's features were completed by a "nurse," followed by the "baby" being formally presented, with photographs taken of the new family. Also in 2001 the company launched a pair of limited edition dolls. The first, She's So Sweet, had a production run of a single day, the second, Walk in the Park, was limited to a one-week period. The birth date and time of birth were marked on each doll. In 2001 the company introduced the Artist Studio Collection, a line of 60 fine-quality dolls aimed at the serious collector or the consumer looking to create an heirloom for the family.

With its doll subsidiary thriving and well positioned for continued growth, the parent corporation was likely to become even more focused on an industry it had entered only by chance.

Principal Subsidiaries

Lee Middleton Original Dolls, Inc.; Bando McGlocklin Small Business Lending Corporation; Middleton (H.K.) Limited; License Products, Inc.

Principal Competitors

Alexander Doll Company; Ashton Drake Galleries; Mattel, Inc.

Further Reading

Evain, Elaine Newell, "Lee Middleton Original Dolls—The Babies That Love You Back!," *Collectors Mart Magazine,* August 2001, p. 32.

Field, Reggie, "Doll Maker Searches for Happy Ending," *Business First-Columbia,* January 13, 1992, p. 1.

Gardner, Robert W., "The Doll Factory," *Ohio Business,* May 1989, p. 24.

Goetgeluck, Sallie, "Fairy Tales Do Come True," *Doll Reader,* March/April 1999, p. 52.

Hoeschen, Brad, "Bando Finds a Doll," *Business Journal-Milwaukee,* May 16, 1997, p. 1.

Koon, Larry, *Lee Middleton Original Dolls Price Guide,* Grantsville, Md.: Hobby House Press, 2000.

Lawder, Dave, "Bando, McGlocklin Overcame Ex-athlete Stereotypes," *Business Journal-Milwaukee,* August 3, 1987, p. 17.

—Ed Dinger

Milacron, Inc.

2090 Florence Avenue
Cincinnati, Ohio 45206
U.S.A.
Telephone: (513) 487-5000
Fax: (513) 487-5057
Web site: http://www.milacron.com

Public Company
Incorporated: 1884 as Cincinnati Screw and Tap Co.
Employees: 7,885
Sales: $1.2 billion
Stock Exchanges: New York
Ticker Symbol: NZ
NAIC: 333512 Machine Tool (Metal Cutting Types)
Manufacturing; 324191 Petroleum Lubricating Oil and
Grease Manufacturing; 327910 Abrasive Product
Manufacturing; 333298 All Other Industrial
Manufacturing; 333319 Other Commercial and
Service Industry Machinery Manufacturing; 333515
Cutting Tool and Machine Tool Accessory
Manufacturing; 333518 Other Metalworking
Machinery Manufacturing; 334513 Instruments and
Related Product Manufacturing for Measuring,
Displaying, and Controlling Industrial Process
Variables

At the dawn of the 21st century, Cincinnati-based Milacron, Inc. (formerly Cincinnati Milacron Inc.), ranked among the world's largest manufacturers of plastics machinery, but up until the late 1990s, it was best known as a machine tool company. The company's slogan, "Helping the World's Leading Companies Make the World's Favorite Products," only hints at its impressive list of customers. From machines to make everything from baby bottles and car seats to sporting goods and toys to auto parts and medical supplies, Milacron's products are used worldwide.

Late 19th-Century Origins

Cincinnati Milacron traces its roots to 1874, when George Mueller inherited his father's small machine shop on Vine Street in Cincinnati and asked his friend, Fred Holz, to be his partner. Initially, the men maintained the elder Mueller's focus on manufacturing parts for sewing machines and repairing small machines. Gradually, however, they began building specialized machinery, including a device that produced screws and the taps and dies that cut threads for them. By 1876, the company largely centered on manufacturing the screw machine, and Mueller and Holz renamed their business The Cincinnati Screw and Tap Company.

Around 1878, when the small company needed a new milling machine for the tap making business and could not afford one, Holz put his machinist background to work and built one with an improved basic design. Soon, other shops began requesting machines, and by 1882, Cincinnati Screw and Tap found itself adding milling machines to its product line. In 1884, the company became incorporated to raise the capital it needed to produce the more costly machines and to finance a move to a larger facility near the Ohio River.

In 1887, Frederick A. Geier, while doing business with the Cincinnati Screw and Tap Co., became excited about this innovative company's potential. Within three months, Geier, then 21 years old, had bought a stake in the company. While Holz concentrated on the technology side of the business, Geier focused his energy in the areas of organization and sales. Believing that a company should focus primarily on one product, Geier favored the production of the milling machine over the company's screw and tap business. In early 1889, the stockholders approved the sale of the screw and tap business to a group of employees. Holz, Mueller, and Geier all stayed with the milling machine business, which became the Cincinnati Milling Machine Company, or the Mill, as employees would come to call it. Two years later, co-founder Mueller sold his one-third interest in the company and retired.

Although the milling machine industry had long been controlled by companies in the eastern United States, the Mill found its niche by emphasizing quality. In 1889, Holz built a cutter grinder that would help shops and factories save money by sharpening cutting tools so they would last much longer. This gave the company a new product to sell with its millers and helped to build the Mill's machine tooling reputation with its customers.

As early as the next year, the Mill had its first export order to a Swedish company. This was the beginning of an export business that would continue to grow and would, in fact, help keep the company afloat during times when the U.S. economy foundered.

One of those troubling times occurred in 1893, when a sharp recession hit, and factories and machine shops stopped placing orders for new equipment. Sales were almost nonexistent, credit was unavailable, and, moreover, the Mill had its capital tied up in building a new plant on Spring Grove Avenue. Nevertheless, the company worked its way out from the slump by taking a chance. When an order for a dozen milling machines came in from a bicycle maker in Indianapolis, who was short of cash and would need nine months to pay, Geier called the employees together and asked them what they wanted to do. The employees decided to take the order; the bicycle maker received his 12 machines and paid for them. The Mill survived and by 1895 was again prosperous. Reportedly, throughout the 1890s, bicycle makers purchased almost half the machine tools made by the company.

New Century, New Plant

During the early 1900s, Holz sold his common stock to Geier and retired from the company. Geier, who had already held controlling interest in the company, was looking to move the company again, this time to a site where the Mill could be as self-reliant as possible with its own foundry and power plant. By 1907, land was purchased in the nearby community of Oakley, financing had been secured for the move, and work on the foundry began. The foundry and power plant were completed in 1908, and, by 1911, the new complex was complete and operational. The new plant had more than six acres of floor space and was the world's largest milling machine factory. Geier's timing had been perfect. The motor car was just becoming popular, and the Mill was ready to provide the tools that the industrial world needed.

The onset of World War I in 1914 brought with it an initially sluggish market for the Mill. However, once the Allies realized the war was going to last for a while, they began to turn to America for machine tools to gear up for war production. In 1916, the U.S. government began its own war-readiness program, which put even heavier demands on American industry, particularly on the machine tool makers. Sales for the Mill were $1.4 million in 1914 and grew to $7 million in 1917, while its work force increased from 310 to 1,270.

Interwar Contraction

By the time the armistice was signed in November 1918 and the postwar ''return to normalcy'' had begun, however, government contracts were being cancelled, and the Mill found itself with a sudden excess capacity. In 1919, in an attempt to temper the cyclical nature of the business, Geier announced a plan to build a warehouse for storing the milling machines produced by the company until a time when orders exceeded capacity. As Geier sought to keep his employees in work year-round, and for the highest possible wages (a strategy known as ''work-spreading''), Mill employees remained generally disinterested in forming unions or becoming involved in strikes during the labor union wars of the early 1920s.

Still, the economic climate during this time remained ominous, and, early in 1921, Geier announced to his workers that the company had out-produced sales by 66 percent. Specifically, the Mill had 561 machines on hand, unsold. The policy of paying employees to make machines that weren't selling did not make business sense, and changes had to be made. Management salaries were cut, and a 15 percent wage reduction was initiated. Employment fell from an average of 1,004 in 1920 to 250 in 1921.

In the midst of this economic downswing, Geier's son, Frederick V. Geier, convinced management that the company should branch out into the production of centertype grinding machines, devices that used wheels to grind metal into round or cylindrical precision parts, such as pistons, valve stems, and bearings. This move, the younger Geier contended, would help absorb overhead and more fully utilize plant capacity. In September 1921, the company bought controlling interest in the Cincinnati Grinder Co. and the following year moved production of the grinding machine to Oakley. In addition, the Mill obtained the rights to key patents on centerless grinding, and formed a subsidiary, Cincinnati Grinders, Inc. With the success of these machines, in 1926, Cincinnati Milling became the nation's largest machine tool company.

When the Great Depression hit, the Mill was able to rely on its export trade to carry it through. Exports, one-fifth of all sales in 1929, grew to represent one-third of sales in 1932. During this time, the Mill continued to ''spread'' work, keeping as many employees on the payroll as possible. Management also worked closely with the Mutual Aid Committee, which was founded in 1916 as an employee insurance association and used as a relief organization for those hardest hit during the Depression.

Changes occurred at the Mill during this era. Traditionally, the company had used agents and distributors to sell machines to customers. In 1931, after providing sales training for gradu-

Key Dates:

1874: Mueller and Holz establish a partnership to make sewing machine parts.
1876: The business, christened The Cincinnati Screw and Tap, focuses on the manufacture of screw machines.
1917: Sales reach $7 million under wartime production.
1941: The company is producing about 8 percent of U.S. machine tools.
1946: First public offering of stock is held.
1952: Construction of a machine tool factory in the Netherlands is completed.
1970: Stockholders approve a name change to Cincinnati Milacron.
1979: The company establishes its own semiconductor materials division.
1984: The Mill is among the world's largest suppliers of silicon wafers for semiconductors.
1992: A quality assurance program called Project Wolfpack is initiated.
1998: Focusing on metalworking and plastics, the company divests its machine tool business and changes its name to Milacron, Inc.
2001: Efforts at restructuring to improve profitability continue as the country recovers from economic recession.

ates of its co-op program with the University of Cincinnati, the Mill put some of its own sales staff in the field and began direct selling. The company formed a wholly-owned sales subsidiary and opened offices in Detroit, Chicago, and Cleveland.

Moreover, instead of guarding its resources and waiting for better days, the Mill continued to invest in research and development. During this time, the company introduced hydraulic-powered machines, broaching machines able to make finer and more precise cuts, and the Dial Type milling machine, which, with its power speed and feed change features, became the industry standard. In 1932, the Mill agreed with Heald Machine Co. of Worcester, Massachusetts, to share engineering, research, and patents. Although both companies produced grinding machines, their machines were used in different applications and therefore complemented one another. A little over 20 years later, after years of working together, the Mill would purchase Heald outright.

First Overseas Subsidiary

In 1934, Frederick A. Geier died of a heart attack. A month later, his son, Frederick V. Geier, was elected president of the company. One of the younger Geier's first projects was to establish a subsidiary in Great Britain to make machines for world markets. In fact, as World War II began, Britain became one of the Mill's major customers, buying $16.5 million worth of machines in 1940.

Because of the increased number of military orders before the war, the machine tool industry was prepared to meet demand once the United States began mobilizing forces. With

forethought, the Mill had decided to expand the company's capacity in 1938 and had also began a formal three-stage training program for workers. This training program became invaluable, as the Mill's work force escalated to a wartime peak of 8,561 employees. By 1941, the company was producing nearly eight percent of America's machine tools.

Throughout the war, the Mill continued its emphasis on research and development. It began exploring the physics of metal cutting as well as ways to increase tool life. Out of this research came the Mill's first synthetic cutting fluid, called Cimcool. During the postwar era, Cimcool rose to become Milacron's most-recognized brand, with a line of thousands of water, oil, and oil-soluble coolants.

In 1943, Geier began meeting regularly with four other key executives in an effort to identify strategies for postwar growth. According to the official company history, the four goals the committee agreed upon were "to extend overseas manufacturing; to broaden machinery product lines; to enter the industrial consumables market; and to develop new technologies." These goals for growth and diversification brought with them the task of finding a way to finance new company endeavors. In February 1946, the Mill raised $3.8 million in new capital when it issued its first public stock offering.

Acquisitions and Diversification in the 1950s–60s

The next ten years brought a variety of acquisitions and the development of new product ideas. Some of these new products included grinding wheels, cutting fluids, and lathes. In 1955, the Mill expanded its move into chemicals, acquiring a company that, among other things, made additives for plastic. By 1957, the Mill was working with glass reinforced plastic components and had formed the Cimastra division to oversee production and sales of the materials. This division began selling molded plastics to different companies, including manufacturers of children's sleds, seats for bowling alleys, and cases for movie projectors.

The 1950s also bore witness to the Mill's expansion in Europe. The company increased its holdings in England by acquiring and expanding plants and foundries in Birmingham and nearby Cannock. In 1952, the Mill began building a machine tool factory in the Netherlands that was completed in 1954.

The electronic era at the Mill began in the late 1950s, as the company became involved with a new technology called numerical control. Using numerically coded instructions on punch cards, the technology allowed computers to control the movements of machine tools and thus had great potential in automating American industry. In 1955, the Mill received a contract from the U.S. Air Force for numerically controlled machines that could produce intricate aircraft parts at high speed. The company continued to improve on its use of the technology, and, in 1966, the Mill introduced a new generation of controls for its machines using miniaturized integrated circuits rather than the cumbersome vacuum tubes and mechanical relays it had relied on. Using its expertise in both plastics and electronics, the company also began producing plastic circuit boards that were used in TV sets, radios, and eventually computers.

As the 1960s came to a close, Cincinnati Milling found it had become a far more diverse company than its name indicated. In

May 1970, the stockholders approved a new name. Cincinnati Milacron capitalized on the continued use of Cincinnati—a city linked with machine tools—while also introducing a new word, Milacron, the roots of which meant "highest precision." Thus, despite the name change, company employees could logically continue to refer to their company as the Mill.

Plastics Machinery Drives Growth in the 1970s

The 1970s became a time of streamlining and redirection for the Mill. Frederick V. Geier retired from his position as chair of the executive committee in 1976 and was given the honorary title of director emeritus. His cousin, Philip O. Geier, Jr., who had served as the Mill's president and then chairperson, also retired during this time, leaving James A.D. Geier in charge as chairperson. Under Jim Geier, the company began focusing its machine tool efforts on computer-controlled equipment, and, perhaps more importantly, a corporate research department was set up to look into non-machine tool products. As an outgrowth of this research, the Mill moved into the plastics machinery business, producing its first plastics injection molding machine in 1968. With expertise in injection molding and extrusion, the Mill worked with E.I. du Pont Co. to perfect a reheat blow molding machine that would revolutionize the way soft drinks were packaged. A fourth molding process called reaction injection molding was also introduced by the Mill. By 1977, the Mill was the largest U.S. maker of plastics machinery.

Also in the 1970s, the Mill intensified its focus on electronically operated machines, venturing into the markets for minicomputers and semiconductors. While its efforts to manufacture and market minicomputers proved disappointing and short-lived, the company had more success with semiconductors, specifically in the development and manufacture of the silicon wafers on which semiconductors were built. Demand for the Mill's silicon epitaxial wafer prompted the company to provide its semiconductor materials division with its own facility in 1979, and, by 1984, the Mill had become the world's largest supplier of this type of wafer. Also during the late 1970s, the Mill became one of the world's first companies to make computer-controlled-industrial robots. These robots, which performed such tasks as spot-welding, became integral to assembly lines at companies like Ford, General Electric, and Volvo.

Restructuring in the 1980s and 1990s

In 1980, the Mill sold its profitable specialty chemical operations to the Thiokol Corporation in order to focus more strongly on its three more closely allied divisions: machine tools, plastics machinery, and industrial specialty products. During the 1980s, the company felt the effects of a severe economic recession that became second only to the Great Depression in terms of loss in the capital goods markets. In addition, the Japanese were giving U.S. machine tool builders some severe competition. The Mill began cost cutting measures, including plant consolidations and early retirement plans. Worldwide employment declined by one-third, and, in 1983, the company reported its first annual loss.

In fact, the Mill reported losses in five of the next ten years. Increasingly tough competition and misdirected business turns took their toll on the Mill. Under the leadership of Daniel Meyer, who succeeded Jim Geier in 1990, a campaign began that would

help fine tune the company for the 1990s. Called Project Wolfpack, this effort utilized the teamwork of employees from different disciplines to cut product development cycles and cost. According to an April 1992 article in *The Cincinnati Enquirer*, each team was charged with improving the quality of Milacron's machines while removing up to 40 percent of the cost and 40 percent of the components. The teams worked together to consider the market needs, feasibility of design concepts to operate machines of the size range being considered, and the availability of the latest technology to perform functions required. Harold Faig, vice-president of the U.S. Plastics Machinery Division said in *The Cincinnati Post* in May 1991, "Our single goal is to offer the best quality, American-made machines with the widest range of features at a competitive price."

The success of the Wolfpack, as well as moves to abandon or sell several money-losing businesses such as robots and semiconductors, helped the Mill return to profitability in 1992. Aligned with the Wolfpack's goals, the Mill committed itself to simpler, lower-priced, globally competitive tools. In 1993, excess capacity in machine tool facilities prompted the Mill to consolidate operations. In October 1994, the Mill's plastic machinery plants in Ohio were named among *Industry Week* magazine's ranking of the ten best plants in America for their performance, production, and customer satisfaction.

Acquisitions in the 1990s set the pace so that almost half the Mill's revenue came from outside the United States in 1995. Its machine tool, plastics technologies, and metalworking technologies divisions each roughly represented one-third of the business, helping to even out the cyclical nature of the business identified so long ago. Due to a continued emphasis on research and development, more than 75 percent of the Mill's 1993 machinery sales consisted of products not sold five years before. A particular focus on consumables—both consumer and industrial—held out the promise of nonstop growth.

Then, in 1998, after more than a century in the machine tool industry, the company divested that segment of its business and simplified its name to Milacron, Inc. The sale of the machine tool division, combined with a variety of other acquisitions and divestitures in the late 1990s, left Milacron's business nearly evenly split between plastics and metalworking. Machinery for the aerospace industry constituted an important growth industry, with revenues in this business category tripling from 1994 to 1996.

Company leaders hoped that global diversification would also insulate them from domestic economic downturns. Acquisitions and joint ventures in Europe, Asia, South America, and elsewhere increased Milacron's international sales from about 30 percent of revenues to more than 45 percent.

"Finding A Better Way"

Milacron's efforts to diversify could not shield it from a recession in the first years of the 21st century. The company's sales declined from over $1.6 billion in 2000 to just under $1.3 billion in 2001, while net earnings plunged from $72 million to a loss of $36 million over the same period. These setbacks prompted another round of restructuring. Over the first two years of the 21st century, Milacron shuttered 18 plants and eliminated 2,200 jobs. In 2001, the company adopted both Six Sigma and Lean programs in an effort to reduce overhead and increase working capital. This austerity program also entailed withholding senior management bonuses for fiscal 2001.

The restructuring continued in 2002 with the divestment of Valenite, a 1,300-employee metal-cutting tool subsidiary. Milacron also shed the overseas metal cutting tool businesses Widia and Werko that same year. The company used the $290 million proceeds of these sales to pay down debt. CEO Ronald Brown noted that the divestments would also refine the company's focus on its plastics processing and industrial fluids operations.

In keeping with what had by this time become part of the corporate culture, Milacron invested heavily in research and development as well as capital expenditures so as to be prepared for a rebound. Chairman, CEO, and president Ronald Brown, who took over from Daniel J. Meyer in May 2001, expressed his hopes for Milacron's future in his presentation to shareholders on April 23, 2002. "It appears the downturn in the manufacturing sector is bottoming out," Brown observed. "We expect to return to profitability in the second half of this year."

Principal Subsidiaries

Cincinnati Milacron Resin Abrasives Inc.; Uniloy Milacron Inc.; Milacron France S.A.S.; Akron Extruders Inc.; Nickerson Machinery Company Inc.

Further Reading

Baker, Don, "Milacron Executives Bonuses Withheld," *Cincinnati Post*, March 29, 2002, p. 10B.
——, "Milacron CEO Sees Rebound Coming," *Cincinnati Post*, April 23, 2002, p. 6C.
——, "Milacron Selling Overseas Unit Cash Will Be Used to Pay Down Debt," *Cincinnati Post*, May 6, 2002, p. 9C.
Bird, Rick, "City's Tool Industry star of Documentary," *Cincinnati Post*, October 17, 2000, p. 6B.
Boehmer, Mike, "Milacron to Build German Plant," *Greater Cincinnati Business Record*, May 14, 1990, p. 1.
Boyer, Mike, "Milacron, Hounded by Foreign Competition, Unleashes Wolves," *Cincinnati Enquirer*, April 20, 1992, pp. 1D, 5D.
——, "Milacron to Acquire Krupp Widia," *Cincinnati Enquirer*, November 30, 1994, p. 6B.
Cincinnati Milacron, 1884–1984: Finding Better Ways, Cincinnati: Cincinnati Milacron, Inc., 1984, 218 p.
Higgins, James V., "New Industrial Robots Get Ready to Take a Hand In Auto Assembly," *Detroit News*, May 3, 2002, p. 1.
Marsh, Peter, "The Americas: Cincinnati Milacron Seeks Alliances to Increase Sales," *Financial Times*, April 30, 1998, p.30.
Miller, Nick, "Milacron Taking on New Look Company Positioned for More Growth," *Cincinnati Post*, April 24, 1996, p. 6B.
——, "Milacron Joins Venture With Indian Firm," *Cincinnati Post*, August 16, 1996, p. 6B.
——, "Milacron Nails $23M Aerospace Deal," *Cincinnati Post*, January 28, 1997, p. 6B.
——, "Milacron to Beef Up Sales, Distribution," *Cincinnati Post*, April 23, 1997, p. 6B.
——, "Milacron Investing in Plastics Research," *Cincinnati Post*, May 21, 1997, p. 8B.
Rawe, Dick, "Milacron Unveils Latest in Plastics Machines," *Cincinnati Post*, May 29, 1991, p. 6A.
Schiller, Zachary, "One Takes The High-End Road, The Other Takes the Low," *Business Week*, May 18, 1992, pp. 100–01.
Smock, Doug, "Milacron Places Its Bets on Electric Machines," *Plastics World*, July 1994, pp. 6–7.
Stammen, Ken, "Milacron Woos Plastic Industry With Electric, High-Tech Molders," *Cincinnati Post*, June 13, 2000, p. 5B.
——, "Meyer Retiring From Milacron Ronald D. Brown Takes Over in May," *Cincinnati Post*, February 10, 2001, p. 10B.
——, "Sluggish Sales Force Milacron To Cut Deeper," *Cincinnati Post*, September 27, 2001, p. 7B.
Uchitelle, Louis, "Companies Spending Money to Save Money," *New York Times*, April 24, 2002, p. C1.
Wood, Roy, "Milacron Sells Valenite Subsidiary," *Cincinnati Post*, June 19, 2002, p. 10C.

—Jennifer Voskuhl Canipe
—update: April Gasbarre

MPW Industrial Services Group, Inc.

9711 Lancaster Road, Southeast
Hebron, Ohio 43025
U.S.A.
Telephone: (740) 927-7890
Toll Free: (800) 827-8790
Fax: (740) 929-1614
Web site: http://www.mpwservices.com

Public Company
Incorporated: 1978 as MPW Industrial Services, Inc.
Employees: 1,400
Sales: $92.2 million(2002)
Stock Exchanges: NASDAQ
Ticker Symbol: MPWG
NAIC: 561720 Custodial Services

MPW Industrial Services Group, Inc. provides industrial cleaning and associated services. While MPW, which stands for Mobile Power Washing, is a public company, its founder, chairman, and CEO, Monte R. Black, owns nearly 60 percent of its stock. With 1,400 employees and 1,200 pieces of major equipment, MPW serves some 800 customers through its headquarters in Hebron, Ohio, and more than 40 operations located in 14 states and Canada. After expanding into new services in the 1990s, MPW has cut back in recent years and now concentrates on three segments. Industrial Cleaning and Facility Maintenance is MPW's oldest area of business. Generally working on-site, the company cleans important operating equipment, its services including dry vacuuming, wet vacuuming, industrial power washing, high pressure water blasting, cryojetic cleaning, and chemical cleaning. The Facility Support division of this business segment cleans industrial facilities, but is much more than a janitorial service. The focus is on contributing to the efficiency and productivity of an operation through effective cleaning. Customers of the segment include the automotive, utility, chemical, pulp and paper, manufacturing, and steel industries. The second of MPW's business segments is Industrial Container Cleaning, primarily devoted to automotive paint manufacturers. The company cleans totes, paint resin containers used in the painting of vehicles. Once thoroughly cleaned, they can be refilled with paint resin and are capable once again of producing a high-quality paint finish. The last business segment is Industrial Process Water Purification. MPW provides water purification trailers, on an emergency or regular basis, catering to the utility, healthcare, manufacturing, and automotive industries. In addition, the company runs an exchange service of small tanks of purified water when smaller quantities are needed.

Company Established in 1972

MPW's founder, Monte Black, was only 20 years old when in 1972 he borrowed $5,000 from his father to buy a truck and a power washer and start a business in Baltimore, Ohio. He called it Central Ohio Mobile Power Wash, and as a one-man operation he washed trucks. Black earned a reputation as a hard worker, showing up early for jobs and following up with customers to ensure satisfaction. As a result, he secured new business through word of mouth, and even decades later most of MPW's new customers came through referrals from current customers. By 1977, Black had six trucks and 14 employees and was successful enough to build his first office. A year later, he reached an important turning point when a friend who worked at American Electric Power advised him that the plant was a potential client for the services offered by Black's company. Black incorporated his business as MPW Industrial Services, Inc. in 1978, as he began to add more trucks to his fleet and purchase the high-tech equipment necessary to offer new cleaning services in factories. He also began to expand his geographical reach.

MPW grew steadily for the next ten years, then Black named William C. Clark to serve as president and chief operating officer (COO). Charged with guiding the company to the next level of growth, Clark aimed to make MPW into America's premier environmental and industrial cleaning service company. Over the next five years, the company doubled in size and revenues, which approached $50 million. In the 1990s, MPW began to expand beyond industrial cleaning. It entered the industrial process water purification business in 1990, then in 1993 became involved in industrial container cleaning, initially working for a single customer on site. By then, in addition to its headquarters in Hebron, MPW had Ohio offices in Cleveland, Youngstown, Toledo, Lima, and Newark. The company had additional operations in

---

Company Perspectives:

MPW is a leading provider of technology-based services to industrial facilities, including industrial cleaning and maintenance, facility management and support services, container cleaning, process water purification, and other specialized services.

Pittsburgh, Pennsylvania; Savannah and Augusta, Georgia; Jacksonville, Florida; and Alliston, Ontario, Canada.

Clark Dies in Helicopter Accident

In October 1993, tragedy struck for Clark's family and MPW. After meeting with customers in Cleveland, Clark and two MPW employees were flying home when the helicopter they were in struck a power line, obscured by fog, and crashed. Clark was pronounced dead on the scene. Black announced that MPW would continue to pursue the goals laid out by Clark and began recruiting a new management team to make that vision a reality. Most of the new executives came from OHM Corporation, a publicly held environmental services company based in Findlay, Ohio. In March 1994, Ira O. Kane was named to replace Clark as president and COO. An attorney, Kane had served as an executive vice-president and director during his ten years at OHM, then in 1993 was named chairman and executive vice-president of NSC Corporation, an asbestos abatement and industrial services company. Less than a year later, he accepted the position at MPW. Two of his colleagues at OHM, Daniel P. Buettin and Brad A. Martyn, joined Kane at MPW in December 1995, after OHM merged with a subsidiary of Waste Management. Buettin became chief financial officer (CFO) and Martyn was named corporate controller. All three men had experience running a public company, and during his employment at Arthur Andersen & Co. Buettin had been involved in the process of taking companies public. They soon convinced Black to take MPW public, which would help the business to expand faster through acquisitions and to be better able to take advantage of the trend in many industries to outsource services. In addition to the cash raised in the initial public offering (IPO), MPW would be able to use stock as a way to fund purchases.

As it prepared its IPO, MPW continued to grow as a business. In 1996, it acquired Weston Engineering to move into industrial air filtration services, important in the painting of vehicles and a complement to the company's existing paint container cleaning operation. Weston added nearly $9 million in annual revenues. This new business segment was augmented a year later with the purchase of the air filtration management services companies of ESI International, which added another $6.7 million in sales. Together the two acquisitions served 35 major auto manufacturing plants. The Industrial Container Cleaning portion of MPW's business, in the meantime, took a major step froward when in 1996 a dedicated facility located in Chesterfield, Michigan, was opened to service a nearby DuPont plant.

MPW Taken Public in 1997

In December 1997, MPW completed its IPO, issuing nearly 4 million shares of stock at $9 per share and netting $32.1

million. A major portion of the money was immediately used to pay down debt, and both cash ($339,000) and stock (37,677 shares) were used in the purchase of a minority stake in Aquatech, a water purification business. It was the first of many deals that MPW would complete over the next two years. In April 1998, MPW added to its industrial container cleaning segment with the acquisition of Vinewood Companies, in the process gaining a major customer in PPG Industries, Inc., which had a master service agreement with Vinewood. Also in that same month, MPW's Industrial Cleaning business was bolstered by the purchase of Straightline Optical Service, a Georgia company that specialized in the alignment of new industrial equipment and realignment of existing machinery. Industrial Cleaning was further strengthened in June 1998 with the acquisition of Maintenance Concepts.

MPW was able to take advantage of its stock to move via acquisitions into another new business segment, Cleanroom Services. Between November 1998 and January 1999, MPW completed six acquisitions in this area, including Support Systems, Envirosafe, TC International, Sureecso, Dryden Engineering, and Biocon. These businesses were then merged into a new subsidiary called Pentagon Technologies Group, Inc. Cleanroom Services—providing contamination-free manufacturing environments for the semiconductor, microelectronics, pharmaceutical, biotechnology, and healthcare industries—appeared to hold great promise for the future, since companies in industries using cleanrooms tended to grow faster than the Rust Belt industries MPW had traditionally served. Already the market for cleaning and related services for cleanrooms was a $3 billion a year business and growing at a 10 percent clip annually. Moreover, the new segment might ease MPW's dependence on the business cycle of its traditional manufacturing customers. It fit in well with MPW's emerging strategy of moving beyond straightforward cleaning services into more lucrative, value-added, technologically-based services. With Pentagon operating out of Fremont, California, the subsidiary also extended MPW's geographic reach.

MPW added to its Industrial Filtration Management business in August 1998 by acquiring Gauthier Enterprises, a Michigan company that served U.S. automakers. In addition to engineering and consulting, the company also acted as a distributor of filters, filtration media, and such ancillary products as brushes, gloves, and equipment covers. Also in August 1998, MPW expanded the Container Cleaning segment by purchasing Tank Management Inc., another Michigan company that served automotive paint manufacturers, in particular DuPont. MPW's water purification segment was supplemented by the December 1998 acquisitions of WTW Systems, as was the Industrial Cleaning segment by the addition of Mid-Ohio Industrial in February 1999.

MPW displayed significant growth since going public, with annual revenues increasing from nearly $73 million in fiscal 1997 to more than $104 million in fiscal 1999. Nevertheless, the price of the company's stock languished. After reaching a peak of $13.88 in June 1998, MPW stock fell as low as $5 and never bounced higher than $12. In April 2000, Black announced his intention to buy MPW's outstanding shares at $8 per share and take the business private once again. In order to pay off the debt incurred in the buyout, Black indicated a willingness to sell some of MPW's assets. In fact, on the very day he made his

Key Dates:

1972: Monte Black establishes Central Ohio Mobile Power Wash.
1978: The company is incorporated as MPW Industrial Services, Inc.
1990: MPW enters the water purification business.
1993: MPW enters the industrial container cleaning business.
1997: The company goes public.
2000: A majority stake in subsidiary Pentagon Technologies is sold.
2001: The company's filtration business is sold.

intentions known, the company announced that it was going to sell a majority interest in Pentagon to Baird Capital Partners. The deal closed in July 2000, and MPW retained a 22.3 percent interest in the business. In the meantime, the effort to take MPW private caused some fallout in the ranks of management. Buettin and Robert J. Gilker, a vice-president, resigned. Kane took over as chief financial officer until a successor, Richard R. Kahle, was hired in September 2000. Black upped his buyback offer to $9 per share, then cut it back to a $8.25 base amount, to be increased depending on how much money certain assets could fetch. In the end, Black became concerned that the additional debt burden that MPW would have to assume might hurt the company, and in October 2000 he withdrew his offer to buy the rest of the business. Owning nearly 60 percent of the stock, he still remained very much in control.

MPW's debt load became even more of a concern as the U.S. economy began to slip into recession in 2001. Several customers declared bankruptcy, resulting in writeoffs for MPW. Moreover, the company was adversely affected by higher costs, cutbacks by customers, and price-cutting by competing firms. The company took steps to meet this challenging business environment with staff cuts and other cost-saving measures. To pay down debt, MPW elected to sell its filter group for approximately $31 million to Clarcor Inc., a Rockville, Illinois, air conditioner and heating filter manufacturer. In addition to debt reduction, the sale reflected a decision to focus on MPW's three remaining business segments.

In the same month that MPW completed the sale of its filter group, Kane resigned as president and COO, citing his desire to "pursue new leadership challenges elsewhere." Only a few weeks later, MPW announced a reorganization of management, part of a larger restructuring plan to restore growth. Black would serve as both CEO and COO, Kahle remained as CFO, James P. Mock was made a vice-president to head the industrial cleaning/facility maintenance segment, and C. Douglas Rockwell became a vice-president in charge of both the industrial water purification segment and industrial container cleaning services. Annual revenues, after topping out at $135 million in fiscal 2000, fell to $98.7 million in fiscal 2001, most of which was due to the sale of Pentagon. Of more concern to the company was a net loss of $15.7 million for the year. Revenues fell further in 2002, to $92 million, but cost-cutting measures helped to return MPW to profitability, posting net income of $2.7 million. As long as its customers were adversely impacted by a struggling economy, however, MPW would feel the ripple effects. The company's long-term prospects nevertheless remained optimistic.

Principal Divisions

Industrial Cleaning and Facility Maintenance; Industrial Container Cleaning; Industrial Process Water Purification.

Principal Competitors

Safety-Kleen Corporation; Flow International Corporation; Philip Services.

Further Reading

Buchanan, Doug, "MPW Bids for Leadership in Misunderstood Industry," *Daily Reporter*, March 20, 1998.
Hoke, Kathy, "Hebron Cleaning Company Plans $34.3 Million IPO," *Business First-Columbus*, October 10, 1997, p. 5.
——, "New Division Fueling MPW's Growth-by-Acquisition Plan," *Business First-Columbus*, November 13, 1998, p. 9.
Krouse, Peter, "MPW Cleans Up Serving Diverse Industries," *Plain Dealer*, June 23, 2000, p40S.
Newpoff, Laura, "Stock's Value, Cost of Staying Public Spurred MPW Offer," *Business First-Columbia*, May 5, 2000, p. 4.

—Ed Dinger

Multi-Color Corporation

425 Walnut Street, Suite 1300
Cincinnati, Ohio 45202
U.S.A.
Telephone: (513) 381-1480
Fax: (513) 381-2813
Web site: http://www.multicolorcorp.com

Public Company
Incorporated: 1916 as Franklin Development Company
Employees: 347
Sales: $72.6 million (2002)
Stock Exchanges: NASDAQ
Ticker Symbol: LABL
NAIC: 323111 Commercial Gravure Printing; 322221
    Coated and Laminated Packaging Paper and Plastics
    Film Manufacturing

Multi-Color Corporation is a leading U.S. manufacturer of printed labels for consumer goods. Multi-Color prints labels for products such as liquid detergents, laundry-care products, beverages, health and beauty aids, motor oil, chewing gum, and food products. The company's customers are some of the largest consumer products companies in the world, including multinational conglomerates such as The Coca-Cola Company, General Foods Corporation, The Procter & Gamble Company, Tropicana, Colgate-Palmolive Company, and The Clorox Company. Multi-Color uses several different technologies to print its specialty labels, most notably the in-mold label process it helped developed. In-mold labels are applied to plastic containers as the containers are being formed in the mold. Multi-Color serves more than 100 customers in the United States, South America, and Latin America.

Origins

Multi-Color, destined to be one of the largest printers of labels for consumer products in the world, began operating in 1916. The company was founded as the Franklin Development Company, whose executives invested in the latest in print tech-

nology at the time, the sheet-fed, three-color press. The company's management was impressed by the innovation, forming a separate company incorporated as the Printing Machinery Co. to manufacture and sell the new presses. Shortly after its founding, Printing Machinery changed its name to MulticolorType and changed its business focus to printing rather than press manufacturing. The company began producing paper labels in 1918, marking the beginning of Multi-Color's involvement in lending identity and shelf appeal to consumer products.

As Multi-Color matured, it developed a client roster comprising some of the largest, most widely recognized consumer products companies in the world. The company served as an integral facet of the marketing programs for ubiquitous brands, allying itself with stalwart concerns such as The Coca-Cola Company, Colgate-Palmolive Company, The Procter & Gamble Company, General Foods Corporation, and The Clorox Company. Multi-Color established its relationship with the world's most prestigious firms early in its history, gaining The Campbell Soup Company and chewing-gum producer Wm. Wrigley, Jr. as customers early in the 1920s.

Over the decades, Multi-Color's customer base expanded, as did the marketing programs developed by its customers. To keep pace with the increasingly sophisticated demands of its customers, the company embraced technological innovations as they came, and, in one important instance, assumed the role of pioneer. During the 1950s, rotogravure printing technology was developed, which would serve as Multi-Color's primary printing technology throughout the 20th century and into the next century. During the 1960s and 1970s, as greater diversity in label design and presentation were required, eight-color presses emerged, forcing Multi-Color to invest in the new technology.

In-Mold Label Technology Is Developed in 1980

On the technology front, no event was bigger than the company's pioneering efforts in 1980. As the decade began, Multi-Color developed the in-mold label. In-mold labels were labels applied to plastic containers as the containers were being formed in the mold. The in-mold label was a plastic with the same chemical characteristics as the container, making the labels more resistant to moisture and easier to recycle. Multi-Color's innovation became the industry standard for those products packaged in plastic bottles such as orange juice jugs, and its importance to Multi-Color's vitality cannot be ignored. Without the company's creation of and entry into the in-mold market, the years ahead, particularly the 1990s, arguably could have been disastrous. The development of in-mold technology in 1980 stabilized the company, providing a crutch upon which the company would lean heavily.

Multi-Color did not begin to stumble noticeably until roughly a decade after the development of in-mold label technology. During the intervening years, the company expanded modestly. In 1985, the company acquired the assets of the label divisions of Georgia-Pacific. Two years later, the 71-year-old company completed its initial public offering of stock. The same year the company completed its entry into the public spotlight, it also established the Multi-Color Graphic Services division, which supplied color separations of labels and engraved cylinders for the company's facilities. In 1990, the company increased its printing capacity by constructing a rotogravure printing plant in Scottsburg, Indiana. The Scottsburg facility served as the site for the company's in-mold label production. Several months after opening the Scottsburg facility, Multi-Color's management began searching for a way to increase the speed of its rotogravure printing process. In 1991, after investigating the prevailing cylinder manufacturing technologies, the company invested in a Japanese-developed technology. Subsequent to this investment, the company established Laser Graphic Systems in Erlanger, Kentucky. From Erlanger, Multi-Color supplied cylinders to the Scottsburg plant and outside customers, achieving vertical integration in its operations.

Problems Surface in the 1990s

By the early 1990s, nearly 80 years of printing labels had shaped Multi-Color into one of the largest concerns of its kind. Despite the company's entrenched position in the industry, particularly its regard in the in-mold label business, there were indications of disturbing financial problems. On the bright side, the company controlled more than 50 percent of the in-mold market, its leadership translating to exponential financial gains. Between 1989 and 1994, Multi-Color's in-mold sales doubled, helping the company to record $65.4 million in annual sales as it entered the mid-1990s. The problem, however, was that the company's annual revenue volume had plateaued by 1994, failing to rise meaningfully from the amount recorded at the beginning of the decade. A decline in conventional label sales was to blame, negating the impressive increases posted by the

company's in-mold business. In one market niche—cigarette wrappers—the decline was drastic, indicative of the financial anemia affecting virtually everything outside in-mold printing. At the beginning of the 1990s, Multi-Color collected nearly $9 million annually from its cigarette wrapper activities. By 1994, the business had been virtually wiped out. To exacerbate the situation, Multi-Color's ability to post a profit was of grave concern. In 1994, the company failed to earn any income, recording a numbing $4.3 million loss.

By the time Multi-Color reported its depressed financial totals for 1994, it already had begun to take action. The company derived half its sales from conventional label sales and the other half from in-mold label sales, a balance Multi-Color's management wanted to maintain in the future. Although Multi-Color was performing admirably in the in-mold market, this market was not big enough to support the company at its extant size. Accordingly, the company's management needed to repair its conventional label business to restore profitability and to enliven revenue growth. As part of its restructuring efforts, the company closed its plant in Lockport, Illinois, selling the facility in the summer of 1993 to Precise Data, a company that printed mail inserts.

Between 1995 and 1996, the company consolidated certain operations, exited some market segments, reduced payroll, and improved efficiency. By the end of 1996, there was tangible evidence of improvement. After two years of losses, the company recorded $2.6 million in operating profit, a nearly $10 million improvement from the loss reported in 1995. Importantly, the company's focus on rejuvenating its conventional label business had not occurred at the expense of its other operations. In Scottsburg, where the company conducted its in-mold activities, production capacity doubled in 1996. Capacity was expected to increase by another 50 percent once a new printing press was delivered in early 1997.

Although there were signs of recovery, Multi-Color continued to struggle as it entered the late 1990s. The company recorded $1.4 million in net income in 1997, but its sales, rather than stagnating, had begun to erode markedly. From the plateau of $65 million in 1994, revenue had slipped to $55.4 million by 1996 before dropping to $48.1 million in 1997. In 1998, the pattern of decline continued. Sales dropped by $500,000, while the nagging problem of profitability resurfaced. During the year, the company eclipsed the disaster of 1994 by posting a $4.4 million loss. Genuine, lasting recovery did not arrive until the last year of the decade, when the company gained a new leader and a new vision for the future.

New Management and Expanded Markets: Late 1990s and Beyond

Francis D. Gerace, the individual who would lead Multi-Color toward vibrant financial growth, joined the company in April 1998. Gerace joined the company as vice-president of operations one month after the $4.4 million loss was announced. He was appointed president and chief executive officer roughly one year later, in May 1999. Gerace implemented a waste elimination program that reduced waste by 30 percent and increased productivity by 40 percent, helping the company reverse its worrisome financial trend. In 1999, Multi-Color

---

Key Dates:

1916: Franklin Development Company is formed.
1918: The company's business focus changes from manufacturing printing presses to printing labels.
1980: Multi-Color develops in-mold label technology.
1999: Buriot International, Inc. is acquired.
2000: Uniflex Corporation is acquired.
2002: Quick Pak Inc. is acquired.

---

registered $1.2 million in net income and generated $49.8 million in revenue, the first time the company's revenue had increased since 1994.

Gerace's greatest contribution to Multi-Color's well being was his decision to enter new markets. He did so through acquisitions, beginning his buying spree roughly six months after he was given command over the company. In December 1999, Gerace acquired Buriot International, Inc., a pressure-sensitive label manufacturer that had been formed in 1996 by France-based Pierre Buriot S.A. The acquisition, which included a two-year-old manufacturing facility, gave Multi-Color access to the pressure-sensitive market for the first time, a vast, $2-billion market that provided ample room for the company's growth. In June 2000, Gerace engineered the acquisition of Uniflex Corporation, a manufacturer of heat-shrink labels and tamper-evident bands with a production facility in Las Vegas and offices in Anaheim Hills, California. The acquisition provided Multi-Color with access to the $300-million heat-shrink market, which, in conjunction with the acquisition of Buriot, added greatly to the company's potential for growth. The in-mold market, by contrast, was estimated to be a $100 million market.

Diversification through acquisition continued under Gerace's rule. For the first time in more than a decade, Multi-Color was recording substantial increases in its annual revenue volume, gains that were attributable to Gerace's desire to enter new markets. At the end of 2001, Multi-Color acquired Premiere Labels Inc., which increased the company's involvement in the pressure-sensitive label market. In June 2002, the company entered another new market by acquiring Quick Pak Inc., a manufacturer of specialty packaging products such as gift packs and special displays for major health and beauty companies, consumer products manufacturers, and national retailers. The acquisition added $10 million in revenue to Multi-Color's an-nual volume and provided entry into packaging services, estimated to be a $1 billion market. Gerace hailed the completion of the acquisition, placing great hopes on the contribution Quick Pak could make toward Multi-Color's fortunes. "I wouldn't be surprised if some day it isn't the largest division in the company," Gerace remarked in an August 16, 2002 interview with *The Cincinnati Enquirer.*

As Multi-Color prepared for the future, the company anticipated completing further acquisitions. Annual sales slipped past $70 million by the end of the company's fiscal 2002 year, providing encouragement that Gerace's diversification program was delivering the desired results. With new growth opportunities raising expectations for progress in the 21st century, the venerable printing firm prepared for a future that promised to take the company in business directions it had not explored in its nearly 90-year history.

Principal Subsidiaries

Uniflex Corporation; Buriot International, Inc.; Quick Pak Inc.

Principal Competitors

Fort Dearborn Company; Schawk, Inc.; Seven Worldwide, Inc.

Further Reading

Boyer, Mike, "Multi-Color Corp. Predicts Bright Future for Subsidiary," *Cincinnati Enquirer,* August 16, 2002, p. D1.

Frazier, Mya, "Multi-Color Aims to Grow Through New Markets," *Business Courier Serving Cincinnati-Northern Kentucky,* December 8, 2000, p. 36.

——, "New CEO Eyes Growth at Label-Maker Multi-Color," *Business Courier Serving Cincinnati-Northern Kentucky,* October 22, 1999, p. 32.

Milstead, David, "Multi-Color Rides Packaging Trend," *Cincinnati Business Courier,* October 10, 1994, p. 3.

"Multi-Color Buying Uniflex," *Cincinnati Post,* March 31, 2000, p. 11C.

"Multi-Color Corp.," *Business First-Columbus,* January 7, 2000, p. 12.

"Multi-Color Corporation," *Wall Street Transcript,* July 30, 2001, p 31.

Sekhri, Rajiv, "Multi-Color Planning $2.5 M Indiana Expansion," *Business Courier Serving Cincinnati-Northern Kentucky,* July 31, 1998, p. 10.

——, "Reorganizing Brightens Multi-Color's Future," *Cincinnati Business Courier,* November 25, 1996, p. 24.

—Jeffrey L. Covell

Neopost S.A.

113, rue Jean-Marin Naudin
92220 Bagneux
France
Telephone: (+33) 1-45-36-3000
Fax: (+33) 1-45-36-3170
Web site: http://www.neopost-group.com

Public Company
Incorporated: 1992
Employees: 3,400
Sales: EUR 800 million ($750 million)(2002)
Stock Exchanges: Euronext Paris
Ticker Symbol: NEO
NAIC: 333313 Office Machinery Manufacturing

Neopost S.A. is Europe's largest and the world's second-largest manufacturer of mailroom equipment and mailing and logistics systems. (Pitney Bowes, of the United States, is world leader.) Based near Nanterre, France, Neopost has been expanding its global market share, which has risen from 15 percent to more than 25 percent, through a number of strategic acquisitions. In 2002, the company finalized its acquisition of the industry's number three player, Ascom Hasler, formerly part of Switzerland's Ascom group. Neopost offers a full range of mailing systems, including mail franking equipment, folding and other document systems, and parcel tracking and other logistics systems equipment. Neopost has also been a pioneer in so-called "e-postage" systems, which allow for Internet-based postage, bar coding, and related products. Forecasts for the market for Internet-based postage systems range from $500 million to $2 billion per year in the United States alone. That market represents Neopost's single largest market, at 43 percent of Neopost's sales of EUR575 million ($550 million) in 2001. France is the group's second biggest market, at 36 percent of sales, while the United Kingdom accounts for 12 percent of sales. Other important markets for Neopost include Germany, Italy (where the company holds a 40 percent market share), and the Benelux countries. Neopost operates subsidiaries in Belgium, Canada, Ireland, Italy, the Netherlands, Spain, the United Kingdom, and the United

States. The company is quoted on the Euronext Paris Stock Exchange and is led by chairman and CEO Jean-Paul Villot.

From Origins in the 19th Century to Industry Leader in the 1980s

Neopost was formed through a management-led leveraged buyout of the then-Alcatel NV's Friden Alcatel mail systems equipment division in 1992. That operation had been established through the merger of Alcatel's mailing and logistics equipment division with the United States' Friden Mailing Equipment Co. in 1979. Both companies had long been involved in the manufacture of mail franking and processing equipment, a market that remained dominated by Pitney Bowes.

Alcatel dated from 1879, originally named Société Alsacienne de Constructions Atomiques, de Télécommunications et d'Electronique, and had been one of France's pioneering telecommunications companies, before being acquired by the CGE (Compagnie Générales d'Electricité) conglomerate in 1966. In 1970, Alcatel launched the world's first digital switching equipment. By then, Alcatel had also become one of Europe's leading manufacturers of postage meters and stamping equipment, a market the company had entered in 1924.

The European market, dominated by postal monopolies, left little room for expansion, and by the late 1970s, Alcatel sought an entry into the huge U.S. market. Yet the U.S. market itself remained restricted to just four companies authorized by the United States Postal Service to produce postage metering equipment. In 1979, Alcatel found an entry when it merged its mailing and logistics equipment division with Friden Mailing Equipment.

Friden had been founded California in 1933 by Swedish-born inventor Carl Friden, who had already a number of patents to his credit, including an early calculating machine. Friden, who had arrived penniless in the United States during World War I, became quite wealthy after selling the patent to his first machine in 1918. With the stock market crash of 1929, however, Friden lost most of his fortune and was forced to start again.

In 1933, Friden founded his own company, the Friden Calculating Machine Company, and began to work on an entirely new

---

Key Dates:

1879: Establishment of Société Alsacienne de Constructions Atomiques, de Télécommunications et d'Electronique, later Alcatel.

1924: Alcatel begins production of postage metering machines.

1933: Establishment of Friden Calculating Machine Company in California.

1956: Friden begins production of postage metering machines.

1979: Alcatel acquires Friden and merges its mailroom and logistics equipment operations as Friden Alcatel; Friden Alcatel launches the first electronic postage metering machine.

1992: Lazard, Freres backs management-led leveraged buyout of Friden Alcatel, which is renamed Neopost.

1998: The company acquires Lirma in Italy.

1999: Neopost goes public on Euronext Paris Stock Exchange.

2000: The company acquires Sima and Primavera in Italy, boosting its market share to 40 percent in that country.

2001: PackageNet is acquired and renamed Simply Packages.

2002: Neopost acquires Ascom Hasler and launches Postage-On-Call online postage meter reset service.

---

calculating machine, one with a design that would not infringe on his previous machine's patents. Friden's company managed to finish its first machine by 1934, winning the company its first order from the U.S. government. Friden continued to develop new equipment, including the first fully automatic calculating machine, introduced in 1936. By the outbreak of World War II, Friden's company had grown to more than 1,300 employees. Friden then turned over its production to support the war effort, winning some $20 million in ordnance contracts.

After its founder's death in 1945, the company continued to develop new machinery, and by the 1950s Friden had grown into a major company in North America, operating sales and service offices throughout the region, with its products distributed internationally as well. By then, however, the birth of the electronics industry and the development of the first computers were beginning to make Friden's calculating machines obsolete. In response, the company turned to a different market, that of postage meters, introducing its first metering machine in 1956.

By the early 1970s, Friden had come to focus on its postage meters, changing its name to Friden Mailing Equipment Co. Yet the United States remained dominated by Pitney Bowes, which held some 95 percent of the market. Lacking the funds needed to make a push for more market share, Friden found itself struggling by the middle of the 1970s. In 1976, the company posted losses of more than $3.5 million on sales of just $15 million. Three years later, however, Friden and Alcatel found each other—the former attracted by the latter's deep pockets; the latter attracted by the former's coveted manufacturing and leasing rights for the U.S. postal meter market.

Growth and Innovation in the 1980s and Early 1990s

Alcatel paid $14 million for Friden, forming Friden Alcatel as a subsidiary of the larger Alcatel group's mailroom products division. Soon after the merger, the company launched a new product that had been in development at Friden for some time—the world's first electronic postage meter. Because the new meter offered more accurate scale and metering capabilities, it was set to revolutionize the industry. Yet the Friden company's original design proved flawed, with a high percentage of meters breaking down, and Friden Alcatel was forced to foot the bill for shipments back to the factory.

With financial backing from its Alcatel parent, however, Friden Alcatel went back to the drawing board, redesigning the electronic meter to produce a more reliable device, while at the same time eliminating nearly one-third of the machine's components. The resulting product enabled Friden Alcatel to begin asserting itself on the U.S. market, boosting its position from a six percent share to a share of 14 percent of the country's market by the mid-1980s. By 1984, Friden Alcatel had become profitable, with sales of more than $60 million. By the end of the decade, the company's sales had topped $100 million. Friden Alcatel's success helped boost Alcatel's mailroom products division to the rank of number two worldwide.

Friden Alcatel continued to innovate in the early 1980s. The emergence of independent postal services, including United Parcel Service and Federal Express, created a new demand for logistics equipment and systems. Friden Alcatel extended its metering equipment into this new area, introducing its All-electronic Shipping & Mailing System in 1982. The following year, the company introduced the scale-based Manifest Shipping system. Then in 1984, the company integrated its shipping system with the growing business application market, linking its logistics and metering systems with computer-based platforms.

Friden Alcatel broke new ground in 1990 with one of the first attempts to link metering systems with telecommunications capacity. By 1991, the company had rolled out its new product, Postage-On-Call, which allowed users—especially small and mid-sized businesses—to refill postage meters over the telephone. That year, the company rolled out another computer-based product, the FriendShip Manifest Shipping system, based on the emerging PC standard.

The Formation of Neopost

By then, Friden Alcatel's parent CIT-Alcatel had undergone a number of significant changes, merging first in 1985 with Thomson Télécommunications, under the name Alcatel, and merging again with ITT Corporation's European telecommunications operations in 1986. That merger created Alcatel NV, based in Belgium, which became the world's second-largest telecommunications company, behind AT&T. Then, in 1987, Alcatel's parent company, CGE, which had been owned by the government since the Socialist-backed nationalization program of the early 1980s, was privatized.

Alcatel began to focus on the fast-growing telecommunications market in the early 1990s, and in 1992 the company sold off its mailroom products division in a management-led leveraged buyout (LBO) backed by merchant banker Lazard, Freres, which acquired a 51 percent stake in the company. Another financial backer of the LBO was BC Partners, which took a 15 percent share. Friden Alcatel—then in the midst of a major promotion campaign, including a sponsorship of the 1992 Olympic Games—maintained its name for the time being.

The acquisition of the Netherlands' Hadewe in 1992 was to lead to the company's new name. Hadewe had been formed in 1924 as a manufacturer of industrial and agricultural machinery; in 1934, Hadewe found success with its first line of stencil duplicators. In 1952, Hadewe released a folding machine, the Prestofold, and by the 1960s had become a specialist in mail and document handling equipment, releasing an inserter, the P14. By 1986, Hadewe had developed a successor to the P14 using the latest in electronic technology, dubbing the product the Neopost System 7. After its acquisition into Friden Alcatel—which adopted the Neopost name for the entire group—Hadewe changed its name to Neopost Industrie and became a central part of the larger group's document handling division.

Neopost set out to increase its presence on the global market for mailroom and logistics systems. In 1994, the company released its Windows-based integrated software package, WinLink. The following year, Neopost debuted Neolink, a service technician dispatch system. Backed by these and other products, Neopost began gaining speed through the mid-1990s, with sales rising from EUR120 million at the time of its LBO to more than EUR365 million by 1997. In that year, the company's ownership structure changed, with BC Partner's paying the equivalent of more than EUR100 million to buy out Lazard, Freres and raise its stake to 88 percent. The move was seen as part of a run-up to a public offering by Neopost.

Internet Focus at the Turn of the Century

With its revenues nearing EUR 400 million at the end of 1998, Neopost made its move to go public early the next year, listing directly on the Euronext Paris main board. The listing proved to be one of the year's most successful, earning the company a spot on *Forbes* magazine's 300 best small companies list.

Neopost used its public offering to help pay down debt from its LBO and to begin expanding its international presence. By then, the company had already achieved significant market share in the primary mailroom equipment markets, with a 64 percent share in France, 25 percent share in the United Kingdom, and seven percent of the U.S. market. Among the company's first targets was Italy, which it had entered in 1998 with the acquisition of Lirma. In 2000, the company acquired two more Italian firms, Primavera and Sima, which enabled it to step up its market share in that country to 40 percent. That year, the company moved to strengthen its reach into the German-speaking markets with an agreement with Frama GmbH, based in Switzerland, to distribute Neopost's newest digital metering system, under Frama's brand name, to the Swiss, German, and Dutch markets.

By then, Neopost had entered a market of a different sort. In 1995, the U.S. Postal Service had laid out the guidelines for the development of the so-called "e-stamp"—that is, equipment capable of permitting the online purchase and onsite printing of stamps. Neopost joined in the race to develop secure and reliable systems capable of meeting the U.S. Postal Service's guidelines, creating a dedicated subsidiary, based in California, named Neopost Online.

Neopost readied its first system, Simply Postage, and began regional testing in 1999. Government approval for a full-scale national rollout came later that same year. Neopost's first system required a special, secured printer; the company was already preparing two additional desktop postage products: PC Stamp, a stand-alone desktop unit that allowed users to purchase and store electronic postage, and Postage Plus, a fully Internet-based postage purchase and printing system that allowed users to print stamps with their own printers.

While analysts expected Internet-based postage to take off in the future—with market estimates ranging from $500 million to as much as $2 billion in the United States alone—immediate reception proved lukewarm, hampered by faulty software. By 2000, two of the earliest entrants in the e-stamp race had folded. Neopost remained, however, enjoying some success with the Simply Postage system, while preparing the rollout of a more reliable PCMail application. Nonetheless, Neopost Online remained a tiny part of Neopost's overall activity.

Neopost continued to expand its presence in the United States, which represented nearly half of the company's total sales. In early 2001, Neopost expanded its logistics systems operations with the acquisition of its own logistics network, PackageNet, a franchise-based network of Internet-linked package pickup and drop-off points. Renamed Simply Packages by Neopost, the service enabled users to compare shipping prices among the U.S. Postal Service, United Parcel Service, Federal Express, and others, and to make online payment and print stamps, then simply drop-off the package at the nearest Simply Package drop-off point for delivery. Following the acquisition, Neopost began plans to extend the network to as many as 15,000 franchises.

The Internet remained at the center of Neopost's U.S. development in 2001, as the company reached an agreement with popular online auction site eBay to promote the Simply Postage package among its users. That year, Neopost acquired Loop One, based in Austin, Texas, which had developed an Internet-based dispatch and tracking system. Neopost also announced the development of a self-service postage kiosk, in partnership with Grumman, which was launched in 2002.

By then, Neopost had taken a new, major step forward when it announced its acquisition of Switzerland's Ascom Hasler, the mailroom equipment subsidiary of Ascom AG, and the number three such operation in the world. The acquisition, which cost Neopost more than EUR216 million, boosted Neopost's global market share to 25 percent, and its U.S. presence to a 16 percent market share. Neopost remained an industry innovator as well, launching in December 2002 its updated Postage-On-Call program and service, which enabled customers to reset their postage meters through the Internet.

Principal Subsidiaries

Satas Neopost S.A.; Neopost France Neopost S.A.; Neopost Industrie; Mail Finance; Neopost Diva; Dynapost; Mailroom

Holding BV (Netherlands); Neopost Industrie BV (Netherlands); Neopost BV Mailroom Holding BV (Netherlands); Neopost Inc. (United States); Neopost Online Inc. (United States); Neopost Leasing, Inc (United States); Neopost Leasing of Canada, Inc.; Neopost Holdings Ltd (United Kingdom); Neopost Ltd Neopost Holdings Ltd (United Kingdom); Neopost Finance Ltd (United Kingdom); Neopost Lirma (Italy); Neopost Sprl (Belgium); Loop One2 (United States).

Principal Competitors

Pitney Bowes Inc.; Siemens Dematic AG; Stamps.com Inc.

Further Reading

Carlsen, Clifford, ''Going After the Big Guys in the Mail-meter Market,'' *San Francisco Business Times*, February 1, 1988, p. 17.

Drouin, Patrice, ''Neopost s'intéresse aux petites entreprises,'' *Les Echos*, April 8, 2002, p. 18.

Giraud, Hélène, ''Neopost rachète le réseau Simply Packages,'' *Les Echos*, February 12, 2001, p. 55.

Lecoeur, Xavier, ''Neopost consolide sa présence en Europe continentale,'' *Les Echos*, February 11, 2000, p. 18.

Maume, David, ''Neopost mise sur l'affranchissement via Internet,'' *L'Usine Nouvelle*, October 14, 1999.

—M.L. Cohen

New World Pasta Company

85 Shannon Road
Harrisburg, Pennsylvania 17112
U.S.A.
Telephone: (717) 526-2200
Fax: (717) 526-2468
Web site: http://www.nwpasta.com

Private Company
Incorporated: 1999
Employees: 1,300
Sales: $400 million (2001)
NAIC: 311823 Dry Pasta Manufacturing

New World Pasta Company is the leading manufacturer of dried pasta in the United States. It sells a variety of long-standing regional brands of pasta, including American Beauty, Skinner, Prince, Creamette, Ronzoni, San Giorgio, and Mrs. Weiss. The company also manufactures pasta for private labels and sells pasta and pasta products to institutional customers such as hospitals and prisons and to the restaurant industry. New World operates five manufacturing plants located in Winchester, Virginia; St. Louis, Missouri; Louisville, Kentucky; Omaha, Nebraska, and Fresno, California. The company also manufactures two brands of pasta, Catelli and Lancia, sold in Canada, and owns two Italian brands, Monder and Albador. New World was formed in 1999 out of Hershey Food Corporation's pasta division. In 2001, New World combined the former Hershey operations with most of the pasta division of Borden. The company is privately held, with about 85 percent in the hands of New York-based investment group Joseph Littlejohn & Levy. An additional 11 percent is owned by the company's largest grain supplier, Miller Milling Company of Minneapolis.

A History of Small Regional Brands

New World Pasta began in 1999 as a private company that had previously been the Hershey Pasta Group, a division of Hershey Foods. Hershey, known for its chocolate and confections, formed the Pasta Group in 1984, but it had been buying up small pasta makers since the mid-1960s. The pasta industry went through rapid consolidation in the mid-1980s, as many large food companies, including Borden, General Foods, and Coca-Cola, echoed Hershey's strategy and snapped up small independent noodle makers. These larger food companies gained market share by acquiring brands with strong regional followings, but no manufacturer succeeded in rolling out a truly national brand. The brands that today make up New World Pasta all began as family-run companies which marketed inside fairly small geographic areas and often claimed intense customer loyalty.

Pasta was known in Italy from at least 1000 A.D., and during the 15th and 16th centuries it was manufactured throughout a growing region by specialized guilds. The making of pasta was increasingly mechanized in the mid-19th century, and in the early years of the 20th century mechanical dryers produced a new kind of hard pasta that could be shipped abroad. As Italians immigrated to the United States, their new homeland became a huge market for imported pasta. In 1913, Italy exported some 70,000 tons of pasta, most destined for the United States. Around this same time, Italian immigrants began setting up their own pasta factories in cities around the country. San Giorgio Macaroni Company was founded in Lebanon, Pennsylvania, in 1914 by a young Italian immigrant named Girolamo Guerrisi. Guerrisi came to the United States when he was 22 years old and worked in the fruit business. Within two years, he had saved enough to buy the Keystone Macaroni Company in Lebanon. He renamed it San Giorgio, and it operated as a regional brand until it was acquired by Hershey in 1966. Another New World Pasta brand, American Beauty, was founded in Kansas City in 1912. Italian immigrant Rocco Sarli began the company, calling it at first the Kansas City Macaroni and Importing Company. In 1916, Sarli's company merged with the Denver Macaroni Company, which used the American Beauty brand name. The Kansas City Macaroni Company developed a large market during the Great Depression, at which time it had the single largest geographic distribution of any American pasta brand. In 1947, the company changed its name to American Beauty. It went on to open new manufacturing plants in Los Angeles and Salt Lake City, and by the mid-1960s American Beauty ran eight plants throughout the West and Midwest. The company remained in the hands of two founding families, the

Sarlis and the Vagninos, through the mid-1960s. In 1977, it was sold to Pillsbury, and in 1984 Hershey acquired it.

The Prince brand was founded at almost the same time as American Beauty and San Giorgio, also by Italian immigrants. Gaetano LaMarco, Guiseppe Seminara, and Michele Cantella, who all hailed from the same village in Sicily, went into business together on Prince Street in Boston in 1912, forming the Prince Macaroni Manufacturing Company. Prince Macaroni had a thriving market in the Italian immigrant community in North Boston. The company expanded in 1917 into a seven-story building which included a railroad yard so that trains bringing grain could unload right inside the factory. Over the next twenty years, the company continued to expand, and in 1939 Prince moved again to a new facility, this time in nearby Lowell, Massachusetts. In 1940, another Sicilian, Guiseppe Pellegrino, began working at Prince. Pellegrino's wife's family had run a pasta factory in Brooklyn, New York, but it was destroyed by fire. Pellegrino was apparently so taken with Prince's fancy new Lowell factory that he moved into it while he saved up enough money to buy the plant. Pellegrino bought a controlling interest in Prince in 1941 and moved to expand its markets outside Massachusetts. During the early 1950s, virtually all of Prince's advertising was in Italian–language newspapers. Pasta was marketed as an ethnic Italian food. It had not yet crossed into the American mainstream and was in fact somewhat looked down upon as a cheap and filling food until its image began to change around the 1980s. Prince, though, began to reach out to non-Italians with radio ads in the 1950s. In 1969, it came up with a memorable television spot featuring a little boy running through his Boston neighborhood to the slogan ''Wednesday is Prince spaghetti day.'' Prince acquired other pasta companies and increased its market well beyond the Boston area in the 1970s. It remained in the hands of the Pellegrino family until 1987.

The Creamette brand of macaroni was first manufactured by the Minnesota Macaroni Company, which was founded in 1916 in Minneapolis. James Williams eventually bought the Minnesota Macaroni Co. with his brother and redesigned the macaroni to have a thinner wall and larger center hole. This new macaroni, named Creamette, cooked faster than other brands, and it became a popular brand across the Midwest. Creamette was run by the Williams family until 1979, when it was sold to Borden.

Skinner was the second pasta brand that Hershey acquired. This company too was founded early in the 20th century, in 1911, in Omaha, Nebraska. The company was formed by two brothers with the not very Italian sounding names of Lloyd M. and Paul F. Skinner. The Skinner brothers made a variety of food products at their company, including what is considered the first powdered fruit drink mix, called Quick-Ade, in the 1920s. The Skinners also pioneered the well-known American breakfast cereal Raisin Bran and manufactured this until 1963, when the company sold its cereal business to the Uncle Sam Breakfast Food Company. The pasta business continued to be run by one of the brothers, then by his son, Lloyd E. Skinner, who took over in 1950. Lloyd E. Skinner led the company in the acquisition of several other regional pasta makers in the 1960s. In 1979, Hershey bought Skinner Macaroni and merged it into its San Giorgio Macaroni unit. Eventually Skinner and San Giorgio formed the core of the Hershey Pasta Group, which was run by C. Mickey Skinner, a cousin of Lloyd E. Skinner. C. Mickey Skinner ran Hershey's pasta business until 1997, when he retired. He came out of retirement in 1999 to run New World Pasta.

Hershey's Pasta Division in the 1970s–80s

These various pasta manufacturers were similar in many ways. Most had been selling pasta under one or two brand names for a long time and had strong customer loyalty for a product that changed little over the years. Consumers were so used to their favorite regional brands that it was very difficult to bring in new brands. Prince, which by 1979 had sales of $100 million and was one of the top three regional pasta makers in the United States, had tried to move into upstate New York in the early 1960s, buying the Meisenzahl Macaroni Co. in Rochester. Meisenzahl had a 25 percent market share in the upstate region. When Prince put its name on the Meisenzahl product, the result was a financial disaster. Even though Prince had a strong following in Boston and other parts of the Northeast, people in upstate New York apparently were unwilling to try it, and the Meisenzahl customer base disappeared.

Nevertheless, many larger food companies had their eyes on the pasta market, seeing great potential for growth. Per capita consumption of pasta in the United States doubled between 1950 and 1980, with most of the increase beginning in the mid-1970s. By 1980, average consumption was about ten pounds per person annually, and food industry analysts thought that figure could go up. Pasta sales could also spur other food business, because it was usually eaten with sauce and cheese. An article in *Forbes* (March 17, 1980) claimed that for every dollar's worth of pasta sold, another $8 to $10 of trimmings were rung up, and the potential market for pasta and pasta-related food items was at that time estimated at almost $10 billion. This potential brought several large contenders into the pasta field, including Pillsbury Co., Coca-Cola, Borden Inc., General Foods, Foremost-McKesson, Inc., and British food giant Ranks Hovis McDougall Ltd.

Some of these companies entered the pasta market only to drop out after a few years. Hershey Foods was one of the few to persist. Hershey had built its reputation on chocolate, but it branched out into other foods, buying San Giorgio Macaroni Co. in 1966. In 1979, it bought Skinner Macaroni and merged it with its existing pasta unit to form San Giorgio-Skinner Inc. In 1984, San Giorgio-Skinner became an operating division of Hershey under the new name Hershey Pasta Group, led by C. Mickey Skinner. That year, the Hershey Pasta Group acquired the American Beauty brand from Pillsbury. Pillsbury had bought the family company in 1977 and closed some of its plants. When Hershey took over the company, American Beauty still had three plants in the West, where it was a leading brand. By the late 1980s, Hershey's pasta brands were contributing almost 10 percent to the company's overall revenue, and sales had risen steadily. Hershey's three brands then controlled about 18 percent of the U.S. pasta market.

Hershey had become the nation's second-largest pasta maker, behind Borden, and there were fewer independent pasta companies left. Two of the biggest pasta makers in the Northeast, Massachusetts-based Prince and New York-based Ronzoni, had been bought up in the 1980s, with Ronzoni going to General Foods in 1984 and Prince to Borden in 1987. In 1990, Hershey Pasta Group acquired Ronzoni from General Foods for an estimated $80 to $86 million. This deal brought Hershey's share of the U.S. pasta market to around 27 percent, close behind Borden, which had just over 30 percent. By 1990, Hershey ran five pasta plants, and it sold a total of nine brands.

Consolidation in the 1990s

Hershey continued to acquire regional pasta companies in the early 1990s. It bought two Ohio manufacturers in 1993, the Ideal Macaroni Co. and the Weiss Noodle Co. The pasta division discussed rolling out one national pasta brand but never did. C. Mickey Skinner, chief executive of the pasta group, claimed in an interview with *Milling & Baking News* (December 2, 1997) that "pasta products purchased today are the same that a mother or grandmother purchased. As long as you provide good, consistent quality at a reasonable value, customers are not likely to change." Though Hershey standardized the raw materials and thickness of a new brand when it acquired it, the company continued to market under the original pasta name. It was not a market category that accepted much innovation, and Hershey's efforts to bring out a microwaveable pasta, for example, did not meet with much success. In some parts of the country, Hershey brands competed directly with each other. For example, in New York, Ronzoni had long been the leading brand, while muscling in on it from the number two spot was another Hershey product, San Giorgio.

Hershey built a new manufacturing plant in Winchester, Virginia, in the 1990s, giving it one of the most modern pasta factories in the world. However, it faced increased competition when a venerable Italian pasta manufacturer, Barilla, decided to build its first plant on American soil. Hershey was able to build some additional business by manufacturing pasta for private

label customers and by making pasta for ingredients in boxed meals sold by other food companies. Pasta consumption in the United States continued to grow throughout most of the 1990s, reaching around 19 pounds per capita annually by 1997, up from about 11 pounds in the mid-1980s.

Creation of New World Pasta

C. Mickey Skinner retired from Hershey in 1997, leaving the leadership of the Hershey Pasta and Grocery Group to Jay F. Carr. Hershey had become the leading pasta manufacturer by that year, but sales were beginning to stagnate. Sales of pasta overall in the United States dropped about 2 percent in 1998 and again in 1999. Hershey stopped putting money into promoting pasta sales, and other general factors contributed to a lessening of the product's popularity. C. Mickey Skinner, looking back on the drop in an article in *Supermarket Business* (February 15, 2000) claimed that the popularity of low-carbohydrate diets had put many consumers off pasta. Moreover, the end-of-the-century stock market boom years enabled more people to eat out in restaurants, crimping grocery sales. For whatever reason, the Pasta and Grocery Group was not doing as well as it had, and in 1999 Hershey Foods decided to spin off the division and concentrate on its core confectionary business. The last available sales data estimated the pasta unit had brought in around $400 million in 1997. In 1999, Hershey agreed to sell the division for $450 million to a group of investors led by the New York firm Joseph Littlejohn and Levy. The new private company took the name New World Pasta, which included all the previous Hershey pasta brands and manufacturing facilities. C. Mickey Skinner came out of retirement to head New World.

The company worked quickly to reverse the fall-off in pasta sales. New World had just over 26 percent of the United States pasta market, and the company initiated new marketing drives to increase its business. New World began promoting its products jointly with Ragu pasta sauce and began bringing out a wider variety of noodle shapes. The company initiated a sophisticated management tool that it said could analyze a supermarket account and recommend what mix of pasta brands the store should carry. And because intense brand loyalty made it difficult to extend marketing of its brands geographically, New World increased production of its non-branded, private-label products. Hershey had not been particularly interested in this end of the market, but New World pursued it as a growth area.

Skinner led the company through its first year then resumed his retirement. The new chief executive was John Denton, who had previously served as CEO of the snack food maker Snyder's of Hanover. In July 2001, the company announced that it was spending $43 million to buy Borden Foods' remaining pasta business. Borden had long been Hershey's prime competitor in the pasta industry, and it held the formidable Prince brand, Creamette macaroni, and several other regional brands. Borden, like Hershey, had decided to get out of the pasta business altogether, and it earlier sold seven brands to competitor American Italian Pasta Co. New World acquired five regional U.S. brands in the deal, plus two more in Canada and two in Italy. The transaction also gave New World five pasta factories, two in the United States, two in Canada, and one in Italy. Altogether, the business New World bought from Borden was estimated to bring in about $210 million. This left New World the undisputed leader in U.S.

pasta sales, and revenue was expected to rise to around $500 million. By mid-2002 the company was still integrating and restructuring the Borden business, adding plant capacity and predicting moderate future growth.

Principal Competitors

American Italian Pasta Co.; Barilla S.p.A.

Further Reading

Alster, Norm, "Remaking Elsie," *Forbes*, December 25, 1989, pp. 106–10.

Bubny, Paul, "Pasta's Brave New World?" *Supermarket Business*, February 15, 2000, p. 45.

Byrne, Harlan S., "Hershey Foods Corp.: It Aims to Sweeten Its Prospects with Acquisitions," *Barron's*, May 6, 1991, pp. 41–42.

Cochran, Thomas N., "Hershey Foods Corp.: Canadian Acquisition Holds Potential for Chocolate Maker," *Barron's*, June 27, 1988, pp. 61–62.

Dodds, Lynn Strongin, "Sweetening Up the Bottom Line," *Financial World*, April 29, 1986, pp. 14–15.

"Hershey Expands Pasta Unit with Ronzoni Acquisition," *Milling & Baking News*, February 13, 1990, p. 12.

"Hershey Foods to Sell Pasta Business," *Candy Industry*, January 1999, p. 13.

Jaffe, Thomas, "A Case of Indigestion?" *Forbes*, March 17, 1980, pp. 57–62.

Kosman, Josh, "JLL Takes a Taste of $450 Million Pasta Co.," *Buyouts*, February 22, 1999.

"New World Pasta Announces New Chief Executive," *Business Wire*, February 4, 2000, p. 1436.

Novak, Janet, "The High-Profit Candy Habit," *Forbes*, June 29, 1987, p. 76.

Paulden, Pierre, "Pasta Deal Hits Wall, Doesn't Stick," *Loan Market Week*, August 5, 2002, p. 1.

Phelps, David, "Creamette Heirs, Norwest Tangle over Trust Losses," *Minneapolis Star Tribune*, November 1, 1999.

Silverman, Gary, "High-Meat Diet Puts a Squeeze on US Pasta," *Financial Times*, June 10, 2000, p. 14.

Sjerven, Jay, "Smooth Transition at Hershey," *Milling & Baking News*, December 2, 1997, p. 1.

"Skinner Sees Pasta Industry in '90s in 'Settling-in Phase,'" *Milling & Baking News*, March 5, 1991, p. 22.

Sulon, Bill, "Harrisburg, Pa.-Area Pasta Maker Buys Borden Brands, Plants," *Knight-Ridder/Tribune Business News*, July 31, 2001.

Tarpey, John P., et al., "The Pasta Pot Is Boiling—But No One Can Serve up a National Brand," *Business Week*, September 9, 1985, pp. 54–58.

—A. Woodward

Nitches
Incorporated

Nitches, Inc.

10280 Camino Santa Fe
San Diego, California 92121
U.S.A.
Telephone: (858) 625-2633
Fax: (858) 625-0746
Web site: http://www.nitches.com

Public Company
Incorporated: 1973 as Beeba's Creations Inc.
Employees: 32
Sales: $29.5 million (2002)
Stock Exchanges: NASDAQ
Ticker Symbol: NICH
NAIC: 422330 Women's, Children's, and Infants'
   Clothing and Accessories

Nitches, Inc. is a San Diego, California wholesale clothing company, catering primarily to women. It both works with retailers to develop clothing lines and develops its own clothing lines for 41 federally registered trademarks, such as Adobe Rose, Body Drama, and Southwest Canyon. Almost all of the garments are manufactured overseas, then imported in bulk to San Diego where they are sorted and packed, and distributed to customers. Nitches' major retail customers include Cavandars, Kohl's, Mervyns, Sears, and Sheplers. Orders are solicited from the company's showrooms in New York and Los Angeles, as well as through 19 independent sales representative organizations.

Founding the Company in 1973

Nitches' founder and longtime chief executive and chairman was Arjun C. Waney, who grew up in a wealthy family in Bombay, India. He came to the United States to study at the University of California at Berkeley, but after leaving school in 1963 was unable to work legally on his student visa. Instead, taking advantage of contacts in his native country, he began to import blouses and shorts from India and sold them to students. After borrowing $80,000 in 1965 he established two specialty import retail chains: Import Cargo Inc. for the European market

and Cost Less Imports Inc. for the West Coast of the United States. The businesses grew rapidly and were acquired by Pier 1 Imports Inc., at one point making Waney Pier 1's second largest shareholder. In 1973 he and a minor partner, Eugene Price, established the predecessor to Nitches, a San Diego apparel importer and wholesale distributorship they named Beeba's Creation.

Beeba's focused on women's fashions, essentially manufacturing knockoffs of popular clothing, using cotton as the primary material. As a result, the company performed better with its spring and summer lines. Most of the manufacturing took place in India, where Waney relied on businesses connected to his family. Not only did his relatives have stakes in many of the plants Beeba's used, they also owned a number of large textile mills. Early on the company was able to sign Penney's as a major customer, at first providing woven goods. (In 1984 Beeba's would begin to supply Penney's with knitwear.) Although outsourcing manufacturing to overseas plants lowered overhead and allowed Beeba's to maintain inexpensive retail prices, the company began to face clothing import restrictions in certain countries in the early 1980s. As a result, Beeba's began to diversify its sources, in particular cutting back on manufacturing in India, which in the early 1980s still accounted for the production of more than 80 percent of the company's goods.

Beeba's annual sales stood at $15 million in fiscal 1980, resulting in net profits of $166,000. Four years later revenues totaled nearly $34 million and net profits exceeded $1 million. The company was now growing so rapidly that it simply lacked the capital to properly fund the business. In 1984 Waney began making preparations to take Beeba's public. The company also had been used as a vehicle for some nonclothing investments, which were now divested in order to make Beeba's a pure-play venture. For instance, Beeba's sold off its stake in The Perfect Pan restaurant chain. In 1985 the initial public offering (IPO) took place, with the company netting almost $6.5 million and insiders more than $3.1 million.

Launching the Body Drama Subsidiary in 1985

Infused with cash, Beeba's made efforts to expand its business in a number of directions. In 1985 it established Body Drama, an idea brought to Waney by Cecelia Post, who then became president of the division. Post's concept was to market sportswear-inspired intimate apparel, such as nightshirts, nightgowns, pajamas, teddies, and robes. The innerwear division relied on two labels, Body Drama and Body Tease. In 1986 Beeba's looked to move beyond its role as an importer and began to invest in manufacturing in Costa Rica, Jamaica, Mexico, and Morocco in order to circumvent import restrictions. By now the company was growing at an impressive clip, topping $94 million in annual revenues for fiscal 1986, a significant improvement over the $46 million posted the year before. Net profits also increased from $1.76 million in fiscal 1985 to $3.2 million in fiscal 1986.

A major customer, Penney's, established an important partnership with Beeba's in the spring of 1987, agreeing to purchase a 20 percent stake in the business at a cost of more than $19 million. Beeba's was expected to be a major factor in Penney's move into the specialty shop business. These shops within the large department stores were to target 18- to 30-year-old working women. Not only was Beeba's to supply 60 percent of the merchandise for these shops, it would be able to take advantage of its ability to sense trends and capitalize on it by influencing the shops' product mix. (In some cases, however, rivals objected to some of Beeba's imports, which they believed too closely resembled their own designs. More than once in the mid-1980s Beeba's was sued for copyright infringement.) Beeba's also looked to Penney's, as well as other major customers such as Wal-Mart and Ross Stores, to support its new men's division, established in mid-1987.

Due to a number of factors, Beeba's momentum stalled during fiscal 1988, resulting in a $4 million net loss on $102.4 million in sales for the year. For one, the company's investments in manufacturing did not work out, with start-up costs running much higher than expected. As the company backed away, shutting down one factory and selling its stake in another, it was forced to take a $5 million writedown. In addition, the fashion industry in general failed to offer new design trends to consumers. A concerted effort to bring back the miniskirt was a costly failure across the board. Beeba's also was hurt by the stock market crash of October 1987, after investing much of the money gained in the sale of stock to Penney's in what management considered safe, short-term securities. The crash also had an adverse effect on retailers, who delayed placing advanced orders on merchandise. As a result, Beeba's was forced to discount its inventory. Beeba's stock dropped in price during the crash, but failed to recover, so that by the spring of 1988 the company was regarded as a ripe takeover candidate, a situation that persisted for more than a year.

In July 1988 Waney stepped aside as CEO of Beeba's, although he retained the chairmanship. Succeeding him was Steven P. Wyandt, who had been an officer of the company since 1985, and prior to that time had served as a consultant. He came to Beeba's with 17 years of experience with Jockey International, White Stores, and Pier 1 Imports. Under his leadership the company quickly took steps to correct the problems that had led to the fiscal 1988 losses. Aside from pulling back from its move into manufacturing and investing its excess cash in commercial paper, Beeba's decided to cater to its larger and more stable customers, such as Wal-Mart. As a result, in fiscal 1989 revenues rebounded, totaling $128.6 million, and the loss of the year before was reversed, with Beeba's now posting a net profit of $4 million.

As impressive as 1989's turnaround may have been, however, Beeba's faced new challenges in 1990, as both the economy and the weather combined to stall the company's momentum. An unseasonably long and cold winter hurt retailers in general, and several of Beeba's customers in particular. Federated Department Stores, Allied Department Stores, and Ames Department Stores filed for bankruptcy protection. Again, Beeba's was left with excess inventory, which it then had to mark down in order to liquidate. Despite posting record sales of $158 million in fiscal 1990, Beeba's once again found itself reporting a loss on the year, this time $3.4 million.

The Body Drama division remained successful and was Beeba's most recognizable line. From its founding in 1985 to 1991 the division experienced a tenfold increase in annual revenues. Beeba's sought to take advantage of Body Drama's position by spinning it off as a public company. Beeba's retained a controlling stake in the business and was also able to charge Body Drama for certain corporate services, but perhaps of more importance was the cash the company realized in the IPO. Much of those proceeds were used to complete a buyback of stock from Penney's, at a price far below what the retailer paid several years earlier. Although Penney's remained a major account, Wal-Mart by now had eclipsed it as Beeba's largest customer, providing 23.8 percent of sales. In fiscal 1991 Beeba's once again bounced back to profitability, recording net income of $2.7 million in spite of revenues that fell to $132.3 million. The success was the result of reducing administrative costs by some $7 million, shutting down a poor performing beachwear line, and cutting inventories from $24.2 million to $9.9 million. With the country suffering through a recession, however, Beeba's immediate future was uncertain.

Beeba's hoped to find renewed success with an emphasis on western wear for younger women and sportswear for larger sizes and children, as well as to make inroads with membership warehouse clubs, but higher cotton prices and economic conditions caused the company to experience steady erosion over the next few years. Body Drama was especially hard hit, leading to losses and the resignation of its CEO-founder. Unable to find a buyer for Body Drama, Beeba's decided to take the company private. A shareholder lawsuit ensued, essentially accusing the parent company of intentionally depressing earnings to lower Body Drama's stock price in order to rebuy the company on the cheap. In the end, the contending parties settled the matter without going to trial. More than just the Body Drama unit was experiencing difficulties, however. In fiscal 1994 Beeba's returned to red numbers, posting a loss of nearly $3.4 million, which led to a complete reorganization of the business.

Company Considering Selling Itself in 1995

Early in 1995 Beeba's retained Wedbush Morgan Securities, a Los Angeles-based investment bank, as a financial adviser to help it find a buyer for its stock or assets. Management ultimately decided to downsize, reducing lower-margin product lines in favor of more profitable ones. In August 1995 Beeba's sold a number of assets, including its junior sportswear line, girls' wear, and maternity woven and knit tops and bottoms lines to Design & Source Holding Co. Ltd. It later sold the remaining inventory of these lines to the buyer at cost, as well as granting an exclusive worldwide license to use the trademarks associated with these products. Also as part of its downsizing efforts, Beeba's moved its administrative and warehouse operations to a much smaller facility. In late 1995, to help make a break from its past, Beeba's changed its name to Nitches, Inc. Waney also began to step even further away from the active running of the business, completely turning over operational control of Nitches to Wyandt. Waney now shifted his focus to his investment fund, Argent Fund Management Limited, which he ran from London where he now lived. Waney remained chairman of Nitches' board for several years, before relinquishing that role as well to Wyandt, although retaining the title of chairman emeritus.

As a result of the company's downsizing efforts, revenues fell from $83.8 million in fiscal 1995 to $54.4 million in fiscal 1996. Net income, however, improved from $214,000 to $1.4 million. The downsizing trend continued in 1997, as revenues fell to $48.4 million, but because of poor dress sales profits were only $195,000. Shortly after its fiscal year ended in August 1997, Nitches sold off its dress product lines. In January 1998 the company also decided to eliminate its activewear product lines. With the loss of some $14 million in revenues contributed by these two lines, Nitches saw its 1998 sales bottom out at $31 million, the company little more than a break-even concern. Nitches began to rebound in fiscal 2000, with the sale of private-label sleepwear helping to offset discontinued lines and boost sales to nearly $40 million. Nitches also recorded a $1.9 million profit for the year. Once again, however, a sluggish economy intervened to blunt the company's growth. Revenues fell by $5.8 million over the previous year, but Nitches was still able to produce net income of $1 million. Poor economic conditions continued in 2002, however, and sales fell below $30 million, leading to further challenges for the company.

Principal Operating Units

Adobe Rose; Body Drama; Newport Blue; Southwest Canyon.

Principal Competitors

Kellwood Company; Liz Claiborne, Inc.; McNaughton Apparel.

Further Reading

Anderson, Michael A., "Beeba Cuts Penney Deal," *San Diego Business Journal,* April 6, 1987.

"Keeping Teens Decked Out in Whatever's Hot," *Business Week,* May 25, 1987, p. 88.

McClain, Tim, "Beeba's Recovers Through Spin-Off and Inventory Cut," *San Diego Daily Transcript,* February 12, 1992, p. 1.

Moin, David, "A Look at Beeba's," *WWD,* December 16, 1987, p. 9.

O'Reiley, Tim, "Beeba's Creations Bids to Go Public," *San Diego Business Journal,* August 19, 1985, p. 3.

Petruno, Tom, "Cautionary Tale of Body Drama," *Chicago Sun-Times,* August 18, 1994, p. 58.

Rutberg, Sidney, "Going Public Was Right Path for Beeba's," *WWD,* January 2, 1986, p. 12.

Svetich, Kim, "Beeba's Creations: Refocused Efforts Sparks a Quick Turnaround," *California Business,* February 1990, p. 14.

—Ed Dinger

Oak Harbor Freight Lines, Inc.

1339 West Valley Highway North
Auburn, Washington 98071-1469
U.S.A.
Telephone: (253) 288-8300
Fax: (253) 288-8301
Web site: http://www.oakh.com

Private Company
Incorporated: 1916
Employees: 1,000
Sales: $96 million (2001)
NAIC: 484122 General Freight Trucking, Long-Distance,
    Less Than Truckload

With 27 dedicated terminals in five western states, more than 1,000 employees, and several strategic partnerships, Auburn, Washington-based Oak Harbor Freight Lines, Inc. has distinguished itself as one of the elite regional carriers in the competitive Less-Than-Truckload segment of the transportation-trucking industry. Steadfast commitment to a careful and steady growth plan and an unremitting focus on building long-term relationships with both customers and employees have enabled Oak Harbor to adjust seamlessly to the tide of deregulation that has coursed through the trucking world over the last two decades. With 2001 revenues of more than $96 million, Oak Harbor is well positioned to thrive despite the ongoing upheaval in the industry as a whole.

Humble Beginnings in the Early 20th Century

Oak Harbor's roots date back to 1916, when Ben Koetje established a company called Oak Harbor Transfer in Oak Harbor, Washington. Originally a one-truck operation devoted to hauling manure for farmers, Koetje's firm branched out into the transport of local agricultural products as well. The trucking industry experienced a sea change in the mid-1930s, when President Franklin Roosevelt—responding to growing concerns about safety and the pitfalls of unfettered competition—signed the Motor Carrier Act of 1935, ushering in an era of extensive regulation. In particular, new entry and rate restrictions ensured

that trucking companies were able to operate in a relatively protected environment in which they could make consistent if not spectacular profits. Seizing on this new opportunity, brothers John and Gus Vander Pol bought out Koetje's company in 1936 for $600 and the assumption of its debt. The following year, their brother Henry joined them in the business, and in 1942, the trio acquired another small transport company called Oak Harbor Freight Lines. The brothers merged the two firms and kept the latter name. Over the next three decades, they slowly expanded Oak Harbor's delivery area into several counties across western Washington. In 1974, Henry bought out his brothers' stake in the company, and the same year Henry's sons Edward and David came to work with their father.

Deregulation in the 1980s

By the late 1970s, the coziness of the trucking industry was being challenged by those who believed that a more "free market" approach would benefit entrepreneurs and consumers alike. Following the momentum created by the deregulation of the airline industry in 1978, Congress passed the Motor Carrier Act of 1980, which President Jimmy Carter signed into law. With barriers to entry reduced and firms more or less free to establish their own pricing and fee structures, a slew of new competitors jumped into the field, while more established firms had to adjust quickly to this brave new world. The initial result of these changes was a period of chaos in the industry. As operating costs soared and profit margins were squeezed, hundreds of trucking companies—both new and old—went bankrupt in the first three years of the 1980s alone. (The industry would never regain its former predictability. Of the 100 largest carriers in 1980, fully 70 of them were to close or merge with competitors over the next two decades.)

Deregulation also led to the bifurcation of the trucking industry, with a split between the "Truckload" and the "Less Than Truckload" (LTL) segments. As the name suggests, the truckload segment encompasses those carriers who transport shipments that generally fill up an entire truck—in other words, the driver need only take the load from point A (the shipper) to point B (the recipient). LTL companies, by contrast, focus on the delivery of smaller loads, which require them to pack each truck with goods for (and from) several different customers. This presents a much more complicated set of logistical challenges and generally requires a more developed infrastructure of networks and terminals. The LTL market, therefore, was comparatively more sheltered from the post-deregulation influx of new market entrants because the nonregulatory barriers to entry in that sector still remained formidable.

As a company that traditionally had dealt with smaller loads, Oak Harbor came down on the LTL side of the divide and thus was relatively better positioned to weather the industrywide storm in the 1980s. The firm had another advantage as well. Throughout its existence, Oak Harbor had devoted itself to nurturing long-term relationships with its customers, catering to their particular needs, and striving to provide the highest possible level of service. Thanks to the strength of many of these relationships, the company was able to set its deregulated prices at a level high enough to ensure the company's continued viability, without fear that its entire customer base would desert it in favor of cut-rate carriers. This stability allowed Oak Harbor to pursue a conservative but steady growth strategy throughout the 1980s, seeking out new customers and bases of operation in the Pacific Northwest region while always remaining grounded in its rural Washington roots. This approach worked well, as Oak Harbor's sales rose from $8 million in 1984 to $25 million in 1990, and its workforce grew to 300 employees.

Growth and Expansion in the 1990s

Oak Harbor entered the 1990s with high hopes. Its revenues had continued to increase despite the softening of the American economy in the late 1980s, and it anticipated further growth in the wake of the Persian Gulf War of 1991. That same year, Oak Harbor expanded its operations beyond the West Coast when it opened a new terminal in Caldwell, Idaho. The four employees there allowed the company to offer next-day delivery service between the Boise area and markets in Seattle, Portland, and other parts of the Pacific Northwest. The move proved to be a sound one, as company revenues climbed to nearly $34 million by 1992 and to more than $38 million the following year.

In an effort to expand its reach still further, Oak Harbor entered into a strategic partnership with Southeastern Freight Lines, Inc., in 1994. Based in Columbia, South Carolina, Southeastern handled shipments within eight southern and southeastern states, including such large markets as Florida, Georgia, and Virginia. Under the terms of the agreement, Southeastern would deliver shipments in its service area that had originated from Oak Harbor's terminals, and Oak Harbor would perform the same service in the Pacific Northwest for shipments originating from Southeastern's territory.

Not long after aligning with Southeastern, Oak Harbor partnered with Preston Trucking, a regional subsidiary of industry titan Yellow Corp., which served markets in the Northeast and upper Midwest. Buoyed by these linkages, Oak Harbor's 1994 revenues exceeded $45 million.

The trucking industry continued to change rapidly during the mid-1990s. In 1995, Washington, along with many other states, deregulated its intrastate trucking market. (The Motor Carrier Act of 1980 had only reached those trucking operations that crossed state lines.) Previously, carriers wanting to make deliveries solely within Oak Harbor's home state needed to jump through a series of regulatory hurdles to be permitted to do so. With deregulation, the presumption shifted in favor of access—a firm could be denied an operating permit only on safety grounds. Having thrived in the wake of interstate deregulation in the 1980s, Oak Harbor was unfazed by this shift. "You'll see some smaller [carriers] go away," Oak Harbor co-president and co-owner Edward Vander Pol told the *Seattle Post Intelligencer,* "the ones who are not very profitable or serve a small geographic area[.]" Oak Harbor fell into neither of these categories. Indeed, after teaming up with another regional carrier, Central Freight Lines, Inc., whose delivery area encompassed eight southern and southwestern states, including Louisiana, Texas, New Mexico, and Colorado, Oak Harbor's reach was virtually nationwide. The company's 1996 revenues topped $55 million.

Continued Growth: Late 1990s and Beyond

The trucking industry was not isolated from the great leaps in technology that were driving so much of the U.S. economy in the second half of the 1990s. From tracking software that allowed customers and shipping firms to pinpoint the location of a particular shipment at any point along its route to algorithmic programs that calculated the most efficient way to route LTL deliveries to multiple customers, technological advances had become a key to turning a profit in the trucking industry. The consequences of failing to keep up could be devastating, as evidenced by the collapse of the Spokane, Washington-based regional LTL carrier Silver Eagle Trucking Co. in 2000. Despite 70 years in the business, Silver Eagle had run into serious computer problems in 1998 and was never able to recover. (Oak Harbor stepped in to pick up much of Silver Eagle's business.)

Oak Harbor invested heavily in information technology throughout the latter part of the 1990s. The company made sure that all of its new truck engines were equipped with a full range of electronic controls and monitoring devices to ensure that its drivers adhered to efficient driving speeds. "Though some drivers would like it otherwise," Oak Harbor's director of maintenance Jack Morris told the electronic newspaper *Transport Topics,* the company's vehicles "are programmed not to exceed 60 miles per hour. Any time you go over 60 miles per hour it costs you money." The company also installed IBM-based dispatch software to allow customer service representatives to transmit orders directly to paging systems in individual trucks, thereby speeding the pick-up and delivery process. Other software allows Oak Harbor personnel to keep close track of delivery times to ensure that drivers do not delay shipments to attend

---

Key Dates:

1916: Ben Koetje founds Oak Harbor Transfer in Oak Harbor, Washington.

1936: Brothers John and Gus Vander Pol buy Oak Harbor Transfer.

1937: Vander Pol brother Henry joins the company.

1942: The Vander Pols acquire another small carrier named Oak Harbor Freight Lines, merge it with Oak Harbor Transfer, and retain the Oak Harbor Freight Lines name.

1974: Henry Vander Pol buys out his brothers' shares of Oak Harbor; Henry's sons Edward and David join the company.

1980: Passage of the Motor Carrier Act of 1980 heralds the deregulation of the trucking industry; Oak Harbor begins to expand its operations across Washington State and further in the Pacific Northwest.

1984: Company revenues top $8 million.

1991: Oak Harbor opens a terminal in the Boise corridor.

1994: Oak Harbor partners with Southeastern Freight Lines, Inc., expanding its geographical reach.

1995: Washington State deregulates its intrastate trucking industry.

1996: Company revenues hit $55 million.

1999: Oak Harbor partners with New England Motor Freight, Inc.; revenues climb to $75 million.

2001: Partnership with Mid-States Express, Inc. expands Oak Harbor's reach in the Midwest; revenues top $96 million.

2002: Oak Harbor makes a major push into the California market with its Rolling Out California initiative.

---

to personal matters. Using the software, ''[w]e might see a truck that sat mysteriously for two hours 337 miles into a trip,'' Morris told the *Commercial Carrier Journal*. ''Hey, isn't that right about where the driver's girlfriend lives?''

This sort of attention to detail helped Oak Harbor achieve a nearly 99 percent on-time delivery record, an essential attribute for profitability. ''If you aren't faster, better, quicker and providing the value the marketplace is looking for,'' Oak Harbor regional sales manager Parker Powell cautioned on the company's web site in the summer of 2001, ''the market will be looking elsewhere.'' Oak Harbor did not have that problem, and the company's 1997 revenues climbed to $65 million. The year 1997 also saw the beginnings of the company's efforts to reach more deeply into the massive California market, with the opening of a terminal in Oakland to serve the San Francisco Bay Area. At the same time, the company expanded its presence in the eastern Washington-Idaho panhandle area with the opening of a dedicated terminal in Spokane, Washington. (Oak Harbor traffic in the region had been handled previously by Spokane-based Grimmer Transfer & Storage.)

Oak Harbor's regional partner Preston Trucking, however, was unable to keep up with the competitive demands of the trucking industry and went out of business in the summer of 1999. To bridge the gap opened up by Preston's demise, Oak

Harbor partnered with the Elizabeth, New Jersey-based New England Motor Freight, Inc. (NEMF), to ensure its continued access to the East Coast. NEMF, the fastest-growing trucking company in the northeastern United States, had a service area encompassing 11 eastern seaboard states from Maine to Maryland, including such powerhouses as New York and Pennsylvania. Oak Harbor Vice-President for Sales and Marketing Steve Hartmann lauded the agreement to *Traffic World*. NEMF's ''culture matched ours,'' he said. ''We're both privately held. The way they approach the customer is the same as ours. We both have very low turnover in our companies. We believe low turnover allows you to have long-term relationships with customers.'' Oak Harbor's 1999 revenues topped $75 million.

The year 2000 was one of strong growth for many of the large players in the trucking industry, as the booming U.S. economy generated an unceasing demand for the shipment of raw and finished goods. For smaller firms, however, that year's spike in the price of diesel fuel after a long period of stability was difficult to overcome. Nearly 3,600 companies across the industry declared bankruptcy that year, even as the largest 100 trucking companies saw their revenues rise by an average of nearly 8 percent. To remain healthy, Oak Harbor boosted its shipping rates and tacked on a fuel surcharge. Its customers proved understanding, and Oak Harbor continued to thrive, expanding its facilities in the San Francisco Bay Area and southern and central Oregon.

With the U.S. economy slumping, 2001 proved to be a trying year across the industry. Fuel costs remained high, and the terrorist attacks of September 11 led to increased carrier expenses in the form of higher insurance premiums and the need to implement enhanced security measures. Although the driver shortage that had plagued the industry through much of the late 1990s was beginning to abate, upward pressure on labor costs remained, and the need to keep up with advances in information technology required significant capital outlays. Oak Harbor, however, was undaunted. Early in the year, it had partnered with Aurora, Illinois-based Mid-States Express, Inc., expanding the company's reach into 11 midwestern and plains states, including Ohio, Illinois, and Nebraska. Reflecting its confidence and strong business prospects, Oak Harbor also expanded its operations in Sacramento, California; Salem, Oregon; and Lewiston, Idaho, that year. The company now had nine Oregon terminals, to go along with two in Idaho, one in Nevada, ten in Washington, and three in California. Revenues for the year reached $96 million.

Despite economic uncertainty, Oak Harbor strode confidently into 2002. To start the year the company announced a marketing partnership with Molerway Freight Lines, Inc., to begin overnight service between Seattle and western Montana. On its web site, Oak Harbor touted the move as allowing the company to ''[p]rovide the most comprehensive coverage of any carrier in the entire Northwest—thereby minimizing unloading and loading time on all shipments by reducing the number of carriers required to reach the Northwest communities.'' In March, the two companies joined forces again to inaugurate overnight shipments between Oak Harbor terminals in Reno and Boise and Molerway destinations in and around Salt Lake City, Utah.

More significant, Oak Harbor spent the spring and summer of 2002 implementing its Rolling Out California project. With this three-phased effort, Oak Harbor intended to offer its customers direct service across virtually the entire state of California, thereby improving transit times between that key state and the rest of Oak Harbor's service area. The kick-off came with the opening of a new terminal in Fresno, California, in April of 2002. The Fresno facility allowed Oak Harbor to inaugurate daily direct service to and from much of California's fertile central valley, as far south as Bakersfield. In mid-July, Oak Harbor expanded its presence in coastal northern California, when it began direct overnight service from many of its Oregon terminals, as well as Olympia, Washington, to the cities of Crescent City, Arcata, and Eureka, California. Finally, and perhaps most significant, Oak Harbor opened a terminal in Los Angeles in August, enabling the company to institute direct service between southern California, including Los Angeles, San Diego, Long Beach, Palm Springs, and Santa Barbara, and its longstanding bases in Washington, Oregon, and Idaho.

This expansion project left Oak Harbor well positioned to take advantage of the collapse in September 2002, of the nation's third largest LTL shipper, Consolidated Freightways, Inc. Consolidated was forced to suspend operations after an insurer refused to extend a surety bond in light of the company's precarious finances. The Vancouver, Washington-based firm had been losing money since 1998, as it could not raise its rates high enough to offset its operating costs. "This is a $2 billion revenue opportunity that hasn't been seen [in this industry] in some time," Standard & Poor's analyst James Corridore told the *Seattle Times*. Consolidated's customers included such giants as Home Depot, General Electric, Costco Corp., and the United States Postal Service. While much of the traffic was expected to go to industry heavyweights such as Yellow Corp. and Roadway Corp., regional carriers like Oak Harbor expected to benefit as well.

Principal Competitors

Arkansas Best, Inc.; Motor Cargo Industries; USFreightways, Inc.

Further Reading

Abry, George, "At Work: Oak Harbor Freight Lines," *Transport Topics: Trucking's Electronic Newspaper,* October 5, 2002.

Anderson, Steven, "Trucking Firm Plans New Terminal," *Idaho Business Review,* June 23, 1997.

Belzer, Michael H., "Technological Innovation and the Trucking Industry: Information Revolution and the Effect on the Work Process," *Journal of Labor Research,* July 1, 2002.

Caldwell, Bert, "Silver Eagle Closes Doors," *Spokesman Review,* March 21, 2000.

Clements, Barbara, "Trucking Earnings Hit a Dip," *Tacoma News Tribune,* May 13, 2001.

Harrell, Lisa, "Oak Harbor Is Hiring About 30 People," *Journal of Business-Spokane,* December 18, 1997.

Monaco, Kristen, "Sweatshops on Wheels: Winners and Losers in Trucking Deregulation," *Journal of Labor Research,* July 1, 2002.

Modeen, Martha, "Consolidated's Freight Sits in Fife, Waiting for Truckers," *Tacoma News Tribune,* September 5, 2002.

Richards, Paul, "Beyond Diagnostics," *Commercial Carrier Journal,* August 1, 2001.

Schultz, John D., "Linking Up," *Traffic World,* October 25, 1999.

Trask, Amy, "CF Shipping at a Standstill," *Seattle Times,* September 4, 2002.

"Trucking Firm Has High Hopes for the Future," *Seattle Times,* March 1, 1991.

Virgin, Bill, "Weighing Effects of Trucking Deregulation Some Price Wars, Fewer Carriers Seen," *Seattle Post-Intelligencer,* January 12, 1995.

Vise, Avery, "The Top 100," *Commercial Carrier Journal,* August 1, 2001.

—Rebecca Stanfel

Onyx Software Corporation

3180 139th Avenue Southeast, Suite 500
Bellevue, Washington 98005-4091
U.S.A.
Telephone: (425) 451-8060
Toll Free: (888) 275-6699
Fax: (425) 451-8277
Web site: http://www.onyx.com

Public Company
Incorporated: 1994
Employees: 450
Sales: $69.4 million (2002)
Stock Exchanges: NASDAQ
Ticker Symbol: ONXS
NAIC: 511210 Software Publishers

Onyx Software Corporation has pioneered the development of customer relationship management (CRM) software in the second half of the 1990s. Its software solutions have enabled companies to manage and access customer information to improve customer service and support as well as sales and marketing efforts. As electronic commerce has become more important, Onyx has shifted its software to Web-based solutions. The company grew rapidly until faced with the slowdown in information technology (IT) investment that began in 2001, when it was forced to lay off a substantial part of its workforce.

Focused on Customer
Management Software: 1994–96

Onyx Software Corporation was founded in 1994 by three former Microsoft Corp. employees: Brent Frei, Brian Janssen, and Todd Stevenson. At Microsoft they worked on internal customer management solutions, which gave them the idea to form their own software company devoted to customer management. Each contributed $50,000 in start-up capital to form the company, which began operations from Frei's home in the nearby town of Issaquah. Frei was Onyx's president and CEO, Janssen its executive vice-president, and Stevenson the chief technical officer.

Onyx introduced its first software product at the beginning of 1995. Initially called EnCompass, the software enabled companies to manage all customer information from a single application by creating a single database for all customer-related data. The software was considered a pioneering development in centralized customer management, a field that later developed into customer relationship management (CRM). EnCompass was able to handle several customer-related functions, including sales, technical support, customer service, and marketing.

EnCompass was created by using Microsoft development tools, and it was designed to run on a Microsoft SQL Server using Windows NT, with clients using Windows 3.x. The software cost $30,000 for a ten-user license. At the time EnCompass was released, Onyx had ten employees—seven of whom were former Microsoft employees.

With the release of version 2.0 in mid-1995, EnCompass was rebranded Customer Center. The new version added quality assurance tools that made customer-related information available to engineering and product development staff. The tools captured information such as product change requests and incorporated them into the product development cycle. In addition, customers were notified when the changes were made. Customer Center 2.0 also added database drivers that made it possible to link it to other SQL Server-based business software.

Onyx grew quickly over the next 18 months. Sales revenue jumped from $2.1 million in 1995 to $9.8 million in 1996. The company gained 65 customers in 1996 for a total of 100 customers. Most of Onyx's customers were medium-sized businesses that had adopted Microsoft's Windows NT operating system. Onyx obtained venture capital financing from Foundation Capital of Menlo Park, California, and grew to 110 employees by the beginning of 1997.

Updated Product Offerings: 1997–98

The overall market for customer relationship management (CRM) software was forecast to grow dramatically, from $738 million in 1996 to $2.2 billion in 2000, according to the Gartner Group. As a result, several larger competitors had moved into the field, such as Siebel Systems, Inc. The company's biggest

Company Perspectives:

Onyx Software Corp. is a global supplier of customer relationship management (CRM) enterprise applications that power a company's entire business world, connecting sales, marketing and service organizations with customers, prospects and partners. Through an innovative mix of Internet technology, strategic services and customer commitment, Onyx helps companies create the seamless, branded customer experience they need to forge competitive advantage and build real business value.

challenge, though, was to find qualified employees as it continued to grow. For 1997 Onyx reported revenue of $19.4 million, nearly double that of 1996, and a net loss of $2.54 million.

Toward the end of 1997 Onyx introduced Onyx Channel Connect, a Web-based application that helped value-added resellers (VARs) of software. By using Channel Connect, VARs could access a software manufacturer's Customer Center database via the Internet to find and report information on sales leads and other sales opportunities. Software companies could use the data from VARs to improve their sales forecasting.

In mid-1998 Onyx introduced version 4.0 of Customer Center. Among the new features of Customer Center 4.0 was computer-telephony integration (CTI), which allowed Customer Center 4.0 to integrate with any CTI-enabled phone switch for improved customer service. Onyx formed partnerships with three CTI companies—WhiteCap, Interactive Intelligence, and Apropos Technology—to facilitate integration with PBXs and automatic call distributors for applications such as call transfers, outbound dialing, and importing customer information onto a service representative's computer screen.

Customer Center 4.0 also offered increased functionality for mobile users through unattended updates. SyncAssistant allowed mobile users to set a time for their portable computer to dial the home server and receive automatic updates of new customer leads and product information as well as e-mail and virus scans.

PC Week magazine noted that while Customer Center cost significantly less than other sales force automation (SFA) applications, a typical installation with 100 concurrent users cost about $450,000, including support costs of about $10,000 per week and a $52,000 annual maintenance fee.

Later in 1998 Onyx acquired EnCyc Inc., a marketing software developer whose main product was the EnCyc Marketing Encyclopedia, which linked marketing database data with productivity tools, Web-based content delivery, and remote access. Onyx also partnered with Trilogy to bundle its Selling Chain sales configuration software with Customer Center for sale to complex markets such as computer systems and airplanes. In addition, Onyx announced that it was bringing out specialized sales and customer-service software suites for financial and healthcare markets. The company planned to introduce similar modules for other specialized fields in 1999.

Going Public and Shifting to Web-Based Solutions: 1999–2000

Onyx went public on February 11, 1999, offering 13 million shares at $13 per share. On the first day of trading the stock opened at $22.75 and closed at $23.625. The company received venture capital backing from Foundation Capital Management and Technology Crossover Management II, both of which were represented on Onyx's board of directors.

In its offering statements the company described itself as a provider of enterprise relationship management (ERM) software solutions that automated key functions to help companies acquire, manage, and retain customers, partners, and other relationships. For 1998 Onyx's revenue jumped to $35.11 million, but its losses widened to $6.98 million, causing concern among some analysts who noted that most software companies were profitable. At the time it went public Onyx had about 300 customers in financial services, high technology, telecommunications, and other fields.

Over the next two years Onyx began shifting to Web-based solutions. In April 1999 the company released Insight 3.0 and Email Agent, two core products in its newly designated e-Service product family, which also included Web Wizards. Insight 3.0 was a knowledge management tool that provided users with the option of customer self-service. It allowed customers, employees, and partners to access information via the Internet at any time. Email Agent automatically responded to customer e-mails 24 hours a day. Web Wizards let customers create, view, and update product service incidents over the Web, thus allowing an organization to provide 24-hour customer service.

In the second half of 1999 Onyx completed beta testing and began shipping the Onyx Enterprise Portal. It was designed to help online businesses better serve their virtual customers by placing functions such as customer support, help desks, and sales force automation within a Web-enabled, server-delivered portal framework. The Onyx Enterprise Portal shipped with a range of integrated Internet content from third-party providers to give users access to account and market profiles, stock quotes, maps, weather, news, and other content. The Enterprise Portal also made it possible to customize content and applications for different departments and individuals. This new approach helped Onyx gain several new customers, including the Seattle Seahawks and Cincinnati Bell Telephone, among others. Pricing for the Enterprise Portal began at $65,000 for ten users. In a related development, Onyx acquired Versametrix Corp., an Internet technology developer for corporate portals, in September.

Meanwhile, Onyx was developing a reputation as a great company to work for and one that was able to attract top talent. It was named one of the "Best Companies to Work for" in Washington by Simpson Hayward Inc., and it topped the list of the Washington Technology Fast 50 as the fastest growing technology company in the state. For 1999 Onyx reported an increase in revenue to $60.6 million. Its workforce grew to about 400 employees.

In the first half of 2000 Onyx enhanced its suite of Web-enabled CRM software with the release of the Onyx Customer Portal and the Onyx Partner Portal, as well as version 2.0 of the

---

Key Dates:

1994: Onyx Software is founded by former Microsoft employees.
1995: Onyx introduces its first customer management software, EnCompass, which is renamed Customer Center later in the year.
1998: Customer Center 4.0 is introduced.
1999: Onyx becomes a public company.
2000: Onyx makes the transition to offering Web-based customer relationship management (CRM) solutions.
2001: Onyx forms numerous alliances with third-party providers to enhance its CRM solutions.
2002: Onyx becomes a recognized provider of CRM solutions for large enterprises.

Onyx Employee Portal. These portals enabled customers, partners, and employees to access customer-related data through a Web browser interface in a single, customizable location. They were part of Onyx's Front Office 2000 suite of applications.

The Onyx Customer Portal let customers place orders, request information, update their personal data, and initiate and track service requests through the same interface. The Onyx Partner Portal facilitated collaborative selling and the sharing of leads among an organization's partners. The Onyx Employee Portal included CRM tools that let users access and manage account information, track sales opportunities, create customer-service queues, and analyze customer data.

In the second half of 2000 Onyx expanded its presence in international markets. In Brazil the company signed up three distributors to begin selling its software in Spanish, English, and Portuguese. In Japan Onyx teamed with Softbank Investment and Prime Systems Corp. to form Onyx Japan, which was majority-owned and controlled by Onyx. Onyx had first established a presence in the Pacific Rim in 1997 with a full-service operation in Singapore and Australia. The company entered the Hong Kong and Malaysian markets in 1999.

Onyx also announced an initiative to provide its CRM software through hosted application service providers (ASPs). The company began recruiting ASPs and formed its first ASP alliance with Allegis Corp. For 2000 Onyx's revenue grew to more than $100 million, and its workforce stood at about 670 employees.

Forming Alliances: 2001–02

Onyx gained specialized consulting capabilities with the acquisition of RevenueLab in January 2001. RevenueLab was a consulting firm that developed revenue acceleration programs for sales and marketing and provided sales-strategy services. Its customer list included several large enterprises, including EDS, John Hancock, Michelin, Microsoft, and Wells Fargo. Following the acquisition Onyx announced a partnership with Microsoft to join forces to sell CRM packages. The partnership initially targeted large financial services companies by offering a package that included Onyx's Investment Management Edition, Microsoft's .Net enterprise servers, and consulting services from Reve-

nueLab. Around this time Onyx improved its financial position with a secondary stock offering. The company sold 2.5 million shares at $13.50 per share, raising more than $31 million.

Onyx continued to form alliances that added new features to its CRM solutions. It announced a partnership with Cognos Inc. that added Cognos's business-intelligence tools to Onyx's software applications. The tools analyzed customer data and helped develop forecasts. An alliance with MindArrow Systems Inc. added the capability to send multimedia eBrochures to customers from within Onyx's e-business portals. The eBrochures were compressed files that included video, audio, graphics, and interactive hyperlinks that could be distributed by e-mail or be downloaded from a Web page. Other companies joining the Onyx partner program in the first half of 2001 included Metrix Inc., whose products addressed the needs of companies with onsite field service and repair centers, and Incentive Systems, Inc., which provided incentive management solutions.

In May Onyx added e-Service to its Enterprise 2001 CRM portal suite. E-Service included three new tools—Email Assistance, Web Assistance, and Chat—that could be incorporated into the company's overall CRM solution. Email Assistance was an automated e-mail response tool that prioritized incoming messages and returned an automated response. Web Assistance was an intelligent online self-service tool that guided customers through their questions, provided automated responses, and upgraded the responses to e-mail or live interaction as needed. Chat enabled companies to deliver information instantly to Web site visitors.

The technology behind e-Service was the result of a partnership with Firepond Inc. A separate partnership with AvantGo Inc. resulted in a real-time, mobile CRM solution for large, field-based sales and service teams, giving them wireless access to customer information.

Even as Onyx was adding new features to its CRM solutions, the company was experiencing the effects of a slowdown in information technology (IT) spending. In April the company laid off 116 employees, or about 17 percent of its workforce. Its first quarter revenue of $28 million was well short of analysts' forecasts of $39 million, and the company's stock price dropped from a 52-week high of $32 to about $6 per share. For the second quarter the company reported revenue of $28.9 million and a net loss of $13.7 million. With third quarter revenue dropping to around $20 million, Onyx announced that it would cut an additional 25 percent of its workforce, or about 150 employees. The base pay of its remaining 460 employees was adjusted to reflect incentive-based compensation tied to the company's profitability. Onyx also scaled back on its office space and put a six-story, 172,000-square-foot building on the sublease market, which resulted in the company paying about $580,000 a month for unused office space.

For 2001 Onyx reported revenue of $97.2 million, with a net loss of $95.5 million. Included in the company's net loss was $51.8 million in severance, excess facilities, and impairments of fixed assets charged, as well as $15.4 million in amortization and stock compensation expenses. In January 2002 Onyx improved its cash position by completing a secondary stock offering that raised about $20.5 million. At the end of the first quarter

Onyx had increased its cash balances to $33.6 million, compared to $15.9 million at the end of 2001.

Meanwhile, Onyx continued to release new versions of its portal-based CRM solutions. Version 3.0 of its Employee Portal was released in the third quarter of 2001, followed by version 3.0 of its Partner Portal in the first quarter of 2002. In mid-2002 Onyx released Onyx Enterprise CRM 4.0, the firm's flagship CRM suite. Version 4.0 was built entirely on standards-based Internet technologies and was completely Web-based.

Faced with a prolonged decline in domestic IT spending, Onyx continued to expand in Asian markets, where IT investment was projected to increase over the next five years. Onyx entered the growing market for CRM in China in September by signing a master reseller agreement with North 22 Solutions Ltd. Another partnership with Asia Bell Company Ltd. gave the company distribution in Thailand. As the third quarter of 2002 drew to a close, Onyx was ranked 195th on *Software Magazine's* Software 500 list and 30th on the Washington State Technology Fast 50 list of fast-growing technology companies. The company also achieved recognition as a provider of CRM solutions for large enterprises.

Principal Competitors

Broadvision, Inc.; E.piphany Inc.; Kana Communications, Inc.; Oracle Corporation; PeopleSoft, Inc.; Pivotal Corporation; SAP AG (Germany); Siebel Systems, Inc.

Further Reading

"Another Microsoft Grad to Hit IPO Trail," *IPO Reporter,* December 21, 1998.

Baker, M. Sharon, "Onyx Lays Financial Groundwork for Growth," *Puget Sound Business Journal,* December 1, 2000, p. 9.

——, "Staffing a Challenge for Fast-Growing Onyx," *Puget Sound Business Journal,* February 7, 1997, p. 12.

Berst, Jesse, "Customer-centric Firm Creates New Growth Area," *PC Week,* January 23, 1995, p. 100.

Bishop, Todd, "High-Tech Is on the Hook," *Puget Sound Business Journal,* September 28, 2001, p. 1.

——, "No Move for Onyx?," *Puget Sound Business Journal,* September 14, 2001, p. 48.

"Business Sense," *PC Week,* September 28, 1998, p. 20.

Callaghan, Dennis, "E.piphany, Onyx Expand CRM Packages," *eWeek,* May 21, 2001, p. 30.

——, "Microsoft, Onyx Link for CRM Push," *eWeek,* February 5, 2001, p. 28.

——, "More Consolidation in CRM Space," *eWeek,* January 22, 2001, p. 18.

Drucker, David, "Onyx Adds Web CRM Tools," *InternetWeek,* April 10, 2000, p. 19.

Frei, Brent, "Taking the Pain Out of Growing," *Nation's Business,* December 1998, p. 8.

Gannon, Michael, "Onyx Software Corp.," *Venture Capital Journal,* April 1, 1999.

Glascock, Stuart, "Onyx Tool Helps VARs, Vendors Close the Loop," *Computer Reseller News,* July 21, 1997, p. 95.

Greenberg, Ilan, "Onyx, Scopus Unveil Customer Service Apps," *InfoWorld,* March 20, 1995, p. 29.

Hatlestadt, Luc, "Onyx Customer Center Focuses on Quality Assurance," *InfoWorld,* June 12, 1995, p. 29.

"Heard on the Street," *Customer Interface,* February 2001, p. 18.

"Hot Market, Top Talent Propel Onyx Software Revenues Skyward," *Puget Sound Business Journal,* September 24, 1999, p. 2A.

Howle, Amber, "Open-Door Policy," *Computer Reseller News,* June 12, 2000, p. 86.

Karpinski, Richard, "Onyx Portal Approach Personalizes CRM," *InternetWeek,* September 6, 1999, p. 58.

——, "Portal Opens for Customer Mgm't," *InternetWeek,* June 28, 1999, p. 15.

Meisner, Jeff, "Onyx Racks up Revenues, Expands Internationally," *Puget Sound Business Journal,* June 29, 2001, p. 66.

"Metrix Partners with Onyx Software," *Canadian Corporate News,* March 29, 2001.

"Microsoft, Onyx Partner on CRM Package," *TechWeb,* January 31, 2001.

"Onyx and Microsoft Push Vertical CRM Limit," *Intelligent Enterprise,* March 27, 2001, p. 64.

"Onyx Eyes Brazil Market," *Puget Sound Business Journal,* June 23, 2000, p. 12.

"Onyx Goes Back to Stock Market," *Puget Sound Business Journal,* February 9, 2001, p. 3.

"Onyx Moves with Incentive," *Customer Interaction Solutions,* May 2001, p. 32.

"Onyx Software, Softbank Investment, and Prime Systems to Create Onyx Japan," *Japan Telecom,* September 2000, p. 10.

"Onyx, Trilogy to Partner, Not Merge," *InfoWorld,* October 12, 1998, p. 57.

"Onyx Warns of Further Cuts," *Puget Sound Business Journal,* August 24, 2001, p. 14.

Park, Clayton, "A Discipline Learned at Microsoft," *Puget Sound Business Journal,* June 27, 1997, p. 35.

"Sales Suite Gains Telephony," *InfoWorld,* July 20, 1998, p. 67.

"Spring Brings a Gallimaufry of Call Center Products," *Call Center Solutions,* April 1999, p. 24.

Sweat, Jeff, "Onyx Gives Employees Easier Access to Customer Data," *InformationWeek,* May 22, 2000, p. 34.

Whiting, Rick, "Customers Come into Focus with Combination Software," *InformationWeek,* February 12, 2001, p. 30.

—David P. Bianco

Orange Glo International

8765 East Orchard Road #703
Greenwood Village, Colorado 80111
U.S.A.
Telephone: (303) 740-1909
Fax: (303) 740-8622
Web site: http://www.greatcleaners.com

Private Company
Incorporated: 1992
Employees: 155
Sales: $330 million (2002 est.)
NAIC: 325611 Soap and Other Detergent Manufacturing;
325612 Polish and Other Sanitation Good
Manufacturing

Orange Glo International manufactures and markets a variety of household cleaning products designed with natural, environmentally safe ingredients. Family owned and operated, the company offers cleaners, polishes, stain removers, and degreasers under the brand names Orange Glo, Orange Clean, OxiClean, and Kaboom. More than 35 products provide the natural cleaning power of orange oil or oxygen. Home care applications include carpets, upholstery, kitchen, bath, laundry and fabric, wood, and glass. Orange oil provides the base for hand and body soaps as well. In addition to offering cleaning accessories, such as mops, sponges, and reusable towels, Orange Glo packages its products into cleaning systems and value kits. Orange Glo products are available through response television infomercials on cable and network stations, via direct mail and the Internet, and at a major supermarkets, drug stores, hardware stores, and mass-market retailers. Top sellers in certain retail sectors include Orange Glo Wood Cleaner & Polish; Orange Clean Tough Acting Degreaser and Multi-Purpose Cleaner; OxiClean Multi-Purpose Stain Remover; and Kaboom Shower, Tub, and Tile Restorer. The company's products are available in 15 countries worldwide and international distribution is promoted through offices in Tokyo, Shanghai, and London.

1980s: Husband and Wife Team Build a Business

Max Appel's concern for human health and the environment motivated him to experiment with natural, non-toxic substances to create safe cleaning products. Not a chemist by training, Appel worked in his Littleton, Colorado, garage, experimenting with orange oil to reformulate a cleaning product he had bought from another company and repackaged to sell. A turpentine-like substance known to have cleansing properties, orange oil provided a base, along with silicone wood protectants. Through trial and error and damage to several kitchen cabinets, Appel created a wood cleaner and polish without harsh solvents or toxic petrochemicals. With each bottle containing oil from 78 Valencia oranges, the product emitted a pleasant aroma.

When development of Orange Glo Wood Cleaner and Polish came to completion, Appel applied his skills as a salesman and his love of networking to promoting the product. In addition to employment as a fundraiser for medical centers and environmental organizations, as a sideline Appel sold a variety of items, such as carpet sweepers and household cleansers, at home shows and state fairs. At first he sold the wood cleaner to friends and acquaintances. In 1986 he demonstrated the product to the general public for the first time at the Arizona State Fair.

Appel demonstrated Orange Glo Wood Cleaner and Polish at state fairs and home shows across the United States and Canada, developing a loyal base of customers through interpersonal selling. These interactions with customers provided the inspiration for product improvement, new product uses, as well as for the development of new products. Customer feedback led Appel to formulate a multipurpose, concentrated degreaser for hard surfaces. Based on an industrial product used to clean brewing vats, Orange Clean Tough Acting Degreaser and Multi-Purpose Cleaner launched in 1988. Sales increased through new and repeat business, coinciding with increased consumer interest in environmentally safe products.

Operating the business as Appel Mountain, Inc., Appel and his wife, Elaine, worked as a team. Purchasing orange oil and other ingredients from suppliers, Max mixed and sold the wood polish and Elaine managed all other operations. Her job included filling and labeling bottles, processing orders, and handling all aspects of shipping. Elaine Appel's experience in tax accounting and inventory management provided a foundation for establishing office and financial procedures. In addition to caring for their four children, the Appels maintained full time jobs until they felt certain that the company would succeed. They knew the business had reached a new level when Elaine, claiming to have a family emergency, left her regular job one day in order to fill customer orders at home.

1992: Business Plan Guides Expansion

The Appels' son Joel, a marketing executive for Quaker Oats in Chicago, provided the impetus for business expansion. Joel, Max, and Elaine each invested $10,000 and reincorporated the company as Orange Glo International in 1992. The three prepared a business plan to account for the production, order-processing, shipping, and financing that would be necessary as the company's market expanded.

The first steps toward expansion were small but significant. In addition to offering cleaning products through direct mail and at home shows, the Appels introduced Orange Glo to the retail market in 1992, making products available through grocery stores. The company's leap into large-scale operations occurred through access to television audiences. When the Home Shopping Network (HSN) featured Orange Glo Wood Cleaner and Polish in 1996, the 4,000 bottles available sold rapidly. Through its regular distribution channels, the company generated sales of $700,000 in 1995; after a few months on HSN sales increased to more than $300,000 per month.

Orange Glo next invested profits in its first infomercial. Long-playing infomercials provided the perfect venue for promoting Orange Glo products; the visual impact of product demonstration and detailed explanation mirrored Max Appel's home show demonstrations. The investment paid off as sales increased to up to $2 million per month. In 1998 Orange Glo generated $12 million in revenues, primarily through response to television advertising.

While Orange Glo worked with talented producers, much credit for the success of the infomercials went to pitchman Billy Mays. Appel and Mays met at a Pittsburgh home show and became friends as their paths crossed at other shows. Mays brought sales experience, including hawking Washomatiks on Atlantic City's boardwalk, to the infomercials. Trained by veteran salesmen along the boardwalk, Mays brought a high-energy, hard-sell style to the two-minute and 30-minute infomercials. Eventually, Mays wrote scripts and produced Orange Glo infomercials as well. Orange Glo spent $400,000 per week on response television advertising, which generated 15,000 orders per week.

In 1997 the company introduced a fabric stain and odor remover that had dramatic appeal in both home show and infomercial demonstrations. OxiClean Stain Remover was based on a commercial degreaser that contained oxygen in the form of a white powder. When warm water was added to the crystals, minuscule bubbles of oxygen traveled to the staining substance and chemically forced organic matter, such as wine, coffee, and dirt, to loosen its grip on fabrics. OxiClean's oxidation process made dirt disappear from the demonstration carpet without scrubbing, as if by magic.

Infomercials supported sales of the company's products at retail outlets through customer familiarity. Between 1997 and 1999 the company obtained shelf space for its products in many regional and national retail chains, including Target, Wal-Mart, Sam's Club, Walgreens, Costco, and others. Orange Glo pursued sales opportunities through a variety of distribution channels, launching a website in 1998. A direct mail campaign in late 1999 sought to reestablish business relations with former customers from a database of 700,000 names.

By outsourcing operations Orange Glo accommodated growth with minimal capital investment. The company began to outsource production in late 1997; two years later five plants in the Midwest manufactured 20 cleaning products. Four call centers handled order processing. As the company outsourced Elaine Appel's responsibilities, she became the human resource manager, developing staff positions as the company grew.

With $86 million in revenues in 1999, Orange Glo ranked number four on *Inc.* magazine's October 2000 list of the 500 fastest-growing private companies. Between 1995 and 1999 revenues at Orange Glo had increased by over 11,000 percent. To celebrate this accomplishment, the Appels rewarded their 45 employees by giving each a 100 dollar bill along with a copy of the *Inc.* article.

New Directions in Early 2000s

As the family business expanded so did family participation in the business. The oldest Appel son, David, joined Orange Glo in 2000. Formerly a partner in Accenture, David's experience in business strategy and international development complemented the skills of other family members. As chairman of Orange Glo, David Appel oversaw company operations, including finance, information technology, supply chain logistics, customer service, human resources, and international development. Though Orange Glo products had been available in overseas markets for several years, with David Appel's involvement the company opened its first overseas offices, in Tokyo in early 2001, in London later that year, and in Shanghai in late 2002.

Linda Appel joined the family business in 2000 as president of European operations. Like all of the Appel children, Linda had helped her parents demonstrate company products at fairs and home shows. After college she worked at Overseas Development Corporation, a think tank, as well as an advertising account manager for Young & Rubicam in New York. From the London office Linda Appel pursued international distribution opportunities throughout Europe.

Key Dates:

1986: Orange Glo Wood Cleaner and Polish is demonstrated to the general public for the first time at the Arizona State Fair.

1988: Orange Clean Multi-Purpose Degreaser is introduced.

1992: Son Joel joins the company and a long-term business plan is developed.

1995: Home show demonstrations and repeat customers produce $700,000 in sales.

1996: Sales soar with product debut on Home Shopping Network.

1997: Orange Glo launches OxiClean Multi-Purpose Stain Remover.

1998: Sales reach $12 million through product demonstrations on late night infomercials.

2000: Daughter Linda and eldest son David join the family business; the Kaboom line of household cleaning products is introduced.

2002: Advertising strategy includes primetime television, magazines, and billboards.

As president and CEO, Joel Appel continued to direct daily operations and North American sales and marketing and to maintain important customer relationships. As vice-president, Elaine Appel handled finances and taxes and nourished staff with sound advice and the occasional batch of fresh-baked cookies. Another daughter, Amy Appel, monitored product placement at retail stores in Florida.

Max Appel continued to develop cleaning products, but more often he worked with consultants. New products included Orange Foam for cleaning greasy dirt, Power Paste, Bar of Oranges hand and body soap, Orange Grove Air Freshener, and Orange for Hands, a heavy-duty liquid soap. The company began to offer cleaning tools, such as terrycloth mops, magnetized brooms, and squeegee cloths. Orange Glo introduced the Kaboom brand of household cleaning products in 2000. Products included Kaboom Shower, Tub and Tile Cleaner, an ammonia-free alternative to harsh bathroom cleaners, and Kaboom All-Purpose Stain Remover. Orange Glo sold the Kaboom line through retail stores and infomercials.

While *Inc.* magazine ranked Orange Glo at number ten on its list of the 500 Fastest Growing Private Companies in 2001, the success of Orange Glo could also be measured in the number of new competitors. Major producers of cleaning products introduced known products with the addition of orange scent or a less potent form of orange oil than that used by Orange Glo. Such products included Pledge Furniture Polish with Orange Oil and Fantastik with Orange. Not necessarily environmentally friendly, these products nevertheless appealed to consumer preferences for pleasant fragrance. As Orange Glo's OxiClean products proved even more popular than orange-based products, national competitors produced versions of oxygen-based products as well.

Moreover, as infomercials continued to play an important role in demonstrating and promoting Orange Glo products, national competitors began to use the infomercial format to promote their retail products, too. Orange Glo responded with a new promotional strategy. In May 2002 Orange Glo began to advertise Orange Clean and OxiClean products on prime-time television. In one commercial, football players wearing pink prom dresses practiced by rolling in blueberry pies; the tagline said, "Millions believe for a reason." The commercials aired during "Will & Grace," "Late Show With David Letterman," and other popular shows.

A second set of television advertisements, released in early 2003, featured Mays, working under an exclusive contract. Bringing his enthusiasm to network television, Mays compared OxiClean as a laundry additive with detergent alone and asked robustly, "You call that clean?" The company initiated billboard and magazine advertising as well, the latter involving placements in *Good Housekeeping, Rosie, Ebony,* and *Better Homes and Gardens.*

In addition to promoting its products through international distribution, response television, and mainstream advertising, Orange Glo developed less visible business opportunities through two new divisions. The Specialty Retailer Division provided support for small retailers, such as in stimulating store traffic. The International Professional Products Division offered Orange Glo products in large industrial sizes to suit those markets. The division provided technical support and training, as well as distributor support.

Principal Divisions

Specialty Retailer Division; International Professional Products Division.

Principal Competitors

The Clorox Company; Earth Friendly Products; The Procter & Gamble Company; S.C. Johnson & Son, Inc.; Seventh Generation, Inc.; Turtle Wax Inc.

Further Reading

Brand, Rachel, "Family Cleans Up with Infomercials," *Rocky Mountain News,* August 17, 2001, p. 5B.

Casabona, Liza, "Orange Appeal," *Supermarket News,* March 25, 2002, p. 51.

"Direct Response Getting Respect: As OxiClean Moves to Stores, Clorox and P&G Try Infomercials," *Advertising Age,* January 20, 2003, p. 4.

"Family-Run Cleaning Products Maker Basks in Orange Glo of Success," *Knight Ridder/Tribune Business News,* January 19, 2003.

Lewis, Pete, "Appel Takes a Successful Bite at Orange Glo Polish," *Denver Business Journal,* June 9, 2000, p. 17B.

McCrea, Bridget, "A Glowing Success," *Response,* December 2001.

Neff, Jack, "OxiClean: Cindy Heller," *Advertising Age,* October 8, 2001, p. S30.

———, "OxiClean Rides Direct to the Top," *Advertising Age,* July 30, 2001, p. 1.

"Orange Glo International Launches New Division," *ICS Cleaning Specialist,* October 2002, p. 67.

Perry, Karen, "Orange Glo International," *Direct,* May 1, 2000, p. S25.

''Retail Entrepreneurs of the Year: Joel Appel,'' *Chain Store Age Executive*, December 2000, p. 114.

Stamler, Bernard, ''Flush with Infomercial Cash, the Company that Makes OxiClean Moves Up to Prime-Time Spots,'' *New York Times*, May 23, 2002, p. C5.

''Staying on Top: OxiClean Finds Success Leads to More Competition,'' *Advertising Age,* January 20, 2003, p. 35.

Schwab, Robert, ''Family Cleans Up with Sales,'' *Denver Post*, June 12, 1999, p. C1.

—Mary Tradii

Organic Valley (Coulee Region Organic Produce Pool)

507 West Main Street
La Farge, Wisconsin 54639
U.S.A.
Telephone: (608) 625-2602
Toll Free: (888) 444-6455
Fax: (608) 625-2600
Web site: http://www.organicvalley.com

Cooperative
Incorporated: 1988
Employees: 220
Sales: $125 million (2002)
NAIC: 112120 Dairy Cattle and Milk Production; 311512
Creamery Butter Manufacturing; 311513 Cheese
Manufacturing; 112310 Chicken Egg Production;
112111 Beef Cattle Ranching and Farming; 112320
Broilers and Other Meat Type Chicken Production;
112210 Hog and Pig Farming; 111998 All Other
Miscellaneous Crop Farming

Organic Valley, formally known as the Coulee Region Organic Produce Pool, or CROPP, is the nation's largest cooperative in the United States made up solely of organic farmers. The cooperative is also the nation's single largest source of organic milk. Marketing under the Organic Valley brand name, the cooperative sells organic milk both for primary consumption and as an ingredient in other foods. It also markets organic cream, butter, cultured cheese, eggs, and juice. Under the Valley Family of Farms brand, the cooperative also sells certified organic beef, pork, and chicken. The cooperative, headquartered in a small town in rural southwest Wisconsin, is made up of more than 500 farmer members in 17 states, representing all areas of the country from coast to coast. More than two-thirds are principally dairy farmers, and the rest raise meat, eggs, vegetables, or citrus crops. Organic Valley's products are sold in all 50 states and in some overseas markets. The cooperative is a large player in what remains a very small niche market. Yet the market for organic foods grew enormously in the 1990s and

is expected to continue in coming decades. Organic Valley saw sales increase dramatically in the late 1990s and early 2000s.

A Small Start

Organic Valley was founded as the Coulee Region Organic Produce Pool (CROPP) by seven farmers in 1988. Coulee is a geologic term for the small valleys that are common in southwest Wisconsin, where the original Organic Valley farmers were located. It was an area hit hard by drought in the mid-1980s, and many small family farms in the region were struggling to survive. George Siemon, currently chief executive of Organic Valley, was one of the founders of the cooperative. Siemon grew up in Florida, then took a bachelor's degree in animal science from Colorado State University. He and his family began running an organic farm in Wisconsin in 1977. The Siemon farm used no pesticides or herbicides on its crops. Most conventional dairy farms treat their animals prophylactically with antibiotics. Siemon and other organic farmers eschewed preventive drugs, and only treated their animals if they were seriously ill. Siemon's cows also grazed on pasture that was free of herbicides and pesticides. Siemon went on to become one of the nation's premier spokesmen for organic methods of farming, and he was deeply committed to this method of agriculture. By the mid-1980s, however, he and other neighboring organic farmers felt that they were not getting a decent price for their milk and crops, and their livelihoods were in jeopardy. Siemon and the others first concentrated their efforts on marketing their organically grown vegetables. But dairy products represented a much bigger market, and the group soon focused on organic milk. The seven founders were all already members of a farming group called the National Farmers Organization). The NFO was founded in 1955 to give family farmers unified bargaining power. The nonprofit group pooled the interests of member farmers and negotiated prices for farm commodities. The seven coulee region farmers formed CROPP under the auspices of the NFO, hoping that their more specialized group would be able to raise the prominence of organic products. July 13, 1988 was the first day the group began shipping milk under the CROPP name.

In 1989 the small cooperative invested in an abandoned creamery in the small town of LaFarge, Wisconsin to serve as

Company Perspectives:

We, the family farmers of Organic Valley are committed to: cooperatively market the finest in certified organic products produced exclusively by our family of farmers; market nutritious, wholesome food as directly as possible to the consumer; establish farmer-determined prices which provide the farmer with enough profit to sustain his family and his farm; encourage a farming future that emphasizes ecological diversity and economic sustainability; enable a healthy human livelihood by providing quality employment, cooperation, organic education, and community growth; practice environmental awareness and cooperative principles in all aspects of production, handling, marketing and operations; promote a respect for the dignity and interdependence of human, animal, plant, soil, and global life.

its headquarters. The group did not have its own milk processing facility, but used existing ones, with safeguards to keep its organic milk separate from conventional milk. To sell its milk, the group hired an outside marketer. But this arrangement did not work out, and CROPP soon developed its own marketing program and its own brand, Organic Valley. The Organic Valley brand debuted in 1989, and this name gradually became better known than CROPP.

For its first five years, the cooperative was able to sell only about half its milk for the premium prices organic milk fetched; the other half had to be sold on the conventional market. Gradually, the group picked up distributors on the East and West Coasts, where it sold primarily through natural food markets. Its products were more expensive than conventional dairy products. Its organic cheese, for example, sold for $6 to $7 a pound retail, about twice the price of other domestic cheese. But a growing number of consumers were willing to pay more for certified organic dairy products, and Organic Valley hung on. The organization's philosophy was to do the best for its member farmers. So CROPP kept its overhead low, and offered high milk prices to members rather than aim to accumulate capital for expansion. The group also had a clear mission to preserve the family organic farm, believing that this was a method of agriculture that helped farmers, consumers, animals, and the land. As its brand became better known and its marketing and distribution more effective, the cooperative saw sales growth of around 20 percent a year. Sales for 1992 stood at around $2 million. Then in 1993 the organic dairy market took off, spurred by a new development in conventional farming.

Surge in Organic Market in the Mid-1990s

By the early 1990s, the overall dairy market in the United States was worth some $75 billion annually. Organic dairy products made up just a tiny slice of that, estimated at around .3 percent. There were only a few nationally distributed brands of organic dairy. Besides Organic Valley, which had strong sales on the coasts, Stonyfield Farm and the Horizon Organic Holding Corporation also had nationwide sales of yogurt, milk, and other products. Some regional producers also had strong sales, such as the California organic dairy Straus Family Creamery.

But the organic dairy market began to boom in 1993, the year the Food and Drug Administration approved an artificial growth hormone for cows called rBGH. rBGH was developed by the pharmaceutical company Monsanto. It was a genetically engineered hormone that stimulated milk production. Cows treated with rBGH were able to give as much as 25 percent more milk daily than cows that did not receive the hormone. The drug was hailed as a boon to farmers, but immediately met with criticism from consumer groups and raised animal rights concerns. Studies of the effects of milk from rBGH-treated cows had been done on rats, but some groups voiced fears that the milk's safety to humans had not been adequately demonstrated. Studies showed that cows given rBGH were more prone to udder infections, which then raised the amount of antibiotics with which cows were treated. Already at that time half of all antibiotics prescribed in the United States went to farm animals. It seemed that rBGH might increase the amount of antibiotics given to cows, amplifying fears of antibiotic-resistant bacteria entering the human food chain.

rBGH caused a storm of controversy. Some states, including Wisconsin and Minnesota, passed legislation requiring that milk from cows treated with rBGH be labeled as such. Monsanto, on the other hand, sued some dairies for labeling their milk rBGH free, contending that the label misled consumers to think milk treated with rBGH was inferior. Milk sales declined more than 3 percent in the year after rBGH was introduced in the United States (though not necessarily because of rBGH fears). But organic milk products began to sell extremely well. Growth at Organic Valley picked up. The group had picked up new farmer members in its first half-dozen years, growing from seven members at its inception to 50 members by the mid-1990s. By the late 1990s, the group was taking in as many as 50 new members in a single year, and Organic Valley had to learn to cope with rapid expansion. Most of the group's farmers ran dairies in Wisconsin, Illinois, Minnesota, and Iowa, but the group's products were being sold in all 50 states and in Japan. By the late 1990s, organic products had moved beyond small natural food stores and were being sold in conventional supermarkets as well. This gave the cooperative many new opportunities. In 1998 Organic Valley reconfigured its marketing arm, adding three positions and splitting the country into three marketing regions. The cooperative also revised its legal structure slightly, to allow nonmembers to buy stock. The cooperative had sales of $28 million that year, a rise of 36 percent over 1997, and a huge jump over the $2 million the group brought in in 1992.

In 1998 the group made its second major capital expenditure, buying up an abandoned creamery in Chaseburg, Wisconsin. Within months of opening, the Chaseburg plant was making as much as 8,000 pounds of organic butter daily. Another new factor that year was Organic Valley's introduction of a flash pasteurization process developed in Europe. The cooperative was the first in the United States to use the technology, which superheated and cooled milk in a one-second process, giving the treated milk a shelf life of 45 days. The Ultra High Temperature (UHT) pasteurizing process allowed Organic Valley to sell its milk in many markets, whereas earlier a shorter shelf life would have been a barrier. Sales continued to barrel ahead, hitting approximately $46 million in 1999. The group had grown to 135 farms, and milk sales were eight times what they were before the introduction of rBGH six years earlier.

Key Dates:

1988: A small group of organic farmers founds a cooperative.
1989: The Organic Valley brand is launched.
1993: Organic milk sales begin an upswing after the introduction of rBGH in conventional dairies.
1998: The group reorganizes to allow nonmember stock ownership.
2003: The group moves to new headquarters.

Expanding the Product Line in the 2000s

George Siemon, Organic Valley's CEO, was an active promoter of organic methods of farming. He served on the U.S. Department of Agriculture (USDA) committee on small farms and was key to the development of national standards for organic certification. Organic food was the fastest growing sector of the retail food market in the 1990s, growing by as much as 24 percent a year over the decade. Overall sales of organic food reached almost $7.7 billion by 2000. Up to 1999, the USDA had prohibited the marketing of meat as organic. But the USDA rescinded the restriction, and Organic Valley began selling a variety of beef, pork, and chicken products. In 2000 the USDA finally released National Organic Standards—a unified federal program for certifying organic foods, which had been ten years in development. The standards assured consumers that products labeled organic had been handled according to strict rules. The national regulations gave protection to organic farmers, since competitors could not claim their products were organic unless they complied with the USDA standards. By 2000 Organic Valley was distributing more than 100 different organic food products, and the group had more than doubled its membership from two years earlier, to more than 300 farmers. Sales for 2001 were slightly less than $100 million. The cooperative kept its profit to between 1 and 1.5 percent of revenue, which allowed it to give its farmers high prices. Although the group sold eggs, meats, and citrus products, Organic Valley continued to be heavily weighted toward dairy farmers. In 2002 Organic Valley was paying its dairy farmers almost twice what conventional farmers were getting for milk— $18.45 per hundred pounds in December 2002, for example, as against $9.74 per hundred pounds that conventional farmers received on the open market at the same time. Organic products,

particularly milk, continued to be hot. An analysis quoted in the *New York Times* (August 1, 1999) predicted that organic dairy products would comprise 2 percent of the overall dairy market by 2005, and Organic Valley's burgeoning sales seemed to bear this out. The group finished 2002 with more than 500 members and sales of $125 million. Revenue for 2003 was expected to top $155 million. The group contracted with 45 different processing plants across the country, and marketing was broken down into five regional groups handled by a sales force of 20. The cooperative's plants in Wisconsin employed some 200 people, and for 2003 Organic Valley planned to spend $4 million on a new headquarters, having outgrown the old creamery it started out in.

Principal Competitors

Horizon Organic Holding Company; Stonyfield Farm, Inc.; Land O' Lakes, Inc.

Further Reading

Hill, Liz, "Organic Cheese Process Brings Change to Factory," *Milwaukee Journal Sentinel,* June 28, 1995, p. G6.

Kades, Deborah, "An Organic Niche," *Wisconsin State Journal,* January 5, 2003, pp. C1–C2.

Killeen, JoAnne, "From Barn Start-Up to Largest Organic Farm Co-Op," *In Business,* September/October 2000, p. 10.

Mitchener, Brandon, "U.S. Sets Standards for 'Organic' Foods in Move to End a Hodgepodge of Rules," *Wall Street Journal,* December 27, 2000.

Murphy, Kate, "More Buyers Asking: Got Milk Without Chemicals?," *New York Times,* August 1, 1999, p. 6.

Oncken, John, "Cross County," *Capital Times* (Madison, Wis.), May 8, 1997, p. 1C.

——, "For Organic Valley, It's Mission Accomplished," *Capital Times,* February 17, 2000, p. 1E.

——, "Small Organic Dairy Co-Op Proves Big Success," *Capital Times,* February 10, 2000, p. 1F.

"Organic Food-Handlers Expert Says Cooperative's Plan Unique to U.S.," *Wisconsin State Journal,* November 26, 1998, p. 4E.

"Organic Valley Introduces Organic Beef, Pork and Poultry," *Frozen Food Digest,* October 1999, p. 12.

Siemon, George, "Quite the CROPP," *Successful Farming,* September 1999, p. 19.

"Udder Confusion," *Economist,* July 3, 1999, p. 70.

—A. Woodward

Paddock Publications, Inc.

155 East Algonquin Road
Arlington Heights, Illinois 60005
United States
Telephone: (847) 427-4300
Fax: (847) 427-1146
Web site: http://www.dailyherald.com

Private Company
Founded: 1898
Employees: 1,033
Sales: $100.7 million (2000)
NAIC: 511110 Newspaper Publishers

Based in the Chicago suburb of Arlington Heights, Paddock Publications, Inc. is a family-owned newspaper publisher. Its flagship publication, *The Daily Herald,* is the third largest newspaper in Illinois, with a circulation of nearly 150,000. Eschewing the Chicago market, the *Herald* serves many of the city's suburbs by publishing a number of community-specific editions, focusing on local events while still offering coverage of national and international events. This strategy has allowed the *Herald* to maintain healthy growth during a time in which most newspapers have suffered severe erosion in circulation. Paddock also operates *Reflejos,* a bilingual Latino newspaper also catering to suburban readers. In addition, the company has significant investments in two Web businesses: DriveChicago .com and chicagojobnetwork.com.

19th-Century Origins

The founder of what would become Paddock Publications was Hosea Cornish Paddock, born in 1852. He became enamored with the newspaper business early in life, starting out as a reporter at the age of 16. He worked for several downstate Illinois newspapers: the *Sterling Gazette,* the *Prophettown Spike,* and the *Morrison Sentinel.* For a time he also tried his hand at teaching school and working as a salesman for Rand McNally, but the newspaper business remained his passion.

At the age of 28, in 1880, he became the editor of the *Plainfield Enterprise* and three years later became a newspaper owner when he acquired a weekly called the *Wheaton Illinoisan.* After five years in operation, however, he was struck by misfortune when a friend defaulted on a loan he had co-signed, forcing him to sell the paper. Paddock briefly owned the *Rochelle Register,* then turned his attention to the town of Waukegan, where he and a partner launched the *Waukegan Register* and challenged the supremacy of the *Waukegan Gazette,* an effort that ultimately failed.

Paddock next moved to Libertyville, where in 1892 he started the *Lake County Independent.* Three years later, a fire in the town's business district destroyed the newspaper office; unfortunately, Paddock had allowed his insurance to lapse only a few days earlier. Salvaging his printing press, he tried to continue publishing out of his home but in the end had to sell what was left of the operation. To support his wife and six children, he returned to teaching school, as well as canvassing the countryside by horse and buggy to sell subscriptions to Chicago newspapers. In 1898, he learned that the *Palatine Enterprise* was for sale by its owner, W.C. Williams. Paddock scraped together $275, and on December 15, 1898, he purchased the weekly newspaper that would one day evolve into *The Daily Herald.*

The *Palatine Enterprise* was renamed the *Enterprise-Register,* and the middle-aged Paddock devoted all his energies into making this attempt at the newspaper business a success despite considerable obstacles. His press was unwieldy, its lever so heavy that it required help from his 16-year-old son to print a page. Paddock then turned to the Chicago Newspaper Union to print the newspaper, but this required hauling heavy pages of hand-set lead type by train into the city. According to company lore, he bribed conductors with movie tickets in order to gain passage with his bulky cargo.

In addition to his other roles, Paddock continued to scour the country for subscribers, charging $1 per year. He was known to sit on a plow or other machinery a farmer might be attempting to use, refusing to leave until he received an answer. If cash was hard to come by, he also proved more than willing to accept produce in payment. Unlike previous ventures, the *Enterprise-*

Register quickly succeeded. Less than a year later, in March 1899, he was able to purchase the *Cook County Herald* in Arlington Heights. He solidified his presence in that community when he eventually acquired the *Arlington News* and a building in town with a printing press, eliminating the need to have his newspapers published in Chicago. Paddock operated his newspapers under the company named H.C. Paddock and Sons, the sons being Stuart and Charles.

H.C. Paddock Sells Out to Sons in 1922

As a newspaper publisher, Paddock established a focus on local news that would endure until this day. He also adopted a cogent motto for the business: "To fear God, tell the truth, and make money." Paddock added to his holdings in the early years of the 1900s, buying a number of weekly newspapers, including the *DuPage County Register,* the *Franklin Park Beacon, and* the *River Grove Herald.* He maintained ownership until 1922, when he sold his interests to his sons Charles and Stuart. Paddock continued to serve as a senior editor until just days before his death at the age of 83 in 1935.

Charles Paddock was in charge of production operations, while brother Stuart was responsible for editorial and business promotion operations. Stuart's sons, Stuart, Jr., and Robert, and his daughter Margie also began to become involved with the newspapers. As boy, Stuart, Jr., worked as a printer's devil, a job that entailed pouring molten lead into the molds that produced type. After graduating from Knox College in 1937, he was hesitant about joining the family business, concerned that it was not large enough to support him and his siblings. Instead, he elected to strike out on his own, hitchhiking to California to find a job. He eventually found himself in Cheyenne, Wyoming, where he spent his last nickel on a sweet roll. Afraid to ride freight trains with the unsavory hobos he encountered, he decided to hitchhike either east or west, depending upon chance to determine which direction he would take. A family heading to Indiana picked him up and took him as far as Iowa, where an aunt was able to give him $20 and return him to Illinois and the family newspaper business. Stuart became an assistant editor as well as a bookkeeper. After a stint in the service during World War II, he once again returned to the company, becoming a board director in 1948. Younger brother Robert also earned a degree from Knox, graduating in 1939. With Stuart in the military, he shouldered a number of responsibilities during the war in addition to his primary role as a sports editor. Margie also went to work for the family enterprise, becoming involved in advertising, and was eventually named a vice-president and assistant treasurer of the corporation.

Paddock Publications was content to remain a collection of small weekly newspapers until 1966, when the Chicago *Sun-Times,* owned by the heirs of tycoon Marshall Field, launched a suburban daily, *The Day.* By this time, Stuart Paddock, Sr. had retired and his brother Charles had assumed control of Paddock

Publications. With Charles' death in 1967 and Stuart's in 1968, it was left to a third generation of the Paddock family to meet the challenge of *The Day.* Stuart Paddock, Jr., purchased the stock owned by his uncle's son-in-law and gained control of the business. He shared ownership of the company with his brother and sister. A close-knit family, they worked together in running Paddock Publications over the ensuing years. In the short term, *The Day* soon proved to be a major threat to the very existence of the company. Despite increasing the publication frequency of the company's newspapers to three times a week, circulation declined by 40 percent within three years, dipping below 20,000. Matters grew so dire at one point that the company was unable to pay Stuart Paddock, Jr.'s Lions Club dues, and he found himself refused entry to a meeting. As he later told an interviewer, "We either had to go daily or die." In March 1969, soon after he became president of Paddock Publications, he oversaw the conversion of the company's weekly newspapers to a five-day-a-week daily called *The Arlington Heights Herald.* The fortunes of the company quickly reversed, and little more than a year later management of *The Day* decided to quit the field, selling out to Paddock Publications. In order to finance the deal, the Paddocks had to bring in some outside investors, who then advised them to sell the operation and turn a tidy profit. Instead, the Paddocks began to buy back the stock, which they eventually put to use in an employee retirement trust. In 1970, Paddock Publications also entered Lake County, where a number of community weekly papers were established.

Arlington Heights Herald *Becomes* The Daily Herald *in 1977*

While the *Herald* began to enjoy steady growth as a daily, the prospects for newspapers in Chicago were not as bright in the early 1970s. The city boasted four dailies, including *Chicago Today,* the *Chicago Tribune,* the *Chicago Sun-Times,* and the *Chicago Daily News.* Combined circulation topped 2.1 million. By the mid-1980s, only two papers remained in business, the *Sun-Times* and the *Tribune,* with a total circulation of less than 1.4 million. The new battleground for subscribers lay in the suburbs, where Paddock Publications was well entrenched. In 1975, a Saturday edition was added to its daily newspaper; in 1977, the *Arlington Heights Herald* changed its name to *The Daily Herald*; and in 1978, a Sunday edition was introduced, making Paddock a major force in the Chicago suburbs. The Lake County weekly papers then went daily in 1984. Moreover, Paddock Publications expanded into DuPage, Kane, McHenry, and Will counties. The *Herald* launched a number of zoned editions targeting individual communities featuring at least one local lead story each day. As a result of these efforts, circulation grew to 73,000, and the *Herald* became Illinois' fourth-largest daily newspaper. Moreover, Paddock Publications published *This Week,* a free shopper with a circulation topping 250,000. To support this increased activity, the company opened a state-of-the-art printing plant.

Despite competition from the large Chicago dailies and rival suburban publishers, Paddock Publications continued to enjoy sustained growth with the *Herald.* By 1991, circulation exceeded 100,000, making it the state's third largest daily newspaper. In large part, this success was a reflection of the Chicago suburbs coming of age. No longer mere bedroom communities living in the shadow of a major city, they were establishing their own identities and special needs, which in turn could be addressed by a local-oriented newspaper. Since the early 1980s, the *Tribune* and *Sun-Times* attempted to follow this significant shift in population by establishing suburban bureaus. The *Herald* strategy was to target high-growth areas, mostly in the western and northwestern Chicago suburbs, then enter the markets by launching zoned editions. By the end of 1997, paid circulation of the *Herald* had reached 132,000.

During the 1990s, Paddock Publications took on the Chicago newspapers in court. In 1993, it sued the two dailies as well as several major syndicates, including the Los Angeles Times-Washington Post News Service, Times Mirror Co., New York Times Syndication Sales Corp., Creator Syndicate, King Features Syndicate, United Media, and Universal Press Syndicate. Paddock Publications charged that the defendants violated the Sherman Antitrust Act because of their contracts that granted exclusive rights to the large newspapers for the most popular features, cartoons, and news services, thereby stunting the growth of smaller newspapers such as the *Herald*. Although Paddock Publications lost the case initially, it pursued the appeals process all the way to the U.S. Supreme Court. In the end, however, the Supreme Court refused, without comment, to consider the case.

In the late 1990s, the three aging Paddock siblings took steps to insure that the newspaper business remained independent and within the family. They created a trust to minimize federal estate taxes, which in many cases force the sale of family businesses. The first of the three children of Stuart Paddock, Sr. to pass away was Margie Flanders in 1997, followed by brother Robert in 1999. In the meantime, Stuart Paddock, Jr. stepped down as CEO of the company, turning over the reins to Daniel E. Baumann. Paddock remained chairman and publisher, and like the Paddocks of earlier times remained quite active in the running of the business well into his eighties.

Baumann had a long history with the *Herald*, starting in 1964 as a reporter. In the 1970s, he became an editor, then rose to the rank of chief operating officer in 1988. Under Baumann's leadership, Paddock Publications turned its attention to the Internet in the late 1990s. It teamed up with the *Chicago Sun-Times* and the *Herald News* of Joliet, Illinois, to create a regional classified advertising Web site in 1999. Although rivals, the newspapers agreed to work together to fend off upstate Internet companies looking to poach on their classified ad business, which accounts for about 40 percent of revenues at most dailies. In 2000, Paddock Publications formed a partnership with the publisher of the *Sun-Times,* Hollinger Publications, and the Chicago Automobile Trade Association to launch DriveChicago.com, a new and used car Web site that offered the auto classified ads of the participating newspapers as well as those of some 650 area auto dealers. On a more traditional front in 2000, Paddock Publications acquired *Reflejos,* a ten-year-old monthly bilingual Latino paper with a circulation of 28,000 in Chicago's suburbs. The company also initiated plans to build a major new printing facility to improve the quality of its publications.

In 2002, Paddock Publications underwent a number of significant changes. Baumann was succeeded as CEO in January by Douglas Ray, who like his predecessor had originally worked as a reporter, joining the *Herald* staff in the early 1970s. Of more significance in 2002 was the passing of Stuart Paddock, Jr., who in April succumbed to congestive heart failure at the age of 86. The growth of the *Herald* under his leadership had been impressive. When he converted the community newspapers into a daily, circulation had fallen to just 11,800. At the time of his death the *Herald* boasted a circulation of 148,856, making it not only the third-largest daily in Illinois but also the 84th largest in the country. His voting control interest in the Paddock Publications now passed to the three-member trust he set up with his brother and sister. Although this arrangement offered the best chance for the *Herald* to remain one of the last family-owned independent newspapers in America, there was no guarantee that market forces, as well as a change in family wishes, might not result in the eventual selling of the business. In the meantime, however, management of Paddock Publications planned to continue its expansion into the Chicago suburbs.

Principal Competitors

Gannett Co., Inc.; Knight Ridder Inc.; The Copley Press, Inc.; Hollinger International Inc.; Tribune Co.

Further Reading

Borden, Jeff, "The Real Newspaper War Is in Surburbs," *Crain's Chicago Business*, November 17, 1997, p. 3.
Comerford, Mike, "Few Changes Expected at Daily Herald," *Daily Herald*, April 23, 2002, p. 1.
Constable, Burt, "The Passing of the Patriarch Stuart Paddock Jr.," *Daily Herald*, April 16, 2002, p.1.
Lazare, Lewis, "Suburban Papers Show Metros How It's Done," *Crains Chicago Business*, September 8, 1986, p. 17.
Moses, Lucia, "Placing Trust in Family Tradition," *Editor & Publisher*, April 29, 2002, p. 9.
Reese, Joel, "Hosea's Dream 100 Years ago," *Daily Herald*, December 14, 1999.

—Ed Dinger

PANTONE

Pantone Inc.

590 Commerce Boulevard
Carlstadt, New Jersey 07072-3013
U.S.A.
Telephone: (201) 935-5500
Toll Free: (866) 726-8663
Fax: (201) 896-0242
Web site: http://www.pantone.com

Private Company
Incorporated: 1962
Employees: 150
Sales: $19 million (2001 est.)
*NAIC:*511140 Database and Directory Publishers; 511120
   Periodical Publishers; 511210 Software Publishers

Pantone, Inc., with its corporate headquarters in Carlstadt, New Jersey, is a private company that over the last four decades of the 20th century built a global reputation as an authority on color and color systems. Using a 1,757-color palate, the company develops, standardizes and forecasts colors for a worldwide clientele. It provides both color systems and the technology that enables industries not only to select colors accurately but also to communicate choices from designers to manufacturers to retailers and thence to customers and other end users. Over the years, the company has expanded its Pantone Matching System concept for use by a variety of industries with color-critical needs, including textile, plastic, and digital technology manufacturers. Its special expertise lies in the development of communication tools for industries and in the adoption of new digital technology to meet the needs of design and production professionals. The company is headed by Lawrence Herbert, who joined Pantone in 1956 and introduced the Pantone Matching System in the early 1960s.

Gaining Momentum under Lawrence Herbert in the 1950s

Pantone's emergence as a major force in color management systems did not start until Lawrence Herbert became part of the company. As a young man, he had an early interest in printing, but that was not the focus of his education. He graduated from Hofstra University with a double major in biology and chemistry. His plan was to go on to medical school, but in 1956 he began working for Pantone on a part-time basis and became so intrigued with his work that he scrapped his idea of pursuing his studies as a physician.

At that point, Pantone was just a small printing company in Manoochie, New Jersey. There were no industry-wide or uniform standards for color printing. Pantone printers in the 1950s employed a basic stock of about 60 different pigments and used them to mix ink colors in an inefficient, trial and error method. Through his knowledge of chemistry, Herbert was able to reduce the stock of pigments to a basic palette of just 12 from which a full range of colored inks could be mixed.

By 1962, Herbert was running the printing half of the business while the company's original owners focused on promoting commercial displays. Although Herbert's division was profitable, theirs was not, and even though they drained off funds from his division, they soon ran up a $50,000 debt. Herbert then bought the printing division from them for $50,000, enough to pay off their debt. The funds for the buyout were provided by a woman who not only put up the money but did it without demanding a financial stake in the company as collateral. The identity of this benefactor has never been disclosed.

1960s: Becoming an International Authority on Color Systems

Under Herbert, Pantone began its development into an international authority on color and color systems. It took the initial step in 1963, when it introduced its first Pantone Matching System Printers' Edition, the basis for it evolution into a company with global prestige and influence. Although Herbert had previously developed a uniform system based on a carefully coded mixing of 12 basic pigments, it was not until he owned Pantone that he began an aggressive campaign to gain wide acceptance of his system. He had also reduced the number of pigments to just ten basic inks, making the generation of a wide array of colors remarkably simple.

Company Perspectives:

Pantone, Inc. is the world-renowned authority on color and provider of color systems and leading technology for the selection and accurate communication of color. The PANTONE Name is known worldwide as the standard language for color communication from designer to manufacturer to retailer to customer. With 40 years of experience, we are the worldwide market leader in color communication and color technology for the graphic design, printing, publishing, textile and plastics industries. Whether you are creating a logo, a product, packaging, an ad, the latest fashion trend or a vision, we have the tools and solutions for keeping your colors accurate and consistent cross-media, around the world. The PANTONE Color language is the most universally understood standard available.

Herbert wrote to 21 major ink producers, describing the Pantone Matching System and offering to license them as manufacturers of the system's ten basic inks. It took less than two weeks for all but one of them to sign on and pay a basic royalty to Pantone. It was an unheralded achievement, but, albeit quietly, it had revolutionized the color printing trade.

The Pantone Matching System soon began providing solutions to some of industry's problems. For example, it helped Kodak solve one that had stemmed from the fact that Kodak used more than one company to print its film packaging. Confronted with film boxes with varying shades of yellow, customers tended to leave the darker shaded ones on retail shelves, thinking the film in them was not as fresh as that in the brighter ones. With Pantone's systems, companies printing the boxes for Kodak all began producing them with the exact same color tone and thereby solved Kodak's niggling problem.

Through the rest of the 1960s, Herbert started to adapt his basic matching system, not just to printing, but also to other industries. In 1964, he launched the Pantone Color Specifier for the design market, and in the next year introduced the first artist materials application of the Pantone Matching System. Pantone also developed new systems and guides in Hebert's first decade as owner, including, in 1968, Pantone's first Four-Color Process Guide and its Color Tint Selector for the design field.

1970s: Entering the Digital World of Computing

It was more of the same during the 1970s, a decade that also saw Pantone sign up some important clients and negotiate at least one major agreement. In 1971, 3M signed on as a Pantone Color Key licensee. Also in that year, Pantone by Letraset Color Markers were introduced in the design field and, in the following year, Pantone and Letraset entered an agreement granting Letraset global rights to produce and market Pantone Graphic Arts Materials, all of which were coordinated to the Pantone Matching System. At that time, too, Pantone entered a licensing arrangement with Day-Glo Color Corporation for the application of its system to fluorescent base colors.

In 1974, Pantone also made its first foray into the digital world of computing when it produced its Color Data System for

computerized ink color formulation and matching. It was a significant step in an area of application that, as computer use burgeoned in the 1980s and beyond, became increasingly important.

Herbert took Pantone private in 1977. In its last year as a public company, Pantone's sales were about $2 million. Thereafter, Herbert did not divulge what the company's sales volume was each year, but by the mid-1980s, Pantone's trade mark appeared on about $500 million work of art supplies, ink, and other art and printing products marketed in over 50 countries.

1980s: Technological Advances and Partnerships

Through the 1980s, Pantone made some significant technological advances and launched new products. Among other things, in 1981 the company introduced its Two-Color Selector and its Color Selector/Newsprint, and in 1982 it launched its Process Color Simulator. In addition, in 1984, Pantone formed a new division, its Electronic Color Systems Division, established to reproduce the company's color standards in a digital system.

By 1985, Pantone had also signed on its first software licensee, Via Video. In the next year, it inked a licensing agreement with Networked Picture Systems, Inc., its first client to adapt Pantone's software designed for the IBM-PC and compatible computers; then, during the following year, 1987, it licensed LaserWare, Inc. as its first customer to adopt a version of the software for use with the Apple-Macintosh platform. Meanwhile, by that same year, the company expanded its Matching System to 747 colors.

Between 1988 and 1990, the company entered into licensing agreements with most of the world's major graphic and design software manufacturers of programs for both Macintosh and IBM-PC compatible computers. In 1988, it also signed up QMS, Inc., as its first printer licensee, and in the next year added NEC Technologies, Océé Graphics, and Tektronix Inc. to its list.

It was also in 1989 that Pantone expanded its Textile Color System to 1,225 colors and, in a cooperative venture with Intergraph Corporation, developed its Color Interface for high-end computer systems. In a venture with another company, Purup Electronics A-S, it also created and introduced The Purup System for designing sophisticated packaging.

By the late 1980s, Pantone had energetically entered a period of partnering with other companies to develop new products. In that respect it was very much in step with what many large companies were doing in a variety of industries, particularly those that could derive benefits in cost and efficiency from outsourcing some part of their operations. The company's co-development of products would continue through the next decade, starting in 1990, when it developed its Professional Color Toolkit in conjunction with Radius Inc. The toolkit consisted of a software library designed to achieve the best Pantone color in Pantone-licensed printers. Meanwhile, several other companies signed on as Pantone software licensees.

1990s: Technological Advances

Over the next few years, with the phenomenal development of the home computer industry, Pantone's role in digital art and

Key Dates:

1956: Lawrence Herbert starts working part-time at a printing company.
1962: Herbert acquires the printing operations from the original owners.
1963: Company introduces its initial Pantone Matching System Printers' Edition.
1977: Herbert takes company private.
2001: Company launches its Pantone TheRightColor division.

design grew by leaps and bounds. In 1991, the company expanded its textile color system to 1,701 colors. It also entered into a new licensing agreement with NeXT Computer Inc., marking the first time that its colors were provided at the system level. That meant that developers for the NeXT platform did not have to build support for Pantone colors into either their software or hardware products. The company also entered new licensing agreements with Ventura Software, Hewlett-Packard, and others, and its colors became available for the UNIX operating system for the first time. Although NeXT, in many ways ahead of its time, would be absorbed by Apple in 1996 and end production, UNIX and its desktop computer versions began to give Microsoft some growing microcomputer operating-system competition as the 1990s wore on.

By 1992, Adobe, Bitstream, Deneba, MultiAd Services, Quark, and Ventura had all announced support for the Pantone color system in their newest software releases. In that year, too, Pantone introduced its color printer test kit, allowing users of Pantone licensed printers to find the closest possible matches to Pantone colors. In that year, the Xerox 4700 color document printer became the first color laser printer to support the full range of Pantone colors, while the Tektronix Phaser IISD was the first dye-sublimation printer to provide similar support for the company's color matching system.

Between 1993 and 1995, Pantone launched several new products and continued to enhance its technology. Among other things, in 1993 it introduced its Open Color Environment (POCE), the first color management system allowing true WYSIWYG color matching. In that year it also introduced its Plastics Color System, a universal plastic color reference system, and ColorUP, a software color management tool for business professionals designed to help them enhance color quality in their reports and presentations. The next year, 1994, Pantone introduced its Color Systems Cross-Reference Software as well as ColorDrive, a desktop color-management program free of specific applications. Next, in 1995, Pantone introduced its Textile Color Swatch Files, its Foil Stamping Color Guide, and its SuperChip, all technical refinements for making color delineation as accurate as possible in different applications of the Pantone systems.

Meanwhile, in the same three-year period, Pantone continued to develop new partnerships and licensing agreements. In 1993 alone, six new companies—AGFA, Aldus, Corel, Gold Disk, Linotype-Hell, and Serif—included support for the Pantone Process Color System in their most recent software releases.

From 1995 to 1998, Pantone continued to produce an array of new products in its partnering and licensing arrangements with other companies, both at home and abroad. Among other things, in 1995 launched Hexachrome for commercial use, secured new licensing agreements with Hewlett-Packard, Lexmark, and Xerox, and entered a distribution pact with Ingram Micro. In the following year, the company received ISO 9002 certification and entered a global distribution agreement with VISU. Next, in 1997, it signed a distribution agreement with ALTO Imaging Group N.V. for the marketing of Pantone's products abroad, published *Color Trends 1998* for graphic and Web design, and released a new version of ColorDrive for Windows. In the following year, 1998, it began shipping ColorWeb Pro, introduced its OfficeColor Assistant, an operating system add-in, and, with Apple, launched a worldwide color seminar series called ''Expand Your Color Universe.''

2000 and Beyond

By the end of the decade, Pantone had expanded its global presence to the point where its name had virtually become synonymous with color management, and almost monthly it strengthened its position through new partnerships and licensing arrangements.

By 2001, Pantone had built its palette to 1,757 colors. Its aim at that point was to have not just professionals but the general public speaking its color language. To that end, it started up TheRightColor division, the focal responsibility of which was to provide a universal, uniform, and precise color language along with technological solutions for industry retailers needing a color standard for enhancing consumer shopping and sharpening their competitive edge through all their marketing channels. TheRightColor solutions adapted the universally used Pantone Textile Color System to their needs. Among other things, the solutions allowed retailers to cut down on the number of merchandise returns stemming from faulty color matches, update their inventory tracking and restocking techniques, and enhance their ability to monitor customer color tastes and thereby make stocking and shelving adjustments to increase sales. The company also formed a partnership with The National Retail Federation for the purpose of providing a better color coding system for electronic marketing applications. Clearly, with the new millennium firmly underway, Pantone's corporate energy remained unabated in what remained an exciting, wide open specialty driven by a rapidly improving technology.

Principal Divisions

TheRightColor.

Principal Competitors

Adobe Systems Incorporated; Agfa-Gevaert N.V.; Creo, Inc.; IKON Office Solutions, Inc.; Imagining Technologies Corporation.

Further Reading

Hoffer, William, "A Wonderful World of Color," *Nation's Business*, September 1986, p. 69.

Maycumber, S. Gray, "Pantone System Breaks the Fabric Color Barrier," *Daily News Record*, October 2, 1989, p. 44.

Nicksin, Carole, "Pantone to Get Customers Involved in Language of Color," *HFN The Weekly Newspaper for the Home Furnishing Network*, March 19, 2001, p. 4.

Whitcher, Joann S., "Hi-Fi Color Sows New Promise," *Graphics Arts Monthly*, May 1998, p. 69.

Wilken, Earl, "Taking Guesswork Out of Color Work," *Graphic Arts Monthly*, December 1998, p. 72.

—John W. Fiero

[P^cM] uitgevers

PCM Uitgevers NV

Herengracht 466
1017 CA Amsterdam
The Netherlands
Telephone: (+31) 20 553 9430
Fax: (+31) 20 623 31 69
Web site: http://www.pcmuitgevers.nl

Private Company
Incorporated: 1970 as Perscombinatie
Employees: 3,883
Sales: EUR 734 million ($700 million)(2001)
NAIC: 511110 Newspaper Publishers; 511120 Periodical Publishers; 511130 Book Publishers

PCM Uitgevers NV is one of the Netherland's leading newspaper and publishing groups. The company holds four of the country's five national newspaper titles, including *De Volkskrant, NRC Handelsblad, Algemeen Dagbald,* and *Trouw.* The company also publishes regional newspapers, notably *Het Parool,* based in Amsterdam. *De Volkskrant* and *Algemeen Dagblad* are the company's two largest-selling newspapers, each with a daily circulation of more than 335,000. *NRC Handelsblad* sells more than 267,000 papers each day, while *Trouw* sells nearly 128,000 papers daily. The company's regional titles reach more than 200,000 customers daily. PCM's other main branch is its books division, which represents some of the most prestigious names in the Dutch publishing world, including JM Meulenhoff, AW Bruna, De Boekerij, Het Spectrum, Unieboek, Standaard, Vassallucci, and Internet book site Boeknet. The company also publishes educational books under the ThiemeMeulenhoff imprint. PCM Uitgevers is a private company and owned at more than 57 percent by Stichting Het Parool (now separated from the *Het Parool* newspaper) and at 22 percent by insurance company Nationale-Nederlanden Levensverzekering Maatschappij NV. The company posted sales of EUR 734 million in 2001. Yet slumping profits, due to a slumping economy and increasing competition from the radio and television sectors for advertising sales, has caused the company to restructure a number of its operations, including

shutting down all of its Internet operations (individual subsidiaries maintain their Web sites without the support of the parent company). In late 2002, the company was also considering spinning off money-losing *Het Parool.*

Origins

The PCM Uitgevers entering the 21st century was the result of a series of mergers as the Netherlands' press and publishing industry consolidated. PCM Uitgevers itself was formed with the merger of newspaper concern Perscombinatie and book publisher Meulenhoff in 1995, followed by the purchase of Reed Elsevier's newspaper divison, Nederlandse Dagsbladunie, in 1996. Yet the company's history represents a large part of the history of Netherlands' newspaper and publishing industries since the 19th century.

The Dutch resistance during the Nazi occupation of the Netherlands during World War II gave rise to a number of important newspapers and magazines of the postwar era. Among these were *Trouw, Vrije Nederland,* and the Amsterdam-based *Het Parool.* The latter had been launched in 1940 at the beginning of the occupation, and by 1943 its founders had already decided to continue publishing the underground paper at war's end. In 1944, even before the Netherlands' liberation, *Het Parool*'s organization began drafting the framework for a private foundation to govern the newspaper. The choice of a non-profit foundation, rather than a corporation, enabled the new paper to distinguish itself from the country's privately owned newspapers, many of which had been stigmatized by their conduct during the war—and their pursuit of profit over morality.

Stichting Het Parool was created in 1945, and the foundation's location remained a secret until the end of the occupation. At first, the foundation was directly responsible for the newspaper's operations. But in the 1950s, it created a new limited liability company, NV Het Parool, which took over the management of the newspaper. While Stichting Het Parool maintain 100 percent ownership of the new company, editorial and managerial functions were now separated from the foundation.

During the 1960s, the Netherlands' newspaper industry entered a period of crisis. The rising popularity of television in the

Company Perspectives:

PCM Uitgevers has as its goal to take a part in maintaining the diversity of opinion in the press in a parliamentary-democratic state and to take part in maintaining the offer of a broad assortment of books. In the recent past, this direction has led to the following strategy: PCM Uitgevers wants to be a leading publishing group in the Dutch language and culture, which, based on strong brands, provides for the need for information, news, opinion, education, culture, leisure, and in this way maintains an interactive, lasting connection with its customers.

country had begun to attract advertisers to the new medium. Many of the country's newspapers were struggling not just to maintain readership, itself on the decline as people turned to the television for their news, but also advertising revenues. By the end of the decade, the situation led to the growing consolidation of the country's newspapers.

Het Parool's turn came in 1968, when it merged with *De Volkskrant* to form a new company, Perscombinatie NV, controlled at 60 percent by Stichting Het Parool. *De Volkskrant* was by then on its way to becoming one of the Netherlands' largest-selling newspapers. That newspaper, however, initially targeted only a smaller part of the Dutch reading public.

Founded in Den Bosch in 1919, *De Volkskrant* had started out as a weekly newspaper. By 1920, the newspaper had begun appearing every other day, until finally in 1921 the newspaper became a daily. Like many of the Netherlands' newspapers, *De Volkskrant* was oriented toward a specific audience segment, namely the growing Catholic workers' movement of the 1920s. In 1932, the newspaper's relationship with that movement was formalized when it was taken over entirely by the Rooms-katholieke Werkliedenverbond (Roman Catholic Workers Union). The new ownership moved the newspaper's headquarters to its own base in Utrecht. From there, *De Volkskrant*, originally focused on its home region, began to address the concerns of the Netherlands as a whole, building up a subscriber base of some 27,000 throughout the country by the outbreak of World War II. The newspaper had also adopted as a subtitle: ''The Netherland's Catholic Newspaper.''

Unlike a number of the country's newspapers—most notoriously, *De Telegraaf*—*De Volkskrant* escaped the stigma of being a war-time newspaper by shutting down its operations for the duration of the Nazi occupation. Where many of the country's pre-war newspapers were forced to close at the end of the war for what widely became viewed as collaborative activities, *De Volkskrant* was able to return to its daily publishing schedule untainted. Led by editor Joop Lücker, *De Volkskrant* quickly grew to one of the country's largest newspapers, with a circulation of more than 100,000 readers. Although still owned by the Roman Catholic Workers Union (by then known as the Katholieke Arbeidersbeweging or KAB), *De Volkskrant* now targeted the broader Catholic reading market.

In the early 1960s, Lücker was replaced by Jan van der Pluijm, who helped transform *De Volkskrant* into a left-leaning,

progressive newspaper. By 1965, *De Volkskrant* had moved to Amsterdam and dropped its subtitle, although remaining under the KAB's ownership. The company's new headquarters placed its directly across the street from *Het Parool*, and by 1968 the two newspapers were sharing common headquarters under parent Perscombinatie. Each newspaper retained its own editorial staff and policy, functioning as independent entities under the same parent. Indeed, *De Volkskrant*, with its strong support of the social, political, and cultural changes occurring at the time, began to grow, and by 1970 had topped 200,000 readers.

Consolidation in the 1970s

Percombinatie grew again in 1975 when it added a new title to its portfolio, that of *Trouw*. That newspaper had been founded in 1943 as an underground paper by members of the Protestant resistance. *Trouw* became a full-fledged newspaper after the war and focused on the Netherlands' Protestant community. In 1965, the newspaper changed its printing schedule, becoming a national daily with the acquisitions of a number of regional newspapers.

By the beginning of the 1970s, however, *Trouw* had begun to expand its editorial policy to include a broader ranger of the Dutch newspaper reading market. This was in keeping with a dominant trend in the newspaper industry: previously, newspapers had been established and set up to support the viewpoint of an ideological or religious movement. In the 1970s, however, and particularly with the creation of the *NRC Handelsblad*, newspapers adopted a more neutral, information-centric approach. The company also became caught up in the atmosphere of consolidation affecting the Dutch newspaper sector at the time, and in 1972 merged with the Kwartetbladen, a grouping of four Protestant-oriented regional evening newspapers.

The acquisition of *Trouw* brought a change in Perscombinatie's ownership, as Stichting Het Parool stepped up its holding to nearly 90 percent. The Perscombinatie grouping enabled its three newspapers to combine much of their operations, including printing and delivery as well as advertising sales, subscription services, and other logistical and commercial areas of operations. Editorial staff and policies, however, remained strictly separated, as the newspapers attracted distinct readership audiences.

Publishing Group at the Turn of the Century

The consolidation of the Dutch newspaper industry had dramatically changed the country's media landscape by the end of the 1970s. Out of more than 80 independent newspaper groups entering the 1950s, there remained only 27. The consolidation drive continued into the 1980s, which saw the emergence of a smaller number of larger media groups, including VNU, Wolters Kluwer, Elsevier (later Reed-Elsevier), and Wegener. By the end of the 1980s, even the larger groups had begun discussing mergers, as was the case with Perscombinatie and Elsevier.

That merger never went through. Instead, Perscombinatie discovered a more surprising partner: in 1994, the newspaper company announced that it had agreed to merge with book publishing group Meulenhoff, which held a portfolio of some of the most prominent names in the Dutch book publishing industry, not least of which was the JM Meulenhoff imprint itself.

Meulenhoff's history stretched back to 1895, when Johannes Marius Meulenhoff set up a business in Amsterdam importing foreign books, which he then distributed to the city's bookstores. By 1904, Meulenhoff had incorporated as Meulenhoff & Co. and had opened an office in The Hague as well. The company remained focused on the import business, taking over two other businesses in The Hague and the Netherlands. In 1906, however, the company published its first translation, which launched Meulenhoff as a publisher. By 1917, the business had been separated into its two parts, with the publishing wing brought under the name JM Meulenhoff & Co.

Over the following decades, Meulenhoff became one of the Netherlands' most prominent and respected publishing names. It had also become one of the largest, notably through a steady stream of acquisitions of other imprints, such as the Unieboek group of publishers, including the AW Bruna imprint, and, in 1986, the Dutch-language catalog from Elsevier, which was placed under a newly created imprint, De Boekerij. By the early 1990s, Meulenhoff had acquired another important book imprint, Bert Bakker, which was followed by the Prometheus

imprint in 1993. By the mid-1990s, Meulenhoff had grown to become the largest publisher in the Netherlands, with a 30 percent share of the market.

The merger between Meulenhoff and Perscombinatie created PCM Uitgevers, a media giant with combined sales of nearly $370 million by the end of 1994. While PCM Uitgevers faced skepticism over the possibility of generating synergies from merging the two different worlds of newspaper and book publishing, the company faced public outcry the following year when it announced its acquisition of the Nederlandse Dagsbladunie (NDU) from Reed Elsevier.

That purchase—motivated in large part as a means of keeping the NDU out of the hands of rival *De Telegraaf*—cost PCM around NFL1 billion (approximately $500 million) and brought the company a new major shareholder in the form of ING Bank, which took a 30 percent share of PCM. The purchase also added some $332 million to PCM's revenues and two additional national newspapers, *NRC Handelsblad*, with origins tracing back to 1822, and *Algemeen Dagbald*, established in 1946, and meant that PCM Uitgevers now controlled four of the five national newspapers in Holland. Yet PCM expressed its commitment to maintaining the editorial independence of all the members of its newspaper portfolio.

PCM's Meulenhoff branch continued its own expansion into the late 1990s, adding the highly regarded imprint Arena in 1997. In 1999, the company added Het Spectrum, among the last of the major independent Dutch publishing houses, which had been founded in Utrecht in 1936. In 2001, the company added a new imprint, Vassallucci.

PCM Uitgevers had ridden high in its status as Dutch newspaper giant in the last half of the 1990s as the soaring economy brought steady rises in advertising revenues. The slowdown in the economy at the turn of the century, however, had cut heavily into advertising spending, while internal tensions at PCM itself were taking their toll; in 1999, the company ousted the head of Meulenhoff, taking over control of that formerly independently managed division, and by 2000 reports began to circulate the company might spin off money-losing *Het Parool*.

By the end of 2001, PCM's difficulties had begun to mount as its net profits collapsed, shrinking back from more than EUR 21 million in 2000 to just EUR 1.5 million in 2001. The company also suffered a setback when it announced that year that it was shutting down its Internet support operation, PIM, which had been set up with an investment of more than EUR 60 million in order to provide support services, including staffing, for the company's newspaper Web sites, as well as to launch the company's own Internet portal services.

PCM Uitgevers' difficulties continued into 2002 amid slumping sales and declining readership. The company had also come to suffer from the opening up of the Dutch television market during the 1990s, which, as in the 1960s, had begun to lure more and more advertisers away from the newspapers. By September 2002, PCM announced that it was restructuring its operations, including cutting back on a number of its staff. At that time, the company also announced its intention to spin off *Het Parool* at an as yet undetermined time. PCM Uitgevers hoped that its reorganization would enable it to regain its momentum as it entered the new century as a Dutch publishing leader.

Principal Subsidiaries

PCM Landelijke Dagbladen BV; NRC Handelsblad BV; Algemeen Dagbald BV; de Volkskrant BV; Trouw BV; PCM Algemene Boeken BV; ThiemeMeulenhoff BV; De Boekerij BV; AW Bruna Uitgevers BV; Uitgeverij JM Meulenhoff BV; JM Meulenhoff Vlaanderen NV; Uitgeverij Arena BV; Meulenhoff Vastgoed BV; Uitgeverij Prometheus BV; NV Standaard Uitgeverij Antwerpen (Belgium); Unieboek BV Houten 100; Eicanos Verlag GmbH Bocholt (Germany); Uitgeverij Het Spectrum BV; Het Spectrum Electronic Publishing BV; BoekNet BV; Uitgeverij Vassallucci BV; Het Parool BV; Weekmedia BV; BV Randstad Publicaties; Gooipers BV; Wiering's Weekbladen BV; Dagbald van Rijn en Gouwe BV; VETA BV; BV De Dordtenaar; Rotterdams Dagbald BV.

Principal Divisions

Newspaper Publishing; Book Publishing; Electronic and Other Media.

Principal Competitors

VNU NV; HAL Holding NV; Wegener NV; De Telegraaf Holdingmaatschappij NV; WPG Uitgevers BV; Sijthoff Pers BV; Verenigde Noordhollandse Dagbladen BV; PZC Holding BV; Biegelaar and Jansen BV.

Further Reading

"Arena Joins Dutch Meulenhoff Group," *Publishers Weekly*, January 27, 1997, p. 17.

Lottman. Herbert R., "Meulenhoff Buying Het Spectrum," *Publishers Weekly*, June 28, 1999, p. 13.

——, "Meulenhoff Expands in New merger," *Publishers Weekly*, August 1, 1994, p. 16.

Van Grinsven, Lucas "Leading Dutch Publisher Kills Web Hub-sources," *Reuters*, September 6, 2001.

Zwaap, René, "De wankelende reus," *De Groene Amsterdammer*, November 11, 2000.

——, "Help, de krant verzuipt!," *De Groene Amsterdammer*, November 17, 2001.

—M.L. Cohen

PHH Arval

307 International Circle
Hunt Valley, Maryland 21030-1337
U.S.A.
Telephone: (410) 771-1900
Toll Free: (800) 665-9744
Fax: (410) 771-1123
Web site: http://www.phh.com

Wholly Owned Subsidiary of Cendant Corporation
Incorporated: 1953 as Peterson, Howell & Heather, Inc.
Employees: 1,200
Sales: $3.6 billion (2001)
NAIC: 53212 Truck, Utility Trailer, and RV
(Recreational Vehicle) Rental and Leasing; 532111
Passenger Car Rental; 532112 Passenger Car Leasing

PHH Arval, formerly PHH Vehicle Management Services, operates as the second-largest fleet management company in the world. As a subsidiary of Cendant Corporation, the firm provides integrated fleet leasing, fleet management, and corporate payment programs through Wright Express, and a variety of services related to fleet vehicle selection, fleet policy, vehicle acquisition and resale, maintenance and fuel management, expense reporting, and accident and risk management. PHH, along with its European partner, Arval PHH, manages over 1.2 million vehicles. PHH's clientele includes corporate, government, and service-related firms. The company serves approximately one-third of the Fortune 500 companies.

Company Origins

The company originated in 1946, when Duane Peterson, Harley Howell, and Dick Heather formed a partnership to manage corporate automobile fleets. They signed management agreements with two companies in their first year: Gibson Art Company and Johnson & Johnson. The assumption was that corporations would save money by hiring a group that specialized in running car fleets, rather than supervising the car rentals and management themselves. The idea was advanced at the time

when postwar cars were just beginning to be produced, and the firm prospered. It was incorporated in 1953 as Peterson, Howell & Heather. By 1955, a Canadian branch had been formed. The first public offering of stock took place three years later. The client list grew to include Honeywell and Du Pont.

Growth Leads to Expansion: 1960s–1980s

After a decade of steady growth, the company was ready to expand and diversify its services. PHH acquired National Truckers Service (NTS) of Texas in 1969 and Homequity, Inc., of Connecticut in 1971. This latter marked PHH's entry into relocation and real estate management services.

Homequity was then the nation's largest provider of such services, which include the appraisal and purchase of homes from workers being transferred and the homes' subsequent resale. The building of company headquarters in Hunt Valley, Maryland, began in 1972. In 1978 the company name was changed to PHH Group, Inc.

During the 1980s, PHH continued its expansion, especially in European markets. In 1980, the company purchased AllStar Petrol Card Ltd. of London. That same year, Jerome W. Geckle, then president and CEO, succeeded John Lalley as chairman. Geckle oversaw a decade of explosive growth. In 1981, PHH International was formed to manage the company's European operations. The following year, business services grew to include aviation management, and over the next several years PHH acquired Aviation Information Services; Aviation Consulting, Inc.; Beckett Flight Management; and Ryan Aviation Corporation. Despite the recession of the early 1980s, PHH had 2,000 corporate clients in 1982 and a record of 24 consecutive years of increased earnings.

Relocation services were expanded in 1984 with the purchase of Transamerica Corporation's relocation service, which was then ranked as the United States' fourth-largest relocater of corporate personnel. PHH also acquired US Mortgage Corporation that year, adding the related service of mortgage lending to the relocation segment. Fleet management thrived in the United Kingdom, where the country's tax structure encouraged such corporate perquisites as company-provided cars. PHH was listed on the London Stock Exchange in 1984 and the Toronto Stock Exchange in 1986.

PHH signed about 100 new fleet clients in 1984, involving almost 50,000 vehicles. The following year, 78 more clients signed on. At this time, just more than half the company's profits came from fleet services. Aviation management was showing a slight return on investment by 1985. The company orchestrated 29,000 corporate relocations in 1985.

While PHH's major competitor at the time—Gelco Corporation—branched out into containers and truck leasing, PHH broadened only into closely related services, such as credit cards for fuel, tire, and battery purchases, and vehicle expense and maintenance control. In addition to scale economies, PHH offered clients the advantages of its close attention to vehicle prices and values, while handling all the tax, title, and insurance paperwork. In 1985, PHH still ranked among the 100 fastest-growing and most profitable major U.S. companies, despite the fact that falling interest rates had reduced its earnings growth rate in 1983.

In 1986, PHH acquired the Avis Leasing domestic fleet operations from Wesray Capital Corporation for about $136 million. Avis added 35,000 cars to PHH's 281,000 cars in the United States and Canada. More than three-quarters of Avis' business was within 200 miles of New York City, but PHH soon widened the range. Also in 1986, PHH formed an office resources management business segment. These services were to include choosing design, construction, and telecommunications firms and sites for new offices and overseeing the purchase and resale of office equipment. To this new segment were added the 1986 acquisitions of Avenue Group, Inc., of Chicago, and Philadelphia's Interspace, Inc.—both office design firms.

PHH continued expansion in Europe in the late 1980s. It acquired CashCard GmbH in 1987, thus moving into fuel management services in Germany. The company also opened offices in Dublin and Paris. The company's name was changed to PHH Corporation in 1988. The following year, profits rose again, despite hard economic times for both the auto and housing industries. PHH sold its aviation management services business this same year.

Growth Slows: Late 1980s–Early 1990s

Company growth slowed considerably during 1988 and 1989, but profits were steady. Longtime chairman Geckle retired in 1990 and was succeeded by Robert D. Kunisch. The company

picked up important new fleet management clients in 1990, including Coca Cola Enterprises and SmithKlineBeecham. PHH Relocation and Real Estate Management Services USA was formed the same year to oversee the PHH businesses in that area. Also formed were the used vehicle service and card service divisions as a complement to fleet management services. Profits dipped slightly in the fiscal year that ended in April 1991, largely due to the worldwide recession. PHH put off geographic expansion of its fleet services in Europe until the economy recovered.

PHH officials decided in 1990 to exit the facilities management services operations because the required investments of assets and time were too great. PHH seemed to know and build on its strengths as a streamlined provider of certain management services. The company spent the majority of the early 1990s revamping its cost structure and disposing of weak performing assets.

By 1995, PHH was operating as a $5.2 billion asset company with a client base of over 3,000 companies in the United States, Canada, and Europe. That year the firm's mortgage services unit formed a joint venture with First Interstate Bancorp to originate and market home mortgage loans. PHH's sales experienced a slight decline in 1995, falling to $2.07 billion. Profits however, increased 11 percent over the previous year.

Changes in Ownership: Late 1990s and Beyond

PHH's success and position in the industry soon caught the eye of HFS Inc., a global consumer services company in the midst of a major acquisition spree. Its holdings included Avis Inc., a string of hotel chains, real estate broker Century 21, and Resort Condominiums International Inc., which was the largest vacation timeshare exchange provider in the world. In November 1996, HFS announced that it would purchase PHH in a $1.7 billion deal. Just as the PHH/HFS merger closed, HFS teamed up with CUC International Inc. to form Cendant Corp., which became the parent company for the PHH group of companies.

During the transition, PHH's original fleet management operations, which had remained among the largest in the United States, became PHH Vehicle Management Services L.L.C. Its relocation and mortgage units took on the Cendant name. In 1999, Cendant sold PHH to Avis Rent A Car Inc. for $1.8 billion. An Avis executive commented on the deal in a 1999 *Automotive News* article, claiming, "PHH and Avis are a natural fit, since both companies principally serve corporate clients and there are a number of opportunities to cross market to each other's customers."

PHH entered the new century on solid ground. By this time, PHH had developed PHH Interactive, a new fleet information management system that allowed customers to control their fleets via the Internet. In late 2000, Avis strengthened PHH's global reach by forming a joint venture with BNP Paribas, a European banking firm that owned Arval, a fleet management firm based in Europe. The venture merged the operations of both companies together, creating PHH Arval in North America and Arval PHH in Europe.

The company's ownership changed yet again in 2001 when Cendant purchased Avis Group Holdings. Operating as part of Cendant's Vehicle Services division, PHH Arval stood well

Key Dates:

1946: Duane Peterson, Harley Howell, and Dick Heather form a partnership to manage corporate automobile fleets.

1953: The firm incorporates as Peterson, Howell & Heather.

1958: The company goes public.

1969: National Truckers Service is acquired.

1971: The firm gains a foothold in relocation and real estate management services market with the purchase of Homequity Inc.

1978: The company changes its name to PHH Group Inc.

1980: PHH acquires London-based AllStar Petrol Card Ltd.

1988: The firm adopts the name PHH Corporation.

1997: HFS Inc. acquires PHH; HFS and CUC International Inc. merge to form Cendant Corporation

1999: PHH is sold to Avis Rent A Car Inc.

2000: The firm merges fleet operations with Europe-based Arval and changes its name to PHH Arval.

2001: Cendant acquires the Avis Group; PHH operates as a Cendant subsidiary.

positioned for future growth. While the company had experienced significant change during the 1990s, it remained committed to its clients and customer service strategy. Indeed, over 300 companies had been using PHH services for over 20 years, a fact that PHH believed was true because of its long-standing focus on customer satisfaction. As the world's second-largest vehicle fleet management firm, PHH Arval would no doubt remain among the leaders in the vehicle fleet industry in the years to come.

Principal Competitors

Enterprise Rent-A-Car; GE Equipment Management; Holman Enterprises.

Further Reading

"Avis Buys Corporate Leasing Unit," *Automotive News*, May 31, 1999.

Brockman, Joshua, "Cendant's Mortgage Unit Grows Quietly, Quickly," *American Banker*, September 29, 1998, p. 1.

Cook, James, "The PHH Factor," *Forbes*, November 4, 1985.

Forty-Five Years of PHH Quality, Hunt Valley, MD.: PHH Corp., 1990.

Graham, Scott, "PHH Site Cuts the Fat, Aims for Efficiency," *Baltimore Business Journal*, September 14, 2001, p. 6A.

"HFS Inc. and PHH Corp. Announce Merger," *Business Wire*, November 11, 1996.

Mulligan, Thomas S., "MD Firm to Handle First Interstate Mortgage Lending," *Los Angeles Times*, September 1, 1995, p. D2.

Pitock, Todd, "The Artful Acquirer," *Journal of Business Strategy*, March–April 1997, p. 16.

Timmons, Heather, "Merger Could Mean More Business for HFS Unit," *American Banker*, June 3, 1997, p. 21.

—Carol I. Keeley
—update: Christina M. Stansell

Prison Rehabilitative Industries and Diversified Enterprises, Inc. (PRIDE)

12425 28th Street North, Suite 103
St. Petersburg, Florida 33716
U.S.A.
Telephone: (727) 572-1987
Toll Free: (800) 643-8459
Fax: (727) 570-3370
Web site: http://www.peol.com or
http://www.pridefl.com

Not-for-Profit Company
Incorporated: 1981
Employees: 360
Sales: $78.5 million (1999)
NAIC: 624310 Vocational Habilitation Job Training
Facilities (Except Schools)

Prison Rehabilitative Industries and Diversified Enterprises, Inc., or PRIDE Enterprises, with headquarters in St. Petersburg, Florida, is a private, not-for-profit manufacturing and services company whose purpose is to train the inmates of Florida's correctional institutions for employment outside those institutions. Listed in *Trend Magazine*'s top 150 private companies in Florida, PRIDE operates about 55 diverse industries in 20 correctional institutions throughout the sate, offering on-the-job training as well as placement services and support for inmates when they are released. Among its various industries are farming, food processing, digital information services, furniture and garment manufacturing, vehicle maintenance and repair, and printing. Specific items and services PRIDE offers, to name but a few, are metal and wooden bookcases, office furniture, bleach, paint, and mattresses as well as janitorial, book binding, and printing services. Although it receives no direct support funding from the State of Florida, PRIDE sells its products to various customers, including not-for-profit businesses, local governments, and public schools; furthermore, under a controversial state statute, Florida agencies are required to purchase products and services made available by PRIDE when the price and quality of its goods and services are comparable to those available from other sources,

including both the private sector and other state agencies. What is not controversial is the fact that over the two decades of its operation, PRIDE has helped Florida achieve a substantial reduction in inmate recidivism and has become a model for similar programs in other states. PRIDE is currently headed by Pamela Jo Davis, who is the corporation's CEO and president. She is also the CEO of Industries Training Corporation (ITC), a holding/management company providing management services to PRIDE as well as Labor Line, a staffing company that finds jobs for former prisoners and others facing barriers to employment.

1979–81: PRIDE Is Approved by the Florida Legislature

The roots of PRIDE go back to 1979, when Florida's legislation authorized the Prison Industry Enhancement Program, which made it possible for correctional institutions to provide prison inmates for work in for-profit industries provided the workers were paid the prevailing wage in those industries and part of wages went towards crime restitution and prison costs. The Florida legislation was hardly unique. In fact, with at least one eye on a need to provide inmates with marketable trade skills before their release, many states already ran prison industries operated by either their departments of correction or some other state agency.

With that authorization for such a program in place, drugstore mogul Jack Eckerd came up with the idea for PRIDE, and in 1981 helped get its enabling legislation passed. However, because some Florida legislators perceived the work program as a potential tax drain, the authorization for PRIDE stipulated that it had to be vested as a private, not-for-profit entity. Thus, PRIDE became one of the first prison work programs to develop without the support of public funds. In fact, except for some early seed money provided by private businesses, from the outset the program was entirely self-supporting.

1982–90: PRIDE Develops Both Its Pre-release and Post-Release Components

For the first few years of its existence, PRIDE concentrated on the development of its pre-release component. Its focus

Company Perspectives:

Missions: To provide a joint effort between the Department of Corrections, the correctional work programs, and other vocational training programs to reinforce relevant education, training, and post-release job placement and help reduce recommitment; to serve the security goals of the state through the reduction of idleness of inmates and provisions of an incentive for good behavior in prison; to reduce the cost of state government by operating enterprises primarily with inmate labor, which enterprises do not reasonably seek to compete with private enterprise; to serve rehabilitative goals of the state by duplicating, as nearly as possible, the operating activities of a free-enterprise type of profit-making enterprise.

was on developing a comprehensive job training program that stressed work in a productive, commercially relevant industry. Starting in 1987, PRIDE put in place its second main component—its post-release component—which extended employment services to released prisoners who had participated in the program while in prison. That PRIDE would help them find jobs on the outside encouraged more prisoners to participate in the program.

1991–96: Low Inmate Recidivism Rate Among PRIDE'S Participants

In 1991, the reins of PRIDE were assumed by Pamela Jo Davis, who brought to her posts as president and CEO considerable experience in private business and public service. Among other accomplishments, she had directed a $100 million Strategic Business Unit for Motorola, Inc., conducted research surveys for *Business Week* magazine, and had helped establish the Latin American office of Dow Chemical Corp. in Coral Gables, Florida.

Under her leadership throughout the 1990s, the performance of PRIDE continued to justify its existence, albeit on a modest scale. The program was not consistent in its growth, however, and in the first half of the 1990s actually shrunk some in its operational size. In the 1991–92 fiscal year, more than 5,700 convicts worked in 43 industries and 13 service operations, logging over 4.5 million hours at 20 state correctional institutions. In contrast, in 1996, at 21 of Florida's 60 state prisons, there were just 4,600 inmates in the program, although, with 4.2 million hours, these logged almost as many hours at work as the participants did in 1991–92.

PRIDE, with sales of $83.2 million, paid its 1996 workers about $1.9 million. It also purchased goods and services from some 3,500 Florida-based companies. Moreover, it gave $797,500 to the state to offset some of the cost of inmate incarceration. It also put $274,653 in the state's crime victim restitution fund. More importantly, based on the criteria described below, the percentage of PRIDE's program participants re-arrested for crimes committed within two years after their release was just 12.7 percent, which was considerably below the national recidivism rate of 60 percent within the same two-year, 1995–96, period.

1997–99: Establishment of RISE

Between 1996 and 1998, PRIDE's employment service helped over 900 of 1,383 former inmates who participated in the program with in-state jobs on the outside. Of those who did get employment through the company's service, 468 got jobs which related to the work training they received under PRIDE while in prison.

In 1997, PRIDE introduced a new methodology designed to measure the re-incarceration rate of former inmates who had participated in its program. The recommitment rate was defined as a return to prison or to community supervision for a new crime occurring within 24 months of an individual's release from prison. Using fiscal 1994 as its baseline, when 2,512 former PRIDE workers were released from prison, the sample study limited its survey to the 619 ex-offenders who had been in the program for six months or more. Just 78, or 12.6 percent of these were recommitted within a two-year period.

By 1997, PRIDE was offering over 400 different "skill paths" to the nearly 2,600 inmates working its 41 industries operating at 20 Florida prisons. In 1996, the inmates earned $1.6 million, of which $242,758 was contributed to the corporations's victim restitution program. At that time, 87 percent of PRIDE's industries were either certified or recognized by relevant accrediting business or trade associations or institutions.

In early 1999, with over 12 years experience in placing released inmate trainees, the company took a new course. It divested its employment services group and created a new affiliate, RISE (Renewed for Industries, Services, and Employment), which, like PRIDE itself, was organized as a 501 (c)(3) corporation. RISE then took on the responsibility of providing former inmates with help finding jobs on the outside, especially meaningful work that was relevant to their in-prison training. The affiliate also took on the task of reducing the number of former PRIDE trainees who became dependent on publically-funded social programs or were again incarcerated.

The leadership of Davis in PRIDE's success in the 1990s was also recognized in 1999. In that year, Governor Jeb Bush named her to the Florida Council of 100, the exclusive group of Floridians honored for their dedicated service to the state. She was also honored as "Business Woman of the Year" by the St. Petersburg Area Chamber of Commerce.

2000–02: PRIDE Retains Wide Public Support

Despite being a success story, over the years PRIDE has proven very controversial and has generated considerable criticism, something that Davis has sporadically faced throughout her tenure as the corporation's chief officer. Much of this criticism stems from the fact that, by federal law, states can keep up to 80 percent of an inmate's pay. Florida has kept 60 percent, with two-thirds of that going toward offsetting incarceration costs and the remainder going into a victim compensation fund. The pay scheme has drawn fire from both labor unions and industry competitors, who have argued that PRIDE and similar prison industry programs have had an unfair advantage because their labor costs are very low. Also, critics continue to harp on the fact that PRIDE and similar programs have what they perceive as additional advantages because they le-

Key Dates:

1979: Florida Legislature authorizes Prison Industry Enhancement Program.
1981: PRIDE is founded as a private, not-for-profit company.
1991: Pamela Jo Davis assumes the posts of president and CEO.
1999: The company forms its RISE (Renewed for Industries, Services, and Employment) affiliate.

gally sidestep competitive requirements. For example, in Florida, except for printing services, any product or service provided by PRIDE remains exempt from the bidding requirements imposed on the private sector by statutory law. Under Section 946.515 of the Florida Statutes, state agencies are legally required to purchase products and services from PRIDE when such products and services are of a comparable price and quality to those available through any other source. The only restriction is that a product must have been made or a service must be provided by prison inmates.

Bitter complaints about the whole prison labor business have resulted from such real and alleged advantages. Among the voices heard was that of Tim Graves of Marietta, Georgia, who claimed that he was driven out of business in 1998 when a federal prison industry beat his company out of missile-shipping container contract by underbidding him. However, PRIDE has convinced many that the program has saved some Florida enterprises. Don Patach is a well-publicized example. Part owner of Maven Furniture Industries in Lakeland, Patach credited PRIDE with saving 80 jobs in the Lakeland area that otherwise would have gone to Mexico. In 1997, on the verge of moving the company's operation to the Yucatan Peninsula because he was unable to hire workers in Florida, he hired prison inmates under PRIDE's program and began operating Maven's sister company, Maven Manufacturing, in the Hardee Correctional Institute.

Still, PRIDE and its counterparts in other states have also drawn vituperative criticism from some prison inmates and former inmates who, in prison and underground newspapers and online forums, have argued that such programs are exploitive and, particularly in the South, are little more than slave labor. In the face of the decline in Florida's recidivism rate, that argument has few supporters among Florida's citizens. Major defenders, like Daniel Webster, who served a term as speaker of the Florida House of Representatives, have argued that PRIDE has had a major positive impact. Quoted in "Big Business in the BIG HOUSE," an article in the Fall 1999 issue of *Georgia Tech Magazine*, Webster observed that the program's "benefit to the public is awesome because those people are not going back to the correctional facility, or causing more havoc—whether it's murder, rape, burglary, destroying property. If you look at the recidivism statistics—even over an extended period of time—

those prisoners in PRIDE usually don't come back. They have a skill that is marketable, and their supervisors know what they can do. We have employers who are signed up to hire them." In short, the program worked and seemed destined to survive its detractors' efforts to put an end to it. Also, the program's ability to meet the outsourcing needs of many businesses had simply offset the complaints from some businesses about the unfair competitive edge enjoyed by PRIDE.

Given the ballooning incarceration rate in the United States, in part driven up by harsher penalties for nonviolent crimes, PRIDE and programs like it seemed likely to experience robust growth. The "war on drugs" during the 1980s and 1990s left federal, state, and local lockups overcrowded. In 2000, 699 out of every 100,000 citizens in the United States were incarcerated in one of those facilities. Moreover, 77 percent of the growth in the number of inmates from 1978 to 2000 involved nonviolent offenses, most notably drug possession convictions. The U.S. rate of incarceration, the highest in the world, is a figure made even more disturbing by the fact that it had more than tripled since 1980. Correspondingly, sales of products and services provided by prison industries rose sharply in that same period. In 1997, for example, 30 states permitted contract prison labor, and it had become big business, as is evidenced by the fact that between 1989 and 1995 prison industry sales nationwide grew from $393 million to $1.81 billion. In addition, the recidivism rate of prisoners involved in PRIDE seemed to be slowing, although hardly at a pace that would at any time soon impact this and kindred programs.

Principal Competitors

CURE (Citizens United for Rehabilitation of Errants); Federal Prison Industries (FPI); Florida Department of Corrections, Special Education Department; Prisoners for Christ Outreach Ministries.

Further Reading

Abend, Jules, "Ex-Inmates Finding Jobs in Apparel with PRIDE," *Bobbin* September 1994, p.128.
Callahan, Norah, "Workin' for the Man: Captive Labor Is Fueled by the War on Drugs," *Razorwire*, July/August 1997.
Elber, Gail, "Prison-Run GIS—Your New Competition?" *Geospatial Solutions*, September 2001.
Hoffman, Thomas, "From the Big House to the Glass House," *Computer World* August 2, 1999, p. 42.
Jenkins, Shawn, "Big Business in the BIG HOUSE," *Georgia Tech Magazine*, Fall 1999.
Lachenauer, Karen, "The Other Workforce: PRIDE Programs Provide Inmates as Temporary Employees to Florida Companies," *Business Journal of Tampa Bay*, July 5, 1999.
Mann, Timothy, "Pride in the Name of Jobs: A New Approach to Offender Job Placement," *Corrections Today* October 1999, p. 110.
Schloegel, Judith, "PRIDE of Florida: A Working Model for Inmates," in *Privatizing Correctional Institutions*, Gary W. Bowman, Simon Hakim, and Paul Seidenstat, eds., Princeton, N.J.: Transaction Publishers, 1993, pp. 105–11.

—John W. Fiero

RealNetworks ⌐

RealNetworks, Inc.

2601 Elliot Avenue, Suite 1000
Seattle, Washington 98121
U.S.A.
Telephone: (206) 674-2700
Toll Free: (888) 768-3248
Fax: (206) (206) 674-2699
Web site: http://www.realnetworks.com

Public Company
Incorporated: 1994 as Progressive Networks, Inc.
Employees: 798
Sales: $188.9 million (2001)
Stock Exchanges: NASDAQ
Ticker Symbol: RNWK
NAIC: 541511 Custom Computer Programming Services;
    511210 Software Publishers

RealNetworks, Inc. develops software used to deliver streaming media, a product type the company pioneered with the introduction of RealAudio in 1995. RealNetworks' software is used to play audio files, such as radio broadcasts and live music, and video files, such as news and multimedia content, over the Internet. The company's product line includes RealJukebox, RealPlayer, RealFlash, RealText, RealPix, and an assortment of other software. The company generates revenue by collecting money from subscribers to its multimedia programming, from Web site operators whose files use RealNetworks' software to play files over the Internet, and from electronics manufacturers whose products use the company's software. The company is led by Robert Glaser, a former vice-president at Microsoft Corporation.

Origins

A native of Yonkers, a middle-class suburb of New York City, Robert Glaser grew up five miles from Yankee Stadium but supported the New York Mets as a child. After the New York Mets, a decided underdog, won the World Series in 1969, the seven-year-old Glaser knew what he wanted to be when he grew up. Glaser wanted to replace Lindsey Nelson, the Mets' announcer. Although he later abandoned his childhood dream, Glaser's affinity for a team perceived as an underdog was indicative of the type of person he became as an adult. His father operated a small printing press in Yonkers, and his mother was a social worker; both described themselves as political activists. Their beliefs were passed to their son, who at age 12 handed out leaflets in support of the United Farm Workers' grape boycott. Glaser excelled in school, performing well enough to earn admittance to Yale University, where he expressed his progressive views in a column called "What's Left" for the university's newspaper. (In a September 3, 2001 interview with *Business Week,* a RealNetworks' board member described Glaser's political beliefs as "usually to the left of Che Guevera"). When he was not writing his column or participating in disarmament demonstrations, Glaser devoted himself to his studies. In this area, he proved to be indefatigable, exiting Yale in 1979 with no less than three degrees: a Bachelor of Arts in economics, a Bachelor of Science in computer science, and a Master of Arts in economics.

After graduating from Yale, Glaser had to make a decision. He could continue his education or go to work for Hewlett-Packard Co. A third option remained, but few of Glaser's friends believed he would join a little-known, start-up software company. Glaser proved his friends wrong, and moved to the Pacific Northwest, where he signed on with Seattle-based Microsoft Corp. At Microsoft, Glaser worked with the development team that produced Microsoft Word, the company's highly successful word-processing application. After working on Microsoft Word, Glaser moved to the company's networking group, before ultimately becoming vice-president of Microsoft's multimedia systems group. Glaser spent a decade at Microsoft, participating in the company's explosive rise to global dominance in the software industry.

Progressive Networks Is Formed in 1994

By the fall of 1993, Glaser was ready to build his own company. He enlisted the help of a college friend, David Halperin, and began hatching plans for the creation of what he envisioned as a culturally progressive media company. By 1994,

Company Perspectives:

RealNetworks is the global leader in Internet media delivery. Combining cutting edge technology with premium content, RealNetworks opens the world of rich digital audio and video to more than 250 million unique registered consumers of our products worldwide. The result is a multimedia experience that is truly revolutionary.

Glaser and Halperin had formed their conduit for delivering socially conscious programming over the Internet, a company they named Progressive Networks. Within months, the founders realized that investors were more interested in the technology that delivered the socially progressive content than the content itself. Accordingly, Glaser and Halperin focused on developing software to deliver media content, which was then in its infancy on the Internet. In the years ahead, Progressive Networks would concentrate on streaming media—technology that delivered audio and video files over the Internet to personal computers.

History was made not long after Glaser started his company. In 1995, Progressive Networks broadcast the first live event over the Internet, a baseball game between the Seattle Mariners and the New York Yankees. The event marked the first streaming event on the Internet. By the end of the year—Progressive Networks' first year of sales—the company had generated $1.8 million in revenues.

By pinning Progressive Networks' fortunes on delivering streaming media, Glaser had thrust himself into a state of uncertainty. At the time he was fashioning his company to be the dominant competitor in its industry, the industry itself had yet to progress beyond infancy. Much of Progressive Networks' success depended on the Internet developing into the vast, content-rich environment that its proponents claimed it would become. By the time Glaser celebrated the successful broadcast of the first streaming media event over the Internet, however, the projected development of the Internet was uncertain. Glaser's hopes also rested on the exponential increase in connection speeds, the much talked-about but uncertain evolution from narrowband to broadband. In order for Progressive Networks' software to deliver high-quality audio and video files, particularly video files, a sufficient percentage of the online community needed to have the ability to forego dial-up modems and replace them with cable modems or digital subscriber lines (DSL's), which could deliver large files at a much faster pace than narrowband connections. The uncertainty inherent in Glaser's business stance made him, in retrospect, a visionary, the appellation earned by those who enter uncharted waters, succeed, and are followed by others.

In the wake of the first streaming media event, Glaser brokered several critical deals. He reached an agreement with his former employer, Bill Gates, to have Microsoft distribute RealAudio with every copy of Internet Explorer (Microsoft's Web browser) in 1996. The deal enabled Glaser to dramatically increase his revenue volume for the year, as Progressive Networks finished its second full year of business with $14 million generated in sales.

In early 1997, Glaser opened up a massive business arena through a technological development. RealVideo was introduced, enabling users to play videos on the Web. Glaser's biggest coup occurred next, ensuring that Progressive Networks would maintain its place in a now-burgeoning market. Gates, belatedly according to some industry pundits, had begun to realize the potential of streaming media. With vast financial resources at his disposal, the Microsoft chairman could afford to pay to strengthen his company's position in the streaming media industry. He paid $75 million for one of Progressive Networks' rivals, a company named VXtreme Inc. Glaser responded quickly, perhaps fearing that he would be squeezed out of the market just as it was gaining financial legitimacy. Glaser knew he would someday face the increasingly influential Microsoft chairman, a feeling he had had since the day he left Microsoft's Redmond headquarters in 1993. As the summer of 1997 approached, Glaser faced his first great test.

Not long after Microsoft acquired VXtreme Inc., Glaser approached the Redmond-based company. In July 1997, negotiations culminated in an agreement that gave Microsoft a 10 percent stake in Progressive Networks, for which Microsoft paid $30 million. The particulars of the deal also included a $30-million licensing agreement. Glaser convinced Gates to pay $30 million to license Progressive Networks' audio and video technology and embed it in Microsoft's player, Windows Media Player. Industry observers applauded Glaser's work in securing the licensing agreement. In a September 3, 2001 interview with *Business Week,* David B. Yoffie, a Harvard Business School professor, succinctly related his perception of Glaser's talks with Gates. "Rob got the better of Bill," he said.

During the months following the licensing agreement, Progressive Networks prepared for its debut in the public spotlight. The company changed its name to RealNetworks, Inc. shortly before filing for an initial public offering (IPO) of stock at the end of September 1997. The company hoped to raise $34.5 million from the offering, providing financial succor at a time when it was sorely needed. Although the company's revenue volume was expanding impressively—the company matched its sales total in 1996 during the first half of 1997—its losses were mounting. By the time the company filed for its IPO, it had accumulated $12.4 million in losses, with more than half of the total incurred during the first half of 1997.

Late 1990s Pits RealNetworks Against Microsoft

By the summer of 1998, Glaser's efforts to stave off an attack from Microsoft had begun to lose their effectiveness. Glaser was receiving reports that the latest version of Windows Media Player was automatically replacing or disabling RealNetworks' playback software. Glaser sensed the inevitable battle with Microsoft had arrived. In this battle, RealNetworks' founder would not be alone. Several weeks before Glaser began hearing the alarming rumors, the federal government had filed an antitrust case against Microsoft. Federal legislators such as Senator Orrin G. Hatch were on the prowl for any evidence of Microsoft's illegal behavior, which provided Glaser with a powerful, sympathetic audience. Senator Hatch encouraged Glaser to testify against Microsoft at a Senate Judiciary hearing, but, according to Glaser, he initially preferred to keep the battle private. He offered to discuss the matter with Gates, hoping

---

Key Dates:

1994: Progressive Networks is formed.
1995: Progressive Networks broadcasts the first live event over the Internet.
1997: Progressive Networks changes its name to RealNetworks, Inc.
1998: The number of registered users of RealNetworks' audio and video software reaches 22 million.
2000: The number of RealNetworks' registered users climbs to 215 million.

Microsoft would make changes that would eliminate the technical problems with RealNetworks' software. Gates and Glaser reportedly exchanged several e-mail messages, but the electronic negotiations collapsed. Glaser had spent ten years at Microsoft during the company's formative period of development, making enough of an impression at the company to earn a place among its elite cadre of vice-presidents. During this period, Gates had hosted Glaser's bachelor party. Gates' final response to Glaser's proposal for a meeting belied the apparent connection between the two executives. As quoted in the September 3, 2001 issue of *Business Week*, Gates' e-mail to Glaser was brusque. ''I've decided that it doesn't make sense for us to meet,'' he wrote. ''I'm not very familiar with our relationship.'' Shortly thereafter, Glaser testified against Microsoft.

Aside from its increasingly contentious relationship with Microsoft, RealNetworks occupied an enviable market position during the late 1990s. By mid-1998, the number of registered users for the company's audio and video software had tripled during the previous 12 months, reaching 22 million. In 1999, the company's sales reached $131 million and, unlike many Internet-reliant companies, RealNetworks recorded a profit for the year, registering a $7 million gain. The company exited the 1990s as the dominant competitor in the $900 million streaming media industry, with more than 85 percent of the streaming content on the Internet being conveyed with its format. As the company entered a new decade, additional pride could be taken from the success of RealJukebox, which, by April 2000, had attracted 29 million users in less than nine months. RealJukebox allowed users who wanted to build and manage digital music collections to record songs from their CD's or download songs from the Internet and then play them on a personal computer, stereo, or portable music player.

As RealNetworks moved toward the end of its first decade of business, there was cause for both joy and concern. By mid-2001, more than twice as many personal computer users used

the company's software as used Microsoft's rival product. Worldwide, 215 million people had registered to use RealPlayer, roughly a ten-fold increase during a three-year period. Further, the company's exclusive content agreements with media companies such as CNN, ABC, and Viacom generated an ever-growing amount of media content—more than 350,000 hours of content per week as RealNetworks entered the 21st century. There was a wealth of statistical information that pointed to RealNetworks ubiquity on the Internet and on personal computers worldwide, but the specter of Microsoft's alleged anti-competitive practices threatened to diminish the company's dominance. The legal battle against Microsoft continued through 2002, its resolution likely to determine the fate of RealNetworks. The vast majority of personal computers in existence used various versions of Microsoft's operating system, the environment in which RealNetworks' software operated. If that environment proved to be hostile to Glaser's software for the long-term, his company faced an arduous, perhaps fruitless, battle for survival.

Principal Subsidiaries

MusicNet, Inc.; MusicNet, Inc.; Xing Technology Corp.

Principal Competitors

America Online, Inc.; Apple Computer, Inc.; Microsoft Corporation.

Further Reading

Baker, M. Sharon, ''RealNetworks Finally Jumps into IPO Whirl,'' *Puget Sound Business Journal*, October 3, 1997, p. 4.

Hill, Julie, ''The Mpeg-Able Dream,'' *Presentations*, July 2001, p. 13.

Johnson, Bradley, ''Rob Glaser: RealNetworks,'' *Advertising Age*, June 1, 1998, p. S23.

Korzeniowski, Paul, ''Streaming Media Battle Takes Shape,'' *Computer Reseller News*, September 21, 1998, p. 108.

Kover, Amy, ''Is Rob Glaser for Real?,'' *Fortune*, September 4, 2000, p. 216.

Marlowe, Chris, ''Three Battle to Be Ubiquitous Media Player,'' *Billboard*, February 19, 2000, p. 60.

Porter, Dianne, ''Field of Streams,'' *Presentations*, November 2000, p. 54.

''Rob Glaser Is Racing Upstream,'' *Business Week*, September 3, 2001, p. EB14.

Tedesco, Richard, ''Robert Glaser,'' *Broadcasting & Cable*, April 12, 2000, p. 6.

''Worldwide Content, Legally: RealNetworks Founder and CEO Rob Glaser Downloads Ideas on Streaming Video, Profits, and Madonna,'' *Fortune*, June 1, 2001, p. 38.

—Jeffrey L. Covell

RHI AG

Wienerbergstrasse 11
A-1100 Vienna
Austria
Telephone: (+43) 1-50213-6124
Fax: (+43) 1-50213-6130
Web site: http://www.rhi-ag.com

Public Company
Incorporated: 1987
Employees: 11,086
Sales: EUR 1.87 billion ($1.5 billion)(2001)
Stock Exchanges: Vienna
Ticker Symbol: RHI
NAIC: 327124 Clay Refractory Manufacturing; 325998
   All Other Miscellaneous Chemical Product
   Manufacturing; 327125 Nonclay Refractory
   Manufacturing; 541330 Engineering Services; 551112
   Offices of Other Holding Companies

RHI AG is the world's top manufacturer of heat-resistant refractory products, with a global market share of some 15 percent and as much as 30 percent of the European and NAFTA markets. The steel industry accounts for the largest share of the company's sales of its ceramics-based refractory products, contributing more than 59 percent of RHI's revenues of EUR 1.87 billion in 2001. The company also sells to the non-ferrous metals, glass, and cement and lime industries, among others, through brand names and products including Radex, Andkerharth, and Grasanit. RHI's refractories materials, grouped under main subsidiary RHI Refractories, are used for controlling the high temperatures involved in such production processes as steel making, copper and aluminum smelting, and the production of cement, lime, and glass. While refractories remains RHI's core product, contributing more than 80 percent of the company's sales, RHI has long manufactured fire-resistant and noise and thermal insulation building materials for the construction industry, especially through its brand name Heraklith, which has long been one of the major insulation brands in Europe. Until 2002, RHI also maintained an engineering division that was chiefly involved with the construction of lime kilns and smelting furnaces for the non-ferrous metals market and air heater systems for the steel industry. This division was sold off as part of the company's restructuring around its core refractories line. RHI, based in Austria and quoted on the Vienna Stock Exchange, faced a difficult year in 2001, as its debt topped EUR 800 million—largely due to the mountain of asbestos liability claims inherited by the company through its U.S. operations, but also because of a slump in the worldwide steel industry. In early 2002 RHI de-consolidated its U.S. businesses, which then filed for bankruptcy. The restructuring of the company was expected to restore its profits and revenue growth by the end of that year.

European Refractories Pioneers

While the origins of RHI can be traced back to the early nineteenth century, the modern group was forged through the merger of a number of important European refractory products manufacturers in the 1990s. The oldest member of the later RHI originated with the establishment of Chamottefabrik F. Didier, in the town of Podejuch, near Stettin, in what was then known as Prussia, in 1834. Founded by Friedrich F. Didier, that company became one of the first in Europe to begin production of refractory bricks.

The development of fire-resistant materials represented an important step in the development of the Industrial Revolution in general and the steel industry in particular, enabling kilns and furnaces to achieve higher heat levels. At the same time, new refractory products became necessary in order to protect smelters, blast furnaces, kilns and the like, making them safer and longer-lasting. By 1888, the Didier-Werke, as it became known, had begun its own research and development program in order to extend its production into a wider range of industrial fireproofing products. By 1932, when the company officially adopted the name Didier-Werke AG, it had become a leading German refractory products producer and one of the leaders in Europe.

The discovery of the fire-resistant properties of magnesite, the carbonate of magnesium, gave a new boost to the refractory products industry in Europe, and especially in Austria. Thanks to its large magnesite deposits, Austria became a leading player in the European refractory products industry and one of the region's primary sources for the mineral. The country's involvement in the refractories trade received its first boost in 1881, when Carl Spaeter discovered an important magnesite deposit near the town of Veitsch, in the Styria region of Austria. Spaeter began mining operations that same year, and by 1886 the mine was sufficiently established to begin production of magnesite for the refractory products industry.

Spaeter's business, designated as Veitscher Magnesitwerke Actien-Gesellschaft in 1899, became the world's first producer of processed magnesite for refractory products. The company itself developed into a major manufacturer of refractory and fireproof products in addition to its mining operation. Veitscher also played a leading role in the development of new magnesite-based refractory products, particularly after the establishment of a dedicated research and development facility in 1935. By the early 1990s, when Veitscher merged with rival Radex-Heraklith Industriebeteiligungs AG (RHI), it had become Austria's second-largest fireproof products maker.

RHI by then formed the heart of what was to become the world's leading refractory products conglomerate. That company had its start at the turn of the century with the discovery of a magnesite deposit at Millstätter Alpe, in Austria's Carinthia region, in 1907. A year later, Emil Winter, an Austrian-American, bought the mining rights to the Millstätter site and founded the Austro-American Magnesite Company. The new company quickly took over the rights to manufacture a new insulation product patented by Robert Scherer in Vienna in 1907. By 1908, Austro-American had begun production of the new material, the so-called wood wool, which combined wood and magnesite to create a lightweight building material that provided insulation and fire-resistant qualities. Previously, buildings required thick walls in order to provide insulation from the cold; the new product, dubbed Heraklith, was to help transform much of Europe's construction industry by enabling the construction of buildings with thinner walls.

Austro-American, which later became known as Österreichisch-Amerikanische Magnesit AG, became a strategic producer of magnesite, while also developing into an important manufacturer of refractory products. The company's insulation division, which remained focused around the Heraklith brand, later diversified into other insulation products, such as the introduction of multi-layer insulation boards featuring polystyrene and Heraklith materials in 1967 and the introduction of expanded polystyrene boards the following year.

Global Market Leader in the New Century

By 1974, Österreichisch-Amerikanische Magnesit had come under the control of the United States' General Refractories Co.,

which folded the company into its organization as its European Division. At that time, the company's business was separated into two divisions, building materials and insulating materials. The latter division was reformed under the name Austrian Heraklith AG. In 1981, that company began production of rock wool insulation products.

General Refractories' struggles through the 1980s led to its divestment of its European Division in 1987. General Refractories itself was acquired by Belmont Industries in 1988, then taken over by AP Green in 1994. The spin off, in what at the time was Austria's largest-ever management buyout, created the newly independent Radex-Heraklith Industriebeteiligungs AG, or RHI. At the same time, Radex-Heraklith went public, listing on the Vienna Stock Exchange. The company's building and insulation materials operations were then brought under subsidiary Heraklith AG.

RHI began a long expansion drive in the 1990s that rapidly expanded its worldwide presence. Among the companies purchases was that of a 50 percent stake in National Refractories of Oakland, California, giving RHI an important foothold in the U.S. market. The company also launched an engineering division, which specialized in the design and construction of kilns and smelting furnaces. Then, in 1991, RHI announced that it had acquired majority control of domestic competitor Veitscher Magnesitwerke AG. By then, RHI had built up sales of more than $400 million. With the addition of Veitsch, RHI's revenues topped $700 million.

Initially, RHI and Veitsch maintained their separate operations and brand names. However, in 1993, the two businesses were merged together to form a new subsidiary of RHI, Veitsch-Radex Aktiengesellschaft für feuerfeste Erzeugnisse. In that same year, RHI added a new fireproofing and insulation subsidiary, Dolomite Franchi. Based in Italy, Dolomite Franchi had been set up in 1919 in response to the embargo placed on Austrian magnesite imports to Italy. Dolomite Franchi replaced magnesite with dolomite and went on to become a leading Italian producer of insulating materials.

In 1994, RHI acquired Germany's Vedag Dachsysteme GmbH, which produced roofing materials, and then led that company on an expansion drive into Eastern Europe, with marketing and sales facilities in Slovakia, the Czech Republic, and Poland. Vedag was later brought under RHI's Insulation division before being spun off in a management buyout in 2001.

RHI turned to Germany again for expansion in 1995, this time acquiring a 57 percent share in Didier-Werke. RHI quickly added Didier to its core refractories subsidiary, creating the new Veitsch-Radex-Didier, or VRD. By 1997, RHI had increased its control of Didier to nearly 90 percent, and to 96 percent in 2002. The addition of Didier transformed RHI into a truly international company, with sales topping EUR 1.5 billion ($1.2 billion) and a global market share of more than nine percent. Didier also extended RHI's U.S. presence with subsidiary NARCO. That company had been founded in 1929 as North American Refractories Co., a manufacturer of fireclay bricks, and had been acquired by Allied Corp. in 1979 before joining Didier in 1989. The addition of NARCO, which was placed under VRD America, enabled RHI to reduce its reliance on the

Key Dates:

1834: Didier-Werke, one of the first company's in Europe to produce fireclay brick, is founded.

1886: Veitscher Magnesitwerke becomes the world's first magnesite processing company.

1908: Austro-American Magnesite Company, later known as Radex-Heraklith, begins magnesite mining and processing along with the production of Heraklith wood wool insulation and fireproofing boards.

1974: The company is acquired by National Refractories Co., and Radex-Heraklith is separated into its building products and insulation divisions.

1987: Radex-Heraklith is spun off from National Refractories in a management buyout, then goes public on the Vienna Stock Exchange.

1991: Radex-Heraklith acquires Veitscher Magnesitwerke.

1995: Fifty-one percent of Didier-Werke, which includes NARCO North American subsidiary, is acquired.

1997: Radex-Heraklith acquires 89 percent of Didier Werke, later boosting its share to more than 96 percent.

1998: Radex-Heraklith changes its name to RHI AG.

2000: Global Industrial Technologies, which includes subsidiary Harbison-Walker, is acquired.

2002: Facing massive asbestos liability claims, RHI's North American subsidiaries file for bankruptcy and are put up for sale.

European market. After the Didier acquisition, the NAFTA market reached 23 percent of RHI's sales, compared with 70 percent of sales from Europe.

In the late 1990s, RHI began restructuring its operations, which included the phase-out of its engineering division. The company also formally changed its name in 1998, to RHI AG, recreating itself as a holding company for VRD, Radex-Heraklith, and other subsidiaries. Then, in mid-1999, RHI seized an opportunity to extend its presence in the North American market. In that year, Global Industrial Technologies Inc., based in Dallas and parent of Harbison-Walker Refractories Co., one of the United States' leading refractory products companies, faced a hostile takeover from WHX Corp. RHI stepped in as a white knight in a deal worth some $500 million. The acquisition was completed in 2000.

The addition of Harbison-Walker, originally founded in Pittsburgh as Star Fire Brick Co. in 1865, boosted RHI's share of the global refractories market past 15 percent, with a market share in the NAFTA region of more than 30 percent. The acquisition also loaded the company down with debt. Nonetheless, the purchase appeared promising, and Harbison-Walker and NARCO were combined into a new company, RHI Refractories America.

By 2001, however, the company's rapid expansion into the North American market left it highly exposed to the sudden economic downturn, and particularly the slump in the steel industry. The company's debt level soared to nearly EUR 900 million; worse yet, RHI suddenly found itself confronted with a mountain of lawsuits stemming from its newly acquired subsidiaries' use of asbestos in the past. The protective clauses that had been put into place in order to limit RHI's exposure to damage claims had become challenged, and the company's U.S. operations were now under direct threat.

RHI attempted to prop up its North American holdings, but by the beginning of 2002 the company's prospects in the region appeared bleak. At the beginning of 2002, the company deconsolidated its U.S. operations. At the same time, NARCO filed for bankruptcy protection and was soon after joined by Harbison-Walker and Global Industrial Technologies as well. By mid-2002, RHI, which had been forced to restructure its financing in order to confront its heavy debt burden, announced its intention to sell off its U.S. operations and to retrench around its core European operations.

RHI reorganized its structure again, shedding its holding company status to take direct control of RHI Refractories. That division now became the company's core business, although RHI maintained its Radex-Heraklith insulation operations as well. The company finally sold off its engineering division as well. By late 2002, RHI's restructuring efforts appeared to have restored the company's stability, as it once again began showing profits. Although RHI's expansion hopes had stumbled in the United States, the company was comforted by its continued status as the world's leading refractory products group.

Principal Subsidiaries

Betriebs- und Baugesellschaft GmbH (Germany); Corrosion Technologies de México SA de C V (Mexico); Corrosion Technology (Peru) SA (Peru); Didier-Werke AG (Germany); Dolomite Franchi SpA (Italy); Dutch MAS BV (Netherlands); Dutch SAPREF BV (Netherlands); Full Line Supply Africa (PTY) Limited (South Africa); GEFRO GmbH (Germany); Gen-X Technologies Inc (Canada); GIX International GmbH (Germany); GIX International Limited (United Kingdom); INDRESCO de México SA de CV (Mexico); INDRESCO UK Ltd (United Kingdom); INTOOL de México SA de CV (Mexico); Latino America Refractories ApS (Denmark); Magnesit Anonim Sirketi Turkey TRL; Oy Tulenkestävät Tiilet AB Finland; Radex West GmbH (Germany); REFEL SpA (Italy); Refmex S de RL de CV (Mexico); Refractarios Green S de RL de CV (Mexico); Refrattari Italiana SpA (Italy); RHI Africa Investment Holdings (Pty) Ltd (South Africa); RHI (Canada) Inc (Canada); RHI Dinaris GmbH (Germany); RHI Finance ApS (Denmark); RHI Refractories Africa (Pty) Ltd (South Africa); RHI Refractories Andino CA (Venezuela); RHI Refractories Asia Ltd (China); RHI Refractories Asia Pacific Pte Ltd (Singapore); RHI Refractories España SA (Spain); RHI Refractories (France) SA (France); RHI Refractories Ibérica SL (Spain); RHI Refractories Italiana srl (Italy); RHI Refractories Liaoning CoLtd (China); RHI Refractories Mercosul Ltda (Brazil); RHI Refractories México SA CV (Mexico); RHI Refractories Nord AB (Sweden); RHI Refractories Spaeter (Site Services) Ltd (United Kingdom); RHI Refractories Spaeter Ltd (United Kingdom); RHI Refractories Spaeter GmbH (Germany); RHI Refractories UK Limited (United Kingdom); SAPREF AG für feuerfestes Material (Switzerland); Veitsch-

Radex GmbH; Didier Ltd (Zambia); Dolomite Franchi GmbH (Germany); Dr-Ing-Petri & Co Unterstützungs-Gesellschaft mbH (Germany); Magnesitwerk Aken Vertriebsgesellschaft mbH (Germany) N; Marion South America SA (Chile); Radex Latinoamérica CA (Venezuela); Refractories Consulting & Engineering Gesellschaft mbH; Rheinischer Vulkan Chamotte- und Dinaswerke mbH (Germany); RHI Argentina SRL (Argentina); RHI Réfractaires Algérie EURL (Algeria); Thor Ceramics Limited (United Kingdom) N-; Dolomite di Montignoso SpA (Italy) E; Lokalbahn Mixnitz-StErhard AG; Società Dolomite Italiana SDI SpA; Stopinc AG (Switzerland); Treuhandgesellschaft Feuerfest mbH (Germany).

Principal Competitors

Cookson Group plc; Mitsui Mining and Smelting Company Ltd.; Wacker-Chemie GmbH; Morgan Crucible Company plc; Lafarge Refractories; Toshiba Ceramics Company Ltd.; Hepworth Ltd.; Plansee Holding AG; Shinagawa Refractories Company Ltd.

Further Reading

Alm, Richard, ''Austrian Company to Buy Global Industrial,'' *The Dallas Morning News*, July 14, 1999, p. 2D.

''Bullig bis barig,'' *Die Presse*, September 11, 2001.

''Feuerfestkonzern RHI mit Riesenverlust,'' *Der Standard*, January 15, 2002.

''The Making of a Refractories Giant,'' *Ceramic Industry*, October 2000, p. 2.

''RHI Faces Massive 2001 U.S. Asbestos-related Loss,'' *Reuters*, January 14, 2002.

''RHI sieht sich wieder feuerfester,'' *Der Standard*, May 29, 2002.

''RHI's US Assets for Sale,'' *Chemical Business Newsbase*, February 4, 2002.

—M.L. Cohen

Ruiz Food Products, Inc.

501 South Alta Avenue
Dinuba, California 93618
U.S.A.
Telephone: (559) 591-5510
Toll Free: (800) 477-6474
Fax: (559) 591-1948
Web site: http://www.ruizfood.com

Private Company
Incorporated: 1967
Employees: 1,000
Sales: $212 million (2001 est.)
NAIC: 311412 Frozen Specialty Food Manufacturing

Privately owned, Ruiz Food Products, Inc. is the market leader in the frozen Mexican food category. Located south of Fresno, California, in the small town of Dinuba, the company produces approximately 200 different items—including burritos, tamales, taquitos, enchiladas, and chimichangas—most of which are packaged under its signature El Monterey label as well as the Ruiz and Prima Rosa brands. Ruiz Food is also the only frozen Mexican food manufacturer to sell in all channels of distribution: retail, convenience store, clubs, vending, industrial, and foodservice. In addition to nationwide distribution in the United States, Ruiz also sells its products in some 20 countries, including Canada, Japan, Panama, and Costa Rica.

Louis Ruiz Launches a Career
During the Depression

Ruiz Food Products was founded by Louis Ruiz and his son, Fred, in 1964. Louis was born in Mexico and moved to Los Angeles as a child. By the age of ten he was already exhibiting an entrepreneurial spirit, working out a deal with a downtown W.T. Grant five-and-dime store: in return for cleaning, he received overstocked or damaged merchandise to peddle. As a young man, he owned a small grocery store, but when America entered World War II he sold the business and joined the Army. After the war, he took a job with the Flintkoke Corporation but soon supplemented his income by selling sweaters door to door. This side venture led

to his once again striking out on his own and opening a small clothing store, which his wife ran while he continued his door-to-door efforts. By the 1950s, he recognized that Mexican food was gaining broad appeal in California and sold his clothing store to enter the tortilla business along with his four brothers. He spent considerable time, as well as all of his capital, in establishing the operation, but when he approached his brothers in 1954 about drawing up a formal operating agreement, they refused. As a result of this family fallout, Ruiz abandoned the business he was so instrumental in creating and went to work in small grocery stores in order to support his family. It was not until 1960 that he was able to launch another business. This time he bought a small truck, rented warehouse space, and began to deliver groceries to farms in the San Joaquin Valley. A high school student at the time, his son Fred also helped out.

Louis Ruiz had not given up on entering the Mexican food business, however, and soon targeted the production of frozen enchiladas. When his son pointed out that they could not hope to compete with the major companies already supplying the market, Louis conceived of a way to differentiate their product: they would use clear plastic packaging so that customers could see the merchandise. In 1964, the Ruizes established the company that would one day become Ruiz Food Products. Working out of a garage in Tulare, California, with little more than a freezer, Mixmaster, kitchen utensils from home, and a small commercial stove, they began to produce cheese and onion enchiladas, borrowing a recipe from Louis Ruiz's wife, Rosie. They also drew on her name for a label: ''Rosita.'' At first, the Ruizes were unable to include meat, a common ingredient in enchiladas, because their rudimentary plant could not meet state or federal standards for meat processing. To placate grocers who complained that their meatless enchiladas appeared to skimp on fillings, they added beans, which resulted in a significant increase in sales. Unfortunately, the clear packaging did not work as anticipated, the film frosting on the inside and obscuring the customer's view of the enchiladas. It would take Louis two years of experimenting with different flours in order to create a tortilla dough that did not cause frost. In the meantime, Fred held two outside jobs and still found the time to take two years of college business courses, gaining knowledge that would prove instrumental in the growth of the family business.

Company Perspectives:

We are committed to delivering quality products and out-standing customer service. Our mission is to be the best frozen Mexican food company in North America.

Incorporation in 1967

During the early years, Ruiz Food was very much a shoe-string affair. Louis took the truck he had used to deliver groceries and refrigerated it by adding an insulated plywood chest. After spending the morning with his son preparing the products, Louis made sales calls and deliveries in the after-noons. In order to accommodate these dual roles, he relied on gas station rest rooms, where he changed from business attire to clothes more suitable for making deliveries. When sales picked up, the Ruizes were able to supplement their limited storage capacity by turning to a commercial freezing plant. Then, in 1967, they found a 1,400-square-foot plant with a large freezer that had been used for poultry processing and was now available to lease. In order to raise the necessary funds to convert the facility and buy additional equipment, they incorporated the business as Ruiz Food Products, and sold 14,000 shares of stock at $1 each to Tulare residents. They retained 14,000 shares for themselves and eventually bought back about half of the public shares, much of which would be used in an employee stock ownership plan.

A business with five employees, Ruiz Food now had a plant that met California inspection standards, but it also had greater costs and cash flow problems. At one point, the company was unsure it could meet its payroll and the situation with creditors became so dire that the Ruizes determined that they might have to close the business in a matter of two weeks. To meet the challenge, they worked seven days a week, but more importantly Louis created a new way to sell a familiar product, tamales. Recalling how vendors in the Southwest used to sell tamales from pushcarts, steamed hot and wrapped in corn husks, he convinced five convenience store owners to allow him to install heating units in order to sell his tamales piping hot. The idea proved to be a instant success with customers and within days the merchants were ordering more tamales. This influx of cash saved the company and allowed it to begin expanding its offerings, including meat enchiladas. Annual revenues that totaled just $40,000 in 1967 reached $500,000 by 1975.

However, Ruiz Food faced yet another critical juncture in its history. When California elected to turn over responsibility for meat processing standards to the U.S. Agriculture Department, the company found that despite having met state standards its facilities fell far short of federal requirements. If the Ruizes wanted to stay in business they had no choice but to build a new plant. With no ready cash on hand and no established credit line, they had the difficult task of raising the $635,000 needed to build and equip a new facility. Louis Ruiz turned to the Small Business Administration (SBA) and was able to convince them that Ruiz Food was sound enough to support a $500,000 direct loan. He was then able to raise the rest of the money by obtaining an SBA-guaranteed loan from an area bank.

In 1977, Ruiz Food, now employing 26 people, opened its new plant in Tulare. Again the company's finances were deli-cately balanced, the Ruizes calculating that they had just seven months to reach a sales level that would sustain the business. It met that target and for the year recorded sales of $700,000. Moreover, Ruiz Food was in a position to take advantage of its ability to meet federal standards. Allowed to conduct interstate business, and with increased production capacity, it was now able to market its products in major markets. As a result, the company expanded its production capabilities and began hiring a large number of workers. By 1982, it formed a human re-sources department as part of its drive to become a major business. In 1983, with 205 employees and annual sales exceed-ing $15 million, Louis and Fred Ruiz received the United States Small Business Persons of the Year Award, which was pre-sented to them by President Ronald Reagan in a Rose Garden ceremony at the White House.

By the late 1980s, Ruiz Food topped $25 million in annual revenues and employed more than 500 people. In October 1988, the company sent letters to Tulare leaders indicating they hoped to relocate the business to a new site where a larger production facility could be constructed to accommodate future growth. According to Fred Ruiz, recounting the episode years later, the city officials were "arrogant, prejudiced, and conde-scending." As a result Ruiz Foods built its new $16.5 million, 203,000-square-foot plant and corporate offices on a 43-acre site in Dinuba, a town of 12,000 people located in northern Tulare County. With greater production capacity, Ruiz Food was able to boost annual revenues to $85 million and employ-ment to some 1,200 in 1992. In that same year, Louis and Fred Ruiz received the National Entrepreneurial Success Award from SBA, and the company was inducted into SBA's hall of fame in Washington, D.C. The following year, Fred Ruiz was named Executive of the Year by *Refrigerated & Frozen Food Magazine*.

Faced with a sluggish economy and increased competition, Ruiz Food was not without challenges in the early 1990s. In order to maintain growth, it retooled its management structure and Fred Ruiz, now heading the business, turned over more control to his management team to permit the company to become less dependent on a single individual. Ruiz Foods also suffered some adverse publicity when the Border Patrol, acting on a tip in an anonymous letter, visited the plant and determined that more than 200 workers were using false work papers. The company charged that the letter was written by former employ-ees at the behest of the local chapter of the United Food and Commercial Workers Union. Regardless of how the matter was initiated, in the end the company was forced to terminate 123 employees, most of whom appeared to be illegal immigrants.

A New President and Ambitious Goals for the Future

In October 1996, Fred Ruiz announced that he was going to once again be more actively involved in the running of the company, whose annual revenues had stalled at the $90 million level and was stung by the departure of a major account. The company's president, David Hejl, resigned "to pursue other opportunities," and Ruiz temporarily assumed his post. After a year-long executive search, a new president, Ricardo Alvarez, was hired to help Ruiz Food reach the next level. Alvarez had some 20 years experience in the food service industry and came to the job with unique qualifications. Born in Chile, he attended high school in Puerto Rico, then earned a bachelor's degree in microbiology at the University of Florida and went on to earn a master's degree and a Ph.D. in food science. During the first eight years of his career, his work involved quality assurance, and he rose to the level of vice-president on the technical side of the food service industry before switching to management. Prior to Ruiz Food, he was president of $300 million Burns Philip Foods.

Alvarez quickly initiated a strategy to grow sales at Ruiz Food. He looked to penetrate markets, such as the Northeast, where the company had a limited presence. He also wanted to improve sales in vending machines, chain stores, and convenience stores, as well as strengthen the company's co-packaging business for other manufacturers. In addition, Alvarez was eager to offer new products, such as stuffed wraps, which were becoming increasingly popular. His efforts were so successful that Ruiz Food enjoyed a 20 percent spike in sales at a time when the industry saw revenues grow at just three percent. Alvarez was scheduled to take over as chief executive officer after three years, but because of his immediate success he assumed the post after one year on the job, becoming the first non-family member to head the business. Fred Ruiz remained committed, however, to keeping the company a family business. Part of Alvarez's job was to groom a third generation of the Ruiz family to one day take control. Two of Ruiz's children, Kim Ruiz Beck in her early 30s and Bryce Ruiz in his early 20s, already held management positions.

In 1999, Ruiz Food finally cracked the $100 million annual sales barrier and established a goal to reach $200 million within five years, with the ultimate target of $500 million. A key to the company's success hinged on product development, introducing new Mexican food items to keep pace with consumer's changing tastes. Although Ruiz Food prided itself on producing authentic Mexican fare, and retained Rose Ruiz to help in developing its recipes, it had always targeted a general market.

As Ruiz Food expanded into overseas markets, it also had to take into account differences between countries as well as regional differences within countries. It was a fine line that the company was able to straddle successfully, as evidenced by its ability to significantly outpace its competitors in growth. To reach its ambitious sales goals, the company announced in 2000 that it was expanding its Dinuba plant by 65,000 square feet.

Alvarez, after achieving impressive results in a short period of time, unexpectedly resigned in August 2001 to take another job. Fred Ruiz once again stepped in to serve as CEO while a search for a new chief executive was conducted. In June 2002, the company settled on John Signorino, who had been the general manager of David & Sons in nearby Fresno. He became available when David & Sons' parent company, Nestlé, decided to sell the business. Signorino brought with him 25 years of experience in the food industry, including stints with Anheuser-Busch and the Nestlé USA divisions of Sunline Brands and Willy Wonka Candy Factory. As had been the case with Alvarez, Signorino was charged with managing the company's ongoing growth while also preparing the way for a new generation of the Ruiz family to assume control. A month after he was hired, as part of a succession plan, Kim Ruiz Beck was named vice-chairman of the company and began to take over some of her father's responsibilities. Fred Ruiz remained the chairman and continued to be actively involved in the business, making it clear that he hoped Ruiz Food reached $500 million in annual sales before he retired. In fiscal 2001, the company fell well short of that mark, with estimated revenues of $212 million. But with a fast growing Hispanic population in the United States and new products such as breakfast items driving domestic sales—as well as an expanding overseas presence, including penetration in relatively untapped Asian markets—Ruiz Food might very well make its chairman's dream a reality.

Principal Competitors

Jose Ole; Goya Foods, Inc.

Further Reading

Ennen, Steve, "It's No Trend: It's Tradition," *Food Processing*, August 200, p. 19.

Heiman, Grover, "Building the No. 1 Small Business," *Nation's Business*, July 1983, p. 22.

Laabs, Jennifer, "Business Growth Driven by Staff Development," *Personnel Journal*, April 1993, p. 120.

Nax Sanford, "Spicy Profit Picture," *Fresno Bee*, September 30, 1998, p. C1.

——, "Mexican Gold," *The Fresno Bee*, May 24, 2000, p. C1.

Reynolds, Kelley, "Ruiz Food Products Hires Outside Family For Top Spot," *Business Journal Serving Fresno & the Central San Joaquin Valley*, September 28, 1998, p. 1.

—Ed Dinger

Salick Health Care, Inc.

8201 Beverly Boulevard
Los Angeles, California 90048
U.S.A.
Telephone: (323) 966-3400
Fax: (323) 966-3680
Web site: http://www/salick.com

Wholly Owned Subsidiary of AstraZeneca plc
Incorporated: 1983
Employees: 1,400
Sales: $176 million (2000)
NAIC: 62149 Other Outpatient Care Clinics

Salick Health Care, Inc. is a unique chain of for-profit outpatient clinics dedicated specifically to cancer care. Salick's eight cancer clinics are affiliated with major hospitals and staffed by the hospital's leading cancer specialists. Salick clinics offer 24-hour care, seven days a week, with the goal of making cancer treatment as comfortable for the patient as possible. The clinics give comprehensive cancer care, which includes psychological counseling for patients and their families as well as onsite radiation physicists, laboratory technicians, nutritionists, pain management specialists, and a host of other professionals trained in diverse aspects of cancer management. The company was named for founder Bernard Salick, M.D., and is now owned by the European drug company AstraZeneca plc.

Personal Crisis Leads to New Business Direction

Bernard Salick was born in New York City in 1939, the son of recent Jewish immigrants from Rumania. Though his family was poor, Salick's parents pushed him to study and aspire for a professional degree. Salick graduated from Queens College in 1960 with a degree in mathematics, then began his medical training at the University of Southern California. Salick earned his M.D. in 1964 and became a specialist in kidney disease with a practice in Beverly Hills. Salick married in 1973 and eventually had three daughters. It was a confluence of a family medical crisis and Salick's burgeoning entrepreneurship that led to the formation of his chain of cancer clinics.

Beginning in 1972, Bernard Salick began using profits from his medical practice to invest in a chain of outpatient kidney dialysis clinics. Though Salick was still paying back student loans, he put what money he could toward the dialysis centers, soon deciding to keep them open 24 hours, seven days a week. Salick sold the dialysis chain in 1975 to a conglomerate called Damon Corp. Damon ran aground in the early 1980s, and so Salick decided to buy back the kidney clinics. Salick got financial backing from Michael Milken of Drexel Burnham Lambert, the notorious trader who was later jailed for insider trading and racketeering. The new company, in 1983, was again under Salick's management and was called Salick Health Care, Inc.

However, Salick abruptly changed his focus from kidney disease to cancer. In 1983, shortly after he had won a contract to operate a dialysis clinic at prestigious Cedars-Sinai Medical Center in Beverly Hills, he learned that a mysterious pain in his middle daughter's knee was actually a particularly deadly cancer. His daughter, Elizabeth, was only six years old when she was diagnosed with a form of bone cancer that killed nine out of ten victims. Salick was immediately plunged into caring for his daughter, and he basically gave up his medical practice. Elizabeth Salick recovered from cancer after surgery and rounds of chemotherapy at both a Los Angeles hospital and at Memorial Sloan-Kettering Cancer Center in New York. Suffering through midnight visits to emergency rooms and sleeping in the hospital hallway because there was no provision for the patient's parents set Dr. Salick thinking about comprehensive cancer care. His dialysis clinics offered round-the-clock care, but there was nothing comparable for cancer. Salick got the backing of Drexel Burnham Lambert and diversified his dialysis business into a new chain of outpatient cancer care clinics. Salick Health Care's first cancer clinic opened at Cedars-Sinai in 1985.

The company was for-profit, which dismayed some members of the medical community who feared patient care might be skimped on. Salick countered that not-for-profit hospitals were often too loosely run, and sloppy management in itself often worked against the patient's best interest. Salick Health Care was determined to run profitably, but it did anything but skimp. Quite the opposite: Salick was called on to justify his clinics' opulent architecture and design as well as such services as valet parking. Drawing on his own family's experience, Salick insisted that cheerful, comfortable surroundings made patients more likely to comply with their physicians and thus led to better patient outcomes. And valet parking was not a frill where extremely sick people were concerned.

Salick Health Care made an initial public offering in March 1985, raising $18 million, and in 1986 raised another $30 million through a bond offering. Salick had revenue of over $21 million in 1987 and brought in over $38 million the next year. By 1989, the company operated seven cancer centers (while still running its dialysis clinics)—two in Southern California, four in Florida, and one in Philadelphia. The clinics worked with top oncologists who were not paid directly by Salick Health Care but remained on the affiliated hospital's staff. The clinics operated mostly in partnership with non-profit teaching hospitals which were known for excellent staff but could not provide the extensive outpatient care Salick could. Salick Health Care was a profitable public company, bringing in net income of around $7 million by 1988. With its stock market backing, Salick could afford to lay out for its clinics in a way that most non-profit hospitals could not, so it seemed to be a comfortable arrangement all around.

Changes in the Early 1990s

By the early 1990s, Salick had expanded to a chain of nine outpatient cancer clinics. It had established itself financially, both as a profitable small-cap company and as a money-saver for hospitals. Though Salick clinics offered extensive care in plush surroundings likened more to a hotel than a hospital, by 1993 the company was estimating one year of cancer treatment at its clinics cost 20 percent less than in a traditional hospital setting. One reason for this seemed to be that Salick patients had such complete outpatient care that they could avoid costly hospitalization. By 1994, Salick ran ten cancer care clinics as well as nine dialysis clinics and was treating close to a million patients annually. Sales had grown to around $100 million. The company expected to grow even more through a venture begun that year that established a first in the health care industry. Salick negotiated a contract with a Florida health maintenance organization, called Physicians Corporation of America (PCA) to treat all the group's cancer patients for a flat annual fee. For something between $10 and $25 per patient in the group, Salick would cover the entire cost of cancer treatment for any sick PCA member. Such an arrangement is known as a "carve-out," when a health maintenance organization contracts out services

for part of its membership group. This was apparently the first time such an arrangement had been made for a specific disease. The *Economist* (July 23, 1994) called Salick Health Care the "world's first full-service disease management firm."

Salick began negotiating a similar deal with an Arizona health maintenance group. The company had shown that, at least so far, it could offer its Cadillac service at a substantially lower cost than traditional hospitals and clinics. It gambled that it could continue to make a profit with the flat-fee arrangement. The company's revenue almost doubled with the PCA deal, and if similar arrangements came off, Salick looked like it would expand very quickly. At this point, Salick sought an investment partner. In 1995, the company sold 50 percent of its shares to the British pharmaceutical and chemical company Zeneca Group PLC for $195 million. The acquisition raised eyebrows, as Zeneca, a $9 billion giant, was a leading manufacturer of cancer-fighting drugs. Both companies proclaimed that there was no conflict of interest, and that Salick physicians would not be pushed to prescribe Zeneca drugs over other treatments. Zeneca explained its interest in Salick as giving it access to Salick's vast database of cancer drug use and treatment outcomes. Under the 1995 agreement, Bernard Salick was to remain as CEO of the company he had founded until at least 1999. Zeneca retained an option to buy the rest of the company after several years.

Subsidiary Company in the Late 1990s and After

Now flush with cash, Salick went on with its expansion plans. The company continued to put together proprietary practice guidelines, which outlined standards of care for specific disease treatments, such as chemotherapy for colon cancer, bone marrow transplants for breast cancer, and the use of anti-nausea drugs. These guidelines helped make care consistent within the clinics. Consistency between different practitioners and clinics was something Dr. Salick had found sadly missing when his daughter was being treated for her bone cancer. The Salick chain persevered in using its immense patient database and its specialists' expertise to come up with clear protocols for each disease. Because the chain was for-profit, it did not share these guidelines with non-Salick physicians, which again angered some in the medical community. Bernard Salick seemed able to use his own charm, bluster, and prestige, plus his clinics' reputation for excellent care, to counter such criticism. The company's next big move was to enter the New York City market. New York was a potentially lucrative area, accounting for some 10 to 15 percent of the $50 billion Americans spent annually on cancer care. The city was also home to four other well-known cancer clinics, including Memorial Sloan-Kettering. Salick worked out an arrangement with St. Vincent's hospital in 1996 to set up a cancer center under its auspices. St. Vincent's was the flagship of New York's non-profit Catholic hospital system, and the deal with Salick sent reverberations all the way up to New York's Cardinal John O'Connor. The Catholic hospital's mission was to serve the poor, and so there were barriers to it contracting with the profit-driven Salick. Yet the agreement brought money into St. Vincent's that it could then use for the indigent, and Salick built a $20 million cancer facility the hospital could not otherwise have afforded.

Moving into New York City was quite a coup for Salick, and the company had plans to expand into satellite clinics through-

Key Dates:

1972: Bernard Salick founds a chain of dialysis clinics in Southern California.
1975: Salick sells the clinics to Damon Corp.
1983: Salick buys back the dialysis clinics from Damon and incorporates as Salick Health Care, Inc.
1985: The company goes public and opens its first comprehensive cancer clinic.
1995: British drug company Zeneca PLC buys 50 percent of Salick.
1997: Zeneca completes its buyout of Salick.
1999: Parent company Zeneca merges with Astra to form AstraZeneca.

out the area. Then in 1997, its half-owner, Zeneca, bought up the other 50 percent of the company it did not already own. Zeneca had had the option to buy the rest of the company within two and a half years from when it purchased half the company in 1995, but it moved up the time frame and made the purchase sooner than expected. It spent $234 million for Salick, which had revenue of $163.5 million for 1996. Though Bernard Salick had an employment contract which was to run for two more years, Zeneca removed him as chairman and CEO. Salick quit rather than take the position of chairman emeritus, and he immediately started a competing firm of cancer and AIDS clinics, Bentley Health Care. Zeneca was by 1997 the number two maker of cancer drugs worldwide, and its sole ownership of a chain of cancer clinics sent up cries of conflict of interest. The company insisted that the data the Salick clinics provided was its most valuable asset and reiterated that it would never pressure doctors to prescribe Zeneca drugs. Under new leadership, the firm continued to make inroads into the New York market, in 1998 forging an alliance with the University Medical Center in Stony Brook, New York, to run its oncology department. Salick also sold off its dialysis clinics and closed several of its cancer centers, including its long-standing one in Philadelphia.

In 1999, Zeneca merged with the Swedish pharmaceuticals company Astra. The new company, now called AstraZeneca PLC, ranked as the fifth-largest drug company in the world. The company was still a leading cancer drug maker, with one of its best known products the breast cancer fighter tamoxifen. The goal of the newly combined company was to become the number one anti-cancer company in the world, developing and marketing cutting edge treatments of all sorts. With the backing of its powerful parent, Salick poured money into its computer and information systems, investing over $20 million between 1999 and 2001 on upgrades. By 2002, the chain consisted of eight comprehensive cancer clinics. The company ran three clinics in Florida, two in New York City, two in the Los Angeles area, and one more in Berkeley, California.

Principal Competitors

Memorial Sloan-Kettering Cancer Center; US Oncology Inc.; Albert Einstein Cancer Center.

Further Reading

Barrier, Michael, "Doing Good, Getting Well," *Nation's Business*, August 1989, pp. 50–3.

Bianco, Anthony, "Bernie Salick's Business Is Cancer," *Business Week*, June 22, 1998, pp. 76–84.

"British Firm Acquires Rest of Salick Health Care Inc.," *Wall Street Journal*, March 28, 1997, p. B4.

Goldberg, Carol, "Outsource Deal at Stony Brook," *Long Island Business News*, August 31, 1998, p. 1A.

Lagnado, Lucette, "Planned New York Center Sends Shivers through Competitors," *Wall Street Journal*, August 12, 1996, pp. B1–2.

Marcial, Gene G., "These Small-Cap Plums Are Ripe for Plucking," *Business Week*, October 3, 1994, p. 116.

Pallarito, Karen, "Salick Bought Out," *Modern Healthcare*, April 21, 1997, p. 20.

Rice, Trudy Thompson, "The King of Cancer," *Hospitals & Health Networks*, March 5, 1997, p. 34.

Rosenthal, Elisabeth, "Maker of Cancer Drugs to Oversee Prescriptions at 11 Cancer Clinics," *New York Times*, April 15, 1997, pp. A1, D4.

Rundle, Rhonda L., "Salick Pioneers Selling Cancer Care to HMOs," *Wall Street Journal*, August 12, 1996, pp. B1–B2.

"Salick's Salve," *Economist*, July 23, 1994, p. 62.

"Tom McKillop; AstraZeneca," *Business Week*, January 8, 2001, p. 71.

Winslow, Ron, "Zeneca Sets Purchase of 50% of Salick for $195 Million; Treatment Data Cited," *Wall Street Journal*, December 23, 1994, p. B5.

"Zeneca to Complete Buyout of Salick," *Modern Healthcare*, March 31, 1997, p. 7.

—A. Woodward

Samuel Cabot Inc.

100 Hale Street
Newburyport, Massachusetts 01950-3504
U.S.A.
Telephone: (978) 465-1900
Fax: (978) 462-0511
Web site: http://www.cabotstain.com

Private Company
Founded: 1887
Employees: 100
Sales: $50 million (2001 est.)
NAIC: 325510 Paint and Coating Manufacturing; 325612
   Polish and Other Sanitation Good Manufacturing

Samuel Cabot Inc. makes wood stains and surface preparation products, mostly for exterior use. The company's product line features cleaners, primers, strippers, varnishes, stains, and waterproofing. It also offers specialized products for decking, siding, and interiors.

19th-Century Origins

In 1877 a 27-year-old chemist, Samuel Cabot, a graduate of both the fledgling Massachusetts Institute of Technology (MIT) and Switzerland's Zurich Polytechnicum, started his own coal-tar dye business in Chelsea, Massachusetts. By saturating felt paper with coal tar imbedded with gravel, the Cabot business made tarpaper, a construction staple at the time. Tarpaper kept flat roofs tight, and flat roofs made for more efficient building. With his business partner, Frederick Nourse, Cabot later focused on the manufacture of fine calcined lampblack. Residual soot accumulated from the burning of oil distilled from coal tar, lampblack had commercial applications including printer's ink, shoe polish, and stove polish. In the fall of 1878 Nourse left the partnership.

Cabot thrived on his chemical curiosity, conducting research to improve existing products and invent new ones. His notebooks contained hints of products that would come many years later. In 1882 an architect uncle asked Cabot if he could develop a product that would preserve shingles from the ever-changing New England weather without hiding the wood's grain. Soon Cabot had developed a formula for creosote stain, which may have been the first preservative stain for exterior wood and was certainly a breakthrough product. By 1884 Cabot's Creosote Shingle Stain was used throughout New England and beyond. The product would go on to become a standard throughout the country due to its combination of durability and preservation.

Around the same time Cabot's father, a doctor, suggested he develop a disinfectant. Samuel created a coal tar disinfectant that became a well-known household product called Cabot's Sylpho-Napthol. Later he developed Cabot's Clear Brick Waterproofing and many other products.

Cabot's business expansion included mineral exploration in western Pennsylvania. He established a carbon black plant there, putting his brother, Godfrey Lowell Cabot, in charge. Later Cabot sold the business to his brother, and by World War I Godfrey L. Cabot, Inc.(later called Cabot Corporation) dwarfed Cabot's own Boston and Chelsea operation, mainly because carbon black became an important ingredient in the vulcanized rubber on America's growing fleet of automobiles.

Believing everything had a useful purpose, Cabot was initially stumped by eelgrass. No one on the Massachusetts shore could think of a use for eelgrass, which got in the way of boats and swimmers, resulting in huge ugly piles of the stuff on the beach. Soon Cabot learned that early settlers had used eelgrass as a crude home insulation. In the summer of 1893 he created a prototype insulation with layers of eelgrass stitched between sheets of heavy paper. The product, Cabot's Quilt, quickly found an eager market and became one of the company's primary products until the mid-1940s.

Cabot caught pneumonia and died suddenly in November of 1906. His 22-year-old son, Samuel Cabot II, took over the business in 1910 after completing graduate studies in chemistry at MIT. On May 13, 1907 the company was incorporated as Samuel Cabot Inc. Disaster struck April 12, 1908, however, when a fire destroyed more than 17 miles of Chelsea streets. Although the Cabot property was a total loss, public and private money poured in and the city was in better shape three years later than it had been before the fire.

Cabot II and Collopaking in 1922

Cabot II's most significant technological contribution to the company was a pigment-grinding process he called collopaking. He patented the process in 1922 and trademarked a family of heavy-bodied stains under the name Cabot's Collopakes. The product had the preservation quality of stain, but also provided the rich covering color of paint.

By 1930 the company had developed a gloss collopake for doors, shutters, and trim. At the same time, the company boasted a range of other products, including lubricating oils, wood putties, wood preservatives, brick and cement waterproofing products, and interior stains.

Collopaking led to the development of Old Virginia Tints, a product line sold with the tagline, "covers like a paint and performs like a stain." This product would remain one of the company's best sellers into the year 2000.

The same technology that produced Old Virginia Tints produced the first titanium-based white house paint, Double-White. This innovation was nearly twice as heavy as other white paints because collopaking allowed for the suspension of a disproportionate amount of finely ground titanium. The company showcased the product after it was used to paint Colonial Williamsburg in Virginia.

Expansion Under Cabot III

Born in 1910, Samuel Cabot III joined the company after graduating from Harvard in 1933. His father actually helped force his involvement in the family business by limiting his son's funding. With the Great Depression on, jobs were scarce, and Cabot III had little choice but to follow his father's footsteps. By the onset of World War II, Cabot III was working as company sales manager and treasurer.

Into the 1940s many of Cabot's main sellers were close kin to products from the company's earliest days. Old products, such as Lampblack, Beehive Pitch, and Cabot's Quilt, continued to bring in major revenue. During World War II, while Cabot III served in the Army Air Corps, Cabot II developed new products. He and his associates created Klengon, a hand cleaner. His black-out paint, used to darken windows to reduce their visibility to German war planes, was mainly sold to U.S. government agencies. In October 1944 Cabot II won a patent on "a method of reducing the visibility of an object when seen against the sky, water or distant background." Total company sales increased every year from 1942 through 1954.

Credit Cabot III for expanding Cabot internationally. He developed considerable business in West Germany and Australia. The company partnered with the Australian firm Kenneth H. Brock & Son Pty. Ltd. (Kenbrock) in 1960. Australian architects used Cabot Stains on red cedar timber imported from Canada and the United States. By 1970, concentrates of all Cabot products were imported to the Kenbrock plant where they were then diluted and canned. By 2000 Cabot would control more than half of the Australian wood care market and sold more stains per capita in Australia than anywhere else.

In 1960 Samuel Cabot Inc. was still a small company, partially because Cabot II had not reinvested profits into the company. Moreover, the company spent little on advertising and marketing outside of New England. Two years earlier, in 1958, Weyerhauser Corporation had purchased Olympic Stains, and soon Olympic surpassed Cabot as the number one selling stain. Believing that Cabot needed a merger to remain competitive, Cabot III inked a deal to sell the company to the O'Brien Company of South Bend, Indiana. However, his father and the company board negated the deal.

Cabot IV in the 1970s–80s

Samuel Cabot IV, born in 1940, took an active position in the company at age 29. His grandfather had died two years earlier, his father was closing in on retirement, and he wanted to serve under his father to learn the business. His early decision to have the company convert to the world standard metric system ended up costing the company when the U.S. move to metrics died. However, he did succeed in installing Cabot's first generation of computers, an IBM System 3.

Cabot IV officially took over in 1977 when the company's annual sales were $3 million and the growth rate was near zero. He promptly hired a new management team that included Tony Faria as vice-president of sales. Faria developed a two-step distribution system in which Cabot forged relationships with independent sales representatives who then re-sold Cabot products to retailers. The new system produced cost-savings by eliminating the need for warehouses.

In the late 1970s the company began limiting its product line and concentrating on its strength: architectural stains. A study of the firm revealed the stains were the only Cabot product that sold in high volume with reasonable profitability. The timing proved fortuitous. Samuel Cabot Inc. focused on stains just as the U.S. market dramatically increased its interest in building with natural materials, particularly often wood.

Later, another internal business analysis concluded that company growth was restricted by the limited product line. In response, Cabot introduced wood cleaners, wood brighteners, primers, strippers, and a flagship product called The Finish, a high-tech paint containing Teflon.

A growing U.S. economy, especially in the construction business, helped lead the business to significant growth in the 1980s. Cabot also created a marketing tool that gathered wide attention. The company published a calendar featuring historic structures that had been treated with Cabot products. The calendars showcased landmarks such as the Paul Revere House, the mission at San Juan Capistrano, the John F. Kennedy Staten

Key Dates:

1877: Samuel Cabot starts a coal-tar dye business.
1882: Cabot develops a creosote stain to preserve wood shingles.
1907: The company is incorporated.
1910: Founder's son, Samuel Cabot II, becomes president.
1922: Cabot II patents the collopaking process.
1942: Sales begin a 12-year annual increase.
1960: Cabot III oversees international expansion, particularly in West Germany and Australia.
1977: Cabot IV becomes company president.
1985: The company launches its first major advertising campaign and builds a new $9 million Newburyport plant.
2000: John Schutz is named president, making him the first non-Cabot to hold that position; Cabot IV remains as chairman.
2001: Company reaches $50 million in annual sales.

Island ferryboat, and buildings at the Baseball Hall of Fame's Doubleday Field. In 1985 Cabot launched its first major advertising campaign, hiring Ingalls, Quinn & Johnson and spending about $700,000 on national media.

The growth of the 1980s enabled Cabot to move out of its deteriorating Chelsea plant and build a new facility in Newburyport, Massachusetts. After more than 100 years in a Chelsea plant, Cabot built a $9 million facility on Hale Street in 1985. The 100,000 square foot factory was the second largest one-story plant ever built in Newburyport. Computers controlled most of the plant's processing, as well as its stock records, shipping, and receiving. Cabot called the factory a model of safety with "explosion proof" electrical equipment, tanks with special flame arrestors, and an air system that changed the air six times an hour in the plant mixing area. Slightly smaller than the former plant in Chelsea, the Newburyport plant doubled the company's production capacity.

Late 1980s Rough Spot

Revenues, which grew steadily throughout most of the 1980s stumbled in 1989 and 1990. The U.S. economy grew soft. Cabot overspent by offering distributors and dealers a costly sales incentive—an all-expenses-paid Caribbean cruise. The market became overstocked with Cabot products, reducing sales until inventories returned to normal levels. Cabot IV also decided to maintain loyalty to independent paint stores and not pursue sales with such home improvement chain stores as Home Depot and Wal-Mart. All these factors contributed to the downturn. The firm avoided layoffs, but trimmed salaries and benefits over a four-year period.

As chain stores drew more market share, the surviving independent retailers began dropping nationally branded stock that could easily be found at the discount chains. To distinguish themselves, the independent retailers stocked independent brands like Cabot, and the company began to experience revenue growth once more. Vice-President of Sales John Schutz stretched Cabot's definition of independents to include the large co-ops, groups of independent retailers who joined together for buying and marketing clout. Cabot's market was especially enhanced by serving the two largest co-ops, True Value (9,000 independent store members) and ACE (6,500 independents).

The 1990s also brought another round of international expansion. Cabot's Australian partner, Orica, began distributing products in New Zealand, New Guinea, and Fiji. Samuel Cabot Inc. signed a license agreement with Chilcorrofin, a Chilean firm in 1996. Berger Paints, a global coatings company, began marketing Cabot products in the Caribbean late that decade.

Mid-1990s and Beyond

In 1994 Schutz's drive to bypass the company's traditional distributor pipeline and offer direct prices to retailers backfired when its largest distributor, a company that brought in 20 percent of Cabot's sales, announced it was dropping the Cabot line. It took a week of serious talks before Schutz succeeded in convincing the distributor to reinstate the line. In February 2000 Cabot promoted Schutz to president, making him the first non-Cabot family member to hold that position.

New products and greater market penetration produced a doubling of company revenues during the last five years of the 20th century. During the time period 1993–2000, the private company reported that its revenues were increasing "at an impressive annual rate." Under the leadership of Cabot IV, the company grew to 12 times its 1975 size, and was an industry leader in the development, manufacture, and distribution of premium-quality interior and exterior wood care products. Samuel Cabot Inc. reached $1.5 billion in annual sales in 2001.

Principal Competitors

Benjamin Moore & Co.; PPG Industries Inc.; The Sherwin-Williams Company; McCormick Paint Works Co.

Further Reading

"Cabot Follows Alternate Path to Growth," *Chemical Market Reporter*, February 19, 2001, p. 9.

Maty, Joe, "The Centenarians," *Paint & Coatings Industry*, January 2000.

McClure, Andrew, "Dukakis Dedicates Cabot Plant," *Newburyport Daily News*, October 10, 1985, p. A13.

——, "Efficiency a Key Ingredient at Newburyport Stain Plant," *Newburyport Daily News*, December 4, 1985, p. D1.

Samuel Cabot Inc.: Quality and Continuity Since 1877, Newburyport, Mass.: Memoirs Unlimited, 2001

Stott, Peter, H., *Samuel Cabot Company*, Boston: Massachusetts Historical Commission, May 1983.

—Chris Amorosino

Schott Corporation

3 Odell Plaza
Yonkers, New York 10701-1405
U.S.A.
Telephone: (914) 968-1400
Fax: (914) 968-4422
Web site: http://www.us.schott.com

Wholly Owned Subsidiary of Schott Glas
Incorporated: 1986
Employees: 3,200
Sales: $400 million (2001 est.)
NAIC: 327210 Glass and Glass Product Manufacturing

Schott Corporation, with its headquarters in Yonkers, New York, is the holding company for the North American subsidiaries of the major German glass manufacturer Schott Glas. Schott Corporation is comprised of 16 divisions—with subsidiaries in the United States, Canada, and Mexico—employing some 3,200 people. It manufactures and distributes specialty glass and glass-related systems for use in electronics, energy, lighting, architecture, home appliances, optics, pharmaceutical, packaging, and transportation, and automotive applications. The North American market contributes 30 percent of the parent corporation's worldwide revenues.

Otto Schott, 19th Century Glass Pioneer

The Schott Corporation derives its name from Otto Schott, who was born in Witten, Germany, in 1851 into a family of glassmakers. His father was a master in the craft of making window glass and became co-owner of a Wastphalia glassworks shortly after the birth of his son. Young Schott was fascinated by the properties of glass and devoted his education to it, eventually earning a doctorate for his study on defects in window glass manufacturing. In 1877, he opened an iodine and saltpeter factory in Spain, where he carried on a number of experiments involving glass-making techniques. Schott gained a place in history by applying scientific principles to the age-old craft of glassmaking and establishing it as a modern technology. He learned that lithium-based glass was especially useful in the production of lenses and in 1879 shared some of his samples

with acclaimed mathematician and physicist Ernst Abbe, who was eagerly searching for glass with better, more consistent optical qualities in order to develop more sophisticated microscopes. At that time, Abbe was dependent on imports from French and British firms.

Abbe had become involved in the manufacture of microscopes when he went to work for German industrialist Dr. Carl Freidrick Zeiss in 1866. Twenty years earlier, Zeiss had opened a workshop to produce optical instruments, including simple microscopes. He made advances in microscopes, introducing the first compound microscope in 1857, and soon gained an international reputation for the quality of his instruments. Believing that in order to make further advances in optical equipment general advances in optical theory would also have to be made, Zeiss hired Abbe, a 26-year-old lecturer at the University of Jena, to serve as a freelance researcher. Within a short time, Abbe became research director of the Zeiss optical works, and within two years invented the apochromatic lens system for the microscope. Abbe's research also established the theory of refraction of light, key to designing precise optical instruments. In 1872, he produced the first microscope built in accordance with scientific principles, ending the days of trial and error experimentation in the industry. By 1875, he became Zeiss' partner, the same year that Schott earned his doctorate from the University of Jena, which was by now a major center for the study of optics. What frustrated Abbe in his research was the inferior optical glass with which he had to work. It would be Schott's contributions in glassmaking that would be the final step in launching the modern era of precise optical instruments.

Otto Schott Opens Glassworks in 1882

After corresponding for some time, Abbe and Schott finally met in 1881 and began working closely together. In 1882, Schott moved to a new glassmaking laboratory located in Jena. Zeiss and Abbe, along with the Prussian state government, were his chief financial backers. Within two years, Schott created new, marketable apochromatic lenses and by 1893 developed borosilicate glass, which was highly resistant to heat and suitable for use in thermometers, laboratory glassware, pharmaceutical tubing, and heat resistant cylinders used in incandescent gas lamps. The demand for the lighting products proved so great that the laboratory was quickly transformed into a full-fledged glassworks. For Zeiss, Schott's improved optical glass meant that his workshop turned into a industrial powerhouse. After Zeiss died in 1888, Abbe became the sole owner of the business and created the Carl Zeiss Foundation in order to fund scientific research as well as share the fruits of the business with employees. Both Zeiss' son Roderich and Abbe turned over their shares of the glassworks to the foundation, and Schott pledged to do the same upon his death. With the rise of socialism after World War I, he transferred his share of the company immediately, although he lived until 1935. With mutual Foundation ownership, the Schott and Zweiss enterprises were linked not only financially and managerially, but their competitive edge was very much dependent on scientific cooperation as well.

The Schott Glassworks grew into an international business, and by the start of the 20th century more than half of its revenues came from imports. By World War I, the company was recognized as the most advanced maker of optical glass in the world. Because it was so expensive to produce, however, optical glass was not highly profitable, leading Schott to also manufacture mass-produced household and laboratory glass products. Up until World War I, the most profitable item, accounting for three-quarters of all revenues, was a gas bulb used in miners' lamps. Not only did the war disrupt the export business, after the cessation of hostilities Schott Glassworks found that many of its erstwhile trading partners resented doing business with a German company and opted instead to rely on lesser quality wares from domestic firms that had cropped up to fill the gap during the war years. Trade restrictions on Germany also proved problematic, and a conversion from gas to electric lamps hurt the company's sale of glass bulbs. Schott Glassworks recovered along with the German economy in the 1920s, with Otto Schott's son Erick assuming control in 1927, but business again fell off with the advent of the Great Depression in 1929.

Schott Glassworks began to rebound in the 1930s, a period during which Adolph Hitler and the Nazi party came to power. The dictatorship was determined to rearm, in violation of the peace treaty that ended World War I, and the glassworks could not avoid becoming part of the Nazi war machine. Its products were deemed indispensable by the military. As a consequence, the glassworks became an allied target during World War II, although it was only late in the war that it suffered serious damage from bombers. With Germany defeated, the Schott Glassworks faced an uncertain future. In April 1945, both it and Zeiss were placed under the command of U.S. Air Force officers. The glassworks, possessing superior technological expertise, attracted a number of Allied experts, including commercial interests. Relations between the United States and Britain with the Soviet Union were already strained, and because both the glassworks and Zeiss were located within the Soviet sphere of influence in Germany, the U.S. military made plans for a partial relocation of the companies in what would become West Germany. Due to an agreement between the victorious powers, however, the Americans were hesitant to remove equipment from the glassworks. Pressed for time, they instead initiated an "intellectual dismantling program." A list of 50 key scientists, technicians, and specialists was drawn up. Although most of the Schott employees were relieved to avoid Soviet occupation, nine of them did not wish to leave their homes and friends. The relocation trip became known in company lore as the "Odyssey of 41 Glassmakers."

Despite their lack of equipment, which had to be left behind in East Germany, and the difficulties in procuring raw materials, the Schott employees, led by Erich Schott, soon began to build a plant in the town of Zwiesel. In Jena, in the meantime, the old glassworks was placed under the control of the Soviet Army, which proceeded to dismantle the plant (and conscript 17 specialists for five-year terms) and shipped it to the USSR to set up production there. The remaining Jena employees managed to restore operations at the old plant, but instead of ownership returning to the Carl Zeiss Foundation, the business was expropriated by the regional government in 1948. As was the case with Germany as a whole, the glass company founded by Otto Schott was now divided by an "iron curtain." For the next several decades, both companies exploited the Schott name, often to the confusion of consumers. In the West, the Schott Group, under Erich Schott's leadership, built new, state-of-the art facilities in the city of Mainz by the early 1950s. In order to return to profitability and once again grow the business, the company manufactured parts for glass television picture tubes. Later in the 1950s, the Schott Group began producing baby bottles, tea glasses, and mugs. It also found new customers in the United States, not only for consumer goods, which would soon include glass-ceramic baking dishes, but also for its original specialty, optical glass, which found applications in the new space program.

In August 1963, the company opened a sales office in New York City in what was then called the Pan Am Building (now the Met Life Building). In 1967, the Schott Group established Schott Glass Technologies, its first manufacturing subsidiary outside of Germany, and two years later opened a 41,000-square-foot plant in Duryea, Pennsylvania, with 55 employees producing precision optical glass to be made into lenses, mirrors, prisms, and windows that could then be utilized in such equipment as cameras, photocopiers, and range finders. The subsidiary became involved in the prescription eyeglass and sunglass market in 1970 when it acquired the Ophthalmic Glass Division of PPG Industries. Business grew steadily, resulting in a major expansion in production, warehousing, and administrative space. With new facilities, Schott Glass Technologies was able to move beyond the manufacture of raw glass and enter specialty optical markets, including color filters, contrast enhancement filters, and CRT faceplates. In 1981, the subsidiary became involved in the glass ceramic and high energy laser glass sectors. It also opened a major development laboratory to foster further diversification efforts.

Schott Corporation Established in 1986

Having outgrown its sales office in the Pan Am Building, as well as needing more warehouse space for its North America business, in 1982 Schott Group opened a facility on a dozen acres of land it purchased in Yonkers, located just north of the Bronx. To better organize its growing North American interests, Schott Group then formed Schott Corp. in 1986, the headquar-

Key Dates:

1882: Otto Schott forms German glassworks.
1945: Schott Glassworks is divided following World War II.
1963: Schott Group opens a New York sales office.
1967: The company's first U.S. manufacturing subsidiary formed.
1982: Schott's sales office is moved to Yonkers, New York, site.
1986: The holding company Schott Corporation is formed.
1989: Canadian and Mexican subsidiaries of Schott are formed.
1995: German Schott companies are reunited.

ters of the holding company located in the Yonkers site. Its growing assets soon included operations outside the United States. In 1989, Schott Canada Inc. was established in Toronto to produce a wide range of products, from consumer goods to specialty optical products. In that same year, Schott Mexicana S.A. de C.V. opened in Mexico City, offering a similar product line to its Canadian counterpart. To accommodate continued growth, Schott Corp. expanded its corporate headquarters in 1991. By now, the holding company controlled three distribution and six production companies. Most of the focus was on the eastern markets of the United States and Canada, but management also began to target the western portion of the continent, opening a regional office in Los Angeles to gain a toehold on the Pacific Coast. Furthermore, the company took steps to begin selling products that Schott Group had been marketing in Europe for the past few years.

The structure of Schott Corp. underwent an ongoing evolution in the 1990s. Two subsidiaries, Schott America Glass & Scientific Products, Inc. and Schott Zwiesel Glass, Inc., were merged into Schott Corp., with the former becoming the Technical Glass Division and the latter the Consumer Glass Division. The Technical Glass Division would supply specialty glass for science and industry, while the Consumer Glass Division was responsible for the production and marketing of Schott Cristal glassware to both the household and institutional markets. In 1992, Schott Corp. formed a joint venture with the West Company to produce packaging products made out of specialty glass for use by the pharmaceutical industry. The enterprise, located in Puerto Rico, was originally the New Jersey-based O'Sullivan Glass Company, founded in 1945. Schott Corp. bought out West in 1995 and renamed the operation Schott Pharmaceutical Packaging Incorporated. Prior to the buyout, Schott Corp. had acquired from the West Company Tri/West Systems Inc., developers of a patented system for producing syringes with pre-filled dosages.

In 1994, Schott Corporation purchased a glass tubing plant located in Parkersburg, West Virginia, from Corning Inc. The facility produced scientific glassware and tubing, and began operating as a subsidiary, Schott Scientific Glass, Inc. In 1996, Schott Corp. added to its holdings Schott Gas Systems, Inc., dedicated to the development and manufacture of high tech burner media and gas burners, used in such applications as glass-ceramic gas cooktops, firelogs, space heaters, and dryers,

as well as in industrial heating systems. In 1997, Schott formed a joint venture with Chicago Miniature Lamp Inc., called Schott-CML Fiberoptics Inc., to complement its other fiber-optic production unit, Schott Fiber Optics Inc., located in Southbridge, Massachusetts. The Southbridge operation would soon take on the sales responsibilities for Schott Corp.'s entry into the automobile air bag equipment business, following the holding company's 1998 acquisition of the glass header business from Colorado-based Coors Ceramics Co. In that same year, Schott Corp. acquired Baron Industries, a Georgia company that produced gaskets and seals for ranges, ovens, and other consumer appliances. To take advantage of the robust data/communications technology sector, Schott Corp. launched a start-up business in 2000 called Schott Communications Technologies Inc. The focus was on producing high-capacity optical interconnects to replace copper wires in short-distance data transfer. With the demand for broadband increasing, the need for such high performance optical products was projected to enjoy significant growth in the coming years.

While Schott expanded in North America, the parent corporation experienced a noteworthy change. In 1980, the competing Schott entities in a divided Germany signed "divorce" papers, with the Schott Group gaining the rights to the "Schott" trademark and the East Germans securing the "Jena Glass" trademark. The split appeared permanent but with the sudden collapse of the Soviet Union later in the decade and the reunification of Germany in 1990, negotiations commenced to reunite the company founded by Otto Schott as well as the Carl Zeiss Foundation. The transaction was complicated but finally, on January 1, 1995, the Jena operation was fully integrated into the Schott Group. The company, already a major player on the international stage, was now even more formidable. Clearly, a major factor in its future growth would hinge on the success of its North American business, coordinated under its Yonkers subsidiary, Schott Corp.

Principal Subsidiaries

Baron Industries Corporation; Schott Scientific Glass, Inc.; Schott Lithotec USA Corporation; Schott Applied Power Corporation; Gemtron Corporation.

Principal Divisions

Technical Glass Division; Schott Home Tech North America; Schott Canada; Schott Fiber Optics; Schott Glass Technologies; Schott Pharmaceutical Packaging; Schott Fostec; Schott Gas Systems; Schott Electronic Packaging.

Principal Competitors

Corning Inc.; Pilkington plc.

Further Reading

Hagen, Antje, "Export Verus Direct Investment in the German Optical Industry," *Business History*, October 1996, p. 1.
From Jena to Mainz—and Back Again, Schott Group, 2000, 27 p.
"Schott Hoists Flag on U.S. Headquarters," *HFD*, November 25, 1991, p. 88.

—Ed Dinger

Selectour SA

6, rue Laferrière
75311 Paris Cedex 09
France
Telephone: (+33) 1 55 07 12 10
Fax: (+33) 1 55 07 12 11
Web site: http://www.selectour.com

Cooperative
Incorporated: 1970
Employees: 1,400
Sales: EUR 1.28 billion ($1.2 billion)(2001)
NAIC: 561510 Travel Agencies; 561520 Tour Operators

Selectour SA is France's leading network of independent travel agencies. The cooperative company groups more than 400 travel agents and 520 agency offices throughout France, producing a total ticketing sales volume of more than EUR 1.28 billion ($1.2 billion) in 2001. Selectour enables independent travel agents to compete against large-scale tourist groups by offering combined purchasing power and extensive support services. Through Selectour, member agencies gain access to a nationally developed marketing and communications program, which includes the publication of market-specific Selectour advertising brochures (such as the "ten lowest-priced vacations", and special "Honeymoon", "European Capitals," and "Seniors" packages). Selectour customers receive company-backed trip cancellation insurance as well as other travel insurance benefits. Selectour also takes charge selecting and negotiating pricing with tour and travel operators, hotels, airlines and car rental companies, enabling the Selectour network to offer high-quality packages at low prices. Since 1999, Selectour has operated in partnership with hotel and vacation resort giant Accor, a partnership that expanded at the end of 2002 with the inclusion of Globalia, the second-largest travel agent network in Spain. Selectour is led by founder and CEO Philippe Demonchy.

Grouping for Strength in the 1970s

Philippe Demonchy operated his own travel agency in Paris in the late 1960s. The French travel and tourism industry was then undergoing a transition. The arrival of jet airplanes, and especially the shift towards larger planes such as the 747, enabled holiday-makers to travel farther in less time, sparking interest in long-distance vacations. The development of the first electronic communications networks, pioneered by SITA in Europe, had set the stage for new ticketing capabilities. At the same time, the French industry saw the rise of a number of powerful tour and travel groups, such as Club Med, Havas, Nouvelles Frontieres and the like.

Demonchy recognized the vulnerability of the independent travel agent confronted by the changing market. In 1970, he launched a new cooperative society, Selectour, with the aim of grouping independent travel agents under a common banner. The group provided its members with greater purchasing power and other advantages, such as the development of tour packages and a shared brand name backed by full-scale marketing efforts. The Selectour network offered advantages to consumers as well, particularly with the institution of the group's cancellation insurance, which enabled customers to receive full refunds, with Selectour absorbing cancellation charges. As the network grew, Selectour also began holding an annual congress, where Demonchy and Selectour management met with Selectour members to discuss the current travel market and prepare for the future. The first annual congress was held in 1978.

Demonchy's idea caught on quickly. Starting with just ten member agencies, Selectour grew rapidly through the 1970s and into the 1980s. By the middle of that decade, Selectour counted more than 200 members and more than 300 agency locations. During that time, Demonchy and Selectour continued to refine the cooperative association's offering, developing a "test" in the form of a game that helped clarify customers' vacation and travel needs, thereby enabling travel agents to prepare packages better suited to customers' needs. Another initiative taken by Selectour was the preparation of video cassettes, which agencies could lend to their customers. Selectour also developed its own holiday insurance packages and took charge of meeting customer complaints.

Business travel was another important area of the cooperative's operation. In support of this market, Selectour developed a "business kiosque" for its member agencies, enabling agencies to take over the entire travel needs of small, mid-sized, and large-scale corporations. The cooperative's ability to buy in bulk gave

Company Perspectives:

To better understand the needs of consumers, it is necessary to put oneself in their place!

Selectour has also based its approach on this fundamental idea. This has enabled the network to anticipate in order to adapt to the needs of its clientele.

member agents access to competitive pricing, an advantage heightened by the creation of the "Club Selectour Affaires," which grouped together the 75 member agencies with the largest business sector activity. The strength of this sub-network enabled Selectour members to compete against the pricing advantages of larger travel groups. At the same time, the independent, entrepreneurial nature of Selectour members proved an attractive feature for many small and mid-sized businesses.

By 1981, the Selectour network accounted for more than FFr2 billion (EUR 300 million) in sales per year. Ticket sales accounted for the nearly 80 percent of Selectour's sales, with just 22 percent represented by tour package purchases. The group saw steady gains through the decade, topping FFr 3.2 billion (EUR 470 million) in 1985 and FFr 4 billion (EUR 600 million) by 1987. By the end of the decade, the Selectour network boasted total revenues of more than FFr 4.2 billion and 320 agencies, making it the third-largest travel group in France.

Yet at the end of the 1980s, the French travel market was changing again, as a number of key players in the industry began a series of mergers. Such was the case with Club Med and Nouvelles Frontieres, as well as with Havas and Wagon Lits. Meanwhile, government-owned Air France, the dominant airline in the French market, had teamed up with Frantour, the tourism arm of French railway agency SNCF, and with tourism group FRAM in early 1989.

By the middle of that year, Selectour moved to join the trend, announcing its own partnership with Air France. The agreement called for the two groups to cooperate on a number of sales initiatives, while Selectour agreed to sign on to the new Amadeus communications network set up by Air France, Lufthansa, SAS, and Iberia. An important feature of the agreement with Air France was the creation of a new company, Selectour Investissement. Held at 76 percent by Selectour, the new company was set up in order to help solve a growing problem for the cooperative: a number of its members were approaching retirement age, many without any successors in place. Selectour Investissement's role was to acquire the agencies of retiring members or to help finance their transition to new member owners. Selectour Investissement was to play an important role in maintaining the coherence of the Selectour grouping over the long term.

Facing New Market Conditions in the 1990s

With the shakeup of the international tourism market in the early 1990s, hit hard by a lingering recession and by plunging travel rates during the Persian Gulf War crisis, competition tightened, making survival for an independent travel agent still more difficult. In France, Selectour's network, which topped 325 agents and nearly 400 agencies by the middle of the 1990s,

faced growing competition from a number of other networks, including Via Voyages, Protravel, and Manor, as well as from the three largest tourism groups operating in the country, namely Havas, Wagon Lit, and American Express.

Selectour managed to keep ahead of the competition. One move that helped the cooperative preserve its competitive edge was its participation in the Woodside Travel Trust, later to become the Radius group, which recreated on a global scale what Selectour had constructed in France. Woodside represented the grouping of some 175 travel agency networks, operating in a total of 53 countries with nearly 3,500 offices and total revenues of some $17 billion. Selectour's membership in the Woodside network not only gave it access to its bulk purchasing advantages but also gave it an edge in winning orders from multinational businesses seeking travel arrangements in France.

With sales of nearly FFr 5 billion (EUR 750 million), Selectour faced new challenges in the middle of the 1990s. For one, more and more of the company's tour package suppliers were opening their own agencies in a move to become integrated organizations. In response, Selectour began developing new travel products, including its own Selectour-branded tour packages, drafted in partnership with third-party tourism groups. In 1995, the cooperative also restructured its commercial offering, separating its operations into two major areas—Selectour Express, for its ticket sales, and Selectour Expert, which took over the company's value-added operations, including business travel, high-end travel, and other services requiring agent assistance.

Selectour also launched a new series of brochures grouping its offerings according to theme, such as "ten lowest prices" or "Immediate Departure," which were joined in 1996 by a new brochure of packages targeting the domestic destinations and a brochure directed specifically at the seniors market. At the same time, the company was also responding to a new market threat, that of online sales. In 1996, Selectour began offering ticket sales through the French online network Minitel. The group also launched its own Web site that year, which provided information on the group's offerings and directed potential customers to the nearest Selectour agent.

Strategic Alliances in the New Century

Selectour moved to counter another growing threat in the late 1990s, as France's large retail groups began rolling out their own travel services. In 1997, the company reached an agreement with the Continent retail group to place Selectour agencies in Continent supermarkets. On another front, business travel had grown to become an important segment of Selectour's operations, representing some two-thirds of its sales—by then, the cooperative's total revenues had topped FFr 6.3 billion (EUR 960 million). Yet the travel market in general, and the business travel market in particular, was undergoing a rapid consolidation. The European travel industry was transforming from largely separate domestic markets into an increasingly cross-continental market.

Faced with competition from a number of larger players—including such recent pairings as Havas and Amex, Jet Tours and Club Med, and Carlson and Wagonlit—Selectour announced its

Key Dates:

1970: Philippe Demonchy founds a cooperative in order to group together independent travel agents under a common banner, Selectour.

1985: Selectour's network grows to nearly 300 agencies and sales of more than FFr2 billion (EUR 300 million)

1989: Selectour forms a partnership with Air France and creates a subsidiary, Selectour Investissements, to ensure the solidity of the agency's network.

1995: Selectour separates its products into two categories, Selectour Express and Selectour Expert.

1996: The company launches a group Web site; a series of catalogs is also launched to target specific market segments.

1999: The company forms a partnership with Accor, which also takes a 50 percent stake in Selectour Investissements.

2002: Spain's Globalia joins partnership with Accor, which is renamed "Alliance de Sud."

intention to pursue its own "technical alliance," a strategy meant to preserve the cooperative's independent status while giving it the size to compete against the new travel heavyweights. The move was all the more needed because Air France had recently exited the Selectour Investissement partnership.

Selectour found its partner at the end of 1999, announcing its partnership agreement with French hotel giant Accor and its Carlson Wagonlit subsidiary. The alliance, which preserved both networks' independence, nonetheless created a common network worth more than EUR 2 billion. (Selectour's own sales had grown to EUR 1.1 billion by the end of 1999). As part of the agreement, Accor also acquired a 50 percent stake in Selectour Investissement.

The partnership with Accor immediately proved successful on both sides—Accor itself registered a 43 percent sales growth over the first year of the partnership, while Selectour's own revenues grew 12 percent, topping EUR 1.4 billion in 2000. By this time, Selectour had recognized a new trend in the French tourism market. Whereas previously a typical French vacation often included several generations of the same family, the French public was now more likely to seek vacations with just their immediate family. Concurrently, the adoption of a law lowering the standard workweek to just 35 hours had begun to encourage short-stay vacations sprinkled throughout the year. Selectour responded by introducing a new "leisure boutique" concept, both in existing stores and in new dedicated agencies, designed to promote and sell short-stay and spur-of-the-moment sales. A feature of the leisure boutique were self-service computer terminals that enabled a customer to locate and purchase their travel arrangements in a matter of minutes.

The cooperative also reacted to another trend, that of the growing importance of Internet-based sales in the travel industry. In 2000, the group added e-commerce capabilities to its Web site, providing a selection of between 200 and 300 tour and travel offers. Internet sales remained nonetheless a small part of the group's sales, as Selectour continued to emphasize the personal services of its network agents.

The success of the Selectour-Accor partnership did not go unnoticed. At the end of 2002, the partners took on a new partner, Globalia, the second-largest travel agents network in Spain, with some 763 branches operating throughout that country and in Portugal. Globalia also owned its own airline, Air Europa, and its own tour operations, Travelplan. With the addition of Globalia, the partnership took on a new name, Alliance de Sud, boasting nearly 2,500 partner agencies and total sales volume of more than EUR 4.75 billion. While taking a place as part of a European travel agency heavyweight, Selectour had successfully held on to its founder's commitment to independence.

Principal Subsidiaries

Selectour Investissement (50%).

Principal Competitors

I Grandi Viaggi SpA; AAA Auto Club South; Leclerc SA; TUI AG; Havas Voyages American Express SAS; American Express Co.; Compagnie Financiere Michelin; Mycal Corp.; Atlantic Express Coachways; Taisei Corp.; Carlson Wagonlit Travel Inc.; Carlson Companies Inc.; Central Japan Railway Co.; Coop Schweiz Genossenschaftsverband; Allkauf SB-Warenhaus GmbH und Co. KG; MyTravel Group PLC; Thomas Cook AG; ACCOR; TUI Deutschland GmbH; Maritz Travel Co.; Kuhne und Nagel AG und Co.; Quelle AG und Co.; Virgin Group Ltd.; Raiffeisen-Landesbank Tirol AG; Grupo Eroski.

Further Reading

Chevilley, Philippe, "L'alliance de Selectour avec Accor concue comme un point de depart," *Les Echos*, December 6, 1999, p. 26.

——, "Le groupement d'agences de voyages Selectour s'apprête à renforcer sa filiale financière," *Les Echos*, December 4, 1995, p. 17.

——, "Selectour veut bâtir un troisième pôle de voyages d'affaires en France," *Les Echos*, December 7, 1998, p. 23.

——, "Selectour veut spécialiser ses agences," *Les Echos*, December 9, 1996, p. 15.

Frances, Patrick, "Marchand de voyages, le dur métier," *Le Monde*, February 14, 1987.

Guerrier, Philippe, "Sélectour insère un espace marchand dans son site," *Journal du Net*, May 26, 2000.

Legrand, Constance, "Selectour lance les 'boutiques de loisirs,' " *Les Echos*, December 4, 2000, p. 24.

Palierse, Christophe, "L'espagnol Globalia rejoint la grande alliance d'Accor dans le tourisme," *Les Echos*, December 12, 2002, p. 22.

—M.L. Cohen

Sherwood Brands, Inc.

1803 Research Boulevard, Suite 201
Rockville, Maryland 20850
U.S.A.
Telephone: (301) 309-6161
Fax: (301) 309-6162
Web site: http://www.sherwoodbrands.com

Public Company
Incorporated: 1985
Employees: 600
Sales: $52.8 million (2002)
Stock Exchanges: American
Ticker Symbol: SHD
NAIC: 311340 Nonchocolate Confectionary
   Manufacturing; 311821 Cookie and Cracker
   Manufacturing

Sherwood Brands, Inc. is a growing manufacturer of niche market candy and confections, and one of the major U.S. producers of seasonal candy and gift baskets. It sells its products through many nationwide retailers, including drugstore chains such as CVS, Walgreens, Eckerd, Long's Drugs, Rite-Aid, and others; grocery chains such as Albertsons, Kroger, Winn-Dixie, and Safeway; mass merchandisers such as Wal-Mart, K-Mart, and Target; and through discount stores, convenience stores, wholesale clubs, and many other outlets. Almost half of Sherwood's revenue comes from the sale of seasonal gift baskets, particularly Easter baskets and Christmas baskets and gift sets. Its remaining sales come from its several brands of candy and confections, which are marketed as premium brands at a value price. Sherwood's brands include Cows and P.B. Cows butter toffee candies; Demitasse biscuits and wafers and Ruger brand wafers and cookies; several kinds of lollipops, including its attention-getting Tongue Tattoo line; Sherwood hard candy; Fruit Burst brand jelly beans; Elana Belgian chocolates; and Kastin's Old Fashioned Candy. The company also provides jelly beans, lollipops, and other candies to private-label suppliers, and makes holiday gift sets with licensed trademarks from Pepsi, World Wrestling Foundation, and the games Monopoly,

Scrabble, and Twister. The company was founded by Uziel Frydman, who retains about 80 percent of the stock of the publicly traded company.

Finding a Niche Market in the Mid-1980s

Uziel Frydman founded Sherwood Brands in 1985 after a full career as a consumer package goods specialist for several global companies. Frydman was raised in Israel, the son of an importer of meats and luxury goods. He earned a degree in civil engineering from the Technion-Israel Institute of Technology in Haifa in 1960, then came to the United States, where he took an MBA at Case Western University in Cleveland, Ohio. Beginning in 1971, Frydman worked at Lever Brothers (Unilever), the international conglomerate manufacturer of various household goods and packaged foods. Frydman worked in that company's planning division until 1977, when he moved to a marketing job at the R.J. Reynolds Tobacco Co. Frydman learned two valuable lessons from his time at these companies. One was the importance of long-range planning. He told *Candy Industry* (March 2002) that "Everything that I do or think extends out two or three years." He prided himself on his ability to see where his company was going several years down the line. At R.J. Reynolds he learned the importance of strong branding, which was so much a part of cigarette sales. Frydman also came to see that, powerful as leaders like Reynolds were, there were always small companies that managed to grab a sliver of the market. When he reached his late 40s, Frydman decided that he wanted to go into business for himself. He began by using his insight into consumer brands to scope out a niche market. When he looked at the candy and confection market, Frydman saw a lot of large contenders such as Hershey and Mars, but these still left room for small, savvy competitors. He decided that the best opportunities in the candy market in the mid-1980s were for premium brands. Frydman founded Sherwood Brands in 1985 in North Carolina, operating on the philosophy that his company would sell premium candy at an affordable price.

Sherwood's first product was a line of Austrian imports, Ruger wafers. These were wafer cookies with a variety of flavored fillings. In Europe, wafer cookies were seen as a premium item, but their reputation in the United States was rather the opposite. Frydman's company set out to change the recipe of the wafers to accord with American tastes, and then to package and market them as more of a high-end, though value-priced, sweet. Sherwood Brands eschewed the traditional European hazelnut filling in favor of vanilla, strawberry, and chocolate. Frydman also tinkered with the chocolate filling recipe to come up with something that tasted less distinctively European and more like other American chocolate goods. Sherwood Brands also revamped the Ruger packaging, opting for a printed, metallized package instead of clear plastic. The dark packaging increased the shelf life and gave the wafers a distinctive look. Sherwood also began importing Demitasse Tea Biscuits, bringing them in from a division of the Dutch company CSM.

Apparently Sherwood's initial marketing foray went well. *Candy Industry* (March 2002) described Sherwood's Ruger wafers as a "runaway success." The company began bringing in other candies. Some early products were the Cows line of caramels and Zed gum. These were two innovative products that managed to stand out from the crowd. Cows caramels used an eye-catching black-and-white cow design on the packaging, and managed to sell well probably because of this. Zed gum represented a new area in the flavor range, advertised as super sour. It also colored the inside of the chewer's mouth, a factor children evidently found attractive.

From Importer to Manufacturer in the Early 1990s

As the business grew, Uziel Frydman hired two of his children to help run it. His son Amir Frydman had earned a degree in marketing from the University of North Carolina and then gone to work in the banking industry. Amir apparently preferred candy to banking, and asked his father to take him on. He became vice-president of marketing and product development and was credited with bringing out some of Sherwood's more unusual brands. Frydman's daughter Anat Schwartz then became executive vice-president of finance. After several years in business, Frydman decided the company would do better in a larger metropolitan area. In 1992 Sherwood Brands relocated to Rockville, Maryland, a suburb of Washington, D.C.

Through the mid-1990s, Sherwood Brands did not make any confections of its own, but imported them or had them made by contract manufacturers. The company had investigated opening its own manufacturing plant, but found the investment too costly. The company's contract manufacturers had been providing good service at a reasonable cost, so there was really no need to change. Then in 1995 the European company that made Sherwood's Demitasse Tea Biscuits was bought out by private investors and began to run under new management. The manufacturer began to compete directly with Sherwood, and the situation soon became unworkable. So at this point Frydman

decided that Sherwood Brands would have to make its own tea biscuits. Frydman's first consideration for opening a manufacturing plant was that it be far from the corporate offices. He looked at possible sites that were at least an hour and a half drive from Rockville, with some as much as three hours away. Frydman was concerned that Sherwood's management would get too caught up in the manufacturing end of the business if it was any closer to Rockville. Ultimately, the company chose a former textile plant in Chase City, Virginia, and by the fall of 1996, Sherwood was marketing its own domestically produced Demitasse Tea Biscuits.

After a lot of trial and error produced a good tea biscuit at an acceptable cost, Sherwood began manufacturing more of its own confections. It next added a caramel and toffee production line, buying equipment from a variety of European and Japanese manufacturers. After investing in the plant and equipment, Sherwood considered going public to raise capital. The firm's prospects seemed good. The overall candy and confection market in the United States grew steadily throughout the 1990s. Domestic shipments of confectionaries went from approximately $9 billion in 1990 to more than $15 billion in 1998. Sherwood's sales had risen to about $18 million by 1998, and though it was a still a small company, it had some very large clients. By 1998 roughly 15 percent of Sherwood's sales were to Wal-Mart, the nation's largest retailer. Another 12 percent of Sherwood's sales went to Wal-Mart's subsidiary Sam's Club. By that year it also had snagged other major nationwide retailers as clients, including the drug chains CVS and Rite Aid, the discount chain Dollar General, and the renowned K-Mart. In 1998 Sherwood Brands made an initial public offering on the American Stock Exchange. Uziel Frydman retained 80 percent of the stock, and the company remained in many ways a family business. But the stock offering allowed Sherwood to raise capital for acquisitions, and would let it use stock as a bargaining chip in future acquisition negotiations. The company made its first acquisition in September 1998.

Entering the Gift Basket Business in the Late 1990s

Fresh with cash from its stock offering, Sherwood Brands bought up a troubled candy maker in Pawtucket, Rhode Island for $4 million. The E. Rosen Co. had operated School House Candy for almost 90 years, and it had manufacturing plants in Pawtucket and Central Falls in Rhode Island and two more in New Bedford and Fall River, Massachusetts. The company was bigger than Sherwood, with sales of about $42 million, and it was one of the leading suppliers of the holiday gift basket market. It also made jellybeans, lollipops, hard candy, and some holiday items, mostly supplying them to big chains like Wal-Mart and K-Mart, which sold them under their store brand names. But E. Rosen, which employed some 400 people in the area, had run into hard times and was unable to pay back a $15 million bank loan. It went into receivership in July 1998, and by September Sherwood had beat out more than a dozen other contenders to buy the business. The business was antiquated and did minimal marketing, although the candy production equipment was modern. Sherwood revamped the packaging and marketing of some of School House's products and managed to make them into new hit candies. School House had been making a kind of lollipop that transferred a tattoo onto the

Key Dates:

1985: The company is founded.
1992: The company moves to Rockville, Maryland.
1998: The company goes public; the company acquires E. Rosen Co.
2002: Manufacturing is consolidated in the Virginia plant.

licker's tongue. But these had gone into generic packaging and not made much of a splash. When Sherwood took over, it jazzed up the Tongue Tattoo suckers and added Space Aliens, Smile Pops, and Valentine Suckers to the line. The product got extensive television coverage at the next year's Candy Expo, and was even spoofed by late-night television talk show host Jay Leno. This gave Tongue Tattoos a much higher profile than it had ever had under School House management.

Another attractive aspect of the E. Rosen acquisition was its gift basket business. At first, Sherwood was interested in the candy manufacturing business only, and Frydman intended to sell off the gift basket division. But when a competitor offered what he thought was a suspiciously high price for the business, Frydman decided to retain it and develop it himself. Knowing nothing about gift baskets, Frydman hired out of retirement Harris Rosen, the former head of the company, and had him teach Sherwood's staff the basics of the business. Frydman quickly realized what a good thing he had bought, particularly because there were so many opportunities to use Sherwood's other products in the holiday baskets. Sherwood retained most of the original gift basket assembly workers in New Bedford, but worked on the design of the baskets with its own professionals. Within three years, holiday gift baskets accounted for almost half of Sherwood's sales. Revenue had risen steeply, up to almost $60 million for 2001.

Other Acquisitions and Growth in the 2000s

Sherwood Brands hoped to pick up a venerable name in American candy in 2000 when it tried to buy the Clark Bar Candy Company. But Clark Bar went into receivership while Sherwood was still negotiating for it, and the deal turned into an auction with several contenders. Sherwood eventually lost out to the New England Confectionary Company. But in preparation for picking up Clark Bar, Sherwood had already bought a new production facility, a 70,000-square-foot space in Keysville, Virginia. The Keysville plant was only about 20 miles from Sherwood's original facility in Chase City. When Sherwood bought E. Rosen, it had vowed to keep the business in Rhode Island, but it had searched fruitlessly for several years for a Rhode Island site to succeed the decrepit School House facilities. Reluctantly, the company gave up on Rhode Island

and moved its manufacturing to the Chase City plant, which it expanded. Nearby Keysville then became a warehouse and distribution center. The company did keep its gift basket assembly plant in New Bedford, though, sometimes bussing in workers from nearby communities at peak production times.

Sherwood's long-range plan included growth through line extensions and new products, and through acquisition. By 2002, the company had added several new products, including Strip-O-Pops lollipops and Fruit Burst jelly beans. It also made another acquisition that year, that of a small candy manufacturer in Brooklyn, New York, called Kastin's. Kastin's brought Sherwood its Kastin's brand Old Fashioned Candy and a seasonal treat, Kastin's Christmas Candy Mixes. Sherwood moved some of Kastin's newer production equipment to its Chase City plant. Sherwood also began bringing out new products through licensing agreements. By 2002 the company had worked out licensing deals with several companies, and it was putting out Pepsi holiday gift sets as well as gift sets based on the games Scrabble, Monopoly, and Twister. In 2002 the company signed up with the California Milk Processor Board to license the well-known "Got Milk?" slogan. Sherwood used the "Got Milk?" tag for a line of calcium and vitamin-fortified caramels in several flavors. Seven caramels contained the calcium equivalent of a glass of milk. The company continued to focus on developing innovative candies and to extend its older brands with new flavors or varieties.

Sherwood also hoped to make more acquisitions. Late in 2002 the company acquired Asher Candy, of New Hyde Park, New York. Sales for 2002 were lower than 2001, reportedly due to weakened economic conditions overall in the United States. But Sherwood expected steady growth in 2003, especially after it finished expanding and consolidating its manufacturing at its Chase City plant.

Principal Competitors

Hershey Foods Corporation; Mars, Inc.; Just Born, Inc.

Further Reading

Beirne, Mike, "Candy Makers Look to Evergreen Licensing Deals to Sweeten Profits," *Candy Industry*, June 10, 2002, p. 16.

Davis, Marion, "New Owner Plans to Revive Ailing Candy Company," *Providence Journal-Bulletin*, September 19, 1998, p. 1A.

Fasig, Lisa Biank, "Firm to Move Candy Manufacturing Group from Rhode Island to Chase City, Va.," *Providence Journal-Bulletin*, January 4, 2002.

Hedgpeth, Dana, "Success Is Sweet for Family Firm," *Washington Post*, January 8, 2001, p. E4.

Pacyniak, Bernie, "The Art of Acquisition," *Candy Industry*, March 2002, p. 8.

——, "Greener Pastures," *Candy Industry*, March 2002, p. 28.

—A. Woodward

air lib

Société d'Exploitation AOM Air Liberté SA (AirLib)

Bureau 324 NBatîment 363BP 854
94551 Orly Aérogare CEDEX
France
Telephone: (+33) 49 79 23 00
Fax: (+33) 49 79 10 10
Web site: http://www.airlib.fr

Private Company
Incorporated: 2001
Employees: 3,400
Sales: FFr 1.7 billion ($229.62 million) (2001 est.)
NAIC: 481111 Scheduled Passenger Air Transportation;
    481112 Scheduled Freight Air Transportation; 481212
    Nonscheduled Chartered Freight Air Transportation;
    481211 Nonscheduled Chartered Passenger Air
    Transportation

Société d'Exploitation AOM Air Liberté SA (AirLib) is France's second largest airline. Formed from the merger of long-haul airline AOM with regional carrier Air Liberté, most of AirLib's business involves flying passengers between Paris and provincial destinations. The company also operates long-haul flights to France's overseas territories.

Origins

AirLib can trace its origins to three companies that all started out as charter airlines: Minerve, Air Outre Mer, and Air Liberté. Air Outre Mer merged with Minerve in 1992 to form AOM French Airlines, which merged with Air Liberté ten years later to form Société d'exploitation AOM Air Liberté SA, or AirLib.

Minerve S.A. was established in June 1975 by René-Fernand Meyer, a former fighter pilot. It began flying to the United States in 1983 and eventually ditched its Caravelle jets for more modern aircraft. In its first dozen years, Minerve's principal source of business was Nouvelles Frontieres, France's largest tour operator. In the late 1980s, Minerve briefly ran a one-plane charter operation in Montreal, Canada, but ran afoul of regulations there requiring 75 percent Canadian ownership of airlines.

Air Liberté was founded in 1987. Led by Lofti Belhassine, its largest shareholder was Groupe Aquarius, the tour operator. Subsidiary Air Liberté Tunisie was sold to the TTS group in the mid-1990s, becoming known as Nouvelair.

Air Outre Mer (AOM) was also formed in July 1987; its purpose, to link France with its overseas territories. AOM's first scheduled commercial flight was between Paris and Reunion Island in the Indian Ocean on May 21, 1990. AOM's major shareholder was the Hotavia Holding Group; its CEO and chairman was René Micaud.

Air Outre Mer had a fleet of three DC-10s and 300 employees in 1991. Air Liberté had 500 employees in 1991. In addition to resorts in southern Europe and the Mediterranean, it flew as far as Bangkok and Montreal. Minerve was slightly larger, with 650 employees. In addition to tourist and cargo charters to the Caribbean, the Indian Ocean, and East Asia, Minerve also conducted maintenance for other companies at its Nimes-Garons maintenance center.

Deregulation and Consolidation in the 1990s

In January 1990, following Air France's takeover of UTA, the country's main private carrier, Air Liberté requested scheduled airline status from the French government. It was flying just four planes at the time but had plans to double its fleet within the year and to have 25 aircraft by the end of 1993.

Minerve, with eleven planes and 900 employees in 1990, also wanted to pick up the routes of UTA and the domestic carrier Air Inter, which Air France was likely to shed to defer anti-competitive criticism from the European Commission in Brussels.

Club Mediterranée bought a 50 percent interest in Minerve in April 1990. It soon also acquired a controlling interest in Air Liberté through the purchase of Groupe Aquarius. The French government eventually awarded Minerve and Air Liberté, both controlled by Club Med, thirteen international routes plus Orly-Nice. However, the Gulf War and a global recession had disastrous effects for both the airline industry and travel business in

Key Dates:

1975: Minerve S.A. is founded.
1987: Air Liberté is founded.
1990: Air Outre Mer begins flying; Club Med acquires a 50 percent stake in Minerve and Air Liberté.
1991: Minerve merges with Air Outre Mer to form AOM French Airlines.
1997: British Airways acquires Air Liberté.
2001: AOM and Air Liberté officially merge; Holco takes over the company and renames it AirLib.

general, and Club Med reduced its holdings in Minerve and Air Liberté in late 1991.

Air Liberté and Minerve were not merged during their brief period with Club Med at the controls. However, on January 1, 1992, Minerve merged with Air Outre Mer to create AOM French Airlines or AOM Minerve (originally, it was to be called Airmust). The combined fleet was just eleven aircraft. Consortium de Realisation (CDR), a unit of the state-owned bank Credit Lyonnais, owned a 70 percent stake and invested $150 million over the next few years to keep the airline flying.

Air Transport World recorded 1994 revenues of $180 million for Air Liberté and $524 million for AOM. In 1995, AOM posted its first profit, FFr31.4 million, on turnover of FFr3.15 billion. Scheduled flights accounted for 73 percent of its business.

AOM carried 2.4 million passengers in 1995. Its long-haul routes stretched to Australia, Peru, Cuba, Los Angeles, and Tahiti; the carrier also connected Paris with Nice in southern France. The carrier operated eight McDonnell Douglas MD-83s and 14 DC-10s. The airline and its subsidiaries, such as maintenance and overhaul unit AOM Industries, employed 2,200 people.

In the mid-1990s, Crédit Lyonnais was undergoing a financial crisis and wanted to unload AOM. Air Liberté seemed a good match. The two airlines were both based at Orly, had similar fleets, and complementary route networks. Although Air Liberté's bid was turned down, in July 1996 the two independents formed a wide-ranging business partnership aimed at helping them compete against Air France and its regional subsidiary, Air Inter Europe, as well as the predicted influx of foreign carriers upon the implementation of the European Union's free trade policy in 1997. AOM and Air Liberté had combined 1995 revenues of $970 million, and the two carried 4.6 million passengers a year.

Foreign Owners 1997–2001

However, Air Liberté was losing money, $180 million in 1995 and $120 million in the fiscal year ending October 31, 1996. In October 1996, British Airways offered £3 million ($5 million) to take over troubled Air Liberté through BA's French subsidiary TAT European Airlines. Other suitors included Virgin Express, Nouvelles Frontieres, and a founding shareholder in Air Liberté, the Rivaud banking group. AOM, itself up for

sale due to the government's 1995 bailout of Credit Lyonnais, also tendered a bid.

Groupe Rivaud shifted its support to the BA bid, agreeing to invest FFr190 million and write off FFr510 million in debt in exchange for a 30 percent share. BA pledged to protect most of Air Liberté's 1,300 jobs, maintain its routes, and invest FFr440 million for a 67 percent stake. This bid was ultimately accepted by the court, and BA took over operations on December 30, 1996.

Though BA's French-based TAT subsidiary remained a separate entity, by the end of 1997 it was no longer flying under its own name, and its operations were being unified with that of Air Liberté. This effectively made Air Liberté the country's second largest carrier after Air France, with a fleet of 39 aircraft. Air Liberté penned code-sharing agreements with several other regional carriers to support its own hub at Paris-Orly and also worked out a surprise feeder traffic deal with American Airlines. In December 1997, Air Liberté added service to Madrid, Barcelona, and Lisbon out of its new secondary hub, Bordeaux. AOM was also building marketing agreements, with Sabena Belgian World Airlines, Swissair, and Air Portugal.

In May 2000, BA sold Air Liberté to the Taitbout-Antibes unit of the Marine Wendel group, which was representing SAirGroup, Swissair's parent company. The French shipping group Bollor had owned a 14 percent share in Air Liberté's immediate parent company Participations Aéronautiques. Air Liberté would be the French component of Swissair's Qualiflyer Group, a pool of several European regional airlines.

SAirGroup also acquired AOM and a third French carrier, Air Littoral, and was combining the three into one unit under the Air Liberté name. These units announced combined losses of $320 million for 2000 while Swissair was hit by a financial scandal at home. In an effort to stem the flow of losses, the three French carriers cut routes, including AOM's new link between Paris and the Swissair hub of Zurich.

AOM-Air Liberté Merge in 2001

AOM-Air Liberté (the two carriers were operating as one) filed for bankruptcy in June 2001 after its owners, Swissair Group and the French investment group Marine Wendel, refused to provide it with additional capital. Swissair was the managing owner, though it held a minority share.

As many as 15 proposals to take over the carrier were submitted. AOM-Air Liberté chairman Marc Rochet pitched a plan for a management buyout of the airline that would save 3,000 of the company's 4,500 jobs, while breaking even in two years. On July 27, 2001, the court selected as the new owners the Holco SAS group of investors, led by former Air France pilot and union leader Jean-Charles Corbet. The Holco plan retained 2,706 jobs out of 4,559 and kept 28 aircraft flying from a fleet of 50.

SAirGroup, which owned 49.5 percent of shares, pledged FFr1.5 billion ($200 million) to release it from future liabilities. Taitbout-Antibes was also released from future liabilities. The French government, shaken by massive layoffs in several industrial sectors, organized a September meeting of several French transportation companies to help find jobs for former Air Liberté employees. However, Air France cancelled plans to take on 580 workers after the September 11 terrorist attacks in the United States.

Corbet was shifting the carrier's strategy away from direct competition with Air France into positive cooperation. Air Liberté would also avoid city pairs served by TGV high-speed trains. Executives instead planned to tackle niche markets, both domestically and abroad, including the November launch of service to Algeria, abandoned earlier by Air France.

September 11 turned the expected FFr460 million loss to a FFr620 million one. Net revenues were estimated at FFr1.7 billion. AirLib continued to try to collect a FFr400 million ($55 million) debt it said it was promised by Swissair for exiting the company.

AOM and Air Liberté were officially merged on September 22, 2001. A new logo was unfurled, its colors of blue and orange said to symbolize the sun shining above the ocean. While taking the name Société d'exploitation AOM Air Liberté SA, the company traded as simply "AirLib."

A comprehensive restructuring plan was announced in January 2002. AirLib was switching to a low-cost approach within France. In March 2002, AirLib announced a new no-frills domestic service along the lines of easyJet and Ryanair, two British Isles carriers who had recently been fighting French authorities for the right to bring the concept to France themselves. The new low-fare service was dubbed AirLib Express and offered connections between Paris and several cities in southern France for one-way fares of EUR 29. It was priced to compete with high-speed rail as well as Air France.

The company cut its flights to French overseas territories in half in the summer of 2002 but planned to start new services to Africa and Italy in the fall. AirLib Express, a low-cost unit with flights from Paris to destinations in southern France, was successful enough to lift the company to an operational break-even point by the end of the year.

Principal Divisions

Grandes Lignes; Lignes Outre Mer; Lignes Régionales.

Principal Operating Units

AirLib Express.

Principal Competitors

Air France; easyJet; SNCF.

Further Reading

Abrahams, Paul, "Air France May Share Routes with Minerve," *Financial Times* (London), January 23, 1990, p. 23.
——, "Air Liberté Seeks Scheduled Airline Status," *Financial Times* (London), Sec. I, January 18, 1990, p. 36.
"Air Lib Forced to Cut Workforce and Fleet," *Financial Times World Media Abstracts,* abstracted from *La Tribune,* November 22, 2001, p. 1.
"AOM-Air Liberté Chairman Marc Rochet Makes Lone Effort to Take-Over the Troubled Air Operator," *Financial Times World Media Abstracts,* abstracted from *Le Monde,* July 20, 2001, p. 14.
Faujas, Alain, "Avec la fusion de Minerve et Air Outre-Mer le Club Mediterranée maintient sa position dans les compagnies aériennes," *Le Monde,* Economie Sec., October 26, 1991.
——, "La compagnie Minerve demande a reprendre des lignes d'UTA et d'Aéromaritime," *Le Monde,* Economie Sec., January 25, 1990.
——, "L'entrée du Club dans la compagnie Minerve; Quand il y a deux pilotes dans l'avion . . .'' *Le Monde,* Economie Sec., April 30, 1990.
Godard, Jean-Marie, "France's AirLib Announces No-Frills Domestic Service," *AP Worldstream,* March 6, 2002.
Hotten, Russell, "Challenge of 'Fly-By-Nights' That Fly All Over," *Times,* April 10, 2002, Bus. Sec., p. 30.
McDonald, Thomas, "Air Liberté Bankruptcy," *Airfinance Journal,* January 2002, pp. 33–5.
Morrocco, John D., and Pierre Sparaco, "British, French Suitors Eye Ailing Air Liberté," *Aviation Week & Space Technology,* October 14, 1996, p. 40.
Nash, Tom, "Club Med's Creative Family," *Director* (London) October 1992, p. 78.
Owen, David, Michael Skapinker, and Ross Tieman, "BA Wins Fight to Take Over Air Liberte," *Financial Times* (London), November 6, 1996, p. 26.
Silbert, Nathalie, "La compagnie AOM est sortie du rouge en 1995," *Les Echos,* February 22, 1996, p. 13.
Sparaco, Pierre, "Air Liberte, AOM Seek New Investors to Stay Aloft," *Aviation Week & Space Technology,* April 16, 2001, p. 47.
——, "AOM Wants Major Slice of French Airline Pie," *Aviation Week & Space Technology,* March 11, 1996, p. 37.
——, "AOM Widens Business Partnerships," *Aviation Week & Space Technology,* March 16, 1998, p. 30.
——, "British Airways to Unify French Subsidiaries," *Aviation Week & Space Technology,* November 11, 1997, p. 60.
——, "French Carriers Struggle for Survival," *Aviation Week & Space Technology,* May 28, 2001, p. 40.
——, "Independent Carriers Join Forces to Challenge Air France," *Aviation Week & Space Technology,* August 5, 1996, p. 44.
——, "New Owners Plan Future for Air Liberte/AOM," *Aviation Week & Space Technology,* August 6, 2001, p. 46.
——, "Revamped French Airline Charts New Course," *Aviation Week & Space Technology,* September 3, 2001, p. 78.
——, "Swissair's Affiliates on the Precipice," *Aviation Week & Space Technology,* July 2, 2001, p. 54.
Sparaco, Pierre, and John D. Morrocco, "Bidders Vie for Share of France's Air Liberté," *Aviation Week & Space Technology,* October 21, 1996, p. 40.
Warburton, Simon, "Swissair's Broken Promise Forces AirLib to Seek Fresh Finance Deal," *Flight International,* November 6, 2001, p. 26.

—Frederick C. Ingram

First in textile services worldwide

Steiner Corporation (Alsco)

505 East South Temple
Salt Lake City, Utah 84102
U.S.A.
Telephone: (800) 408-0208
Fax: (801) 363-5680
Web site: http://www.alsco.com

Private Company
Incorporated: 1912 as American Linen Supply Co.
Employees: 12,000
Sales: $712 million (2001)
NAIC: 812330 Linen and Uniform Supply

Headquartered in Salt Lake City, Steiner Corporation is the holding company for Alsco, the acronym for the American Linen Supply Company. The company was founded in Lincoln, Nebraska, in 1889, by George A. Steiner and incorporated in 1912 under the original name American Linen. From its incarnation as a towel delivery service, American Linen quickly became a pioneer in the commercial and industrial laundry businesses, or textile services. Still true to its original motto, "It pays to keep clean," Steiner remains a third generation, family-owned private company with some 70 facilities around the world.

The First Generation: 1889–1946

The linen supply industry did not yet exist in 1889 when George A. Steiner, at the age of 15, started his own part-time towel delivery service in Lincoln, Nebraska. In those days it was customary for a business to wring a wet towel through a wooden roller and hang it to dry for the next use; a change of linen was a rare luxury.

George Steiner made an initial investment of $50.80 to buy the towel delivery route from Lincoln Steam Laundry. Two years later he invited his younger brother, Frank M. Steiner, to join him in equal partnership, picking up clean towels from the laundry, delivering them to local businesses, and collecting dirty towels for return to the laundry. It was a watershed moment and became part of the American Linen legend when the Steiner brothers sold a grocery store clerk on the idea of receiving a crisp clean apron every morning in exchange for the work-soiled one he was wearing. After striking this groundbreaking deal, the Steiner brothers' towel business soon became "Lincoln Towel and Apron Supply." As the business grew, the boys continually upgraded their means of delivery, from hand- to bicycle- to horse-drawn cart.

The local economy of Lincoln was particularly affected by the economic depression of the 1890s. Steiner weathered three years of declining business before he decided in 1895 to reestablish his linen supply in Salt Lake City, where the economic conditions were more favorable. Inspired by his brother's entrepreneurial spirit, Frank Steiner moved to Minneapolis in 1896 to start a towel business there. During these early years, both of the Steiner brothers funneled the majority of their earnings back into the company, and it grew steadily. George tended to excel in the role of office manager, while Frank's talent was as the company salesman.

The company built its first industrial laundry plant in Salt Lake City in 1910 and was incorporated under the name American Linen Supply Company in 1912, with George Steiner as president and a listed value of $150,000. Branches in Ogden, Utah, Minneapolis and St. Paul, Minnesota, and Chicago were incorporated separately that same year. By this time American Linen was supplying linens to butcher shops, bars, restaurants, groceries, offices, barber shops, hotels, and stores.

In 1918, in response to increased pressure throughout the industry from health officials over the unsanitary conditions created by the public roller towel, 21-year-old Frank G. Steiner, George's son, developed and patented his first original product, a continuous towel dispensed by a specialized cabinet. In 1922 the Steiner Sales Company was founded in Salt Lake City to manage the production and sales of the cabinets. The invention proved such a popular and effective improvement that by 1948 it was in use all across the United States and would continue to be used into the 21st century.

Following World War I the Steiner brothers dedicated themselves to the goal of bringing American Linen to national prominence. In 1930 the founding brothers recapitalized their

Salt Lake City and Ogden corporations in order to publicly rectify the increased worth of the companies and to strengthen their borrowing power. The Salt Lake branch was now valued at $1.5 million. While the recapitalization positioned the company for accelerated expansion, the onset of the Great Depression limited this. Still, during these years the Steiners maintained their intensive sales efforts and, having entered the decade debt-free, the company endured the hard times with relative ease. Even in the lean years, expansion was not halted altogether: by the time World War II broke out, American Linen's operations had proliferated to Los Angeles, Portland, Oregon, Milwaukee, and New York City.

Consolidation and Expansion: 1946–59

George A. Steiner died in 1946, less than seven years after his brother Frank. In 1948 the disparate American Linen branches were consolidated under a new name: on June 1st, American Linen Supply Company (Alsco) was incorporated in the state of Nevada. The action dissolved the disparate companies in Salt Lake City, Ogden, Los Angeles, Portland, Milwaukee, Chicago, Minneapolis, St. Paul, Hibbing, and New York, replacing American Linen's multicorporate structure with one that was unified under a single name and the centralized leadership of the parent corporation's president, F.G. Steiner. Chicago became the company's national headquarters. With the merger, management hoped, American Linen would benefit from increased buying and borrowing power, better-leveraged sales efforts, and more fluid communication throughout the company. All of these improvements would facilitate the rapid expansion that was to follow.

In the ten years following the consolidation, the American Linen Supply Company opened 16 new branches and nearly tripled its sales. Some of the new branches were built from the ground up, but most were the result of acquisition and rebuilding—the purchase of modest, family-run linen supply and laundry businesses which were subsequently upgraded and equipped with the latest machinery and Steiner-proven business practices. Some of the company's most ambitious expansion was forged in Canada, and in 1949 Alsco extended its reach beyond North America by establishing a branch in Rio de Janeiro, Brazil.

The Brazil plant was the result of F.G. Steiner's tireless expansion efforts and his sense that there was limited business left to be gained in the United States after World War II. However, the fledgling operation in Brazil presented a significant cash drain for the company, and it was not soon profitable. In addition, Steiner had bought a large paper mill in Albany, New York, in order to manufacture paper for a new paper towel cabinet he had invented, and this operation also required seemingly endless infusions of the company's resources. After a period of growing dissent over Steiner's management decisions, the Alsco board became irreparably factionalized, and a decision was made in 1959 to split the business into two companies: George R. and Lawrence McIvor, the sons of Frank M. Steiner, assumed control of 22 plants in the Midwest and Canada, with headquarters in Minneapolis; F.G. Steiner and his own son Richard stayed at the helm in Salt Lake City, retaining control of 19 western plants, those in Milwaukee and Chicago, plus the operation in Brazil and another international effort in Cologne, Germany. The Minneapolis faction continued to operate under the name American Linen Supply Company, while the Salt Lake group changed their name, effective January 1, 1960, to Steiner American Corporation. Richard, then still in his 30s, became president of Steiner American, with his father F.G. as chairman of the board.

Expansion and Diversification: 1960s–80s

After the split F.G. Steiner was more determined than ever to continue in the vigorous pursuit of expansion. To accomplish this the company maintained conservative fiscal policies and concentrated on building up its net working capital. Within five years father and son had tripled the volume of business Steiner American had started with in 1959; they built new plants, including five of industrial capacity, and established 17 new branches, 11 of them domestic and six international.

In anticipation of increased international business, a company was formed in Lausanne, Switzerland, in 1960, to hold all of Steiner American's assets outside the United States and Canada. In the coming years Steiner would command enterprises in Brazil, Italy, Spain, Mexico, Argentina, Australia, and South Africa. Steiner's international pursuits were threefold: in addition to the linen supply branches and plants that were run by the Foreign Linen Supply Division, the American Uniform Company (whose ownership was divided evenly between Salt Lake City and Minneapolis) was establishing plants to manufacture uniforms and other textile products; further, the Steiner Company Division, directed by Robert L. Steiner, was focused on international manufacturing and distribution of paper products and cloth-towel cabinets. In 1974 Steiner Company Lausanne was renamed Steiner Company International.

In 1964 Steiner American moved to disentangle its industrial operations from linen supply by creating a wholly owned subsidiary, the American Industrial Service Company (AIS), to manage the five industrial plants. Alongside linen supply, Steiner American also continued to develop its paper interests. This facet of the business was led by F.G.'s son Richard. In November 1967, Steiner American opened new international headquarters in Salt Lake City, where the company would continue to reside more than 30 years later.

Key Dates:

1889: 15-year-old George Steiner buys the delivery route of Lincoln Steam Laundry in Lincoln, Nebraska, for $50.80.

1895: Steiner moves the business to Salt Lake City, Utah.

1896: A second branch of the business is established in Minneapolis.

1912: The company is incorporated under the name American Linen.

1918: Steiner patents the first continuous roll towel cabinet to replace the condemned public roll towel.

1935: Minneapolis Linen Supply Co. is established to manufacture uniforms.

1948: All individual American Linen companies are consolidated under the American Linen Supply Company.

1960: Company is renamed Steiner American Corporation.

1976: Steiner American is renamed Steiner Corporation.

1988: U.S. branches of Steiner Corporation revert to the original name, American Linen Supply.

2000: Richard Steiner, Sr., steps down, yielding control of Steiner to his two sons, Robert and Kevin.

2002: Alsco launches an international rebranding effort whereby American Linen, American Industrial, American Cleanroom Garments, and Servitex are all combined under the name Alsco.

The years from 1965 to 1968 showed solid earnings for Steiner American, and the company's financial base continued to strengthen. In addition to investing in geographic expansion, the company also used its capital to diversify its interests. And while the legacy of international expansion belonged to F.G. Steiner, the legacy of diversification would belong to son Richard. Diversification was becoming a trend in American business, and Steiner also perceived the need to guard against antitrust sentiments, as well as a possible slow-down in the linen supply industry. Under Richard Steiner's leadership, then, Steiner American explored a range of other industries through acquisitions and investments: food processing, fiberglass manufacturing, equipment leasing, leveraged equipment leasing, real estate development, banking, and filter manufacturing. As quoted in *From Small Beginnings,* Richard Steiner remarked on his approach to diversification, "If there's a good deal, we'll take it regardless of the area. We'll add to either our diversified or our linen supply interests if it's profitable." True to Richard's vision, by 1989 fully one third of Steiner's revenues came from businesses outside the linen supply industry.

In the years after the 1959 split, the Minneapolis contingent of American Linen also forged ahead and grew rapidly, tripling the number of branches it held in the United States and Canada by the 1970s. Under the leadership of George R. and Lawrence M. Steiner, Minneapolis American Linen also expanded internationally, establishing interests in Belgium and Puerto Rico. During these years, American Linen plant equipment was upgraded and new technology was introduced. In 1969 a Paper Division was created to distribute paper towels, napkins, and

tissue in the Minneapolis area. In 1979 George R.'s son Larry became president and George R. became chairman of the board.

A Second Century of Business: 1990 and Beyond

In the 1990s and the early years of the 21st century, Alsco faced increased competition from big national companies who were seeking to gain a share of major textile service markets. These companies included Cintas Corp. of Cincinnati; Aramark Corp. of Philadelphia; G & K Services, Inc., of Minnetonka, Minnesota; Tartan Textile Services of Abilene, Texas; and Angelica Corp. of Chesterfield, Missouri. In the face of these challengers, Alsco felt increased pressure to offer the most competitive prices as well as to gain new and maintain existing accounts.

In 1997, according to *Forbes* magazine, Alsco achieved $585 million in sales. Over the next four years, this number would climb 22 percent, to $712 million, earning the company a position as the 430th largest private company in the United States according to *Forbes'* 2002 rankings. At the Ogden, Utah, plant alone, Alsco was processing more than 20,000 pounds of laundry per day, or 4.5 million pounds per year, by 2002.

With decades of sustained growth, Alsco found that it had outgrown many of its operating facilities and needed to expand. Also, stricter environmental controls and increased consciousness over the polluting effects and heavy water usage of industrial laundry plants forced Alsco to upgrade its facilities to conserve water and recycle industrial solvents. Among other upgrades, Alsco doubled the size of a plant in Spokane, Washington, in 1993; in 2000, in Boise, Idaho, Alsco moved into a new building, tripling its operating space and adding new equipment, including a water re-use system. Further, in 2001 Alsco began construction of a $25.2 million state-of-the-art plant in Chicago.

In December 2000 77-year-old Richard R. Steiner stepped down from his positions as president and CEO of the Steiner Corporation, yielding control of the company to his two sons, Robert and Kevin. Though it was unusual for a company to have co-chief executives, Robert and Kevin, great grandsons of the founder, George Steiner, represented a unique leadership opportunity for the company: Robert was considered the adventurous one while Kevin had a meticulous mind for details. Both had been involved with the family business since the age of eight, when they began working in the linen plants, and their ability to work together was long-proven.

By the beginning of the 21st century, Alsco employed some 12,000 workers in eight countries. Its offerings included everything from sheets, towels, and uniforms to dust control mop heads, reusable incontinence products, and numerous washroom and hygienic products. These extensive and diverse operations were carried on by different subsidiaries under a variety of names. Confusion often resulted from the lack of a single operating name, and some branches even experienced difficulty closing global contracts. To remedy this, Alsco launched an international rebranding effort in March, 2002, whereby American Linen, American Industrial, American Cleanroom Garments, and Servitex were all combined under the name Alsco. Under the umbrella of one name, Alsco hoped to build a globally integrated communications platform and to convey its long tradition of quality products at a global level, while continuing to operate as a network of local businesses able to relate to its customers as neighbors. Backed by over a century of success in an industry whose growth potential was seen as virtually unlimited, Alsco seemed to be taking the necessary steps to assure its continued dominance.

Principal Subsidiaries

American Uniform Company; American Industrial SVC; American Linen; National Filter Media Corporation.

Principal Competitors

Aramark Corporation; Cintas Corporation; G & K Services, Inc.

Further Reading

Arrington, Leonard J., *From Small Beginnings: A History of the American Linen Supply Company and Its Successors and Affiliates,* Salt Lake City: Steiner, 1991.

Carlson, Brad, ''American Linen Eyes Expansion in Medical, Industrial Markets,'' *Idaho Business Review,* March 11, 2002, p. A3.

Oberbeck, Steven, ''Steiner Leaves Sons to Co-Pilot Firm,'' *Salt Lake Tribune,* December 20, 2000, p. C6.

Spielman, Fran, ''Subsidy Persuades Plant to Stay in City,'' *Chicago Sun-Times,* May 9, 2001, p. 34.

Troester, David, ''Alsco Cleaning Up; Ogden Plant Celebrates 100 Years,'' *Standard-Examiner* (Ogden, Utah), May 12, 2002.

—Erin Brown

Stollwerck AG

Stollwerckstrasse 27-31
D-51149 Cologne
Germany
Telephone: (49) (2203) 43-0
Fax: (49) (2203) 43-319
Web site: http://www.stollwerck.de

Public Company
Incorporated: 1839 as Franz Stollwerck
Employees: 4,776
Sales: EUR 750.6 million ($737.2 million) (2001)
Ticker Symbol: G.STL
NAIC: 31132 Chocolate and Confectionery
Manufacturing from Cacao Beans; 311821 Cookie and
Cracker Manufacturing

Stollwerck AG is one of Germany's largest chocolate manufacturers. Stollwerck sells brand name chocolate under many different brand names, including the most well-known brands "Sarotti," "Sprengel," "Gubor," "Alpia," and "Stollwerck." The company also makes chocolate products for others under private labels—including that of Germany's number one food discounter, Aldi—and produces and markets a range of cookies. Based in Cologne, Stollwerck runs eight production plants in Germany, Belgium and Switzerland and maintains sales offices in France, Spain, and Italy. About 70 percent of Stollwerck's sales are generated in Germany, the world's second-largest market for chocolate, in which the company has a market share of about 13.5 percent. The Swiss cocoa empire Barry Callebaut AG owns almost all of Stollwerck's share capital and is planning to delist Stollwerck shares from public trading.

Origins in the 19th Century

Company founder Franz Stollwerck started out as a baker. The son of a wool spinner, he learned the baker's craft in his hometown of Cologne. As was common among craftspeople in early 19th century Europe, Stollwerck sought to expand his knowledge of his trade by traveling outside his native region. His trip led him to southern Germany, Switzerland, and France. After he had returned to Cologne, the 24-year-old got married in 1839 and rented a small bakery in the southern part of the city. Right from the beginning, Stollwerck offered his customers a broad range of baked goods, including sweet delicacies from other countries, sophisticated fruit cakes, marzipan, and chocolate.

Stollwerck prospered as a maker of pastries and candies. One of his products, *Kölner Brustbonbon*, was a candy that served as a remedy for cold symptoms and breathing problems. This item soon turned into a bestseller. Although he was not the only one selling cough drops and other "medicines" as a side business, Stollwerck's commercial success drew the attention of Cologne's pharmacists. In 1845, they asked the local authorities to forbid the non-pharmacist from selling medicinal products. Stollwerck brought the case to the Prussian government, which issued a decree allowing bakers to sell various home remedies that did not require a doctor's prescription. On top of that, Prince Friedrich von Preußen, who resided in Dusseldorf, made Stollwerck a supplier to his court.

In the following decades, Stollwerck's business continued to grow as he expanded the distribution network for his *Brustbonbons*. By 1864, about 900 representatives sold his "healthy candies" in Germany. The business also began to extend beyond Germany's borders. Stollwerck founded sales offices in most European countries as well as in New York. A master marketer, he introduced "picture chocolates" that featured images of a variety of things, including flowers, butterflies, and Cologne's cathedral.

Stollwerck was not only involved in baking and candy manufacturing, but also in hospitality and culture. In the 1840s, he opened a café in his house where people could also enjoy a glass of wine or liquor until late at night. This establishment was frequented by Cologne's bohemians. In 1847, Stollwerck opened a second café in the same street. Named at first "Café Royal," it was renamed *Deutsches Kaffeehaus*—"German coffee house"—two years later and became a popular hangout for Cologne's intellectuals and politicians. A few years later, Stollwerck turned the coffee house into a vaudeville-type theater, and he subsequently invested in a brand-new hall in the south-

Company Perspectives:

We are an international company with a long tradition and we look back on a successful company history. Thus, for the future, too, we feel an obligation to our shareholders to secure a permanent growth that is in line with market requirements creating added value. Our major business is the production and international marketing of our chocolate products of premium quality. Our distinctive brand portfolio provides extensive and versatile business activities from premium quality to value for money. The centre of all our activities is the consumer/customer, whose needs and requirements are decisive for us. A trustful co-operation with clear targets and responsibilities charcterize our company's policy. Therefore, motivated, commited and innovative employees are the solid base for a successful future.

ern part of Cologne's old-town. The *Königshalle*—"King's Hall"—seated 2,400 people and could be used for theater performances, concerts, or balls. However, the new venue was not widely accepted, and Stollwerck closed it down in the 1860s, remodeling it into a factory for producing candies, chocolate, liquor, and even Cologne's famous perfume, *Eau de Cologne* or *Kölnisch Wasser.*

Innovations in Production, Marketing, and Distribution after 1870

Stollwerck successfully reigned over his enterprise for twenty years. Then, one by one, beginning in 1860, his five sons (Albert Nicolaus, Peter Joseph, Heinrich, Ludwig, and Carl) entered the business, which was renamed Franz Stollwerck & Söhne in 1869. However, conflicts arose between the strong-willed company founder and his sons, who founded their own company, Gebrüder Stollwerck, in November 1871. Two years later, the Emperor of Austria made Gebrüder Stollwerck a vendor to his court. When Franz Stollwerck died in 1876, the two companies were merged. By that time, Stollwerck was an established manufacturer with a wide range of products. The demand for chocolate had exploded in the preceding decades, replacing candies as the company's mainstay. Stollwerck now made 375 different chocolate products. Besides chocolate, the company offered about 150 varieties of candies and 80 varieties of cookies. Stollwerck also manufactured fruit preserves and jellies as well as crystallized and caramelized fruits. In addition, the company sold tea and imported items from Japan and China.

In the second half of the 19th century, Stollwerck mechanized its production facilities. In 1865, the company moved to another location, where chocolate manufacturing was modernized. The people passing by the factory were even able to watch how the chocolate was made. Of all the Stollwerck brothers, Heinrich Stollwerck was the one who most pushed the company's mechanization forward. He was a talented inventor who devised steam-powered machines to produce chocolate products that had formerly been made by hand. Heinrich Stollwerck also built his own equipment, including a giant furnace and a machine with five rolls for flattening masses of chocolate.

The advent of vending machines in the 1880s revolutionized the distribution of chocolate and candies, and Ludwig Stollwerck pursued this means of purveying the company's products. The company established over 10,000 such machines throughout Germany. By 1893, the number had reached 15,000 throughout Europe. Another 4,000 Stollwerck vending machines were installed in New York. As with many commercial innovations, the automated selling of sweets was not embraced by everyone, and Stollwerck was accused of unfair competition, disturbing the day of the Lord, and facilitating over-indulgence in candy on the part of children. These objections notwithstanding, Stollwerck's "steel salesmen" were a highly successful means of distributing the company's products. To prevent people from using slugs in order to get the candy of their choice, Stollwerck developed its own device for coin-verification.

Vending machines were not the only means of promoting Stollwerck's chocolate. Ludwig Stollwerck introduced a "miniature picture series" and paid well-known artists of the time, among them Max Liebermann and Adolph von Menzel, for creating these images. Between 1896 and 1899, Stollwerck sold over 50 million such collectors items. On top of that, the company sold about 100,000 collector's albums per year. In 1903, Stollwerck even hired Thomas Edison to help promote their chocolate. The "speaking audio records" Edison developed for the company were made from pure chocolate and became a bestseller. Music lovers with a sweet tooth were able to choose from 300 different melodies sung by popular artists. After listening to their favorite tune, they could simply eat the record.

Two World Wars Interrupt International Expansion

The first decade of the 20th century was a particularly prosperous one for the chocolate maker. In 1902, Stollwerck was transformed into a public company. In the years thereafter, Stollwerck evolved as an international enterprise with sales offices in many parts of the world and production plants in London, Vienna, and the United States. Stollwerck's American subsidiary, Stollwerck Brothers Inc., became America's second largest chocolate manufacturer. In 1908, Stollwerck's cookie production was moved to Berlin. Between 1911 and 1913, the company greatly expanded its facilities at Cologne. However, the onset of World War I in the summer of 1914 interrupted Stollwerck's success story. As a result of the war, the company lost all of its foreign subsidiaries. In the United States, Stollwerck Brothers Inc. was seized and auctioned off for one and a half million dollars in 1919. The meager compensation payments by the German government could hardly make up for such enormous losses. Stollwerck, like many other German manufacturers that did not profit from the war, found itself financially and organizationally weak in a fragile economic environment. The 1920s and 1930s brought even more hardship. In the early 1920s, the German economy was hit hard by the rapid devaluation of its currency, brought about mainly by the irresponsible financial practices of the German government. The hyperinflation of 1923 was followed by the worldwide economic depression that began at the end of the decade.

In 1930, Stollwerck bought out the large German cocoa and chocolate manufacturer Reichardt. Taking over Reichardt's high debt placed another strain on Stollwerck's finances. Finally, the company's financial position became so weak that

Key Dates:

1839: Franz Stollwerck opens a small bakery in Cologne.
1869: The company is renamed Franz Stollwerck & Söhne.
1876: Franz Stollwerck's five sons manage the company after his death.
1902: Stollwerck is transformed into a public company.
1906: The brand name ''Alpia'' is registered as a trademark.
1919: The company's subsidiary in the United States is lost after World War I.
1930: Stollwerck acquires cocoa and chocolate maker Reichardt.
1931: Deutsche Bank becomes Stollwerck's majority shareholder.
1949: Stollwerck resumes operations after World War II.
1972: Hans Imhoff is elected chairman of Stollwerck's advisory board of directors.
1979: Stollwerck takes over German chocolate manufacturer Sprengel.
1991: The company buys the eastern German chocolate factory Thüringer Schokoladenwerk.
1998: Stollwerck acquires Sarotti from Nestlé.
2001: Hans Imhoff retires; Stollwerck's eastern European subsidiaries are sold to Kraft Foods.
2002: Swiss Barry Callebaut AG acquires Stollwerck.

German bank Deutsche Bank had to come to the rescue. The Stollwerck family gave up managing the company and sold its shares to the bank, which were then offered publicly. Deutsche Bank kept a majority stake in Stollwerck while the rest of the shares were distributed widely. In the fall of 1939, Germany's National Socialist government under Adolf Hitler started another war. Stollwerck struggled with the increasing pressure of government restrictions on the production of chocolate and other sweets and found it more and more difficult to buy the necessary raw materials. This time the takeover of Reichhardt paid off, since Stollwerck received a double-portion of the rationed cocoa. By 1942, however, more than half of Germany's chocolate factories had been closed down. Ultimately, half of Stollwerck's production facilities and office buildings were destroyed by bombs in the last years of the war.

In mid-1949, Stollwerck resumed operations. The company reorganized its administration, rebuilt and modernized its production plants, and made its comeback as a major player in Germany's chocolate industry during the postwar economic boom of the 1950s. In the 1960s, however, the company had to face new challenges. The former seller's market had become a buyer's market. Customers became more demanding. In the middle of the decade, the German government revoked the existing price restrictions on chocolate. Competition among chocolate makers intensified. Stollwerck's management was not able to cope with the new market demands soon enough to prevent another downturn in the company's history. In the business year 1970–71, Stollwerck incurred losses in the millions, and the company's majority shareholder Deutsche Bank was feverishly looking for a strategic partner with the financial strength to rescue Stollwerck from collapse. However, none of the large German chocolate makers showed any interest. It seemed more likely that they were eagerly waiting for one of their competitors to disappear from the marketplace.

A New Era Begins with Hans Imhoff

In 1971, entrepreneur Hans Imhoff entered the picture at a time when Stollwerck's prospects for survival were at a low point. Imhoff had not only built the largest wholesale food operation in the Rhineland south of Cologne but had also set up and successfully run his own chocolate manufacturing plant. As a child, he had grown up near Stollwerck's chocolate factory in Cologne and was enchanted by the sweet smells hovering around the plant. In 1972, after many difficulties, Hans Imhoff—with the help of Deutsche Bank's Alfred Herrhausen—became Stollwerck's new chairman of the advisory board. With a personal loan that enabled him to take over the bank's 46.5 percent stake in the struggling company, Imhoff initiated a radical reorganization program. The number of products made by Stollwerck was cut by over 80 percent, from about 1,000 to 190. Stollwerck's workforce shrunk by two-thirds, from 2,011 down to 705, between 1971 and 1975. As a result, the company recovered within just a few years. When Imhoff took over, Stollwerck's balance sheet showed DM6.4 million in losses. In 1975, the company reported a profit of DM6.9 million. In the same year, Stollwerck started building a brand-new production plant and headquarters in Cologne's suburb of Porz. Imhoff sold the old premises to the German Rueger group and, as a part of that deal, took over Rueger's 36 percent share in Stollwerck.

In the following 25 years, Imhoff continuously worked on Stollwerck's growth and on expanding its reach. The company acquired many other chocolate manufacturers and expanded into both western and eastern Europe. In 1979, Stollwerck took over Sprengel, one of Germany's oldest chocolate makers. Three years later, the company acquired the Belgian chocolate bar manufacturer Jacques Chocolaterie. After the reunification of East and West Germany, Stollwerck bought Thüringer Schokoladenwerk, the largest chocolate factory in the eastern part of the country, and invested heavily in modernizing it during the next ten years. The disintegration of the former Eastern Bloc opened the markets of eastern Europe, in which Imhoff—although aware of the high risk—saw equally high potential for growth. By 1996, Stollwerck owned two of the largest chocolate and cookie factories in Hungary and chocolate manufacturing plants in Poland and Russia, making the company the number one maker of chocolate bars in all three countries. In the late 1990s, Stollwerck was able to acquire two other major chocolate brands. In 1998, the company got lucky when Dutch food giant Nestlé decided to dispose of ''Sarotti,'' one of Germany's leading manufacturers of premium chocolate. One year later, Stollwerck acquired the premium chocolate brand ''Gubor.'' Stollwerck's export business soared and the company sold its sweets in the United States again, as well as in Japan and China. As a result, sales increased from about DM100 million in 1971 to DM1.52 billion in 1998.

Up until the late 1990s, Hans Imhoff was in firm control of every part of Stollwerck's operations. In 1993, he saw a childhood dream come true when he presented in Cologne's city-center a brand-new chocolate museum for which he had paid

DM53 million out of his own pocket. One of the main attractions was a ''chocolate fountain'' where visitors could taste the warm chocolate pouring out. In the late 1990s, Imhoff transferred 30 percent of his 95 percent stake in the company held by Imhoff Industrie Holding GmbH to a nonprofit foundation, while the other 65 percent was transferred to a family trust. During the 1990s, Stollwerck operated in a tougher environment with stagnating markets, growing competition, and rising cost for raw materials. The Russian crisis in the late 1990s hit Stollwerck hard, but Imhoff paid the DM30 million in losses out of his own pocket to keep the roughly 2,600 stockholders happy.

The year 2001 was a turning point for Stollwerck. Hans Imhoff retired at age 79 after leading the company for 30 years. Stollwerck's eastern European subsidiaries were sold to American food giant Kraft Foods Inc. for DM350 million. Stollwerck was planning to use the cash to strengthen its position in Germany and western Europe and to push the three core brands ''Sarotti,'' ''Alpia,'' and ''Sprengel.'' In spring 2002, the world's leading producer of cocoa and chocolate products, Swiss Barry Callebaut AG, acquired a 96 percent stake in Stollwerck from Hans Imhoff. Barry Callebaut, which was majority-owned by Klaus J. Jacobs, the heir of an old German coffee dynasty, planned to integrate Stollwerck into its organization within two years and to delist the company's shares from public trading.

Principal Subsidiaries

Sarotti GmbH; Stollwerck AG Werk Berlin; Stollwerck AG Werk Hannover; Thüringer Schokoladewerk GmbH; Wurzener Dauerbackwaren GmbH; Jacques Chocolaterie S.A. (Belgium); Chocolat Alprose S.A. (Switzerland); Stollwerck Werbe- und Marketing GmbH; Stollwerck Log-Trans Spedition GmbH.

Principal Competitors

Kraft Jacobs Suchard; Alfred Ritter GmbH & Co. KG; Nestlé Deutschland AG; Cadbury; Lindt & Sprüngli; Hershey Foods Corporation; Ferrero OHG mbH.

Further Reading

''Callebaut Opens New Markets with Stollwerck Buy,'' *Candy Business,* May–June 2002, p.6.

Chwallek, Andreas, ''Erfolg im Ausland; Hans Imhoff verfolgt ehrgeizige Ziele in Russland,'' *Lebensmittel Zeitung,* January 28, 2000, p. 56.

Jaspert, Werner, ''Hans Imhoff; Mister Stollwerck unter Dampf,'' *Süddeutsche Zeitung,* February 29, 1992.

——, ''Hans Imhoff Personalien,'' *Süddeutsche Zeitung,* February 2, 2001, p. 26.

Joest, Hans-Josef, *150 Jahre Stollwerck—Das Abenteuer einer Weltmarke,* Cologne, Germany: Stollwerck AG, 1989, 172 p.

Klein, Petra, ''Stollwerck-Deal perfekt,'' *Lebensmittel Zeitung,* May 31, 2002, p. 18.

Kuske, Bruno, *100 Jahre Stollwerck. Geschichte 1839–1939,* Cologne, Germany: Stollwerck AG, 1939, 165 p.

Olah, Peter, ''Prolonged Ownership Dispute Seen as Damaging Stollwerck,'' *Europe Intelligence Wire,* November 25, 2002.

Sieger, Heiner, ''Stollwerck; Der Schokoladenkönig,'' *Focus Magazin,* February 1, 1993, p. 122.

—Evelyn Hauser

Strayer Education, Inc.

1025 15th Street Northwest
Washington, D.C. 20005
U.S.A.
Telephone: (202) 408-2424
Fax: (202) 289-1831
Web site: http://www.strayereducation.com

Public Company
Incorporated: 1996
Employees: 960
Sales: $92.9 million (2001)
Stock Exchanges: NASDAQ
Ticker Symbol: STRA
NAIC: 611410 Business and Secretarial Schools

Strayer Education, Inc. is the education services holding company for Strayer University, which was founded in Baltimore, Maryland, in 1892, then under the name Strayer Business College. Strayer University is a proprietary institution of higher learning that offers undergraduate and graduate degree programs in accounting, business administration, and computer information systems to a student body comprised mostly of working adults. Strayer has 20 campus locations in the Washington, D.C., area, Virginia, Maryland, and North Carolina and an annual enrollment of more than 16,500 students. By putting a premium on convenience and flexibility for students with other scheduling commitments and by continually updating curriculum to provide the most practical and current skills for professional advancement in the ever-changing marketplace, Strayer has become one of the most successful and fastest-growing proprietary institutions in the United States.

A Proprietary School Takes Root: 1892–1958

Strayer's Business College was founded in 1892 in Baltimore, Maryland, by Dr. S. Irving Strayer. Prior to founding the business school, Strayer had spent years developing a shorthand method that improved upon the then widely popular Pitman system. First copyrighted in 1890, ''Strayer's Universal Shorthand'' became one of the main courses of study at the new school. With an original focus on secretarial skills, the other primary course of study was bookkeeping.

Shortly after the school was opened, a typewriter distributor named Thomas W. Donoho contributed significant financing and all the needed typewriters to the school in exchange for half ownership. Donoho became president and general administrative officer of the college in 1902. Donoho immediately began to make strides toward the development, improvement, and expansion of the school. After an extensive survey, he implemented revisions and refinements to the various courses of study, the textbooks, and the quality of the teaching faculty. Also under Donoho's leadership, Strayer opened two more branches in 1904, one in Washington, D.C., and one in Philadelphia. Donoho went on to buy the Washington, D.C., and Baltimore campuses from Irving Strayer in 1910, extending his presidency to both schools. Thomas W. was the first of three generations of Donohos to serve as president of the college.

From the beginning, Strayer emphasized its commitment to making its educational opportunities available to industrious individuals at whatever hours those individuals had available for study. To this end, a night school was established to accommodate students who held jobs during the day. Strayer set out to characterize itself as a rigorous institution and to distance itself from other business colleges that offered perhaps cheaper or quicker, but also less thorough, training. Strayer's commitment to placing its graduates in employment situations led to the development of close affiliations with businesses who would come to rely on the college for the direct recruitment of new employees from its roster of graduates.

In 1929, a separate school, the Strayer College of Accountancy, was founded and licensed to grant degrees by the Board of Education of the District of Columbia. This school was governed by its own board of trustees but operated in conjunction with the business college for almost 25 years, until the two schools merged in 1959 under the newly incorporated Strayer Junior College.

Building Academic Credibility: 1960s–1980s

Strayer had been known primarily for training in accounting and secretarial skills, but after its incorporation as Strayer

Junior College in 1959, the school began to broaden the range of its courses. For instance, the school added programs in court reporting and health facilities management—two areas where, it was speculated, demand for qualified personnel was growing faster than supply.

Further, Strayer launched a major endeavor to modernize its curriculum in September 1964 by adding data processing as a degree prerequisite for their accounting programs. The school invested significant funds to rent and install IBM equipment in new laboratory environments where students could receive instruction and practice using actual data processing machines. As quoted in the Strayer Junior College newsletter, *Strayer Topics*, in April of 1964, Chairman of the Board Murray T. Donoho said, ''Anybody working for an organization of any size in the next five years will be in the midst of automation. We consider Data Processing to be an absolute necessity today, if our students are to be considered adequately educated for modern administrative positions.'' Strayer was the first accounting degree program in the Washington, D.C., area to incorporate automation into its curriculum. Data processing courses were also offered to students pursuing business administration and executive secretarial degrees. This innovation was just one instance of Strayer's commitment to continual innovation in the interest of always providing its students with a competitive edge in the job market of the present and future.

By 1969, Strayer enrolled approximately 1,500 students and employed 32 full-time faculty members and 52 part-time instructors. Having received licensure to award bachelor of science degrees, Strayer became a four-year institution and was renamed Strayer College. By 1974, Strayer was fully accredited and gained full legitimacy as a four-year institution. By September of 1977, Strayer's enrollment had reached a record high. The total enrollment of 1,775 represented a 14 percent increase over the previous year.

In 1980, Dr. Charles E. Palmer was elected Chairman of Strayer's Board of Directors. Palmer brought extensive experience to the Strayer board: he had headed nine proprietary private business colleges and associate degree-granting junior colleges of business in North Carolina, South Carolina, Virginia, and the Washington, D.C., area; he had also served as the leader of a number of educational and civic organizations and co-authored 11 McGraw-Hill-published accounting and business textbooks. Strayer made significant strides in credibility and growth during Palmer's ten-year leadership.

In 1981, Strayer became the first proprietary school in the country to receive regional accreditation when it was so endorsed by the Commission of Higher Education of the Middle States Association. That same year, Strayer received approval from the State Council of Higher Education for the state of Virginia to open a campus in Arlington, Virginia. This approval marked the beginning of a period of geographic expansion for Strayer.

In 1989, the ownership and presidency of Strayer changed hands when Ron K. Bailey bought the college from Charles E. Palmer. Ron Bailey had received his bachelor of science degree from Strayer College and returned to the college shortly thereafter in 1974 as a part-time instructor of business courses. In a short period of time, Bailey joined the leadership of the company. Bailey was serving as Strayer's executive vice-president in 1989 when he was presented with a chance to buy the college. The total selling price in 1989 was $5 million.

There were several reasons why for-profit education was such an attractive business. In exchange for offering students flexible hours, an accelerated degree path, and a near 100 percent acceptance rate, for-profit schools were generally able to charge higher tuition than most public state schools. Tuition and fees for Strayer were, on average, more than three times higher than those at state universities. Also, for-profit schools, with their emphasis on job training rather than a broad liberal arts education, were able to operate with significantly lower overhead and labor costs: campus facilities were less extensive, and because classes were predominantly taught by part-time instructors, the cost of personnel—a university's most significant operating cost—was dramatically lower. The trick for Strayer, as Ron Bailey knew, was to maintain a vigilant commitment to cost controls while continuing to distinguish the school as a provider of top-quality educational services.

When he took over the presidency, Bailey accelerated Strayer's program of regional expansion and committed himself to further broadening Strayer's curriculum and degree programs and to improving the caliber of its faculty. By 1991, Strayer had added campus locations in Huntington Metro, Potomac Mills, Manassas, Loudoun, Fredericksburg, and Takoma Park.

Feeding Off the High-Tech Boom in the 1990s

The exponential growth of Strayer coincided closely with the high-tech boom of the 1990s. As computer skills became a crucial requirement for more and more jobs, so demand for computer education began to burgeon. Similarly, as the bull market continued for technology-related stocks, so analysts began to favor the stocks of for-profit education companies. Analysts were also keen on for-profit education companies because they were deemed to be relatively recession-proof: when the economy slumped, they speculated, people who were laid off tended to go back to school to improve their skills and better their employability.

In addition to following the most direct avenues for expansion, Strayer developed a subsidiary interest in 1995 when it introduced the Strayer Education Loan Program as an alternative source of student funding to government-sponsored loans. The wholly owned subsidiary was named Education Loan Processing, Inc. (ELP). The program was able to service loans at a lower cost than the government and thereby offer students highly competitive terms and interest rates. Tailored specifically to meet the loan needs of working adults, ELP served the dual purpose of further accommodating Strayer's valued students while increasing the company's tuition revenues through earned interest on loans. ELP was good for Strayer students and good for Strayer business at the same time.

Key Dates:

1892: Strayer Business College is founded in Baltimore, Maryland, by Dr. S. Irving Strayer.

1904: Branches of Strayer Business College are opened in Washington, D.C., and Philadelphia.

1910: The Washington, D.C., and Baltimore campuses are purchased from Irving Strayer by associate founder Thomas W. Donoho.

1928: The Strayer College of Accountancy is established.

1959: Strayer Junior College is incorporated and becomes the umbrella under which the Business College and the College of Accountancy operate.

1969: Strayer Business College gains licensure to award bachelor of science degrees and is renamed Strayer College.

1974: Strayer College receives accreditation by the Association of Independent Colleges and Schools.

1981: Strayer receives approval to offer its programs in the state of Virginia, which marks the beginning of a period of expansion.

1987: Strayer College is authorized to award master of science degrees.

1989: Ronald K. Bailey, then administrative vice-president, buys Strayer College from Charles Palmer.

1996: Strayer Education, Inc. is established as the holding company for Strayer College, and an initial public offering is made.

1998: Strayer College is awarded university status by the District of Columbia.

2000: New Mountain Capital, LLC and DB Capital Partners purchase a controlling stake in Strayer Education, Inc.

In 1996, Strayer Education, Inc., was established as the parent company of Strayer College in order to take the business public. Trading on the NASDAQ Stock Exchange under the ticker symbol STRA, Strayer raised $30 million with its initial public offering, selling three million shares for $10 per share. Nine months later, Strayer returned to the market for a secondary offering of 1.15 million shares. This time the stock sold for $21.75 per share, a more than 100 percent gain since the initial offering.

In July 1997, Dr. Donald Stoddard was appointed president of Strayer College. Ron K. Bailey continued as president and CEO of Strayer Education, Inc.; relinquishing the presidency of the college enabled him to devote his full energies to guiding the strategic growth of the corporation. Stoddard, who had worked extensively in the field of higher education, assumed responsibility for maintaining the quality of education at the college. At this time, Strayer had built an enrollment of over 8,000 students at nine campuses in Washington, D.C., Virginia, and Maryland.

With solid leadership in place and the significant capital raised from stock sales, Strayer was ready to expand in three strategic directions. First, the company would continue to expand its regional presence, opening a new campus every year for five years. Second, Strayer would increase the program offerings of its Internet-based "school," Strayer Online. Finally, the company would continue to expand the courses tailored for its corporate and government clients.

In July 1997, with 48 percent of its students majoring in computer information systems, Strayer leadership was acutely aware of the fast-increasing demand for computer training. Computer skills were needed not only by students seeking to enter the job market or change careers but also by the established employees of many corporations. Strayer had already begun offering onsite computer training courses for corporations like AT&T and federal agencies like the Internal Revenue Service. These affiliations were particularly lucrative, because Strayer was paid for teaching the courses without having to provide equipment or facilities. To solidify its stake in the computer education industry, Strayer formed a new, wholly owned subsidiary called Professional Education, Inc. (ProEd). ProEd was designed to offer a specialized professional development curriculum whereby students could build a wide range of technical skills needed for success in the increasingly computer-driven corporate world.

Strayer also courted the demand for computer and business-related courses by adding new degree programs. In 2000, the university gained approval from the District of Columbia Education Licensure Commission to offer programs for a master of science degree in communications technology, as well as associate in arts degrees in computer networking and acquisition and contract management.

In January 1998, Strayer Education, Inc. received a significant endorsement for its ongoing efforts to improve its faculty and educational resources and expand its degree programs when the college was granted university status. This promotion—rare for a proprietary institution—conferred new respectability on Strayer, and with the company on the verge of a major expansion, it could not have come at a better time.

New Ownership Accelerates Growth: 2000–02

Strayer faced significant changes as it headed into the new millennium. The company signed an agreement in November 2000 with a group of investors headed by a New York investment firm that specialized in education companies, New Mountain Capital, LLC. Under the agreement, New Mountain Partners and co-investor DB Capital Partners, the private equity component of Deutsche Bank AG, purchased a controlling stake in Strayer Education, Inc. The price of this investment was $150 million.

Further, Ron K. Bailey, who owned 52 percent of the company, retired from Strayer, selling the bulk of his stake in the company. Bailey was succeeded as president and CEO by Robert S. Silberman, who had joined New Mountain Capital a few months earlier. In addition, Steven B. Klinsky, New Mountain Capital's founder and CEO, became the non-executive chairman of Strayer's Board of Directors. The deal was finalized in March of 2001.

Silberman intended to increase shareholder value at Strayer by stepping up the company's rate of organic growth (in the form of increased enrollment and new educational sites), along with considering selective strategic acquisitions. While Bailey's growth strategy had called for opening one new campus per year, Silberman planned to accelerate this to three new sites per year. The cost of adding numerous new facilities was not as great as one might think. As Silberman told the *Washington Post* on July 9, 2001, each new campus required an investment of only $1 million, half of which went to the necessary equipment and the other half of which was used to cover losses until the school began to pay for itself. Further, 75 percent of faculty were part-time adjunct professors who were paid on a strictly per-class basis, and students paid all tuition up front. As Silberman put it, "It's a great business. It has positive cash flow, and it's not capital intensive." After proliferating up and down the east coast, Silberman planned to establish Strayer as a nation-wide institution. Further, Silberman saw the opportunity to grow enrollment by recruiting more foreign students to "attend" Strayer classes online.

In March 2002, Strayer was granted regulatory approval to open campuses and offer courses in North Carolina. This was a significant gain for Strayer, as the demographics of North Carolina looked promising, and as it represented the company's first entry into a state beyond the realm of its established geographic footprint. Strayer's first three North Carolina campuses were opened that year, two in the Charlotte area and one in Raleigh-Durham, and the company acknowledged provisional plans to open six more campuses in the state within the next few years. At the same time, Strayer had established alliances with more than 80 corporations and government institutions to provide training to their employees. The challenge for Strayer was to maintain a high level of academic quality and integrity while continuing to expand across the nation. With over 100 years of experience and no sign of demand abating for working adult education, Strayer confidently projected its own success into the foreseeable future.

Principal Subsidiaries

Strayer University; Education Loan Processing (ELP); Professional Education, Inc. (ProEd).

Principal Competitors

Apollo Group Inc.; Corinthian Colleges Inc.; DeVry Inc.

Further Reading

"ABCs of Education Stocks," *Business Week,* September 24, 2001, p. 128.

Atkinson, Bill, "For-Profit Schools Stand Tall as Investments," *Baltimore Sun,* April 6, 1998, p. 11C.

Knight, Jerry, "Wall Street Looks to Make Dollars Off Scholars," *Washington Post,* October 26, 1996, p. F29.

——, "Learning from Strayer's Ron Bailey," *Washington Post,* July 9, 2001, p. E01.

McTague, Jim, "Strayer Education's Lofty Growth Plans Mirror the Expanding Market for Professional Training," *Barron's Online,* August 5, 2002.

Morey, Ann, "The Growth of For-Profit Higher Education," *Journal of Teacher Education,* September, 2001, p. 300.

Soley, Lawrence, "Higher Education . . . or Higher Profit; For-profit Universities Sell Free Enterprise Education," *Institute for Public Affairs,* September 28, 1998, p. 14.

—Erin Brown

The Sumitomo Trust & Banking Company, Ltd.

5-33, Kitahama 4-chrome
Chuo-ku
Osaka 540-8639
Japan
Telephone: (06) 6220-2121
Fax: (06) 6220-2043
Web site: http://www.sumitomotrust.co.jp

Public Company
Incorporated: 1925
Employees: 5,154
Total Assets: ¥16.7 trillion ($124 billion)(2002)
Stock Exchanges: Osaka Tokyo London
Ticker Symbol: 8403
NAIC: 523991 Trust, Fiduciary, and Custody Activities;
    52211 Commercial Banking

The Sumitomo Trust & Banking Company, Ltd., a member of the Sumitomo keiretsu or group of companies, operates as an independent financial concern offering asset management and custodial services as well as traditional commercial banking services. During the 1990s, Sumitomo Trust faced distinct challenges related to Japan's faltering economy and the high rate of nonperforming, or bad, loans. Amid major restructuring of the Japanese banking sector, Sumitomo Trust remains independent, unlike many of its competitors whose merger activity has created a handful of large megabanks.

Sumitomo Trust's Origin

Sumitomo Trust is one of many companies that bear the name Sumitomo. Sumitomo, originally a copper producer, was one of Japan's conglomerates. By subsidizing new ventures with existing operations, Sumitomo branched into numerous businesses, including transport and warehousing, insurance, engineering, and banking.

Sumitomo established a successful banking subsidiary in 1912. The Sumitomo Bank was eager to enter trust banking, but was prevented by financial regulations from doing so. Sumitomo circumvented the regulations by creating another subsidiary, the Sumitomo Trust Company.

Established in 1925, the Trust was actually a spinoff of the Sumitomo Bank, staffed at first with bank personnel. Although technically it was an independent corporation, Sumitomo Trust was controlled by other companies in the Sumitomo group. As a "captive" subsidiary, it functioned as the group's private trust bank, becoming an important link in an increasingly complex financial organization that included commercial banking, insurance, and corporate finance.

PostWar Challenges

Sumitomo Trust benefited greatly from Japan's strong industrial growth during the 1930s. But at the same time the government was ruled by a military clique which, threatened by the power of huge industrial groups like Sumitomo, favored their dissolution. This inclination, however, was strongly tempered by the government's reliance on their industrial might for its massive armament program.

During World War II, Sumitomo Trust was forced to obey strict instructions from the government. When the war ended in 1945, the occupation authority ordered a complete breakup of the Sumitomo group. This meant that Sumitomo Trust's ties with other group companies had to be cut completely. Each company was purged of managers who overtly supported the war, and each was forced to change its name.

The Sumitomo Trust returned to business in 1948 as the Fuji Trust & Banking Company. As a result of new financial regulations, primarily the Commercial Banking Law, Fuji Trust also was permitted to engage in limited banking activities. In 1950 the company was authorized to deal in foreign exchange, and the following year started trusteeships for investment trusts.

Restoring the Sumitomo Name: 1952

In 1952 industrial laws were liberalized and the company was allowed to change its name back to Sumitomo. In addition, the former Sumitomo companies were permitted to hold minority shares in each other and to conduct regular strategy meetings.

Company Perspectives:

Our mission is to be an indispensable financial institution in Japan, capitalizing on our management autonomy and our business model and gaining support from our stakeholders, including our shareholders and customers.

In an effort to maintain leadership in the industry, Sumitomo Trust consistently pioneered new forms of trust management. In 1952 it introduced loan trusts, and in 1957 began pension-trust management.

The company grew steadily during the 1960s, just as it had in its early years. The Trust had many profitable middle-market clients, but its primary sources of business were affiliated Sumitomo companies; it was again, in many ways, the private trust bank for the Sumitomo group.

In 1973, after setting up foreign offices in New York, London, and Los Angeles, Sumitomo Trust opened an international department to gather intelligence on capital markets. The establishment of this department marked the beginning of Sumitomo Trust's interest in developing a solid international financial network. This was later expanded, with offices in Europe, the Middle East, Australia, and elsewhere in Asia and the Americas.

It was not until the early 1980s, however, that Sumitomo Trust became highly active in international markets, becoming more aggressive in marketing its services to third parties with little or no association with other Sumitomo companies. The Trust's business expanded accordingly, and by 1987 it was the second largest trust and banking company in Japan.

The company soon outgrew the limited opportunities of its close association with the Sumitomo group, and during the late 1980s it began to forge new relationships with foreign banks and securities dealers. In 1987, it created a securities lending services subsidiary in the United States.

During the 1980s and early 1990s, Sumitomo Trust & Banking remained closely associated with the Sumitomo group—its four largest shareholders were Sumitomo companies. It continued to focus on international finance and maintaining its efficient management structure. As the 1990s progressed, however, Sumitomo Trust faced many challenges brought on by the faltering Japanese economy and bad loans.

Problems Arising in Japan's Banking Sector: 1990s

As the company's assets began to deteriorate, Sumitomo Trust began a restructuring effort in 1992 that included layoffs, a slowdown in new branch openings, and cost cuts related to capital spending. The firm's financial situation continued to worsen with pretax profits falling by 6.1 percent in 1992 and then by 30.7 percent in 1993.

A significant factor related to Sumitomo Trust's faltering bottom line was the firm's exposure to bad or nonperforming loans. Housing loan companies were established in Japan in the 1970s by commercial banks to handle residential mortgage

Key Dates:

1925: The Sumitomo Trust Company is established.
1948: The company returns to business after the war as Fuji Trust & Banking Company.
1952: The firm is allowed to change its name back to Sumitomo Trust; loan trusts are introduced.
1973: Sumitomo Trust opens an international department to gather intelligence on capital markets.
1987: By now, the company is the second largest trust and banking company in Japan.
1994: Pretax profits fall by 30.7 percent due to bad loan write-offs.
2000: Japan Trustee Services Bank is created as a joint venture with Daiwa Bank.

lending, a business service that a bank could not provide. During the 1980s, however, Japan began changing its laws, which allowed banks to offer mortgage lending themselves. To deal with the changing laws, the housing loan companies sought out the commercial real estate market during the 1980s and began lending at breakneck speed. When the Japanese property market collapsed in the late 1980s, housing loan companies and the major commercial banks that funded them were left with large amounts of bad loans. In fact, in 1994 the *Financial Times* reported that nearly 60 percent of housing company loans were bad. Sumitomo Trust felt the effects of the crisis in 1994 when Nippon Mortgage Co., one of its largest debtors, declared bankruptcy with nearly US$1.2 billion in debt owed to the firm. As such, Sumitomo Trust—and the majority of Japan's large banks—spent the 1990s writing off bad loans.

In the late 1990s, Japan began to restructure its financial sector in an attempt to get its major banks back on track. The Financial Reconstruction Commission (FRC) began to force Japan's largest banks to merge and form business alliances and also laid the groundwork for new banking regulations. Sumitomo Trust became its target in 1998 when the government pushed it into merger talks with the Long-Term Credit Bank of Japan (LTCB), a bank in financial ruin. Sumitomo Trust remained independent, however, as LTCB was nationalized, renamed Shinsei Bank, and then sold to U.S.-based Ripplewood Holdings LLC in 2000.

Looking Ahead in the New Millennium

Sumitomo Trust held on to its independence into the new millennium. While it continued to write off bad loans, it appeared to weather the financial storm better than its competitors. In fiscal 2001, it was the only Japanese bank whose credit costs did not exceed net business profit—this was the first time in eight years that the firm reported such results. Foreign investors held a 16.6 percent stake in the firm, a greater share than any other Japanese banking concern—and its share performance was higher than the industry average. As the company claimed that its independence could be maintained because of its solid management system, it continued to seek out key alliances that would improve profitability and increase market share. Sumitomo Trust forged one such alliance with Daiwa Bank—now called Resona Holdings Inc.—in 2000 when it created Japan Trustee Services Bank in a joint venture.

The company announced its Revised Plan for Restoring Sound Management in August 2001. As part of this initiative, Sumitomo Trust planned to increase net profit and focus on its core trust business in order to increase the percentage of fee income to gross profit—27 percent in 2001—to 50 percent by 2005. While Japan's financial and banking sectors continued to restructure under intense global scrutiny, Sumitomo Trust management was confident that the company would achieve future success.

Principal Subsidiaries

The Sumishin Shinko Company Ltd.; Sumishin Business Service Company Ltd.; STB Personnel Service Co. Ltd.; STB Investment Corp.; Sumishin Loan Guaranty Company Ltd.; Sumishin Guaranty Company Ltd. (98.8%); Japan Trustee Services Bank Ltd. (50%); Businext Corp. (40%); The Sumitomo Trust Finance Ltd. (Hong Kong); Sumitomo Trust and Banking S.A. (Luxembourg); STB Finance Cayman Ltd.; FCSC Corp.; STB Cayman Capital Ltd.; STB Preferred Capital (Cayman) Ltd.; Sumitomo Trust Banking Co. (United States).

Principal Competitors

Resona Holdings Inc.; Mitsui Trust Holdings Inc.; Mizuho Asset Trust & Banking Co.

Further Reading

"Bad Loan Disposal by Japan's Trust Banks Doubles Forecasts," *AsiaPulse News,* May 24, 2000.

Baker, Gerard, "Japan's Banks Get Tough on Debt," *Financial Times* (London), July 13, 1994, p. 32.

Bremner, Brian, "Cleaning Up Japan's Banks—Finally," *Business Week,* December 17, 2001.

Bremner, Brian, and Emily Thornton, "Bad Banks: Why Japan's Pols Are Paralyzed," *Business Week,* October 5, 1998.

Rowley, Anthony, "Japanese Bank Merger Talks Spark Rumours Over FRC's Role," *Banker,* February 1999, p. 6.

——, "LTCB Becomes Japan's Test Case for Mergers," *Banker,* September 1998, p. 6.

"Sumitomo Trust Eyes Deep Cut in Costs," *Jiji Press Ticker Service,* October 8, 1992.

—update: Christina M. Stansell

tamedia:

Tamedia AG

Werdstrasse 21
8021 Zurich
Switzerland
Telephone: +41 1 248 50 41
Fax: +41 1 248 50 61
Web site: http://www.tamedia.ch

Public Company
Incorporated: 1933 as Tages-Anzeiger für Stadt und
Kanton Zürich AG
Employees: 1,982
Sales: SFr 756.1 million ($490.39 million) (2001)
Stock Exchanges: Zurich
Ticker Symbol: TAG
NAIC: 511110 Newspaper Publishers; 323119 Other
Commercial Printing; 511120 Periodical Publishers;
511130 Book Publishers

Tamedia AG is Switzerland's second largest media and publishing group. Publisher of that country's second largest newspaper, *Tages-Anzeiger Zeitung,* Tamedia has spread its interest to cover a variety of newspaper, magazine, radio, television, and Internet interests. The company also owned independent Swiss television station TV3, which shut down at the end of 2001. The company's losses at TV3 were in large part responsible for depressing the company's revenues, down to SFr 756 million in 2001 from nearly SFr 820 million the year before, while the company dipped into the red in 2001. Tamedia's operations are divided into three primary divisions. Print Media, which includes the newspapers *Tages-Anzeiger,* the Sunday morning paper *Sonntags Zeitung,* business newspaper *Finanz und Wirtschaft,* and shares in *Zurich Express* and *Berner Zeitung,* and magazines titles such as *Annabelle, Facts, Du, Spick,* and *Schweizer Familie.* The Electronic Media division includes the company's TeleZüri television station, radio stations Radio 24 and Radio Basilisk, and control of Belcom, which owned Tele24, another failed independent television station. The Electronic Media division also includes the company's Internet operations, which consist primarily of the Win-

ner family of web sites. The third Tamedia division, Services, represents the company's in-house printing operations, Tamedia Drukzentrum, Waser Druck, and Regor AG. Tamedia went public on the Zurich stock exchange in 2000, yet two-thirds of the company's shares remain under the control of the Coninx family, which has owned the company since the beginning of the 20th century.

Newspaper for a New Town at the Dawn of the 20th Century

The creation of the city of Zurich—formed by combining 11 formerly independent towns in 1893—opened the opportunity for a new newspaper to serve the new city's socially diverse population. In that year, Wilhelm Girardet, a publisher in Germany, and Swiss editor Fritz Walz joined together to launch a Zurich newspaper, the *Tages-Anzeiger,* owned by Wilhelm Girardet & Co. After giving the paper away for free during its first month, the company began signing up subscribers. By the end of its second month, *Tages-Anzeiger* boasted 25,000 subscribers and a circulation base of more than 43,000 readers. Walz's role in the company's success was recognized at the end of the decade, when the company changed its name to Girardet, Walz & Co., but remained a partnership.

In 1904, *Tages-Anzeiger* launched an illustrated weekly supplement, *Zeitbilder,* because printing restrictions at the time made it difficult for the company to incorporate text and images on the same page. *Zeitbilder* was to remain a *Tages-Anzeiger* institution for nearly 60 years, continuing into the 21st century as *Das Magazin.*

A new era for the company began when Otto Coninx, also from Germany, married Girardet's daughter Berta. Because Girardet had tapped his own son to take over his publishing company, Otto Coninx, who had worked as an editor, was placed in charge of *Tages-Anzeiger* in 1905.

Girardet, Walz & Co. reincorporated as a limited liability company in 1912, although the company was still based in Germany. By 1917, the company's newspaper had reached a circulation of 84,000. The turbulent social and political climate over the postwar period led to a decline in circulation, yet by the mid-1920s, sales of *Tages-Anzeiger* had started to pick up again. By then, Otto Coninx had gradually gained ownership control of the company. In 1926, the company incorporated as a Swiss company and Coninx himself took on Swiss citizenship.

The company changed its name to Tages-Anzeiger für Stadt und Kanton Zürich AG in 1933. By then, the company had branched out beyond its daily newspaper, adding a publishing subsidiary Regina Verlag in 1927 and acquiring the publishing rights to *Das Schweizer Heim,* a magazine that was to be a forerunner of the company's later success, *Schweizer Familie,* the rights to which were acquired in 1933.

Switzerland's neutrality during World War II shielded Tages-Anzeiger, which saw its daily newspaper circulation rise past 100,000 in the early 1940s. By 1950, circulation neared 125,000 copies. The company also had grown to include the second generation of the Coninx family, notably through the addition of Otto Coninx-Wettstein, who took over as managing director upon his father's death in 1956.

Tages-Anzeiger remained the centerpiece of the company into the 1960s, as circulation topped 200,000 by the end of the decade. A number of format changes had helped in the newspaper's success, such as the adoption of a new layout and subtitle (*Non-Partisan Swiss Daily Newspaper*) in 1962, and the adoption of an early morning delivery schedule. After exchanging the *Zeitbilder* supplement for the new color TA7 supplement in 1963, the company introduced a separate classified ads section in 1966. The following year, the company began publishing a weekly international edition of the paper.

Diversified Print Offerings in the 1980s

Tages-Anzeiger started the 1970s on a roll, with its circulation soaring past 230,000 by 1973. In 1971, the company merged *Schweizer Heim* into *Schweizer Familie,* which helped boost circulation of the newly expanded magazine to more than 300,000 copies by 1974. Yet the company's fortunes were hit by the recession of that decade, as ad spending dropped drastically. Nonetheless, Tages-Anzeiger pushed on with its own expansion plans, notably with the construction of a new printing facility, which was ready in 1975. In 1978 the company began construction on another printing plant, on Zurich's Bubenbergstrasse.

The third generation of the Coninx family took over the company by the end of the 1970s and led the group on a more ambitious expansion in the next decade. A new weekly supplement was added to *Tages-Anzeiger* in 1978, called *Wochenprogramm.* That supplement was converted to a magazine format under a new title, *Züri Tip,* in 1983.

Tages-Anzeiger's diversification built up steam in the early 1980s. In 1981, the company began publishing a youth-oriented—and advertising-free—magazine, *Spick.* That year, also, the company acquired popular women's magazine *Annabelle.* The next year, the company added a second women's title, *Femina,* the German-language edition of which was combined with *Annabelle* to create *Annabelle-Femina.* That year, Tages-Anzeiger also bought a controlling stake in rival newspaper *Tagblatt der Stadt Zürich.*

The company moved its newspaper printing to the new Bubenbergstrasse works in 1984, bringing the company into the offset printing era. The new technology led the company to redesign *Tages-Anzeiger*'s layout again in 1985, adding more graphics as well as adopting block pagination. With its expanded printing capacity, Tages-Anzeiger then prepared a new newspaper, a Sunday morning paper called *Sonntags Zeitung,* which was launched in 1987 in partnership with *Berner Zeitung.* Also that year, Tages-Anzeiger acquired printing and magazine group Conzett & Huber, and its popular youth-culture magazine *Du.*

The following year the company acquired another printing company, Waster Druck, and founded a new nonfiction book publishing subsidiary, Werd Verlag. The company then separated the *Tages-Anzeiger Magazin* from the newspaper, relabeling it as *Das Magazin* and placing it under direction of its own editorial staff. *Das Magazin* then became the supplement for *Berner Zeitung* as well.

In 1990, Tages-Anzeiger, Berner Zeitung, and Neuste Nachrichten formed the Swiss Combi advertising pool. The company then purchased a controlling share of regional newspaper publisher Bremgartner Bezirks Anzeiger, which brought the company's newspaper division outside of Zurich for the first time. That year marked the company's entry into the media sector, with the purchase of stakes in Metex AG, Schlosser Film AG, and Condor Production AG, as well as a controlling share of radio and TV advertising sales group Radiotele AG, later reduced to a minority position, before selling out entirely at the end of the decade.

Swiss Media Company for the New Century

In 1993, as the company continued to diversify its activities, Tages-Anzeiger adopted a new name, Tamedia AG. In that year, the company joined in the creation of another advertising pool partnership, Swiss Pool. The company's advertising interests expanded again the following year with the acquisition of 50 percent of Press Publicité SA. In 1994, also, Tamedia made its first move into broadcasting, with the acquisition of a one-third stake in private Zurich regional television broadcaster TeleZüri.

New titles for the mid-1990s included *Facts,* a news magazine, and *Ernst,* a youth-oriented newspaper, both introduced in 1995. *PCTip,* originally published in partnership with International Data Group as another *Tages-Anzeiger* supplement, was

Key Dates:

1893: *Tages-Anzeiger* is founded as a daily newspaper by German publisher Wilhelm Girardet and editor Fritz Walz, in establishing the partnership Wilhelm Girardet & Co., based in Germany.

1899: The name is changed to Girardet, Walz & Co.

1905: Otto Coninx marries Berta Girardet and becomes head of Tages Anzeiger.

1926: The company becomes a Swiss corporation and Otto Coninx, who now owns the company, becomes a Swiss citizen.

1927: The company founds subsidiary Regina-Verlad and acquires the publishing rights to *Das Schweizer Heim.*

1933: The company changes its name to Tages-Anzeiger für Stadt und Kanton Zürich AG; the company acquires the rights to Schweizer Familie.

1962: The company introduces the first major layout change of *Tages-Anzeiger.*

1981: The company begins publishing *Spick,* a youth-oriented magazine; the company acquires the publishing rights to *Annabelle* magazine.

1987: The company launches *Sonntags Zeitung,* published on Sundays.

1990: The company begins media interests with the acquisition of Metex and other production companies, as well as a share in Radiotele AG.

1993: The company changes its name to Tamedia AG.

1994: The company acquires one-third of TeleZüri regional television station.

1995: The company launches *Facts,* a news magazine, and *Ernst,* a newspaper for young adults.

1998: The company launches TV3, a private television station, in partnership with Scandinavian Broadcasting System SA, with broadcasting starting in 1999.

2000: Tamedia goes public on the Swiss stock exchange.

2001: Tamedia acquires Belcom Holding AG, giving it full control of TeleZüri and Tele24; the company shuts down TV3.

2002: The company begins charging fees for viewing the online version of *Tages-Anzeiger.*

taken over entirely as the newspaper launched a dedicated computer section in 1996. The following year, Tamedia took its first steps into the Internet, with a participation in the PressWeb-operated jobs site, SwissClick.

Tages-Anzeiger took on a new layout in 1997, and added a new supplement, *Alpha,* a jobs section focused on the management-level jobs market. The following year the *Ernst* newspaper was converted as a *Tages-Anzeiger* supplement. In that year, the company bought a new women's magazine, *Orella,* which was reformatted as *Annabelle Creation.* The year 1998 also marked the formation of television network TV3, in partnership with Scandinavian Broadcasting System SA. TV3 marked a new attempt to break government-owned Swiss Broadcasting Corporation's (SBC) monopoly on the Swiss television broad-

casting market. The company also purchased a 25 percent stake in private Zurich radio station Radio Zürisee.

The following year, Tamedia boosted its television position again when it increased its position in TeleZüri to 50 percent. In 1999, also, Tamedia increased its Internet holdings when it pulled out of the PressWeb partnership and instead created a new subsidiary, Winner AG, which began developing a series of web sites under the Winner brand name. Tamedia enhanced its Internet operations in 2000 with a partnership with Swisscom's Bluewin, the country's leading Internet service provider. That year marked the first full year of broadcasting of TV3, the first private television station in Switzerland to offer a full programming schedule.

At the end of 2000, TV3 appeared to be winning over a share of the Swiss viewing public, with an emphasis on entertainment programming, including such popular fare as ''Big Brother'' and ''Who Wants to Be a Millionaire.'' Meanwhile, Tamedia had increased its newspaper portfolio with the acquisition of *Finanz und Wirtschaft,* a twice-weekly business specialty with a circulation of 55,000.

The year 2000 marked the end of an era as the Coninx family, now in its fourth and fifth generations, announced its decision to launch Tamedia as a public company, placing some 20 percent of the company's shares on the Swiss stock exchange. The Coninx family also announced its intention to divest all of its interest in the company by the end of the decade.

In November 2001, Tamedia announced that it was acquiring control of Belcom Holding AG, giving it full control of TeleZüri AG as well. The purchase, which forced Tamedia to sell off its stake in Radio Zurisee to satisfy antitrust requirements, also placed Belcom's struggling Tele24 national television franchise under Tamedia. Yet by then, Tamedia's own television empire was fading fast, as the company's audience shares were shrinking, dragging down advertising revenues. With losses at the station mounting to SFr 186 for the year, the company was forced to pull the plug at the end of December—its final broadcast schedule featured the film *Titantic.* The Swiss television market, which faced heavy competition from nearby German-language broadcasters in Germany, seemed unable to support an advertising-supported rival to the SBC.

By mid-2002, the damage caused by the TV3 collapse became clear, as the company was forced to post a loss for the year amid shrinking revenues. Nonetheless, Tamedia remained committed to its strategy of developing itself as a cross-media group for its second century. In July 2002, the company joined the trend toward fee-based web sites when it announced the introduction of reading fees for its online *Tages-Anzeiger* site.

Principal Subsidiaries

BD Bücherdienst AG (72%); Service Zentrum Buch SZB AG (24%); Belcom Holding AG; Radio 24 AG Zurich; TeleZüri AG 3 Zurich; Belcom AG Zurich; Takeoff-Communications AG; Zürichvision AG 4 Zurich (66.6%); Betriebsgesellschaft SonntagsZeitung (85%); Bevo AG Berne (25%); Bonus Medien AG Zurich; Condor Communications AG (70%); DMT Marketing Support AG; Facts-Media AG; Presse Publicité Rep SA (50%); Regor AG; Tages-Anzeiger Verlag AG; TA-Internet

Holding AG; Winner AG (84.5%); Verlag Finanz und Wirtschaft AG; Verlags-AG Sonntags Zeitung (85%); Waser Druck AG; Südostschweiz Pressevertrieb AG.

Principal Competitors

Ringier AG; Basler Zeitung AG; AG fur die Neue Zurcher Zeitung; Berner Tagblatt Mediengruppe; AZ Medien AG; Limmatdruck AG; LZ Medien Holding; Zollikofer AG; Der Bund Verlag AG; Huber und Co AG; Zurichsee Medien AG; Edipresse SA.

Further Reading

Blassel, Frederic, ''L'ambassadeur du changement,'' *Webdo,* August 31, 2000.

Hall, William, ''TA Media Offering Set to Value Group at SFr2.5bn,'' *Financial Times,* Sept 18, 2000, p. 32.

Maupin, Michael, ''Off the Air for Tele24,'' *Swiss News,* November 2001, p. 22.

''Readers Charged for Online Newspaper,'' *EuropeMedia,* July 16, 2002.

''Tamedia Closes Tough IPO as Actelion Seeks SFr400m,'' *Euroweek,* Oct 6, 2000 p. 20.

''Tamedia: Turbulences et nouvelle rotative,'' *Presse Romande,* July 2002.

''Weak Outlook for Tamedia,'' *Swissinfo,* October 10, 2001.

—M.L. Cohen

Tetra Pak International SA

70 Avenue Général-Guisan
Case Postale 446
CH-1009 Pully/Lausanne
Switzerland
Telephone: (41) 21 729 2111
Fax: (41) 21 729 2244
Web site: http://www.tetrapak.com/

Wholly Owned Subsidiary of Groupe Tetra Laval
Incorporated: 1951 as AB Tetra Pak
Employees: 20,200
Sales: EUR 7.6 billion ($8.15 billion) (2001)
NAIC: 322212 Folding Paperboard Box Manufacturing;
   322215 Nonfolding Sanitary Food Container
   Manufacturing; 322221 Coated and Laminated
   Packaging Paper and Plastics Film Manufacturing;
   333993 Packaging Machinery Manufacturing

Tetra Pak International SA makes laminated containers such as juice boxes. For decades identified with its unique tetrahedral dairy packaging, the company's product line has grown to include hundreds of diverse containers. It is a leading supplier of plastic milk bottles. With its sister companies, Tetra Pak claims to be the only provider of complete systems for processing, packaging, and distributing liquid foodstuffs worldwide. Tetra Pak products are sold in more than 165 countries. The company describes itself as a partner in developing its client's concepts rather than as a mere vendor. Tetra Pak and its founding dynasty have been notoriously secretive about profits; parent company Tetra Laval is controlled by the family of Gad Rausing, who died in 2000, through Netherlands-registered Yora Holding and Baldurion BV. The company reported 94.1 billion packages sold in 2001.

Origins

Dr. Ruben Rausing was born on June 17, 1895 in Raus, Sweden. After studying economics in Stockholm, he went to America in 1920 for graduate studies at New York's Columbia University. There, he witnessed the growth of self-service grocery stores, which he believed would soon be coming to Europe, along with a heightened demand for packaged foods. In 1929, with Erik Åkerlund, he established the first Scandinavian packaging company.

Development of a new milk container began in 1943. The goal was to provide optimal food safety while using a minimum amount of material. The new containers were formed from a tube that was filled with liquid; individual units were sealed off below the level of the beverage inside without introducing any air. Rausing reportedly got the idea from watching his wife Elizabeth stuffing sausages. Erik Wallenberg, who joined the firm as a lab worker, is credited with engineering the concept, for which he was paid SKr 3,000 (six months of wages at the time).

Tetra Pak was founded in 1951 as a subsidiary of Åkerlund & Rausing. The new packaging system was unveiled on May 18 of that year. The next year, it delivered its first machine for packaging cream in tetrahedral cartons to Lundaortens Mejeriförening, a dairy in Lund, Sweden. The 100 ml container, which was covered in plastic rather than paraffin, would be named Tetra Classic. Before this, European dairies typically dispensed milk in bottles or in other containers brought by customers. Tetra Classic was both hygienic and, with individual servings, convenient.

The firm continued to focus exclusively on beverage packaging for the next 40 years. Tetra Pak introduced the world's first aseptic carton in 1961. It would become known as Tetra Classic Aseptic (TCA). This product was different in two important ways from the original Tetra Classic. The first was in the addition of a layer of aluminum. The second was that the product was sterilized at a high temperature. The new aseptic packaging allowed milk and other products to be kept several months without refrigeration. The Institute of Food Technologists called this the most important food packaging innovation of the century.

Tetra Pak set up a Japanese subsidiary in 1962. It took six years to turn a profit but would soon be one of the company's most successful regions, generating annual sales of about ¥40 billion in the early 1980s. The rectangular Tetra Brik made its commercial debut in 1963. Tetra Rex, introduced in 1965, had a pointed top.

Company Perspectives:

We commit to making food safe and available, everywhere. We work for and with our customers to provide preferred processing and packaging solutions for food. We apply our commitment to innovation, our understanding of consumer needs, and our relationships with suppliers to deliver these solutions, wherever and whenever food is consumed. We believe in responsible industry leadership, creating profitable growth in harmony with environmental sustainability, and good corporate citizenship.

The rest of the packaging company, apart from Tetra Pak, was sold off in 1965. During this decade, a joint ownership arrangement between Hans and Gad Rausing, sons of the founder, was put in place.

Building with a Brik in the 1970s–80s

Tetra Brik Aseptic (TBA), a rectangular version, debuted in 1968 and sparked dramatic international growth. The TBA would account for most of Tetra Pak's business into the next century. Borden Inc. brought Brik Pak to U.S. consumers in 1981 when it began using this packaging for its juices. At the time, Tetra Pak's worldwide revenues were SKr 9.3 billion ($1.1 billion). Active in 83 countries, its licensees were putting out more than 30 billion containers a year, or 90 percent of the aseptic package market, reported *Business Week*. Tetra Pak claimed to pack 40 percent of Europe's dairy packaging market, reported Britain's *Financial Times*. The company had 22 plants, three of them for making machinery. Tetra Pak employed 6,800 people, about 2,000 of them in Switzerland.

In 1981, the company relocated its headquarters to Lausanne, Switzerland, mostly for tax reasons. Research and development facilities remained in Sweden. In 1984, much of the company's assets were transferred to a holding company registered in the Netherlands.

Tetra Pak's ubiquitous coffee-cream packages, often seen at restaurants, were by then only a small portion of sales. The Tetra Prisma Aseptic carton, eventually adopted in more than 33 countries, would become one of the company's greatest successes. This octagonal carton featured a pull-tab and a range of printing possibilities. Tetra Fino Aseptic, launched in Egypt, was another successful innovation of the same time period. This inexpensive container consisted of a paper/polyethylene pouch and was used for milk. Tetra Wedge Aseptic first appeared in Indonesia. Tetra Top, introduced in 1991, had a resealable plastic top.

By 1990, the company was selling 50 billion containers a year. There were some setbacks, however. It dropped a paper and plastic bottle for carbonated beverages due to the rising cost of plastic. There was also concern about Tetra Pak's impact on the environment. Unlike glass or plastic bottles, the laminated containers could not be sterilized and reused. In 1990, the company introduced a recycling program for its drink cartons in Canada, which converted used containers into a "superwood" plastic material.

Acquisition of Alfa-Laval in 1991

In 1991, Tetra Pak acquired Alfa-Laval AB for SKr 16.25 billion ($2.5 billion) in Sweden's largest takeover deal to date. Another Swedish multinational corporation, Alfa-Laval was a world leader in industrial and agricultural equipment, particularly dairy equipment. This allowed Tetra Pak to develop entire processing and packaging solutions for clients, a capacity that came to be increasingly in demand.

The deal drew intense anti-competitive scrutiny from the European Commission, which was already handing Tetra Pak an EUR 75 million ($89 million) fine for abusing its market dominance in Italy. The takeover nevertheless went through.

After the merger, Tetra Pak announced plans to return its headquarters to Sweden. Group Tetra Laval was created on January 1, 1993, with three divisions. Alfa-Laval's liquid packaging machinery was absorbed into Tetra Pak, the largest unit.

Gad and Hans Rausing were credited with transforming their father's milk carton firm into a leading global packaging company. They became wealthy in the process. The brothers had moved to England in the early 1980s and were considered to be the richest people in the country. One survey estimated their personal fortune at £4 billion ($6.4 billion).

In August 1995, Gad Rausing bought out the interest of Hans Rausing, who had retired from active management in early 1993. Terms were not officially disclosed, but it is estimated the 50 percent share in the company sold for $7 billion, making it Europe's largest private buyout ever, reported the *Financial Times*. The paper reported that a group of Swiss banks based the valuation on that of U.S. competitor International Paper, capitalized at slightly more than one times sales.

Hans Rausing preferred to focus on his farms in England and Portugal. His children were not interested in carrying on the business, while Gad Rausing's sons Finn and Jorn were active in management.

Tetra Pak accounted for more than 70 per cent of Tetra Laval's total 1997 revenues of SKr 15.5 billion. Slowing growth in Western Europe, Tetra Pak's biggest sales region, was being offset by emerging markets. By this time, Tetra Pak had invested $100 million in China and up to $50 million in Russia. Latin America was another area of rising demand. Besides geographic expansion, the company was aiming to aggressively grow its plastic bottling business, which the company had entered in 1994. Its research and development efforts were tackling the question of bottling beer in plastic. Tetra Pak launched a £1 billion bid for French plastic packaging group Sidel in 2001.

Gad Rausing died in 2000, leaving ownership of the Tetra Laval empire to his children—Jorn, Finn, and Kristen. When he sold his share of the company to his brother in 1995, Hans Rausing also agreed not to compete with Tetra Pak until 2001. He emerged from retirement backing a Swedish packaging company, EcoLean, devoted to a new biodegradable "Lean-Material" made primarily of chalk. Rausing acquired a 57 percent stake in the venture, which had been formed in 1996 by Åke Rosen.

Key Dates:

1929: Erik Åkerlund and Dr. Ruben Rausing form Scandinavia's first food packaging company.
1951: AB Tetra Pak is established in Sweden.
1961: First aseptic packaging is introduced.
1968: Tetra Brik Aseptic, the company's most enduring product, is launched.
1981: The company's headquarters is moved to Switzerland.
1991: Tetra Pak acquires Alfa-Laval.
1993: Groupe Tetra Laval is formed.
1995: Gad Rausing buys out brother Hans.
2000: Gad Rausing's children take over the company after his death.

Tetra Pak continued to introduce innovations. In 2002, the company launched a new high-speed packaging machine, the TBA/22. It was capable of packaging 20,000 cartons an hour, making it the fastest in the world. Under development was the Tetra Recart, the world's first carton able to be sterilized.

Principal Divisions

Carton Ambient; Carton Chilled; Plastics; Processing Systems.

Principal Competitors

Crown Cork & Seal Company Inc.; International Paper Company; RPC Group plc.

Further Reading

Benson, Ross, "He's Making 1 Million a Day But Still Haggles Over the Cost of a Few Tomatoes," *Daily Mail* (London), January 29, 2001, p. 43.

Brown-Humes, Christopher, "Deal Leads to Change of Control at Tetra Laval," *Financial Times*, August 23, 1995, p. 18.

Burt, Tim, "Tetra Pak Shapes Up for Plastic Push," *Financial Times*, December 16, 1998, p. 28.

"Carton Unit Still Dominant Within Group," *Financial Times*, December 16, 1998, p. 28.

"Cash Rich Group Sees Rise of 9.5%," *Financial Times*, December 16, 1998, p. 28.

Cinquante ans d'innovation, Romont, Switzerland: Tetra Pak Group, 2002.

Couzens, Gerard, "Dad's Tetra Pak Invention Made Billions . . . He Got £300," *Sunday Mirror* (London), February 11, 2001, p. 31.

Done, Kevin, "Tetra Pak Shifts Partial Ownership from Sweden," *Financial Times*, July 19, 1984, p. 21.

"Fabulous Wealth of the Rausing Dynasty," *Financial Times*, December 16, 1998, p. 28.

Foo Choy Peng, "Tetra Pak Boosts Its Profile on Mainland," *South China Morning Post*, April 17, 1997, p. 4.

Hill, Andrew and John Thornhill, "Packaging Crusader Wraps Up Merger Deal," *Financial Times*, May 24, 1001, p. 23.

Karnani, Roop, "A White Revolution at Tetra Pak," *Business Today* (India), July 7, 2000, p. 50.

Lawson, Dominic, "Swedish Packager Milks Old Markets," *National Post*, February 8, 2001, p. C13.

McIvor, Greg, "Balancing Risk and Reward: Doing Business In Russia," *Financial Times*, March 6, 1998, p. 31.

"Packaging Industry Has Strong Trio," *Financial Times*, May 25, 1983.

Shick, Nicole, "Le poumon Tetra Pak," *La Gruyère*, October 24, 2000.

Slavin, Terry, "Leader of the Pack," *Observer*, August 5, 2001, p. 5.

Smith, Charles, "Early Arrival Pays Off," *Financial Times*, July 5, 1982, p. 11.

Taylor, Robert, "Tetra Pak Returns Base to Sweden," *Financial Times*, August 21, 1991, p. 18.

"Testing a New Paper Package for Liquids," *Business Week*, April 6, 1981, p. 92.

—Frederick C. Ingram

Tommy Hilfiger Corporation

11/F, Novel Industrial Building
850-870 Lai Chi Kok Road
Cheung Sha Wan
Kowloon
Hong Kong
Telephone: (852) 2216-0668
Fax: (852) 2312-1368
Web site: http://www.tommy.com

Public Company
Incorporated: 1992
Employees: 4,900
Sales: $1.87 billion (2002)
Stock Exchanges: New York
Ticker Symbol: TOM
NAIC: 315223 Men's and Boys' Cut and Sew Shirt
(Except Work Shirt) Manufacturing; 315224 Men's
and Boys' Cut and Sew Trouser, Slack, and Jean
Manufacturing; 315232 Women's and Girls' Cut and
Sew Blouse and Shirt Manufacturing; 315234
Women's and Girls' Cut and Sew Suit, Coat, Tailored
Jacket, and Skirt Manufacturing; 315999 Other
Apparel Accessories and Other Apparel
Manufacturing; 44819 Other Clothing Stores; 53311
Lessors of Nonfinancial Intangible Assets (except
Copyrighted Works)

Tommy Hilfiger Corporation markets menswear, womenswear, and childrenswear designed by Tommy Hilfiger. Hilfiger sells a complete line of clothing from socks to shirts, swimwear, jackets, pants, belts, wallets and ties, as well as sleepwear, golf clothes, eyewear, cosmetics, bedding, and home furnishings. The company operates 15 specialty stores, ten Tommy Jeans stores, a Tommy Hilfiger Children's store, and a dual concept store. Hilfiger also operates 102 company outlet stores that offer branded products as well as out-of-season merchandise. Tommy Hilfiger products, which bear the well known red, white, and blue logo, can also be found in department stores and are marketed in over 55 countries across the globe.

Origins

Though the company was not incorporated until 1992, its history properly begins with the fortunes of its namesake, Thomas Jacob (Tommy) Hilfiger. Born in Elmira, New York, in 1951, Hilfiger started his first clothing business while still in high school. He and two friends invested $300 in used blue jeans and sold them out of an Elmira basement. Hilfiger never attended college but built up the blue jean business into a chain of seven upstate New York stores called People's Place. People's Place sold jeans, bell bottom pants, and other clothing, as well as candles, incense, and posters. The stores were successful enough to afford Hilfiger a Porsche, but they were poorly managed. In 1977, People's Place was forced to declare bankruptcy. Hilfiger moved to Manhattan and tried to find work as a clothing designer. Though he had no formal training, he had designed and sold vests and sweaters for People's Place. He worked freelance and then started a sportswear company that went out of business after only one year. He eventually found work designing jeans for Jordache.

In 1984, Hilfiger was contacted by Mohan Murjani, an Indian textile magnate. Murjani owned the license to Gloria Vanderbilt jeans and had helped spark the craze for designer jeans in the 1970s. Murjani had an idea to update the popular ''preppy'' look associated with designer Ralph Lauren and give it a younger and more mass appeal. He chose Hilfiger to design the line for his firm, Murjani International. In the beginning, however, marketing was much more important than the actual clothes.

First Marketing Campaign in 1985

The line of Tommy Hilfiger clothing debuted in the fall of 1985 with an ad campaign that featured no clothes but declared that Hilfiger was a designer on par with Ralph Lauren, Perry Ellis, and Calvin Klein. The ads did little more than insert Hilfiger's name in the pantheon. Yet this was somehow effective. The brashness of the strategy attracted attention in the fashion industry and caused comment by Johnny Carson and

Company Perspectives:

The Tommy Hilfiger Corporation is dedicated to living the spirit of the American dream. We believe: the spirit of youth is our greatest inspiration; resourcefulness is the key to value and excellence; in making quality a priority in our lives and products; by respecting one another we can reach all cultures and communities; and by being bold in our vision we continually expand our boundaries.

other notables. The first ads were centered around New York City, using print and outdoor media. By 1987, the Hilfiger line was attracting more national attention with advertisements in *People*, *USA Today*, *Newsweek*, *GQ*, *Sports Illustrated*, and other publications. The entire advertising budget for Hilfiger clothing was only $1.4 million, and ads appeared infrequently. They made a splash, however, with double-page spreads, and because they featured words, logos, or Hilfiger's face, and no images of clothes or models, they stood out from other fashion advertisements. George Lois, who helped create the ads for the firm Lois, Pitts, Gershon, Pon/GGK, claimed in a March 1988 *Marketing and Media Decisions* article that he could not make Hilfiger's clothes "look any better than anyone else's," and therefore the ads sold "an idea" and not the particular fashion. According to one survey, after only two years of his ads, Hilfiger had succeeded in convincing 68 percent of sampled New Yorkers to name him as one of the top four or five important designers. Sales also attested to the brilliance of the marketing strategy. In 1986, Hilfiger brand clothing was available in 60 department stores and 25 specialty shops and brought in $32 million in retail sales. A year later, retail sales had more than doubled, to $70 million.

Though clever advertising turned Hilfiger from an unknown into a top-selling designer, it was not only the mystique of the ads that accomplished this. The clothing was for the most part casual—khaki pants and a big polo shirt being the quintessential Hilfiger outfit. There was a little more flippancy in the cut and colors than the more staid Ralph Lauren style that Murjani had set out to imitate, and the clothes retailed for a bit less than similar designer togs. Hilfiger clothes fit the trend towards more casual work clothes—many offices in the 1980s were instituting casual Fridays—so this particular niche was expanding. Hilfiger clothes became staples of college men and others in the 20- to 35-year-old age group. The clothes were well-made, well-priced, similar to an existing fashion but with enough difference to stand out, and the offbeat ad campaign ignited a craze for them.

Expanding the Label: Late 1980s

By the late 1980s, Murjani International was troubled financially. The company had also licensed Gloria Vanderbilt and the Coca-Cola brand of clothing and seemed unable to focus adequately on the Hilfiger brand, which was growing enormously. In 1988, Tommy Hilfiger, Mohan Murjani, and two others formed a new company, called Tommy Hilfiger Co. Inc., buying out Murjani International. The deal was complicated, and it took the new company almost a year to finally purchase back from

Murjani the rights to the Tommy Hilfiger name. In the meantime, the company found a new financial backer in Hong Kong businessman Silas Chou. Chou's firm, Novel Enterprises, was one of the largest sweater manufacturers in Asia, and the company was willing to invest money in Tommy Hilfiger Company to allow it to expand. The new principles were Chou, Hilfiger, and two former Ralph Lauren executives, Lawrence Stroll and Joel Horowitz. Mohan Murjani was out. With Chou's extensive contacts in the Asian garment industry, the new company not only designed but manufactured Hilfiger clothing, using Asian factories that produced low-cost, high-quality goods.

Chou was eager to push the Hilfiger line to greater availability. Sales for the new company were only $25 million its first year, so they had fallen off quite a bit from the Murjani days. Yet Chou insisted on renting a luxurious midtown Manhattan office space as New York headquarters, surmising that things would quickly get better. They did. In the fall of 1992, the company made an initial public offering (IPO) on the New York Stock Exchange at $15 a share. Within a few months, the stock was selling at $25. Revenue for 1992 was $107 million, an astonishing increase that justified Chou's hopes. Hilfiger became a Wall Street darling, with steadily increasing earnings. In November 1993, a secondary stock offering brought in $70 million. The company used this cash to expand its in-store shops and to develop new outlet stores, which would sell past-season Hilfiger garments at reduced prices.

Mid-1990s Successes

Hilfiger's sales went up and up, from $107 million in 1992 to $138 million in 1993 and $227 million in 1994. There were close to 500 Tommy Hilfiger sections within department stores by the mid-1990s. About half the company's revenues came from sales at three big department store chains: Dillard's, Federated, and May. Another 15 percent of sales came from the discount chains T.J. Maxx and Marshalls, which sold the outdated stock at lower prices. Hilfiger began opening its own freestanding shops as well, debuting in Stamford, Connecticut, and Columbus, Ohio.

By 1994, it seemed everyone knew who Hilfiger was. President Clinton wore Hilfiger designs, as did the Prince of Wales, rock stars Michael Jackson, Elton John, and Snoop Doggy Dogg. Perhaps the most fanatic fans of Hilfiger designs were urban youths who gave the preppy look a new twist. Hip ghetto kids began taking the essentially suburban Hilfiger clothes and wearing them in extra large sizes in eclectic mixes with sports gear. Drooping pants from which Hilfiger logo underwear peeked out was one peculiar fashion. The designer noticed the street trend and responded by making extra-large sizes labeled "giant," using brighter colors, and attaching bigger and bolder logos. It was apparently what the people wanted, and sales soared. Hilfiger had achieved a remarkable level of mass appeal, with everyone from bike messengers to CEO's dressed in his designs.

Sales and earnings kept going up dramatically. The company used its profits to expand in various ways. Between 1994 and 1995 Hilfiger Corporation added over 200 in-store men's shops. The company had introduced boys' clothes in sizes 8 to 20, and when this line was successful it introduced a line for boys in sizes 4 to 7 in spring 1995. The company had close to 500 in-store boys' shops, and planned to add more. Hilfiger licensed its name to Cypress Apparel to make robes and sleepwear and to other manufacturers licensed scarves, handkerchiefs, umbrellas, and a line of golfing clothes. Hilfiger had a presence in Japan, with 36 shops inside Japanese department stores by 1995. Also in that year, the company launched 12 in-store shops across Central and South America. A new fragrance line, produced through a licensing agreement with Estee Lauder, also sold well.

Hilfiger slowly built more freestanding stores, with six full-price and 16 discount outlet stores open by 1995. The company had to move cautiously on its own stores in order not to appear to compete with the Hilfiger shops operated by its best customers, the large department chains.

Plans to launch a line of women's clothing started and stopped. There had been an unsuccessful attempt to make womenswear when Hilfiger designs were backed by Murjani International. The designer acknowledged that he had taken on too much too soon, and womenswear was dropped. It was a logical extension of the brand's popularity, however, and potentially enormously profitable. In March 1994, Tommy Hilfiger Corporation hired Jay Margolis as its new president and vice-chairman, with the specific task that he develop a womenswear line. Little over a year later, however, the company announced that it would not develop the women's line, and Margolis resigned. The company declared that bringing out its own womenswear would be prohibitively expensive, and the new plan was to find a competent licensee. The company eventually licensed womenswear to Pepe Jeans International. Hilfiger chairman Silas Chou owned the Pepe Jeans brand, and the company already produced a men's jeans line for Hilfiger. The women's line came out in the summer of 1996 at more than 400 major department store shops. Like Hilfiger menswear, the women's line was mostly sportswear and aimed for the same casual wear-to-work niche. The company also put out a women's perfume, "Tommy Girl," through a licensing agreement with Estee Lauder. In other expansions, the line of boyswear was extended down into toddler and infant clothes.

Sales for 1996 were close to $500 million, and the company's earnings increased over 60 percent. Hilfiger stocks had

at times been the highest traded apparel stocks on Wall Street, and investors seemed to love the company's strong growth. The danger to investors, of course, was that the enormously popular Hilfiger brand would suddenly turn stale. Fashion stocks tended to be unpredictable because apparel's success was mostly dependent on a fickle public. Still, Tommy Hilfiger Corporation still seemed capable of continued expansion. Profit margins were widening, something investors looked at as an indicator of soundness. Moreover, the trend toward casual work clothing that Hilfiger had first taken advantage of was still running. One industry survey indicated that over 20 percent of offices were casual every day, not just on Friday. Workers were spending money on nice casual clothes such as Hilfiger designs, and so there did not seem to be a looming end to the clothing's popularity. Also, though Hilfiger Corporation had brought out its women's line, its staple was still menswear, traditionally more stable than women's apparel. Hilfiger designs were also priced well. General consumers typically spent less than $50 on individual items of clothing, and most Hilfiger apparel was in that range. Nevertheless, Hilfiger was perceived as high quality. The company had not watered down its appeal by making the brand available at lower-end chains such as Penney's and Sears. By 1997, the company was just beginning to expand into European markets. A huge flagship store was under construction in London, and presumably there was much market potential overseas.

Tommy Hilfiger Corporation had taken a virtually unknown designer and declared him a dean of menswear on par with industry leaders Calvin Klein, Ralph Lauren, and Perry Ellis. Remarkably, consumers bought the idea and bought the clothing. A dozen years after the company's brash inaugural ads, the clothing was selling more strongly than ever, not only in the United States but in Japan, Europe, and Central and South America. The combination of guileful advertising, shrewd management, and a truly appealing and useful product brought the company to a strong global level by the mid-1990s.

Battling Competition in the New Century

In fact, Hilfiger's success would continue throughout the late 1990s before coming to an abrupt halt in 2000. In 1998, the firm acquired its Canadian licensee, Tommy Hilfiger Canada, and also a portion of Pepe Jeans USA for $1.15 billion. It also launched a series of new products including a home furnishings line, the Hilfiger Athletics Fragrance for men, and an infant and toddlers line. Sales for the year climbed to $847 million and then skyrocketed to $1.63 billion just one year later. During 1999, the company moved into the bath and body products market, and also began offering a girls' line, color cosmetics, the Freedom fragrances, and also came out with a line of women's handbags.

The competitive nature of the fashion industry, however, caught up with Hilfiger in 2000. Stock price plummeted as the company announced that its profits for the fiscal year would fall. A 2000 *Fortune* magazine article summed up the company's problems, commenting that "Tommy rested on its red, white, and blue laurels too long. New trendier brands (think Fubu) dominate urban fashion, while Tommy's clothes fill bargain bins at Bloomingdale's and Macy's." The article went on to state that "Hilfiger tried a host of makeover strategies that were belated and misguided.'' These strategies included a lackluster women's sportswear line that was supported by sponsorships of the Mary J. Blige and Sheryl Crow music concerts. These sponsorships however, did little to bolster sales of the women's line, which saw the addition of both golf and swim apparel during 2000.

After customers complained that the womenswear line was too trendy and did not fit well, Hilfiger revamped the line, going back to its basic preppy modern look. The company also brought in a slew of industry veterans, including Lynn Kohlman, a former Donna Karan executive, and Camilla Nickerson, a fashion editor from *Vogue* to get the division back on track. Success in this section of the market was crucial, as its menswear division was suffering from weakening sales. In fact, Bloomingdale's—with the exception of the 59th Street location in New York—pulled the Tommy menswear line from its brand lineup in 2001.

During 2001, a women's intimate apparel line and plus-size line was introduced. The company also generated publicity that year when Lauren Bush, the niece of President George W. Bush, began modeling Hilfiger clothing. The company's efforts appeared to pay off, and by June of that year sales in both women's and junior's sportswear and jeans was exceeding company forecasts.

During fiscal 2002, overall sales declined slightly, while net income increased by 2.7 percent to 134.5 million. Though Hilfiger's impressive growth had slowed dramatically from the 1990s, the company remained a popular and well-known brand. Along with traditional advertising, the company choose to tout its image using unique methods, including the purchase of the sponsorship rights to Long Island's Jones Beach Theater, one of the most successful amphitheaters in the United States, and the sponsorship of a 50-foot sailing vessel. The ship was named the Tommy Hilfiger Freedom America yacht and would be racing in the challenging 27,000-mile, nine-month endurance ''Alone Around'' race that would launch in New York City in September 2002. For Tommy Hilfiger Corp., remaining afloat in the highly competitive, ever-changing fashion industry would no doubt prove to be just as challenging.

Principal Subsidiaries

Tommy Hilfiger U.S.A., Inc.; Tommy Hilfiger Wholesale, Inc. (United States); Tomcan Investments Inc. (United States); Tommy Hilfiger Canada Inc.; Tommy Hilfiger Canada Retail Inc.; Tommy Hilfiger Canada Sales Inc.; Tommy Hilfiger Retail, LLC (United States); TH Retail, LLC (U.S.); Tommy Hilfiger Retail (UK) Company; Tommy Hilfiger Licensing, Inc. (United States); Tommy Hilfiger Hungary Ltd.; Tommy Hilfiger 485 Fifth, Inc. (United States); Tommy.com, Inc. (United States); Tommy Hilfiger E-Services, Inc. (United States); Tommy Hilfiger (Eastern Hemisphere) Limited (British Virgin Islands); Tommy Hilfiger (India) Limited; New Bauhinia Limited (British Virgin Islands); Tommy Hilfiger (HK) Limited;

Wellrose Limited; THHK Womenswear Limited; THHK Jeanswear Limited; THHK Menswear Limited; THHK Junior Sportswear Limited; THHK Childrenswear Limited; T.H. International N.V.; Tommy Hilfiger Europe B.V. (Netherlands); TH UK Ltd.; TH Deutschland GmbH (Germany); TH Italia SRL (Italy); TH Belgium NV; TH France SAS; Hilfiger Stores BV (Netherlands); Hilfiger Stores SAS (France); Hilfiger Stores GmbH (Germany); Hilfiger Stores Ltd. (United Kingdom).

Principal Competitors

Calvin Klein Inc.; The Gap Inc.; Polo Ralph Lauren Corporation.

Further Reading

Alson, Amy, ''7th Avenue's Bad Boy,'' *Marketing & Media Decisions,* March 1988, pp. 79–82.

Borden, Mark, ''Why Tommy Hilfiger Tanked,'' *Fortune,* May 29, 2000, p. 52.

Bradford, Stacey L., ''Tommy Who?'' *Financial World,* March 18, 1997, pp. 41–44.

Brady, Jennifer L., ''Hilfiger Head Sees Huge Growth for Women's Line,'' *Women's Wear Daily (WWD),* October 3, 1996, p. 5.

Brown, Ed, ''The Street Likes Hilfiger's Style,'' *Fortune,* May 29, 2000, p. 52.

Conant, Jennet, ''A Flashy Upstart,'' *Newsweek,* October 6, 1986, p. 68.

Cropper, Carol, ''Designing Earnings,'' *Forbes,* February 1, 1993, p. 105.

Doebele, Justin, ''A Brand Is Born,'' *Forbes,* February 26, 1996, pp. 65–66.

Dolbow, Sandra, ''Tommy Hilfiger Sailing Through Spring 2003,'' *Brandweek,''* August 19, 2002, p. 42.

Fallon, James, ''Lauren Bush Stumps for Tommy Hilfiger,'' *WWD,* March 2, 2001, p. 19.

Gibbons, William, ''Confirm New Firm to Make, Market Tommy Hilfiger Apparel,'' *Daily News Record,* November 29, 1988, p. 7.

Green, Michelle, Kristina Johnson, and Benilda Little, ''With Brash Advertising and a $20 Million Boost, Tommy Hilfiger Takes on Seventh Avenue Titans,'' *People,* July 7, 1986, pp. 89–90.

Hochswender, Woody, ''Prep Urban,'' *Esquire,* March 1996, pp. 131–32.

Lockwood, Lisa, ''Tommy Dances to the Beat at the Beach,'' *WWD,* May 6, 2002, p. 5.

——, and Kristen Larson, ''Tommy's Back: Women's Takes Off,'' *WWD,* June 27, 2001, p. 1.

''Margolis Resigns As Hilfiger Plans to License Women's,'' *Daily News Record,* June 2, 1995, p. 2.

Norton, Leslie P., ''Hot Pants,'' *Barron's,* October 17, 1994, pp. 17–18.

Palmieri, Jean E., ''Bergdorf's Santacroce Joining Hilfiger,'' *Daily News Record,* May 30, 1997, p. 2.

Ryan, Thomas J., ''Tommy's Biz Still Playing Happy Tune,'' *Daily News Record,* May 25, 1995, pp. 1–2.

——, ''Hilfiger Net Climbs 24.6% in 4th Quarter,'' *Daily News Record,* June 4, 1997, p. 1.

Tyrnauer, Matthew, ''It's Tommy's World,'' *Vanity Fair,* February 1996, pp. 108–13, 150–51.

—A. Woodward
—updated by Christina M. Stansell

Triumph Motorcycles Ltd.

Jacknell Road
Hinckley
Leicestershire LE10 3BS
United Kingdom
Telephone: (+44) 1 455 251 700
Fax: (+44) 1 455 251 367
Web site: http://www.triumph.co.uk

Private Company
Incorporated: 1906 as Triumph Engineering Co. Ltd.
Employees: 650
Sales: £165 million ($250 million) (2002 est.)
NAIC: 336991 Motorcycle, Bicycle, and Parts
   Manufacturing; 423110 Automobile and Other Motor
   Vehicle Merchant Wholesalers

One of the oldest names in motorcycle manufacturing, Triumph Motorcycles Ltd. is also one of the youngest—while production of the first Triumph motorcycles began in 1902, in its present incarnation the company has been in business only since 1990. Triumph's motorcycle production facilities in Hinckley, England, had to be completely rebuilt after the original plant was destroyed by fire early in 2002. The plant is capable of producing up to 50,000 units per year; a second plant has been in the works and is expected to open in 2003. The private company's sales are estimated at more than £165 million ($250 million) per year, with the United States representing the company's biggest market. Triumph is entirely owned by John Bloor, who is also head of Bloor Holdings, a real estate development company. Bloor's total investment in Triumph, which only began to break even at the turn of the century, is estimated to range between £70 and £100 million. Triumph also sells a line of Triumph-branded clothing and accessories.

Making Motorcycles at the Turn of the 20th Century

Nuremberg, Germany native Siegfried Bettmann emigrated to the town of Coventry, England, in 1883. A year later, at the age of 20, Bettmann founded his own company, the S.

Bettmann & Co. Import Export Agency, in London. Bettmann's original products were bicycles, which the company bought and then sold under its own brand name. Bettmann also distributed sewing machines imported from Germany.

In 1886, however, Bettmann sought a new, more universal name for his company, and the company became known as the Triumph Cycle Company. A year later, the company registered as the New Triumph Co. Ltd., now with financial backing from the Dunlop Tyre Company. In that year, Bettmann was joined by another Nuremberg native, Mauritz Schulte.

Schulte encouraged Bettmann to transform Triumph into a manufacturing company, and in 1888 Bettmann purchased a site in Coventry using money lent by his and Schulte's families. The company began producing the first Triumph-branded bicycles in 1889. Meanwhile, the popularity of the bicycle and invention of the internal combustion engine had led a number of inventors to begin experimenting with the first motorcycle designs. By 1898, Triumph decided to extend its own production to include motorcycles.

By 1902, the company had debuted its first motorcycle—a bicycle fitted with a Belgian-built engine. The following year, as its motorcycle sales topped 500, Triumph opened a subsidiary, Orial TWN (Triumph Werke Nuremberg) in Germany in order to produce motorcycles for that market as well. During its first few years producing motorcycles, the company based its designs on those of other manufacturers. In 1904, Triumph began building motorcycles based on its own designs and in 1905 debuted its first completely in-house designed motorcycle. By the end of that year, the company had produced more than 250 of that design.

Triumph reincorporated as Triumph Engineering Co. Ltd. in 1906. By then production had doubled, and in 1907, after the company opened a larger plant, production doubled once again to 1,000 bikes. Triumph had also launched a second, lower-end brand, Gloria, produced in the company's original plant.

By 1909, production of the Triumph brand had topped 3,000 per year, and the company added new, updated designs, including the popular Roadster model. The outbreak of World War I

Key Dates:

1884: German immigrant Siegfried Bettmann sets up S. Bettmann Import Export Agency in London and begins distributing bicycles under Bettmann name.

1886: The company changes its name to Triumph Cycle Company.

1888: Triumph buys a factory in Coventry to begin producing bicycles.

1889: The company moves its headquarters to Coventry.

1902: The first Triumph motorcycles go into production using a Belgian engine.

1903: A manufacturing subsidiary is created in Nuremberg, Germany, to produce Triumph motorcycles for the German market.

1905: The first fully company-built motorcycle is produced.

1915: Switching to wartime production, the company produces 30,000 "Trusty Triumph" motorcycles for the Allies during the World War I.

1923: The first Triumph car model, the 10/20, is launched.

1929: Triumph's German subsidiary is spun off as a separate company, which continues to make Triumph motorcycles until the 1950s.

1936: Triumph car and motorcycle operations are broken up into two companies; Jack Sangster, who owns Ariel motorcycles, buys the motorcycle division.

1939: Triumph Cars goes bankrupt and is acquired by Standard Motor Company.

1940: The company switches to wartime production, building over 50,000 motorcycles for the Allies.

1950: The Thunderbird model debuts.

1951: Triumph is acquired by the BSA Group, which also makes BSA motorcycles.

1954: Marlon Brando rides a Triumph Thunderbird in the film *The Wild One.*

1958: The Bonneville, hailed as the greatest motorcycle of all time, is introduced.

1969: Triumph production peaks at nearly 48,000 motorcycles.

1972: Norton-Villiers-Triumph (NVT) is created in an effort to rescue the British motorcycle industry.

1973: After NVT chairman announces the closure of the Triumph plant; its workers stage an 18-month sit-in, shutting down production.

1974: Meriden Motorcycle Cooperative is created with government backing and production soon resumes at the Triumph plant.

1983: Triumph goes bankrupt, and its brand and manufacturing rights are acquired by John Bloor.

1990: Bloor opens a state-of-the-art plant in Hinckley and unveils new Triumph models.

1991: The company begins full-scale production of new models.

1995: Triumph returns to the U.S. market, distributing through Triumph USA subsidiary set up the year before.

2000: The company relaunches the Bonneville and approaches the break-even mark.

proved a boost of sorts for the company as production was switched to support the Allied war effort. More than 30,000 motorcycles—among them the Model H Roadster, often cited as the first modern motorcycle—were supplied to the Allies. The Roadster's nickname, the "Trusty Triumph," provided an early promotional push for the company.

Following the war, Bettmann and Schulte fell out over a disagreement, with Schulte wishing to replace bicycle production with a move into the automobile market. Schulte was replaced by Col. Claude Holbrook—who, in fact, agreed with Schulte. By the early 1920s, the company was prepared to launch its first motor car, the model 10/20, which came to market in 1923. Triumph continued to manufacture bicycles, however.

By the mid-1920s, Triumph had grown into one of Britain's leading motorcycle makers, with a 500,000-square-foot plant capable of producing up to 30,000 motorcycles each year. With its models winning top honors at many of the races held during the period, Triumph also found its bikes in high demand overseas, and export sales became a primary source of the company's revenues, although for the United States, Triumph models were manufactured under license. The company found its first automotive success with the debut of the Super Seven car in 1928.

When the Great Depression hit in 1929, Triumph spun off its German subsidiary as a separate, independently owned company. The Nuremberg firm continued to manufacture motorcy-

cles under the Triumph brand until 1957. In 1932, Triumph sold off another part of the company, its bicycle manufacturing facility. By then, Triumph had been struggling financially, and Bettmann had been forced out of the chairman's spot. In 1933, Bettmann retired from the company.

Renamed Triumph Co. Ltd., the company enjoyed success from both its motorcycle and car sides through the 1930s. In 1936, however, the company's two components became separate companies—the Triumph automobile operation went bankrupt in 1939 and was acquired by the Standard Motor Company. The motorcycle operation fared better, having been acquired in 1936 by John Sangster, who also owned the rival Ariel motorcycle company. That same year, the company began its first imports into the United States, which quickly grew into the company's single most important market.

World War II and After

Production of civil models came to a halt once again as Triumph converted to wartime production at the beginning of World War II. The company supplied more than 50,000 motorcycles to the Allied forces despite a bombing raid on Coventry that had destroyed the company's manufacturing facility in 1940. Production was moved to a new site in Meriden, which was to remain the company's base until the 1980s. The company also began producing lightweight generator motors for Britain's Royal Air Force.

Triumph returned to civilian production in 1946, although military production of its motorcycles continued for some time as well. The company was to base its newest models on the generator motor design, which led to the development of the acclaimed Thunderbird. Launched in 1950, the Thunderbird was hailed as the world's first "superbike," capable of reaching speeds of 100 mph (and also inspiring the development of the Ford Thunderbird automobile). In addition, the company introduced at this time the first of its three-cylinder engines (most motorcycles had either two or four cylinders), which became a company hallmark.

By then, Triumph—which had been bought by the BSA Group in 1951 for £2.5 million—had put into place its own dedicated distribution subsidiary for the U.S. market, Triumph Corp., based in Maryland. Known as TriCor, the subsidiary helped nearly triple U.S. imports of Triumph motorcycles in just a year. With the success of the 1954 film *The Wild One,* which featured Marlon Brando riding a clearly identified Thunderbird, Triumph became one of the hottest-selling motorcycle brands in the United States.

While continuing to roll out successful motorcycle models in the mid-1950s, Triumph extended its production into a line of scooters. In 1958, however, Triumph unveiled a new model, the Bonneville, named after the track where the model had set a new speed record. The Bonneville, which inspired the Pontiac Bonneville car model, was to become regarded as one of the greatest motorcycles ever built. The movies once again proved a new source of publicity, as Steve McQueen rode off on a Bonneville in the 1961 film *The Great Escape.*

By the middle of the 1960s, the United States had come to account for some 80 percent of Triumph's production, which reached its all-time peak in 1969, with nearly 47,000 motorcycles produced that year. By then, however, Triumph, like the rest of the British motorcycle manufacturing industry, was already past its prime.

Collapsing in the 1980s

In the 1950s, the British motorcycle industry had been the world's largest, producing three out of every five motorcycles sold worldwide. Yet English manufacturing methods had not kept pace with those used elsewhere in the world—especially in Japan, whose motorcycle manufacturers, including Honda, Suzuki, Yamaha, and Kawasaki, had begun to impose themselves not only on the road but on the racetrack as well.

Japanese mass production techniques enabled these new brands rapidly to build up their share in the market, offering good quality and low pricing. Triumph, meanwhile, had become haunted by a reputation for its low production quality, the result of a lack of investment in its manufacturing base. The U.S. market, the world's largest, had during this time grown from just 50,000 motorcycles per year in the 1950s to more than two million per year at the beginning of the 1970s—growth inspired in large part by Triumph itself.

By 1971, the BSA Group was losing money, and in 1972 the group began cutting back on its personnel. In 1973, in an effort to salvage the country's motorcycle industry, the British government engineered a merger among Triumph and two other

manufacturers, creating Norton Villiers Triumph (NVT), controlled by Norton chairman Dennis Poore. By the end of that year, Poore had announced the company's decision to shut down the Triumph facility in Meriden, putting some 3,000 employees out of work.

The Triumph employees went on strike, entering an 18-month sit-in that ended production at the Meriden plant. NVT relaunched production of some Triumph models at its other sites in 1974. That year, the Labour-party led government created the Meriden Motorcycle Cooperative, owned by the plant's workers and backed by a government load of £5 million. The Meriden Co-Op resumed production of Triumph motorcycles in 1975.

The co-op never quite took off, however, despite a £1 million order for 2,000 motorcycles from GEC, designed to help stabilize the company. NVT hardly fared better. In 1977, the company sold the rights to the Triumph name to the Meriden Co-Op, and then went bankrupt. The Meriden Co-Op limped on, building up more than £10 million in debt. Despite the government's waiver of its debts, and the co-op's conversion into a worker-owned limited company, Meriden continued to fail, and by 1983 had run out of money.

Reborn in the 1990s

In 1983, the Triumph name and manufacturing rights were quietly purchased by John Bloor, a plasterer turned real estate magnate who had become one of the United Kingdoms's wealthiest individuals. Bloor, who had little interest in motorcycles, had for some time wanted to start up a manufacturing business. Touring the Meriden plant, which was slated for demolition in 1984, Bloor became interested in Triumph, and particularly its still highly regarded brand name.

Due to the fact that the company's manufacturing plant and its designs were too far out of date to compete against the now-dominant Japanese makers, Bloor did not relaunch Triumph immediately. Instead, production of the Triumph Bonneville was licensed to a small plant in Devon, which produced the model on a limited scale until 1988. In the meantime, Bloor set to work assembling the new Triumph, hiring several of the group's former designers to begin work on new models. Bloor took his team to Japan on a tour of its competitors' facilities and became determined to adopt Japanese manufacturing techniques and especially new-generation computer controlled machinery. In 1985, Triumph purchased a first set of equipment to begin working, in secret, on its new prototype models. By 1987, the company had completed its first engine. The following year, the company purchased a new site in Hinckley and began construction of a new, state-of-the-art facility, completed in 1990.

In that year, Triumph returned to the worldwide motorcycle scene with the launch of six new models. Full-scale production began in 1991, as the company, now with nearly 100 employees, produced some 1,200 motorcycles. Bloor, who continued to bankroll the company's development from his own fortune, had correctly judged that the Triumph name remained a strong marketing tool, and by the end of 1991 the company had begun shipping to Germany, then Holland, Australia, and France. The company also shrewdly kept many of the original Triumph model names from its heyday. By 1992, the company's production had already topped 5,000 motorcycles.

The new Triumphs were not only winning praise for their design innovation but for their high quality as well. Sales and production continued to surge, topping 8,000 in 1993. By 1995, the company was already reaching the 15,000-unit capacity of its existing facility, as orders came in from more than 25 countries. In 1997, in order to meet growing demand, Triumph initiated an expansion of the Hinckley plant.

Triumph initially avoided entering the U.S. market because its production facilities were not yet able to meet the expected demand. In 1995, however, Triumph reentered the United States, launching an updated version of its famed Thunderbird. The company also took a leaf from Harley Davidson's book, launching a line of Triumph-branded clothing and accessories. The United States proved a ready market for the company, fueled in part by Triumph's willingness to allow dealers to offer test rides—something most motorcycle manufacturers refused.

Triumph relaunched another legendary model in 1996, the Daytona, which surprised the industry by outselling its comparably classed rival from Honda. Meanwhile, the company moved to take advantage of a growing shift in the motorcycle market away from youthful customers to a more affluent clientele of 35–50 year-olds attracted by Triumph's retro styling. In 2000, the company relaunched its legendary Bonneville, the success of which boosted the company's total production to 33,000 units by 2001. The company was also finally beginning to break even, on sales that had risen to an estimated £165 million ($250 million). Bloor's own investment in the company was said to have totaled as much as £100 million.

In February 2002, as the company was preparing to celebrate its 100th anniversary as a motorcycle maker, its main factory was hit by fire, which destroyed most of its manufacturing capacity. Nevertheless, the company, which by then numbered more than 300 employees, quickly rebuilt the facility and returned to production by September of that year. Furthermore, Triumph began plans to build a new, cutting-edge manufacturing facility, which was expected to open in 2003. John Bloor was not only credited with reviving an industry legend, he had also proved that high-quality, state-of-the-art manufacturing remained possible in Britain in the new century.

Principal Subsidiaries

Triumph Motorcycles Inc. (USA).

Principal Competitors

Honda Motor Company Ltd.; Bayerische Motoren Werke AG; Suzuki Motor Corp.; Harley-Davidson Motor Co.; Kawasaki Heavy Industries Ltd.; Kyocera Corp.; Yamaha Motor Company Ltd.; Ducati Motor Holding SpA.

Further Reading

Brown, Roland, "Wheeling Back in Triumph," *Independent*, April 19, 1997, p. 20.
Brown, Stuart F., *Fortune Small Business*, April 2002, p. 48.
"Company Triumphs Through Adversity," *Newsletter*, December 21, 2002.
Harris, Alan, "A Global Triumph," *Evening Telegraph*, July 8, 2002, p. 15.
McDiarmid, Mac, *Triumph: The Legend*, London: Smithmark Publishing, 1997.
Tipler, John, *Triumph Motorcycles*, Thrupp, England: Sutton Publishing, 2000.

—M.L. Cohen

Tubby's, Inc.

43191 Dalcoma Drive, Suite 6
Clinton Township, Michigan 48038
U.S.A.
Telephone: (586) 416-1900
Toll Free: (800) 752-0644
Fax: (586) 416-1639
Web site: http://www.tubbys.com

Private Company
Incorporated: 1968
Employees: 68
Sales: $10 million (2002 est.)
NAIC: 53311 Lessors of Nonfinancial Intangible Assets
    (Except Copyrighted Works); 722211 Limited-Service
    Restaurants

Tubby's, Inc. operates a chain of more than 100 submarine sandwich restaurants in Michigan, Florida, and Iowa, all but three of which are owned by franchisees. The firm's outlets, which range from small takeout-only locations to larger dine-in sites, feature a menu of more than 20 sandwiches that are served grilled. Among the most popular choices are steak and cheese and the Tubby's classic, a blend of different meats and cheese. Some Tubby's restaurants also serve premium ice cream and pizza. The company is controlled by the family of its founder, Richard Paganes, and is headquartered near its stronghold of Detroit.

Beginnings

The first Tubby's restaurant was opened in the winter of 1968 in St. Clair Shores, Michigan, a suburb of Detroit. The company's founder, 21-year old Richard Paganes, had learned the restaurant business while working at a place called Dan's Giant Subs, where he began to dream about opening his own shop. On Christmas Eve, 1967, his car had a flat tire in front of a building that was for rent. Inspired by the location, he decided to take the plunge and scraped together $8,000 to buy equipment and supplies.

Early the next year, Paganes opened his 600-square foot restaurant for business, selling carry-out food only. He offered a menu of 25 different submarine sandwiches, which ranged in price from 75 cents to $1.45. Among the choices were a steak and cheese sub and the "Tubby's Famous" variety, made with three different meats and cheese. What made Paganes' shop different was the fact that the submarines were grilled rather than served cold.

The restaurant was a success, and over the next several years three more locations were opened. To help run the operation, Paganes enlisted the help of several of his siblings, including his brother Robert, who helped formulate many of the company's sandwich recipes. In 1972, Tubby's began using a distinctive logo, which was based on a popular cartoon character.

Growth continued throughout the early 1970s, with a total of 12 shops in operation by 1977. December of that year saw the firm incorporate as Tubby's Sub Shops, Inc. and shortly afterwards begin to franchise its restaurant concept. The first franchised site was opened in Madison Heights, Michigan. Over the next several years more were added, including a number of dine-in restaurants, as well as the chain's first drive-through, located in Westland, Michigan. Tubby's also began to sell franchises outside of the state during this period.

Initial Public Offering in 1986

In March of 1986, the growing Tubby's began selling its stock publicly on the over-the-counter market. By this time, 50 sub shops were in business, none of which were owned by the corporation itself. All but two were located in southeastern Michigan. Tubby's still utilized a menu of 25 different sandwiches, and some restaurants now offered made-on-the-premises ice cream. Ten stores were also experimenting with home delivery service.

In the summer of 1986, Tubby's bought Ricky's Dairy Bar and Luxury Grill Ltd., which had two 1950s-style hot dog and ice cream restaurants in the Detroit area. The company began to franchise the Ricky's concept, and a number of new locations were opened over the next four years.

In 1990, Tubby's merged with a NASDAQ-traded corporation, Stuff Your Face, Inc., which had three restaurants in New Jersey that featured the sub-like Stromboli sandwich. After the merger, the reconfigured company took the name Tubby's, Inc. Richard Paganes was named chairman and CEO, while his brother J. Thomas Paganes was named president. Brothers P. Terrance Paganes and Robert M. Paganes were also given executive positions with the firm and made board members.

In 1991, Tubby's brought in a new president and CEO, Alexander Bardy. Over the next several years he laid ambitious plans for growth, including the development of new store concept, called Tubby's/Cafe Express, that would be located at Sears stores in shopping malls. The first experimental outlets were all company-owned. The venture was financed by a $250,000 private stock placement.

1994: Bardy Ousted and Restructuring Follows

Bardy's efforts to develop new initiatives were consuming large amounts of cash, however, and the company soon began to suffer from growing quarterly losses. In August of 1994, the Tubby's board ousted Bardy and appointed Robert Paganes as his replacement. The move was swiftly followed by implementation of an austerity program that included layoffs of seven corporate-headquarters employees, pay cuts of 20 to 40 percent for those at the top, and abandonment of the Tubby's/Cafe Express concept. Bardy was also sued by the company over a stock option worth 1.325 million shares, though he quickly countersued. Losses for 1994 totaled $920,000 on sales of $3.7 million. It was the third consecutive year of red ink.

In early 1995, a group of disgruntled stockholders and franchisees held an "alternative shareholders meeting," which resulted in a demand that two of the Paganes brothers return 1 million shares of stock which each had purchased at half-price during the winter. The company defended the sales, claiming they had kept the firm from being delisted by the NASDAQ exchange. Tubby's meanwhile had launched a health-conscious menu and a new advertising campaign that were credited with boosting sales. The company was also buying sites and building new stores itself, then selling them to franchisees, which cut the time needed to open a new store by several months. The cost of opening a Tubby's was estimated at $110,000 to $115,000, which included equipment, an initial marketing budget, and the $15,000 franchise fee that was paid to Tubby's, Inc. Franchisees also paid the firm a royalty of 4 percent of gross sales and an additional 3.5 percent to help cover advertising costs.

The company's new austerity measures were proving a success, and during the mid-1990s Tubby's returned to profitability. In 1996, the firm announced plans for national expansion. Development agreements were reached during the year to open stores in Arizona, Florida, and Ohio. Experiments were also under way to locate scaled-down Tubby's shops in service stations and at other non-traditional sites. CEO Robert Paganes stated that the company's goal was "to be the third largest submarine chain in the world."

In early 1997, Tubby's opened a shop in Edmonton, Alberta, Canada, the first of 30 restaurants planned for that country over the next five years. In 1998, as it celebrated three decades in business, the company unveiled a new logo and launched a subsidiary, SUBperior Distribution Systems, Inc., to wholesale supplies to franchisees. A reverse stock split was effected to raise the share price, which was in the 25 to 30 cent range, below the newly instituted NASDAQ minimum of $1. The one to ten split reduced the number of outstanding shares from 26 million to 2.6 million. The year 1998 also saw stores opened in St. Louis, Missouri, and Indianapolis, Indiana, and the settlement of a lawsuit by a former investor and board member for $265,000. Revenues for the year reached $7.4 million, double the figure of just four years earlier.

Return to Private Ownership

At the end of 1998, Tubby's hired an investment relations firm to boost its image on Wall Street. Plans to merge with Interfoods of America, Inc. of Florida were announced soon afterwards, but the deal fell through in the spring of 1999 when Interfoods decided to seek a different method of getting a NASDAQ listing, its primary motivation for the deal. After the merger fell apart, Tubby's management decided to go private by buying back 2 million outstanding shares. Robert and Peter Paganes and company secretary Vincent Tatone, who each owned 150,000 shares, retained their stakes and took control of the firm. The $2.3 million buyback, financed by Comerica Bank, was completed in early 2000. By this time the chain had grown to 94 stores in Michigan, Florida, and Nebraska. Development agreements for Arizona, Texas, Pennsylvania, Ohio, Indiana, and Canada had been terminated due to failure to meet agreed-upon schedules for opening restaurants. After taking Tubby's private, the firm's management announced it would no longer seek national penetration and would concentrate on building business within Michigan.

During 2000, and into 2001, the company worked on developing the Tubby's brand to fight off new competition from Quizno's Corporation of Denver and Panera Bread Company of Missouri, both of which had recently doubled their presence in the Detroit area. Tubby's 100th store, opened in Macomb Township, Michigan, sported a new design that featured high ceilings and a colorful interior. The restaurant also offered pizza, a first for the chain. Forty percent of Tubby's sales came in the evening, and the company hoped the new menu choice would increase sales during this time period. The declining price of pizza-making equipment made the option attractive to franchisees, and if the pizza experiment proved successful it was expected to be added chain-wide.

In early 2002, Tubby's announced it was seeking to open up to three dozen new stores throughout Michigan. Advertisements run on television in March and April seeking new franchisees drew a strong response, and more spots were planned for later in the year.

```
┌─────────────────────────────────────────────────────┐
│                    Key Dates:                        │
│                                                       │
│  1968:  Richard Paganes opens a sandwich shop in St. Clair
│         Shores, Michigan.                            │
│  1972:  Tubby's, with four locations, introduces a new logo.
│  1978:  The company begins franchising restaurants.  │
│  1986:  Tubby's goes public and acquires Ricky's Dairy
│         Bar & Luxury Grill.                          │
│  1990:  Tubby's merges with Stuff Your Face, Inc., and the
│         company's moves to the NASDAQ.               │
│  1991:  New CEO Alexander Bardy begins to lay plans for
│         expansion.                                   │
│  1994:  Bardy is removed by Tubby's board; mounting │
│         losses lead to restructuring.               │
│  1995:  Healthy menu options are introduced and an up-
│         dated ad campaign is launched.              │
│  1996:  New outlets begin opening that will extend the fran-
│         chise into Ohio, Florida, Arizona, Missouri, Indi-
│         ana, and Canada.                            │
│  1998:  SUBperior Distribution Systems, Inc. is formed to
│         service franchisees; Tubby's logo is revised.│
│  2000:  The company returns to private ownership after
│         Interfoods merger falls through.            │
│  2002:  Tubby's refocuses on Michigan and begins running
│         TV ads seeking franchisees.                 │
└─────────────────────────────────────────────────────┘
```

After some 35 years, the submarine sandwich shops of Tubby's, Inc. remained popular in the company's home base of southeastern Michigan. Several attempts at national expansion and a period of public ownership had proven less than successful, but Tubby's appeared to be back on track with a renewed focus on regional development.

Principal Subsidiaries

Tubby's Sub Shop Advertising, Inc.; The SubLine Company, Inc.; Tubby's Company Stores, Inc.; Tubby's Sub Shops, Inc.; SUBperior Distribution Systems, Inc.

Principal Competitors

Doctor's Associates, Inc. (Subway); The Quizno Corporation; Blimpie International, Inc.; Panera Bread Co.

Further Reading

Barkholz, David, "Looking for Big Growth: Tubby's Contemplates Secondary Stock Offer," *Crain's Detroit Business*, August 16, 1993, p. 2.

Bunkley, Nick, "Tubby's to Add Shops Outside of Metro Detroit," *Detroit News*, May 10, 2002.

Kosdrosky, Terry, "Tubby's Hopes New Image Boosts Stock," *Crain's Detroit Business*, December 7, 1998, p. 3.

——, "Tubby's May Go Private," *Crain's Detroit Business*, December 13, 1999, p. 2.

——, "Tubby's New Look, Menu Throw a Pie at Local Rivals," *Crain's Detroit Business*, January 22, 2001, p. 17.

Papiernik, Richard L., "Tubby's Trims Costs, Changes Strategy After '94 Fiscal Loss," *Nation's Restaurant News*, April 10, 1995, p. 14.

Stopa, Marsha, "Leaner Tubby's Back to Its Bread and Butter," *Crain's Detroit Business*, October 31, 1994, p. 1.

——, "Promises of Profitability: Tubby's Inc. Resurfaces, Ready to Expand," *Crain's Detroit Business*, June 17, 1996, p. 2.

——, "Shareholder Beef Getting Attention at Tubby's," *Crain's Detroit Business*, May 15, 1995, p. 1.

——, "Sub-Sandwich Chain Surfaces as Area Competitor," *Crain's Detroit Business*, June 12, 1995, p. 30.

——, "Tubby's Cleans Plate and Puts on New Face," *Crain's Detroit Business*, January 26, 1998, p. 64.

——, "Tubby's Hopes Meatier Profits Will Beef Up its Future," *Crain's Detroit Business*, April 24, 1995, p. 30.

Walkup, Carolyn, "Tubby's Subs Targets Nontraditional Sites," *Nation's Restaurant News*, April 11, 1994, p. 7.

—Frank Uhle

Unitika Ltd.

Osaka Center Building
4-1-3, Kyutaro-cho, Chuo-ku
Osaka 541-8566
Japan
Telephone: (06) 6281-5695
Fax: (06) 6281-5697
Web site: http://www.unitika.co.jp

Public Company
Incorporated: 1889 as Amagasaki Spinners Ltd.
Employees: 1,345
Sales: $1.9 billion (2002)
Stock Exchanges: Tokyo Osaka
Ticker Symbol: 3103
NAIC: 325211 Plastics Material and Resin Manufacturing

Through its many subsidiaries, Unitika Ltd. operates as a leading manufacturer in the Japanese fibers and plastics industry. The company began a major restructuring effort in the late 1990s and spun off its main fiber and textiles businesses, creating subsidiaries Unitika Textiles Ltd. and Unitika Fibers Ltd. The firm's main business segments include its High Polymers division, which produce films, resins, synthetics, vinylon fibers, polyester and nylon, cotton nonwoven fabrics, and biodegradable plastic products. Unitika also has holdings involved in water treatment facilities, incinerators, air pollution prevention, chemicals, advanced materials, and biotechnology.

Early History

Unitika was created in 1969 out of the merger of the Nichibo and Nippon Rayon companies. Until 1964, the former was known as the Dainippon Spinning Company, which formed, along with Toyobo and Kanegafuchi, the dominant triumvirate in Japan's interwar spinning industry. Dainippon itself emerged at the end of World War I out of the amalgamation of five separate concerns initiated by Amagasaki Spinners Ltd., and it is this last company which is therefore regarded as the founder of the present company.

Cotton-spinning was the chosen vehicle for Japan's industrialization in the last quarter of the 19th century, remaining until World War II the nation's most important single industry and the spearhead of its successful attempt to create a modern industrialized economy capable of competing with those of the West. Although spinning mills had existed in Japan since the 1860s, it is generally agreed that it was the establishment in 1882 of the famous Osaka Spinning Company which began the spectacular growth of Japan's indigenous cotton-spinning industry.

The Osaka mill was both sufficiently large-scale and powerful—driven by steam, and with 10,000 spindles—to be able to compete with the mills of Britain and the United States, and its success set a pattern for mill development in the ensuing two decades. The reorganization of the nation's capital in the 1880s, along with the emergence of a powerful merchant-banking class, especially in the Osaka area, were the other necessary ingredients for the expansion of the industry. Among the numerous spinning companies established in this period was Amagasaki Spinners Ltd., set up in 1889 in Hyogo province by a group of Osaka merchants and bankers.

By 1895, the company was ranked as one of the dozen largest spinning concerns in the country, with over 27,000 spindles. During this decade the company discarded mule frames in favor of the more efficient ring frames to enhance its productive capacity of coarse-grade cotton yarn. Amagasaki's factory workers were typical of those of the cotton-spinning industry of the day—young women recruited from the provinces who lived in the company's own dormitories. Their relative docility and—by Western standards—meager pay helped provide the company with a distinct cost advantage over foreign competitors. However, the extremely rapid expansion of the industry produced severe shortages of skilled labor and led to the phenomenon of labor piracy among competing firms. In order to combat this, the industry set up the Japan Cotton Spinners' Association in 1882, and this body remained for the next 50 years the governing body of the industry as a whole and the vehicle for governmental intervention in it. The Association's effectiveness in the latter respect was soon displayed when over-production in the final years of the 1890s led to an enforced cut-back in production, the first of many such cutbacks to affect the spinning industry in the decades to come.

Key Mergers and Production Innovations: 1900s–30s

By the early years of the 20th century, the industry had become characterized by an excessive number of competing companies. Although the Sino-Japanese War of 1895–96, the Russo-Japanese War of 1904–05, and especially World War I stimulated the industry by opening up new opportunities in China, Korea, and Formosa (later Taiwan), it was clear that rationalization was necessary. A series of mergers in which Amagasaki figured prominently was initiated in the industry. The company absorbed the Toyo Textile Company in 1908, the Tokyo Spinning Company in 1914, the Nihon Spinning Company in 1916, and finally in 1918 the Settu Spinning Company. The new giant composite, now with mills all over the country, was named the Dainippon Spinning Company. The merger process appears to have had the effect of bringing to an end what one industry historian, S. Yonekawa, has called "a period of trial and error" in the company's management and operational spheres.

The financial crisis of 1920 affected Dainippon severely, but the management cooperated with the other large spinning firms in a far-sighted policy of using financial reserves built up in the profitable war years to avert a total breakdown in the yarn and fiber markets. From this experience, Dainippon learned the importance of guarding itself against price fluctuations in raw cotton, and during the 1920s and 1930s the company adopted a number of measures—such as "hedge-selling," whereby the company sold raw cotton on a cotton exchange in amounts equal to their cotton holdings to offset any losses on the purchases—to lessen such risks. Dainippon further protected itself from the notorious vagaries of the cotton market by diversifying into synthetic fiber production, and to this end set up the Nippon Rayon Company in 1926.

As a result of the amalgamation process of the previous decade, Dainippon in the 1920s had a somewhat complex management structure composed of departments based on its various products. A modern divisional system did not emerge until after 1945. Dainippon was, however, notable for its innovative work on production processes. A company engineer, Kasuo Imamura, who had joined the new Dainippon after the absorption of the Settu Spinning Company in 1918, developed the new, efficient ECO-type high-draft spindle which was to become the most favored type of spindle in the industry as a whole. Dainippon was quick to take advantage of Toyota's revolutionary automatic looms after 1926 to increase efficiency in production

and thereby enable it to reduce the size of its work force. The company's Sekigahara plant was the first in the country to employ the more efficient unit drive, whereby each unit had its own power source, for all of its operations in 1932. Innovations such as these enabled Dainippon to maintain its position in the inter-war decades as one of the industry's leading operations despite such setbacks as the enforcement in 1929 of the Revised Factory Law (1923), which ended the profitable all-night work system known as "midnight labor," and the Great Depression that followed, during which the company had to discharge half of its labor force.

Surviving the War Years

In the mid-1930s, the Japanese textile industry replaced that of Britain as world leader. The threat from Japan was felt to be so grave that protectionist measures were taken by Britain and the United States against the Japanese, severely affecting export-dependent companies such as Dainippon. The position of the firm and of the industry as a whole was further threatened in the second half of the decade when the imposition of sanctions against Japan by the Western democracies checked the supply of raw cotton from India and the United States, thereby forcing reductions in cotton-yarn production. The year 1937 saw the first government-imposed controls on prices, and for the next eight years virtually every aspect of the company's operations came under increasing governmental scrutiny and control. During 1940–41, the spinning industry was reorganized into 14 so-called units in an attempt to place it on a strengthened war-footing. Dainippon managed to remain intact, constituting one of the 14 units. A further series of amalgamations took place in 1943, culminating in the emergence of a grouping known as the "Big Ten" spinners, but once again Dainippon retained its corporate integrity despite this imposed aggregation. For the spinning industry, the war years were harsh ones, bringing government-imposed ceiling prices, the rationing of increasingly scant supplies of raw cotton, the turning over of mills to munitions production, and their subjection to Allied aerial attack in the latter stages of the conflict. By the time of Japan's surrender in 1945, the industry was a shadow of its former self.

After the surrender, Dainippon found itself subject to the ordinances of the Supreme Commander for the Allied Powers (SCAP), some of which were designed to force the break-up of large multi-product firms such as Dainippon by stripping away their non-spinning activities. Fortunately for Dainippon and the other members of the "Big Ten," SCAP revised these plans. In 1949, the industry was allowed to return to private trade, although SCAP maintained a close supervisory control in some areas. For example, production controls were not lifted until 1951.

With the return of Japanese sovereignty, the Ministry of Trade and Industry (MITI) embarked on a series of plans to resuscitate the industry, deciding that textile manufacturing should shift its emphasis from cotton to synthetic and chemical products in view of the latter's greater foreign earnings potential. Thus, it was that the 1950s saw Dainippon and the other majors expand their synthetic yarn production.

The Korean War gave the Japanese economy a very significant boost, stimulating recovery in the fibers industry as in many others. From the mid-1950s, Dainippon and the other

Key Dates:

1889: Amagasaki Spinners Ltd. is established.
1918: By now, Toyo Textile Company, Tokyo Spinning Company, Nihon Spinning Company, and the Settu Spinning Company have been acquired; the company adopts the Dainippon Spinning Company name.
1926: Nippon Rayon Company is formed.
1945: The industry falls under control of the Supreme Commander for the Allied Powers (SCAP).
1949: SCAP allows the industry to return to private trade.
1964: Dainippon renames itself Nichibo.
1969: Nichibo and Nippon Rayon companies merge to form Unitika.
1975: A recession forces the company to close two cotton staple mills and reduce synthetic fiber production.
1989: The company pays its first dividend in 13 years.
1994: The firm exits the rayon filament production market.
1999: Unitika spins off its fiber and textiles businesses as part of a major restructuring effort.

majors entered upon a 15-year period of high growth. Symptomatic of the company's restored fortunes was its 1965 establishment of Nippon Ester Co., Ltd. in a joint venture.

A Recession Leads to Diversification: 1970s–80s

However, the 1969–72 Japan-U.S. textile negotiations, and even more the oil shock which followed in 1973, brought an abrupt end to this prosperity. Steep rises in raw materials, labor, and fuel costs, plus growing competition from the newly industrializing countries of Northeast and Southeast Asia, combined to present a serious threat to Unitika's competitiveness abroad and its home market in Japan. Dainippon had renamed itself Nichibo in 1964 and Unitika in 1969 on the merging of the Nichibo and Nippon Rayon Companies.

The recession forced Unitika to close down two of its cotton staple mills in 1975 and reduce synthetic fiber production. In the same year, the company announced plans to work in concert with Toyobo (Toyo Boseki Kaisha) and Kanebo (Kanegafuchi Boseki Kaisha) to help pull the industry out of the recession. The one bright spot was polyester filament, for the production of which Unitika received permission to open a plant at Sabae in a joint venture with Kanebo.

Nevertheless, it was clear that Unitika had to diversify away from fibers production, and from this period dates the company's movement into non-fiber activities, although the benefits of this diversification was at least a decade away. In the later years of the 1970s, the company experienced a continued decline in the profitability of its business. Consequently, it withdrew in 1977 from a joint cotton-spinning venture in Singapore. In the next year, it was the first of the industry's large firms to cut its work force by making 650 employees redundant: declining profitability meant there was little revenue to invest in increasing productive capacity, so cost-reduction by this method was the company's chosen response to the recession.

Further measures to bolster the fiber business included the voluntary production cutbacks in which the company took part in the late 1970s and early to mid-1980s; this action was designed to raise low product prices, and mutual inter-company mill inspections were put in place in order to enforce the cutbacks.

Unitika saw that if it was to survive it had to develop new value-added high-technology products. An example of this kind of development was the commercialization in 1979 of a special type of nylon filament designed to reduce static electricity in work garments. The company also embarked on the internationalization of its operations by involvement in technology licensing agreements and a new round of joint ventures abroad, on this occasion in Hong Kong, Italy, and the United States.

In 1981, in a further bid to improve production efficiency in the fibers business, Unitika announced plans to replace some 1,000 of its looms with 400 of the most up-to-date machines. Two years later, the company joined with seven other leading firms in forming a Research and Development Association to speed up and reduce the cost of development of more efficient production methods. One project was the design of a new cotton-spinning machine up to 17 times as productive as existing models.

However, these and other moves could not prevent the post-1985 rise in the value of the yen that caused further decline in the profitability of the important export sector. In 1986, Unitika announced plans to shed some 800 employees in an effort to reduce the size of its work force by the end of the decade. The impact of a strong yen on export competitiveness again underlined the necessity of rapidly expanding the non-fibers business, which in 1991 amounted to about 33 percent of total sales, while simultaneously concentrating on the equally rapid development and commercialization of high-value, high-technology products in the mainstay yarns sector.

The company's cost-cutting and diversification efforts led to profits in 1989, enabling the company to resume its dividend payment to shareholders for the first time since 1977. By this time, Unitika's non-textile businesses were experiencing steady growth, its recent acquisitions were beginning to pay off, and key product launches—including Solar, a heat retaining fiber—were successful.

Restructuring in the 1990s and Beyond

The 1990s initiated a period of change and restructuring for Unitika as the company continued to develop new products and expand into new territories during the first half of the decade. In 1991, the company established a women's clothing material company based in France with Dollfus Meig et Cie. It also formed subsidiaries in Indonesia, Hong Kong, and Thailand. Unitika's financial success, however, came to a halt in 1994 when the company posted losses due to the increase of imports into the region. The firm's textiles division experienced a sales drop of 14.5 percent while its nontextiles business experienced a 6.6 percent gain. That year, the company exited the rayon filament production market and began to make sweeping changes within its textiles division, closing several plants and cutting jobs.

While Unitika worked at restructuring operations, it faced many challenges. Japan's economy began faltering in the late 1990s, consumer spending dropped, and competition increased. As a result, Unitika's sales fell during 1997 and 1998 and profits were hard to come by. As such, the company made a strategic move in 1999 and spun off its textiles and fibers business. As part of this streamlining effort two new subsidiaries were created—Unitika Textiles Ltd. and Unitika Fibers Ltd.

After nearly a decade of unsteady profits, Unitika management was forced to adopt a new business plan in 2000 that included cutting the number of its subsidiaries drastically. By this time, the company's holdings included 92 different businesses, and Unitika hoped to halve that number by 2003. As part of this new direction, the company focused on five main operating units related to synthetic fibers, polymers, the environment, functional materials, and life and health.

Profits and sales continued to fall into 2002, due in part to increased competition and weak global economies. Sales dropped by 11 percent over fiscal 2001 while the company posted net income of $10 million, a 66 percent drop over the previous year. As profits and sales continued their downward trend, Unitika revamped expansion efforts. Plans to construct a new spun-bond facility were dropped, and the company instead looked to make improvements to existing machinery.

Unitika was certain its survival depended on its ability to diversify its holdings in a cost efficient manner. The company continued with its strategy—which was started in the late 1970s—and focused on developing new value-added high-technology products as well as non-fiber products. Unitika's future fortunes, however, remained dependent on the firm's ability to turn that strategy into a reality.

Principal Subsidiaries

Brazcot Limitada (Brazil); Unitika do Brasil Industria Textil Limitada (Brazil); Thai Nylon Co. Ltd. (Thailand); Kian Dai Wools Co. Ltd. (Hong Kong); P.T. Unitex (Indonesia); Unitika America Corporation (U.S.); Unitika Hong Kong Ltd.; South Overseas Fashion Ltd. (Hong Kong); Unitra (Indonesia); Inner Mongolia Donghao Cashmere Products Co. Ltd. (Inner Mongolia); PT Emblem Asia (Indonesia); Tusco (Thailand); Unitika Textiles Ltd.; Unitika Fibers Ltd.

Principal Competitors

Dainippon Ink and Chemicals Inc.; Kuraray Co. Ltd.; Toray Industries Inc.

Further Reading

"Cost-Cutting Decides Japanese Synthetic Fiber Firms' Earnings," *AsiaPulse News*, November 21, 2002.

"Teijen, Unitika to Set Up Polyester Venture in Thailand," *Japan Economic Newswire*, October 31, 1996.

"Unitika Group Net Profit Fell Shrinks 30.8%," *Japan Economic Newswire*, November 20, 2001.

"Unitika Group Net Profit Fell 26.5% in Fiscal 1st Half," *Japan Economic Newswire*, November 20, 2002.

"Unitika Lessens Expansion Strategy," *Nonwovens Industry*, June 2002, p. 14.

"Unitika Logs 1st Recurring Profit Loss in 10 Yrs," *Jiji Press Ticker Service*, May 27, 1994.

"Unitika Paying 1st Dividend in 13 Years," *Jiji Press Ticker Service*, February 1, 1989.

"Unitika Spins Off Fiber Business," *Nonwovens Industry*, November 1999, p. 6.

"Unitika's Profit Slumps on Weaker Sales," *Jiji Press Ticker Service*, May 22, 1998.

"Unitika to Halve Number of Subsidiaries by March 2003," *AFX Asia*, September 13, 2000.

"Unitika, Two French Firms to Start Textile Company," *Japan Economic Newswire*, March 5, 1991.

—D. H. O'Leary
—update: Christina M. Stansell

United to Improve
America's Health®

VHA Inc.

220 East Las Colinas Boulevard
Irving, Texas 75039-5500
U.S.A.
Telephone: (972) 830-0000
Toll Free: (888) 842-3375
Fax: (972) 830-0012
Web site: http://www.vha.com/public

For-Profit Cooperative
Incorporated: 1977 as Voluntary Hospitals of America
Employees: 1,250
Sales: $394 million (2001)
NAIC: 421450 Medical, Dental, and Hospital Equipment
and Supplies Wholesalers; 421490 Other Professional
Equipment and Supplies Wholesalers

VHA Inc. is a leading purchasing cooperative for community-owned, nonprofit healthcare institutions. VHA had 2,200 members in its nationwide alliance at the time of its 25th anniversary in 2002. These included leading institutions such as Cedars-Sinai Health System and the Mayo Foundation, and range in size from small 50-bed hospitals to integrated healthcare systems. The group is active in 48 states (minus Utah and Nevada) and represents a quarter of the country's community-owned hospitals.

VHA was created in the late 1970s to help nonprofit hospital groups attain the same purchasing discounts as corporate hospital systems. In 2003, VHA found itself on *Fortune*'s list of the "100 Best Companies to Work For"—for the fourth year in a row.

Origins

In the 1970s, for-profit hospitals owned by investors were consolidating into large, multihospital healthcare systems with tremendous buying power. Community-owned facilities were unable to command the same huge discounts of suppliers.

An experimental, seven-member alliance of not-for-profit hospitals sprang out of a 1973 meeting of industry executives at the Hospital Research and Development Institute in Port St. Lucie, Florida. Launched in 1974, Hospital Shared Services failed, being unable to secure the necessary time commitments from its members.

As *Modern Healthcare* recalled, the topic came up as four healthcare industry CEOs had dinner one evening in September 1976 during the American Hospital Association's annual meeting in Dallas. Participants included Pat Groner (Baptist Hospital, Pensacola), M.T. Mustian (Tallahassee Memorial Regional Center), Duncan Moore (Moore-Trinity Regional Hospital, Iowa), and Allen Hicks (Community Hospitals of Indiana). During the impromptu discussion, these four agreed on the need for another purchasing alliance for nonprofit hospitals. Hicks shared the idea with two more CEOs, Stanley Nelson (Henry Ford Hospital, Detroit) and Wade Mountz (Norton Children's Hospitals, Louisville, Kentucky), when they met in Arizona for the Healthcare Executive Study Society the next spring.

An enlarged group of up to 30 executives began meeting at Chicago's O'Hare Airport to revive the concept. These meetings soon resulted in the creation of Voluntary Hospitals of America Inc., which was registered as a Delaware corporation on October 19, 1977. According to company founder Pat Groner, the name choice was influenced by that of Hospital Corporation of America (HCA), a leading for-profit group. "Voluntary hospitals" refers to hospitals operated by religious or other nonprofit groups.

The group continued to meet in Chicago and elected Wade Mountz as chairman and Nelson as president. Robert Kitzman, business manager at Nelson's hospital, Henry Ford, became VHA's first employee. In 1978, the Delaware company was merged into a new VHA cooperative in Illinois. VHA was reincorporated in Delaware after the state's laws changed to allow more members.

VHA signed a major supply agreement with American Hospital Supply Co. (AHS) in 1979, which held price increases to half the (then considerable) rate of inflation in anticipation of increased volume. The next year, four medical supply houses sued VHA for antitrust violations because of this arrangement; VHA ultimately prevailed in a federal appeals court, however, which reversed a lower court's ruling in 1983. In 1980, VHA awarded the country's largest forms contract to date. The group had 37 members at the time.

Relocating to Texas in 1982

Stanley R. Nelson was VHA's first president and chief executive officer. Donald Arnwine, president on a volunteer basis since 1980, became VHA's first full-time, paid CEO in January 1982. Arnwine had been CEO of West Virginia's Charleston Area Medical Center, a charter shareholder. In March 1982, VHA opened new offices in Irving, Texas, a site chosen due to the convenience of nearby Dallas-Fort Worth International Airport.

Five full-time employees were hired in 1982, and the group began to grow rapidly. A number of Regional Health Care Systems were established in the mid-1980s, beginning with VHA Minnesota—later called VHA Upper Midwest—which began with 17 hospitals. By the early 1990s, there would be a total of 29 regional offices, which were set up as separate, locally owned nonprofits. Non-shareholding hospitals could become partners in these regional companies, receiving full membership benefits, save voting rights.

A for-profit subsidiary, VHA Enterprises (VHAE), was established in 1983. The next year, VHA initiated a private-label program under the VHA Plus brand—the first among purchasing alliances.

In 1985, the dedicated purchasing subsidiary VHA Supply Co. was created following the announcement of the merger of AHS, VHA's main supplier, with HCA. HCA, a leading for-profit hospital chain, had acquired VHA charter hospital Wichita's Wesley Medical Center in December 1984. "These events . . . make people aware of how big the stakes are and make the case that large systems will dominate the industry," said Arnwine in *Modern Healthcare.*

VHA Enterprises soon teamed with Aetna Life Insurance Co. to create a managed care organization: PARTNERS National Health Plan. The venture lost $51.8 million, however, in its first four years. VHA also began developing assurance and risk and claims management programs. VHA Insurance Services Inc. and VHA Insurance Co. Ltd. started operations in 1987.

The group's corporate structure was streamlined in 1988. That September, Arnwine resigned as CEO; Mountz and Boise Cascade Corp. founder Robert Hansberger were interim replacements. VHA founder Gordon Sprenger (Allina Hospitals and Clinics, Minneapolis) became chairman of the board. Money-losing VHA Enterprises began selling off assets.

VHA closed the 1980s with about 834 members, 650 of them hospital clients—roughly a third of the amount served by the leading for-profit group, American Healthcare Systems (AHS). VHA purchased $2.3 billion worth of supplies in 1989.

Streamlining in the 1990s

In 1990, VHA returned to its original structure, a cooperative, allowing it to distribute a share of profits to partners as well as shareholders. VHA began calculating how much value it returned to members in the form of cash distributions and supply-cost savings. In 1991, the figure was $278 million.

Also in 1990, VHA Enterprises sold its 50 percent share in the PARTNERS managed care initiative to Aetna for $26 million in cash and the assumption of $34 million in debt. (VHA also got an $8 million bonus for its members' continued participation.) Two years later, VHAE was dissolved, after developing 18 business ventures in nine years.

Robert O'Leary, CEO at St. Joseph Health System in California, had taken over as VHA's chief executive in 1990. He left in June 1991 to lead American Medical International. C. Thomas Smith, formerly president of Yale-New Haven Health Services Corp., became VHA's next president and CEO.

The group's name was formally changed from Voluntary Hospitals of America to VHA Inc. in April 1994. "It enables us to move beyond the misunderstood concept of 'voluntary' and the limiting word 'hospitals,'" CEO C. Thomas Smith told shareholders. "United to Improve America's Health" was the company's new slogan.

At the same time, a restructuring program was launched to streamline the group's structure. The number of regional offices was reduced from 29 to 18; many of these were converted to wholly owned subsidiaries of VHA.

VHA enjoyed much growth and success in the late 1990s. A total of 22 shareholders were added in 1997, bringing the number of shareholder and partner organizations to 464. Membership grew 14.6 percent to 1,650.

A joint venture with University HealthSystem Consortium (UHC) created the industry's largest supply company. Called Novation, it began operations in January 1998, and soon racked up sales of $11 billion a year. One combined pharmacy contract alone was worth $3.9 billion.

Vha.com, launched in August 1997 as VHAseCURE.net, grew to accommodate a user base of more than 35,000. This innovative extranet connected 97 percent of VHA shareholders and partners. The online health information source www.Laurus Health.com was launched in 1998 with three pilot members. Within a year, it had grown to include 50 healthcare systems and 105 hospitals.

VHA joined another significant online venture in mid-1999. HEALTH*vision,* Inc. was created to combine the web-based products and resources of VHA with those of Eclipsys Corporation, which provided IT solutions to more than 1,400 healthcare provider organizations.

Key Dates:

1977: Voluntary Hospitals of America is formed.
1979: VHA signs a huge purchasing deal with supplier AHS.
1980: VHA awards the country's largest forms printing contract to date.
1982: Offices open in Irving, Texas.
1983: VHA Enterprises (VHAE) is established.
1984: The VHA Plus private-label brand is rolled out.
1985: VHA Supply Co. is formed; PARTNERS HMO/PPO plan is created with Aetna.
1987: VHA's Insurance operations begin.
1990: VHAE sells half interest in PARTNERS to Aetna.
1992: VHAE is dissolved.
1994: The company name is changed to VHA Inc.; regional offices are restructured.
1997: Vha.com is launched.
1998: A supply company, Novation, is formed with UHS.
1999: HEALTH*vision* online resource is formed with Eclipsys Corporation.
2002: VHA has 2,200 members at the time of its 25th anniversary.

VHA announced that its members realized $5 billion in value from their participation in the cooperative during the 1990s. At the same time, it was being named one of the "100 Best Companies to Work For" by *Fortune* magazine.

VHA estimated that it returned $1.15 billion in value to members in 2000. Novation attained $15.6 billion in purchasing volume. Within a year it had grown to include more than 80 manufacturers and distributors and more than 400 VHA and UHC hospitals.

25 in 2002

VHA had 2,200 members in its alliance at the time of its 25th anniversary in 2002. Of these members, 700 were partici-

pating in the Marketplace@Novation e-commerce venture with UHC. *Modern Healthcare* magazine named VHA CEO Tom Smith as one of the 25 most influential healthcare leaders of the preceding 25 years.

Principal Operating Units

VHA Central, LLC; VHA Central Atlantic, LLC; VHA Consulting Services; VHA East Coast, LLC; VHA Empire State, LLC; VHA Georgia Inc.; VHA Gulf States Inc.; VHA Metro, LLC; VHA Michigan Inc.; VHA Mid-America, LLC; VHA Mountain States, LLC; VHA New England Inc.; VHA Northeast, LLC; VHA Oklahoma/Arkansas, LLC; VHA Pennsylvania Inc.; VHA Southeast Inc.; VHA Southwest Inc.; VHA Upper Midwest, LLC; VHA West Coast, LLC.

Principal Competitors

AmeriNet; MedAssets HSCA, Inc.; Premier, Inc.

Further Reading

Montague, Jim, "The Process: How BJC Health System Chose a Single Alliance," *Materials Management in Health Care,* September 1995, p. 18.
——, "When Hospital Networks Form, Alliances Feel the Aftershocks," *Materials Management in Health Care,* September 1995, pp. 18, 20, 22.
"100 Best Companies to Work For," *Fortune,* January 20, 2003.
Scott, Lisa, "VHA Posts Profit, Shortens Name," *Modern Healthcare,* April 25, 1994, p. 8.
"Three Who Helped Forge Today's VHA," *Modern Healthcare,* April 22, 2002, p. 16.
Wagner, Mary, "Purchasing Groups Vie for Control and Clout," *Modern Healthcare,* June 25, 1990, p. 27.
"Working on a Vision, Mission; Growth, Changes and Challenges Have Been Constants During VHA's First Quarter-Century," *Modern Healthcare,* Supplement: VHA at 25, April 22, 2002, p. 6.

—Frederick C. Ingram

Vossloh AG

Vosslohstrasse 4
D-58791 Werdohl
Germany
Telephone: (49) 2392 52-0
Fax: (49) 2392 52-219
Web site: http://www.Vossloh.com

Public Company
Incorporated: 1909 Vossloh KG
Employees: 5,583
Sales: EUR 854.4 billion ($804.5 million) (2000)
Stock Exchanges: Frankfurt am Main Düsseldorf
Ticker Symbol: VOS
NAIC: 33651 Railroad Rolling Stock Manufacturing;
   332999 All Other Miscellaneous Fabricated Metal
   Product Manufacturing; 335121 Residential Electric
   Lighting Fixture Manufacturing; 335129 Other
   Lighting Equipment Manufacturing

Vossloh AG is the world market leader for switch systems and fasteners of railway tracks. The company's Vossloh Rail Systems division manufactures railway fastening products for all types of railways for any load and climate which are being used in 65 countries. Every third railway switch in the world comes from Austria-based VAE AG, a company in which Vossloh and VOEST-Alpine Stahl AG together hold 90 percent of the shares. Vossloh Schienenfahrzeugtechnik division makes diesel-powered locomotives and, together with Britsh Angel Trains Limited, offers part of them for lease. The company's traffic management systems division Vossloh System-Technik develops and implements software for railroad-based traffic management and passenger information systems for train stations and airports. Vossloh also offers safety diagnosis and maintenance services for railroad vehicles and makes noise suppression systems for railways and wheel set maintenance machinery. While the company's activities connected with railroad transportation account for about two-thirds of its revenues, its lightning technology division Vossloh-Schwabe—which makes electrical components such as transformers, sockets, ignitors and capacitors for a variety of lamps as well as LED lamps, displays, and chips—accounts for the other third. Headquartered in Werdohl, Germany, Vossloh has over 65 production facilities and subsidiaries around the globe. The Vossloh family owns 35 percent of the company's shares, and German life insurer Deutscher Herold Lebensversicherungs AG has an 11-percent stake.

Blacksmith Workshop Evolved into Factory in the 19th Century

In 1848, when Germany was in upheaval against the feudal system, Eduard Vossloh—written ''Voßloh'' in German—was born in Werdohl, a small town in Westphalia that belonged to Prussia. His father slipped into poverty in those economically depressed years and—out of desperation—emigrated to the United States, where he died six months after arriving, around 1852. Vossloh's mother barely managed to keep him and his three brothers and sisters alive. In 1861, she married again, and Eduard Vossloh started working at his stepfather's blacksmith workshop before and after school, which he attended regularly for only two years. Vossloh went on to work as an apprentice for another blacksmith in a nearby town, often for 15 hours a day. The construction of the Ruhr-Sieg-Railroad in 1961 fueled Werdohl's development into a center of the metal processing and manufacturing industry.

In 1869, the young man—although always weak and sick—was drafted into the Prussian Army. In the summer of 1870, just after Vossloh had made it through the tough months of military training, France declared war on Prussia, and his division was called to the battlefield. He was seriously wounded and sent back to his hometown for recovery, called back again in early 1871 despite his weak health, and finally came back home after the defeat of France three months later. In 1872, after he was able to walk without crutches again, 24-year-old Vossloh began to work in the family's blacksmith workshop. The pension he received as a war invalid was not sufficient to support a family. He married in 1873, and his first three sons were born between 1875 and 1882. There was not much demand for his blacksmith business, so Vossloh took a job as a locksmith and got into selling hardware. Eventually, however, he returned to working as a blacksmith. During this time, he was suffering from various serious health problems, until his doctor forbid him to do physically demanding work. After selling most of his inventory, Vossloh was still left with considerable debt. But he kept the tools to make small hardware products and hired an assistant. The endeavor did not turn a profit.

In 1883, Vossloh took a leap of faith by bidding to manufacture metal lock rings for the Royal Prussian Railroad. The rings were used to buffer the railroad track from vibrations and transfer them to the lower part of the rail construction. Being a war invalid turned out to his advantage, and Vossloh was granted the order. It turned the company's fate around. Lacking the resources to carry out the order, Vossloh found help from Rudolf Kugel and Carl Berg, whose company Kugel & Berg delivered on credit the necessary wire to construct metal lock rings. After the Prussian Railroad had paid for the order, Vossloh paid the workers he had hired, as well as Kugel & Berg for the raw materials. New orders followed, and the enterprise finally took off.

In 1888, the Vossloh family moved out of the small house in the inner city to a new house with a workshop on their property near Werdohl's train station. The blacksmith workshop was expanded and so was its range of products. Besides lock rings and metal plates for the railroad, the firm EDUARD Vossloh, which was officially registered at the new Altena county registry, started manufacturing hardware products such as metal hooks and curtain rails. New machines were added, and the workshop turned into a small factory. After the death of his first wife at age 43 in 1894, the company founder was struggling with severe health problems again. He remarried after a year but never recovered his former strength. In 1899, the Vossloh family moved into a new residential complex built on a hill to ease the company founder's health problems. Nevertheless, the patriarch died in the same year.

Second Vossloh Generation Takes Over in 1900

The company founder left behind five children: his oldest son Eduard, Jr., who had worked at the firm Brockhaus & Löwen; Wilhelm, the second oldest, who received a formal education in commerce; Karl, the third oldest son, who went to high school and studied civil engineering; 15-year-old Ernst, who worked as an apprentice to a locksmith; and Vossloh's only daughter, Hermine, who was twelve years old. Eduard Vossloh had determined that his four sons carry on the family business in the same legal form until Hermine reached maturity. For the time being, the three oldest Vossloh brothers took over the management of the family business. They based their decisions and work ethics on the same philosophy as their father did. He viewed his enterprise as a God-given means to build a sustain-

able existence for his family. Consequently, Vossloh's major purpose was to provide a living for the Vossloh family—not to pile up money for its own sake.

In 1909, Hermine turned 21 years old, and Vossloh was transformed into a Kommanditgesellschaft, a firm with at least one limited liability partner who was not involved in management, the Kommanditist. In that role, Hermine had a limited liability stake of 60,000 Marks in the company. Despite many obstacles and difficult times, Vossloh entered a period of solid growth. The engineer Karl Vossloh expanded the company's product range by developing new metal parts used in the railroad industry. In 1911, a modern iron forge was erected. With the onset of World War I in 1914, the family business employed about 240 people. During the war, civil production was replaced by the manufacture of grenade shells.

Fire in 1917 Maintains the Company's Independence

The year 1917 could have been the last year of Vossloh's independence. It was then that Rheinische Stahlwerke Duisburg, a large steel maker from the Ruhr, was interested in taking over Vossloh. At a time when many smaller manufacturers in the iron and steel processing industry were being gobbled up by larger players with more competitive strength, the Vossloh management decided to explore possible advantages of such a move. However, when a fire caused major damage, the two potential partners could not come to an agreement about who would have to pay for the excess loss not covered by insurance and further negotiations were canceled.

After the war ended, the demand for forge products dropped. Vossloh, as a rather small player in a market which was dominated by the giant steel makers from the Ruhr, decided to give up the manufacture of forge metal products that demanded a high input of raw material. Instead, the Vossloh brothers decided to focus on small metal parts and to set up a small sheet metal plant as well as a new facility for making wires and pipes to provide the necessary raw material. In 1919, EDUARD Vossloh KG acquired a factory for making decorative metal elements in Lüdenscheid, located southeast of Dortmund. The manufacture of aluminum silverware was ceased, while the existing production of sockets for Edison-light bulbs was expanded.

The 1920s began with a major change in the company's legal structure. In 1920, three limited liability companies were established, each led by one of the three oldest Vossloh brothers. One of them headed the production plants in Werdohl, one the Lüdenscheid factory, and one was responsible for marketing and sales. The three oldest Vossloh brothers each held a 30 percent stake in the family business, while the remaining 10 percent was divided equally between Ernst and Hermine Vossloh. EDUARD Vossloh KG ceased to exist.

After the devastating hyperinflation in the early 1920s, which the company survived, the Reichsmark became Germany's new currency, and the country's economy stabilized. In 1924, Vossloh acquired a wood processing plant in Dillenburg, near Gießen, that enabled the company to expand its range of decorative products to include such items as wooden hooks and curtain rails. The company also had a share in the Kassel-based firm Appel & Pfannschmidt, a manufacturer of brass products

Key Dates:

1872: Eduard Vossloh starts working at the family blacksmith workshop.

1883: The Royal Prussian Railroad awards Vossloh an order to make lock rings for rails.

1899: The company founder, dies and his sons take over the business.

1909: Vossloh KG is formed.

1919: The company acquires a production plant in Lüdenscheid.

1920: Vossloh KG is split into three limited liability companies.

1927: Karl Vossloh develops the "high tension lock ring."

1930: The three Vossloh companies are reunited under the umbrella of Vossloh-WERKE G.m.b.H.

1951: Vossloh family members form the Familiengemeinschaft Vossloh GbR.

1967: Vossloh is granted the general production license for a new railroad track fastener.

1986: Burkhard Schuchmann becomes new CEO of Vossloh.

1990: Vossloh goes public.

1996: The company takes over Deutsche System-Technik GmbH.

1998: Vossloh buys diesel locomotive maker SIEMENS Schienenfahrzeugtechnik and a 90 percent majority in the Austrian VAE group together with Austrian steel maker VOEST-Alpine Stahl.

2002: The company announces that its lighting division is up for sale.

that was owned by Hermine Vossloh's husband Nikolaus Appel. To attract qualified workers, Vossloh maintained more than 60 company-owned apartments that were rented at low prices to Vossloh employees. In 1927, Karl Vossloh developed the "high tension ring," which—made from a better quality steel—soon became the standard used in German and other European railroad tracks.

Between 1921 and 1927, Vossloh focused on strengthening the company's distribution channels. Appel & Pfannschmidt marketed Vossloh products in and around Kassel. A new distribution partner was found in Hamburg and a sales subsidiary, Metallgesellschaft METAG, set up in Cologne. By the late 1920s, Vossloh had developed a network of sales offices in Germany, including offices in Königsberg, Breslau, Munich, and Frankfurt/Main, as well as in the Netherlands and Belgium. In 1927, Eduard Vossloh, Jr.'s son-in law, Wilhelm Bomnüter, joined the company. After Eduard, Jr.'s death at age 53 in 1929, the three Vossloh companies were reunited under the umbrella of Vossloh-WERKE G.m.b.H. in 1930.

World War II and the German Economic Miracle

During the worldwide economic depression between 1929 and 1933, demand for Vossloh products dropped significantly. The smaller iron and steel processing industry in the Sauerland,

as the region east of the Ruhr where Vossloh was located was called, was pulled into a tough price competition with the iron and steel giants of the Ruhr. Many smaller subsidiaries associated with them were shut down, and 19 mid-sized enterprises in the region went bankrupt. Vossloh's diverse product range—including sockets for Edison light bulbs, light and doorbell switches, and electrical outlets—found a huge market, and the company's financial reserves also proved to be a big advantage. After the National Socialists took over power in 1933, the German economy was more and more regulated by the government, which increasingly forced the production of war-related goods. Before and during the war, Vossloh products were in high demand. The occupied territories in the Soviet Union were equipped with new railroad tracks to transport war supplies, since the existing railroad tracks were much wider than Germany's. Vossloh's lock rings were also used in railroad-based vehicles. Because so many men of working age were taken into the military, German women and foreign female forced laborers assembled the light sockets that were especially needed after many production facilities for war materials were moved underground to caves and old mines. Shortly before the war ended, a bomb destroyed the warehouse and office building at Vossloh's Werdohl headquarters.

While the war left Vossloh's production facilities untouched, the British military government confiscated part of them as reparations. After Vossloh was granted a production permit in 1946, the company started a race to keep up with an ever-growing demand. The German railroads had to be rebuilt and houses had to be fixed and equipped with lighting. The currency reform in the three German zones occupied by the Western Allies triggered a new economic upswing which, under the Christian Conservative Chancellor Konrad Adenauer and his visionary Minister of Economic Development Ludwig Erhard, and with the financial aid from American Marshall Plan funds, accelerated into an unprecedented boom that became known as the German Wirtschaftswunder ("economic miracle"). By 1950, more than 700 people worked at the three Vossloh facilities. A new plant was erected in Lüdenscheid for the manufacture of sockets for the new fluorescent lights, which became immensely popular in the 1950s and 1960s. Another novelty was the Doppelspannagel, an elastic W-shaped metal nail invented in England that over time replaced the screw-based attachment of the railroad tracks to the wooden ties and for which Vossloh acquired a license. In 1951, the ever expanding number of Vossloh family members agreed to form a private legal entity—the Familiengemeinschaft Vossloh GbR—to ensure a joint decision-making process among the many family shareholders. In the same year, the company sued German car maker Volkswagen, who registered a logo containing the letters V and W that was very similar to Vossloh's. Although the company had used its trademark for two decades, the German trademark authority—the Patentamt—granted Volkswagen the right to use the "VW" logo on its cars. Over the following decades, Vossloh developed a new trademark based on the company name.

Between 1950 and 1964, the economic boom caused wages and salaries to skyrocket. Besides buying cars, washing machines, and television sets, Germans redecorated their homes, which boosted Vossloh's interior decoration business. By the end of the 1960s, the company was confronted with a serious shortage of workers. Instead of attracting new workers to the old locations, however, Vossloh's management decided to expand geographically. A brand-new production plant was built in 1961 in Selm, near Dortmund, where space and workers were readily available, and the company's facilities expanded many times thereafter. In the same year, the first production facility abroad was established in Sarsina, a small Italian town in the province of Forli where Wilhelm Bomnüter's son Diethelm had met the town's mayor when he studied Italian. Finally, a new plastic-processing plant was set up near Lüdenscheid between 1964 and 1966. In 1967, the West German railway, Deutsche Bundesbahn, started experimenting with a new railroad track fastener, the Spannklemme, an invention of German Bundesbahn director Hermann Meier. Vossloh was awarded the general production license for the Spannklemme, which over the following decades became the standard for the European railroad industry.

Family Business Becomes a Global Public Enterprise in the 1990s

During the Wirtschaftswunder years, the second Vossloh generation had handed over responsibility for the family business to the third. Wilhelm Vossloh died in 1952. In 1958, Karl Vossloh's son Hans became the company's new CEO. Two years later, his father and his uncle Ernst died. In 1980, Wilhelm Bomnüter was succeeded by his son Diethelm as CEO of Vossloh-Werke. The early 1980s started out with a recession in Germany that especially affected Vossloh's lighting and decoration divisions. Automation helped cut cost but was not sufficient. Vossloh's management decided to focus on the two main locations, Werdohl and Lüdenscheid, and close down the production plants in Selm and Dillenburg. These measures led to significant layoffs, shrinking Vossloh's workforce from 1,300 at the beginning of the 1960s to about 750 in 1984. However, the company's profits still declined, and Vossloh started looking for help from experienced top managers outside the Vossloh family. After two outside managers proved unsuccessful in turning around the company, Burkhard Schuchmann, a 43-year-old Berliner who had successfully helped to take Munich-based Hans Knürr KG public as a member of the executive management board, became Vossloh CEO in March 1986. Hans Vossloh in turn became chairman of the advisory board, a position in which he remained until 1994, when he became honorary chairman and stayed actively involved in the business by coordinating and representing the Vossloh family group of shareholders, which counted more than 80 members by 1998.

Backed by the Vossloh family, Schuchmann took on the challenging task of transforming the mid-sized family enterprise into a public company with a strong financial footing, a competitive portfolio of products and services, and a global reach. In 1990, Vossloh shares were publicly traded for the first time at the stock exchange in Düsseldorf and later in the decade in Frankfurt/Main. In 1992, Diethelm Bomnüter resigned as a member of the executive board.

In 1990, the year when the two German states reunited, Vossloh acquired companies in eastern Germany. The sudden demand for railroad fasteners from the former East German railway company Deutsche Reichsbahn, as well as from other eastern European railways that were modernizing their infra-

structure, boosted the company's sales. At the same time, Vossloh's home decoration division did not turn up the desired profits, partly due to the cyclical nature of that business. The interior decoration market was highly dependent on fashion cycles that were picking up speed, demanding rising cost for design and marketing. When another recession hit the industry in the mid-1990s, Vossloh sold the business to the Italian Arquati group in 1997. The lighting division, which in the late 1980s was strengthened by the takeover of the German Schwabe group and by 1996 accounted for almost half of Vossloh's revenues, also slipped into a recession in the late 1990s, mainly due to a slump in the construction industry. Vossloh tried to counteract by investing in new technologies such as LED technology through the takeover of the German Wustlich Group in 2000, and in lighting control systems through a new subsidiary, as well as by restructuring the division to cut back cost. However, in April 2002, Vossloh announced that its lighting division was for sale.

Vossloh's CEO Schuchmann emphasized the company's sole focus was to be on the railway and transport division for which he saw a bright future. He was the driving force that relentlessly strengthened the company's market position and pushed forward its transition from manufacturer to integrated service provider. The takeover of the German firms Hegenscheidt GmbH and Hoesch Maschinenfabrik GmbH in the mid-1990s made Vossloh the world's leading manufacturer of machinery for refurbishing railroad vehicle wheels. Vossloh also acquired parts of DST Deutsche System-Technik GmbH, which had developed electronic traffic management and information systems, after the firm filed for bankruptcy. This company was then integrated into a newly established systems technology division, Vossloh System-Technik. Finally, the takeover of SIEMENS Schienenfahrzeugtechnik in 1998 made Vossloh a leading manufacturer of diesel locomotives in Europe. In the same year, Vossloh, together with Austrian steel maker VOEST-Alpine Stahl AG, bought a 90 percent majority in the Austrian VAE group, the world market leader of railroad switches. In 1999, Vossloh acquired British York-based Comreco Rail Ltd., an engineering firm that developed traffic flow planning and management software for railroad companies. Another deal with British Angel Trains Limited, a subsidiary of the Royal Bank of Scotland Group that took over 3,600 railroad vehicles from state-owned British Rail after its privatization in 1995, set Vossloh on track to exploit the emerging trend that railroad companies would rather lease than purchase rolling stock. The two companies agreed to set up a joint venture which would mainly buy diesel locomotives made by Vossloh and lease them to European railroad companies. Vossloh also entered the field of railroad vehicle maintenance, directly offering maintenance and repair services; at the same time, the company rented the necessary workshops—fully equipped—to others, or even set them up at client locations as far as China. Vossloh planned to use the expected cash inflow from the sale of its lighting business for acquisitions that would further strengthen the company's leading market position in the highly profitable field of railroad related products and services. Although Vossloh had become a truly global company with subsidiaries all over the world, reunited German railroad company Deutsche Bahn, which heavily depended on public funding, remained one of its major customers.

The Vossloh family had managed to keep a voting majority throughout the 1990s. However, the family's influence eventually declined. At the time of the IPO in 1990, the Vossloh family kept a 72 percent stake, which declined to 55 percent in 1992 due to a raise in share capital. By 1997, the Vossloh family's stake had shrunk to about 40 percent and was reduced to 35 percent by 2000. However, through a liaison with German life insurance company Deutscher Herold Lebensversicherungs AG, whose 11 percent share in Vossloh was pooled with the holdings of the Vossloh family, the descendants of company founder Eduard Vossloh were still in control of Vossloh. However, they were likely to loose that position in the future, due to further raises in the company's share capital.

Principal Subsidiaries

Vossloh-Schwabe GmbH (Germany); Vossloh Schienenfahrzeugtechnik GmbH (Germany); VAE Holding (Deutschland) GmbH (Germany); Vossloh Rail Systems GmbH (Germany); VAE Eisenbahnsysteme GmbH (Austria); VAE Holding GmbH (Austria; 50%); Vossloh-Schwabe France S.A.r.l.; Weichenwerk Brandenburg GmbH (Germany); Vossloh-Schwabe Italia S.p.A. (Italy); Hegenscheidt-MFD GmbH & Co. KG (Germany); Butzbacher Weichenbau GmbH & Co. KG (Germany); Vossloh-Schwabe Elektronik GmbH (Germany); VAE Nortrak Cheyenne Inc. (United States); VAE Nortrak Inc. (United States); VAE Nortrak Ltd. (Canada); Vossloh Systemelektronik GmbH (Germany); VAE Aktiengesellschaft (Austria; 90.6%); Elektrobau Oschatz GmbH & Co. KG (Germany; 70%); Vossloh Wehrdohl GmbH (Germany); Hegenscheidt-MFD Corporation (United States); Vossloh System-Technik GmbH (Germany); JEZ Sistemas Ferroviaros S.L. (Spain; 50%); Vossloh-Schwabe Española S.L. (Spain; 90%); Vossloh-Schwabe UK Ltd. (United Kingdom); Vossloh-Wustlich Opto GmbH & Co. KG (Germany; 80%); Vossloh-Schwabe Australia Pty. Ltd. (Australia); Vossloh-Schwabe Pte. Ltd. (Singapore); Vossloh-Schwabe Skandinavien AB (Sweden); Vossloh-Schwabe, Inc. (United States).

Principal Competitors

ALSTOM; DaimlerChrysler AG; General Electric Company.

Further Reading

"Börsenneuling Vossloh nutzt seine Marktnischen," *Süddeutsche Zeitung*, May 10, 1991.
"Ende des Übernahmekampfs um die VAE," *Neue Zürcher Zeitung*, June 30, 1998, p. 28.
"Familie Vossloh auf dem Rückzug," *Süddeutsche Zeitung*, May 12, 1992.
Rose, Stefanie, and Matthias Bringmann, *Vossloh Zeiten-Vom Beginn bis zur Gegenwart*, Werdohl, Germany: Vossloh AG, 2001, 114 p.
"Vossloh bereitet sich gut auf weitere Übernahmen vor," *Süddeutsche Zeitung*, May 31, 1994.
"Vossloh erreicht Vorjahresergebnis nicht," *Frankfurter Allgemeine Zeitung*, December 15, 2001, p. 19.
"Vossloh erwartet Impulse durch Investitionen der Deutschen Bahn," *Frankfurter Allgemeine Zeitung*, December 15, 2000, p. 21.
"Vossloh geht auf Einkaufstour," *Süddeutsche Zeitung*, May 25, 1993.
"Vossloh: 1996 kein weiteres Umsatzwachstum," *Frankfurter Allgemeine Zeitung*, December 5, 1995, p. 22.
"Vossloh strukturiert die schwächelnde Lichttechnik-Sparte um," *Frankfurter Allgemeine Zeitung*, December 10, 1999, p. 19.
"Vossloh vermietet künftig Lokomotiven gemeinsam mit Angel Trains," *Frankfurter Allgemeine Zeitung*, July 15, 2000, p. 17.
Wintermann, Jürgen H., "Vossloh konzentriert sich auf die Verkehrs- und Bahntechnik," *Die Welt* (online version), April 25, 2002.

—Evelyn Hauser

WHITNEY

W.A. Whitney Company

650 Race Street
Rockford, Illinois 61101-1434
U.S.A.
Telephone: (815) 964-6771
Fax: (815) 964-3175
Web site: http://www.wawhitney.com

Division of Esterline Technologies Corporation
Incorporated: 1907
Employees: 250
Sales: $38 million (2001 est.)
NAIC: 333990 All Other General Purpose Machinery
Manufacturing

Located in Rockford, Illinois since 1907, W.A. Whitney Company is a leading international manufacturer of metal fabrication equipment. Other manufacturers use the systems and tooling made by W.A. Whitney to punch and cut sheet metal and thick metal plates. Some of the company's cutting and punching systems involve thermal technology (plasma and lasers) to cut precisely through metals of great thickness. Although W.A. Whitney serves customers in a number of different industries, manufacturers of heavy construction and agricultural equipment comprise a significant share of its customer base. A division of Bellevue, Washington-based Esterline Technologies Corporation, W.A. Whitney has several international sales offices. W.A. Whitney of Canada Ltd. is located in Brampton, Ontario. As part of Esterline Technologies (HK) Ltd., Whitney's China/HK Office is located in T.S.T., Kowloon, Hong Kong. Finally, W.A. Whitney de Mexico S.A., based in Tlalnepantla, Mexico, serves customers in Latin America.

Humble Beginnings: 1907–49

W.A. Whitney Corporation stems from the efforts of William Andrew Whitney, a distant relative of legendary American inventor Eli Whitney. Whitney was born in Burns, New York on June 9, 1863. In the 1880s his family relocated to Stillman Valley, Illinois. Whitney received his first patent—for a fold-up wheelbarrow—in the mid-1880s. His second patent was for a hand-

operated ticket punch used by train conductors. Whitney then developed a lock nut, which led to the establishment of the American Lock Nut Co. in approximately 1902. Based in Oregon, Illinois, this enterprise was a partnership between Whitney and C.D. Etnyre.

Although his lock nut venture proved unsuccessful, Whitney's inventive spirit remained very much alive. By 1906, he had patented another hand punch and relocated to Rockford, Illinois, where he established the W.A. Whitney Manufacturing Co. in August 1907. This new venture was a partnership with three other men: C.D. Ballentine, William L. Keeney, and Frank VanderBogart. Using parts made by other manufacturing firms, William Whitney designed a series of punching hand tools (the No.1, No. 2, and No. 4 punches) and the company marketed them via direct mail.

Due to a variety of circumstances, by 1911 ownership of W.A. Whitney was completely in the hands of VanderBogart and a man named N.A. Merlin. After relinquishing his interest in W.A. Whitney, William Whitney established the Whitney Metal Tool Co., which later became known as Roper Whitney. However, he was more of an inventor than a businessman. By 1918, Whitney had exited the hand tool business and returned to Oregon, Illinois, where he ran a small machine shop until 1924. Following this, he entered into a period of semi-retirement.

In 1918, VanderBogart moved W.A. Whitney to 715 Park Avenue in Rockford. From this location, the company continued to assemble and market hand punches. Seven years later, VanderBogart retired and the George H. Spengler Co. acquired W.A. Whitney. The Spengler Co. actually had been granted a license to sell Whitney's products in 1924 and had long supplied Whitney with many of the parts used in the assembly of its hand punches. By 1928, W.A. Whitney had moved to the Spengler Co.'s building at 636 Race Street. Remaining in the same general vicinity, Whitney would later move to 650 Race Street. These sites are located in the heart of the city's old Water Power district, where a millrace used water from the Rock River to supply local industry with affordable electric power.

Aside from several new machines that were introduced in the 1930s—namely the #4B and 91 series press—the 1930s and

1940s constituted a relatively quiet period in W.A. Whitney's history. However, it was during this time period that William A. Whitney passed away in Rockford at the age of 82. At the time of his death in July 1945, William Whitney had 19 different patents to his name. In addition to the folding wheelbarrow, lock nut, and various hand punching tools, Whitney's inventions included ball bearings, universal joints, and check hooks.

As the July 20, 1945, *Rockford Morning Star* explained, Whitney's punches were used "in nearly every shipyard and aircraft factory in the country. He also had patented several types of shears. His inventions ranged from machinery to a folding baby carriage. Some of his inventions were used in the construction of the Chrysler building and other skyscrapers." According to an early historical profile, Whitney "was remembered by his grandchildren as a very happy-go-lucky type of individual with the cares of his past life behind. Even in his old age he would spend many hours at a drawing board in his barn just trying out ideas."

Transition and Preparation: 1950–59

As early as 1954, W.A. Whitney remained a very small company with only three part-time employees. That year, sales totaled approximately $150,000. However, things would soon change. In the mid-1950s Robert H. Spengler, grandson of George H. Spengler, was looking to hire an entry-level manufacturing engineer. During a meeting with Harry Conn, then chief engineer at Chicago-based Scully-Jones and Co., Conn recommended that Spengler hire one of his own employees for this position—a young man named Ted Brolund. As Spengler once recalled, Conn described Brolund as "one of the three best young engineers that I have ever had work for me." Brolund was interested in returning to his native city of Rockford and Conn allowed him to leave Scully-Jones and work for the George H. Spengler Co. and W.A. Whitney.

Brolund would go on to become the company's leading engineer. He was instrumental in making W.A. Whitney the first company to incorporate the use of hydraulics in punching tools. Registering 19 patents during his first 13 years with the company, Brolund designed a number of products including coper-notcher-benders, duplicators, gang punches, large panel presses, portable hydraulic punches, and shears. Brolund's accomplishments did not go unnoticed. In approximately 18 years time, he was successively promoted to vice-president of international operations, vice-president of manufacturing, and finally executive vice-president in 1973.

In 1957, Robert H. Spengler, grandson of George H. Spengler, was appointed president and treasurer of W.A. Whitney. The following year, the company constructed its very first manufacturing plant. This was an important step toward making W.A. Whitney an independent company. Although plans were first established to separate W.A. Whitney from the George H. Spengler Co. during the mid-1940s, manufacturing and sales continued to operate as two separate companies under the same ownership until January 1961, when W.A. Whitney officially became its own, self-sustaining organization. At this time George E. Spengler and George P. Spengler, son and grandson of founder George H. Spengler, assumed ownership of the George H. Spengler Co. Harold C. Spengler and Robert H. Spengler, also son and grandson of George H. Spengler, took control of W.A. Whitney.

Expansion and Modernization: 1960–69

Through the late 1950s, W.A. Whitney had focused mainly on the marketing of small hydraulic punches and hand tools. An important development took place in 1961 that set the stage for a different future. Harry Conn, who had recommended Ted Brolund to Robert H. Spengler several years before, joined W.A. Whitney as its vice-president and general manager. He possessed sales ability, management skills, engineering know-how, and the vision to achieve great things. Conn received his formal education in mechanical engineering from the Lewis Institute and Armour Tech. Early in his career he worked as an engineer for a number of companies, including Buick, Harvester Co., International Harvester, John Deere, and Studebaker. Prior to working for W.A. Whitney Conn served as methods engineer and tool designer for the LaSalle Engineering Co. of Chicago, chief engineer of LaSalle Engineering Co. of New York City, and chief engineer for Scully-Jones and Co.

Together, Brolund and Conn had a major impact on W.A. Whitney's future. The company introduced new products, including a sheet metal duplicator in 1962. A number of portable metalworking tools followed in 1963. Customers were able to take these to remote job sites like bridges, where it was necessary to punch great numbers of holes. One of these products was a hydraulic, 70-ton Web punch that, according to the March 20, 1963, *Rockford Morning Star* was capable of punching "a 1-inch diameter hole through ⅞-inch thick plate of mild steel." These developments benefited the company considerably. By 1963, sales had mushroomed to $1 million and the company's employees numbered 50. That year, Harry Conn was appointed president of W.A. Whitney. Robert H. Spengler was named W.A. Whitney's chairman, and also president of W.A. Whitney Canada.

A number of industry firsts were achieved at W.A. Whitney during the mid-1960s. In 1965, the company pioneered the application of numeric controls to sheet metal punching machines. In 1968, Whitney developed the Beamline Punching Unit—a machine capable of punching angle iron, I-beams, and structural steel. In order to obtain much needed capital for expansion, the Spengler family sold W.A. Whitney to New York-based Esterline Technologies Corp. in October 1969. At the time, Esterline was a $70 million firm involved in the areas of atomic energy, instrumentation, and metalworking. As part of the acquisition, Conn agreed to remain as Whitney's presi-

Key Dates:

1907: Inventor William Andrew Whitney—along with C.D. Ballentine, William L. Keeney, and Frank VanderBogart—starts W.A. Whitney Manufacturing Co. to manufacture punching hand tools for which Whitney holds various patents.

1918: By this time, Whitney has exited the hand tool business and opens a small machine shop, which he operates until 1924.

1925: George H. Spengler Co. acquires W.A. Whitney Manufacturing Co., which had come under the ownership of Frank VanderBogart and N.A. Merlin around 1911.

1945: William A. Whitney dies at the age of 82, having 19 patents to his name, including those for the folding wheelbarrow, lock nut, ball bearings, and various hand punching tools.

Mid-1950s: Ted Brolund is hired as manufacturing engineer for W.A. Whitney; Brolund registers numerous patents vital to the company's growth.

1958: The company builds its first manufacturing plant.

1961: W.A. Whitney separates from the George H. Spengler Co.; Harold C. Spengler and Robert H. Spengler, son and grandson of George H. Spengler, are given control of the company.

1963: Sales reach $1 million; Harry Conn is appointed president.

1969: W.A. Whitney is sold by the Spengler family to New York-based Esterline Technologies Corp. and operates as a subsidiary of Esterline's Machine Tool Group.

1974: Ted Brolund replaces Harry Conn as president, becoming president and CEO in 1978.

1980: The company begins using plasma to cut sheet metal and unveils its 661 Punch/Plasma Combination machine.

1992–93: Sales increase by 20 percent.

1998: Dr. Joe Mayer assumes the leadership position at Whitney upon Ted Brolund's retirement.

1999: PartHANDLER load/unload system is launched.

dent for five years. Whitney became a subsidiary of Esterline, organized under the company's Machine Tool Group. At the time of the acquisition, Whitney employed 267 workers and had expanded its international reach with branches in Birmingham, England; Mexico City, Mexico; and Torino, Italy.

On The Cutting Edge: 1970 to the 21st Century

During the early 1970s, W.A. Whitney rolled out a number of new products, including the 6115 N-C Platemaster, which was "the largest single station numerically controlled plate punching, notching, and nibbling machine on the market," according to an article in the August 1, 1971, *Rockford Morning Star*. The 6115 N-C Platemaster was built for a market that included bridge builders, construction equipment manufacturers, perforators, railroad equipment companies, ship builders, manufacturers of steam power equipment, structural steel fabri-

cators, and utilities. In 1972, the company unveiled more products that were designed to save employees in the machine tool and metalworking industries time and effort. Among these were the 838-CP-N-C Contourmaster and the 845-A Clipmaster.

In 1974, several noteworthy things took place at W.A. Whitney. Ted Brolund replaced Harry Conn as president. Conn remained with the organization as chairman. In addition, the company reached a milestone by giving its Numerically Controlled Punching Unit the ability to perform plasma cutting. In 1978, Conn retired from W.A. Whitney. Once again, Brolund was Conn's successor. In addition to becoming W.A. Whitney's president and CEO, he also became group executive of Esterline. In the latter role, Brolund assumed responsibility for five Esterline companies. At the time of the leadership change, Conn affirmed what he had told Robert Spengler in 1955. Of the more than 3,000 scientists and engineers he had employed over the course of his career, Conn named Brolund as the best in a local news article.

In 1976, W.A. Whitney made plans to spend $1 million on the construction of a new assembly building and the renovation of an existing facility. In addition, a number of older structures on its property were demolished and additional space for parking was added. By the late 1970s, W.A. Whitney's products had evolved considerably. Leading the way was its numerically controlled hydraulic plasma arc fabricator. Reaching temperatures of 42,000 degrees Fahrenheit, this device was capable of cutting "half-inch-thick stainless steel on a contour at 400 inches a minute," according to a news article by Dean Todd.

Similar innovations continued in the 1980s. In 1980, the company began using plasma to cut sheet metal and unveiled its 661 Punch/Plasma Combination machine. In 1982, W.A. Whitney celebrated its 75th anniversary. The company had exploded in size since 1907, occupying manufacturing space in excess of 450,000 square feet on an 11-acre campus. During its anniversary year, Whitney continued to improve its product offerings. That year the company added a robotic tool changer to its punching units. In addition, the National Machine Tool Builders Association recognized W.A. Whitney's sales and promotional efforts by presenting the company with two awards in its marketing communications competition. W.A. Whitney ended the decade by selling two machines to the government of India for almost $2 million. The machines were to be used for the production of railroad cars by New Delhi-based Rail Coach Factory.

Things continued to go well at W.A. Whitney during the 1990s. Between 1992 and 1993, the company's sales rose 20 percent, according to Ted Brolund in the April 21, 1994, *Rockford Register Star*. That year, Whitney was marketing its TRUECut Oxygen Plasma Cutting System, which used oxygen to make cuts in sheet metal that rivaled laser technology. At this point in history, Whitney's top customers included the likes of J.I. Case and Caterpillar.

A number of new product introductions took place in the mid- to late 1990s. Whitney introduced its 3400 RTC (Rail Tool Changer) in 1996. The following year, it unveiled its 1524 CNC Fabricator with Panelgage 1000 Series Control and received ISO 9001 certification. In 1998, Whitney introduced its new PlateLASER cutting machine for plate more than five-eighths of an inch thick. In March 1998, W.A. Whitney announced a $3 million, 250,000-square-foot expansion effort. The project included an addition with classrooms and a technical/demonstration center where Whitney customers and employees could learn about the company's products.

Another major development took place on June 30, 1998. On that day, Ted Brolund retired from W.A. Whitney and became the company's senior consultant for a period of two years. Dr. Joe Mayer, who formerly served as vice-president of operations at Hartford, Connecticut-based Trumpf (a competitor of W.A. Whitney), succeeded him. In the August 1998 issue of *BusinessProfile Magazine*, Mayer commented: "I don't think the customer will see any radical changes in how the company operates. Ted and I share a lot of the same values, like quality, teamwork, the integrity with which we would like to do business, a focus on goals and the vision."

Building on the successes of Ted Brolund, Joe Mayer continued to lead W.A. Whitney in a positive direction. In 1999, the company unveiled its PartHANDLER load/unload system, as well as its PlateLASER 6000. As W.A. Whitney entered the 2000s, its latest products included the PlateLASER-II and the Model 3400 RTC-60 Punch/Plasma Fabricating Center. Beginning with simple hand punches, W.A. Whitney's products have continually evolved over the years, providing customers with better ways to cut and punch metals with more speed, precision and accuracy.

Principal Operating Units

W.A. Whitney de Mexico S.A.; W.A. Whitney of Canada Ltd.

Principal Competitors

Trumpf Company.

Further Reading

"Conn Named Head of W.A. Whitney," *Rockford Morning Star*, March 20, 1963.

Kleczkowski, Linda, "W.A. Whitney . . . Innovators in Metal Fabricating Machinery," *BusinessProfile Magazine*, August 1998.

Marshall, Ruth, "George E. Spengler Dead After Illness," *Rockford Morning Star*, August 19, 1970.

"New York Firm Buys W.A. Whitney Corp.," *Rockford Register Republic*, October 23, 1969.

Rogers, Cathy, "Whitney Survives as a Diamond in Rough Times," *Rockford Register Star*, August 29, 1982.

"Ted Brolund . . . President of W.A. Whitney: Forty-One Years of Innovative Contributions," *BusinessProfile Magazine*, June 1998.

"W.A. Whitney Corp. 60th Anniversary," *Rockford Register Republic*, February 15, 1968.

"Whitney Begins Expansion Work," *Rockford Register Star*, March 10, 1998, 1C.

"Whitney Observes 75th," *Rockford Journal*, September 1, 1982.

"Whitney Rites on Saturday," *Rockford Morning Star*, July 20, 1945.

—Paul R. Greenland

Warrantech Corporation

150 Westpark Way
Euless, Texas 76040
U.S.A.
Telephone: (817) 354-0095
Fax: (817) 436-6151
Web site: http://www.warrantech.com

Public Company
Incorporated: 1983
Employees: 457
Sales: $37.30 million (2001)
Stock Exchanges: Over-The-Counter
Ticker Symbol: WTEC
NAIC: 541990 All Other Professional, Scientific and
    Technical Services; 561110 Office Administrative
    Services

Warrantech Corporation operates as a third-party administrator of extended warranty services, providing its services to distributors, manufacturers, and retailers. Warrantech does not pay the claims covered by its contracts. Instead, the company locates insurance companies that underwrite the warranty-extension and product-replacement contracts it sells. The company's business is divided into two divisions—automotive, which operates domestically, and consumer products, which operates both domestically and internationally. Warrantech's automotive business consists of marketing and administering vehicle service programs that offer coverage for terms ranging between three months and 84 months. The company's consumer products segment develops, markets, and administers extended warranties and product replacement plans for a range of household appliances and consumers electronics, such as televisions and computer equipment. Part of Warrantech's consumer products division also includes home warranties, which cover the mechanical breakdown of home systems such as plumbing, heating, and air-conditioning systems. The company's international segment markets and administers both automotive and consumer products services overseas. Through foreign subsidiaries, Warrantech operates in Puerto Rico, Guatemala, Chile, and Peru.

Origins

When Joel San Antonio and William Tweed founded Warrantech in 1983, it represented an unusual career change. The pair managed Little Loraine Ltd., a company that San Antonio had founded in 1975. For the next seven years, San Antonio served as president of Little Loraine, hiring Tweed in 1976 to serve as his vice-president. The two executives remained at Little Loraine until August 1982, when they began developing plans for Warrantech, a third-party contract extension and warranty vendor. Considering that Little Loraine produced women's apparel, the foray into the warranty and contract extension business was a tangential move by San Antonio and Tweed. The career change proved to be a lasting one, however, occupying the two executives' attention for the ensuing two decades.

Warrantech's service contracts, extended warranties, and replacement contracts typically covered terms ranging from three months to 84 months. The company operated as a third-party administrator, acting on behalf of dealers and insurance companies. In its role as a third-party administrator, Warrantech's responsibilities excluded either performing repairs or providing replacement products. Independent, authorized repair facilities or dealers provided such services. The cost of the repairs or the replacement products was typically incurred by the insurance companies.

The services provided by Warrantech varied according to the type of contract offered by the company. During its first decade of business, the company operated in two business segments: automotive and consumer products. Through its automotive segment, Warrantech marketed and administered vehicle service contract (VSC) programs to automobile and motorcycle dealers, leasing companies, and repair facilities. A VSC was a contract between the dealer and the consumer that offered coverage for a term ranging between three months and 84 months. Warrantech processed VSC's produced by a dealer and administered the paying of claims according to the terms of the VSC, costs that were borne by insurance companies. Warrantech's consumer products segment developed, marketed, and administered consumer product extended warranties and product replacement plans developed for household appliances, televisions, computers and home office equipment, as well as a number of other electronics products.

It took several years for Warrantech to begin recording any appreciable growth. By 1988, five years after the company's founding, its sales amounted to a mere $6.2 million, a fraction of the revenue volume Warrantech would record in a few short years. The company's fifth year of business marked a turning point, the year in which the company began to register substantial growth. The year also marked San Antonio's appointment as Warrantech's chairman. San Antonio had served as president and chief executive officer of Warrantech since its inception. When he was selected as chairman, he retained his post as chief executive officer but passed the presidential duties to Tweed, who had served as the company's vice-president since its inception.

Warrantech's rapid revenue growth during the late 1980s occurred largely because the company began greatly expanding it customer base. Before the company began fleshing out its roster of clients, it drew the bulk of its revenue from automobile contracts, which included servicing the business of automobile manufacturers such as BMW of North America. Although automobile contracts served as Warrantech's main source of revenue, the business segment did not provide the company with a wealth of opportunities for expansion. The company's consumer products segment offered such opportunities, providing the company with the means to pursue a path of expansion. In the years ahead, automobile contracts would continue to account for the majority of Warrantech's revenue, but its greatest growth would be achieved through consumer products contracts, which covered traditional products such as televisions and videocassette recorders, as well as more esoteric products, such as laser pointers and mood rings.

Late 1980s Expansion

As Warrantech aggressively sought more consumer products customers, it also expanded its business through acquisitions. In 1989, when San Antonio also was appointed chairman and chief executive officer of Warrantech's principal operating subsidiaries, the company acquired Dealer Based Services Inc., a Euless, Texas-based automobile service contract supplier. In 1991, the company also acquired a controlling stake in Minnehoma Insurance Co. The acquisitions represented only one facet of the company's broad-based strategy for building its service-contract business. To invigorate contract sales, the company implemented training programs and specialized marketing tools, including contract forms and point-of-purchase displays. More significantly, the company formed a 35-employee division based in Fort Worth, Texas. Called Warrantech Direct, the division was formed in 1990 to strengthen the company's telemarketing efforts.

As Warrantech's tenth anniversary neared, its annual revenue totals began to increase with decided vigor. By 1990, sales had grown to $30 million, far more than the $6.2 million recorded two years earlier. In 1991, sales leaped to $56 million. Of the total registered in 1991, $40 million was collected from the company's automobile contracts, with the balance derived from the company's consumer products contracts. The company's client base, after several years of concerted expansion, included catalog retailers such as Sharper Image and Damark. The company also had forged business relationships with traditional retailers, such as department store operators Stern's and Abraham & Strauss and mass merchandisers such as Tops Appliance. The company conducted business with specialty electronics chains as well, such as the 11-store chain RogerSound Labs Inc. Warrantech gained RogerSound as a customer in 1986. By the beginning of the 1990s, RogerSound's management, led by president and chief executive officer Murray Dashe, was convinced of Warrantech's value as a third-party warranty company. In a December 23, 1991 interview with the trade publication *HFD—The Weekly Home Furnishings Newspaper,* Dashe noted, "They're [Warrantech] a quick-moving company that can act in a more entrepreneurial mode, and they're not hamstrung like many larger companies."

Warrantech completed its first decade of existence occupying a favorable market position. Although the company's sales declined to $50.6 million in 1992, the mood at company headquarters in 1993 was buoyant. The company found itself facing less intense competitive pressures during its tenth anniversary, as the number of its rivals diminished. In a March 8, 1993 interview with *HFD—The Weekly Home Furnishings Newspaper,* San Antonio shared his observation of the dwindling number of competitors vying for market share. "Three or four years ago, there were about 25 warranty companies at the Consumer Electronics Show," he remarked. "At the last show there were four."

The reduction in competition left Warrantech in the position to grow, a stance that the company assumed with an aggressive posture. To take advantage of the situation, the company made several moves that pointed to its commitment to growth. In Dallas, the company began developing a sales-training complex, a 5,000-square-foot facility that represented a $250,000 investment. Warrantech also began marketing new service-contract products and expanded its telemarketing staff, increasing Warrantech Direct's staff to more than 60 employees. Nevertheless, the most significant event of the year arrived through a joint venture agreement.

In early 1993, Warrantech signed an agreement with American International Group, Inc. (AIG), an $18 million-in-annual-sales insurance company with operations in 130 countries. Under the terms of the agreement, Warrantech operated as the administrator of service contracts and AIG provided the underwriting. As part of the agreement, AIG purchased a 20 percent stake in Warrantech, paying $6.4 million to consummate its affiliation with the third-party warranty company. To spearhead the company's new overseas business, Warrantech International Ltd. was established in Northampton, England, where the company began offering three- and five-year contracts covering consumer electronics, major appliances, home office products, and computers. The warranties were sold on a private label basis or under the new Warrantech International brand.

The ultimate goal of Warrantech International was to lead its parent company's expansion into other parts of Europe and other continents. As the 1990s progressed, Warrantech International fulfilled its objective, transforming Warrantech into a multinational concern.

Warrantech in the 21st Century

Warrantech's geographic reach was extended into Canada, Puerto Rico, and Latin American by the time the company exited the 1990s. By this point in the company's development, it was regarded as a leader and innovator in the field of service contracts and extended warranties, holding sway as one of the largest independent service-contract companies in the United States. In addition to expanding geographically, the company also had expanded the range of services it provided. For example, the company entered the real industry by providing home warranties, which were administered through a subsidiary, Warrantech Home Service Co.

As the company's 20th anniversary approached, there were numerous reasons to suggest that the arrival of the milestone would find the company's management in a celebratory mood. In June 2001, Warrantech renewed a long-term contract with one of its major consumer products clients, BrandsMart USA. In December 2001, the company renewed a long-term contract with another major consumer products client, Ultimate Electronics, Inc. In July 2002, the company renewed its third major contract, signing a three-year extension of its business agreement with Micro Center, the Hilliard, Ohio-based retail arm of Micro Electronics Inc., a leading provider of computers and peripheral products.

On the heels of the contract extension with Micro Center, Warrantech announced it was relocating its corporate headquarters. In August 2002, the company signed a ten-year lease agreement in the city of Bedford, Texas. Warrantech announced it was moving to a new 56,700-square-foot facility that was expected to house its executive, marketing, and administrative personnel. The new facility was also designed to house a direct-marketing operation capable of containing a 400-seat call cen-

ter. Warrantech executives anticipated moving into the new facility in October 2002, giving the company a new home for its 20th anniversary.

Principal Divisions

Automotive; Consumer Products.

Principal Subsidiaries

Warrantech Consumer Product Services, Inc.; WCPS of Florida, Inc.; Warrantech Automotive, Inc.; Warrantech Automotive of California, Inc.; Warrantech Automotive Risk Purchasing Group, Inc.; Warrantech Automotive of Florida, Inc.; Warrantech Direct, Inc.; Warrantech (UK) Limited; Warrantech International, Inc.; WCPS of Canada, Inc.; Warrantech Automotive of Canada, Inc.; Warrantech Europe PLC (England); Warrantech Additive, Inc.; Warrantech Home Service Company; Warrantech Caribbean Ltd. (Cayman Islands); Warrantech Home Assurance Company; Repairmaster Canada, Inc.; WCPS Direct, Inc.; WHSC Direct, Inc.; Warrantech International de Chile; VEMECO, Inc.

Principal Competitors

Automobile Protection Corporation; Federal Warranty Service; BancTec, Inc.

Further Reading

Greenberg, Manning, "Warrantech Looks Beyond Mere Survival," *HFD—The Weekly Home Furnishings Newspaper*, March 8, 1993, p. 55.

"Home Warranty Company Adds Mortgage Protection," *Mortgage Servicing News*, April 2002, p. 10.

Seavy, Mark, "Warrantech Names ComponentGuard in $35 Million Counter Claim Action," *HFD—The Weekly Home Furnishings Newspaper*, Jan 28, 1991, p. 87.

"Warrantech-AIG Pact," *HFD—The Weekly Home Furnishings Newspaper*, January 11, 1993, p. 178.

"Warrantech Corp.," *Market News Publishing*, July 15, 2002.

"Warrantech Corp.," *Market News Publishing*, August 13, 2002.

"Warrantech Widens Service-Contract Array," *HFD—The Weekly Home Furnishings Newspaper*, December 23, 1991, p. 84.

—Jeffrey L. Covell

Wegener NV

Laan van Westenenk 4, 7336 AZ Apeldoorn
Postbus 26, 7300 HB Apeldoorn
The Netherlands
Telephone: (+31) 0 55 538 88 88
Fax: (+31) 0 55 538 85 00
Web site: http://www.wegener.nl

Public Company
Incorporated: 1903
Employees: 8,080
Sales: EUR 973 million ($957.6 million) (2001)
Stock Exchanges: Euronext Amsterdam
Ticker Symbol: WEG
NAIC: 511110 Newspaper Publishers; 511120 Periodical
  Publishers; 511140 Database and Directory
  Publishers; 541820 Public Relations Services; 551112
  Offices of Other Holding Companies

Wegener NV is one of the Netherlands' leading newspaper publishing groups. The company claims the number one spot in the regional newspaper segment, with a 58 percent market share. Wegener, which also publishes and distributes a long list of free door-to-door newspapers, claims a 28 percent share of the total newspaper market in the Netherlands. In addition to its newspaper publishing activities, which are centered primarily on the Netherlands but also extend into Flemish/Dutch-speaking Belgium, Wegener has been building a strong presence in the European direct marketing segment through primary business unit Wegener Direct Marketing. In addition to the Netherlands, this division operates subsidiaries in France (through a 90 percent share of Sopres), Belgium, the United Kingdom (through the Dudley Jenkins Group), Hungary, and Scandinavia, with operations in 13 European countries. Known as Wegener Arcade during the late 1990s, the company has repositioned itself to focus on its core direct marketing and newspaper publishing activities, disposing of a number of operations, including its Arcade music group, its television holding—The Music Factory, sold to MTV in 2001—and a string of technical and trade journals. The company maintains a small presence in the local radio market through its Radio 10 group, which includes Radio 10 Gold, Jazzradio FM, and Love Radio. Wegener publishes a limited range of magazines, including *Golfers Magazine, Golf Journaal, Golf Nieuws,* and *Party.* The company has also built an extensive presence on the Internet, with a vast range of Web sites for its various newspapers. Other company activities include a cartography unit and publishing of local community guides. Listed on the Euronext Amsterdam Stock Exchange, Wegener posted sales of more than EUR 973 million ($950 million) in 2001.

Regional Publisher at the Turn of the 20th Century

Wegener's origins can be traced back to the turn of the twentieth century, when Johan Frederik Wegener founded a newspaper in the Netherlands' Apeldoorn in 1903. Wegener called his newspaper the *Nieuwe Apeldoornsche Courant*—because there was already an "old" *Apeldoornsche Courant.* Yet Wegener soon took over that paper as well, merging its expanded operation under the *Nieuwe Apeldoornse Courant* banner (the Dutch spelling system was simplified following World War II). Starting with just one subscriber, Wegener built up a thriving local business.

In 1930, the Wegener company made its first acquisition, purchasing Rotterdam-based *Het Zuiden,* a free door-to-door newspaper. That purchase was to become the cornerstone of a later Wegener specialty. Over the next decades, the company, which became known as the Wegener Couranten Concern, continued to add other titles, including door-to-door titles in the small towns of Tiel and Veenendaal. Wegener also branched out into magazine publishing, with titles including *Rijdend Nederland,* focused on the auto market.

By the early 1960s, however, Wegener faced disaster, particularly as losses mounted in the company's magazine publishing division. Led until then by the Wegener family, the company turned to outsider Gerard Spanhaak in 1964. A former journalist, Spanhaak had joined the company as an editor for the *Nieuwe Apeldoornse Courant* in 1953, becoming editor-in-chief in 1958.

Spanhaak was credited with laying the foundation of Wegener's later success. Taking the helm of the company in 1962, Spanhaak quickly sold off its money-losing magazine division and began plotting a strategy to keep the company afloat. In order to survive, Wegener needed to grow and achieve sufficient economies of scale—in 1962, the company's annual revenues amounted to just NFL 5 million, and the company's share of the Dutch newspaper market was less than 1 percent. Yet acquiring other newspapers in order to build up the company's core division would have been too costly for the cash-strapped, family-owned company.

Instead, Spanhaak pointed the company toward building scale in a more accessible market, that of small-scale door-to-door publications. The company adopted what Spanhaak himself described, as reported by the *Apeldoornse Courant*, as "a fairly aggressive policy for taking over newspapers." Over the next several years, the company acquired a number of small papers, targeting especially the Betuwe and Veluwe regions.

Wegener's acquisition drive took off especially after 1969, when the company went public on the Amsterdam Stock Exchange. In 1970, the company grouped just four newspaper titles in the Gelderland region, good for a total circulation of just over 47,000. But by 1972, Wegener had taken over some twenty door-to-door newspapers. The company had also entered the direct marketing market as an extension to its door-to-door business. The company's operations, however, had come to rely too heavily on the advertising-driven door-to-door market. In 1974, the company was able to address that imbalance by acquiring the Drents-Groninger Pers, which gave the company a number of new regional newspapers.

Spaanhak, who retired in 1982, prepared his largest expansion move in 1981, when the company successfully acquired the Utrechts Nieuwsblad holding company, beating out rival Elsevier and its Nederlandse Dagbladunie newspaper subsidiary. That acquisition marked the beginning of Wegener's development into one of the Netherland's leading newspaper publishing groups.

By 1988, the company had boosted its holdings to more than 17 regional newspapers, with total circulation of nearly 330,000. The company's revenues of that year, which topped NFL262 million (approximately $130 million), made Wegener one of the rising stars of the Dutch publishing firmament, with a market share of nearly 6 percent. In that year, the company merged with fellow newspaper group Koninkljke Tijl NV, changing its name to Wegener-Tijl. That acquisition also helped boost the company's catalog of trade journals and magazines, including titles such as *Weekblad Motor* and *Automobile Klassiek*.

Regional Publishing Leader for the New Century

Wegener continued targeting new acquisitions in the early 1990s. In 1992, the company acquired the *Oostelijke Dagblad Combinatie,* which boosted the company's portfolio of regional newspapers to 30, with total circulation of 600,000. By then, Wegener's market share neared 13 percent. The company was also expanding elsewhere, boosting its direct marketing division to market leadership and diversifying its publishing offering with the acquisition of Surrlan Beheer BV, which specialized in publishing maps and other cartographic products, as well as publishing municipal guidebooks.

In 1994, Wegener added Sijthoff Pers, publisher of the *Haagsche Courant* and other regional papers. That acquisition, which gave the company coverage across the Netherlands, led the company to realign its portfolio, selling off its holdings in the northernmost regions of the country. At the same time, the company reorganized its newspaper titles into five regional "clusters," merging its portfolio of titles under five primary titles, *Apeldoornse Courant, Gelders Dagblad, Arnhemse Courant, Deventer Dagblad,* and *Overijssels Dagblad.* In 1996, the company converted most of its newspaper titles to morning editions, making them more competitive in the crowded Dutch newspaper market. In 1997, Wegener added another local newspaper to its holdings, the *Zeeuwse Courant.*

By then, Wegener, led by chairman C. Appeldoorn, had attempted to step beyond publishing into the broader media arena by buying up music group Arcade, which, apart from music recording and publishing, operated one of the Netherlands' largest music retail chains, the Music Store, as well as a television station, TMF or The Music Factory, and several radio stations grouped under the Radio 10 name. The Arcade acquisition led Wegener to change its name to Wegener Arcade, as its sales now topped NFL1.4 billion (EUR 679 million).

Yet the marriage between Wegener and Arcade quickly proved an uneasy one, and by 1999 Wegener had begun selling off nearly all of its Arcade-related holdings, keeping little more than the Radio 10 radio station group. By 2000, the company was able to shorten its name to Wegener NV. The failure of the Arcade experiment led Wegener, under new chairman Jan Houwert, to redefine itself for the coming new century. The company refocused itself around two principal operations: publishing a core of regional newspapers and door-to-door titles—the company had sold off most of its magazine titles the year earlier, then sold its trade journals in 2000—and its various direct marketing activities, which were united into a single division, Wegener Direct Marketing, in 2000.

By then, that division was boosted with the acquisition of Dudley Jenkins Plc, one of the leading direct marketing groups in the United Kingdom, in a deal worth more than $120 million. The company had also begun expanding its direct marketing operations elsewhere in Europe, notably into Belgium and France through a 45 percent stake in Belgium's Sopres group, acquired in 1997. By 2001, the company had increased its position to a controlling share of more than 70 percent.

Key Dates:

1903: Johan Frederik Wegener founds *Nieuwe Apeldoornsche Courant* in Apeldoorn, Netherlands.
1930: *Het Zuiden,* a free door-to-door paper in Rotterdam, is acquired.
1964: Gerard Spanhaak is named editor-in-chief and reorients company into door-to-door market.
1969: Wegener goes public on the Amsterdam Stock Exchange and begins an acquisition drive.
1974: Regional newspaper group Drents-Groninger Pers is acquired.
1981: Utrechts Nieuwsblad newspaper group is acquired.
1988: The company merges with Koninklijke Tijl and changes its name to Wegener Tijl.
1992: Wegener Tijl acquires *Oostelijke Dagblad Combinatie,* boosting regional newspaper portfolio to 30 papers.
1994: Wegener Tijl acquires Sijthoff Pers, owner of the *Haagsche Courant* and other regional papers.
1996: Arcade music group is acquired, and Wegener Tijl changes its name to Wegener Arcade.
1999: Wegener Tijl begins selling off Arcade-related holdings and acquires Dudley Jenkins Plc, a leading UK direct marketing group, and VNU's newspaper division.
2000: Wegener Tijl changes its name to Wegener NV and acquires Koba in France and ExSample in the Netherlands; all direct marketing operations are grouped under Wegener Direct Marketing.
2001: Wegener NV acquires Wij-Speciaal Media in the Netherlands and 25 percent of Idata in France.

Yet the company's largest acquisition had come in 1999 with the purchase of the Dutch publishing group VNU's newspaper division, which included the Brabantse Dagbladen group as well as a range of free door-to-door newspapers. The acquisition, at a cost of some EUR 700 million, boosted Wegener's circulation by more than 800,000 and its revenues to more than EUR 975 million. The company was on its way to becoming the clear leader in the regional newspaper market, with a 58 percent share of that segment, and a 28 percent share of the overall newspaper market.

Wegener continued adding on to its newspapers titles, acquiring 11 door-to-door titles in the south of the Netherlands from H.J. Willems in 2000. Yet, with little room for further growth in the Netherlands, the company stepped up its investments in its direct marketing wing at the turn of the century. As with its newspaper portfolio, Wegener complemented its internal growth with a new acquisition program, which included the acquisition of France-based Koba and ExSample Media BV of the Netherlands, in 2000, then Wij-Speciaal Media of the Netherlands and the "Scandinavian Baby Bag" operations from Sweden's NIDAB in 2001. In that year, the company also acquired a 25 percent stake in France's IData, with a provision to extend its ownership to 75 percent by 2003.

Wegener had a difficult year in 2001 as a result of a poor economic climate, as well as increasing competition for advertisers, which saw its revenues slip back to EUR 973 million, while the company's profits plunged. The company expected to recover in 2002, however, through tighter cost controls. With circulation levels of more than 1.7 million, Wegener, which had begun preparations for celebrating its 100th anniversary, had come a long way from its beginning as a one-subscriber newspaper company.

Principal Divisions

Publishing; Direct Marketing.

Principal Subsidiaries

Brabants Dagblad BV; Dagblad Tubantia/Twentsche Courant BV; Dudley Jenkins Group Plc (United Kingdom); Eindhovens Dagblad BV, Eindhoven; ExSample Media BV; Interlanden Spreigroep BV,; Party Publishing BV; RDMS Direct Marketing BV; Sijthoff Pers BV, Rijswijk; Uitgeversmaatschappij De Gelderlander BV; Uitgeversmaatschappij Zuidwest-Nederland BV; Uitgeverij Provinciale Zeeuwse Courant BV; Wegener Direct Marketing Belgium, Brussel NV; Wegener Direct Marketing France SA; Wegener Hungary Direct Marketing KFT; Wegener Direct Marketing Nederland BV; Wegener DM Services BV; Wegener eMedia BV; Wegener Falkplan BV; Wegener Golf BV; Wegener Huis-aan-Huiskranten Nederland BV; Wegener Huis-aan-Huiskranten Oost BV; Wegener Huis-aan-Huiskranten Zuid BV; Wegener Informatie Centrum/WIC Media; Wegener Publicatie Services; Wegener Radio en Televisie BV; Wegener Scandinavia AB (Sweden); Wegener Uitgeverij Gelderland-Overijssel BV; Wegener Uitgeverij Midden Nederland BV; Wij Special Media BV.

Principal Competitors

VNU NV; HAL Holding NV; De Telegraaf Holdingmaatschappij NV; PCM Uitgevers NV; WPG Uitgevers BV; Sijthoff Pers BV; Verenigde Noordhollandse Dagbladen BV; PZC Holding BV; Biegelaar and Jansen BV.

Further Reading

Bosveld, Johan, "Wegener slaat grote slag op postmarkt," *Apeldoornse Courant*, July 9, 2002.
Horlings, André, "Van één abonnee naar 1,3 miljoen," *Deventer Dagblad*, March 13, 2000.
Jagger, Suzy "Dudley Jenkins agrees pounds 80m bid," *The Daily Telegraph*, January 14, 1999.
Van Aartrijk, Steven, "Wegener verlaagt prognose voor hele jaar 2002," *De Financieele Nieuwsdienst*, August 14, 2002.
Van Amelsvoort, Herman, "Gerard Spanhaak 1919–2002: Motor achter expansie Wegener," *Apeldoornse Courant*, July 30, 2002.
Yorgey, Lisa A., "Starting at Ground zero," *Target Marketing*, May 2001, p. 30.
"Wegener Sees Flat 2001 Net Profit Before Extras," *Reuters*, April 24, 2001.

—M.L. Cohen

WMS Industries, Inc.

800 South Northpoint Boulevard
Waukegan, Illinois 60618
U.S.A.
Telephone: (847) 785-3000
Fax: (847) 785-3058
Web site: http://www.wmsgaming.com

Public Company
Incorporated: 1946 as Williams Manufacturing Company
Employees: 838
Sales: $175 million (2002)
Stock Exchanges: New York
Ticker Symbol: WMS
NAIC: 334310 Audio and Video Equipment
    Manufacturing; 713290 Other Gambling Industries

WMS Industries, Inc. operates as a designer, manufacturer, and marketer of video and mechanical reel spinning slot machines and video lottery terminals (VLTs). Formerly one of the world's largest pinball manufacturers, WMS retooled in the late 1990s to focus exclusively on the gaming industry. Its most popular games are based on "Monopoly," "Hollywood Squares," the television show "Survivor," "Pac-Man," "Scrabble," and "Pictionary." The company serves the U.S. casino gaming industry and also has sales offices in Canada, Australia, Spain, and South Africa.

Early History: 1930s–40s

The modern pinball industry took off during the Depression era, and Harry Williams was one of the industry's first great game designers. In 1929, Williams graduated from Stanford University; five years later, his name was important enough to be a selling point in advertisements. Working for Los Angeles-based Pacific Amusements Company, Williams designed the first electromechanical pinball machine in 1933. That game, called "Contact," featured two solenoid-powered contact holes, which gave points when the pinball landed in them. The solenoid quickly became an industry standard, used to operate a variety of features on the pinball playing field. "Contact" was also the first pinball machine to feature electrically generated sound when Williams attached a doorbell to the machine. These innovations created boom years for the entire industry through the Depression.

While working for Pacific Amusements, Williams also designed games for other pinball makers, including Bally and Rock-Ola in Chicago. Williams was responsible for several more important innovations, including the kicker, the pedestal tilt, and pendulum tilt mechanisms. For years, pinball had been, for the most part, a game of chance, as the player had little influence over the course the ball took. Williams's designs were among the first to introduce skill elements to the game. He was also instrumental in introducing the first replay feature, allowing the player to compete for extra balls and free games, rather than prizes. This would be important for the entire industry, as more and more communities and states outlawed pinball as a game of chance.

Williams moved to Chicago, the center of the coin-operated amusements industry, in 1936, and for the next several years designed games for Bally, Rock-Ola, and other pinball manufacturers. World War II came close to shutting down the pinball industry, however, as raw materials made it impossible to build new machines. The war would later prove important to the industry in another way, as American GIs brought pinball machines to other countries, opening an international market that at times rivaled the market in the United States. In 1941, Williams joined with Lyn Durant, a designer who also had worked for Bally and Exhibit, to form the United Manufacturing Company. Their business was almost entirely in reconditioning and redesigning old machines.

Postwar Boom Leading to Innovation

Williams left United at the end of the war and in 1946 founded the Williams Manufacturing Company in Chicago. The most significant moment of the pinball industry's history occurred the following year, when another company, Gottlieb, introduced the first pinball machines featuring flippers. This innovation allowed the player greater control of the ball, transforming the game at last from a game of chance to one of skill. Through its early history, pinball had been banned at various

Company Perspectives:

WMS' mission is to create the most entertaining gaming products in the world and service its customers with an uncompromising passion for quality. All of our employees embrace our core values of innovation, tenacity, passion, quality, and integrity and are guided by the fundamental principle of teamwork.

times virtually everywhere in the United States. (San Francisco was the only community that had never banned the game; pinball prohibitions remained in force until the late 1970s in many other communities, including New York City.) As a game of chance that offered prizes and cash rewards, early pinball also suffered from its link to gambling and organized crime.

Williams, joined by Sam Stern, a former operator and distributor of coin-op amusement machines, brought out his first flipper pinball machine—called "Sunny"—in 1947. The postwar boom in the American economy created a huge demand for new pinball machines, and with raw materials once again in ready supply, manufacturers were soon making and selling thousands of units of each model they created. During the 1950s and 1960s, pinball boomed, dominated by Gottlieb. For most of this time, Williams and Bally would vie for second place. This era also saw the rise of another Chicago company, soon to become important for the Williams company. In 1948, the Seeburg Corporation, begun in 1903 as a piano maker and through the 1930s and 1940s a competitor with Wurlitzer for the jukebox market, brought out the first jukebox, offering 100 selections. By the end of the next decade, Seeburg's jukeboxes captured 70 percent of the jukebox market. Seeburg would retain its leading position for the next two decades.

Harry Williams retired back to California in 1959 and Sam Stern took over Williams Manufacturing. In the following year, Stern retooled the company's manufacturing facilities. By then, Seeburg, which had revenues of nearly $30 million in 1960, had started an aggressive expansion campaign beyond the jukebox market. In 1958, it entered the vending machine business, selling cigarettes, and in the early 1960s expanded its vending machine business to include cigars, soft drinks, hot coffee, soup, candy, milk, and laundry products. Seeburg also went into the home music field, selling transistorized musical equipment and home stereo equipment.

Changes in Ownership: 1960s–70s

Meanwhile, Seeburg continued to sell its 100- and now 200-selection jukeboxes, retaining its market lead. A series of acquisitions, coupled with new product development, helped raise Seeburg's revenues to $76 million by 1964. In May of that year, Seeburg acquired Williams Manufacturing, reorganizing it as the Williams Electronics Manufacturing division. Late in 1964, Williams Electronics acquired United Manufacturing (led by Lyn Durant who did not like flippered pinball), which manufactured other types of coin-op amusement games, such as shuffle alleys. Williams paid $1.2 million for United and Sam Stern remained as president of the Williams division.

Seeburg consolidated its six manufacturing facilities into a new one million-square-foot facility in Chicago in 1965. With its Qualitone division, Seeburg manufactured hearing aids, and the company also moved into background music systems, including extensive copyright holdings used in its own recordings. In addition to making electronic organs through its 1963 Kinsman Manufacturing Co. acquisition, in 1965 and 1966 Seeburg acquired three more companies to make it one of the largest musical instrument manufacturers in the country. These three were Kay Musical Instrument Co., which made guitars, basses, and cellos; Gulbransen Co., which made quality pianos and organs and featured a 1,100-dealer distribution network; and N.H. White Co., which made band instruments under the King brand name. Revenues for 1965 reached $89 million, although profits dropped to absorb the costs of consolidating its manufacturing facilities. The following year, revenues jumped again to nearly $115 million. During this time, Louis Nicastro joined Seeburg as vice-president. By 1968, Nicastro had risen to become Seeburg's president. In that year, Seeburg was acquired by Commonwealth United Corp. of New York for $12 million.

Commonwealth, which produced films and television programs, had started up in 1967 with $6 million in revenues. From the start, Commonwealth launched a series of acquisitions—including Seeburg—that would raise its revenues to $155 million in its second year of operations. One year later, however, Commonwealth was in trouble, coming up short on cash for another acquisition. In 1969, Commonwealth lost some $60 million. Nicastro, who had joined Commonwealth's board but then returned to run Seeburg, became president and CEO of Commonwealth in 1970.

One year later, Nicastro spun off Commonwealth's main subsidiary, Seeburg, as Seeburg Industries, Inc. In that year, Commonwealth had posted a $1.6 million loss on sales of $54 million, while its Seeburg subsidiary had seen a $3.3 million profit on $53 million in sales. Under the reorganization plan, Nicastro, together with several partners, purchased Seeburg for $2.75 million, while assuming $9 million of Consolidated's debts of about $13 million. As Nicastro told *Business Week* at the time, "Nobody's delighted to accept any deal we propose. It's only the realization that the alternatives are worse." The spin-off was completed by 1973.

Nicastro moved Seeburg's headquarters to New York, where it would remain until 1990. By 1976, the new Seeburg's revenues had once again risen to more than $125 million. In 1977, Seeburg was renamed Xcor International. At this time, the pinball industry was undergoing a revolution of sorts with the introduction of the first solid-state pinball machines. Featuring far more exciting play than electromechanical machines, solid state quickly became the industry standard, and by 1977, Williams Electronics followed industry leader Bally—which grabbed 70 percent of the then-$75 million market—and converted all of its machines to the new technology. By 1980, Williams was selling more than 60,000 pinball machines per year. Although Williams remained profitable, however, it was not enough to prevent Xcor losses of $1.5 million in 1977. Revenues dropped through the next year, although Xcor managed to record a $5 million profit. But in 1979, Xcor once again posted a loss, now of $2.5 million. In that year, Xcor faced a $33

Key Dates:

Key Dates:

1933: Harry Williams designs the first electromechanical pinball machine.
1941: Williams joins with Lyn Durant to form the United Manufacturing Company.
1946: Williams establishes the Williams Manufacturing Company.
1964: The firm is acquired by Seeburg Corp. and reorganized as the Williams Electronics Manufacturing Division.
1968: Commonwealth United Corp. purchases Seeburg.
1973: Louis Nicastro completes a spin-off of Seeburg Industries Inc.
1977: Seeburg is renamed Xcor International.
1980: Nicastro orchestrates a spin-off of Williams Electronics.
1988: Williams acquires Bally Manufacturing Co.'s pinball and video arcade game unit; the company officially adopts the name WMS.
1992: WMS enters the VLT market.
1998: The firm spins off its video game business.
1999: WMS exits the pinball market.
2001: Brian R. Gamache is named CEO.

million debt with only $1.8 million in shareholder equity. Meanwhile, a new revolution was looming: the video arcade.

Birth of the Video Arcade Market: Late 1970s–Early 1980s

Begun with "Pong" in the early 1970s, video arcade games grew to a $70 million market by 1977. Its boom years, however, were to follow shortly. In 1979, Bally Manufacturing Co. brought out the industry's first great hit, "Space Invaders," which was soon followed by Atari's "Asteroids." By 1981, the video arcade market would grow to $650 million. The boom would be too late to salvage Xcor, however. The Seeburg division declared Chapter 11 bankruptcy in 1979. In 1980, Nicastro moved again to spin off his most profitable subsidiary, now Williams Electronics, which acquired about $18 million of Xcor's debt. Nicastro remained as chairman and CEO of both Williams and Xcor. Williams went public, selling 5 million shares at $12.25 per share; its shareholders, including Gulf & Western, kept four million shares. Nicastro also attempted to enter the burgeoning Atlantic City casino business by buying the Sands Hotel, but was rebuffed. Instead, Williams looked to Puerto Rico, purchasing a controlling interest in a new hotel-casino complex there. Xcor quickly faded from view, posting losses of $3.9 million on revenues of nearly $24 million in 1982.

Meanwhile, business boomed for Williams. Whereas the video arcade business hurt pinball sales for most manufacturers, Williams's pinball sales actually grew, to $80 million in 1981, giving it the industry lead for the first time. But most important to Williams was its first entry into the video arcade. Its game, "Defender," introduced in 1981, was a smash success, becoming one of the top-selling arcade games of the time, with 50,000 machines ordered in its first year alone. Williams' revenues

soared to $150 million in 1981—some $110 million of which came from sales of Defender. By then the coin-op industry had grown to a $4 billion market. To accommodate demand for its video arcade machines, Williams scaled back pinball production, to as low as 2,300 machines in 1983. Nevertheless, Williams machines continued to top pinball sales, with five of the top nine selling machines in the early 1980s.

By the summer of 1982, however, the video market slowed. Despite the successes of such games as "Pac Man," "Galaxian," "Space Invaders," "Defender," and "Asteroids," the industry was unable to come up with strong follow-up games. The recession of the early 1990s also contributed to the slowing sales of video arcade machines. Williams attempted to introduce a pinball-video hybrid, called "Hyperball," which in large part failed. Its sales began to dry up, dropping to $136 million in 1982. But the following year, the bottom fell out of the video market. Revenues from its amusement games fell by $65 million. Williams was unable to take up the slack with pinball sales. Despite about $39 million in revenues added by its hotel casinos, Williams lost $14 million on revenues of $57.5 million in 1984. Williams stock, which had risen to $29 per share three years earlier, fell to $2 per share.

Losses continued through the next year. But by 1986, Williams's fortunes had turned again. Renewed interest in pinball, and successes with new pinball machines such as "Comet" and "Space Shuttle," set up the Williams 1986 introduction of one of the great pinball machines of all time, "High Speed," which posted initial orders of more than 7,500 machines. Williams casino holdings continued to do well, with its Condado Plaza in San Juan, Puerto Rico adding $11 million in revenues and operating profits of almost $4 million, bringing Williams a 1986 net profit of $3 million on revenues of $105 million.

Williams acquired Bally Manufacturing Co.'s pinball and video arcade game unit in 1988 for $8 million, giving Williams an 80 percent share of the pinball market, which in turn had grown to account for more than 20 percent of the $5 billion coin-op game industry. Under the Williams, Bally, and Midway names, Williams pinball production grew to about 35,000 by the turn of the decade; approximately 48 percent of its machines were now being shipped overseas. The company was renamed WMS in 1988, as its casino holdings grew to provide more than 40 percent of company revenues. Two years later, the company moved back to Chicago to be closer to its core gaming division. It also doubled its research and development (R&D) spending, to about $1.5 million per game, a move that would prove crucial to its success in the coming years.

Entering New Markets: Early to Mid-1990s

In the 1990s, WMS moved into the home video game market, granting an exclusive licensing contract to Acclaim. Despite the success of WMS-designed titles such as "Mortal Kombat" and "NBA Jam," WMS licensing fees were meager compared with the earnings enjoyed by Acclaim. When that contract ended in 1995, WMS—which had acquired Tradewest Inc. and related companies for $15 million in 1994—began to market its video games through its newly formed Williams Entertainment Inc. subsidiary. In 1995, WMS also entered a joint venture with Nintendo of America Inc. as the exclusive creator and distributor of games for that company's new 64-bit video game system. The 1995 release of "Mortal Kombat 3" sold 250,000 copies in its first three days, bringing in around $15 million in just one weekend.

WMS next entered the VLT market in 1992, and soon after began producing casino gaming machines for the exploding casino industry. By 1995, WMS was licensed to manufacture and distribute its casino machines in 12 states, including Nevada and New Jersey, as well as in Australia and Canada, and its casino games had grown to an estimated $26 million in revenues. In that year, overall revenues jumped to $385 million, with sales in 1996 projected to reach $550 million. WMS faced a setback in late 1995 when it failed in an attempt to acquire Bally Gaming International, losing out to Las Vegas-based Alliance Gaming Corp.'s hostile takeover bid. Nevertheless, the company's troubled past seemed far behind it, and WMS's future in casino gaming machines appeared strong. As Neil Nicastro, company president and son of Louis Nicastro, told the *Chicago Tribune:* "There is not much we haven't ended up leading after entering."

A New Focus for the New Millennium

The shape of WMS would change dramatically, however, during the remaining years of the 1990s and into the new millennium. The company's first move came in 1996 when its hotel and casino operations in Puerto Rico were divested as a result of poor results brought on by strict Puerto Rican gaming laws. The decision signaled the company's strategy of focusing on its core businesses at the time, which included coin-operated amusement games, home video games, and most important, its gambling equipment line. In fact, it is the latter that was to become the focus of WMS's operations. In 1997, the firm launched its most successful video slot machine, Reel 'em In. One year later, the company decided to jettison its video game business. By this time the pinball market also had deteriorated, forcing WMS to leave the market that its founder—known as the father of pinball—had entered back in the 1940s.

WMS hit the mark with its restructuring and by 2000, the company held the number two spot in the U.S. slot machine market—behind Nevada-based International Game Technology Inc. Sales increased dramatically from 1999 to 2001, climbing from $126.56 million to $263.7 million. Nicastro, having transformed WMS into leading gaming equipment concern, resigned as CEO in 2001, leaving Brian R. Gamache to follow in his footsteps.

During fiscal 2002, sales and profits fell off due in part to technology setbacks. As such, the company set forth an aggressive technology improvement plan that included hiring new product development management. Despite faltering sales, the firm remained optimistic about future success. It launched new games based on "Hollywood Squares," "Pac-Man," and "Survivor," and also created the "Puzzle Pays" series and "Rapid Roulette." The firm also acquired Big Foot Software Research and Development LLC, a progressive system designer. WMS had indeed come a long way from its roots as a pinball wizard. Management, however, appeared confident that it had hit the jackpot in the gaming industry.

Principal Subsidiaries

WMS Games Inc.; WMS Gaming Inc.; WMS Gaming (Nevada) Inc.; WMS Gaming (Canada) Ltd.; Fun House Games Inc.; Lenc-Smith Inc.; Williams Electronics Games, Inc.; WMS Finance Inc.; WMS Gaming International, S.L. (Spain); WMS Gaming Australia PTY Ltd.; WMS Gaming Africa (Pty) Ltd. (South Africa); WMS Gaming do Brasil, Ltda. (Brazil); Big Foot Software Research & Development, LLC.

Principal Competitors

Alliance Gaming Corporation; Aristocrat Leisure Ltd.; International Game Technology Inc.

Further Reading

Ackerman, Elise, "The Pinball Wizard Blues," *U.S. News & World Report,* November 15, 1999, p. 56.
Barnfather, Maurice, "Tilt?," *Forbes,* March 2, 1981, p. 42.
Borden, Jeff, "Game Maker Ends Bet on Puerto Rico Casinos," *Crain's Chicago Business,* March 4, 1996.
——, "WMS Betting That Grown-Ups Want to Play," *Crain's Chicago Business,* May 20, 1996, p. 3.
Byrne, Harlan S., "The Mystery of Williams Electronics," *Barron's,* April 7, 1986, p. 30.
Franklin, Stephen, "Pinball Power Puts Money into the Slots," *Chicago Tribune,* May 9, 1994, p. B9.
Mehlman, William, "Williams Seen Benefiting from Video Game Shakeout," *Insiders' Chronicle,* February 21, 1983, p. 1.
Murphy, Lee H., "WMS Is Passing Go with Slot Machines," *Crain's Chicago Business,* August 28, 2000, p. 4.
Natkin, Bobbye Claire, and Steve Kirk, *All About Pinball,* New York: Grosset & Dunlap, 1977.
"New Player in the Video Game," *Financial World,* August 15, 1981, p. 22.
"A Spinoff to Break a Fall," *Business Week,* September 25, 1971, p. 38.

—M.L. Cohen
—update: Christina M. Stansell

WPS Resources Corporation

WPS Resources Corporation

700 North Adams Street
P.O. Box 19001
Green Bay, Wisconsin 54307-9001
U.S.A.
Telephone: (920) 433-4901
Fax: (920) 433-1526
Web site: http://www.wpsr.com

Public Company
Incorporated: 1883 as Oshkosh Gas Light Company
Employees: 2,856
Sales: $2.67 billion (2002)
Stock Exchanges: New York
Ticker Symbol: WPS
NAIC: 22111 Hydroelectric Power Generation; 221112
    Fossil Fuel Electric Power Generation; 221113
    Nuclear Electric Power Generation; 221119 Other
    Electric Power Generation; 221122 Electric Power
    Distribution

WPS Resources Corporation (WPSR) was created in 1993 to act as a utilities holding company. Its four main subsidiaries include Wisconsin Public Service Corporation (WPSC), Upper Peninsula Power Company (UPPCO), WPS Power Development Inc. (PDI), and WPS Energy Services Inc. (ESI). WPSC, whose history can be traced back to the 1860s, provides electricity and natural gas to nearly 700,000 customers in Wisconsin and Michigan, while UPPCO serves over 50,000 customers in Michigan's Upper Peninsula. These two regulated units account for the majority of company earnings. PDI and ESI operate in the non-regulated energy sector—PDI develops and maintains electric generation facilities and ESI acts as an energy supply and services company in Illinois, Maine, Michigan, Ohio, and Wisconsin.

Early History: 1860s–1920s

Wisconsin Public Service traces its origins to Oshkosh Gas Light Company, the successor company to a franchise that had been taken out in 1868 to sell coal gas, which was used for lighting, to the citizens of Oshkosh. The franchise had lain dormant for about five years when E.P. Sawyer, a businessman whose previous experience had been in the lumber industry, acquired it in 1883 and reincorporated it under the name Oshkosh Gas Light. In 1885, the company received a franchise to sell electricity in Oshkosh, putting it into direct competition with Oshkosh Electric Light and Power. The two companies merged in 1907.

In these early years, the electrical utility industry in the United States little resembled its current state, in which a relatively small number of large companies are granted state-regulated franchises to produce and sell power in large geographic areas. Instead, a bewildering array of strictly local companies took out franchises to provide electricity and coal gas to small areas on a small scale. However, as the merger between Oshkosh Gas Light and Oshkosh Electric Power suggests, this began to change after the turn of the century, when the industry underwent a period of rapid consolidation and centralization of power.

In 1911, a Milwaukee engineer named Clement Smith joined with his brother-in-law, utility lawyer George Miller, to found Wisconsin Securities Company with the purpose of operating it as a utilities holding company. They quickly acquired Green Bay Gas and Electric Company, Green Bay Traction Company, and Northern Hydro-Electric Power Company. In 1922, Wisconsin Securities acquired Oshkosh Gas Light from the estate of E.P. Sawyer, changed its name to Wisconsin Public Service Corporation, and merged it with the other companies that it had acquired, which by now included Sheboygan Gas Light Company, Calumet Service Company, and Manitowoc and Northern Traction Company. Wisconsin Securities had also founded Peninsula Service Company to supply electricity to Door County in 1920; it, too, was merged into WPSC.

This rapid consolidation among electrical utilities did not escape notice and drew fire from some reform-minded journalists. *New Republic* magazine, for instance, published two books during the 1920s critical of current trends in the industry, one of which mentioned WPSC as a brief example. However, the desire to gain monopolistic control of regional markets for electrical power was not the sole factor at work, perhaps not even the most important one. The attrition rate for the small power companies that characterized the early days of the industry was quite high, and those small companies were not likely to have the capital to invest in new power plants. In the case of Wisconsin Securities, the owners of Green Bay Gas and Electric, Green Bay Traction, and Northern Hydro-Electric Power asked Clement Smith and George Miller for help after cost overruns from a hydro-electric plant they were building threatened to bankrupt them. Thus, a certain amount of consolidation was not only inevitable but healthy for the industry and necessary for maintaining consistency of service.

More mergers and acquisitions followed the creation of WPSC. In 1924, the company bought small electric companies operating in the towns of Brillion, Mishicot, and De Pere. The next year, it acquired all the assets of Northeastern Power Company, including its subsidiaries Riverview Motor Bus Company; Oslo Power and Light Company; Denmark Power and Light Company; Green Bay Park Railway Company; Northern Light, Heat, and Power Company of Suring; and Wabeno Lighting Company.

As some of the names of the acquired Northeastern Power subsidiaries suggest, WPSC operated public transportation at this time in addition to supplying electricity. Electric companies had long been in this line of business, a natural consequence of the fact that they produced the electricity that made trolley cars run. After World War I, street railways were widely replaced by buses, which were more flexible and less expensive to operate. From the 1920s through World War II, WPSC operated transportation systems in Green Bay, Wausau, Merrill, and, briefly, in Menominee and Marinette.

A Change in Ownership: Late 1920s

Just after the Northeastern Power acquisition, WPSC was itself acquired by H.M. Byellsby, an electrical engineer who had worked for the Edison and Westinghouse Electric Corporation before going into business himself, designing and building power stations and hydro-electric plants for utility companies. Byellsby immediately turned over control of WPSC to Standard Gas and Electric, a public utility holding company that he had founded in 1910. As a result of the move, Clement Smith stepped down as president in 1926.

In 1927, Standard Gas and Electric acquired another large electrical utility, Wisconsin Valley Electric Company. Like WPSC, Wisconsin Valley Electric had grown rapidly through a series of mergers and acquisitions and was selling electricity to the towns of Merrill, Stevens Point, Tomahawk, Antigo, Rhinelander, and Waupaca when Standard Gas and Electric won a bidding war to acquire it. Though a successful and growing company, Wisconsin Valley Electric operated hydro-electric plants exclusively and ran into trouble in winter because of ice and low water on the Wisconsin River. In 1933, Standard Gas and Electric decided to merge its two main subsidiaries, so that WPSC's steam turbine plants could pick up Wisconsin Valley Electric's wintertime slack.

During World War II, WPSC's public transportation systems saw increases in ridership due to gas rationing and reduced automobile production. However, wartime shortages also made running bus lines difficult, despite the increases in business. For instance, the company's fleet in Green Bay was forced to bring an old 1925 Reo bus out of mothballs and press it into service. It was christened the Queen Marie, and a slogan painted on her side declared that she would be retired again "When the clock strikes peace!" After the clock did, in fact, strike peace, bus ridership declined as gasoline rationing ended and private cars returned to the roads. In 1951, WPSC divested its bus lines in Wausau and Merrill, and they began independent operation under the name Wausau Transit Lines.

Growth and Expansion as a Public Company: 1950s–80s

WPSC also gained independence of a sort in the 1950s. In 1952, Standard Gas and Electric divested its entire stake in the company. Common stock was distributed to WPSC's preferred stockholders. The following year, Wisconsin Public Service was listed on the Midwest and New York Stock Exchanges for the first time.

In the 1960s, natural gas became an increasingly important fuel source, and WPSC responded by expanding its operations in that area. The company had been selling natural gas to its customers since 1950, just after the first pipeline from the Hugoton Field in the Oil Patch of Oklahoma and Texas to the Upper Midwest was built. In 1961, it made a move to control the means of distribution when it acquired two natural gas franchises, Merrill Gas Company and Oneida Gas Company. By 1963, over half of the homes in WPSC's service area were heated with gas, and by the mid-1970s natural gas sales would account for about 30 percent of the company's operating revenues.

In 1967, the firm acquired the electrical distribution system for the municipality of Kewaunee, which had been owned by the city. That year, the company also took its first plunge into the age of nuclear energy when it broke ground on a nuclear plant nine miles south of Kewaunee, on the shores of Lake Michigan. The Kewaunee nuclear plant, which did not begin operation until 1974 (once safety and environmental concerns had been assuaged), was built and operated by WPSC but was in fact a joint venture between three Wisconsin utility companies. WPSC owned 41.2 percent, with Wisconsin Power and Light Company holding 41 percent and Madison Gas and Electric Company 17.8 percent.

In 1970, the company consolidated its corporate offices. True to its roots as an amalgamation of many small, local companies, WPSC had long operated out of offices scattered among the cities of Green Bay, Milwaukee, and Oshkosh. For decades, the firm had used a stately old mansion in Milwaukee as one of its headquarters—which made little sense, since the city lay outside

Key Dates:

1883: E.P. Sawyer buys a franchise and reincorporates it under the name Oshkosh Gas Light Company.

1907: Oshkosh Gas Light merges with competitor Oshkosh Electric Light and Power.

1911: Clement Smith and George Miller create Wisconsin Securities Company to act as a utilities holding company.

1922: Wisconsin Securities acquires the firm and changes its name to Wisconsin Public Service Corporation.

1926: H.M. Byellsby acquires Wisconsin Public Service and turns over control of the company to Standard Gas and Electric.

1933: Standard Gas merges its two main subsidiaries: Wisconsin Public Service and Wisconsin Valley Electric Co.

1952: Standard Gas divests its entire stake in the company.

1953: The firm goes public.

1974: The Kewaunee nuclear plant begins operation.

1993: WPS Resources Corp. is created to act as a holding company.

1997: The company acquires the Upper Peninsula Energy Corp.

2001: Wisconsin Fuel and Light Company merges with Wisconsin Public Service.

the company's operating area, except that Clement Smith had acquired the house from his brother-in-law. In 1970, the old Milwaukee mansion was vacated, and operations were consolidated at a new corporate headquarters in Green Bay.

In 1973, WPSC left the public transportation business entirely. Its Green Bay lines had been losing money since the 1950s, and the company finally sold its operations to the city of Green Bay that year. Its Green Bay bus system notwithstanding, WPSC prospered during the 1970s. In 1975, it posted revenues of $219.9 million, its best sales year ever. Its most important customer was the paper industry, which accounted for 15 percent of the company's electricity sales, and renewed strength among paper companies operating mills in northeastern Wisconsin meant increased demand for WPSC's main product. The company's reliance on the paper industry continued to serve it well into the 1980s, giving it a solid base of industrial demand.

In 1992, WPSC's contacts with the paper industry resulted in a joint venture seeking to find an efficient, ecologically sound way to generate electricity. That year, the company signed an agreement with Rhinelander Paper Company to build a 90 to 100 megawatt power plant that would be fueled by low-sulfur coal and paper mill waste. The firm began using more low-sulfur coal in its power plants in the 1990s in order to comply with state and federal air pollution laws.

Success in a Changing Industry: 1990s and Beyond

By this time, WPSC had established a record of good financial performance. Between 1975 and 1992, its revenues tripled.

This growth pattern was impressive, considering that the relatively modest city of Green Bay was its largest urban market. It benefited from the presence of large industrial customers in its area of operations, showing that an electrical utility could prosper and grow large by hanging around small towns. In late 1993, the firm adopted a holding company structure, forming WPS Resources Corporation to oversee subsidiary operations, which at the time included WPSC, WPS Energy Services Inc., WPS Power Development Inc., Packerland Energy Services Inc., and WPS Communications Inc. The restructuring continued into 1995, when Packerland was merged into ESI and WPS Communications was folded into WPSC's operations.

Deregulation brought change to the utilities industry in the United States during the latter half of the 1990s. In 1995, the Wisconsin Public Service Commission outlined a plan for restructuring of the state's electrical utility sector. By 2000, however, it was clear that the state would not open its industry to retail competition in the near future. Instead the Commission focused on infrastructure improvements aimed at strengthening the state's electrical service. The Commission passed two legislative acts in 1998 and 1999 related to generation, distribution, and transmission, and, as a major utility operator in the state, WPSR was required to follow these acts. As part of Wisconsin Act 9, for example, the company would be subject to lessened statutory restrictions when making non-utility investments if it transferred its transmission assets to a state transmission company. In January 2001, it did just that when it allowed American Transmission Company to take over its transmission holdings.

WPSR maintained focus on both its regulated and non-regulated businesses during this time period. The firm bolstered its regulated holdings with the purchase of the Upper Peninsula Energy Corporation in 1997. It also merged Wisconsin Fuel and Light Company into its WPSC subsidiary. The company's non-regulated subsidiaries continued to grow, mainly by purchasing generation facilities and by moving into deregulated regions. In 2000, the firm began supplying customers in Maine. One year later, WPSR moved into Ohio when the state allowed competition in its retail electric market.

The firm's strategy of balancing its regulated and non-regulated businesses appeared to pay off. In 2001, the company reported its 43rd consecutive year of increasing dividends. Revenues had also climbed steadily, rising from $1 billion in 1999, to $2.67 billion in 2001. The company secured $112.5 million in net income during 2002—a 45 percent increase over the previous year. As WPSR faced tough economic times in 2003, the company continued to eye the future with optimism. It set plans in motion to build a 500-megawatt coal-fired plant near Wausau, Wisconsin, and purchased the De Pere Energy Center from Calpine Corp. With a long-standing history of success behind it, WPSR appeared to be well positioned for growth in a changing industry.

Principal Subsidiaries

Wisconsin Public Service Corp.; Upper Peninsula Power Co.; WPS Power Development Inc.; WPS Energy Services Inc.

Principal Competitors

Alliant Energy Corporation; Wisconsin Energy Corporation; Xcel Energy Inc.

Further Reading

Bergquist, Lee, "Green Bay, Wis., Utility WPS Resources to Buy Pennsylvania Power Plant," *Milwaukee Journal Sentinel*, May 25, 1999.

Campanella, Frank W., "Profits Generator," *Barron's*, March 29, 1982.

Hawkins, Jr., Lee, "Power Plant Construction Part of Effort to Close Supply, Demand Gap," *Milwaukee Journal Sentinel*, September 26, 2002.

——, "Quarterly Earnings Rise 40 Percent for Energy Holding Company WPS Resources," *Milwaukee Journal Sentinel*, October 30, 2002.

Hillert, Mark, and Paul Davis, *Wisconsin Public Service Corporation: 100 Years—1883–1983—A Century of Service*, Green Bay: Wisconsin Public Service Corporation, 1983.

"Maine's Main Supplier," *Electric Light & Power*, January 2000, p. 25.

"Wisconsin Public Service Generating Higher Net," *Barron's*, August 30, 1976.

"WPS Buys From Calpine," *Electric Light & Power*, June 2002, p. 2.

"WPS Files for Storage Facility," *Oil Daily*, November 29, 1999.

"WPS Resources to Acquire Upper Peninsula Energy," *New York Times*, July 12, 1997, p. 35.

—Douglas Sun
—update: Christina M. Stansell

Zebra Technologies Corporation

333 Corporate Woods Parkway
Vernon Hills, Illinois 60061-3109
U.S.A.
Telephone: (847) 634-6700
Toll Free: (800) 423-0422
Fax: (847) 913-8766
Web site: http://www.zebra.com

Public Company
Incorporated: 1969 as Data Specialties Inc.
Employees: 2,000
Sales: $450 million (2001)
Stock Exchanges: NASDAQ
Ticker Symbol: ZBRA
NAIC: 333293 Printing Machinery and Equipment
    Manufacturing; 334418 Printed Circuit Assembly
    (Electronic Assembly) Manufacturing; 334613
    Magnetic and Optical Recording Media
    Manufacturing; 334119 Other Computer Peripheral
    Equipment Manufacturing

The mysterious series of lines and numbers called bar coding has provided a thumbprint of products since the 1970s, conveying instant information on model, price, weight, and dozens of other product characteristics. As a manufacturer and international distributor of bar code and automatic identification labeling, Zebra Technologies Corporation develops and builds thermal bar code label and receipt printers, card printers, radio frequency identification smart label printers and encoders, and a variety of related supplies. The company caters to a wide variety of industries including consumer goods, manufacturing, automotive, healthcare, electronics, and warehousing and distribution. In 2002, Zebra was named one of *Forbes* magazine's "200 Best Small Companies in America."

A Shaky Start: 1969

In 1969 engineers Edward L. Kaplan and Gerhard Cless contributed $500 each to found Data Specialties Inc., a manu-

facturer of high-speed electromechanical products such as hole-punching and tape-reading machines. Kaplan had graduated with honors from the Illinois Institute of Technology and received a prestigious National Defense Education Act fellowship (which he relinquished after deciding not to earn a Ph.D.), while Cless had attended the University of Esslingen in Germany, where his mechanical engineering skills had earned him ten patents. While employed full-time as project engineers at Teletype Corp., they began to design machinery after hours.

After a client expressed interest in their work, they pooled their savings and came up with two punch machine prototypes using paper tape. Receiving an order for 500, Kaplan and Cless borrowed $20,000 to produce the machines and worked nights in a Chicago loft to complete the order. Hiring 15 part-time workers to assemble parts during the day and on weekends, Kaplan and Cless then received a second, multimillion-dollar order for 2,000 machines from a client in the banking industry in response to an ad they had placed in a Florida trade publication.

Thrilled, Kaplan and Cless quit their day jobs and pushed hard to complete the initial order—of which only a fraction were finished and paid for. As the remainder of the machines awaited assembly, the client suddenly canceled. Kaplan and Cless then concentrated on designing machines for the second contract, creating a revolutionary punch machine that could print passbook and bookkeeping entries as well as customer receipts, all at the same time. They later discovered, however, that the client wanted only the prototypes so it could manufacture the machines on its own; the client then sued the engineers for breach of contract when they would not hand them over. Unable to afford any retaliatory legal action, Kaplan and Cless were forced to relinquish the machines' designs in return for the lawsuit being dropped.

Citing the incident as "devastating but one of those lessons that can't be taught," Kaplan and Cless were left with a loft full of parts for 475 punch machines and no money from their first three months of business. The two hammered out a new $1.5 million business plan to design and produce printing machinery, then set about raising the necessary capital. Able to come up with only $70,000, they hired themselves out as consultants and continued working on a paper punch machine to collect data while attached to other instruments. The partners decided that Kaplan would handle the management, marketing, and money side of Data Specialties' business and Cless the technological aspects. Kaplan then borrowed his father's car for a jaunt to the East Coast to drum up business. After eating and sleeping in the car the entire trip, the partners were almost ready to give up, but decided they would give their venture another two weeks before calling it quits. Within days an order came in from an Ohio-based division of Monsanto Corp., followed by two more orders in the next several weeks.

By the end of 1970, Data Specialties Inc. was located in Highland Park, Illinois, and had reached revenues of $90,000; in 1971 total sales climbed by 360 percent to $330,000. Then Bell and Howell Co. came calling with a major contract, contingent upon inspection of Data Specialties Inc.'s manufacturing plant—which did not exist. Thinking fast, the engineers took apart already-assembled machines and spread them throughout their 1,320-square-foot office space, hired a secretary and workers to reassemble the machines for the day, and enlisted their wives to call every ten minutes impersonating customers. Their creativity and virtual factory paid off, as Bell and Howell and many other clients signed with Data Specialties over the next few years, eventually earning the company a 50 percent share of the paper tape punch and related machinery market.

Focus on Bar Coding: 1980s

When the paper tape industry began to falter due to new technology like bar coding, the partners decided to pursue the latter. Although bar coding had been around since the 1970s, the industry was still in its infancy, with just a handful of competitors. The odd-looking black and white stripes were first favored by grocers using UPC (Universal Product Code) labels as a means of speeding up the check-out and payment process; then bar codes caught on in the retail clothing industry. Data Specialties introduced its first bar code printer, The Zebra, at a Dallas trade show in 1982, and despite some minor glitches, the machine was far more advanced than those of competitors. "It had the capability to create on-demand bar coding," Cless explained, "that could revolutionize the industry." The fledgling company began selling its wares to businesses, especially healthcare and pharmaceutical companies, at home and overseas.

In 1986, to combat scanning problems due to poor resolution from off-shaped or uneven-surfaced products, the company built its first "thermal transfer" printer using heated printer heads that melted characters from a waxy ribbon onto labels made from paper, plastic, foil, or other smooth materials. Unlike standard bar codes, thermal transfer labels were able to withstand temperatures as high as 400 degrees Fahrenheit or as

cold as minus 110 degrees Fahrenheit. Although there were other printing processes using heat, thermal transfer did not require specially treated labels, lasted much longer, and soon became an industry standard for affixing labels to items of all shapes and sizes—such as U.S. Steel's strip steel coils and bars and hospitals' blood bags and specimens.

With the success of its Zebra printer and other products, Kaplan and Cless changed the company's name from Data Specialties to Zebra Technologies Corporation in 1986. Over the next few years, the company began transferring its Japanese manufacturing (which began in the early 1980s through a partnership) back to the United States, to maximize profit and decrease product defect rates. While manufacturing in Japan had initially been beneficial, the fall of the dollar by nearly half, government embargoes, and import duty increases had taken their toll on Zebra, and both Kaplan and Cless wanted to regain control of their manufacturing. Yet the years in Japan had given Zebra an important technological edge, which when combined with Cless's German background and their location in the United States, gave the company a valuable international orientation.

Success Leads to an Early 1990s Public Offering

The next year Kaplan and Cless's hard work was recognized when the company was awarded the prestigious 1988 High Technology Entrepreneur Award from Peat Marwick Main & Co., a Chicago-based accounting and consulting firm. Zebra finished the year with $30 million in sales and income of $5.5 million; the following year, 1990, sales jumped nearly 30 percent to $38 million. In 1991 the partners decided to take their company public, and in August 1991 Zebra successfully completed an initial public offering of 2.8 million shares at $15.50 each; within hours, the stock traded at $18. By year's end in 1991 analysts estimated the bar code industry at $380 million with Zebra having captured more than 25 percent of the market. There were more than 23,000 of Zebra's bar code printing systems installed at some 5,000 sites worldwide, pumping the company's net sales up to $45.6 million, including nearly 36 percent from international sources. As Zebra prospered the company increased its funding in R&D proportionately, spending nearly $2.4 million.

By 1992 Zebra was considered the premier manufacturer of high-performance demand printing materials used in factory assembly lines to label a wide variety of consumer goods. With more than 30,000 machines installed worldwide, Zebra's product line of 20 thermal-transfer printing systems and 12 different symbologies had earned a reputation for excellence as well as durability, especially in harsh conditions. As a result, Zebra was ranked number seven on *Forbes*'s "200 Best Small Companies" in November. The company then ended the year with net sales of $58.7 million and earnings of $11.8 million, due in part to its increasing supplies business, which accounted for a quarter of 1992's sales. By the end of that year 90 percent of Zebra's operations were housed at its 67,000-square-foot Vernon Hills facility, which added another 37,000 square feet to accommodate the growth.

In March 1993, Zebra's second public offering of 2.6 million shares (at $22.75 each) went off without a hitch. The company now had 45,000 machines in circulation, and Zebra's

Key Dates:

1969: Edward L. Kaplan and Gerhard Cless establish Data Specialties Inc.
1982: The firm introduces The Zebra, its first bar code printer.
1986: The company changes its name to Zebra Technologies Corp.
1991: Zebra goes public.
1995: The firm purchases Vertical Technologies Inc.
1998: The firm merges with Eltron International Inc.
2000: Comtec Information Systems is acquired.

engineers began looking in another direction. Although its printers were intricately crafted, high-performance machines (which became known as the trademarked Performance Line), the company continued to research ways to make their printers more technologically advanced, less expensive, and accessible to a wider client base. In general, Zebra's customers were divided into two market segments and two subdivisions—the first between the industrial and retail markets (nearly 90 percent of retailers used bar codes, while only 20 percent of the industrial market had been tapped in 1993), and the second between clients whose primary purpose was compliance with bar-coding standards versus those who used the bar codes for the detailed information the labels could provide about production, including tracking inventory and routing deliveries.

Whereas some clients easily spent more than $10,000 for a sophisticated, custom-made printer (prices ranged from about $1,600 to $12,000), others required as many as a dozen printers and supplies for factory assembly lines. With this in mind, in 1993 Zebra launched its Value-Line of economically priced products, consisting of completely reengineered and redesigned printers and accessories. Although the technology of the entry-level Value-Line was still state-of-the-art, the products themselves were smaller and easier to assemble (with the number of parts reduced by up to 40 percent), lightweight (due to their use of structural plastic), manufactured in up to 25 percent less time, and, consequently, lower-priced by nearly half. When the Stripe S-300 and S-500 were introduced in the fall of 1993, sales were impressive. Yet romancing the mid- to lower-priced market did not affect Zebra's higher-end markets—its specialized Performance Line machines continued to be purchased by its regular clients (which mainly consisted of Fortune 500 companies) and steadily attracted new ones as well.

Continuing Growth in the Mid-1990s

While laser and ink-jet technology became hot topics of discussion in the bar code industry, Zebra's thermal transfer printing continued to reflect record gains: 1993's net sales rose to $87.4 million and income increased to $18.2 million, both well over the 27 percent in sales and 19 percent in profits predicted by analysts. Stock value, too, increased to $23.25 per share, and Zebra raised its R&D spending to $4.6 million to fine-tune its product line still further. Except for a setback in 1994's second quarter after manufacturing slowed due to extreme weather and the California earthquake, Zebra's growth continued unabated—again with record high sales of $107.1 million (up 22.5 percent from 1993), helped in part by the introduction of new products and significantly by an increase of almost 53 percent in international sales (which accounted for about 40 percent of Zebra's total sales). New products included an accessory called the Verifier, which identified unscannable or faulty labels; the STRIPE cutter, which sliced labels as they were printed for immediate application; and several new label surfaces resistant to not only excess heat and cold, but to abrasions, chemicals, light, and moisture.

As the bar code industry saw its best year yet in 1994, due to clients like Kmart, Wal-Mart, and Lowe's, who demanded merchandise with bar coding—the company achieved number one status with its popular and durable Performance Line in the higher-priced market while possessing a healthy 33 percent share (second only to Datamax Corp. with a 40 percent share) in the economy segment. By the end of the first quarter in 1995, Zebra's overseas sales grew by 89 percent as a result of a weakened dollar and increased penetration of markets in the United Kingdom and other countries. Operations in High Wycombe and Preston, England, helped speed delivery to the company's international customers. The High Wycombe facility, completed in 1994, consisted of 17,000 square feet and became Zebra's international headquarters, while the operation in Preston, near Manchester, occupied nearly 20,000 square feet and served as the company's European distribution center. Back in the United States, Zebra built a 50,000-square-foot addition to its manufacturing facility and added another 11,500 square feet to its corporate headquarters in Vernon Hills. As square footage expanded worldwide, the company's workforce approached a new high of 500.

By mid-1995 Zebra's $119.5 in sales had doubled from just three years earlier and the company was ranked number 72 on *Business Week*'s list of "100 Best Small Corporations and Hot Growth Companies" in May. Zebra invested $5.8 million (up 26 percent from 1993) into R&D to explore new possibilities in engineering and design as well as materials and adhesives. The company's internal structure was overhauled after several senior employees left to work for competitors. With very little long-term debt and plenty of cash and marketable securities (estimated at more than $54 million), the increasingly acquisition-minded Kaplan began hinting at diversification when he told *Equities Magazine Inc.,* "We're not married to the thermal transfer printer market." In July 1995, Kaplan and Cless purchased the Utah-based Vertical Technology Industries, a company specializing in bar code software. Kaplan turned day-to-day operations over to new president Jeffrey Clements (former CEO of Miller Fluid Power Corp.) while Cless continued in his role as executive vice-president of engineering and technology.

With distribution in 60 countries throughout Africa, Asia, Europe, the Middle East, the Pacific Rim, and Central, North, and South Americas, Zebra Technologies' bar code printers had produced labels for a myriad of products, including millions of Microsoft's floppy diskettes, Motorola's cellular phone batteries, Philips Consumer Electronics' audio and video components, and even postage stamps and labels in 35 post offices in Taipei. "We have never seen a company that could not benefit from our technology," Kaplan told *Fortune* in 1993, and he and his partner Cless have been proved right repeatedly since founding their company in 1969.

Acquisitions and Product Expansion: Late 1990s and Beyond

As the new millennium approached, the partners made several key moves to solidify the company's position in the industry. In 1996, the company announced that it would merge with California-based Eltron International Inc., a manufacturer of desktop bar code label and plastic card printers. The deal was completed in 1998, giving Zebra access to both a broader distribution market and additional product development staff. It also positioned Zebra as the leading bar code printer manufacturer, with new customers including United Parcel Service Inc. and FedEx Corp. Sales in 1998 grew to $339.6 million and continued to increase, reaching $481.5 million in 2000.

Zebra's solid financial results left it well positioned to make additional acquisitions. Comtec Information Systems Inc., a portable and mobile printer manufacturer, was the company's next major purchase. Eyeing the portable and wireless printer market for its growth potential, Zebra was quick to add the Rhode Island-based firm to its holdings in April 2000. This deal proved lucrative as a majority of the firm's growth during 2001 stemmed from Comtec's operations.

Zebra continued its growth strategy even as the U.S. economy faltered during 2001. Sales fell for the first time in its history, dropping to $450 million. The firm's planned acquisition of Fargo Electronics also fell through when it was met with opposition by the Federal Trade Commission. Nevertheless, Zebra continued to invest in expansion and product development and looked to penetrate new growth markets, including healthcare and homeland security. The latter was especially important as airports across the globe made security a key priority after the terrorist attacks that occurred on September 11, 2001. By 2002, more than 50 airports used Zebra products to print secure identification cards and security badges.

As part of its international expansion efforts, the company established a mobile printing business based in Europe during 2001 and planned to aggressively pursue opportunities in Eastern Europe, the Asia Pacific region, and Latin America. Zebra launched its first wireless tabletop printer at this time and focused on its product development related to wireless technology. The company also increased its sales in the postal, banking, and hospitality and travel industries.

Sales picked up during 2002 in both North America and international regions, and management expected a return to growth. Even with its drop in sales during 2001, Zebra was recognized by both Forbes and Deloitte & Touche for its overall growth and financial strength. The firm also was awarded Business Finance Magazine and Hyperion Solution's "2002 Vision Award," which was based on business performance management. As a well respected industry leader, Zebra's future looked promising.

Principal Competitors

Axiohm Transaction Solutions Inc.; Datamax Corporation; Intermec Technologies Corporation.

Further Reading

"Bar-Code Firm Will Go Public," *Chicago Tribune,* July 13, 1991, p. 3.

"Eltron International and Zebra Technologies to Merge," *New York Times,* October 17, 1996, p. D4.

"The Generalist vs. The Specialist: How to Decide Which Printer Is Best for Your Application," *Modern Office Technology,* February 1992, p. 44.

Hamilton, Walter, "Zebra Tech Links Success to Entering Key New Markets," *Investor's Business Daily,* July 14, 1995.

Jones, Sandra, "Zebra Gets Ready to Earn Its Stripes," *Crain's Chicago Business,* February 21, 2000, p. 3.

Koprowski, Gene, "Zebra Technologies Also Targets Small Firms," *Crain's Chicago Business,* July 22, 1996, p. 9.

Lyons, Daniel J., "Bar-Code Printers Produce Coded Labels," *PC Week,* January 6, 1992, pp. 77, 80.

Maclean, John N., "Weak Earnings Sink Zebra Stock," *Chicago Tribune,* April 23, 1994, p. 1.

——, "Zebra Says Ribbon Woes Are Ending," *Chicago Tribune,* May 11, 1994, p. 3.

Marcial, Gene G., "Bar-Coding the World," *Business Week,* July 31, 1995, p. 71.

Moskal, Brian S., "Zebra Tames New-Product Development," *Industry Week,* September 6, 1993, pp. 19–20.

Murphy, Lee H., "Bar Code Specialist Zebra Hunting for Acquisitions," *Crain's Chicago Business,* May 28, 2001, p. 30.

O'Maolchoin, Sean, "Zebra Finds Its Stripes in Bar Codes," *Equities Magazine Inc.,* April 1995.

Palmer, Ann Therese, "Different Stripes," *Chicago Tribune,* January 3, 1993, pp. 1, 6, 7.

——, "Zebra Looks to Management Revamp to Help Bolster Growth," *Crain's Chicago Business,* March 6, 1995, p. 42.

——, "Zebra Strategies Anything But Tame," *Chicago Tribune,* April 13, 1992, pp. 1, 6.

Rae, Sriknmar S., "Tomorrow's Rosetta Stones," *FW,* November 22, 1994, pp. 70–72.

Ringer, Richard, "Market Place: Zebra Technologies Finds a Downside in Its Prosperity," *New York Times,* August 2, 1993, p. C4.

Sherrod, Pamela, "4 High-Tech Innovators Honored," *Chicago Tribune,* November 21, 1988, p. B1.

Sietz, Patrick, "Zebra Tech Stands Out in Jungle," *Investor's Business Daily,* November 25, 2002.

Teitelbaum, Richard S., "Companies to Watch: Zebra Technologies," *Fortune,* January 25, 1993, p. 105.

"Zebra Acquires Eltron," *Transportation & Distribution,* August 1998, p. 16.

Zipser, Andy, "Where Stripes Are," *Barron's,* January 20, 1992, pp. 42–43.

—Taryn Benbow-Pfalzgraf
—update: Christina M. Stansell

Zions Bancorporation

One South Main Street
Salt Lake City, Utah 84111
U.S.A.
Telephone: (801) 524-4787
Fax: (801) 524-4805
Web site: http://www.zionsbancorporation.com

Public Company
Incorporated: 1955 as Keystone Insurance and
    Investment Co.
Employees: 8,124
Total Assets: $24.3 billion (2001)
Stock Exchanges: NASDAQ
Ticker Symbol: ZION
NAIC: 52211 Commercial Banking

Through its various subsidiaries, the Salt Lake City-based Zions Bancorporation provides a full range of banking and related services in Arizona, California, Colorado, Idaho, Nevada, New Mexico, Utah, and Washington. Its primary holding, Zions First National Bank, operates 150 branch offices, 214 ATM's, and has assets of $8.5 billion. All together, Zions' collection of banks has over 400 branch offices. The company has grown quickly since the early 1990s by acquiring other banks and expanding existing operations.

Keystone Insurance and Investment Co., the precursor to Zions Bancorporation, was incorporated in Utah in 1955 by a group of investors for the purpose of acquiring the Lockhart Corporation. In addition to Lockhart's financial holdings, during the next few years Keystone purchased an insurance agency and about 120 acres of land in an industrial park. When Keystone went public in 1960, it was worth about $2 million.

In 1960, a group of investors, the chief of which was Keystone, purchased a controlling share of Zions First National Bank. A holding company, Zions First National Investment Co., was incorporated in Nevada to own the bank. The holding company's name was changed to Zions Utah Bancorporation in 1965. The holding company went public in 1966 when existing

stockholders sold their shares. In 1971, Zions Utah Bancorporation merged into Keystone, with Keystone becoming the surviving company. Keystone subsequently changed its name to Zions Utah Bancorporation.

Zions chief holding, Zions First National Bank, was a leading local bank in Salt Lake City. Prior to the buyout by Keystone and its associates, the bank was principally owned by the Latter-day Saints Church. Renowned Mormon leader Brigham Young had started the bank in 1873 to serve the church and local community. Throughout the late 1800s and through the mid-1900s, Zions had close ties to the Mormon Church, taking deposits from, and providing loans to, church members as well as handling many of the church's financial transactions.

Growth Under Simmons' Direction: 1960s–80s

The group of investors that bought out the church's ownership interest in First National in 1960 was headed by Roy W. Simmons. Simmons was a Mormon with a strong banking background. Both his father and grandfather had worked in banking and had served as officers of the competing First National Bank of Layton, near Salt Lake City. Under Simmons's direction, First National prospered during the 1960s and 1970s. Besides emphasizing its core Salt Lake City market, the bank expanded into rural Utah and eventually amassed a regional network of branches throughout the northern part of the state.

By the 1980s, First National had cemented a position as the second largest banking organization in the state of Utah, earning Simmons a reputation as a savvy banker and businessman. "Roy has an uncanny knack for figures and sizing up a situation," Lawrence Adler, president of the Utah Bankers Association, told *Knight-Ridder/Tribune Business News,* adding, "He's a banker from the old school."

In addition to running one of the region's most successful banks during the 1960s and 1970s, Simmons successfully helped raise his family, sending four sons to Harvard. One of his sons, Harris, would follow in the footsteps of the three generations before him. Harris Simmons was born in 1955, about five years before his father lead the buyout of First National and assumed leadership of the bank. He began his banking career at

Company Perspectives:

Our goal is to create value. Value for our customers. Value for the communities we serve. Value for our employees. And, most importantly, value for our shareholders. Creating shareholder value must be a preeminent objective, since the support of our owners, whose capital has been entrusted to us, is essential to our very existence as an independent enterprise. The creation of enduring shareholder value requires that we achieve consistently superior risk-adjusted returns on capital, and that we achieve healthy, strong earnings growth.

age 16 as a teller filing canceled checks. When he returned from Harvard, he went to work with First National and was named assistant vice-president at Zions Utah Bancorporation in 1981.

Although Zions achieved steady gains during the 1960s and 1970s, it was during the 1980s that the bank would realize its heady expansion. Zions' success was due in part to management strategies and in part to trends in the banking industry. By the late 1970s, banks began to feel competition from non-bank financial institutions. The new competitors were vying for consumer dollars that had traditionally gone to bank deposits and were also competing as lenders and financiers. Because of restrictive bank industry regulations passed through Congress in the wake of a flurry of bank failures during the Depression era, banks had been functioning at a disadvantage to their competitors. But during the mid 1960s and early 1970s, Congress eliminated some of the restrictions and created a variety of favorable tax incentives for specific banking activities. During that period, a number of bank holding companies like Zions were created to take advantage of deregulation and to begin participating in a number of non-banking-related financial markets.

Opportunities and Challenges: Mid- to Late 1980s

Nevertheless, Zions and other banks suffered because of interstate banking restrictions. For example, General Motors was free to offer consumer financing for its vehicles throughout the United States, thus benefitting from various economies of scale. In contrast, most of the activities of Zions and other bank holding companies were confined to a single state or region. In the mid-1980s, Congress allowed bank holding companies to engage in interstate banking. That legislation, combined with other banking industry dynamics, set the stage for a period of rampant growth that would double Zions' size by the mid-1990s.

By the time interstate banking regulations were loosened, the industry was already experiencing rapid consolidation. The new legislation only served to intensify the trend. The percentage of U.S. assets held by commercial banks dropped from about 37 percent in the late 1970s to 25 percent by the late 1980s. That reduction left many competitors scrambling for business. To survive, banks began merging to achieve economies of scale. The number of independent banking entities in the United States dropped from about 13,000 in 1983 to less than 10,000 by 1990. Meanwhile, the number of multi-bank holding companies like Zions grew from about 300 to around 1,000.

Augmenting the consolidation trend was the fact that computers and electronic banking devices were increasingly making it easier for banks like Zions to operate across broad regions. Thus, Zions' growth strategy in the 1980s was relatively straight forward. It wanted to acquire smaller competitors and integrate them in the Zions Utah Bancorporation system. Besides working to improve the performance of the banks it purchased, Zions' managers would reduce aggregate operating costs by amassing a large network of branches in a multi-state region. The savings would result from economies of scale related to marketing, reporting, and management overhead at the executive level.

Harris Simmons assumed his father's position as president of Zions Bancorporation in 1986. Roy Simmons became chairman of the company and retained his chief executive title. In January 1986, Zions entered the Arizona banking market by opening a commercial loan branch of its Zions First National Bank in Phoenix. The branch started out with one man, Clark Hinckley, in a hotel room and expanded rapidly with Zions' financial backing. In October 1986, Zions purchased Mesa Bank and changed the name of its Arizona operations to Zions First National Bank of Arizona. Zions added a third branch to its Arizona operations with the 1987 acquisition of Camel Bank. Also in 1987, the holding company shortened its name to Zions Bancorporation reflecting expansion efforts outside of Utah.

After adding millions of dollars of assets to its portfolio in Utah, Nevada, and Arizona, Zions Bancorporation seemed to be growing at a healthy clip going into the late 1980s. Unfortunately, souring commercial real estate markets and general economic malaise in the late 1980s hurt Zions and many other banks. But problems at Zions were compounded by a downturn in the local copper industry.

Though some of Zions' properties remained profitable, the company struggled through the late 1980s. Zions' Nevada and Arizona operations sustained profitability, generating combined earnings of about $1.8 million in 1986 and $2 million in 1987. In contrast, Zions of Utah stumbled. It posted a profit of $24 million in 1986, but then reported a loss of $14.1 million in 1987. The next year brought a loss of $17.9 million. The losses were so bad that Roy Simmons suspended his $191,000 chairman's salary in 1988 and cut his officer's pay. Nevertheless, Zions continued to pay dividends to its shareholders throughout the slump.

As many of its competitors became mired in nonperforming real estate loans, Zions recovered in 1989 as local markets perked up and its loan portfolio improved. Zions' net income rose to nearly $18 million, and the company stepped up its acquisition efforts. Because the banking industry was in such a slump during the early 1990s and capital was hard to come by, Zions was presented with several good investment opportunities. Harris Simmons became chief executive in 1991. Under his direction, the bank cautiously took advantage of several of those opportunities.

Acquisitions and New Markets in the Early 1990s

Among Zions' most notable acquisitions during the early 1990s was National Bancorp of Arizona, a $435 million institution based in Tucson. That purchase made Zions the seventh largest banker operating in the state. Zions moved up a notch in the rankings with the subsequent purchase of $107 million Rio Salado Bancorp. That purchase gave Zions a total asset base of about $630 million in Arizona by 1993 and extended its reach into Phoenix, Tucson, and Flagstaff. Although it emphasized expansion in Arizona, Zions added holdings in Utah as well. Similarly, Zions expanded its Nevada State Bank in Las Vegas, increasing its total number of branches to 19 by early 1994.

Perhaps Zions' most interesting purchase during the early 1990s was Discount Corporation of New York, a dealer in U.S. government securities. Observers questioned the deal, but Simmons believed it was a shrewd move. "I spent a couple of days explaining to analysts and stockholders that we weren't crazy," Simmons told *Knight-Ridder/Tribune Business News*. The subsidiary allowed Zions to begin repackaging and securitizing the loans that it made, rather than selling them in secondary markets. Most banks sell the home mortgages that they make to an investment house, which packages several mortgages and sells them as securities. The investment house makes money on the sales and the originating banks continue to make money servicing the loans. By bringing the securitizing process in-house, Zions was able to reap profits from both sides of the business. Discount Corporation made Zions one of only two primary dealers in government securities headquartered in the western United States. And it complemented Zions' expanding lending operations related to student loans, mortgages, credit card receivables, and other consumer financing.

The Discount Corporation acquisition revealed Simmons's penchant for innovation. For example, Zions was one of only a few lenders that had chased the accounts receivable lending business. Zions would extend credit to customers on the backing of the accounts receivables of their business. Viewing it as labor intensive, most banks shunned the niche. However, Zions set up a separate division to serve the market and found much new business in the mid-1990s. Another area where Zions was a recognized innovator was in opening branch offices in grocery

stores. The bank was also one of the first to begin securitizing small business loans.

Although Zions changed radically during the 1980s and early 1990s, one part of its business that did not change was its tie to the Mormon Church. Many people still thought of Zions as the "Mormon Bank" in the mid-1990s because of its long-time affiliation with the church. The church continued to be one of Zions' largest single customers. Zions had a separate "missionary remittance office" that handled electronic transfer funds to missionaries at the Mormon Church's 285 worldwide missions.

Besides expanding through acquisition, increasing its fee services, and innovating new profit centers, Zions achieved significant gains during the 1990s by streamlining internal operations and tightening controls. The combined results of Zions' strategy was strong revenue growth and even greater profit gains, suggesting a bright future for the holding company. As Zions Bancorporation's asset base grew from $3 billion in 1989 to nearly $4.5 billion in 1993, the company's net income surged to $26.6 million in 1990 and to $53 million in 1993. By 1994, Zions was operating about 125 branches in its three states and was involved in negotiations to acquire other banks in Arizona and Utah. In addition, it provided insurance, data processing, credit, and consumer lending services through several subsidiaries.

Success and Growth Continue: Mid-1990s and Beyond

By 1995, brokerage firm Dean Witter Reynolds had ranked Zions as the best-performing regional bank in the United States. During that year, the company's stock price almost doubled based on the company's return on equity. The success continued into 1996 as net income reached $101.3 million. Southern Arizona Bank was acquired that year, and the company also established Zions Agricultural Finance to originate and service loans for the Federal Agricultural Mortgage Corporation.

Zions' acquisition strategy continued into the latter half of the 1990s and into the new millennium. Tri-State Bank, with branches in Montpelier and Paris, Idaho, was purchased in 1997 along with Sun State Capital Corporation and California-based GB Bancorporation, whose holdings included Grossmont Bank. Overall, the company expanded its reach from three states to seven. Zions moved aggressively into Colorado during 1998, buying a host of small banks, including Kersey Bancorp, Citizens Banco Inc., and First National Bank of Alamosa.

The firm also eyed California for its growth potential. As such, Sumitomo Bank of California was added to its arsenal in 1998 along with First Pacific National Bank. Sumitomo, First Pacific, and Grossmont Bank were then merged together and renamed California Bank and Trust. The new subsidiary stood as the fifth-largest commercial bank in California with assets of $6 billion.

In 1999, Zions laid the groundwork for perhaps its most significant deal to date. By teaming up with First Security Capital Markets Inc.—the largest banking company in Utah— Zions planned to create the 20th-largest bank holding company in the United States, with assets of $40 billion. The merger was thwarted however, after First Security reported a major drop in its first quarter earnings during 2000. Zions' shareholders rejected the proposed deal shortly thereafter.

The failed merger did little to dampen Zions' spending spree. During 2001, the company added the following companies to its holdings: Draper Bancorp, Eldorado Bancshares Inc., the Arizona branches of Pacific Century Financial Corp., Minnequa Bancorp (a Utah-based branch of Washington Federal Savings), a municipal finance advisory business, and icomXpress, a workflow and electronic process management solutions provider. IcomXpress was renamed Lexign and became a key component of Zions' e-commerce business segment.

Zions' strategy appeared to pay off. Between 1996 and 2000, the firm's revenue had nearly doubled, and during 2001 the firm was named Utah's top revenue growth company by MountainWest Venture Group. The company was also added to Standard & Poor's 500 Index that year as net income soared to $283 million, increasing nearly 75 percent over the previous year.

During 2002, the company faced challenges related to a slowing economy. Zions' e-commerce unit was hit especially hard as technology spending fell off. As such, its Digital Signature Trust unit was sold. Cuts were also made at its Lexign division, and the firm toyed with the idea of a possible divestiture. Despite this setback, management remained positive about the company's future. While Zions' stellar growth appeared to have momentarily slowed, the financial services company was positioned to remain a leader among its peers for years to come.

Principal Subsidiaries

California Bank & Trust; The CommerceBank of Washington; National Bank of Arizona; Nevada State Bank; Vectra Bank Colorado; Zions First National Bank.

Principal Competitors

Bank of America Corporation; Washington Mutual Inc.; Wells Fargo & Company.

Further Reading

Anderson, Gary L., "Corporate Profile for Zions Bancorporation," *Business Wire*, June 24, 1994.

Crockett, Barton, "Zions' Chief Makes Believers Out of Skeptics," *American Banker*, September 27, 1995.

——, "Zions' Low-Key Chief Churns Out Profits While Rewarding Shareholders," *American Banker*, December 21, 1995, p. 7.

Deters, Barbara, "Salt Lake City, Utah, Bank Finds Plenty of Opportunity," *Knight-Ridder/Tribune Business News*, February 6, 1994.

Mandaro, Laura, "After Failed Deal, Zions Buys and Buys," *American Banker*, December 29, 2000, p. 1.

——, "Cost-Cutting Zions Is Rethinking Tech Plans," *American Banker*, September 24, 2002, p. 1.

Marios, Michael B., "Zions Bancorporation, First Security Announce Merger Worth $5.9 Billion," *Bond Buyer*, June 8, 1999, p. 32.

Max, Jarman, "Zions Pushing Receivables Loans," *Arizona Business Gazette*, November 22, 1991, p. 6.

Mitchell, Lesley, "Utah's Zions Bancorporation Expands Its Presence in Colorado," *Salt Lake Tribune*, May 2, 1998.

——, "CEO of Utah-Based Zions Bancorporation Opts to Forgo Bonus for 1999," *Salt Lake Tribune*, April 19, 2000.

O'Brien, Pat, "Zions First Finds Niche Among Big Banks in Local Marketplace," *Business Journal-Phoenix & the Valley of the Sun*, July 18, 1988, p. 9.

Rave, Jodi, "Zions Bancorporation Reports Gains for 1997," *Salt Lake Tribune*, January 27, 1998.

"Zions Bancorporation Is Honored As Top Revenue Growth Firm in Utah," *Standard Examiner*, October 31, 2001.

—Dave Mote
—update: Christina M. Stansell

Zoom Technologies, Inc.

207 South Street
Boston, Massachusetts 02111
U.S.A.
Telephone: (617) 423-1072
Fax: (617) 338-5015
Web site: http://www.zoom.com

Public Company
Incorporated: 1977
Employees: 214
Sales: $43.7 million (2001)
Stock Exchanges: NASDAQ
Ticker Symbol: ZOOM
NAIC: 334210 Telephone Apparatus Manufacturing;
    334418 Printed Circuit Assembly (Electronic
    Assembly) Manufacturing

Zoom Technologies, Inc. is a leading designer, manufacturer, and marketer of dial-up modems, cable and digital subscriber line (DSL) modems, wireless local area network (LAN) products, home phoneline networking devices, and a variety of data communication products. Its products—sold under the Zoom, Hayes, and Global Village names—are found in over 3,000 U.S. computer retail locations and in over 5,000 international locations. The company was one of the first manufacturers of faxmodems and voice faxmodems and stood at the forefront of emerging trends in computer connectivity during the late 1990s and into the new century. During 2002, the company changed its corporate name from Zoom Telephonics to Zoom Technologies and moved the jurisdiction of its incorporation from Canada to Delaware. Zoom Technologies conducts its business through its wholly owned subsidiary, Zoom Telephonics.

Early History

During the late 1960s, Frank B. Manning and his roommate, Peter R. Kramer, would stay up late into the night discussing how to start their own business. After graduating with doctorates from the Massachusetts Institute of Technology (MIT) in

the mid-1970s, the two young men decided that the timing was finally right. Taking a suggestion from T. Pat Manning, Frank's brother, the ambitious entrepreneurs settled on a product idea that they thought would be marketable and inexpensive to produce. The company was incorporated and began operations in March of 1977 under the name of Zoom which, according to the founders, would symbolize the quick growth of the business.

Manning and Kramer could not have started their business under more auspicious circumstances. The company's first product, dubbed the Silencer, was a switch that could be easily installed on a phone to keep it from ringing. This simple yet revolutionary idea lessened the frustration of callers who continually dialed a number when the phone was off the hook expecting to get through after a few attempts. The introduction of the Silencer fortunately coincided with the breakup of AT&T's monopoly of the telephone equipment industry. Marketed in such magazines as *Esquire, Vogue,* and *Playboy* as the perfect solution for an undisturbed ''romantic evening at home,'' the new product was welcomed in newly opened independent phone stores selling non-AT&T equipment.

Although the Silencer generated approximately $200,000 during the company's first few years of operation, Frank Manning and Peter Kramer knew that they would have to expand their product line in order to remain in business. While the two were students at MIT, they had designed an automatic dialer that would continuously dial a busy phone number. Avid tennis players, Manning and Kramer had originated the idea in order to get tennis court reservations at the campus courts, which only took reservations on a first-come, first-served basis beginning at noon. Confident of the dialer's success, Manning devoted himself to its electronic design and programming while Kramer concentrated on the mechanical design and packaging.

During the late 1970s, both Sprint and MCI entered the long distance business, attempting to attract customers by offering discounted long distance service. However, AT&T was the only company that could offer ''one-plus'' long distance dialing. Sprint and MCI were required to make customers dial an access code and a security code before the actual telephone number, which brought the total number of digits necessary to dial any long distance phone number to a minimum of 23, and some-

Company Perspectives:

The age of broadband is upon us, and Zoom is ready. We are ready with a line of advanced cable and DSL modems, and with wireless and home phoneline networking products that make it easy for people to use and share their broadband line to the Internet. We are ready with a thorough commitment to high-volume Internet access products so we can meet the needs of our customers, both end-users and channel partners. We are strong in dial-up modems, and we plan to get stronger. And we will use our expertise and channels as a springboard to success in broadband.

times even more. Aware of the potential demand for a product that would make using discount services like Sprint and MCI practical, in 1980 Zoom introduced the Demon Dialer. For use in both the home or office, the Demon Dialer could memorize and dial 176 telephone numbers, of up to 32 digits each. Recognized by the telecommunications industry for its innovative design and market potential, the Demon Dialer won the design award at the 1981 Consumer Electronics Show. More importantly for Zoom, however, the new product helped sales leap from $200,000 to an impressive $6 million annually.

Retrenchment and Reorganization

With the success of the Demon Dialer, Zoom not only began to hire more people and stock large amounts of inventory, but Manning and Kramer decided to go into debt in order to finance Zoom's projected expansion. The budding company hit their first major stumbling block when equal access within the telephone industry ended AT&T's monopoly on one-plus dialing and customers became free to choose their one-plus long distance carrier. It was no longer necessary to dial 23 digits to save money and the Demon Dialer became obsolete overnight. Sales dropped precipitously from $6 million to $1.5 million from 1984 to 1986, and the company lost nearly $1 million during each of those years. Manning and Kramer were forced to get rid of unused inventory, rearrange the financing for their debt payments, and reduce the number of Zoom employees from 56 to 16.

With the insight that separates the successful entrepreneur from the amateur investor, Manning and Kramer had already started to diversify Zoom's product line in 1983. By a stroke of good luck, a field applications engineer who worked for National Semiconductor had developed and designed a 300 baud modem for one of Apple Computer's first products. Aware of Zoom's reputation as a new and innovative company, he approached Manning and Kramer with the proposal that Zoom license, manufacture, and market his original design. Without much income from sales, however, Manning and Kramer convinced the Massachusetts Technology Development Corporation, a quasi-public venture capital company, to underwrite the cost of manufacturing and selling the new product.

In 1983, Zoom introduced the new product based on the licensing agreement. Dubbed the Networker, it was Zoom's first modem product, but, with the personal computer industry on the verge of expansion, the two entrepreneurs thought it expedient

to take a chance on the new technology. The Networker was more successful than Manning and Kramer could ever have imagined. As the company's annual sales volume for dialers continued its downward spiral, the modem business started to grow—and grow dramatically. Unable to arrange sufficient retail distribution for its modem, Zoom hit upon the idea of selling their product through direct mail advertising. With their successful modem, Zoom began to garner a higher profile in the telecommunications industry. Soon the company was able to forego its reliance on direct mail and focus on selling modems to distributors, personal computer manufacturers, and high-volume retail stores.

By 1985, Zoom began to design and market its own line of modems. Since the issue of compatibility was uppermost on everyone's mind, especially with IBM introducing its personal computer during the same year, the modems at Zoom were designed to provide a high level of compatibility and related enhancements, including such features as Demon Dialing. Sold at reasonable prices, Zoom's modems quickly captured a large share of the market. In just three years, sales at the company had surpassed the $5 million mark, almost all of which had been generated from the design and sale of new modems. By 1989, sales had topped the $8 million milepost and, in 1990, the company began trading shares on the NASDAQ exchange. During the same year, sales jumped to just over $13 million, and in 1991 sales skyrocketed to approximately $25 million.

International Expansion and the Emergence of the Internet

With the growth of the company through sales of modems, and in control of a significant share of the market, Manning and Kramer decided it was time to expand the company's product line overseas. As the communications network among personal computer users began to grow, the demand for high-technology, state-of-the-art, faxmodem products also rose. People found that they could keep in regular contact with their business associates, even between the most remote locations around the world, as long as they had a reliable source of electricity and a faxmodem. Zoom established distribution channels and sales offices in Belgium, Finland, Germany, Hong Kong, Italy, Korea, Poland, Portugal, Spain, and the United Kingdom. The company's major European distributors included Criterium, Computer 2000 and its Frontline division, and Northamber. Zoom's major European retail customers included Schadt and Vobis. In the Far East, the company's major distributor of its faxmodems was Nippon Polaroid, one of the largest retail stores for software and computer support technology. By 1994, Zoom reported that its international sales accounted for nearly 20 percent of its total revenues.

With the rise in interest in on-line services, personal computer users were increasingly looking for easy and quick connections to the Internet. This development alone created an enormous demand for high-speed modems. High volume production shifted from modems with a top transmission of 2400 bps in 1987 to a maximum transmission speed of 28,800 bps by 1995. The primary advantage in increasing transmission speed was that the less time it took to transmit text files and graphics, the less expensive phone call costs would be. In addition, high speed transmission modems facilitated data intensive applica-

Key Dates:

1977: Frank B. Manning and Peter R. Kramer establish Zoom Telephonics.

1980: Zoom launches the Demon Dialer.

1983: The company introduces the Networker, its first modem product.

1986: Sales drop to $1.5 million as the Demon Dialer becomes obsolete.

1990: Zoom goes public.

1991: Sales reach $25 million based on rising modem sales.

1994: By now, international sales account for nearly 20 percent of revenues.

1996: Tribe Computer Works is acquired.

1999: Zoom acquires Hayes Corp.

2002: The company incorporates in Delaware and changes its name to Zoom Technologies, Inc.

tions such as World Wide Web browsing, remote access to corporate computer networks, and video telephony.

Recognizing the ever-increasing demand for modem-related technologies, Manning and Kramer decided to concentrate entirely on developing products to meet the needs of consumers. Zoom developed modems that provided a range of services. These included functions that digitalized incoming voice signals, stored them in memory, and then retrieved and sent these signals through the telephone network to a remote computer or person. The company's advanced modems could facilitate two-way voice conversations between employees working on the same project but in different locations. The advances in computer software during the early and mid-1990s also increased the demand for high speed transmission modems. Microsoft's introduction of its Windows 95 included capabilities such as remote access, faxing, and Internet access that could only be used with a high speed transmission modem such as Zoom's ComStar. ComStar's key features included a top data speed of 28,800 bps, voice mail, full-duplex speakerphone, VoiceView, Caller ID, Plug & Play, Internet Software, and a maximum fax speed of 14,400 bps.

The Mid-1990s

By the end of fiscal 1995, Zoom had sold over 920,000 faxmodems on the North American continent alone. New products and savvy marketing techniques helped to expand the company's market share. One of its most successful new product marketing methods was the Zoom Business Products Line. Created specifically to meet the demands of institutional and corporate users, the company introduced the Zoom/Multiline, a collection of eight non-related high transmission faxmodems packaged in a single case. For use in situations that require multiple modems in a high-density, low-power format, and with remote access capabilities, this line of products was an immediate success.

At the beginning of 1996, Zoom renewed its commitment to developing highly innovative products and product enhancements. New products included ISDN modems, a communica-

tion service that permitted current phone lines to transmit data digitally; simultaneous voice and data capabilities that allowed two people using personal computers to engage in a conversation at the same time as data is being transferred; combined faxmodem/LAN PCMCIA cards, which combined both faxmodem and LAN capabilities in one card and allowed one PCMCIA slot in a notebook computer to serve both functions; and multi-line faxmodems, to be used for bulletin boards, UNIX servers, and LANs that employ a variety of modems. Also in 1996, Zoom entered into an agreement with Hewlett-Packard and Rockwell to design and develop a product that would allow a printer to function as a fax receiving device, whether or not the computer is turned on.

In the mid-1990s, Zoom also reached agreements with numerous high volume retailers in the personal computer market to sell its products, including Best Buy, Circuit City, Computer City, Office Depot, OfficeMax, Staples, and Wal-Mart. In January 1996, Zoom had secured the second largest amount of retail space set aside for modems throughout North America. In 1995, nearly 20 percent of the company's total revenue was generated from sales at the high volume retailer Best Buy, which was located in most urban and suburban areas across the United States.

As sales for the company continued to increase, Zoom management became convinced that the time was right for the implementation of an acquisition program. In July 1996, Zoom purchased Tribe Computer Works, a private corporation based in California that manufactured remote access systems and routers for branch office environments such as banks. In 1995, the remote access systems market grew by an astounding 120 percent, and Zoom was well placed to sell remote access products in the high volume retail stores already distributing the company's products.

By now, Zoom had received recognition from such eminent publications as *Forbes* magazine, *Financial World, Fortune, PC World, Windows Magazine, ComputerLife, NetGuide, Windows User,* and *PC Professionell* in Germany. Best Buy awards had come from such distant countries as the United Kingdom and Brazil. With such rave reviews from sources all over the world, Manning and Kramer, still managing the company's development and direction in the mid-1990s, were confident that Zoom's best years lay ahead.

The Broadband Age: Late 1990s and Beyond

Indeed, the latter half of the 1990s proved to be boom years for technology-related and Internet-based companies. By 1998, the new standard for dial-up modems shifted to V.90 and K56flex, which allowed to users to connect to the Internet at 56,000 bps. Zoom spent heavily on developing new products that were compatible with this standard. In October 1998, the firm's Zoom FaxModem 56K Dualmode received an Editor's Choice award from *CNET,* beating out competitor 3Com Corp. Zoom also continued its acquisition program in 1999 with the purchase of Hayes Corp. The deal added a host of new modems to Zoom's product arsenal and gave the company access to Hayes' DSL and cable modem development facilities.

Zoom entered 2000 focused on its dial-up modems as well as its new broadband products. The popularity of broadband—

high speed digital Internet access that was significantly faster than a dial-up modem—grew rapidly during the early years of the new millennium. Considered the wave of the future, broadband became the focal point of many companies' business strategies. In fact, the majority of Zoom's research and development spending during 2000 went towards developing broadband-related products. The company chose, however, to remain a premier dial-up modem provider as well—unlike competitor 3Com who exited the dial-up arena in 2000.

The company introduced new V.92 dial-up modems in 2000. V.92 was a new standard in dial-up access that increased possible upload speed to 48,000 bps. Zoom president and CEO Manning commented on the company's direction in an October 2000 press release, claiming that ''industry analysts agree that dial-up modems will be the most popular way of accessing the Internet through 2010 and beyond. Zoom is committed to Internet access, and V.92 is an important part of that commitment. Along with cable modems, DSL modems, and advanced network products that link multiple users to the Internet, dial-up modems will continue to be important to Zoom.'' According to market research firm Instat/MDR, over 86 million analog modems were sold during 2001. That number was estimated to have increased to 89 million during 2002.

As Zoom kept pace with changing technology during the late 1990s and into the new century, its bottom line felt the crunch of falling modem prices. The firm began posting losses in 1997, and during 2001 sales fell by nearly 27 percent over the previous year as the firm reported a net loss of $18.3 million. The company cut spending and jobs as a result of a slowing economy and falling retail demand for its dial-up modems. Its share price tumbled from $15 in March 2000 to below one dollar in early 2003. As a result, the company's stock was moved from the main NASDAQ trading platform to a market for small-cap stocks. In early 2002, the company changed the jurisdiction of incorporation from Canada to Delaware and adopted a new corporate name, Zoom Technologies, Inc. The company continued to conduct business through its Zoom Telephonics subsidiary.

In January 2003, the firm began shipping its Zoom CableModem 5041 to Best Buy stores, hoping to cash in on increasing demand for broadband modems. Despite the challenges it faced, Zoom remained optimistic about its future. Whether or not Zoom could achieve the level of success it had secured during the early 1990s, however, remained to be seen.

Principal Subsidiaries

Zoom Telephonics Inc.

Principal Competitors

3Com Corporation; Motorola Inc.

Further Reading

Bray, Hiawatha, ''Boston's Zoom Telephonics Aims to Keep its Core Business in Analog Modems,'' *Boston Globe*, January 27, 2003.

Brown, Bruce, ''Zoom/FaxModem V.34X,'' *PC Magazine*, October 24, 1995, p. 403.

Farrell, Craig S., ''Review: Leading 28,8K Notebook Modems Pass Muster,'' *Computerworld*, July 8, 1996, p. 86.

Laville, Stacy, ''Remote Access Expansion Plans Flurry of Buyouts,'' *PC Week*, June 24, 1996, p. 121.

——, ''Volume Rises For Voice/Data Modems At Comdex,'' *PC Week*, November 6, 1995, p. 6.

Pickering, Wendy, ''New V.34-Based Modems Join The Comdex Crowd,'' *PC Week*, November 14, 1994, p. 26.

Robinson, Earle, ''Zoom/FaxModem V.34X,'' *PC Magazine*, March 14, 1995, p. 271.

Sparks, Debra, ''The Second Time Around,'' *Financial World*, May 24, 1994, p. 59.

Wildstrom, Stephen H., ''Thoroughly Modern Modems,'' *Business Week*, July 31, 1995, p. 18.

Yang, Jae, ''Zoom/FaxModem VFX 28.8,'' *PC Magazine*, September 13, 1994, p. 308.

''Zoom Ships First V.92 Modems,'' *Business Wire*, October 26, 2000.

''Zoom Telephonics Responds to 3Com,'' *Canadian Corporate Newswire*, March 23, 2000.

''Zoom Telephonics Turns Fax Machines Into Scanners,'' *PC Week*, March 6, 1995, p. 35.

—Thomas Derdak
—update: Christina M. Stansell

INDEX TO COMPANIES ─────────────────────────────

Index to Companies

Listings in this index are arranged in alphabetical order under the company name. Company names beginning with a letter or proper name such as Eli Lilly & Co. will be found under the first letter of the company name. Definite articles (The, Le, La) are ignored for alphabetical purposes as are forms of incorporation that precede the company name (AB, NV). Company names printed in bold type have full, historical essays on the page numbers appearing in bold. Updates to entries that appeared in earlier volumes are signified by the notation (upd.). Company names in light type are references within an essay to that company, not full historical essays. This index is cumulative with volume numbers printed in bold type.

Fab 9, **26** 431

Fabbrica D' Armi Pietro Beretta S.p.A., 39 149–51

Fabco Automotive Corp., **23** 306; **27** 203

Faber-Castell. *See* A.W. Faber-Castell Unternehmensverwaltung GmbH & Co.

Fabergé, Inc., **II** 590; **III** 48; **8** 168, 344; **11** 90; **32** 475; **47** 114

Fabri-Centers of America Inc., 15 329; **16 197–99; 18** 223; **43** 291

Fabrica de Cemento El Melan, **III** 671

Fabtek Inc., **48** 59

Facchin Foods Co., **I** 457

Facit, **III** 480; **22** 26

Facom S.A., 32 183–85; 37 143, 145

Facts on File, Inc., **14** 96–97; **22** 443

FAE Fluid Air Energy SA, **49** 162–63

Fafnir Bearing Company, **13** 523

FAG Kugelfischer Georg Schafer AG, **11** 84; **47** 280

Fagersta, **II** 366; **IV** 203

Fahr AG, **III** 543

Fahrzeugwerke Eisenach, **I** 138

FAI, **III** 545–46

Failsafe, **14** 35

Fair Grounds Corporation, 44 177–80

Fair, Isaac and Company, 18 168–71, 516, 518

Fairbanks Morse Co., **I** 158, 434–35; **10** 292; **12** 71

Fairchild Aircraft, Inc., 9 205–08, 460; **11** 278

Fairchild Camera and Instrument Corp., **II** 50, 63; **III** 110, 141, 455, 618; **6** 261–62; **7** 531; **10** 108; **11** 503; **13** 323–24; **14** 14; **17** 418; **21** 122, 330; **26** 327

Fairchild Communications Service, **8** 328

The Fairchild Corporation, **37** 30

Fairchild Dornier GmbH, 48 167–71 (upd.)

Fairchild Industries, **I** 71, 198; **11** 438; **14** 43; **15** 195; **34** 117

Fairchild Semiconductor Corporation, **II** 44–45, 63–65; **III** 115; **6** 215, 247; **10** 365–66; **16** 332; **24** 235; **41** 201

Fairclough Construction Group plc, I 567–68

Fairey Industries Ltd., **IV** 659

Fairfax, **IV** 650

Fairfield Communities, Inc., 36 192–95

The Fairfield Group, **33** 259–60

Fairfield Manufacturing Co., **14** 43

Fairfield Publishing, **13** 165

Fairmont Foods Co., **7** 430; **15** 139

Fairmont Hotels and Resorts Inc., **45** 80

Fairmont Insurance Co., **26** 487

Fairmount Glass Company, **8** 267

Fairport Machine Shop, Inc., **17** 357

Fairway Marketing Group, Inc., **24** 394

Fairway Outdoor Advertising, Inc., **36** 340, 342

Faiveley S.A., 39 152–54

Falcon Drilling Co. *See* Transocean Sedco Forex Inc.

Falcon Oil Co., **IV** 396

Falcon Products, Inc., 33 149–51

Falcon Seaboard Inc., **II** 86; **IV** 410; **7** 309

Falconbridge Limited, IV 111, 165–66; **49 136–39**

Falconet Corp., **I** 45

Falley's, Inc., **17** 558, 560–61

Fallon McElligott Inc., 22 199–201

Falls Financial Inc., **13** 223; **31** 206

Falls National Bank of Niagara Falls, **11** 108

Falls Rubber Company, **8** 126

FAME Plastics, Inc., **18** 162

Family Bookstores, **24** 548. *See also* Family Christian Stores, Inc.

Family Channel. *See* International Family Entertainment Inc.

Family Christian Stores, Inc., 51 131–34

Family Dollar Stores, Inc., 13 215–17

Family Golf Centers, Inc., 29 183–85

Family Health Program, **6** 184

Family Life Insurance Co., **II** 425; **13** 341

Family Mart Group, **V** 188; **36** 418, 420

Family Restaurants, Inc., **14** 194

Family Steak Houses of Florida, Inc., **15** 420

Famosa Bakery, **II** 543

Famous Amos Chocolate Chip Cookie Corporation, **27** 332

Famous Atlantic Fish Company, **20** 5

Famous-Barr, **46** 288

Famous Dave's of America, Inc., 40 182–84 4

Famous Players-Lasky Corp., **I** 451; **II** 154; **6** 161–62; **23** 123

Famous Restaurants Inc., **33** 139–40

FAN, **13** 370

Fancom Holding B.V., **43** 130

Fannie Mae, 45 156–59 (upd.)

Fannie May Candy Shops Inc., **36** 309

Fansteel Inc., 19 150–52

Fantastic Sam's, **26** 476

Fanthing Electrical Corp., **44** 132

Fantle's Drug Stores, **16** 160

Fantus Co., **IV** 605

Fanuc Ltd., III 482–83; **17 172–74 (upd.)**

Fanzz, **29** 282

FAO Schwarz, **I** 548; **46 187–90; 50** 524

Faprena, **25** 85

Far East Airlines, **6** 70

Far East Machinery Co., **III** 581

Far Eastern Air Transport, Inc., **23** 380

Far West Restaurants, **I** 547

Faraday National Corporation, **10** 269

Farah Incorporated, 24 156–58

Farben. *See* I.G. Farbenindustrie AG.

Farbenfabriken Bayer A.G., **I** 309

Farberware, Inc., **27** 287–88

Farbro Corp., **45** 15

Farbwerke Hoechst A.G., **I** 346–47; **IV** 486; **13** 262

Farine Lactée Henri Nestlé, **II** 545

Farinon Corp., **IV** 38

Farley Candy Co., **15** 190

Farley Industries, **25** 166

Farley Northwest Industries Inc., I 440–41

Farm Credit Bank of St. Louis/St. Paul, **8** 489–90

Farm Electric Services Ltd., **6** 586

Farm Family Holdings, Inc., 39 155–58

Farm Fresh Foods, **25** 332

Farm Journal Corporation, 42 131–34

Farm Power Laboratory, **6** 565; **50** 366

Farmcare Ltd., **51** 89

Farmer Bros. Co., 52 117–19

Farmer Jack, **16** 247; **44** 145

Farmers and Mechanics Bank of Georgetown, **13** 439

Farmers and Merchants Bank, **II** 349

Farmers Bank of Delaware, **II** 315–16

Farmers Insurance Group of Companies, 23 286; **25 154–56; 29** 397

Farmers' Loan and Trust Co., **II** 254; **9** 124

Farmers National Bank & Trust Co., **9** 474

Farmers Petroleum, Inc., **48** 175

Farmers Regional Cooperative, **II** 536

Farmland Foods, Inc., IV 474; **7** 17, **7 174–75**

Farmland Industries, Inc., 39 282; **48 172–75**

Farnam Cheshire Lime Co., **III** 763

Farrar, Straus and Giroux Inc., 15 158–60; 35 451

FAS Acquisition Co., **53** 142

FASC. *See* First Analysis Securities Corporation.

Fasco Consumer Products, **19** 360

Fasco Industries, **III** 509; **13** 369

Faserwerke Hüls GmbH., **I** 350

Fashion Bar, Inc., **24** 457

Fashion Bug, **8** 97

Fashion Co., **II** 503; **10** 324

Fasquelle, **IV** 618

Fasson. *See* Avery Dennison Corporation.

Fast Air, **31** 305

Fast Fare, **7** 102

Fastenal Company, 14 185–87; 42 135–38 (upd.)

FAT KAT, Inc., **51** 200, 203

Fata European Group, **IV** 187; **19** 348

Fateco Förlag, **14** 556

FATS, Inc., **27** 156, 158

Fatum, **III** 308

Faugere et Jutheau, **III** 283

Faulkner, Dawkins & Sullivan, **II** 450

Fauquet, **25** 85

Favorite Plastics, **19** 414

FAvS. *See* First Aviation Services Inc.

Fawcett Books, **13** 429

Fay's Inc., 17 175–77

Fayette Tubular Products, **7** 116–17

Fayva, **13** 359–61

Fazoli's Systems, Inc., 13 321; **27 145–47**

FB&T Corporation, **14** 154

FBC. *See* First Boston Corp.

FBO. *See* Film Booking Office of America.

FBR. *See* Friedman, Billings, Ramsey Group, Inc.

FC Holdings, Inc., **26** 363

FCBC, **IV** 174

FCC. *See* Federal Communications Commission.

FCC National Bank, **II** 286

FCI. *See* Framatome SA.

FDIC. *See* Federal Deposit Insurance Corp.

Fearn International, **II** 525; **13** 293; **50** 293

Feather Fine, **27** 361

Featherlite Inc., 28 127–29

Feature Enterprises Inc., **19** 452

Fechheimer Bros. Co., **III** 215; **18** 60, 62

Fedders Corporation, 18 172–75; 43 162–67 (upd.)

Federal Barge Lines, **6** 487

Federal Bearing and Bushing, **I** 158–59

Federal Bicycle Corporation of America, **11** 3

Federal Cartridge, **26** 363

Federal Coca-Cola Bottling Co., **10** 222

Federal Communications Commission, **6** 164–65; **9** 321

Federal Deposit Insurance Corp., **II** 261–62, 285, 337; **12** 30, 79

Federal Electric, **I** 463; **III** 653

Minnesota Cooperative Creamery Association, Inc., **II** 535; **21** 340

Minnesota Linseed Oil Co., **8** 552

Minnesota Mining & Manufacturing Company, **I** 28, 387, **499–501**; **II** 39; **III** 476, 487, 549; **IV** 251, 253–54; **6** 231; **7** 162; **8** 35, **369–71** (upd.); **11** 494; **13** 326; **17** 29–30; **22** 427; **25** 96, 372; **26 296–99** (upd.)

Minnesota Paints, **8** 552–53

Minnesota Power & Light Company, **11 313–16**

Minnesota Power, Inc., **34 286–91** (upd.)

Minnesota Sugar Company, **11** 13

Minnesota Valley Canning Co., **I** 22

Minnetonka Corp., **II** 590; **III** 25; **22** 122–23

Minntech Corporation, **22 359–61**

Minn-Dak Farmers Cooperative, **32** 29

Minolta Camera Co., Ltd., **III 574–76**, 583–84

Minolta Co., Ltd., **18** 93, 186, **339–42** (upd.); **43 281–85** (upd.)

Minorco, **III** 503; **IV** 67–68, 84, 97; **16** 28, 293

Minstar Inc., **11** 397; **15** 49; **45** 174

Minton China, **38** 401

The Minute Maid Company, **I** 234; **10** 227; **28 271–74**, 473; **32** 116

Minute Tapioca, **II** 531

Minuteman International Inc., **46 292–95**

Minyard Food Stores, Inc., **33 304–07**

Mippon Paper, **21** 546; **50** 58

MIPS Computer Systems, **II** 45; **11** 491

Miracle Food Mart, **16** 247, 249–50

Miracle-Gro Products, Inc., **22** 474

Miraflores Designs Inc., **18** 216

Mirage Resorts, Incorporated, **6 209–12**; **15** 238; **28 275–79** (upd.); **29** 127; **43** 82

Miramar Hotel & Investment Co., **IV** 717; **38** 318

Mirant, **39** 54, 57

Mircali Asset Management, **III** 340

Mircor Inc., **12** 413

Mirrlees Blackstone, **III** 509

Mirror Group Newspapers plc, **IV** 641; **7** 244, 312, **341–43**; **23 348–51** (upd.); **49** 408

Mirror Printing and Binding House, **IV** 677

Misceramic Tile, Inc., **14** 42

Misr Airwork. See AirEgypt.

Misr Bank of Cairo, **27** 132

Misrair. See AirEgypt.

Miss Erika, Inc., **27** 346, 348

Miss Selfridge, **V** 177–78

Misset Publishers, **IV** 611

Mission Energy Company, **V** 715

Mission First Financial, **V** 715

Mission Group, **V** 715, 717

Mission Insurance Co., **III** 192

Mission Jewelers, **30** 408

Mississippi Chemical Corporation, **8** 183; **IV** 367; **27** 316; **39 280–83**

Mississippi Drug, **III** 10

Mississippi Gas Company, **6** 577

Mississippi Power & Light, **V** 619

Mississippi Power Company, **38** 446–47

Mississippi River Corporation, **10** 44

Mississippi River Recycling, **31** 47, 49

Missoula Bancshares, Inc., **35** 198–99

Missouri Book Co., **10** 136

Missouri Fur Company, **25** 220

Missouri Gaming Company, **21** 39

Missouri Gas & Electric Service Company, **6** 593

Missouri-Kansas-Texas Railroad, **I** 472; **IV** 458

Missouri Pacific Railroad, **10** 43–44

Missouri Public Service Company. See UtiliCorp United Inc.

Missouri Utilities Company, **6** 580

Mist Assist, Inc. See Ballard Medical Products.

Mistik Beverages, **18** 71

Mistral Plastics Pty Ltd., **IV** 295; **19** 225

Misys PLC, **45 279–81**; **46 296–99**

Mitchel & King Skates Ltd., **17** 244

Mitchell Construction, **III** 753

Mitchell Energy and Development Corporation, **7 344–46**

Mitchell Home Savings and Loan, **13** 347

Mitchell Hutchins, Inc., **II** 445; **22** 405–06

Mitchell International, **8** 526

Mitchells & Butler, **I** 223

Mitchum Co., **III** 55

Mitchum, Jones & Templeton, **II** 445; **22** 405

MiTek Industries Inc., **IV** 259

MiTek Wood Products, **IV** 305

Mitel Corporation, **15** 131–32; **18 343–46**

MitNer Group, **7** 377

MITRE Corporation, **26 300–02**

Mitre Sport U.K., **17** 204–05

MITROPA AG, **37 250–53**

Mitsubishi Aircraft Co., **III** 578; **7** 348; **9** 349; **11** 164

Mitsubishi Bank, Ltd., **II** 57, 273–74, 276, **321–22**, 323, 392, 459; **III** 289, 577–78; **7** 348; **15** 41; **16** 496, 498; **50** 498. See also Bank of Tokyo-Mitsubishi Ltd.

Mitsubishi Chemical Industries Ltd., **I** 319, **363–64**, 398; **II** 57; **III** 666, 760; **11** 207

Mitsubishi Corporation, **I** 261, 431–32, 492, **502–04**, 505–06, 510, 515, 519–20; **II** 57, 59, 101, 118, 224, 292, 321–25, 374; **III** 577–78; **IV** 285, 518, 713; **6** 499; **7** 82, 233, 590; **9** 294; **12 340–43** (upd.); **17** 349, 556; **24** 325, 359; **27** 511

Mitsubishi Electric Corporation, **II** 53, **57–59**, 68, 73, 94, 122; **III** 577, 586; **7** 347, 394; **18** 18; **23** 52–53; **43** 15; **44 283–87** (upd.)

Mitsubishi Estate Company, Limited, **IV 713–14**

Mitsubishi Foods, **24** 114

Mitsubishi Group, **V** 481–82; **7** 377; **21** 390

Mitsubishi Heavy Industries, Ltd., **II** 57, 75, 323, 440; **III** 452–53, 487, 532, 538, **577–79**, 685, 713; **IV** 184, 713; **7 347–50** (upd.); **8** 51; **9** 349–50; **10** 33; **13** 507; **15** 92; **24** 359; **40 324–28** (upd.)

Mitsubishi International Corp., **16** 462

Mitsubishi Kasei Corp., **III** 47–48, 477; **8** 343; **14** 535

Mitsubishi Kasei Industry Co. Ltd., **IV** 476

Mitsubishi Kasei Vinyl Company, **49** 5

Mitsubishi Marine, **III** 385

Mitsubishi Materials Corporation, **III 712–13**; **IV** 554; **38** 463

Mitsubishi Motors Corporation, **III** 516–17, 578–79; **6** 28; **7** 219, 348–49; **8** 72, 374; **9 349–51**; **23 352–55** (upd.); **34** 128, 136; **40** 326

Mitsubishi Oil Co., Ltd., **IV 460–62**, 479, 492

Mitsubishi Paper Co., **III** 547

Mitsubishi Rayon Co. Ltd., **I** 330; **V 369–71**; **8** 153

Mitsubishi Sha Holdings, **IV** 554

Mitsubishi Shipbuilding Co. Ltd., **II** 57; **III** 513, 577–78; **7** 348; **9** 349

Mitsubishi Shokai, **III** 577; **IV** 713; **7** 347

Mitsubishi Trading Co., **IV** 460

Mitsubishi Trust & Banking Corporation, **II 323–24**; **III** 289

Mitsui & Co., Ltd., **I** 282; **IV** 18, 224, 432, 654–55; **V** 142; **6** 346; **7** 303; **13** 356; **24** 325, 488–89; **27** 337; **28 280–85** (upd.)

Mitsui Bank, Ltd., **II** 273–74, 291, **325–27**, 328, 372; **III** 295–97; **IV** 147, 320; **V** 142; **17** 556. See also Sumitomo Mitsui Banking Corporation.

Mitsui Bussan K.K., **I** 363, 431–32, 469, 492, 502–04, **505–08**, 510, 515, 519, 533; **II** 57, 66, 101, 224, 292, 323, 325–28, 392; **III** 295–96, 717–18; **IV** 147, 431; **9** 352–53. See also Mitsui & Co., Ltd.

Mitsui Gomei Kaisha, **IV** 715

Mitsui Group, **9** 352; **16** 84; **20** 310; **21** 72

Mitsui House Code, **V** 142

Mitsui Light Metal Processing Co., **III** 758

Mitsui Marine and Fire Insurance Company, Limited, **III** 209, **295–96**, 297

Mitsui Mining & Smelting Co., Ltd., **IV 145–46**, 147–48

Mitsui Mining Company, Limited, **IV** 145, **147–49**

Mitsui Mutual Life Insurance Company, **III** 297–98; **39 284–86** (upd.)

Mitsui-no-Mori, Ltd., **IV** 716

Mitsui O.S.K. Lines, Ltd., **I** 520; **IV** 383; **V 473–76**; **6** 398; **26 278–80**

Mitsui Petrochemical Industries, Ltd., **I** 390, 516; **9 352–54**

Mitsui Real Estate Development Co., Ltd., **IV 715–16**

Mitsui Shipbuilding and Engineering Co., **III** 295, 513

Mitsui Toatsu, **9** 353–54

Mitsui Trading, **III** 636

Mitsui Trust & Banking Company, Ltd., **II** 328; **III** 297

Mitsukoshi Ltd., **I** 508; **V 142–44**; **14** 502; **41** 114; **47** 391

Mitsuya Foods Co., **I** 221

Mitteldeutsche Creditbank, **II** 256

Mitteldeutsche Energieversorgung AG, **V** 747

Mitteldeutsche Privatbank, **II** 256

Mitteldeutsche Stickstoff-Werke Ag, **IV** 229–30

Mitteldeutsches Kraftwerk, **IV** 229

Mity Enterprises, Inc., **38 310–12**

Mixconcrete (Holdings), **III** 729

Miyoshi Electrical Manufacturing Co., **II** 6

Mizuno Corporation, **25 344–46**

Mizushima Ethylene Co. Ltd., **IV** 476

MJB Coffee Co., **I** 28

MK-Ferguson Company, **7** 356

MLC. See Medical Learning Company.

PEPCO. *See* Portland Electric Power Company *and* Potomac Electric Power Company.

Pepe Clothing Co., **18** 85

Pepper Hamilton LLP, 43 300–03

Pepperell Manufacturing Company, **16** 533–34

Pepperidge Farm, **I** 29; **II** 480–81; **7** 67–68; **26** 56–57, 59

The Pepsi Bottling Group, Inc., 40 350–53

PepsiCo, Inc., I 234, 244–46, 257, 269, **276–79**, 281, 291; **II** 103, 448, 477, 608; **III** 106, 116, 588; **7** 265, 267, 396, 404, 434–35, 466, 505–06; **8** 399; **9** 177, 343; **10** 130, 199, 227, 324, **450–54 (upd.); 11** 421, 450; **12** 337, 453; **13** 162, 284, 448, 494; **15** 72, 75, 380; **16** 96; **18** 65; **19** 114, 221; **21** 143, 313, 315–16, 362, 401, 405, 485–86; **22** 95, 353; **23** 418, 420; **25** 91, 177–78, 366, 411; **28** 271, 473, 476; **31** 243; **32** 59, 114, 205; **36** 234, 237; **38 347–54 (upd.); 40** 340–42, 350–52; **49** 77

Pepsodent Company, **I** 14; **9** 318

Perception Technology, **10** 500

Percy Bilton Investment Trust Ltd., **IV** 710

Percy Street Investments Ltd., **IV** 711

Perdigao SA, 52 276–79

Perdue Farms Inc., 7 422–24, 432; **23 375–78 (upd.); 32** 203

Perfect Circle Corp., **I** 152

Perfect Fit Industries, **17** 182–84

Perfect-Ventil GmbH, **9** 413

Performance Contracting, Inc., **III** 722; **20** 415

Performance Food Group Company, 31 359–62

Performance Technologies, Inc., **10** 395

Perfumania, Inc., **22** 157

Pergamon Holdings, **15** 83; **50** 125

Pergamon Press, **IV** 611, 641–43, 687; **7** 311–12

Perini Corporation, 8 418–21; 38 481

Perisem, **I** 281

The Perkin-Elmer Corporation, III 455, 727; **7 425–27; 9** 514; **13** 326; **21** 123

Perkins, **I** 147; **12** 90

Perkins Bacon & Co., **10** 267

Perkins Cake & Steak, **9** 425

Perkins Engines Ltd., **III** 545, 652; **10** 274; **11** 472; **19** 294; **27** 203

Perkins Family Restaurants, L.P., 22 417–19

Perkins Oil Well Cementing Co., **III** 497

Perkins Products Co., **II** 531

Perl Pillow, **19** 304

Perland Environmental Technologies Inc., **8** 420

Permal Group, **27** 276, 513

Permaneer Corp., **IV** 281; **9** 259. *See also* Spartech Corporation.

Permanent General Companies, Inc., **11** 194

Permanent Pigments Inc., **25** 71

Permanente Cement Company, **I** 565; **44** 152

Permanente Metals Corp., **IV** 15, 121–22

Permian Corporation, **V** 152–53

PERMIGAN, **IV** 492

Permodalan, **III** 699

Pernod Ricard S.A., I 248, **280–81; 21 399–401 (upd.)**

Pernvo Inc., **I** 387

Perot Systems Corporation, 13 482; **29 375–78**

Perret-Olivier, **III** 676; **16** 120

Perrier, **19** 50

Perrier Corporation of America, **16** 341

Perrier Vittel S.A., **52** 188

Perrigo Company, 12 218, **387–89**

Perrin, **IV** 614

Perrot Brake Co., **I** 141

Perrow Motor Freight Lines, **6** 370

Perry Brothers, Inc., **24** 149

Perry Capital Corp., **28** 138

Perry Drug Stores Inc., **12** 21; **26** 476

Perry Ellis International, Inc., 16 37; **41 291–94**

Perry Manufacturing Co., **16** 37

Perry Sports, **13** 545; **13** 545

Perry Tritech, **25** 103–05

Perry's Shoes Inc., **16** 36

Perscombinatie, **IV** 611

Pershing & Co., **22** 189

Personal Care Corp., **17** 235

Personal Performance Consultants, **9** 348

Personal Products Company, **III** 35; **8** 281, 511

Personnel Pool of America, **29** 224, 26–27

Perstorp AB, I 385–87; **51 289–92 (upd.)**

PERTAMINA, IV 383, 461, **491–93,** 517, 567

Pertec Computer Corp., **17** 49; **18** 434

Pertech Computers Ltd., **18** 75

Perusahaan Minyak Republik Indonesia, **IV** 491

Peruvian Corp., **I** 547

Pet Food & Supply, **14** 385

Pet Foods Plus Inc., **39** 355

Pet Incorporated, I 457; **II** 486–87; **7 428–31; 10** 554; **12** 124; **13** 409; **14** 214; **24** 140; **27** 196; **43** 217; **46** 290

Petco Animal Supplies, Inc., 29 379–81

Pete's Brewing Company, 18 72, 502; **22 420–22**

Peter Bawden Drilling, **IV** 570; **24** 521

Peter, Cailler, Kohler, Chocolats Suisses S.A., **II** 546; **7** 381

Peter Cundill & Associates Ltd., **15** 504

Peter Gast Shipping GmbH, **7** 40; **41** 42

Peter J. Schmitt Co., **13** 394; **24** 444–45

Peter J. Schweitzer, Inc., **III** 40; **16** 303; **43** 257

Peter Jones, **V** 94

Peter Kiewit Sons' Inc., I 599–600; **III** 198; **8 422–24; 15** 18; **25** 512, 514

Peter Norton Computing Group, **10** 508–09

Peter Paul/Cadbury, **II** 477, 512; **15** 221; **51** 158

Peterbilt Motors Co., **I** 185–86; **26** 355

Peters-Revington Corporation, **26** 100. *See also* Chromcraft Revington, Inc.

Peters Shoe Co., **III** 528

Petersen Cos., **52** 192

Petersen Publishing Company, 21 402–04

Peterson Furniture Company, **51** 9

Peterson, Howell & Heather, **V** 496

Peterson Soybean Seed Co., **9** 411

Petit Bateau, **35** 263

La Petite Academy, **13** 299

Petite Sophisticate, **V** 207–08

Petoseed Co. Inc., **29** 435

Petrie Stores Corporation, 8 425–27

Petrini's, **II** 653

Petro-Canada Limited, IV 367, **494–96,** 499; **13** 557; **50** 172

Petro/Chem Environmental Services, Inc., **IV** 411

Petro-Coke Co. Ltd., **IV** 476

Petro-Lewis Corp., **IV** 84; **7** 188

Petroamazonas, **IV** 511

Petrobas, **21** 31

Petrobel, **IV** 412

Petrobrás. *See* Petróleo Brasileiro S.A.

Petrocarbona GmbH, **IV** 197–98

Petrocel, S.A., **19** 12

Petrochemical Industries Co., **IV** 451

Petrochemicals Company, **17** 90–91

Petrochemie Danubia GmbH, **IV** 486–87

Petrochim, **IV** 498

PetroChina Company Ltd., **46** 86

Petrocomercial, **IV** 511

Petrocorp. *See* Petroleum Company of New Zealand.

Petroecuador. *See* Petróleos del Ecuador.

Petrofertil, **IV** 501

PetroFina S.A., IV 455, 495, **497–500,** 576; **7** 179; **26 365–69 (upd.)**

Petrogal. *See* Petróleos de Portugal.

Petroindustria, **IV** 511

Petrol, **IV** 487

Petrol Ofisi Anonim Sirketi, **IV** 564

Petrolane Properties, **17** 558

Petróleo Brasileiro S.A., IV 424, **501–03**

Petróleo Mecânica Alfa, **IV** 505

Petróleos de Portugal S.A., IV 504–06

Petróleos de Venezuela S.A., II 661; **IV** 391–93, **507–09,** 571; **24** 522; **31** 113

Petróleos del Ecuador, IV 510–11

Petróleos Mexicanos, IV 512–14, 528; **19** 10, **295–98 (upd.); 41** 147

Petroleum and Chemical Corp., **III** 672

Petroleum Authority of Thailand, **IV** 519

Petroleum Company of New Zealand, **IV** 279; **19** 155

Petroleum Development (Qatar) Ltd., **IV** 524

Petroleum Development (Trucial States) Ltd., **IV** 363

Petroleum Development Corp. of the Republic of Korea, **IV** 455

Petroleum Development Oman LLC, IV 515–16

Petroleum Helicopters, Inc., 35 334–36; 37 288; **39** 8

Petroleum Projects Co., **IV** 414

Petroleum Research and Engineering Co. Ltd., **IV** 473

Petrolgroup, Inc., **6** 441

Petroliam Nasional Bhd. *See* Petronas.

Petrolite Corporation, 15 350–52

Petrolube, **IV** 538

Petromex. *See* Petróleos de Mexico S.A.

Petromin Lubricating Oil Co., **17** 415; **50** 416

Petronas, IV 517–20; 21 501

Petronor, **IV** 514, 528

Petropeninsula, **IV** 511

Petroproduccion, **IV** 511

Petroquímica de Venezuela SA, **IV** 508

Petroquimica Española, **I** 402

Petroquisa, **IV** 501

PETROSUL, **IV** 504, 506

Petrotransporte, **V** 511

PETsMART, Inc., 14 384–86; 27 95; **29** 379–80; **41 295–98 (upd.); 45** 42

Petstuff, Inc., **14** 386; **41** 297

Pettibone Corporation, **19** 365

Petzazz, **14** 386

157; **25** 55; **26** 384; **28** 246–47; **30** 188–89

Revson Bros., **III** 54

Rewe-Beteiligungs-Holding National GmbH, **53** 179

Rewe Group, **37** 241

Rewe-Liebbrand, **28** 152

Rex Pulp Products Company, **9** 304

Rex Re Insurance Ltd., **51** 143

REX Stores Corp., 10 468–69; 19 362

Rexall Drug & Chemical Co., **II** 533–34; **III** 610; **13** 525; **14** 547

Rexall Drug Co., **50** 487

Rexall Sundown, Inc., **37** 340, 342

Rexam PLC, 32 380–85 (upd.); 45 337; **50** 122

Rexel, Inc., 15 384–87

Rexene Products Co., Ltd., **III** 760; **IV** 457

Rexham Inc., **IV** 259; **8** 483–84

Rexnord Corporation, I 524; **14** 43; **21 429–32; 37** 30

Reycan, **49** 104

Reydel Industries, **23** 95–96

Reyes Holdings, Inc., **24** 388

Reymer & Bros., Inc., **II** 508; **11** 172

Reymersholm, **II** 366

The Reynolds and Reynolds Company, 17 142, 144; **50 376–79**

Reynolds Electric Co., **22** 353

Reynolds Metals Company, II 421–22; **IV** 11–12, 15, 59, **186–88; IV** 122; **12** 278; **19 346–48 (upd.); 21** 218; **22** 455; **25** 22

RF Communications, **II** 38

RF Micro Devices, Inc., 43 311–13

RF Monolithics Inc., **13** 193

RHC Holding Corp., **10** 13; **13** 364; **27** 11

RHD Holdings, **23** 413

Rhee Syngman, **I** 516; **12** 293

Rheem Manufacturing, **25** 368; **52** 398–99

Rhein-Elbe Gelsenkirchener Bergwerks A.G., **IV** 25

Rheinelbe Union, **I** 542

Rheinisch Kalksteinwerke Wulfrath, **III** 738

Rheinisch Oelfinwerke, **I** 306

Rheinisch-Westfalische Bank A.G., **II** 279

Rheinisch-Westfälischer Sprengstoff AG, **III** 694

Rheinisch-Westfälisches Elektrizatätswerke AG, **I** 542–43; **III** 154; **IV** 231; **V** 744; **25** 102

Rheinische Aktiengesellschaft für Braunkohlenbergbau, **V** 708

Rheinische Creditbank, **II** 278

Rheinische Metallwaaren- und Maschinenfabrik AG, **9** 443–44

Rheinische Wasserglasfabrik, **III** 31

Rheinische Zuckerwarenfabrik GmbH, **27** 460

Rheinmetall Berlin AG, 9 443–46

Rheinsche Girozentrale und Provinzialbank, Düsseldorf, **II** 385

Rheinstahl AG, **IV** 222

Rheinstahl Union Brueckenbau, **8** 242

Rheintalische Zementfabrik, **III** 701

Rhenus-Weichelt AG, **6** 424, 426

RHI AG, 53 283–86

RHI Entertainment Inc., **16** 257

Rhino Entertainment Company, 18 457–60; 21 326

RHM. *See* Ranks Hovis McDougall.

Rhodes & Co., **8** 345

Rhodes Inc., 23 412–14

Rhodesian Anglo American Ltd., **IV** 21, 23; **16** 26; **50** 31

Rhodesian Development Corp., **I** 422

Rhodesian Selection Trust, Ltd., **IV** 17–18, 21

Rhodesian Sugar Refineries, **II** 581

Rhodia SA, 38 378–80

Rhodiaceta, **I** 388–89

Rhokana Corp., **IV** 191

Rhône Moulage Industrie, **39** 152, 154

Rhône-Poulenc S.A., I 303–04, 371, **388–90,** 670, 672, 692; **III** 677; **IV** 174, 487, 547; **8** 153, 452; **9** 358; **10 470–72 (upd.); 16** 121, 438; **21** 466; **23** 194, 197; **34** 284; **38** 379

Rhymey Breweries, **I** 294

Rhymney Iron Company, **31** 369

Rhythm Watch Co., Ltd., **III** 454; **21** 121

La Riassicuratrice, **III** 346

Rica Foods, Inc., 41 328–30

Ricard, **I** 280

Riccar, **17** 124; **41** 114

Riccardo's Restaurant, **18** 538

Rice Broadcasting Co., Inc., **II** 166

Rice-Stix Dry Goods, **II** 414

Riceland Foods, Inc., **27** 390

Rich Products Corporation, 7 448–49; 38 381–84 (upd.)

Rich's Inc., **9** 209; **10** 515; **31** 191

Richard A. Shaw, Inc., **7** 128

Richard D. Irwin Inc., **IV** 602–03, 678; **47** 102

Richard Hellman Co., **II** 497

Richard Manufacturing Co., **I** 667

Richard P. Simmons, **8** 19

Richard Shops, **III** 502

Richard Thomas & Baldwins, **IV** 42

Richards & O'Neil LLP, **43** 70

Richards Bay Minerals, **IV** 91

Richardson Company, **36** 147

Richardson Electronics, Ltd., 17 405–07

Richardson-Vicks Company, **III** 53; **8** 434; **26** 383

Richardson's, **21** 246

Richfield Oil Corp., **IV** 375–76, 456

Richfood Holdings, Inc., 7 450–51; 50 458

Richland Co-op Creamery Company, **7** 592

Richland Gas Company, **8** 349

Richmon Hill & Queens County Gas Light Companies, **6** 455

Richmond American Homes of Florida, Inc., **11** 258

Richmond Carousel Corporation, **9** 120

Richmond Cedar Works Manufacturing Co., **12** 109; **19** 360

Richmond Corp., **I** 600; **15** 129

Richmond Paperboard Corp., **19** 78

Richmond Pulp and Paper Company, **17** 281

Richton International Corporation, 39 344–46

Richway, **10** 515

Richwood Building Products, Inc., **12** 397

Richwood Sewell Coal Co., **17** 357

Ricils, **III** 47

Rickards, Roloson & Company, **22** 427

Rickel Home Centers, **II** 673

Ricky Shaw's Oriental Express, **25** 181

Ricoh Company, Ltd., III 121, 157, **159–61,** 172, 454; **6** 289; **8** 278; **18** 386, 527; **19** 317; **21** 122; **24** 429; **36 389–93 (upd.)**

Ricolino, **19** 192

Riddell Inc., **33** 467

Riddell Sports Inc., 22 457–59; 23 449

Ridder Publications, **IV** 612–13, 629; **7** 191

Ride, Inc., 22 460–63

Ridge Tool Co., **II** 19

Ridgewell's Inc., **15** 87

Ridgewood Properties Inc., **12** 394

Ridgway Co., **23** 98

Ridgway Color, **13** 227–28

Rieck-McJunkin Dairy Co., **II** 533

Riedel-de Haën AG, **22** 32; **36** 431

Rieke Corp., **III** 569; **11** 535; **20** 361

The Riese Organization, 38 385–88

Rieter Holding AG, 42 315–17

Rieter Machine Works, **III** 638

Rig Tenders Company, **6** 383

Riggin & Robbins, **13** 244

Riggs National Corporation, 13 438–40

Right Associates, **27** 21; **44** 156

Right Management Consultants, Inc., 42 318–21

Right Source, Inc., **24** 96

RightPoint, Inc., **49** 124

RightSide Up, Inc., **27** 21

Rijnhaave Information Systems, **25** 21

Rike's, **10** 282

Riken Corp., **IV** 160; **10** 493

Riken Kagaku Co. Ltd., **48** 250

Riken Kankoshi Co. Ltd., **III** 159

Riken Optical Co., **III** 159

Riklis Family Corp., 9 447–50; 12 87; **13** 453; **38** 169; **43** 355

Riku-un Moto Kaisha, **V** 477

La Rinascente, **12** 153

Ring King Visibles, Inc., **13** 269

Ring Ltd., **43** 99

Ringier America, **19** 333

Ringkopkedjan, **II** 640

Ringling Bros., Barnum & Bailey Circus, **25** 312–13

Ringnes Bryggeri, **18** 396

Rini-Rego Supermarkets Inc., **13** 238

Rini Supermarkets, **9** 451; **13** 237

Rinker Materials Corp., **III** 688

Rio Grande Industries, Inc., **12** 18–19

Rio Grande Oil Co., **IV** 375, 456

Rio Grande Servaas, S.A. de C.V., **23** 145

Rio Grande Valley Gas Co., **IV** 394

Rio Sportswear Inc., **42** 269

Rio Sul Airlines, **6** 133

Rio Tinto plc, 19 349–53 (upd.); 27 253; **42** 395; **50 380–85 (upd.)**

Rio Tinto-Zinc Corp., **II** 628; **IV** 56, 58–61, 189–91, 380; **21** 352

Rioblanco, **II** 477

Riordan Freeman & Spogli, **13** 406

Riordan Holdings Ltd., **I** 457; **10** 554

Riser Foods, Inc., 9 451–54; 13 237–38

Rising Sun Petroleum Co., **IV** 431, 460, 542

Risk Management Partners Ltd., **35** 36

Risk Planners, **II** 669

Rit Dye Co., **II** 497

Ritchie Bros. Auctioneers Inc., 41 331–34

Rite Aid Corporation, V 174–76; **9** 187, 346; **12** 221, 333; **16** 389; **18** 199, 286; **19 354–57 (upd.); 23** 407; **29** 213; **31** 232; **32** 166, 169–70

Rite-Way Department Store, **II** 649

Riteway Distributor, **26** 183

Rittenhouse and Embree, **III** 269

INDEX TO INDUSTRIES

Index to Industries

CONGLOMERATES

ENTERTAINMENT & LEISURE

FINANCIAL SERVICES: NON-BANKS

HEALTH & PERSONAL CARE PRODUCTS

INFORMATION TECHNOLOGY

INFORMATION TECHNOLOGY
(*continued*)

Logitech International SA, 28
LoJack Corporation, 48
Lotus Development Corporation, 6; 25 (upd.)
The MacNeal-Schwendler Corporation, 25
Macromedia, Inc., 50
Madge Networks N.V., 26
MAI Systems Corporation, 11
Maxtor Corporation, 10
Mead Data Central, Inc., 10
Mecklermedia Corporation, 24
Mentor Graphics Corporation, 11
Merisel, Inc., 12
Metatec International, Inc., 47
Metro Information Services, Inc., 36
Micro Warehouse, Inc., 16
Micron Technology, Inc., 11; 29 (upd.)
Micros Systems, Inc., 18
Microsoft Corporation, 6; 27 (upd.)
Misys plc, 45; 46
MITRE Corporation, 26
The Motley Fool, Inc., 40
National Semiconductor Corporation, 6
National TechTeam, Inc., 41
Navarre Corporation, 24
NCR Corporation, III; 6 (upd.); 30 (upd.)
Netscape Communications Corporation, 15; 35 (upd.)
Network Associates, Inc., 25
Nextel Communications, Inc., 10
NFO Worldwide, Inc., 24
Nichols Research Corporation, 18
Nimbus CD International, Inc., 20
Nixdorf Computer AG, III
Novell, Inc., 6; 23 (upd.)
Océ N.V., 24
Odetics Inc., 14
Onyx Software Corporation, 53
Opsware Inc., 49
Oracle Corporation, 24 (upd.)
Oracle Systems Corporation, 6
Packard Bell Electronics, Inc., 13
Parametric Technology Corp., 16
PC Connection, Inc., 37
PeopleSoft Inc., 14; 33 (upd.)
Perot Systems Corporation, 29
Pitney Bowes Inc., III
PLATINUM Technology, Inc., 14
Policy Management Systems Corporation, 11
Portal Software, Inc., 47
Primark Corp., 13
The Princeton Review, Inc., 42
Printrak, A Motorola Company, 44
Printronix, Inc., 18
Prodigy Communications Corporation, 34
Progress Software Corporation, 15
Psion PLC, 45
Quantum Corporation, 10
Quark, Inc., 36
Racal-Datacom Inc., 11
Razorfish, Inc., 37
RCM Technologies, Inc., 34
RealNetworks, Inc., 53
Red Hat, Inc., 45
Renaissance Learning Systems, Inc., 39
Reuters Holdings PLC, 22 (upd.)
The Reynolds and Reynolds Company, 50
Ricoh Company, Ltd., III
RSA Security Inc., 46
SABRE Group Holdings, Inc., 26
The Sage Group, 43
The Santa Cruz Operation, Inc., 38
SAP AG, 16; 43 (upd.)
SAS Institute Inc., 10

SBS Technologies, Inc., 25
SCB Computer Technology, Inc., 29
Schawk, Inc., 24
Seagate Technology, Inc., 8
Siebel Systems, Inc., 38
Sierra On-Line, Inc., 15; 41 (upd.)
SilverPlatter Information Inc., 23
SmartForce PLC, 43
Softbank Corp., 13; 38 (upd.)
Standard Microsystems Corporation, 11
STC PLC, III
Steria SA, 49
Sterling Software, Inc., 11
Storage Technology Corporation, 6
Stratus Computer, Inc., 10
Sun Microsystems, Inc., 7; 30 (upd.)
SunGard Data Systems Inc., 11
Sybase, Inc., 10; 27 (upd.)
Sykes Enterprises, Inc., 45
Symantec Corporation, 10
Symbol Technologies, Inc., 15
Synopsis, Inc., 11
System Software Associates, Inc., 10
Systems & Computer Technology Corp., 19
Tandem Computers, Inc., 6
TenFold Corporation, 35
Terra Lycos, Inc., 43
The Thomson Corporation, 34 (upd.)
3Com Corporation, 11; 34 (upd.)
The 3DO Company, 43
Timberline Software Corporation, 15
Transaction Systems Architects, Inc., 29
Transiciel SA, 48
Triple P N.V., 26
Ubi Soft Entertainment S.A., 41
Unilog SA, 42
Unisys Corporation, III; 6 (upd.); 36 (upd.)
United Business Media plc, 52 (upd.)
UUNET, 38
Verbatim Corporation, 14
VeriFone, Inc., 18
VeriSign, Inc., 47
Veritas Software Corporation, 45
Viasoft Inc., 27
Volt Information Sciences Inc., 26
Wang Laboratories, Inc., III; 6 (upd.)
West Group, 34 (upd.)
Western Digital Corp., 25
Wind River Systems, Inc., 37
Wipro Limited, 43
Wolters Kluwer NV, 33 (upd.)
WordPerfect Corporation, 10
Wyse Technology, Inc., 15
Xerox Corporation, III; 6 (upd.); 26 (upd.)
Xilinx, Inc., 16
Yahoo! Inc., 27
Zapata Corporation, 25
Ziff Davis Media Inc., 36 (upd.)
Zilog, Inc., 15

INSURANCE

AEGON N.V., III; 50 (upd.)
Aetna, Inc., III; 21 (upd.)
AFLAC Incorporated, 10 (upd.); 38 (upd.)
Alexander & Alexander Services Inc., 10
Alleghany Corporation, 10
Allianz Aktiengesellschaft Holding, III; 15 (upd.)
The Allstate Corporation, 10; 27 (upd.)
AMB Generali Holding AG, 51
American Family Corporation, III
American Financial Corporation, III
American Financial Group Inc., 48 (upd.)
American General Corporation, III; 10 (upd.); 46 (upd.)

American International Group, Inc., III; 15 (upd.); 47 (upd.)
American National Insurance Company, 8; 27 (upd.)
American Premier Underwriters, Inc., 10
American Re Corporation, 10; 35 (upd.)
N.V. AMEV, III
Aon Corporation, III; 45 (upd.)
Assicurazioni Generali SpA, III; 15 (upd.)
Atlantic American Corporation, 44
Aviva PLC, 50 (upd.)
Axa, III
AXA Colonia Konzern AG, 27; 49 (upd.)
B.A.T. Industries PLC, 22 (upd.)
Baldwin & Lyons, Inc., 51
Bâloise-Holding, 40
Benfield Greig Group plc, 53
Berkshire Hathaway Inc., III; 18 (upd.)
Blue Cross and Blue Shield Association, 10
Brown & Brown, Inc., 41
Business Men's Assurance Company of America, 14
Capital Holding Corporation, III
Catholic Order of Foresters, 24
The Chubb Corporation, III; 14 (upd.); 37 (upd.)
CIGNA Corporation, III; 22 (upd.); 45 (upd.)
Cincinnati Financial Corporation, 16; 44 (upd.)
CNA Financial Corporation, III; 38 (upd.)
Commercial Union PLC, III
Connecticut Mutual Life Insurance Company, III
Conseco Inc., 10; 33 (upd.)
The Continental Corporation, III
Empire Blue Cross and Blue Shield, III
Enbridge Inc., 43
Engle Homes, Inc., 46
The Equitable Life Assurance Society of the United States Fireman's Fund Insurance Company, III
ERGO Versicherungsgruppe AG, 44
Erie Indemnity Company, 35
Farm Family Holdings, Inc., 39
Farmers Insurance Group of Companies, 25
The First American Corporation, 52
First Executive Corporation, III
Foundation Health Corporation, 12
Gainsco, Inc., 22
GEICO Corporation, 10; 40 (upd.)
General Accident PLC, III
General Re Corporation, III; 24 (upd.)
Gerling-Konzern Versicherungs-Beteiligungs-Aktiengesellschaft, 51
Great-West Lifeco Inc., III
Gryphon Holdings, Inc., 21
Guardian Royal Exchange Plc, 11
Harleysville Group Inc., 37
HDI (Haftpflichtverband der Deutschen Industrie Versicherung auf Gegenseitigkeit V.a.G.), 53
The Home Insurance Company, III
Horace Mann Educators Corporation, 22
Household International, Inc., 21 (upd.)
Jackson National Life Insurance Company, 8
Jefferson-Pilot Corporation, 11; 29 (upd.)
John Hancock Financial Services, Inc., III; 42 (upd.)
Johnson & Higgins, 14
Kaiser Foundation Health Plan, Inc., 53
Kemper Corporation, III; 15 (upd.)
Legal & General Group plc, III; 24 (upd.)
The Liberty Corporation, 22

LEGAL SERVICES

MANUFACTURING

MATERIALS

PAPER & FORESTRY

PERSONAL SERVICES

RUBBER & TIRE

TELECOMMUNICATIONS

TOBACCO

TRANSPORT SERVICES

WASTE SERVICES

GEOGRAPHIC INDEX

Geographic Index

Algeria

Entreprise Nationale Sonatrach, IV

Argentina

Aerolíneas Argentinas S.A., 33
YPF Sociedad Anonima, IV

Australia

Amcor Limited, IV; 19 (upd.)
Australia and New Zealand Banking Group
  Limited, II; 52 (upd.)
Billabong International Ltd., 44
Bond Corporation Holdings Limited, 10
Boral Limited, III; 43 (upd.)
Brambles Industries Limited, 42
Broken Hill Proprietary Company Ltd., IV;
  22 (upd.)
Carlton and United Breweries Ltd., I
Coles Myer Ltd., V; 20 (upd.)
CRA Limited, IV
CSR Limited, III; 28 (upd.)
Elders IXL Ltd., I
Foster's Brewing Group Ltd., 7; 21 (upd.)
Foster's Group Limited, 50 (upd.)
Goodman Fielder Ltd., 52
John Fairfax Holdings Limited, 7
Lend Lease Corporation Limited, IV; 17
  (upd.); 52 (upd.)
News Corporation Limited, IV; 7 (upd.);
  46 (upd.)
Pacific Dunlop Limited, 10
Pioneer International Limited, III
Qantas Airways Limited, 6; 24 (upd.)
TABCORP Holdings Limited, 44
Telecom Australia, 6
Telstra Corporation Limited, 50
Westpac Banking Corporation, II; 48 (upd.)
WMC, Limited, 43

Austria

Andritz AG, 51
Austrian Airlines AG (Österreichische
  Luftverkehrs AG), 33
Bank Austria AG, 23
BBAG Osterreichische Brau-Beteiligungs-
  AG, 38
Gericom AG, 47
Glock Ges.m.b.H., 42
Julius Meinl International AG, 53
Lauda Air Luftfahrt AG, 48
ÖMV Aktiengesellschaft, IV
Österreichische Bundesbahnen GmbH, 6
Österreichische Post- und
  Telegraphenverwaltung, V
RHI AG, 53
VA TECH ELIN EBG GmbH, 49
Voest-Alpine Stahl AG, IV
Zumtobel AG, 50

Bahamas

Sun International Hotels Limited, 26
Teekay Shipping Corporation, 25

Bangladesh

Grameen Bank, 31

Belgium

Almanij NV, 44
Bank Brussels Lambert, II
Barco NV, 44
Belgacom, 6
C&A, 40 (upd.)
Cockerill Sambre Group, IV; 26 (upd.)
Delhaize "Le Lion" S.A., 44
Generale Bank, II
GIB Group, V; 26 (upd.)
Interbrew S.A., 17; 50 (upd.)
Kredietbank N.V., II
PetroFina S.A., IV; 26 (upd.)
Roularta Media Group NV, 48
Sabena S.A./N.V., 33
Solvay & Cie S.A., I; 21 (upd.)
Tractebel S.A., 20
NV Umicore SA, 47
Xeikon NV, 26

Bermuda

Bacardi Limited, 18
Frontline Ltd., 45
Jardine Matheson Holdings Limited, I; 20
  (upd.)
Sea Containers Ltd., 29
Tyco International Ltd., III; 28 (upd.)
White Mountains Insurance Group, Ltd., 48

Brazil

Banco Bradesco S.A., 13
Banco Itaú S.A., 19
Companhia Vale do Rio Doce, IV; 43
  (upd.)
Empresa Brasileira de Aeronáutica S.A.
  (Embraer), 36
Lojas Arapua S.A., 22
Perdigao SA, 52
Petróleo Brasileiro S.A., IV
TransBrasil S/A Linhas Aéreas, 31
VARIG S.A. (Viação Aérea Rio-
  Grandense), 6; 29 (upd.)

Canada

Abitibi-Consolidated, Inc., V; 25 (upd.)
Abitibi-Price Inc., IV
Air Canada, 6; 23 (upd.)
Alberta Energy Company Ltd., 16; 43
  (upd.)
Alcan Aluminium Limited, IV; 31 (upd.)
Algo Group Inc., 24
Alliance Atlantis Communications Inc., 39
Bank of Montreal, II; 46 (upd.)
Bank of Nova Scotia, The, II
Barrick Gold Corporation, 34
BCE Inc., V; 44 (upd.)
Bell Canada, 6
BFC Construction Corporation, 25
Biovail Corporation, 47

Bombardier Inc., 42 (upd.)
Bramalea Ltd., 9
British Columbia Telephone Company, 6
Campeau Corporation, V
Canada Packers Inc., II
Canadair, Inc., 16
Canadian Broadcasting Corporation (CBC),
  The, 37
Canadian Imperial Bank of Commerce, II
Canadian National Railway System, 6
Canadian Pacific Railway Limited, V; 45
  (upd.)
Canadian Utilities Limited, 13
Canfor Corporation, 42
Canstar Sports Inc., 16
CanWest Global Communications
  Corporation, 35
Cinar Corporation, 40
Cineplex Odeon Corporation, 6; 23 (upd.)
Cinram International, Inc., 43
Cirque du Soleil Inc., 29
Clearly Canadian Beverage Corporation, 48
Cognos Inc., 44
Cominco Ltd., 37
Consumers' Gas Company Ltd., 6
CoolBrands International Inc., 35
Corby Distilleries Limited, 14
Corel Corporation, 15; 33 (upd.)
Cott Corporation, 52
Creo Inc., 48
Discreet Logic Inc., 20
Dofasco Inc., IV; 24 (upd.)
Dominion Textile Inc., 12
Domtar Inc., IV
Dylex Limited, 29
Echo Bay Mines Ltd., IV; 38 (upd.)
Enbridge Inc., 43
Extendicare Health Services, Inc., 6
Falconbridge Limited, 49
Fortis, Inc., 15; 47 (upd.)
Four Seasons Hotels Inc., 9; 29 (upd.)
GEAC Computer Corporation Ltd., 43
George Weston Limited, II; 36 (upd.)
Great-West Lifeco Inc., III
Groupe Vidéotron Ltée., 20
Harlequin Enterprises Limited, 52
Hemlo Gold Mines Inc., 9
Hiram Walker Resources, Ltd., I
Hockey Company, The, 34
Hudson Bay Mining and Smelting
  Company, Limited, The, 12
Hudson's Bay Company, V; 25 (upd.)
Husky Energy Inc., 47
Hydro-Québec, 6; 32 (upd.)
Imasco Limited, V
Imax Corporation, 28
Imperial Oil Limited, IV; 25 (upd.)
Inco Limited, IV; 45 (upd.)
Intrawest Corporation, The, 15
Irwin Toy Limited, 14
Jean Coutu Group (PJC) Inc., The, 46
Jim Pattison Group, The, 37
Kinross Gold Corporation, 36
Kruger Inc., 17

625

Germany

NOTES ON CONTRIBUTORS ————————————————

Notes on Contributors

AMOROSINO, Chris. Connecticut-based freelance writer.

BIANCO, David. Freelance writer, editor, and publishing consultant.

BRENNAN, Gerald E. Freelance writer based in California.

BROWN, Erin. Freelance writer.

BRYNILDSSEN, Shawna. Freelance writer and editor based in Bloomington, Indiana.

COHEN, M. L. Novelist and freelance writer living in Paris.

COVELL, Jeffrey L. Seattle-based freelance writer.

DINGER, Ed. Bronx-based freelance writer and editor.

FIERO, John W. Freelance writer, researcher, and consultant.

GASBARRE, April Dougal. Michigan-based freelance writer.

GREENLAND, Paul R. Illinois-based writer and researcher; author of two books and former senior editor of a national business magazine; contributor to *The Encyclopedia of Chicago History* (University of Chicago Press) and *Company Profiles for Students*.

HALASZ, Robert. Former editor in chief of *World Progress* and *Funk & Wagnalls New Encyclopedia Yearbook*; author, *The U.S. Marines* (Millbrook Press, 1993).

HAUSER, Evelyn. Researcher, writer and marketing specialist based in Arcata, California; expertise includes historical and trend research in such topics as globalization, emerging industries and lifestyles, future scenarios, biographies, and the history of organizations.

HENRY, Elizabeth. Freelance writer and editor based in Maine.

INGRAM, Frederick C. Utah-based business writer who has contributed to *GSA Business, Appalachian Trailway News,* the Encyclopedia of Business, the *Encyclopedia of Global Industries,* the *Encyclopedia of Consumer Brands,* and other regional and trade publications.

MONTGOMERY, Bruce P. Curator and director of historical collection, University of Colorado at Boulder.

ROTHBURD, Carrie. Freelance writer and editor specializing in corporate profiles, academic texts, and academic journal articles.

STANFEL, Rebecca. Freelance writer and editor based in Montana.

STANSELL, Christina M. Freelance writer and editor based in Farmington Hills, Michigan.

TRADII, Mary. Freelance writer based in Denver, Colorado.

UHLE, Frank. Ann Arbor-based freelance writer; movie projectionist, disc jockey, and staff member of *Psychotronic Video* magazine.

WOODWARD, A. Freelance writer.